THE ALPHABET OF THE
SAINTS

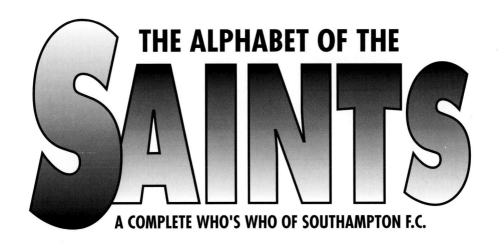

A COMPLETE WHO'S WHO OF SOUTHAMPTON F.C.

By DUNCAN HOLLEY & GARY CHALK

Published by
ACL & POLAR PUBLISHING (UK) LTD

DEDICATED TO THE MEMORY OF

Steve Mills and Austin Hayes

First published in Great Britain by
ACL Colour Print & Polar Publishing (UK) Ltd
2 Uxbridge Road, Leicester LE4 7ST
England

Copyright ACL & Polar 1992

ISBN 0 9514862 3 3

Edited by
Julian Baskcomb & Julia Byrne

Printed by
ACL Colour Print & Polar Publishing (UK) Ltd
2, Uxbridge Road, Leicester LE4 7ST
Telephone: (0533) 610800

Photographs are courtesy of:
Southern Evening Echo, David Munden Photography and Empics.
The majority of the remaining photographs are from the private collection of the authors or from albums owned by various Southampton supporters or individual players. We have been unable to trace the sources of these pictures, but any photographer involved is cordially invited to contact the publishers in writing providing proof of copyright.

Cover photographs:
Front: (Clockwise): Mick Channon, Terry Paine, Bert Lee, Matthew Le Tissier, Ted Bates, Mike Keeping.
Back: Charlie McGibbon, Ron Davies, Alex Glen.

FOREWORD
by Ted Bates

WITHOUT players there can be no football club. Some inevitably are more gifted than others. This book tells in great detail of those that either started their careers with Southampton Football Club or joined us along the way. It also shows that whatever their ability there is always a level at which a player can contribute. For some it is a starting point for management, as in my case, and personally there was no finer satisfaction than to see men that I signed for the Saints as youngsters, such as Terry Paine, Martin Chivers and Mick Channon, go on and eventually play for their country.

Footballers play before the supporters of their time. As most supporters are football managers at heart, I am sure when they scan through the pages of this book they will get considerable enjoyment from recalling happy memories from the names and deeds recorded in it.

How times change. The first transfer deal I did for the Club was with the help of our Supporters' Club. Without any money at the time I wanted to buy Jimmy Shields from Sunderland who was available for £1,000. At my request the Supporters' Club lent the money and I duly signed him in the North East in July 1956 on my way to Scotland with my wife as part of our summer holiday. At the following A.G.M. and after speaking to the supporters, I became acutely aware of how vitally important it was to spend the Club's money wisely whenever entering the transfer market. I was a very relieved young manager when Jimmy justified the expenditure by scoring 18 goals for us in his first season.

Moving on, the best transfer activity that I presided over came about in the close season of 1959. At the time I felt that if we were to get anywhere we needed drastic changes and with this in mind I put 14 players on the transfer list. Ted Drake, then manager of Chelsea wanted to buy my centre-forward Charlie Livesey, and I decided to let him go to them in exchange for Cliff Huxford plus £12,000. I then bought George O'Brien from Leeds for £6,000 and Dick Connor from Grimsby for £4,000. Cliff had all the characteristics to make a great captain while George was a brilliant finisher. Dick was a bubbly personality who oozed confidence which reflected in his team work. All three immediately settled into the side and 1959-60 was a truly memorable season with the club winning the Third Division championship and scoring 106 goals along the way.

The most money I ever spent was £75,000 for Brian O'Neil but he was well worth it. When I heard he was available I travelled to Burnley and conducted the negotiations for the transfer with Chairman Bob Lord in a meat factory which he ran. Brian was a true competitor, winning the ball and then playing it, making sure to always give 100 per cent - quite a character. I have managed several very good players over my 18 years at the Dell; Mick Channon for one was recommended to me by a supporter who also thoughtfully enclosed in his letter the details of where the young Channon would be playing on the Saturday. Bill Ellerington watched him and confirmed that he was good enough to become an apprentice so I travelled to Orcheston on the Sunday morning; it turned out to be a very worthwhile visit for this Club as Swindon's manager Bert Head arrived at Mick's house on the Monday morning just 24 hours too late.

Of all the players though, the best I ever had was Terry Paine. He was gifted with a perception on the field second to none and his great control and skill on the ball enabled him to be one of the most accurate crossers and passers in the game. His 160 goals with many of them vital for us, showed that he was not only a maker but also a taker of goals. To think that I only persuaded him to sign for us a day before he was due to travel to Arsenal for a trial.

A football club is indeed fortunate when they have fans such as Duncan Holley and Gary Chalk who have put so much time and care into the compilation of its history. I am sure there is something inside this book that will be of interest to all Saints fans young and old, as they discover the fascinating details of the lives of the many individuals who have passed through the Club since its beginning in 1885. I sincerely wish this book well.

PLAYERS AND DAYS GONE BY......
Action from a Saints v Sheffield United
match at The Dell in December 1938.

CONTENTS

Saints' solid defensive pair
John McGrath and Jim Steele in action
against Crystal Palace in April 1972.

INTRODUCTION

OCTOBER 1991 marked the hundred year anniversary of Southampton Football Club's involvement in the English (F.A.) Cup and as such their first truly nationally competitive fixture.

Up until October 1891 the club (originally known as Southampton St. Mary's) had spent the six years prior to its formation, playing friendlies and Hampshire Cup matches. Some of those early players remained long enough to play in early F.A. Cup ventures and their biographies are included here. In October 1894 St. Mary's became a league team with their entry into the Southern League, which in those days, was as strong as its Northern rival, the Football League. In 1920 there was an en masse movement by the southern clubs to join the Football League and for the first time the country had a truly national league to complement the F.A. Cup. This book contains a biography of every single man who played at least one game in either the F.A. Cup 1891-1991; Southern League 1894-1920, Football League 1920-1991, League Cup 1960-1991, and the various European Cup competitions 1969-1991.

In preparing these biographies we were faced with some dilemmas. Did we for instance, include heights and weights which of course vary from year to year and are thus unreliable. As this publication is intended to be exhaustive we decided to, wherever possible, list the players' physical "vital statistics", taken if possible at the onset of careers. Dates of joining the clubs and leaving are given whenever known, although these will not in some cases coincide with the seasons played statistics which are given next to the players positions. Take for instance a player who joined the club in September 1946 but did not make his debut until February 1949 and then played his last game in September 1952. He will be down as having played from 1948-53, making his first appearance during the 1948-49 season and his last during the 1952-53 season. Substitute appearances are listed separately and are not included with full appearances. This is because a forward who makes five outings from the substitutes' bench, each lasting a few minutes, and fails to score, would end up with misleading figures of 5 games 0 gls. Therefore we prefer to list his figures as 0 (5) apps. 0 gls. and similarly when debuts are given we prefer to list full debuts. (Pre-1965 substitutes were not allowed and our method does help to keep comparisons of players analyses from different eras in perspective). Of course our method is not foolproof as, for instance, Steve Moran (who first scored when coming on as a substitute) will be listed as scoring before making his debut. Conversely, Alan Shearer is credited with becoming the youngest player ever to score a hat-trick in the First Division, and has this feat considerably enhanced by the fact that it occurred on his full debut.

Finally in an effort to make 700 plus biographies not seem repetitive and, in a further effort to evoke an atmosphere from bygone days, we have quoted, if possible, contemporary characterisations taken from the press of the day. Thus some portrayals may appear old-fashioned and archaic but do at least give, we hope, a "period feel" to our work. If anyone disagrees or can add to these biographies we will be delighted to accept further information. It is always interesting to discover what players went on to achieve after leaving the Dell as one of the commonest questions posed by fans interested in the club's history is, "Whatever happened to so and so?". We hope that this book will go some way to answering that question.

Duncan Holley and Gary Chalk
Southampton November 1991

ACKNOWLEDGEMENTS

One of the delights of compiling a book such as this is the pleasures of uncovering a hitherto forgotten photograph from long ago or, alternatively, an unknown and unpublished snippet of information. Gary and I have spent most of the last four years traipsing around the country, meeting old players, talking about their careers and persuading them to loan us their treasured photos and scrapbooks. It would have been ideal if we could produce a likeness for every one of the 700 plus players featured in this publication but we fear the discovery of a portrait of some players who maybe played just a few games and have been dead for half a century may now be beyond feasibility. Nevertheless, included here are many photos not seen before in modern times, most of them plucked from the lovingly compiled collections of the men themselves. We would like to thank all ex-players of Southampton F.C. who willingly agreed to meet us, and particular gratitude is expressed to those who entrusted their photographs to us. The Saints moved to the Dell in 1898 which was also the year that an evening Sports Echo appeared on the streets of Southampton. Fortunately for us, someone at the Echo Office had the foresight to bind these early periodicals and they survive to this day offering an invaluable source of reference. Without the assistance of the Southern Evening Echo and permission to use their vast catalogue of photographs, this book would certainly not have been worthwhile.

For that reason special thanks to Peter Ashton, Sheila Ballantyne and Phil Rood. Gary and I are also indebted to exiled Saints fan and 'football statistician extraordinaire' Mike Davage, who, despite being up to his neck in research on an epic publication of his own, has taken the time to provide us with not only a critical eye but also a wealth of extra information. Andrew Murray is another fan who deserves special mention as he has willingly made available from his huge collection of programmes and handbooks anything we required. Likewise Mr. Richard Humphries M.B.E., a childhood supporter from the 1920's, who has permitted us not only a priceless forage amongst his massive library of Southampton newspaper cuttings but has also given us a unique insight from a fan's point of view of the pre-war days at the Dell. Once again undying thanks to our typist-come-chief critic Louise Westwick, our proof reader, and back-up critic Robin Holley. We'd also like to acknowledge a debt of gratitude to Ann Chalk and Trevor Jelly, Ray Mursell, Gill Hall, Dave Coyne, Frank Grayer, Dave Juson, Rob Jex and Eric White - authors of '100 years of Brentford F.C.', Laorna Parnell and C. Pickford at the Football League H.Q., Mike Conroy and Mike Gannaway for listening to the moans in the Tea Bar, Toby Keleher, Paul Wilkinson, Jane Watt, Malcolm Robinson, Jim Creasy, Ian Garland, Ron Meston, Alan Futter, Fred Ollier, John Harkus, 'Felix' Baker, Neil Jenkinson, Les Laney, the late Sid Clarke, George Jewett, Ken Prior, Steve McBride, Chris Lewis, Chris Arundale, Keith Baker, Karen Smith, Jamie Horton, Derek Murray and Leigh Edwards. Last, but not least, our sincere thanks to Ted Bates for kindly agreeing to provide a foreword for the book.

ADAMS, Michael Richard

Role: Full-back 1988-
5'7" 10st.10lbs.
b. Sheffield 8 November 1961

CAREER: Gillingham app. Aug 1978, pro Nov 1979/Coventry City July 1983/Leeds United Jan 1987/SOUTHAMPTON Mar 1989.

Debut v Arsenal (h) 25.3.89

Micky Adams started his professional life as a left-winger but converted to a left midfield role at Leeds. His favoured position, however, is in the left-back position and soon after his move to the Dell he ousted Derek Statham to become first choice in the number 3 shirt. The former England Youth international cost the Saints £250,000 but despite being plagued by a series of niggling injuries since his arrival he has been good if not spectacular value. His main rival for the left-back spot has been Francis Benali but 1990-91 ended with Micky firmly ensconced in the driving seat.

Appearances:
FL: 52 (1) app. 0 gls.
FAC: 2 app. 0 gls.
LC: 6 app. 0 gls.
Total: *60 (1) app. 0 gls.*

ADAMS, William

Role: Full & half-back 1927-36
5'9" 12st.0lbs.
b. Tynemouth 3 November 1902
d. Southampton 15 March 1963

CAREER: Sunderland Colliery/Guildford United July 1925/SOUTHAMPTON Mar 1926/West Ham United Aug 1936/Southend United Jan 1937.

Debut v Stoke City (h) 27.8.27

Bill Adams had a tentative start to his footballing life at the Dell, making his debut in August 1928 and then having to wait over three years until his next first team outing! Once settled however, Bill soon displayed a wholehearted attitude and became club captain during the 1931-32 season. He joined West Ham United for £500 in 1936 and although he had only netted 3 goals in over 200 games for the Saints he nevertheless must have been delighted to score on his Hammers debut against his old club. After a brief spell at Southend United, Bill returned to Hampshire late in 1937 and ran the Half Way Inn at Chandlers Ford for 26 years.

Appearances:
FL: 196 app. 3 gls.
FAC: 9 app. 0 gls.
Total: *205 app. 3 gls.*

Micky Adams

Bill Adams accepts a good luck charm from a young fan prior to an FA Cup tie with Birmingham in 1935.

AFFLECK, David Roy

Role: Centre-half 1937-39
6'0" 12st.11lbs.
b. Coylton 26 July 1912
d. Stoke-sub-Haddon, Somerset 11 August 1984

CAREER: Crosshouse Castle Rovers/Notts County July 1932/Bristol City May 1934/Clapton Orient July 1935/SOUTHAMPTON May 1937/Southampton Police during World War 2/Yeovil Town June 1946

Debut v Bradford (a) 11.9.37

Although born in Ayrshire, Dave Affleck's first taste of professional League football came with Notts County. He joined the Saints in the close season of 1937 and his heading ability, coupled with some incisive tackling, reportedly attracted the attentions of top London clubs, Tottenham Hotspur and Chelsea. Unfortunately for Dave the war interrupted his career at this crucial stage and he enlisted into the police war reservists, becoming a regular member of the successful Southampton Police XI. Thirty three years old by the time the hostilities ended, Dave was given a free transfer to Yeovil Town and settled down to live in Somerset.

> **Appearances**:
> *FL: 61 app. 0 gls.*
> *FAC: 1 app. 0 gls.*
> **Total:** *62 app. 0 gls.*

AGBOOLA, Reuben Omojola Folasanje

Role: Defender 1980-85
5'9" 11st.2lbs.
b. Camden 30 May 1962

CAREER: SOUTHAMPTON app July 1978/pro Apr 1980/Sunderland Jan 1985 (Charlton Athletic-loan-Oct-Dec 1986) (Port Vale-loan-Nov 1990).

Debut v Manchester United (a) 29.11.80

Reuben Agboola was one of many products from the highly successful London Selection Centre and his quick and alert defending was put to good use when the sweeper role was introduced, with good effect, in 1983. It was something of a surprise when he was allowed to join Sunderland, but he has since failed to hold down a regular first team place at Roker Park. In April 1991 Reuben won an international cap when he played for Nigeria against Benin.

Appearances:
FL: 89 (1) app. 0 gls.
FAC: 7 app. 0 gls.
LC: 10 app. 0 gls.
Eur: 5 app. 0 gls.
Total: *111 (1) app. 0 gls.*

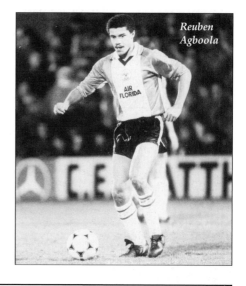

Reuben Agboola

ALLEN, Thomas

Role: Goalkeeper 1920-28
6'1" 11st.4lbs
b. Moxley 1 May 1897
d. Castle Bromwich 10 May 1968

CAREER: Wednesbury Old Park/Bilston United/Hickmans Institute F.C./ Wolverhampton Wanderers (during WW1)/ Sunderland May 1919/ SOUTHAMPTON May 1920/ Coventry City June 1928/ Accrington Stanley July 1932/ Northampton Town Sept 1933/ Kidderminster Harriers Aug 1934.

Debut v Gillingham (a) 28.8.20

Tommy Allen's arrival at the Dell coincided with the club's first season as a Football League club and an added bonus was that he cost nothing as Sunderland had forgotten to include his name on their end-of-season retained list. Sunderland's loss was certainly Southampton's gain as Tommy became the backbone of a defence that, in the 1921-22 season, conceded only 21 goals in 42 games - a national record for sixty years and a club record to this day. A tall, slightly built man, his agility was often described as "miraculous" and his 291 League appearances is yet another club record for a custodian. After retiring from football he settled in Coventry.

Appearances:
FL: 291 app. 0 gls.
FAC: 32 app. 0 gls.
Total: *323 app. 0 gls.*

❏ **Saints Note** - *Tom's slender build was frequently the target of friendly fun in the dressing-room. Players in the bath after a match would often cry in mock alarm: "Look out, the plug's pulled - we don't want to lose Tom down the drain!"*

ANDERSON, Alexander Ferguson

Role: Full-back 1949-52
b. Monifieth 15 November 1921

CAREER: Dundee East Cragie
Juniors/Hibernian (trial)/East Fife/
St. Johnstone/Forfar Athletic/
SOUTHAMPTON trial Nov 1949, pro. Jan
1950/ Exeter City June 1952.

Debut v Chesterfield (h) 1.4.50

Alex Anderson originally came to the Dell on
trial but within two months had impressed
enough to be given a contract. Despite winning
initial praise from fans and press alike, he was
unable to make the number 2 shirt his own,
mainly because his rival contemporaries were
Len Wilkins and Bill Ellerington. In the late
1980's Alex was known to be living in Dundee,
Scotland and working as a postman.

> **Appearances:**
> *FL: 20 app. 0 gls.*
> **Total:** *20 app. 0 gls.*

Alex Anderson

ANDREWS, Arthur

Role: Half-back 1919-20
b. Sunderland 1 April 1891
d. Southampton 24 September 1964

CAREER: Sunderland Rovers/Blackpool Nov
1913/Harland & Wolff/SOUTHAMPTON
Aug 1919/Harland & Wolff 1920/Southampton
Post Office/Cowes c.s.1922/Lymington.

Debut v Southend United (h) 8.11.19

A boiler-maker by trade, Arthur Andrews
moved to the Southampton area during the
First World War to work in the shipyards of
Harland & Wolff. Considered one of the fastest
half-backs in North Eastern League soccer
before his move South, he fitted in well in the
works' team that took part in the South Hants
War League in 1918. His impressive showing
earned him the offer of a playing contract at
the Dell in August 1919 and he forced his way
into the side by November. His professional
career though was unfortunately short; after
only twelve minutes of an F.A. Cup tie at West
Ham United he attempted a fierce tackle, only
to suffer a broken leg. Released by the club in
May 1920 he returned to work in the shipyards
whilst playing regularly in Hampshire League
soccer.

> **Appearances:**
> *SL: 10 app. 0 gls.*
> *FAC: 2 app. 0 gls.*
> **Total:** *12 app. 0 gls.*

ANDREWS, Ian Edmund

Role: Goalkeeper 1989-
6'2" 12st.0lbs.
b. Nottingham 1 December 1964

CAREER: Nottingham Forest assoc. schoolboy/
Mansfield Town apprentice 1980/Leicester City
Sept 1981 (Middlesbrough-loan-Jan 1984)
(Swindon Town-loan-Jan 1984)/ Celtic July 1988
(Leeds United-loan-Dec 1988)/ SOUTHAMPTON
-loan-Dec 1989 transfer Feb 1990.

Debut v Derby County (h) 10.3.90

An England Youth international, Ian Andrews
looked to be yet another fine custodian
discovery from the renowned goalkeepers'
stable at Filbert Street. Unfortunately, after
some inspirational early performances, Ian
suffered an alarming fall in confidence which

Ian Andrews

coincided with Leicester City's slip from the top flight in 1987. After losing his place to Paul Cooper he moved to Parkhead for a fee of £300,000 but his spell with Celtic was spent mainly as understudy to Pat Bonner. Manager Chris Nicholl, anxious to find cover for Tim Flowers, had been trying to sign Ola By Rise, the Norwegian international but, when problems arose with a work permit, turned instead to Ian, initially bringing him to the Dell on loan. A fee of £200,000 made the transfer permanent and within a month Ian had made a steady debut in the 2-1 defeat of Derby. Unfortunately it all started to go horribly wrong in his next match away to Wimbledon when one or two basic errors cost the Saints a couple of points. The pattern continued in his next match at home to United and, with Ian's fragile confidence in shreds, Nicholl recalled Tim Flowers. In 1990-91 Ian, or "Archie" as he is known to the fans, made only one appearance and incredibly made another expensive howler that cost the team a point at Queen's Park Rangers. Ian now stands at the crossroads of his career with his future at the Dell looking very uncertain.

Appearances:
FL: 4 app. 0 gls.
Total: *4 app. 0 gls.*

ANDREWS,
Leonard Thomas Alford

Role: Forward 1912-19 & 1921-24
5'9" 11st.4lbs.
b. Reading 9 December 1888
d. Southampton 21 January 1969

CAREER: Reading University/Reading Oct 1909/SOUTHAMPTON c.s.1912/Reading July 1919/SOUTHAMPTON Aug 1921/Watford Aug 1924

Debut v Northampton Town (h) 4.9.12

Len Andrews was the Saints' most consistent forward in the three seasons leading up to the Great War, having been signed from Reading in 1912. A clever and able forward who could play in all the front positions, he particularly excelled on the left. A noted penalty-taker, he missed only twice out of 22 kicks and had the reputation of a man who could hit the ball harder, and more accurately, with his left foot than any other player in the game. During the war Len joined up and was promoted through the ranks to Regimental Sergeant Major with the 5th Battalion Royal Wiltshire Regiment serving in Mesopotamia. He returned to play for Reading but re-signed for the Saints and helped them to win their way up to Division Two in 1922. His enthusiasm carried him through another two seasons before he ended his career with a brief spell at Watford. In his early days Len trained as a teacher but in 1925 he decided to become an insurance salesman in Southampton.

Appearances:
FL: 59 app. 3 gls.
SL: 105 app.
32 gls.
FAC: 16 app.
5 gls.
Total: *180 app. 40 gls.*

❏ **Saints Note -**
Len was an outstanding bowls player and won honours at Southampton and County level.

Len Andrews

*Manny
Andruszewski*

ANDRUSZEWSKI,
Emmanuel Franciszek

Role: Defender 1974-80
5'10" 10st.9lbs.
b. Eastleigh 4 October 1955

CAREER: SOUTHAMPTON app Sep1972
pro Oct 1973/Tampa Bay Rowdies May
1979/Waterlooville/Luton Town (trial) Oct
1981/SOUTHAMPTON Jan 1982/A.F.C.
Bournemouth (trial) July 1982/Aldershot Aug
1982/Andover c.s.1983/Grimsby Town (trial)
Sept 1983/Houston Dynamos summer 1984/
Netley Sept 1984.

Debut v West Bromwich Albion (a) 1.2.75

Manny Andruszewski was an
uncompromising tackler who was at his best
given a particular opponent to shadow. His
finest game was against Birmingham City in
the League Cup in August 1978 when he
shackled Trevor Francis to such effect that the
Saints were able to notch a memorable 5-2
victory. He suffered from never having a
prolonged run in the first team and a £150,000
transfer took him to the United States where
illness soon forced his return. He briefly
reappeared at the Dell as cover in 1982 but,
after a spell at Aldershot, went back to the
States, this time to play indoor soccer.

Appearances:
FL: 82 (1) app. 3 gls.
FAC: 7 (1) app. 0 gls.
LC: 6 app. 0 gls.
Eur: 2 app. 0 gls.
Total: *97 (2) app. 3 gls.*

ANGELL, James William

Role: Half-back 1906-07
b. Bitterne, Southampton January qtr 1883
d. Romsey 4 January 1960

CAREER: Peartree/Woolston Alma/
SOUTHAMPTON c.s.1902/Bitterne Guild/
Eastleigh Athletic/Thornycrofts (coach) 1919/
Arsenal (scout)/ Norwich City (scout)/South-
ampton 'A' (manager) 1937/Romsey Town
(manager) 1945, (chairman) 1954, (president)
1956/Hampshire F.A. Council member 1948-55

Debut v Brentford (a) 29.9.06

Probably better known in Southampton for the
building firm which bears his name, Jim
Angell joined the Saints from local minor
football in 1902. Whilst a reserve player he
won three Hampshire Senior Cup Winners'
medals but had to wait until September 1906
before making three consecutive Southern
League appearances. In 1920 he was coaching
the famous Thornycrofts side that took
Burnley to an F.A. Cup replay and later, after
World War Two, he took over the reins at
Romsey.

Appearances:
SL: 3 app. 0 gls.
Total: *3 app. 0 gls.*

ANGUS, William John

Role: Forward 1893-96
b. Blythswood, Glasgow 1 December 1868

CAREER: Third Lanark/Ardwick Aug 1892/
SOUTHAMPTON St. Mary's 1893
Debut v Uxbridge (h) 4.11.1893 FAC

Previously on the books of Division Two side
Ardwick (later Manchester City), Jack Angus
had made nine League appearances before
migrating south in 1893. A deft and aggressive
forward, Jack became the first ever Saints
player to be sent off when he was over zealous
in a Hampshire Senior Cup tie against
Freemantle in February 1894. He scored in the
club's inaugural game in the Southern League
and was a prominent member of the side until
he quit the area in November 1895.

Appearances:
SL: 16 app. 7 gls.
FAC: 7 app. 4 gls.
Total: *23 app. 11 gls.*

ARMSTRONG, David

Role: Midfield/defender 1981-87
5'8" 11st.5lbs.
b. Durham 26 December 1954

CAREER: Middlesbrough am Sept 1968, app. July 1970, pro. Jan 1972/SOUTHAMPTON Aug 1981/ Sheffield Wednesday July 1987/A.F.C. Bournemouth July 1987/Netley Central Sports coach July 1989/Andover commercial manager Jan 1991, manager Feb 1991 (combining both jobs), resigned Apr 1991/ A.F.C. Bournemouth community officer July 1991.

Debut v Wolverhampton Wanderers (h) 1.9.81

Although David Armstrong cost the Saints a record £600,000 the fans never begrudged a single penny as the six seasons he spent at the Dell coincided with some of the club's finest moments. Left-sided and primarily a midfield or defensive player he also showed a healthy appetite for goal-scoring. Twice he finished a season scoring 15 League goals, - impressive statistics for a mid-fielder. During his spell at the Dell he augmented his original England appearances versus Australia by gaining two further caps against West Germany in 1982 and Wales in 1984, with his versatility arguably costing him further appearances in an England shirt. Injuries and contractual problems led him to Hillsborough for 48 hours before second thoughts provoked a final League move to Bournemouth. The Dean Court fans were, though, to be disappointed, as a serious injury effectively ended David's League career within a few months.

Appearances:
FL: 243 app. 69 gls.
FAC: 17 app. 4 gls.
LC: 23 app. 6 gls.
Eur: 6 app. 1 gl.
Total: *289 app. 80 gls.*

David Armstrong

ARMSTRONG, Kenneth Charles

Role: Defender 1983-84
6'2" 13st.7lbs.
b. Bridgenorth 31 January 1959

CAREER: Beith Juniors/Kilmarnock June 1977/ SOUTHAMPTON June 1983 (Notts County-loan-Mar 1984)/Birmingham City Aug 1984/ Walsall Feb 1986.

Debut v Nottingham Forest (a) 27.8.83

Born in Shropshire, Ken Armstrong grew up in Scotland and joined Kilmarnock in 1977 before moving to the Dell six years later for a fee of £25,000. Powerfully built he seemed an ideal replacement for the recently departed Chris Nicholl and, playing alongside Mark Wright,

Ken Armstrong

At the time Johnny Arnold signed for the Saints in 1928 he was qualifying as a professional cricketer for Hampshire and it was reputed that as soon as Arthur Chadwick, the Saints' manager, saw him play he said, "I have a star here". A star he certainly was, as not only did he create a Saints' record by scoring 21 goals in the 1931-32 season from the left-wing, but eventually he was to represent his country at both football and cricket - a rare feat in those days and unheard of nowadays. Unfortunately for Saints fans his one England cap was gained one month after leaving the Dell for Craven Cottage in a double transfer with Mike Keeping that cost Fulham £5,000. The war ended his footballing career but he continued to open the batting for Hampshire until 1950. He played 396 matches for the county, scoring 21,831 runs and notched 34 and 0 on his single appearance for England. He also played for Oxfordshire. After retiring from cricket Johnny became a first class umpire, enjoying 20 years at the wicket and also ran the Criterion Public House in St. Mary's for several years.

Appearances:
FL: 106 app. 46 gls.
FAC: 4 app. 0 gls.
Total: *110 app. 46 gls.*

❏ **Saints Note** - *During the early war years, Johnny had the unusual job of packing the tobacco and cigarettes which were to be sent abroad for the troops.*

quickly formed a formidable central partnership in a defence that only conceded two goals in the opening eight games of the 1983-84 season. But Ken seemed to lose confidence on the heavier pitches and a loan period at Notts County was followed by a £100,000 transfer to Birmingham. The move to St. Andrews was not a happy one as he sustained a serious leg injury which, after a transfer to Walsall, finished his career. In 1991, Ken was believed to be living in Lithingow, West Lothian.

Appearances:
FL: 26 app. 0 gls.
LC: 2 app. 0 gls.
Total: *28 app. 0 gls.*

ARNOLD, John

Role: Forward 1928-33
5'8" 10st.8lbs.
b. Cowley 30 November 1907
d. Southampton 3 April 1984

CAREER: Cowley Elementary/Oxford Schools/Oxford City/SOUTHAMPTON Sept 1928/Fulham Feb 1933/SOUTHAMPTON during World War Two.

Debut v Millwall (h) 1.4.29

Johnny Arnold

BAILEY, Robert

Role: Centre-half 1892-93

CAREER: SOUTHAMPTON St. Mary's 1892.
Debut v Newbury (h) 15.10.1892 FAC

Bob Bailey's first game for St. Mary's came in a friendly at Newbury on October 1st 1892 and the Hampshire Independent summarised his performance as "useful" and agreed that "he truly warranted his selection for a red and white shirt". Given his senior debut a fortnight later in the first qualifying round of the F.A. Cup, coincidentally against Newbury, Bob only remained in the Southampton area for a few months and thus had a short lived career in the "red and white".

> **Appearances:**
> *SL: 0 app. 0 gls.*
> *FAC: 2 app. 0 gls.*
> **Total:** *2 app. 0 gls.*

BAINBRIDGE, John Robert

Role: Forward
1907-10
5'11" 11st.2lbs.
*b. Seaham, Sunderland
April qtr 1880
d. Sunderland
17 January 1960*

CAREER: Silksworth/Sunderland Royal Rovers/Glossop May 1903/Reading c.s. 1904/ Portsmouth c.s. 1906/ SOUTHAMPTON May1907/Hartlepool c.s. 1910.
Debut v Luton Town (h) 2.9.07

John Bainbridge came to the Dell in the summer of 1907 having had considerable Southern League experience with his previous two clubs. A reliable performer, his right wing partnership with Frank Jefferis drew favourable comparisons with the famed duo of Wood and A. Turner seven years earlier. Ill health ended his Dell career and he returned to his native North East where, after playing briefly for Hartlepool, he reverted to his original occupation of coal miner.

> **Appearances:**
> *SL: 84 app. 20 gls.*
> *FAC: 10 app. 4 gls.*
> **Total:** *94 app. 24 gls.*

BAIRD, Ian James

Role: Forward
1982-85
6'0" 12st.9lbs.
b. Southampton 1 April 1964

CAREER: Bitterne Saints/St. Mary's College/ SOUTHAMPTON app. July 1980 pro. Apr 1982 (Cardiff City-loan-Nov 1983) (Newcastle United-loan-Dec 1984)/ Leeds United Mar 1985/Portsmouth June 1987/Leeds United Mar 1988/ Middlesbrough Jan 1990/ Heart of Midlothian July 1991.
Debut v West Ham United (a) 26.2.83

Ian Baird was an England Schoolboy International who quickly developed into a strong bustling centre-forward. He made a big impact in the reserves but struggled to do the same for the first team and two loan spells with Cardiff and Newcastle were followed by a £100,000 transfer to Leeds. Ian was more successful at Elland Road and helped them to reach the F.A. Cup semi-final in 1987. It was a surprise when he was allowed, therefore, to move to Fratton Park as Alan Ball attempted to bolster Portsmouth's attack in preparation for their return to Division One. His stay at Portsmouth was beset by injury and

Ian Baird

Charlie Baker

disciplinary problems and Leeds re-signed him in March 1988 before reselling him to Middlesbrough for half a million pounds in January 1990. Shortly after Lennie Lawrence arrived as the new manager at Ayresome Park he moved on again in July 1991, joining Scottish outfit Hearts for £350,000.

Appearances:
FL: 20 (2) app. 5 gls.
LC: 1(1) app. 0 gls.
Total: *21 (3) app. 5 gls.*

BAKER, Charles

Role: Forward 1894-96
b. Stafford 1870

CAREER: Stafford Rangers/Stoke Apr 1889/ Wolverhampton Wanderers Aug 1892/Stoke Jan 1893/SOUTHAMPTON St. Mary's c.s.1894.

Debut v Chatham (h) 6.10.1894

Charlie Baker moved south to join Saints at the commencement of the club's first season of Southern League soccer in 1894. The team captain, his surges down the right wing made him a favourite with the Southampton public. A neat dribbler, he had a firm command over the ball and could centre with precision. He announced his retirement in April 1896 and was presented with a gold watch by the club before he returned to Stafford to pursue a shoemaking trade.

Appearances:
SL: 33 app. 11 gls.
FAC: 9 app. 6 gls.
Total: *42 app. 17 gls.*

BAKER, Graham Edgar

Role: Midfield 1977-82 & 1987-90
5'9" 10st.8lbs.
b.Southampton 3 December 1958

CAREER: Merry Oak School/Southampton Schools/SOUTHAMPTON app. Sept 1975, pro. Dec 1976/Manchester City Aug 1982/ SOUTHAMPTON May 1987 (Aldershot-loan-Mar 1990)/Fulham Aug 1990.

*Debut v Blackpool (h) 12.11.77 * (scored on debut)*

When Southampton played Blackpool at home in a Division Two match in November 1977 the cameras were there to capture Graham Baker scoring after only 58 seconds of a dream debut. Capitalising on this auspicious start Graham won not only a regular place in the Saints midfield but England Under-21 recognition in 1980 against Norway and Romania. He was sold to Manchester City in 1982 for £225,000 which McMenemy needed to help pay for the arrival of Peter Shilton. Graham's career fluctuated at Maine Road, not helped by a succession of injuries, and Chris Nicholl brought him back to the Dell on a free transfer. After a further three seasons, during which time he was in and out of the team, Graham joined Fulham, again, on a free transfer.

Appearances:
FL: 168 (5) app. 31 gls.
FAC: 7 (1) app. 1 gl.
FL: 13 (2) app. 4 gls.
Eur: 2 app. 0 gls.
Total: *190 (8) app. 36 gls.*

BAKER, Stephen

Role: Defender 1980-88
5'5" 10st.5lbs.
b. Newcastle 16 June 1962

CAREER: Wallsend Boys Club/ SOUTHAMPTON app. July 1978, pro. Dec 1979 (Burnley-loan-Feb 1983)/Leyton Orient Mar 1988/A.F.C. Bournemouth trial Aug 1991/perm. Sept 1991.

Debut v Ipswich Town (a) 13.5.81

Chris Nicholl welcomes Graham Baker back to the Dell in May, 1987.

Steve Baker

Tynesider Stephen Baker arrived at the Dell as a 16 year old after being spotted playing for the renowned Wallsend Boys Club. Despite having an impressive debut in the last game of the 1980-81 season, Steve struggled in the First Division and in 1988 he joined Leyton Orient for £50,000, his tenacity helping to keep them out of Division Four the following year.

Appearances:
FL: 61 (12) app. 0 gls.
FAC: 5 app. 0 gls.
FL: 15 (1) app. 0 gls.
Eur: 4 app. 0 gls.
Total: *85 (13) app. 0 gls.*

BALL, Alan James

Role: Midfield 1976-83
5' 6" 10st. 5lbs.
b. Farnworth 12 May 1945

CAREER: Farnworth Grammar/Bolton Wanderers am Dec 1960/Blackpool app. Sept 1961, pro. May 1962/ Everton Aug 1966/ Arsenal Dec 1971/ SOUTHAMPTON Dec 1976 /Philadelphia Fury May 1978/ Vancouver Whitecaps June 1979/Blackpool player-

manager Feb 1980/SOUTHAMPTON March 1981/ Eastern Athletic (Hong Kong) Oct 1982/Bristol Rovers Jan 1983/Portsmouth Youth team coach c.s.1983, manager May 1984-July 1988; first team coach until Jan 1989/ Colchester United coach Apr 1989/Stoke City coach Oct 1989, manager Dec 1989/resigned February 1991/Exeter City manager Aug 1991.
Debut v Plymouth Argyle (a) 27.12.76

One of the select Englishmen to possess a World Cup Winners' Medal, Alan Ball arrived at the Dell specifically to help mould an F.A. Cup-winning side into a team that could gain promotion from Division Two. McMenemy realised that Alan's natural qualities of leadership, coupled with an astute footballing mind, were just what the Saints needed and almost inevitably, the following season, Southampton, inspired by Alan Ball, regained their place amongst the top clubs. The next two seasons were then spent teaching his immaculate passing and visionary skills to the fledgling Steve Williams, whilst Saints reached the final of the League Cup and consolidated their position in the First Division. In the summer of 1980 he was tempted by an offer from one of his old clubs to be their player/manager but his spell at Bloomfield Road proved to be an unhappy one. McMenemy, the perfect managerial foil to the fiery midfielder, offered him the chance to line up alongside Channon, Keegan and Watson back at the Dell and, with 246 England caps between them, they helped Saints take the First Division by storm. Unfortunately, in the

Lawrie McMenemy signs Alan Ball in December 1976.

final run-in the old legs grew weary and Alan in particular, now aged 37, was feeling the strain. After a brief flurry in Hong Kong and at Bristol Rovers he reluctantly hung up his boots only to re-surface at Fratton Park as youth team coach. Within a year he became Pompey's manager and, within three years, the famous chimes were once more heard in Division One. Unfortunately Portsmouth's return was all too brief and with relegation came the inevitable sacking, but Alan Ball was never a man to remain in the shadows too long and in December 1989 he became manager of Second Division strugglers Stoke City but was unable to stop them dropping into the Third Division. Things did not work out at the Victoria Ground and in February 1991 Alan turned his back on football to take over a public house in Maidenhead, but within a few months he was persuaded by the Exeter City board to take over as their new manager.

Appearances:
FL: 195 app. 11 gls.
FAC: 18 app. 2 gls.
LC: 15 app. 0 gls.
Eur: 6 app. 0 gls.
Total: *234 app. 13 gls.*

❑ **Saints Note** - *Alan Ball is one of a very small number of players who have made 100 League appearances for four different clubs. He won 72 England caps, was twice transferred for an all British record and won one championship medal with Everton.*

BALLARD, Edgar Albert

Role: Full-back 1947-51
b. Brentford 16 June 1920

CAREER: Hayes/Brentford am Sept 1943/Leyton Orient am Apr 1946, pro. Apr 1946/SOUTHAMPTON June 1947/Leyton Orient Aug 1952/Snowdown Colliery June 1953-56/Hastings United 1956-57/Ashford Town player/manager June 1957-58, manager 1958-62/Hastings United secretary/manager 1962-65.

Debut v West Ham United (h) 31.1.48

Ted Ballard initially joined Saints as a half-back but soon found himself as understudy to Alf Ramsey. Although able to play both right and left-back, he failed to make either position his own and was given a free transfer in the

Ted Ballard

close season of 1951. He re-signed for Orient but never made their first team. Later he became the landlord of the Clarence Public House in Hastings where he stayed for a few years before becoming a franchise officer for Green Shield Stamps in the early 1970's. In April 1991 Ted by now retired lives in St. Leonards-on-Sea and enjoys supporting Arsenal from the comfort of his armchair.

Appearances:
FL: 45 app. 0 gls.
FAC: 2 app. 0 gls.
Total: *47 app. 0 gls.*

BAMFORD, Harold W.

Role: Half-back 1908-11

CAREER: Bitterne Guild/SOUTHAMPTON c.s.1908.

Debut v Luton Town (a) 9.1.09

Harry Bamford was a product of Hampshire County football and signed for Saints from local side Bitterne Guild. His three seasons at the Dell were spent mostly in the reserves, acting as cover for Trueman and Robertson, and he decided to retire from professional football in 1911 to continue his career as a Southampton schoolmaster.

> **Appearances:**
> *SL: 7 app. 0 gls.*
> **Total:** *7 app. 0 gls.*

BANGER, Nicholas Lee

Role: Forward 1990-
5' 8" 10st. 6lbs.
b. Southampton 25 February 1971

CAREER: Mansbridge & Southampton Schools/Bassett Comets/SOUTHAMPTON trainee July 1987, pro. April 1989.

Debut v Rochdale (h) LC 9.10.90
* (scored on debut)

Hailing from Swaythling, Nicky Banger emerged from Dave Merrington's youth team to become an overnight sensation when he netted three goals on his senior debut for the club. With the Saints holding a first leg lead of five goals, the manager decided to rest Le Tissier and Wallace for the return Rumbelows League Cup match at home to Rochdale and blood Nicky who had recently hit a streak of goal-scoring form in the reserves. The young forward responded by running himself into the ground in an effervescent performance that culminated in a memorable hat-trick. Surprisingly, Nicky was not to be given a full league match in the ensuing season but, with time still very much on his side and the 1991 close season departure of Rodney Wallace, he should soon become a lot more visible in the first team.

Appearances:
FL: 0 (6) app. 0 gls.
LC: 1 app. 3 gls.
Total: *1 (6) app. 3 gls.*

The Saints' reserve side of 1909-10.
*Back row (left to right): W Bulpitt (Director), H Rainsley, WC Rundle, F Grayer, AJ Goodchild, WG Smith, **Harry Bamford**, G Carter. Middle row: E Arnfield (Secretary), S Smith, T Clark, WE Toomer, P Prince, S Shearer, F Jordan, G Rainsley (Trainer). Front: WB McDonald, ECR Christmas.*

Nicky Banger scored a hat-trick on his senior debut for the Saints, against Rochdale in the Rumbelows League Cup.

BARLOW, Thomas Henry

Role: Forward 1902-03
5'9" 10st.0lbs.
b. Bolton January qtr 1875

CAREER: Halliwell Rovers/Bolton Wanderers May 1898/SOUTHAMPTON May 1902/ Bolton Wanderers May 1903/Millwall Aug 1904/Atherton Church House 1905.

*Debut v Brentford (h) 6.9.02 * (scored on debut)*

Previously with First Division side Bolton Wanderers, Tom Barlow journeyed south in May 1902. The directors considered him to be "a capture" and the local press declared him to be "a player who combined good ball control and distribution with legitimate trickery." Tom scored twice on his debut and impressed to the extent that he was selected to play in an international trial, representing the South versus the North at Tottenham in 1903. It was a blow to all concerned when he grew home-sick and was granted a transfer back to Burnden Park.

Appearances:
SL: 22 app. 6 gls.
FAC: 3 app. 1 gl.
Total: *25 app. 7 gls.*

BARRATT, Josiah

Role: Forward 1919-22
5'8" 11st.10lbs.
b. Bulkington 21 February 1895
d. Coventry April 1968

CAREER: Nuneaton Town/Leicester Fosse Dec 1916/Birmingham City Feb 1917/ SOUTHAMPTON May 1919/Birmingham City Mar 1922/Pontypridd June 1923/Lincoln City June 1924/Bristol Rovers May 1926.

Debut: Exeter City (h) 30.8.19

A wartime guest player during the 1918-19 season when he had been serving with the Royal Berkshire Regiment, Joe Barratt was transferred to the Dell from Birmingham in May 1919. His creative, storming runs down the right flank were most effective as Saints made the successful transition between the Southern League and Division Three of the Football League. A crowd pleaser, Joe, inexplicably, always insisted on playing with a piece of straw in his mouth and when he moved back to Birmingham, along with Fred Foxall, his departure was much mourned by the fans. Joe ended his playing days at Bristol Rovers and resurfaced, after the Second World War, at Coventry City where he helped coach the youngsters, although whether he had relinquished his straw habit is not recorded!

Appearances:
SL: 41 app. 5 gls.
FL: 52 app. 2 gls.
FAC: 8 app. 1 gl.
Total: *101 app. 8 gls.*

BARRETT, Albert Frank

Role: Half-back 1924-25
5'10" 11st.7lbs.
b. Stratford, London 11 November 1903
d. Cape Town, South Africa 8 December 1989

CAREER: Park School/Fairburn House Lads/Middlesex Wanderers/Leytonstone 1921/West Ham United Nov 1921/SOUTHAMPTON Feb 1925/Fulham June 1925/Leytonstone coach 1937.

Debut v Derby County (h) 14.3.25

Albert Barrett proved to be one of those that got away. He arrived at the Dell in February

1925 having won England Schoolboy honours in 1917 and amateur recognition in 1924 but, despite this excellent pedigree, he failed to impress the Dell management. A move to Craven Cottage effectively

Albert Barrett

relaunched Albert's career as he went on to make nearly 300 League appearances for Fulham over a ten year period. In 1929 he won his full England cap versus Ireland and although he represented his country just the once , Fulham's gain was undoubtedly Southampton's loss. After coaching Leyton-stone in 1937 he trained as an accountant and emigrated to South Africa in 1954.

Appearances:
FL: 1 app. 0 gls.
Total: *1 app. 0 gls.*

BARRETT, Uriah John

Role: Goalkeeper 1894-96
b. Watton Bassett, Wiltshire April qtr 1874
d. Redhill, Surrey January qtr 1934

CAREER: Alma/SOUTHAMPTON St. Mary's Mar 1894.

Debut v Chatham (h) 6.10.1894

Jack Barrett joined St. Mary's in March 1894 having played local parks football with junior side Alma. He succeeded the club's very first goalkeeper Ralph Ruffell to become the initial custodian to appear between the posts in the Southern League. After only three games he lost his place to Williamson and, although he was reinstated at the start of the 1895-96 season, he left the club in October 1895 after again losing his place, this time to Tom Cain. In 1896 he decided to quit football to concentrate on a professional career in cricket but he never made it to county status. He was also a shoemaker by trade. He died relatively young reputedly from blood poisoning,with his illness apparently stemming from being struck on the leg by a cricket ball.

Appearances:
SL: 7 app. 0 gls.
Total: *7 app. 0 gls.*

BATES, Edric Thornton

Role: Inside Forward 1937-53
5'9" 11st.0 lbs.
b. Thetford, Norfolk 3 May 1918

CAREER: Cardiff Schools/Thetford Thursday XI/Thetford/Hertfordshire County XI/ Norwich City am Oct 1935, pro. Sept 1936/ SOUTHAMPTON May 1937 (Northampton and Follands during WW2), Southampton coach May 1953, manager Sept 1955.

Debut v Swansea (a) 27.12.37

When Tom Parker became Southampton's manager in 1937 he did not forget a young lad he had left behind at his previous club, Norwich. Within months the young Ted Bates followed Parker to the Dell and so began his unbroken association with the club that has lasted to this day. The youthful inside forward forced his way into a regular place in Saints' forward line before he was twenty and his promising career looked ready to take off until the war rudely interrupted events. Serving in the army, Ted still managed the odd game with the Saints as well as playing for Northampton and Follands. Returning full time as soon as he had been demobbed, Ted struck up a lethal partnership with Charlie Wayman, more than making up for Charlie's lack of height with his own powerful heading ability. Ted's retirement from playing was not unconnected with the club's relegation into Division Three and within two years he was appointed first team manager with the task of lifting the club back into the Second Division. History records Saints storming to promotion in 1960 helped by a blend of youngsters such as Paine and Sydenham and older pros such as Reeves and Conner. Ted continued his careful team building and six years later triumphantly led Southampton to the virgin pastures of the top flight. Difficult days lay ahead and Ted had his hands full keeping the Saints from an early slide back into the anonymity of the Second Division. By the time he retired in 1973 he had not only survived seven eventful seasons but had become the League's longest serving manager. A seat on the board was just reward for a man whose name, more than any other, has become synonymous with Southampton Football Club.

Appearances:
FL: 202 app. 64 gls.
FAC: 14 app. 1 gls.
Total: *216 app. 65 gls.*

❏ **Saints Note** - *Ted Bates comes from a particularly sporting family - his father, Billy, played cricket for Yorkshire and Glamorgan and football for Leeds City and Bolton. His grandfather, Willie, played cricket and rugby for England and once performed the hat-trick for England against Australia in 1882-3.*

BEANEY, William Ronald

Role: Defender 1972-75
5'9" 12st.2lbs.
b. Southampton 29 May 1954

CAREER: SOUTHAMPTON app. Aug 1969, pro. June 1972 (Reading-loan-Oct 1974)/ Waterford Feb 1975/Washington Diplomats June 1975/Totton Aug 1975/Swansea City trial Sept 1975/Poole Town Oct 1975/Dorchester Town Feb 1978/Poole Town Aug 1980/ Follands/Andover Oct 1983/Netley Central Nov 1984, manager Feb 1985.

Debut v Chelsea (a) 21.4.73

Billy Beaney was a local product who did not improve on his considerable early promise. He was loaned to Reading and spent the summer of 1975 playing in the United States. His enthusiasm for the game is reflected in a whole list of non-league local clubs he has since represented.

Billy Beaney

Appearances:
FL: 2 (1) app. 0 gls.
Total: *2 (1) app. 0 gls.*

BEARE, George

Role: Forward 1906-07
5'7" 10st.10lbs.
b. Southampton 2 October 1885

CAREER: Shirley Warren/Southampton c.s.1906/Blackpool May 1908/Everton Nov 1910/Cardiff City June 1914/Bristol City Nov 1921/Cardiff City Sept 1922.

Debut v Bristol Rovers (h) 27.4.07

George Beare was a local discovery invited to join Saints in the summer of 1906 having previously turned out for local side, Shirley Warren. A "quick touch-line dribbler", he performed with some merit in the reserves and was rewarded with his Southern League debut in the last game of the 1906-07 season. Unable to break into the team the following year, it fell to Football League side Blackpool to resurrect George's career and he went on to regularly score goals for Everton, Cardiff and Bristol City. A northern journalist wrote of George in 1921, "if he did not enjoy playing football he would probably have been one of our leading music hall comedians, as he is an expert card manipulator, a trick cyclist of no little repute and an excellent billiards player."

Appearances:
SL: 1 app. 0 gls.
Total: *1 app. 0 gls.*

BEATTIE, George

Role: Forward 1947-48
b. Aberdeen 16 June 1925

CAREER: Rosemount (Aberdeen)/ SOUTHAMPTON Aug 1947/Gloucester City Dec 1948/Newport County Sept 1950/Bradford Park Avenue July 1953/Tonbridge player-coach July 1955/Dursley Town player-manager June 1959.

Debut v Fulham (a) 11.10.47

George Beattie arrived from Scottish non-league soccer but was only to make one appearance for the Saints, mainly due to the arrival of Charlie Wayman. He drifted into non-league football but Newport rescued his career and he scored 24 league goals in 113 appearances for the Welsh club. He had over 50 games for Bradford Park Avenue before returning to the non-league scene. In 1991 George was living in Newport, Monmouthshire.

Appearances:
FL: 1 app. 0 gls.
Total: *1 app. 0 gls.*

George Beare

BEAUMONT, William Edward

Role: Centre-half 1910-11
5'9" 12st.0lbs.
b. Ashton in Makerfield, Lancashire October qtr.1883
d. Portsmouth, Hampshire 19 November 1911

CAREER: Swindon Town/ Portsmouth Sept 1907/ SOUTHAMPTON Oct 1910.

Debut v Brentford (a) 29.10.10

Bill Beaumont had cost Portsmouth £75 when he joined from Swindon and he repaid them by performing consistently for three seasons. A motor engineer by trade, he was on the verge of retiring from the game in 1910 when Southampton made him an offer he gratefully accepted. He continued his full-time trade in Portsmouth, training every night at Fratton Park and only made contact with Saints on match days. Never a brilliant player, he was, nonetheless, versatile and could operate anywhere in the half-back line. Bill left the club and retired from the game in the summer of 1911 but within months had died after contracting pneumonia.

Appearances:
SL: 27 app. 0 gls.
FAC: 1 app. 0 gls.
Total: *28 app. 0 gls.*

BEDFORD, Noel Brian

Role: Forward 1955-56
5'11" 11st.8lbs.
b. Ferndale 24 December 1933

CAREER: Beddau Youth Club (South Wales)/ Reading Apr 1954/SOUTHAMPTON July 1955/Bournemouth Aug 1956/Queen's Park Rangers July 1959/Scunthorpe United Sept 1965/Brentford Sept 1966/Atlanta Chiefs Apr

George Beattie

1967/Bexley United Nov 1968.

Debut v Southend United (h) 24.3.56

Signing Brian Bedford from Reading was one of George Roughton's last acts before vacating the Saints' managerial position and, when Ted Bates bought Jimmy Shields the following year, Brian duly moved on to Bournemouth. Queen's Park Rangers paid £750 to acquire his services and his 163 goals in 258 League games repaid his fee many times over. Moves to Scunthorpe and Brentford were followed by a spell in the United States and, overall, Brian's League record of 231 League goals in 399 games suggest a premature release from the Dell. After his return from Atlanta in 1967, Brian found

Brian Bedford

himself banned from playing by the F.A. due to the fact that the American Football Association was then non-affiliated. It took a year for Brian to successfully appeal against the ban and he then finished his playing days with Bexley United. Afterwards he became a professional tennis coach and, in April 1991, was still registered with the Lawn Tennis Association. He now lives in West London and is employed by Queen's Park Rangers as a maintenance engineer at Loftus Road.

Appearances:
FL: 5 app. 2 gls.
Total: *5 app. 2 gls.*

BELL, Edward Inkerman

Role: Forward 1906-08
b. Gibraltar 1886

CAREER: South Farnborough/Crystal Palace trial/SOUTHAMPTON Mar 1907/South Farnborough c.s. 1908/Portsmouth Feb 1911.

Debut v Queen's Park Rangers (h) 13.4.07

Edward Inkerman Bell was the son of a soldier in the 7th Regiment, explaining not only his impressive middle name but the fact that, with the family based at Aldershot, his early football was played at Arthur Turner's old club South Farnborough. Like Arthur, Edward was a right-winger but there the similarity ended for he was not in the same class. He later had four Southern League games for Portsmouth at the tail end of the 1911-12 season.

PROMINENT FOOTBALLERS.

E. BELL,
SOUTHAMPTON.

Appearances:
S.L. 4 app. 0 gls.
Total: *4 app. 0 gls.*

BELL, Mark Dickson

Role: Forward 1902-03
5'8" 12st.2lbs.
b. Edinburgh 8 February 1881.

CAREER: Rosebery F.C. Juniors/Edinburgh
St. Bernards/Heart of Midlothian Oct 1900/
SOUTHAMPTON May 1902/Heart of
Midlothian Apr 1903/Fulham May 1904/
Clapton Orient Aug 1907/Leyton c.s.
1910/Fulham Oct-Dec 1915.

Debut v Kettering Town (a) 18.10.02

Awarded his Scottish international cap in 1901
versus Wales, Mark Bell had played all his
football in Edinburgh preceeding his move south
to join Saints in May 1902. Whilst at Hearts he
had won a Cup Winners' Medal in 1901 and was
regarded as a nippy forward, equally at home on
either wing. Plagued by injuries, Mark only
managed nine games for the Saints but his six
goals lifted them to the championship before he
decided to return to Hearts in April 1903. Twelve
months later he was playing for Fulham, helping
them obtain two consecutive Southern League
championships and he spent the rest of his
playing career in London before emigrating to
Australia in 1919.

> **Appearances:**
> *SL: 9 app. 6 gls.*
> *FAC: 3 app. 1 gl.*
> **Total:** *12 app. 7 gls.*

BENALI, Francis Vincent

Role: Full Back 1988-
5'9" 11st.0lbs.
b. Portswood, Southampton 30 December 1968

CAREER: Bellemoor School/Southampton &
Hampshire Schools/Windsor United/
SOUTHAMPTON app. July 1985, pro. Jan 1987.

Debut v Tottenham Hotspur (a) 25.10.88

Francis Benali started out as a forward but
with elevation to first team status came his
conversion to the left-back position. Naturally
aggressive and a stern tackler, his area of
weakness is his distribution when going
forward and this fault has at times earned him
the wrath of the crowd. Franny is, however,
nothing if not a battler and his commitment to
the club's welfare cannot be doubted. With a

Francis Benali

little more thought and concentration he could
yet become a permanent fixture in the side.

> **Appearances:**
> *FL: 35 (12) app. 0 gls.*
> *FAC: 5 app. 0 gls.*
> *LC: 7 (4) app. 0 gls.*
> **Total:** *47 (16) app. 0 gls.*

BENNETT, Paul Reginald

Role: Defender 1971-76
6'0" 12st.6lbs.
b. Southampton 4 February 1952

CAREER: Taunton's School/
SOUTHAMPTON app. July 1968, pro. Nov
1969/Reading July 1976/Aldershot Aug
1979/Road Sea Southampton c.s.
1982/Salisbury c.s. 1987/Eastleigh Oct 1988,
manager Apr-July 1989/Andover Oct 1989.

Debut v Tottenham Hotspur (h) 22.4.72

Local lad Paul Bennett was educated at
Taunton's school before joining the Saints
ground staff. He developed into a sturdy,
tough-tackling defender very much in the
same mould as John McGrath, the man he
followed into the senior side. With the arrival
of the Mel Blyth-Jim Steele central partnership,

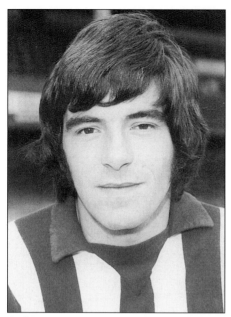

Paul Bennett

Paul suddenly found himself in the reserves and joined Reading in the summer of 1976. After 195 League games at Elm Park he moved to Aldershot where again he made over 100 League appearances.

Appearances:
FL: 116 app. 1 gl.
FAC: 7 app. 1 gl.
LC: 8 app. 0 gls.
Total: *131 app. 2 gls.*

❑ **Saints Note** - *When Paul made his debut against Tottenham at the Dell in April 1972, the man he was marking, Martin Chivers, had, coincidentally, attended the same Southampton school whilst to make matters even more unusual the Spurs centre-half, Mike England, and the Saints centre-forward, Ron Davies, were also ex-pupils of the same North Wales school!*

BENNETT, Robert

Role: Full Back 1912-13
b. Belfast

CAREER: Glentoran/SOUTHAMPTON March 1913

Debut v Norwich City (a) 19.4.13

Bob Bennett became a Saints player soon after his move to the area from his native Ireland. In his only Southern League game at Norwich, the Saints were to suffer a 3-0 defeat which could have been a lot worse as the Canaries hit the woodwork on nine occasions!

Appearances:
SL: 1 app. 0 gls.
Total: *1 app. 0 gls.*

BENSON, Robert William

Role: Full-back 1904-05
5'9" 12st.8lbs.
b. Whitehaven 9 February 1883
d. Highbury, London 19 February 1916.

CAREER: Dunstan Villa/Shankhouse/ Swalwell F.C./Newcastle United Nov 1902/ SOUTHAMPTON Sept 1904/Sheffield United May 1905/Woolwich Arsenal Nov 1913.

Debut v Brighton & Hove Albion (h) 1.10.04

The circumstances of Bob Benson's engagement as a Southampton player were rather unusual. It was decided, soon after the commencement of the 1904-05 season, that the team was weak in the right back position and an official of the club was sent to the North East to hunt for a player. His quest led him to the Newcastle area where he heard of a young miner who, due to fierce competition, had been crowded out of Newcastle's first team. After interviewing Benson and agreeing a fee of £150 with the Magpies, the official triumphantly returned South with his "catch". Bob's form was immediately impressive; big and bold, he was a terror to opposition forwards, often snuffing out their moves with his sense of anticipation. He also developed an unorthodox method of

PROMINENT FOOTBALLERS.

R. BENSON.

penalty taking. After having a team-mate place the ball on the spot he would run from inside his own penalty area belting the ball towards the goal. The wisdom of such a tactic was debatable as he never actually converted a penalty for the Saints although, after a £150 transfer to Sheffield United, it is recorded he perfected his run-up somewhat! At Bramall Lane Bob was an F.A. tourist to South Africa in 1910 and continued to impress when, following his transfer to Arsenal in 1913, he won an England cap. Upon the outbreak of war he retired from playing and found employment in a munitions factory but, in February 1916, was persuaded to play for Arsenal as a late substitute. He collapsed during the game, after bursting a blood vessel, and died in the Highbury dressing room soon afterwards.

Appearances:
SL: 19 app. 0 gls.
FAC: 3 app. 0 gls.
Total: *22 app. 0 gls.*

BERNARD, Eugene Henri Georges

Role: Goalkeeper 1936-37
5'10" 11st.0lbs.
b. Southampton 3 June 1914
d. Southampton 31 August 1973

CAREER: Taunton's School/ SOUTHAMPTON am Nov 1933/Winchester City/Ryde Sports/Southampton 'A' team manager 1945-46/Bitterne Nomads 1946/ Southampton 'A' team coach 1952.
Debut v Chesterfield (h) 29.8.36

Eugene Bernard was an amateur goalkeeper who made two appearances at the beginning of the 1936-37 season when regular goalkeeper, Bert Scriven, was indisposed. A bad hand injury precipitated his retirement from League football but he did turn out for the Saints on several occasions during the war and, in 1946, he was appointed coach to the club's youngsters. He later worked in the insurance business.

Appearances:
FL: 2 app. 0 gls.
Total: *2 app. 0 gls.*

BERRY, Michael James

Mike Berry

Role: Full Back 1974-75
5'8" 10st.8lbs.
b. Lambourn 14 February 1955

CAREER: SOUTHAMPTON app. July 1971, pro. Oct. 1973/ Western Suburbs (Sydney) Jan 1977.

Debut v Cardiff City (h) 22.4.75

Mike Berry's only two League games for the Saints came at the tail end of the 1974-75 season and, with Peter Rodrigues arriving in the close season, chances of a regular first team place evaporated. He was released in January 1977 to emigrate to Australia where he joined the semi-professional Western Suburbs team in Sydney.

Appearances:
F.L. 2 app. 0 gls.
Total: *2 app. 0 gls.*

BEVIS, William Ernest

Role: Forward 1937-47
5'5" 9st.11lbs.
b.Warsash 29 September 1918

CAREER: Gosport Borough/Portsmouth am Feb 1934, pro. July 1936/SOUTHAMPTON June 1937/Winchester City Sept 1947/Cowes 1949/Winchester City 1951/Warsash 1952.

Debut v Aston Villa (h) 4.9.37

Billy Bevis joined Portsmouth as a fifteen year old amateur but failed to make a significant impression at Fratton Park and was relieved to have his career revived by Tom Parker. The Saints' manager's faith in the little right winger was quickly justified as Billy made 68 pre-war League appearances, the highlight being a spectacular hat-trick at Swansea in April 1939. Billy joined the merchant navy as a petty officer gunner during the war and had an eventful time, being torpedoed three times, mined once and spending seven days adrift. After being demobbed in November 1945, Billy returned to the Dell but, after a further 14 games, decided to retire from League football

Billy Bevis

despite an offer from Plymouth. Reverting to his love of the sea, Billy became a yachtsman whilst continuing to turn out for Winchester and Cowes. In 1991 he was living just outside Southampton in Park Gate.

Appearances:
FL: 82 app. 16 gls.
FAC: 5 app. 2 gls.
Total: *87 app. 18 gls.*

❏ **Saints Note** - *When Billy was rescued, after spending seven days floating adrift in the Atlantic, he was staggered to recognise one of his rescuers as former Saints colleague, reserve goalkeeper Alec Warnock! Billy's war-time exploits led to him being awarded the D.S.M. presented at Buckingham Palace by King George VI.*

BINDER, Thomas Edwin

Role: Forward 1912-14
b. Weldon, Northamptonshire
26 January 1889.
d. Caldecott, Leics. 23 August 1969.

CAREER: Kettering/
SOUTHAMPTON am. Mar
1913, pro. June
1913/Kettering c.s.1914.

Debut v Norwich City (a)
19.4.13

Although only an amateur
when he joined Saints from
Kettering, Tom Binder made
his debut within a month and
was, soon after, promoted to
professional status. However,
holding down a regular position proved to be
above him and, after featuring regularly in the
Southern Alliance League during 1913-14, Tom
returned to Kettering.

Tom Binder

> **Appearances:**
> *SL: 10 app. 1 gl.*
> **Total:** *10 app. 1 gl.*

had nonetheless made 43
First Division appearances
when Ted Bates, rarely one to
overspend, gladly parted
with £6,000 to acquire
Ken's services. Initially the
money seemed well spent
as Saints won seven out of
their final ten League
games to finish sixth in
Division Three (South)
therefore qualifying to join
the newly formed Third
Division proper. Struggling
to maintain his form the
following year, Ken
eventually lost his place to
Terry Simpson and was
freed in the ensuing close
season to Chelmsford. His
career later enjoyed a brief
renaissance with Bangor City, his second non-
league team, as they enjoyed a memorable run
in the European Cup Winners' Cup.

> **Appearances:**
> *FL: 34 app. 3 gls.*
> *FAC: 2 app. 0 gls.*
> **Total:** *36 app. 3 gls.*

BIRCH, Kenneth Joseph

Role: Half-back 1957-59
5'9" 11st.9lbs.
b. Birkenhead
31 December 1933

CAREER: Birkenhead Boys/
Bebington Hawks/Everton
Aug 1951/Army (Royal Tank
Corps)/SOUTHAMPTON Mar
1958/Chelmsford City July
1959/Bangor City Aug 1960/
Benoni (Johannesburg) player-
manager Jan 1963.

Debut v Northampton Town
(a) 15.3.58

Although originally a
schoolboy centre-forward,
it was to be in the right-half
position that Ken Birch
made his Everton and
Southampton debuts. Never
a regular at Goodison, he

Ken Birch

BIRD, Frederick Charles

Role: Half-back 1907-08
b. Weymouth, Dorset
April qtr 1884

CAREER: Rushden/
SOUTHAMPTON Dec
1907.

Debut v Brighton & Hove
Albion (a) 18.3.08

Bird's brief and largely
anonymous spell at the
Dell spanned just three
months. Having moved
from Northamptonshire
side Rushden, his one
League appearance came at
Brighton in March 1908
when he replaced the
injured Johnston.

> **Appearances:**
> *SL: 1 app. 0 gls.*
> **Total:** *1 app. 0 gls.*

BISHOP, Alfred Ernest

Role: Forward 1926-27
5'10" 11st.7lbs.
b. Aston July qtr 1906

CAREER: Royal Air Force/Southampton trial
Jan 1923/St. Albans City 1925/
SOUTHAMPTON Aug 1926/Cradley Heath
St. Lukes June 1927/ Barrow May 1928/
Cradley Heath St. Lukes Nov 1928.
Debut v Bradford City (h) 4.9.26

Alf Bishop came to Southampton's attentions
while he was playing representative soccer
with the Royal Air Force and he subsequently
played seven consecutive games early on in
the 1926-27 season, appearing in both inside-
forward positions. His failure to find the net,
and the rise to prominence of Dick Rowley,
dispatched Alf to the reserves where he made
23 appearances before his contract was
cancelled in January 1927. He later briefly
returned to League football with Barrow.

> **Appearances:**
> *FL: 7 app. 0 gls.*
> **Total:** *7 app. 0 gls.*

BLACK, Ian Henderson

Role: Goalkeeper 1947-50
6'0" 12st.4lbs.
b. Aberdeen 27 March 1924

CAREER: Aberdeen Boys Brigade/Aberdeen
St. Clements/(Aberdeen, Chelsea &
Southampton during W.W.2)/
SOUTHAMPTON Dec 1947/Fulham July
1950/Bath City July 1959/Canterbury City
Aug 1962/Brentford coach mid 1960's.
Debut v Leeds United (a) 3.1.48

Ian Black has two special reasons to be
remembered at the Dell. Firstly, he remains the
only man this century to win a Scottish cap
whilst a Southampton player and secondly, he
is the only goalkeeper to concede fewer goals
than the number of games played (95 goals in
97 games). Ian had guested for Southampton
during World War Two and, as he had found
employment as a mechanic in the town
following his demob, he was keen to sign on
for the club. Bill Dodgin was equally eager to
enlist the young Scot as Southampton's

Ian Black

permanent custodian and had to use all his
powers of persuasion plus a thousand pounds
to sway a reluctant Aberdeen into releasing
him. Within a few months he was to win what
transpired to be his only Scottish cap, against
England in April 1948. (Although Scotland lost
2-0 Ian had little to do in the match and
consequently failed to impress). Ian's
inspirational presence between the posts
formed the perfect platform for a talented
Saints side that were to come so
heartbreakingly close to Division One in three
consecutive seasons. He followed Bill Dodgin
to Craven Cottage in the summer of 1950 and
went on to play 263 League games for Fulham.
On one occasion, whilst playing for Fulham
against Leicester City in August 1952, Ian
sustained an injury that forced him to
relinquish his goalkeeper's jersey for an
outfield position and, remarkably, he headed
Fulham's goal as they sank to a 6-1 defeat.

Upon his retirement from League football,
Ian concentrated on running a sports shop

business while developing a keen interest in bowls which led to him representing his adopted county, Surrey. Today he lives in Tolworth and helps run an indoor bowls club.

Appearances:
FL: 97 app. 0 gls.
FAC: 7 app. 0 gls.
Total: *104 app. 0 gls.*

BLACKBURN, Arthur

Role: Full-back 1900-01
5'11" 12st.7lbs.
b. Blackburn 1877

CAREER: Mellor/Blackburn Rovers Mar 1895 /Wellingborough c.s.1898/Blackburn Rovers c.s. 1899/SOUTHAMPTON May1900/ Blackburn Rovers c.s. 1901.

Debut v Luton Town (a) 1.9.00

Secured as a Southampton player in the summer of 1900 Arthur Blackburn was playing in Rovers' reserve eleven whilst keeping fit by voluntarily working on the renovation of a church. Blackburn were reluctant to part company with their young full-back but the financial inducements offered by Southampton were enough to persuade Arthur to try his luck in the south. Strongly built, he never gave less than one hundred per cent but at times his play was too impetuous to be reliable. An ankle injury also plagued his season at the club and once he lost his place in November it was never regained and subsequently he returned to Ewood Park. Arthur was later known to have coached in Rotterdam, Holland.

Appearances:
SL: 9 app. 0 gls.
Total: *9 app. 0 gls.*

❏ **Saints note** - *Arthur's brother Fred played outside-left for West Ham and Blackburn and won two England caps in the 1901-02 season.*

BLACKMORE, William J.

Role: Forward 1912-13
b. Southampton

CAREER: Adelaide/SOUTHAMPTON c.s. 1912/Woolston Sept 1913/ Southampton 1919/Harland & Wolff 1920.

Debut v Northampton Town (a) 12.9.12

Bill Blackmore arrived at the Dell having previously featured in the local junior league with Adelaide. He was initially impressive in the reserves and in September 1912 was drafted into the first eleven at outside right. Throughout the rest of the season Bill made fleeting appearances in the right-wing berth but, in a struggling team, consistency was hard to come by and the following September saw him back in local junior football with Woolston. With the outbreak of the Great War, Bill returned to the Dell, to give valuable service right up until the 1919-20 season when he assisted the reserves in the South Eastern League.

Appearances:
SL: 7 app. 0 gls.
FAC: 2 app. 0 gls.
Total: *9 app. 0 gls.*

BLAKE, John Joseph

Role: Forward 1906-1920
5'10" 11st.4lbs.
b. Belchamp Walter October qtr. 1882
d. Southampton 23 February 1931

CAREER: C.E.Y.M.S./ Ilford/Tottenham Hotspur 1905 in Western League/Cowes/ SOUTHAMPTON am. 1905, pro.1908/ Thornycrofts Mar 1920.

Debut v Millwall (h) 6.10.06
* *(scored on debut)*

Joe Blake was a draughtsman by trade. A Cowes player, he guested for Southampton's second team on

Joe Blake

several occasions in 1905 and it wasn't until transferring his employment to the Thornycrofts shipyard that he was to play on a regular basis for Saints. Equally at home on either wing, Joe posed many problems to opponents. He was fleet-footed, could dribble the ball with skill and, most importantly for a winger, was able to centre the ball with pin point exactness. He remained a regular member of the side until 1915, when due to the war effort his services were required on a larger scale at Thornycrofts. During the hostilities Joe played mainly for the works side although periodically he appeared in a Saints' shirt and in 1919 he resumed his career at the Dell, making a single appearance before being transferred to Thornycrofts in March 1920.

Appearances:
SL: 148 app. 13 gls.
FAC: 6 app. 0 gls.
Total: *154 app. 13 gls.*

BLAKE, Mark Christopher

Role: Defender 1985-89
6'0" 12st.4lbs.
b. Portsmouth 17 December 1967

CAREER: Wildern & Southampton Schools/ SOUTHAMPTON app. July 1984, pro. Dec 1985 (Colchester United-loan-Sept to Oct 1989) (Shrewsbury Town-loan-Apr 1990), transferred Aug 1990.

Debut v Tottenham Hotspur (a) 5.5.86

An England Youth International, Mark was given his debut when an injury crisis had virtually eliminated all regular defenders from consideration for the last game of the 1985-86 season. With Mark Wright still not fully recovered from a broken leg, Mark kept his place for the opening six games of the next season but a 5-1 defeat at Old Trafford signalled a return to the reserves. From then on Mark struggled to become a regular and, although sound enough, he lacked that extra bit of pace which is often the difference between an average and a good defender. In the summer of 1990 Mark joined Asa Hartford's Shrewsbury for a fee of £100,000.

Appearances:
FL: 18 app. 2 gls.
FAC: 3 app. 0 gls.
LC: 2 app. 0 gls.
Total: *23 app. 2 gls.*

Mark Blake

BLUFF, Edgar Underwood

Role: Forward 1904-06
5'7" 11st.2lbs.
b. Attercliffe, Sheffield June 1881

CAREER: First Army Corps/Reading (trial) Feb 1903/SOUTHAMPTON Apr 1904/Sheffield United Sept 1905/ Birmingham Dec 1907/St. Helens Town c.s. 1908.

Debut v Wellingborough Town (h) 24.9.04

Edgar Bluff joined the Yorkshire Light Infantry in March 1900 and served for four years until the Saints, anxious to acquire his full-time services, paid for his discharge. His army discipline and training served him in good stead and, introduced to the side in September 1904, he displayed a natural goalscoring ability. His heading was a strong feature of his game and he formed an exciting partnership with Fred Harrison which resulted in recognition by the England International selectors as first reserve in a match against Ireland in 1905. Just after the commencement of the 1905-06 season, Edgar was transferred to Sheffield United, and although reluctant to leave he was persuaded that the move to his home town would further his career. After representing Sheffield versus Glasgow his form fell away and he was never the force at Bramall Lane that he was at the Dell. A year at Birmingham was then followed by a spell in Lancashire with St. Helens Town.

Appearances:
SL: 27 app. 10 gls.
FAC: 3 app. 3 gls.
Total: *30 app. 13 gls.*

BLYTH, Melvin Bernard

Role: Defender 1974-77
6'1" 11st.11lbs.
b. Norwich 28 July 1944

CAREER: Norwich City am/Great Yarmouth/ Scunthorpe United Nov 1967/Crystal Palace July 1968/SOUTHAMPTON Sept 1974 (Crystal Palace-loan-Nov 1977)/Margate July 1978/Millwall Nov 1978/Andover Sept to Oct 1982.

Debut v Bristol City (a) 21.9.74

Saints paid £60,000 for Mel Blyth in September 1974 and he quickly became a favourite with the fans. A cool and commanding figure in defence, he was voted the supporters' Player of the Year (1974-75) and quickly formed an effective partnership with Jim Steele that was to be the mainstay of Saints' victorious F.A.

Robert Blyth

Cup run of 1976. Chris Nicholl's arrival in the summer of 1977 signalled the end of 33-year-old Mel's stint at the Dell and he completed his League career at Millwall. Although an electrician by trade, Mel later became a driving instructor, however, by the time he attended a reunion of the 1976 FA Cup team, in November 1990, he was running his own building firm.

Appearances:
FL: 104 (1) app. 6 gls.
FAC: 15 app. 0 gls.
LC: 2 app. 0 gls.
Total: *121 (1) app. 6 gls.*

BLYTH, Robert Roberts Taylor

Role: Forward 1922-23
5'8" 11st.6lbs.
b. Muirkirk, Scotland 2 June 1900

CAREER: Portsmouth Apr 1921/ SOUTHAMPTON Jan 1922.

Debut v Derby County (h) 9.12.22

Mel Blyth

Robert Blyth arrived at the Dell after making 10 appearances in a Pompey shirt and had a brief run in Saints' first team when Charles Brown was injured. He had left the club by the end of the 1922-23 season for pastures unknown.

Appearances:
FL: 8 app. 0 gls.
FAC: 1 app. 0 gls.
Total: *9 app. 0 gls.*

❏ **Saints note** - *Robert's Uncle William was a Portsmouth player between 1903-05 whilst his father, Bob Blyth, was a player between 1899 and 1901 and then player-manager between 1901-1903.*

Tommy Bogan

BOGAN, Thomas

Role: Forward 1951-53
b. Glasgow 18 May 1920

CAREER: Blantyre Celtic/Renfrew Juniors/ Hibernian 1944/Glasgow Celtic 1946/Preston North End Sept 1948/Manchester United Aug 1949/Aberdeen Mar 1951/SOUTHAMPTON Dec 1951/Blackburn Rovers Aug 1953/ Macclesfield Town June 1954.

Debut v Barnsley (h) 22.12.51

Tommy Bogan was Sid Cann's last signing for the Saints and he struggled to make an impression in his 21 month stay at the Dell. He had had his finest seasons immediately after the war with Celtic when he made 34 League appearances and represented the Scottish League. After giving up football Tom was employed in the newspaper industry with the Daily Express and the Manchester Evening News.

Appearances:
FL: 8 app. 2 gls.
FAC: 1 app. 0 gls.
Total: *9 app. 2 gls.*

❏ **Saints note** - *Tom probably has the shortest international record of all time, having been selected to represent Scotland in a war time international he was carried off injured after just 60 seconds! Tom also has Sir Matt Busby as a relation, having married his niece.*

BOND, Kevin John

Role: Defender 1984-88
6'0" 13st.7 lbs.
b. West Ham 22 June 1957

CAREER: A.F.C. Bournemouth app July 1972/Norwich City am June 1974, pro Apr 1976/Seattle Sounders Feb 1981/Manchester City Sept 1981/SOUTHAMPTON Sept 1984/ A.F.C. Bournemouth Aug 1988.

Debut v Queen's Park Rangers (h) 29.9.84

Kevin Bond's first three English League clubs were Bournemouth, Norwich and Manchester City and his life as a professional footballer cannot have been made easy by the fact that his often controversial father, John, was the manager of each club when Kevin made his debuts.

Kevin Bond

Overcoming the inevitable jibes he assumed a confident approach to the game and gained England 'B' team honours before having a spell in the N.A.S.L. with Seattle Sounders. Lawrie McMenemy paid a bargain £60,000 for Kevin in September 1984 and he quickly became not only a fixture in the defence but team captain during the 1986-87 season. A move to Bournemouth, a club he had originally joined as an apprentice, was followed by a serious injury which threatened to end his career but happily he fought back into first team contention.

Appearances:
FL: 139 (1) app. 6 gls.
FAC: 11 app. 0 gls.
LC: 18 app. 0 gls.
Total: *168 (1) app. 6 gls.*

❏ **Saints note** - *It could safely be said that Kevin was good in the air, as he gained his private pilots licence in 1987!*

BOULTON, Colin Donald

Role: Goalkeeper
1976-77
5'10" 11st.7lbs.
b. Cheltenham
12 September 1945

CAREER: Charlton Kings/ Gloucestershire Police/Derby County Aug 1964 (SOUTHAMPTON-loan-Sept 1976)/Tulsa Roughnecks Mar 1978/Los Angeles Aztecs May 1979/Lincoln City July 1980.

Debut v Burnley (a) 11.9.76

Colin Boulton

Colin Boulton came to Southampton on loan from Derby, a club he had served admirably. Although small in stature as goalkeepers go, he more than made up for this in agility. Three seasons in the N.A.S.L. were followed by a spell at Lincoln but a leg injury finally forced him out of the game and he became a policeman.

Appearances:
FL: 5 app. 0 gls.
Total: *5 app. 0 gls.*

BOWDEN, James William

Role: Half-back 1906-07
5'8" 11st.12lbs.
b. Wolverhampton August 1880
d. Wolverhampton 25 May 1951

CAREER: Yardley Methodists/Erdington
F.C./Handsworth Rovers/Aston Villa am Jan
1903/West Bromwich Albion June
1904/SOUTHAMPTON Aug 1906/ Grimsby
Town Aug 1907/Hyde United Mar 1909/
Stourbridge/ (retired 1916).

Debut v Swindon Town (a) 1.9.06

James Bowden was installed as the club's
regular centre-half for the 1906-07 season and,
although handicapped by a lack of height,
impressed the fans with his stylish neatness
when in
possession. For
reasons unknown
he moved to
Grimsby but only
enjoyed nineteen
games for the
Mariners before
dropping into
non-league
football.

   Appearances:
   SL: 29 app. 0 gls.
   FAC: 2 app.
   0 gls.
   Total:
   31 app. 0 gls.

❏ **Saints note -**
*James Bowden had
a lucky escape prior
to joining the
Saints when he was
involved in a
shooting accident
and a bullet passed
through his left
arm.*

*Right:
James Bowden
Above:
Oswald Bowden*

BOWDEN, Oswald

Role: Forward 1938-39
5'10" 11st.7lbs.
b. Byker, Newcastle 7 September 1912
d. Newcastle 20 May 1977

CAREER:
Newcastle United
Swifts/Newcastle
United am. Oct
1929/Derby
County May 1930
/Nottingham
Forest June 1935/
Brighton June
1937/
SOUTHAMPTON
June 1938.

Debut v Tottenham Hotspur (h) 27.8.38

Oswald Bowden had spent most of his
League career playing in the reserves
and his season at the Dell was to prove
no exception as he had only two first
team outings compared to 25 games
for the seconds. Freed in the close
season prior to the outbreak of WW2
he never played League soccer again.

   Appearances:
   FL: 2 app. 0 gls.
   Total: *2 app. 0 gls.*

BOWEN, Lionel Francis William

Role: Full-Back 1936-37
5'10" 11st.7lbs.
b. Sholing, Southampton
31 December 1915

CAREER: Sholing School/Sholing St.
Mary's/Crystal Palace am/
SOUTHAMPTON am Sept 1934, pro
Oct 1934/Metropolitan Police
1937/Winchester City.

Debut v Barnsley (a) 24.4.37

Lionel Bowen was locally born but
managed to arrive at the Dell via
Crystal Palace with whom he was an
amateur. Although he joined the Saints

Lionel Bowen

in September 1934 he had to wait two and a half years, during which time he made 91 London Combination appearances, before having two first team outings at left back. During the summer of 1937 Lionel applied, and was accepted, to join the Metropolitan Police training college so beginning a long and meritorious career in the force that saw him eventually reach a high rank in the Hampshire Constabulary.

Appearances:
FL: 2 app. 0 gls.
Total: *2 app. 0 gls.*

❏ **Saints note** - *During the war Lionel was on the night-time beat and had cause to admonish a man who had had 'one too many'. He was amused to recognise the inebriated reveller as none other than Billy Boyd his one-time Dell team mate.*

BOWMAN, Thomas

Role: Half-back 1901-04
5'8" 11st.8lbs.
b. Tarbolton, Strathclyde 26 October 1873
d. Southampton 27 August 1958

CAREER: Annbank 1891/Blackpool June 1896/Aston Villa Oct 1897/

SOUTHAMPTON May 1901/ Portsmouth May 1904/Eastleigh Athletic c.s. 1909-retired 1912.

Debut v New Brompton (h) 7.9.01

Scottish born, Tommy Bowman came to the Dell in May 1901 with a fine reputation which had been gained over three seasons at Villa Park as a strong determined centre-half. A "fixture" in the Saints half back line for three years, he missed only five League games within that period and was an ever-present in the championship side of 1904. Described as "hard to beat" Tommy became the cornerstone of a fine Saints team that started the 1900's in much the same successful fashion as they had finished the 1890's. In 1904 he made the short move along the south coast to join local rivals Portsmouth and then dropped out of top class soccer to join Eastleigh Athletic in 1909. A boiler scaler by trade, Tommy later worked for many years in Southampton Docks.

Appearances:
SL: 88 app. 2 gls.
FAC: 13 app. 1 gl.
Total: *101 app. 3 gls.*

❏ **Saints note** - *Tommy Bowman represented the Anglo-Scots versus the Scots in 1902.*

Billy Boyd

BOYD, William Gillespie

Role: Forward 1936-37
5'7" 10st.11lbs.
b. Cambuslang, Scotland 27 November 1905
d. Bristol 14 December 1967

CAREER: Regent Star/Larkhill Thistle/Clyde
1930/Sheffield United Dec 1933/Manchester
United Feb1935/Workington Dec 1935/
Luton Town Jan 1936/SOUTHAMPTON July
1936/Weymouth Aug 1937.

Debut v Chesterfield (h) 29.8.36

Billy Boyd began his working life as a tube
fitter in a Clyde shipyard and, whilst playing
for junior side Larkhill Thistle, scored over two
hundred goals in just three seasons. Such
prodigious scoring led to a contract with
Clyde, the first of six League clubs for whom
he was to play. By the time Billy reached
Southampton he was past his prime and,
perhaps because he was renowned for having
an erratic temperament, it was not surprising
that his sojourn at the Dell was short.

Appearances:
FL: 19 app. 7 gls.
Total: *19 app. 7 gls.*

BOYER, Philip John

Role: Forward 1977-81
5'8" 10st.4lbs.
b. Nottingham 25 January 1949

CAREER: Musters Road School, Nottingham/
Rushcliffe Representative XI/Derby County
app. Aug 1965, pro Nov 1966/York City July
1968/A.F. C. Bournemouth Dec 1970/Norwich
City Feb 1974/SOUTHAMPTON Aug 1977/
Manchester City Nov 1980/Bulova (Hong
Kong) Feb 1982-Apr 1983/Grantham July
1983/Stamford/Shepshed Charterhouse/
Grantham Dec 1985 player-manager, resigned
Feb 1987/Spalding.

Debut v Brighton & Hove Albion (h) 20.8.77

Philip Boyer must be one of the few men in
football who can question Brian Clough's
judgement as a manager as he was freed from
Derby by Clough as a 19-year-old without ever
making the Rams' first team. At York, Phil, or
"Charlie" as he was nicknamed, formed a
partnership with Ted MacDougall that was to
blossom and flourish at Bournemouth,
Norwich and finally Southampton. Arriving at
the Dell to replace Mick Channon, Phil's neat
and intelligent forward play paid immediate
dividends and he was top goalscorer as Saints
finished runners-up in Division Two. In
1979-80, in harness with Channon, Phil scored

Phil Boyer

41

three hat-tricks on his way to netting 23 League goals, making him Division One's top scorer. Kevin Keegan's arrival precipitated Phil's departure to Manchester City for £220,000 (Saints making a profit of £90,000), but an injury ended his League career soon after his arrival. Phil has since scouted for Northampton Town, Blackpool and more recently (1991) Maidstone United.

Appearances:
FL: 138 app. 49 gls.
FAC: 11 app. 5 gls.
LC: 13 app. 7 gls.
Total: *162 app. 61 gls.*

❏ **Saints note** - *Like Alan Ball, Phil is one of a select number of players to make over 100 League appearances for four different clubs and he was also the first Norwich City player to win an England cap whilst at Carrow Road. His appearance, which was to be his only full England international, was against Wales in March 1976.*

BOYES, Kenneth Cecil

Role: Forward 1919-22
5'9" 11st.0lbs.
b. Southampton 17 November 1895
d. Eastleigh 6 October 1963

Ken Boyes

CAREER: SOUTHAMPTON am May 1914, pro. Oct 1919/Bristol Rovers June 1922/Poole July 1923/Weymouth July 1924/Southampton Civil Service c.s.1925/Pirelli General until 1940.
Debut v Reading (a) 22.10.19

A member of Hampshire County Cricket Club's ground staff, Ken Boyes became an amateur footballer in May 1914. His love of sports found ample expression throughout his service in the First World War when he not only represented his battalion at cricket and football but was also the regimental sprinting champion. Picking up his football career in October 1919, this time as a professional, Ken found his first team opportunities at the Dell limited somewhat due to the form shown by Moore and Foxall and moved to Bristol Rovers on a free transfer. He made just two appearances in one season for the Rovers before entering non-league football. In 1928 he became Pirelli General's groundsman, overseeing the laying of the Dew Lane pitch, a position he held until retirement in 1960.

Appearances:
FL: 4 app. 0 gls.
SL: 4 app. 1 gl.
Total: *8 app. 1 gl.*

❏ **Saints note** - *Ken's younger brother Stuart played 474 matches for Hampshire County Cricket Club as well as touring India, Burma and Ceylon with the M.C.C. In 1938 he took 9-57 in an innings for Hampshire against Somerset.*

BRADBURN, George

Role: Centre-half 1919-22
5'10" 12st.11lbs.
b. Wolverhampton April qtr 1894

CAREER: Walsall 1914/SOUTHAMPTON May 1919/Walsall May 1922.
Debut v Cardiff City (a) 6.9.19

A pre-war player for Walsall, George Bradburn moved south upon the outbreak of the Great War and was employed at the Whitehead Torpedo Works in Weymouth. He played in the Garrison League throughout the war and made one guest appearance wearing Southampton colours in 1917. At the war's conclusion he returned to Walsall but was secured by Southampton on a permanent basis in May 1919. He was a strong, rugged centre-

George Bradburn

Arthur Bradford

Arthur Bradford was one of the most loyal players ever to appear on the books of Southampton Football Club and, when he left in 1936, only Albert Shelley and Stan Woodhouse had made more appearances. Ideally built for a centre-back role Arthur's versatility was put to good use and in emergencies he would even play in goal. The club gave him two benefits in recognition of his outstanding service and when he retired from League football he remained in town to run The Plume of Feathers public house in St. Mary's street. Arthur played one season for Cowes, winning a Hampshire Senior Cup Winners medal, before finally hanging up his boots.

Appearances:
FL: 305 app. 6 gls.
FAC: 14 app. 1 gl.
Total: *319 app. 7 gls.*

BRADLEY, John

Role: Forward 1946-48
5'10" 12st.7lbs.
b. South Kirkby 27 November 1916

CAREER: South Kirkby Colliery/Huddersfield Town Nov 1935/Swindon Town Aug 1936/ Chelsea June 1938/SOUTHAMPTON May 1939/(guest for Reading, Luton Town, Blackpool, Millwall, Aldershot, Rotherham during World War Two)/Bolton Wanderers Oct 1947/Norwich City Nov 1950/Great Yarmouth player-manager July 1952-55.

Debut v Newport County (h) FAC 5.1.46.

Jack Bradley moved to the Dell just prior to the outbreak of war and had to wait some seven years until he made his official League debut in the opening game of the 1946-47 season. Big and strong, Jack had a powerful left foot that he put to good use during his short spell with the Saints. His goal scoring record attracted the attention of numerous bigger clubs and he was sold to Bolton in an £8,000 deal that saw William Wrigglesworth move in the opposite

half and immediately challenged Alec Campbell for the first team berth during the club's last season as a Southern League club. Eventually Campbell forced his way back into the team and, after making only six first team appearances in two seasons, George was, at his own request, given a free transfer back to Walsall.

Appearances:
SL: 28 app 0 gls.
FL: 6 app. 0 gls.
FAC: 3 app. 0 gls.
Total: *37 app. 0 gls.*

❑ **Saints note** - *Whilst in Southampton Reserves George was twice selected to represent the Southern League - against the Welsh League in September 1921 and against the Central League in March 1922.*

BRADFORD, James Arthur

Role: Half-back 1923-36
5'11" 12st.0lbs.
b. Walsall 3 July 1902
d. Southampton 13 April 1944

CAREER: Bloxwich All Saints/Talbot Stead Tube works/SOUTHAMPTON am Sept 1922, pro Nov 1922/Cowes c.s.1936.

Debut v Crystal Palace (a) 18.4.24

Jack Bradley

direction. He later spent twenty-seven years as a publican in the Norwich area and today lives on the East Anglian coast.

Appearances:
FL: 49 app. 22 gls.
FAC: 6 app. 3 gls.
Total: *55 app. 25 gls.*

❏ **Saints note** - *Jack's father, Martin played for Grimsby, Sheffield Wednesday and Bristol Rovers, while his uncle James was on the books of Stoke, Liverpool and Reading.*

BRADLEY, W. J.

Role: Forward 1912-13
5'8" 12st.0lbs.
b. Liverpool

CAREER: 8th Hussars (Tidworth)/ SOUTHAMPTON April 1913/Andover 1914.
Debut v Reading (h) 12.4.13

A soldier based at Tidworth, W. Bradley assisted his regiment to win the Cavalry Cup just two days before making his debut for the Saints in April 1913. Infused with plenty of dash he showed a fair degree of promise but his army commitments restricted his availability and his appearances in a red and white shirt during the 1913-14 season were all in the reserve team. During the war years he appeared in Saints colours at regular intervals, scoring seven times in ten South Hampshire War League games during the 1917-18 season.

Appearances:
SL: 3 app. 1 gl.
Total: *3 app. 1 gl.*

BREWIS, John Thomas

Role: Forward 1931-37
5'8" 11st.4lbs.
b. Tynemouth 21 April 1907
d. Portsmouth 5 April 1975

CAREER: West Stanley Aug 1928/Newark Town Aug 1929/York City July 1930/ SOUTHAMPTON Mar 1932/Newport (I.O.W.) c.s. 1937.
Debut v Oldham Athletic (a) 19.3.32

Tom Brewis was signed from York by George Kay and in his five years at the Dell he was in

Tom Brewis

and out of the team without ever truly establishing himself. The highlight of his spell at Southampton was the scoring of a fine hat-trick against Manchester United in September 1932. Tom was not a tall man but had the knack of hanging in the air to head improbable goals and, in the 1932-33 campaign, he netted a creditable ten times in 31 appearances. In the last few years before the outbreak of World War Two he assisted Newport before joining the Navy in 1939. He survived the war and later became a hotelier, running the Durham Hotel in Northam, Southampton.

Appearances:
FL: 118 app. 18 gls.
FAC: 1 app. 0 gls.
Total: *119 app. 18 gls.*

BRIGGS, Fred

Role: Forward 1938-39
5'9" 11st.0lbs.
b. Rotherham 15 August 1914
d. Rotherham October 1985

CAREER: Mexborough Town/Wombwell 1932/Rotherham United May 1932/Reading June 1935/ SOUTHAMPTON May 1938/ (Fulham, Wrexham, Watford, Accrington Stanley during World War Two).
Debut v Newcastle United (a) 24.9.38

Tom Parker signed Fred Briggs on a free transfer from Reading in an effort to find a goalscorer to complement Harry Osman. Fred settled in quickly and his 14 goals in 36 games meant he finished the 1938-39 season as Saints' top scorer. He stayed at the Dell for one wartime season but moved to Wrexham sometime in 1940. He later guested for Fulham, Watford and Accrington Stanley but never re-appeared in post-war League soccer.

Fred Briggs

Appearances:
FL: 36 app 14 gls.
FAC: 1 app. 0 gls.
Total: *37 app. 14 gls.*

BRITTLETON, Samuel

Role: Forward 1909-10
5'8" 11st.0lbs.
b. Winsford July qtr. 1885

CAREER: Stockport County Aug 1905/Preston North End Feb 1908/Chorley 1908/ SOUTHAMPTON c.s.1909.

Debut v Queen's Park Rangers (a) 25.9.09

The younger brother of the renowned John Brittleton, the Sheffield Wednesday and England forward, Sam was signed from non-league Chorley. His acquisition had been made from under the noses of some of the League's big clubs including Manchester City who had been arguing with Chorley over the size of the fee. Sam's form was to fluctuate during his season at the Dell. Sometimes brilliant, sometimes hopeless, he consequently found himself in and out of the team and, not surprisingly, moved back to the north of England in the summer of 1910. The Southern League granted him a free transfer in March 1911 although he never appeared in senior football again.

Appearances:
SL: 17 app 3 gls.
Total: *17 app. 3 gls.*

Thomas Broad

BROAD, Thomas Higginson

Role: Forward
1924-25
5'10" 12st.0lbs.
b. Stalybridge 31 July 1887
d. 1950's

CAREER: Redgate Albion/Denton Wanderers/ Openshaw Lads Club/Manchester City (trial) 1904/West Bromwich Albion Sept 1905/ Chesterfield Feb 1908/Oldham Athletic May 1909/Bristol City May 1912/Manchester City Mar 1919/Stoke May 1921/ SOUTHAMPTON July 1924/Weymouth Sep 1925/Rhyl Athletic c.s.1926.

Debut v Stockport County (a) 11.10.24

Thomas Broad has the dubious distinction of being the oldest man ever signed by the Saints, arriving at the Dell just three and a half weeks short of his 37th birthday. He provided right wing cover for Bill Henderson during the 1924-25 season and then moved to Weymouth in the summer.

Appearances:
FL: 9 app. 0 gls.
Total: *9 app. 0 gls.*

Sam Brittleton

BROOKS, Richard

Role: Full-back 1912-14
5'10" 12st.8lbs.
b. Reading

CAREER: Kings Royal
Rifles/Royal Garrison
Artillery (Essex) 1908/
Eastleigh Athletic 1910/
Reading Mar 1911/
SOUTHAMPTON Aug
1912.

Debut v Brentford (a)
21.3.13

After leaving the army
Richard Brooks found
employment at Eastleigh
Railway works and,
playing for Eastleigh
Athletic in the Hampshire
League, attracted the
attention of Reading. He
moved to the Dell in 1912
and was a strong, burly
full-back with, at times,
an inclination to be over-
exuberant. He rejoined
the army upon the
outbreak of the war,
surviving to once more
don a Saints shirt during
the 1919-20 season when
he featured in the
reserves.

Appearances:
SL: 19 app. 0 gls.
Total: *19 app. 0 gls.*

Richard Brooks

BROPHY, Harry Frank

Role: Forward & Half-back 1938-39
6'0" 12st.0lbs.
b. Leicester 22 October 1916

CAREER: Islington Schoolboys 1929-33/
Arsenal am 1933, pro May 1936 (Canterbury
Waverley (Kent League)-loan)/Margate 1935-
36 (Arsenal nursery)(Brighton & Hove Albion-
loan-Sept 1936)/SOUTHAMPTON May 1938/
(Follands, Bradford Park Avenue,
Huddersfield Town, Fulham, Crystal Palace
during World War Two)/Nuneaton Town

1945/Corinthian F.C. (Brisbane)
1949/ Queensland and Australia
team coach 1952-56/Mauritius
manager-coach 1957-59/Hakoah
Sports (Melbourne) coach
1961/Hellenic F.C. (Brisbane)
coach 1961/Sydney F.C. Prague
manager-coach 1962.

Debut v Tottenham Hotspur (h)
*27.8.38 * (scored on debut)*

Harry Brophy tasted glory as a
schoolboy when he captained
Islington to success in the 1931
English Schools Shield and his
maturity was duly noted by
Arsenal who offered him terms
in 1933. Whilst on loan at
Brighton in 1937 he broke a leg
(coincidentally in a tackle with
Fred Briggs who he was later to
partner in the Southampton
forward line), and Arsenal
decided to terminate his
contract. Fortunately, when at
Highbury, Harry had caught the
eye of Tom Parker and the
Saints' manager moved quickly
to secure his free transfer in May
1938. Although a half-back he
made his debut in the number 9
shirt against Tottenham in the
opening game of the 1938-39
season and scored. He netted in
the next two games, became
injured and then reappeared
two matches later at left-half.
Later the same season he was
also to occupy the right-half,
centre-half and full-back positions, proving his
versatility. Upon the outbreak of war Harry
initially enlisted in the Police Force but later
decided to join the
Merchant Navy
where, serving on
the hospital ship, 'St.
Andrew', he spent
five days in Dunkirk
during the
evacuation. He
emigrated to
Queensland in 1949

Harry Brophy

and proceeded to make a sizeable contribution to the development of Australian soccer. Following a brief stint coaching in the Indian Ocean with the Mauritius national team he returned to England in 1960 to gain coaching qualifications at Lilleshall before once more deciding to try his luck with a variety of club sides in Melbourne, Sydney and Brisbane. In 1989 he moved back to England and now lives in Bedford where his passion for football remains undimmed.

Appearances:
FL: 37 app. 5 gls.
FAC: 1 app. 0 gls.
Total: *38 app. 5 gls.*

BROWN, Albert

Role: Forward 1901-03
5'11" 12st.6lbs.
b. Tamworth, Staffs April qtr. 1879

CAREER: Atherstone Star/Tamworth/Aston Villa Feb 1898/ SOUTHAMPTON May 1901/Queen's Park Rangers Oct 1902/Preston North End May 1904/Blackpool March 1906.

Debut v New Brompton (h) 7.9.01

Having been secured from Aston Villa together with Tommy Bowman in 1901, Albert Brown soon considerably enhanced his reputation as a goalscorer at Southampton. Nicknamed "the Tamworth sprinter", Albert was thought at the time to be the "fastest forward in the kingdom" and, considering he was the owner of a powerful shot and was supported by the celebrated skills of the Turners on either wing, his rise to nationwide fame was mercurial. A hat-trick was not an unusual event for Albert and he entered the Southampton record

COPE'S "CLIPS" CIGARETTES

No. 416.—BROWN Southampton
Noted Footballers

books in December 1901 when he notched seven out of a total of eleven goals against Northampton Town at the Dell. As well as securing a record which stands to this day, he went on to score 25 goals in almost as many matches during the 1901-02 season adding, for good measure, another four goals in the F.A. Cup run to the final. He sustained an injury during the following summer and struggled to regain his place from newcomer Jack Fraser. After just one League outing he was, surprisingly, sold to Queen's Park Rangers in the October, and he eventually wound up his career with two Lancashire clubs. Albert's date of death is unknown, but in 1941 he was living in Birmingham.

Appearances:
SL: 26 app. 25 gls.
FAC: 8 app. 4 gls.
Total: *34 app. 29 gls.*

BROWN, Arthur Charles

Role: Goalkeeper 1910-12
b. Cowes July qtr. 1888

CAREER: Hartley College/SOUTHAMPTON am 1906/Cowes am/Portsmouth am 1907/SOUTHAMPTON am c.s. 1910/ Wanderers (Nova Scotia) 1912.

Debut v Brighton & Hove Albion (h) 24.9.10

Arthur Brown (*left*) signed on for Southampton in 1906 while still a student at Hartley College. He had subsequent spells at Cowes and Portsmouth before registering with the Saints once more and this time he made the first-team goalkeeping position his own with some outstanding performances. In 1912 he was selected as reserve goalkeeper for the British Olympic team in Stockholm. Soon afterwards he terminated his association with the club to emigrate to Canada where he took up a position as Chief Civil Engineer on a £6 million dock scheme in Halifax, Nova Scotia.

Appearances:
SL: 39 app. 0 gls.
FAC: 2 app. 0 gls.
Total: *41 app. 0 gls.*

BROWN, Charles

Charlie Brown

Role: Forward 1919-24
5'7" 10st.10lbs.
*b. Stakeford 14 January
1898
d. Southampton 2
February 1979*

CAREER:
Stakeford United/
SOUTHAMPTON Mar
1920/Queen's Park Rangers Aug 1924/Poole
F.C. Aug 1926/ Supermarine Sports Oct 1927.
Debut v Plymouth Argyle (a) 17.4.20

Charlie Brown was signed from North Eastern
side Stakeford and partnered Dominy and
Moore in Saints' last three matches as a
Southern League side. Competing with Barratt
for the outside-right position his most
consistent season was 1922-23 by which time
his rival had departed for Birmingham.
Charlie's quick, crafty wing play had a subtle
way of drawing a defence before centring, but
playing before the Dell crowd seemed to
unsettle him and most of his best games for the
Saints came in away matches. He enjoyed two
good seasons at Queen's Park Rangers before
returning to the Southampton area to live.
Charles was employed at Vosper Thornycroft
Ltd. in 1936 until his retirement in 1967.

Appearances:
*SL: 3 app. 0 gls.
FL: 80 app. 6 gls.
FAC: 10 app. 0 gls.*
Total: *93 app. 6 gls.*

BROWN, Edward

Role: Forward 1950-52
5'10" 11st.2lbs.
b. Preston, Lancashire 28 February 1926

CAREER: Preston North End Aug 1948/
SOUTHAMPTON Sept 1950/Coventry City
Mar 1952/Birmingham City Oct 1954/Leyton
Orient Jan 1959/Scarborough player-coach
Feb 1961/Stourbridge player-manager
1964-65/Wigan Rovers player-manager and
pools promoter July 1965/Broughton
Amateurs manager.

Debut v Leeds United (h) 9.9.50

Born and brought up in Preston, Eddie Brown

initially spent two years in Guernsey in the
hope of becoming a religious teacher but
returned to his home town in August 1948. He
presented himself at Deepdale one day and
said: "I am a centre-forward". Preston took
him at his word and he scored a hat-trick on
his debut for the 'A' team. After thirty-six
League games Eddie arrived at the Dell in an
exchange deal that sent Charlie Wayman in the
opposite direction and cannot have been
envied as he attempted to win over the
heartbroken Saints' faithful. Fortunately, not
only was Eddie an extrovert but he had no
little skill to match and, helped by his pace and
deadly left foot, came close to emulating his
revered predecessor's scoring achievements.
Unfortunately for the fans, Eddie failed to
settle in the South and was granted a transfer
to Coventry. He later gained an F.A. Cup
runners-up medal with Birmingham in 1956
and finished his career with a League analysis
of 189 goals from 399 matches. In December
1990 Eddie was living back in Preston while
working for the family carpet firm as a sales
representative. He maintains his interest in
football by coaching Broughton Amateurs
who, five years ago, became the only side in
Lancashire to have completed the Amateur
Cup and League double.

Appearances:
*FL: 57 app. 32 gls.
FAC: 2 app. 2 gls.*
Total: *59 app. 34 gls.*

*Eddie
Brown*

BROWN, George Samuel

Role: Full-back 1909-10
b. Longfleet St. Mary's January qtr 1883.

CAREER: Longfleet St. Mary's/
SOUTHAMPTON Mar 1910/Longfleet St.
Mary's c.s. 1910.

Debut v Bristol Rovers (a) 26.3.10

A fisherman by profession, George Brown had
won Dorset County honours before arriving at
the Dell in March 1910 for a trial period. A tall,
weighty and muscular full-back, he acquitted
himself well in his two games and, although he
was considered up to scratch, George himself
decided to resume his career at sea and re-
signed from his local team. In January 1911 he
was given an England amateur international
trial at Nunhead but unfortunately failed to
sufficiently impress the selectors.

Appearances:
SL: 2 app. 0 gls.
Total: *2 app. 0 gls.*

BROWN, Gordon

Role: Forward 1959-61
5'10" 11st.6lbs.
b. Ellesmere Port 30 June 1933

CAREER: Ellesmere Port Boys/Cheshire
Schools/Ellesmere Port Town/
Wolverhampton Wanderers Sept 1951/
Scunthorpe United Dec 1952/Derby County
Jan 1957/SOUTHAMPTON Mar 1960/Barrow
July 1961/Southport Jan 1964/Morecambe
1964/Burneyside (Westmoreland League)
manager 1965-67.

*Debut v Tranmere Rovers (h) 19.3.59 * (scored on
debut)*

Gordon Brown was signed from Derby just
before the transfer deadline in 1959 and scored
two vital goals in Saints' final surge to the
Division Three championship. The first of
those two came on his debut at home to
Tranmere Rovers and the second priceless
strike came the following week when he
scored the only goal at Loftus Road against
Queen's Park Rangers. He was an England
Youth International and had promised much
early on but, like so many, had to settle on
finishing his career in the lower divisions.

Appearances:
FL: 8 app. 2 gls.
Total: *8 app. 2 gls.*

❏ **Saints note** - *When Derby signed Gordon from
Scunthorpe United in 1957 the £5,150 transfer fee
was paid by the Derby County Supporters
Association.*

BROWN, Harry

Role: Forward 1905-06 & 1910-13
b. Northampton November 1883
d. Basingstoke 9 February 1934

CAREER: St. Sepulchre's F.C./Northampton
Town 1902/West Bromwich Albion Nov 1903/
SOUTHAMPTON April 1905/Newcastle
United May 1906/Bradford Park Avenue Oct
1907/Fulham Mar 1908/SOUTHAMPTON
Sept 1910/Woolston Nov 1913.

Debut v Northampton Town (a) 23.9.05

Harry Brown's arrival at the Dell followed two
seasons of League experience with West
Bromwich Albion where he was regarded as a
clever ball player. He had a deceptive style
which often disconcerted his opponents and
gave colleagues either side of him
opportunities in front of goal. A goalscorer in
his own right, Harry found the net with
frequency during his first spell at the Dell,
notching up 10 League and four cup goals. In
May 1906, offered tempting terms by
Newcastle United, he moved to St. James' Park
for a fee of £380. A brief but successful spell
with the Magpies, (eight goals in 24 games),
was followed by stays at Bradford and Fulham
before he decided to return to Southampton to
buy the Kingsland Tavern in St. Mary's Street.
He re-signed for the Saints and, although he
had slowed a little since 1906, he still
possessed his clever touches and served the
club for a further three seasons until retiring in
1913. During the war he worked in Motor
Transport and afterwards took a greengrocers'
shop in Padwell Road. In 1933 he developed a
virus that attacked his optic nerve causing him
to lose his sight. Within a few months the
illness spread and he died in February 1934
aged only 50.

Appearances:
SL: 72 app. 26 gls.
FAC: 9 app. 5 gls.
Total: *81 app. 31 gls.*

BROWN, Peter Barry

Role: Forward 1953-58
5'7" 9st.3lbs.
b. Andover 13 July 1934

CAREER: Andover Old Boys/
SOUTHAMPTON Jan 1952/R.A.M.C.
Crookham (National Service) 1952/Wrexham
July 1958/Poole Town July 1960/Dorchester
May 1962/Andover July 1963.
Debut v Norwich City (a) 30.4.54

Peter Brown signed as a part time professional
in 1952 but national service interrupted his
career until 1954 when he became a full time
player. Never establishing himself in the first
team, Peter found more success at Wrexham
where he scored nine times in 33 League
games. A sign-writer by trade, Peter dropped
into non-league football in 1960.

Appearances:
F.L. 16 app. 3 gls.
Total: *16 app. 3 gls.*

❏ **Saints note** - *Peter's son Kevan was on the
Saints books in the mid-eighties, later playing 37
League games for Brighton.*

Peter Brown

BROWN, Robert

Role: Forward 1897-98
b. Lancashire

CAREER: Burton Wanderers July 1894/
SOUTHAMPTON May 1897/Queen's Park
Rangers c.s.1898.
Debut v Tottenham Hotspur (a) 18.9.97

Bob Brown was given a trial with
Southampton having travelled south from
Lancashire with Arthur Chadwick. Despite
being described in the local press as an
"average type of player", he ousted Jimmy
Yates from the outside-right berth for a long
period in the 1897-98 season and played in the
F.A. Cup semi-final replay against Nottingham
Forest. He moved to London in the close
season, signing for Southern League rivals
Queen's Park Rangers.

Appearances:
SL: 12 app. 2 gls.
FAC: 1 app. 0 gls.
Total: *13 app. 2 gls.*

BROWNING, Donovan Albert

Role: Full-back 1936-38
5'9" 11st.6lbs.
b. Ashley 9 May 1916

CAREER: New Forest Schools/New Milton
1934/SOUTHAMPTON May 1935.
Debut v Coventry City (h) 28.12.36

Don Browning came from a farming family
and progressed from Hampshire League
soccer to sign professional terms at the Dell in
1935. He found it hard to maintain any
consistency
and, coupled
with the fact
that he suffered
a serious knee
injury in 1937,
he found
himself transfer
listed at £500 in
May 1938.
During 1938-39
he made just six
appearances for
the reserves and
was freed in

Don Browning

May 1939. In 1991, Don was farming 5,000 acres in Dorset and is a season ticket holder at the Dell.

Appearances:
FL: 26 app. 0 gls.
Total: *26 app. 0 gls.*

❏ **Saints note** - *A talented cricketer, Don was once a member of Hampshire County Cricket Club's groundstaff.*

BROWNING, Robert Ernest

Role: Forward 1912-13
5'10" 11st.11lbs.
b. Kettering, Northamptonshire July qtr 1888

CAREER: KetteringTown/Queen's Park Rangers c.s. 1910/SOUTHAMPTON Feb. 1913 /Brentford c.s. 1913.

Debut v West Ham United (a) 15.2.13

The Sports Echo described Bob Browning as "a clever forward with an accurate shot" and the Southampton directors hoped that with his arrival the problem inside-left position had been solved. However, his goalscoring form, shown previously with Queen's Park Rangers, never materialised and within a few months he found himself back in West London as the result of a move to Brentford.

Appearances:
SL: 6 app. 0 gls.
Total: *6 app. 0 gls.*

BRUTON, Leslie Hector Ronald

Role: Forward 1923-26
5'9" 11st.6lbs.
b. Foleshill 1 April 1903
d. Coventry 2April 1989

CAREER: Foleshill/SOUTHAMPTON Nov 1922/Peterborough c.s. 1926/Raith Rovers Nov 1927/Blackburn Rovers May 1929/Liverpool Feb 1932/Leamington Town July 1933/Coventry City's training staff.

Debut v Bristol City (h) 6.10.23

Leslie Bruton was signed for just £15 from the Coventry non-league side Foleshill but failed to make much of an impression in his three years at the Dell. It seems, however, that he was a late

Leslie Bruton

developer for, after spells in Southern and Scottish Leagues, Blackburn Rovers paid £10,000 for him. Linking up with his namesake and England international Jack Bruton, Leslie scored 23 times in 38 appearances before transferring to his final League club Liverpool in 1932.

Appearances:
FL: 7 app. 0 gls.
Total: *7 app. 0 gls.*

BUCHANAN, Robert John

Role: Forward 1896-99
5'9" 12st.7lbs.
b. Johnstone, Paisley, Scotland 1868
d. Southwark Jan qtr. 1909

CAREER: Johnstone/Abercorn/Sunderland Albion/Burnley May 1892/Woolwich Arsenal Sept 1894/SOUTHAMPTON c.s.1896/ Sheppey Utd. c.s.1899.

*Debut v Chatham (h) 19.9.1896 *(scored on debut)*

The Southampton public immediately took to Bob Buchanan following his move from Woolwich Arsenal and his never-give-up attitude earned him the nickname of 'Death or Glory Bob'. His willingness to chase a lost cause enabled him to score some unlikely goals, including the ones that knocked out Leicester Fosse and Newcastle in the 1898 F.A. Cup run. Ever-present during his first season at the County Ground, he spent three seasons with the Saints before joining Sheppey in 1899. On retiring from the game he settled in South East London but died prematurely in 1909 from unknown causes.

Appearances:
SL: 41 app. 21 gls.
FAC: 16 app. 12 gls.
Total: *57 app. 33 gls.*

BUCKENHAM, William Elijah

Role: Forward 1909-11
6'0" 12st.0lbs.
b. Exeter January qtr 1888
d. Plumstead 9 June 1954

CAREER: Wood Street School (Plumstead)/ Plumstead Park Villa/Plumstead Melrose/ Farnham/86th Battery Royal Artillery (Aldershot)/Woolwich Arsenal Nov 1909/ SOUTHAMPTON Dec 1909/12th Brigade Royal Field Artillery 1910.

*Debut v Reading (h) 30.4.10 * (scored on debut)*

A Hampshire County player, Bombardier Bill Buckenham served with the Royal Artillery at Aldershot as well as holding dual registrations with Arsenal in the Football League and with Southampton in the Southern League. He scored in his first two outings but then failed to find the net in his subsequent four appearances and he eventually decided to concentrate on a career in the Army.

Appearances:
SL: 6 app. 2 gls.
Total: *6 app. 2 gls.*

BUCKLEY, A.

Role: Forward 1913-14
5'9" 11st.4lbs.
b. Birmingham

CAREER: Bath City/ SOUTHAMPTON Jan 1914.

Debut v Bristol Rovers (h) 24.1.14

A Buckley

Jim Bullock

A. Buckley made his Southampton debut in the centre-forward position just three days after being registered with the Saints. He played several reserve games and then joined up at the outbreak of the First World War, never to be heard of again.

Appearances:
SL: 1 app. 0 gls.
Total: *1 app. 0 gls.*

BULLOCK, James

Role: Forward 1924-28
5' 8" 11st.6lbs.
b. Manchester 25 March 1902
d. Stockport 9 March 1977

CAREER: Manchester City Mar 1922/Crewe Alexandra Feb 1924/SOUTHAMPTON Aug 1924/Chesterfield June 1929/Manchester United Sept 1930/Dundalk June 1931/Llanelly July 1932/Hyde United June 1933.

Debut v Stockport County (a) 11.10.24

Jim Bullock was, for a centre-forward, rather small but he possessed a knack for scoring goals. During his spell at Southampton he was overshadowed by Bill Rawlings but, whenever called upon, always performed creditably as figures of 13 goals in 33 appearances suggests. His high rate of scoring in the reserves was staggering as, over five years, he notched 166 goals in 208 games, a record that has never been threatened since. In June 1929 he was signed by his old team mate Alec Campbell, then manager of Chesterfield, and continued to score goals with some regularity.

Appearances:
FL:. 33 app. 13 gls.
FAC: 1 app. 0 gls.
Total: *34 app. 13 gls.*

BUNDY, William

Role: Forward 1902-03
b. Eastleigh January qtr. 1883
d. Eastleigh 8 December 1945

CAREER: Eastleigh Guild 1898/ SOUTHAMPTON Sept 1902/Eastleigh Athletic Jan1904/Woolston/Eastleigh Athletic until Feb 1922.

*Debut v Reading (h) 14.2.03 * (scored on debut)*

Bill Bundy was a product of Hampshire League football and joined Southampton's second string for the start of the 1902-03 season. The club being blessed at the time with a number of top class forwards, it took a serious injury crisis to create an opening in the first team for Bill but he rose to the occasion by scoring in the 4-1 demolition of Reading. He was never rewarded with another senior game and returned to the Hampshire League with Eastleigh Athletic where, apart from a brief sojourn to Woolston, he spent the next twenty years.

Appearances:
SL: 1 app. 1 gl.
Total: *1 app. 1 gl.*

BURLEY, Benjamin

Role: Forward 1933-34
5'7" 11st.0lbs.
b. Sheffield 2 November 1907

CAREER: Darnall Road School/Netherhope Institute/Woodhouse Mill United/Sheffield United am Nov 1931, pro Oct 1932/

SOUTHAMPTON Sept 1933/Grimsby Town June 1934/Norwich City June 1935/ Darlington May 1938/Chelmsford City July 1939/ (Southend, Millwall, Brighton, Queen's Park Rangers and Crystal Palace during World War Two) Chelmsford City secretary June 1951.

Debut v Bradford (a) 28.4.34

Before arriving at the Dell Ben Burley had won Sheffield and Yorkshire honours but, despite being a stocky and thrustful winger, was only to make two appearances on the left wing for the Saints. At Grimsby he met with more success playing 22 games in their First Division side before moving to Carrow Road. After the war, having obtained his F.A. Coaching Badge, he coached in Holland and later returned to live in East Anglia.

Appearances:
FL: 2 app. 0 gls.
Total: *2 app. 0 gls.*

BURNS, Francis

Role: Full-back 1972-73
5' 9" 10st.10lbs.
b. Glenboig 17 October 1948

CAREER: St. Augustine's School/ Coatbridge/Manchester United am June 1964, pro Oct1965/SOUTHAMPTON June 1972/ Preston North End Aug 1973/Shamrock Rovers 1981.

Debut v Derby County (h) 12.8.72

Francis Burns was a talented left-back who, whilst at Old Trafford, won a Scottish cap and managed to make 111 League appearances despite undergoing three cartilage operations. Ted Bates paid £50,000 for him in the close season of 1972 but a further cartilage operation, a thigh injury and the emerging form of

Francis Burns

Steve Mills in the reserves, led to Burns moving to Preston the following year. He enjoyed several successful seasons at Deepdale before finishing his career in Eire.

Appearances:
FL: 20 (1) app. 0 gls.
LC: 3 app. 1 gl.
Total: *23 (1) app. 1 gl.*

BURNSIDE, David Gort

Role: Forward 1962-65
5'9" 11st.4 lbs.
b. Bristol 10 December1939

CAREER: Kingswood School/Bristol & District Schools/Bristol City am/West Bromwich Albion am Dec 1955, pro Feb 1957/ SOUTHAMPTON Sept 1962/Crystal Palace Dec 1964/Wolverhampton Wanderers Sept 1966/Plymouth Argyle Mar 1968/Bristol City Dec 1971/Colchester United Mar 1972/Bath City manager May 1972/Walsall coach c.s. 1973/Minehead Jan 1974/Cadbury Heath Jan 1975/Bridgewater Town player-manager Apr 1975/Taunton Town/Walsall assistant-manager/F.A. Coach (West Region) Oct 1979/ England Youth manager 1983.

Debut v Leeds United (a) 29.9.62

David Burnside was signed for £17,000 from West Bromwich Albion where he had won two England Under-23 caps and acquired nationwide fame for his incredible ball-juggling abilities. In October 1957, during half-time at a West Bromwich Albion v C.D.S.A. (Russia) friendly, he performed his "tricks" live on television whilst in 1960 he entered the Sunday Despatch's heading competition to keep the ball in the air. He managed 495 clean headers without a break and, although this was well short of the world record, it clearly demonstrated David's ball skills. He quickly settled at the Dell, his artistry playing a memorable role in Saints' 1963 F.A. Cup run. A knee injury received at Newcastle in September 1963 disrupted his progress although he seemed to be regaining his form when he was, surprisingly, sold to Crystal Palace for £12,000. He travelled widely afterwards and eventually became part of the national set-up when he was appointed England Youth Team manager in 1983. In December 1990 David was living in Bristol and still managing England Youth. He was also the F.A.'s regional director in the South West programme for excellence.

Appearances:
FL: 61 app. 22 gls.
FAC: 7 app. 4 gls.
LC: 2 app. 0 gls.
Total: *70 app. 26 gls.*

❏ **Saints note** - *David's father was so keen for his son to develop his football skills that he had floodlights installed in the back garden to enable the youngster to practice on the darker evenings.*

David Burnside, player and coach

BURRIDGE, John

Role: Goalkeeper 1987-89
5'11" 12st.11lbs.
b. Workington 3 Dec.ember1951

CAREER: Workington app. Apr 1967, pro Jan 1970/ Blackpool Apr 1971/Aston Villa Sept 1975 (Southend United-loan-Jan 1978)/Crystal Palace Mar 1978/Queen's Park Rangers Dec 1980/Wolverhampton Wanderers July 1983 (Derby County-loan-Sept 1984)/ Sheffield United Oct 1984/SOUTHAMPTON Aug 1987/Newcastle United Oct 1989/Hartlepool trial July 1991/Falkirk trial Aug 1991 (Hibernian loan Aug 1991).

Debut v Watford (h) 17.10.87

When Peter Shilton left the Dell, Chris Nicholl was left without any experienced cover for Tim Flowers and so, remembering John Burridge from his Villa Park days, paid £25,000 to Sheffield United to acquire the experienced custodian. The Saints were 'Budgie's' tenth League club in seventeen years and his enthusiasm and confidence were soon put to the test when Tim Flowers suffered a loss of form. His fervour for fitness,

combined with an infectious *joie de vivre* , produced an immediate rapport with the fans who especially loved his pre-match warm up routines. After two seasons of marshalling Saints' somewhat unpredictable defence he declined a new contract and took his invaluable influence to Newcastle. In April 1991 Ossie Ardiles, recently installed as Newcastle's manager, gave John a free transfer.

Appearances:
FL: 62 app. 0 gls.
FAC: 4 app. 0 gls.
LC: 7 app. 0 gls.
Total: *73 app. 0 gls.*

BURROWS, Thomas

Role: Goalkeeper 1904-11
6'2" 12st.4lbs.
b. Portsmouth 1886

CAREER: Hill Lane/St. Mary's Swifts/ SOUTHAMPTON 1904/Merthyr Town c.s. 1911.

Debut v Queen's Park Rangers (h) 29.4.05

Tom Burrows

Tom Burrows was employed at Steven's shipyard on Weston Shore before embarking on a soccer career in 1904 and was a tall, able deputy goalkeeper to George Clawley, providing a safe and sound pair of hands when called upon. His future looked promising until a nasty injury in October 1906 preceded a temporary loss of form, enabling Herbert Lock to move up upon Clawley's retirement. After three years as Lock's deputy, Tom finally gained regular recognition in 1909 and made 48 consecutive appearances in the Southern League. After an indifferent season in 1910-11 he moved to Wales to assist Merthyr Town where he was virtually an ever-present up until the outbreak of war.

Appearances:
SL: 84 app. 0 gls.
FAC: 3 app. 0 gls.
Total: *87 app. 0 gls.*

John Burridge

BUSHBY, Thomas William

Role: Half-back 1946-47
5'10" 11st.8lbs.
b. Shildon 21 August 1914

CAREER: Timothy Hackworth School/
Durham County Schools/Shildon Amateurs/
Southend United am Sept 1933, pro Oct 1934/
Portsmouth June 1939/(guest for Southampton
& Chelsea during World War Two)/
SOUTHAMPTON Sept 1946/Cowes 1947/
Sarisbury coach 1954.
Debut v West Bromwich Albion (a) 5.10.46

Bill Bushby joined cup-holders Portsmouth from
Southend in June 1939 as cover for captain
Jimmy Guthrie who was fighting for his life after
a car crash. Guthrie's full recovery, and the
outbreak of war, led Bill to Follands in
Southampton where he worked for the duration
of the hostilities. Follands had a fine soccer team
which included two future Saints managers, Bill
Dodgin and Ted Bates, and it was Dodgin who
signed Bill at the start of the 1946-47 campaign.
In May 1947 he was offered terms by Aldershot
but decided to retire from professional football
and once more took employment at Follands.

Bill Bushby

> **Appearances:**
> *FL: 2 app. 0 gls.*
> **Total:** *2 app. 0 gls.*

❏ **Saints note** - *Bill's only two games for the
Saints both took place in Birmingham, one at The
Hawthorns and his second at St. Andrews.*

BUTT, Leonard George

Role: Half-back 1920-22
5'6" 10st.4lbs.
b. Freemantle, Southampton 20 December 1893

CAREER: Weston School/Malmesbury United/
Shirley St. James/SOUTHAMPTON Apr 1912/
Thornycrofts 1919/SOUTHAMPTON Aug
1920/Bournemouth June 1922/Cowes 1927.
Debut v Brentford (a) 30.10.20

Growing up in Edwardian Southampton, Len
Butt spent the majority of his boyhood either
watching the Saints at the Dell or cheering on
Hampshire at the County Ground. When not
spectating he was usually playing and, while
participating in a match on Southampton
Common, he was noticed by Saints player Bert

Lee and invited to the Dell for a trial. Joining
the professional ranks in April 1912, Len spent
the next two years as a reserve player and,
when war broke out in 1914, had yet to make a
first team appearance. Len immediately joined
up with the 5th Hampshire Regiment and
spent much of the next four years serving in
India where he played plenty of top class
cricket but little football. Upon returning to
Southampton at the conclusion of the war, Len
found work at Thornycrofts, who then boasted
one of the finest non-league footballing teams
in the South. (Within a year they reached the
first round proper of the F.A. Cup and held
mighty Burnley to a draw). Len was paid ten
shillings a game and, showing that his sojourn
in India had not dulled his skills, once more
was visited by Bert Lee (now the Saints trainer)
who proposed that he rejoin the Saints.
Thornycrofts were not amused at this piece of
poaching and promptly sacked Len who,
fortunately, had been offered a full-time
contract at the Dell. Len's second spell with the
Saints was more productive and, playing at
half-back, he made 18 first team appearances
between 1920 and 1922. He was small for a
half-back but his quickness into the tackle
earned him the nickname of "Badger Butt"
from the fans who also appreciated his
wholeheartedness. Unfortunately for Len, also
at the club over this period were Bert Shelley,

Alec Campbell and Bill Turner whose form in the half-back line was so formidable that Len was only called upon when injuries struck. He joined Bournemouth on a free transfer in 1922 and, within a year with Len as Captain, the Cherries gained admittance to Division Three of the Football League. After hanging up his boots Len became mine host at The Sailors Home public house in Bevois Street and in 1935 attended Southampton's silver jubilee dinner held at the South Western Hotel. In December 1990 Len, still sprightly, celebrated his 97th birthday which makes him the oldest living Saint and the only player still alive who signed for the club when they were still in the Southern League.

Len Butt

Appearances:
FL: 17 app. 0 gls.
FAC: 1 app. 0 gls.
Total: *18 app. 0 gls.*

❏ **Saints note** - *In 1932 while playing for Cowes in the Hampshire Senior Cup Final against Newport, Len found himself up against two more ex-Saints players in the formidable shape of Bill Rawlings and Arthur Dominy. Interest in the game was immense and a crowd of over 20,000 witnessed an eventual Newport victory.*

BYRNE, Anthony Brendan

Role: Defender 1966-74
5'7" 9st.10 lbs.
b. Rathdowney 2 February 1946

CAREER: Millwall Aug 1963/ SOUTHAMPTON Aug 1964/Hereford United Aug 1974/Newport County Mar 1977/ Trowbridge Town player-coach July 1979.

Debut v Manchester United (a) 18.4.67

Born in Ireland, Tony Byrne came to England in 1958 with his family and played one League game for Millwall prior to joining the Saints. Before he played in the first team he suffered a broken leg sustained in a reserve match in April 1966, but overcame this set-back to make his debut in front of 54,000 fans at Old Trafford a year later. He was slightly built for a defender and, although quick and diligent, struggled to carve a permanent niche in Southampton's notoriously robust rearguard. His stay at the Dell encompassed a decade during which time he won 14 Eire caps and made over 100 first team appearances before he joined Terry Paine at Hereford. In 1991 Tony was working as a foreman at Hereford Golf Course.

Appearances:
FL: 81 (12) app. 3 gls.
FAC: 8 (1) app. 0 gls.
LC: 6 app. 0 gls.
Eur: 6 app. 0 gls.
Total: *101 (13) app. 3 gls.*

BYRNE, Michael Patrick

Role: Goalkeeper 1903-05
5'10" 11st.8lbs.
b. Bristol April qtr 1880

CAREER: Bristol Rovers1902/
SOUTHAMPTON c.s.1903/Chelsea Aug 1905/
Glossop May 1907.
Debut v Swindon Town (h) 23.1.04

A former soldier with the Irish Guards,
Michael Byrne was signed to act as George
Clawley's deputy and as such was only to
make five appearances in his two seasons with
the club. In 1905 Chelsea signed him as
understudy to their famous goalie, "Fatty"
Foulke but a dislocated shoulder heralded a
short-lived move to Glossop. He eventually
returned to Bristol to live and found
employment with the Imperial Tobacco
Company.

> **Appearances:**
> *SL: 5 app. 0 gls.*
> **Total:** *5 app. 0 gls.*

CAIN, Thomas

Role: Goalkeeper
1895-96
5' 11" 12st.0lbs.
*b. Sunderland
October qtr 1872
d. 1952*

CAREER: Hebburn Argyle/Stoke City Nov
1893/Everton Apr 1894/SOUTHAMPTON
St. Mary's Oct 1895/Grimsby Town Apr 1896/
Hebburn Argyle Oct 1896/West Stanley Jan 1897.
Debut v Clapton (a) 19.10.1895

Tom Cain had experienced League soccer with
Stoke and Everton before his move to the
Antelope Ground in October 1895. He
underwent a goalkeeper's nightmare on his
debut, conceding seven goals at Clapton but
overcame this setback to help Saints to a
satisfactory season. His move to Grimsby in
April 1896 created a club record as the fee
involved was £20.

> **Appearances:**
> *SL: 10 app. 0 gls.*
> **Total:** *10 app. 0 gls.*

CALLAGHER, John

Role: Centre-half 1924-25
5' 11" 12st.0lbs.
*b. Glasgow 3 April 1898
d. Blackpool 25 January 1980*

CAREER: St. Rochs (Glasgow)/Bury June 1921/
SOUTHAMPTON Apr 1924/Wigan Borough
June 1925/Norwich City June-Nov 1926.

*Debut v Stoke
(a) 1.9.24*

John Callagher
arrived at the
Dell with
Stanley
Woodhouse in
1924 in a deal
that saw Bill
Turner move in
the opposite
direction to
Bury. Unlike
Woodhouse,
John failed to
settle in the south

Tony Byrne

John Callagher

and although offered a retaining wage in May 1925, he declined and was placed on the transfer list at his own request. The following month he joined Wigan Borough for a fee of £400 and later became a fireman in Blackpool where, in 1938, he received a bravery award.

Appearances:
FL: 1 app. 0 gls.
Total: *1 app. 0 gls.*

CAMPBELL, Alistair Kenyon

Role: Centre-half 1908-09 & 1919-26
6' 2" 12st.0lbs.
b. South Stoneham, Southampton 29 May 1890
d. Cosham 16 June 1943

CAREER: King Edward VI School/ SOUTHAMPTON 1908/Glossop May 1909/ SOUTHAMPTON Jan 1914/(guest for West Ham United during World War One/Poole F.C. July 1926/Chesterfield manager 1927.

Debut v Millwall (a) 27.2.09

Born of Scottish parents, Alec Campbell attended King Edward VI Grammar School where he captained both the football and cricket elevens. Whilst still at King Edwards he played for England (at amateur level) in a soccer international versus Holland, the only known occasion a schoolboy has represented his country at that level. He made his senior Southampton debut in February 1909 and quickly emerged as one of the club's brightest-ever prospects but, unfortunately for Saints, in September the same year he, together with several other amateur internationals, decided to join Mr. Hill-Wood's team at Glossop. His spell in Derbyshire encompassed four seasons but he returned to the Dell in January 1914 only for the war to interrupt his progress. During the hostilities Alec guested for West Ham and the East London club offered him tempting terms to move to Upton Park but, as he had been offered a directorship with a company of Fruit Importers, he decided to stay with Southampton. He became the club's first captain at the resumption of normal post-war football and became a distinctive figure on the pitch with his "telescopic legs" providing ample scope for contemporary cartoonists. Undoubtedly one of the club's best-ever centre halves, Alec played for the Saints until 1926 when he joined Poole, helping them through the qualifying rounds of the F.A. Cup to meet Everton at Goodison Park. In 1927 he became, briefly, manager at Chesterfield before giving up the game for good. During World War Two he served as an officer in the Royal Artillery but tragically contracted pneumonia and died in Queen Alexandra's hospital, Cosham, in June 1943. His name is recorded on the war memorial at South Stoneham Crematorium.

Alec Campbell

Appearances:
SL: 19 app. 2 gls.
FL:157 app. 13 gls.
FAC: 23 app. 0 gls.
Total: *199 app. 15 gls.*

❏ **Saints note** - *Alec Campbell played seven matches for Hampshire County Cricket Club in 1908 and 1909 appearing as a right hand batsman.*

CAMPBELL, Francis Stephen

Role: Half-back 1931-35
5' 10" 12st.0lbs.
b. Camlachie 3 March 1907

CAREER: Irvine Meadow/SOUTHAMPTON July 1931/Newport (I.O.W.) 1935.
Debut v Tottenham Hotspur (h) 7.9.31

Although twenty-four years of age by the time he arrived at the Dell, Frank Campbell's only previous soccer experience had been in the Scottish Intermediate League with Irvine Meadow. Nevertheless he developed into a strong, forceful half-back, quickly adapting to life in the English Second Division. It was particularly unfortunate that first a fractured thigh and then, more perniciously, a knee injury that developed into chronic arthritis, eventually curtailed a most promising career. He played briefly on the Isle of Wight with Newport whilst employed at Follands but later moved to Hatfield to work in the aircraft industry.

Appearances:
FL: 86 app. 5 gls.
FAC: 3 app. 0 gls.
Total: *89 app. 5 gls.*

Frank Campbell

CARNABY, Thomas Easton

Role: Centre-half
1938-39
6' 0" 11st.12lbs.
*b. Newsham
25 December 1913
d. Hendon July
qtr. 1971*

CAREER: New Delaval United/ Blyth Spartans 1933/SOUTHAMPTON May 1938/ Southampton War Reserve Police 1939/ Andover August 1947.
Debut v Tottenham Hotspur (a) 24.12.38

Tom Carnaby

A brawny centre-half, Tom Carnaby was signed from non-league football in 1938 and provided cover for Dave Affleck in the last season before World War Two. He kept fit by turning out for the Police throughout the hostilities and then signed on for Andover in 1947.

Appearances:
FL: 14 app. 0 gls.
FAC: 1 app. 0 gls.
Total: *15 app. 0 gls.*

CARR, James Edward Charles

Role: Forward 1923-26
5' 8" 11st.0lbs.
*b. Maryhill, Glasgow 19 December 1893
d. Harrow 26 June 1980*

CAREER: Watford Orient/ Watford 1908/ West Ham United 1914/(Portsmouth & Kilmarnock during World War One) Reading 1919/ SOUTHAMPTON June 1923/ Swansea May 1926/Southall 1927.
Debut v Bury (a) 25.8.23

Jimmy Carr

Jimmy Carr was introduced to League football by Watford at the age of 16 and played for Portsmouth during the 1916-17 war-time season while he was an army private. However, it was at Reading that he really burst into prominence forming an exciting partnership with Len Andrews, which, in 1923, was resumed at the Dell. Despite a knee operation in 1924, Jimmy's contribution to the team from the left wing was invaluable, not least during the run to the F.A. Cup semi-finals during the 1924-25 season. With his mid-thirties approaching he now took the unusual step of placing an advertisement in the "Athletic News" stating that he wanted to 'assist a club outside the League in exchange for a business'. The advert must have produced results for after a brief spell at Swansea he became the proprietor of The Red Lion Hotel at Southall, Middlesex.

Appearances:
FL: 86 app. 10 gls.
FAC: 10 app. 0 gls.
Total: *96 app. 10 gls.*

CARTER, George

Role: Full Back 1891-94
b. Hereford 1867
d. Southampton 23 June 1945

CAREER: Nil Desperandum F.C. (Hereford)/ Hereford & Herefordshire County XI/ SOUTHAMPTON St. Mary's Oct 1887, reserve team manager 1901-15.

*Debut v Warmley (a) 3.10.91 F.A.C. * (scored on debut)*

George Carter was an exceptional sportsman from Hereford who had represented his native county at both football and cricket. He was posted to Southampton as an employee of the Ordnance Survey Office in London Road and introduced to the St. Mary's side in October 1887. The story goes that Ned Bromley the club's captain greeted the newly arrived player with the question "Where do you play as a rule, Mr. Carter?", George replied: "Full-back", and from that day onwards until his retirement that was to be his position. A gentleman and a generous opponent George succeeded Bromley to the captaincy in 1888 and led the club to firstly Junior and then Senior Cup successes. He captained the team in their first ever "national cup tie" at

Warmley in October 1891 and remained a virtual ever-present up until December 1893 when he damaged a leg in a match. When he retired the following May, George's distinguished service to the club was rewarded with a gold watch and a cheque. He continued to serve Southampton by shouldering responsibility for the club's second string and "discovered" men such as Harrison, Jefferis and Dominy. Standing down in 1915, George was made a life member of Southampton Football Club. George also displayed his versatility as a sportsman when, as a member of the Southampton Amateur Swimming Club, he represented Hampshire at water polo. He remained employed with the Ordnance Survey for forty years, retiring in 1927.

Appearances:
FAC: 6 app. 1 gl.
Total: *6 app. 1 gl.*

CARTER, Robert

Role: Forward 1908-10
5' 6" 10st.7lbs.
b. Hendon, Sunderland
d. Sunderland 1927

CAREER: Stockport County 1904/Burslem Port Vale Jan 1905/Fulham Mar 1908/ SOUTHAMPTON Mar 1909.

Robert Carter

Debut v Bristol Rovers (h) 20.3.09

Nicknamed "Toddler" because of his small stature, Bob Carter was recruited from Fulham and proved to be a lively and very nippy forward who was most at home on the wing. His feet were so small that his boots could easily have fitted into those of Frank Thorpe, yet his size helped him to be very elusive and effective in front of goal. Illness prevented him taking up his place for the start of the 1910-11 season and, although he returned to reserve team action in October, Bob never regained full fitness and returned to Sunderland where a generation later his son Raich was to make such a name for himself.

Appearances;
SL: 41 app. 12 gls.
FAC: 2 app. 0 gls.
Total: *43 app. 12 gls.*

Jimmy Case

CASE, James Robert

Role: Midfield 1984-1991
5' 9" 12st.7lbs.
b. Liverpool 18 May 1954

CAREER: Garston Woodcutters/South
Liverpool 1971/Liverpool May 1973/Brighton
& Hove Albion Aug 1981/SOUTHAMPTON
Mar 1985/A.F.C. Bournemouth June 1991.

Debut v Tottenham Hotspur (a) 23.3.85

Jimmy Case was Lawrie McMenemy's last
signing and at £30,000 was undoubtedly his
best. Many Dell critics, still smarting at the
transfer of Steve Williams, felt that Jimmy was
past his 'sell-by date' and if Brighton didn't
value him at more than £30,000 why should he
be of any benefit to Saints? The fans had not
taken into account Jimmy's Liverpool pedigree
or an incredible fitness level that saw him, in
1991, become the oldest outfield player in the
First Division. At Anfield Jimmy won four
league titles, three European cups, one
U.E.F.A. trophy and a League Cup Medal. He
joined Brighton as a £450,000 makeweight
when Mark Lawrenson moved in the opposite
direction and played a
large part in the
success story at the
Goldstone Ground in
the early eighties.
Soon after his arrival
at the Dell,
McMenemy's parting
legacy had become
club captain and new
manager Chris Nicholl
could consider himself
fortunate to have
inherited such a
model professional.
Over the next six years
Jimmy lost none of his
bite in the tackle, and
if he slowed a touch it
was more than
compensated for by his broadening vision and
finely polished passing skills. He was Saints
Player of the Year for the 1989-90 season and
in December 1990 won praise when he made
his (long overdue) debut on the international
stage when picked to play for the Football
League against the Irish League. Without him
in the team the progress of Le Tissier, Shearer
and Wallace would not have been so swift and

it will be odd if and when he finally retires
that he does not receive a multitude of
managerial opportunities. As it turned out
Saints' new manager decided against retaining
his talents and within 24 hours of Ian
Branfoot's arrival Jimmy resumed his travels
along the South Coast by way of a free transfer
to Dean Court.

Appearances:
FL: 213 (3) app. 10 gls.
FAC: 15 app. 1 gl.
LC: 34 app. 2 gls.
Total: *262 (3) app. 13 gls.*

CASSELLS, Keith Barrington

Role: Forward 1981-83
5' 10" 11st.12lbs.
b. Islington, London 10 July 1957

CAREER: Wembley Town/Watford Nov 1977
(Peterborough-loan-Jan 1979)/Oxford United
Feb 1980/SOUTHAMPTON March 1982/
Brentford Feb 1983/Mansfield Town Aug
1985.

Debut v Swansea City (a) 13.4.82

Keith Cassells

Keith Cassells joined
Southampton from
Oxford at the same
time as Mark Wright,
with Lawrie
McMenemy
describing his
acquisition as a
"gamble". Although
he showed flashes of
skill, Lawrie's flutter
never really paid off
in the First Division
and Keith returned to
his native London to
play for Brentford. He
later had four seasons
at Mansfield Town
scoring 52 League
goals before joining
the Police Force.

Appearances:
FL: 13 (6) app. 4 gls.
FAC: 1 app. 0 gls.
LC: 5 app. 1 gl.
Eur: 2 app. 0 gls.
Total: *21 (6) app. 5 gls.*

CATLIN, Norman John

Role: Forward 1935-37
5' 8" 10st.0lbs.
b. Liverpool 8 January 1918
d. Posted missing 29 May 1941

CAREER: Bitterne Boys Club/Arsenal am. Oct
1931/SOUTHAMPTON am. June 1933, pro.
Jan 1935/Ryde Sports 1937/Southampton
part-time pro. 1938/Bitterne Nomads 1940.

Debut v Swansea (a) 28.12.35

Norman Catlin made nationwide sporting
headlines when, as a schoolboy playing in
Southampton, he scored 17 goals in an English
Schools Shield match. In all he scored 62 goals
in just 13 matches as Southampton Boys went
all the way to the final in 1932. Such prolific
goalscoring attracted the attention of Arsenal,
who signed him on amateur terms, and he was
duly capped for England Schoolboys before
deciding to sign as a professional for
Southampton on his seventeenth birthday.
Mysteriously Norman never really developed
into the player everyone expected; he certainly
found his slight build a disadvantage and his
League career ended in March 1937 whilst
aged only 19. Later the same year he joined the
Cunard White Star Company as a clerk
although in 1938 he agreed to help Saints out
on a part-time basis if needed. Joining the
Royal Navy on the outbreak of World War
Two he lost his life when H.M.S. Gloucester
was sunk in action off Crete in 1941.

Norman Catlin

> **Appearances:**
> *FL: 6 app. 0 gls.*
> **Total:** *6 app. 0 gls.*

CAVENDISH, Sidney William

Role: Forward 1899-1902
b. Overseal October qtr 1876
d. Salisbury July qtr. 1954

CAREER:
Overseal/SOUTHAMPTON May
1898/Freemantle c.s.1902/
Southampton Wanderers during
1902/Freemantle again/
Clapton Orient c.s.1904/Salisbury
City c.s. 1906, later trainer.

Debut v Gravesend (h) 6.1.1900
* (scored on debut)

Sid Cavendish was discovered, together with
John Joyce, playing with Staffordshire side
Overseal and in his first season at the Dell he
scored 22 goals for the reserves. His debut for
the first team came in a memorable 8-0 win
against Gravesend in which he scored, but he
was unable to build on this auspicious start. A
gentlemanly player, often winning
esteem and respect from
many of his opponents, he
moved into the
Hampshire League with
Freemantle. After a
period helping Clapton
Orient achieve League
status, Sid settled in
Salisbury and became
associated with the
City side as a
player and trainer
for well over 20
years.

Appearances:
SL: 9 app. 2 gls.
Total: *9 app. 2 gls.*

Sid Cavendish

CHADWICK, Arthur

Role: Centre-half 1897-1901
5′ 8″ 12st.3lbs.
b. Church July qtr. 1875
d. Exeter 21 March 1936

CAREER: Church/Accrington/Burton Swifts
May 1895/SOUTHAMPTON May1897/
Portsmouth May 1901/Northampton Town c.s.
1904/Accrington c.s.1906/Exeter Apr 1908,
manager c.s.1910-Dec 1922/Reading manager
Jan 1923-Apr 1925/Southampton manager
Oct 1925-Apr 1931.

Debut v Sheppey United (a) 2.10.97

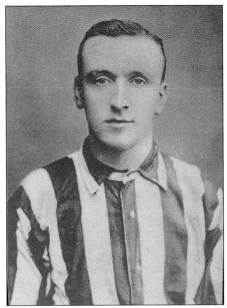

Arthur Chadwick

Little was known of Arthur Chadwick when
he signed for Saints in 1897 except that he was
a Lancashire man who favoured the right-half
position. Initially his displays were criticised
by the fans but before his first season had been
far advanced he had been moved to the centre-
half position and from then on his rise was
rapid. A powerful and efficient defender,
Arthur reached his peak at the turn of the
century and, after helping Saints to the final of
the 1900 F. A. Cup, was rewarded with two
England caps against Scotland and Wales.
Moving along the coast in 1901 he helped
Portsmouth win the Southern League
Championship the following year before
joining Northampton Town. He finished his
playing career at Exeter in 1910 and
immediately became their manager until the
beginning of 1923 when he assumed control at
Reading. When he took over the reins at the
Dell in October 1925 he was the first ex-player
to become manager and he found immediate
success by guiding the team to the 1927 F.A.
Cup semi-final. Soon after, the club embarked
on a policy of selling rather than buying and
Arthur grew disillusioned, resigning on the
16th April 1931 to end a long association with
the game. He left the area to live in Exeter and
it was whilst watching a match at Exeter's
ground that he collapsed and died in 1936.

Appearances:
SL: 81 app. 6 gls.
FAC: 15 app. 0 gls.
Total: *96 app. 6 gls.*

❑ **Saints note** - *In January 1899 versus Sheppey
United, Arthur became the first Saint to be sent off
in a League match.*

David Chadwick

CHADWICK, David Edwin

Role: Forward 1961-66
5' 6" 9st.8lbs.
b. Ootacamund, India 19 August 1943

CAREER: Priestlands School/Lawrence Boys Club/SOUTHAMPTON am May 1959, pro Oct 1960/Middlesbrough July 1966/Halifax Town Jan 1970/Bournemouth Feb 1972 (Torquay-loan-Dec 1972)/Gillingham Sept 1974/Dallas Tornado c.s. 1975/Fort Lauderdale Strikers 1977/Atlanta Chiefs coach 1980/Fort Launderdale Strikers coach 1983/ Minnesota Strikers coach 1984.

Debut v Bristol Rovers (h) 4.11.61

Despite becoming the youngest player ever to appear for Saints reserves in October 1959, David Chadwick's six professional seasons at the Dell were spent totally in the shadows of Terry Paine and John Sydenham. A £10,000 transfer to Middlesbrough blew away the cobwebs and he made over 100 League appearances before joining Halifax Town. In the mid-seventies he moved to the States, finding success as a well respected coach.

> **Appearances:**
> *FL: 25 app. 1 gl.*
> *LC: 1 app. 0 gls.*
> **Total:** *26 app. 1 gl.*

CHADWICK, Edgar Wallace

Role: Forward 1900-02
5' 7" 11st.6lbs.
b. Blackburn, Lancashire 14 June 1869
d. Blackburn 14 February 1942

CAREER: Little Dots F.C. 1884/Blackburn Olympic 1886/Blackburn Rovers c.s.1887/ Everton July 1888/Burnley May 1899/ SOUTHAMPTON Aug 1900/ Liverpool May 1902/Blackpool May 1904/ Glossop May 1905/Darwen c.s.1906/retired 1908/The Hague and Haarlem F.C. (Holland) 1908/ England amateur team coach November 1908.

*Debut v Luton Town (a) 1.9.1900 * (scored on debut)*

A former England international, and cousin of Arthur, Edgar Chadwick had already distinguished himself at the highest level of English football before joining the Saints in

Edgar Chadwick

August 1900. Nicknamed "Hooky", his frequent trick was to run with the ball parallel with the goal line drawing the goalkeeper in the direction of the post, and then hooking the ball into the opposite corner of the net. His left-wing partnership with Alf Milward (renewed from their Everton days) was an outstanding feature of the club's success story during the first two seasons of the century. In May 1902 he sought fresh fields, but as Burnley held his Football League registration he had to pay them £35 to release him to join Liverpool. In 1908, having wound up his career at Darwen, he coached in Germany and also for the Dutch F.A. while simultaneously instructing The Hague and Haarlem sides. He was also the England Amateur International team coach in November 1908 before returning to Blackburn to ply his original trade of baker. In December 1923 Edgar applied for the vacant manager's job at Blackpool but after being on a short list of two he lost out to Major Frank Buckley.

> **Appearances:**
> *SL: 52 app. 18 gls.*
> *FAC: 9 app. 6 gls.*
> **Total:** *61 app. 24 gls.*

CHALK, Norman William

Role: Centre-half 1937-39
6' 0" 11st.12lbs.
b. Bitterne, Southampton 28 October 1916

CAREER: Bitterne C. of E. School,
Southampton & Hampshire Schools/Obelisk
Rovers/Woolston Wednesday/
SOUTHAMPTON am May 1937, pro Sep.
1937/Southampton Police.

Debut v Plymouth Argyle (a) 7.5.38

Norman Chalk

Born locally,
Norman Chalk
captained
Southampton
Schools, gained
County Schoolboy
honours and went
on to join the
Saints in the
summer of 1937.
Strong and
rugged, he was
given his debut in
the last game of
the 1937-38 campaign but spent most of the
following year in the reserves and asked the
club to release him from his contract to pursue
a career with the Police. Retiring from the
Force in 1969, Norman found part-time
employment as an office assistant with a firm
of Southampton solicitors whilst continuing to
live locally.

> **Appearances:**
> *FL: 5 app. 0 gls.*
> **Total:** *5 app. 0 gls.*

CHANNON, Michael Roger

Role: Forward 1965-77 & 1979-82
6' 0" 12st.11lbs.
b. Orcheston 28 November 1948

CAREER: Shrewton/Amesbury Secondary
Modern/Salisbury & Wiltshire Schools/
SOUTHAMPTON app Mar 1964, pro Dec.
1965/Manchester City July 1977/
SOUTHAMPTON Sept 1979/ Caroline Hills
(Hong Kong) 1982/Newcastle United Aug
1982/Bristol Rovers Oct 1982/Norwich City
Dec 1982/Portsmouth Aug 1985/Finn Harps
1986.

*Debut v Bristol City (h) 11.4.66 * (scored on debut)*

Legend has it that Mike Channon was spotted
by Bill Ellerington playing in his native
Wiltshire, and although Swindon were keen to
acquire his signature the fact that large parts of
his childhood had been spent on the Milton
Road terraces helped Ted Bates persuade him
to join the staff at the Dell. Mike made his
reserve debut in September 1964 whilst still
two months short of his sixteenth birthday
and, portentously, scored, as he did on his full
debut which came in Saints' final acceleration
to Division One status in 1966. Although
frequently appearing to spend more time on
his bottom than his feet Mike's talents were
obvious and in January 1968 Ted Bates decided
to sell Martin Chivers to Spurs, knowing full
well that in Mike he had a player more than
capable of taking his place. Fortunate to have
Terry Paine and Ron Davies as
contemporaries, Mike's progress was
mercurial, as his pace, forceful running and
skilful determination blazed a trail through the
First Division. Sir Alf Ramsey picked him nine
times for the Under-23's before awarding him
his full cap in October 1972 against Yugoslavia
and he went on to play 46 times for England
(45 times as a Saint), score 20 goals and captain
the team. Coveted by all the games' major
clubs, Mike remained at the Dell, his loyalty
being rewarded by his winning an F.A. Cup
winners medal in 1976. However, with Saints
seemingly unable to regain promotion and
growing stale in the Second Division, he chose
to move to Manchester City for a fee of

Mike Channon

£300,000. His subsequent two year stint at Maine Road was not particularly auspicious and he was happy to be repatriated to the Dell where he forged exciting partnerships with Phil Boyer and Kevin Keegan. In 1981-82, with Saints playing perhaps their best ever football, Keegan and Channon were irrepressible and for a while Saints led the League for the first time in their history. Surprisingly Lawrie McMenemy released him in the close season and his subsequent three successful years at Norwich City, and a swansong year at Portsmouth proved the Saints' manager a little premature in his judgement. Mike Channon will be remembered not only for his dashing, swashbuckling surges but for his refreshing, almost cavalier, attitude both on and off the pitch that has since seen him appear regularly both on the radio and television. He now lives in West Hampshire where he breeds and trains race horses.

Appearances:
FL: 507 (3) app. 185 gls.
FAC: 40 (2) app. 18 gls.
LC: 28 app. 11 gls..
Eur: 16 app. 9 gls.
Total: *591 (5) app. 223 gls.*

❏ **Saints note** - *Mike's 185 League goals remain an all-time record for Southampton Football Club.*

CHARLES, Alfred

Role: Forward 1936-37
5' 9"
b. Trinidad, West Indies 1912

CAREER: Burnley Nov 1933/Nelson 1934/ Darwen 1935/Stalybridge Celtic/ SOUTHAMPTON Jan 1937/Stalybridge Celtic.
Debut v Bradford City (a) 9.1.37

Alf Charles was born in Trinidad and originally came to England with the 1932 West Indies Cricket team acting as Captain Learie Constantine's batman. Initially Alf had secured a contract with Burnley, failing to make their first team, but latterly signed on for Stalybridge Celtic where he settled in well and established an impressive scoring record. When he arrived at the Dell at the beginning of 1937 he came with a reputation for being a 'clever inside forward either on the left or right', and was reputedly wanted by a whole host of First Division clubs. Alf certainly had many strings to his bow (he was by trade a professional magician) but on the pitch he seemed to leave his wizardry in the dressing room and he made only one first team appearance - a 2-2 draw at Bradford. He was placed on the transfer list at £350 and was soon on his way back to Stalybridge. Alf was the first black player to represent the Saints.

Appearances:
FL: 1 app. 0 gls.
Total: *1 app. 0 gls.*

CHARLES, Robert John

Role: Goalkeeper 1959-61
6' 0" 13st.0lbs.
b. Southampton 26 December 1941

CAREER: Woolston & Southampton Schools/ SOUTHAMPTON am May 1958, pro Apr 1959/Weymouth Aug 1961.
Debut v Shrewsbury Town (a) 28.9.59

Alfred Charles

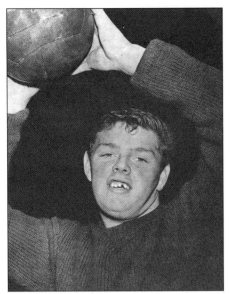

Bob Charles

As a schoolboy Bob Charles played a major part in Southampton's successful run in the England Schools Trophy in 1957. He subsequently won England schoolboy honours and was in the same England Youth team as Nobby Stiles and Geoff Hurst. He made his Saints debut before his eighteenth birthday and at the time was the youngest goalkeeper in the Football League. With such a pedigree Bob should have had a long and successful career in the game but he lacked the required discipline and tended to put on weight. Having moved to Weymouth he had the misfortune to suffer a badly broken elbow which confirmed a premature end to his playing days. Bob has since remained in Southampton and runs a car sales business.

Appearances:
FL: 26 app. 0 gls.
FAC: 6 app 0 gls.
Total: *32 app. 0 gls.*

CHARLTON, William

Role: Centre-forward 1931-32
b. Eastleigh 4 June 1912

CAREER: Peter Symonds School, Winchester/ St. Edmunds Hall, Oxford University/ SOUTHAMPTON am. Dec 1931/Hull City am.

Nov 1934/Wimbledon am. Aug 1935/Queen's Park Rangers May 1936/Barnet/Leyton 1938. (Also played for Corinthians and Middlesex Wanderers).
Debut v Preston North End (h) 16.1.32

Bill Charlton was a gifted centre-forward who, whilst at Oxford, won his Blue and signed as an amateur for the Saints. Unfortunately his studies interfered with his availability and eventually took him away from the area. He was given an England amateur cap in 1936 and signed professional terms with Queen's Park Rangers for whom he scored ten times in 18 League outings. After the war Bill became a headmaster in a London school and now lives in Barnes.
    Bill won four England amateur caps and scored a hat-trick in one game against Ireland.

Appearances:
FL: 2 app. 1 gl.
Total: *2 app. 1 gl.*

CHATTERLEY, Lawson Colin

Role: Defender 1973-75
6' 0" 11st.7lbs.
b. Birmingham 15 February 1945

CAREER: Birmingham Schools/Aston Villa app Aug 1960, pro Feb 1962 (Doncaster Rovers-loan-Mar 1971)/Northampton Town Sept 1971/ Grimsby Town Feb 1972/ SOUTHAMPTON Mar 1974/Torquay player-coach Feb 1975/ Chicago Sting (USA) coach 1978/Southampton coach 1979/Sunderland coach July 1985/ manager Clump Inn, Southampton/Poole Town manager June 1987/Reading coach June 1988/Southampton youth development Jan 1990/Southampton coach July 1991.
Debut v Burnley (a) 22.4.74

Lew Chatterley was an England Youth International who played over 150 games for Aston Villa before Lawrie McMenemy, then manager of Doncaster, signed him on loan. Lew followed McMenemy to Grimsby and then Southampton and played the last two games of Saints' 1973-74 relegation season. As the team struggled to shine in the Second Division, Lew became the butt of the crowd's frustration and he moved to a player-coach position at Torquay. He settled in Devon and took a guest house in the area only to be lured back into football, firstly as a coach in Chicago

Lew Chatterley

and then as McMenemy's right hand man back at Southampton. In 1985 he chose to accompany Lawrie to Roker Park, despite being in contention for the vacant manager's job at the Dell, but unfulfilled expectations at Sunderland precipitated his resignation. In 1990 he returned to the Dell as a youth development officer and in July 1991 became Ian Branfoot's right hand man resuming a partnership that had originally started at the Dell and had continued at Reading.

Appearances:
FL: 7 (2) app. 0 gls.
LC: 0 (1) app. 0 gls.
Total: *7 (3) app. 0 gls.*

CHEREDNIK, Aleksey

Role: Full-back 1989-
5' 9" 11st.7lbs.
b. Pamir, U.S.S.R. 12 November 1960

CAREER: Pamir 1979/Dnepropetsk 1983/
SOUTHAMPTON trial December 1989,
transfer March 1990.

Debut v Queen's Park Rangers (h) 3.4.90

Aleksey Cherednik had been capped thirteen

times by Russia and won a gold medal in the 1988 Seoul Olympics before coming to the attention of Chris Nicholl. His club Denepropetsk played at the Dell in a pre-season friendly in August 1989 and, although Aleksey was working his way back to full fitness and only appeared as a second-half substitute, he caught the eye of the Southampton dug-out. "Glasnost" had signalled the relaxation of previous stringent regulations for players moving from Russia and despite Denepropetsk being involved in the European Cup quarter-finals, £300,000 was enough to persuade them to let Aleksey become the first Russian to ply his trade in the English First Division. Understandably, he has since found it awkward to adapt to the English game and, with the Saints defence unsettled, has found himself in and out of the side. Jason Dodd's impressive and unexpected form at right-back has not helped Aleksey's cause, although it has been something of a mystery to Saints fans why the Russian has not been tried in a midfield role which would certainly seem more suited to his style of play.

Appearances:
FL: 19 (4) app. 0 gls.
FAC: 1 app. 0 gls.
LC: 3 app. 0 gls.
Total:
23 (4) app. 0 gls.

CHIVERS, Martin Harcourt

Role: Forward 1962-68
6' 1" 12st.2lbs.
b. Southampton 27 April 1945

CAREER: Foundry Lane School/Taunton Grammar/C.P.C. Sports May 1961/SOUTHAMPTON Sept 1962/Tottenham Hotspur Jan 1968/Servette, Switzerland July 1976/Norwich City July 1978/Brighton & Hove Albion Mar 1979/Dorchester Town player-manager Aug 1980/Vard, Norway player-coach 1981/Barnet Oct 1982.

Debut v Charlton Athletic (h) 8.9.62

Martin Chivers initiated his Southampton career by writing and asking for a trial and, after a brief spell with C.P.C. Sports, Saints' nursery side, made his full debut aged 17. He was a powerful, long-striding forward with an eye for goal and, with Terry Paine loading the gun, Martin fired most of the bullets in the club's successful quest for First Division football. Playing alongside Ron Davies, Martin quickly confirmed his position as one of the country's top young strikers and rumours of his unrest at the Dell soon had the country's foremost clubs licking their lips and checking their bank balances. His departure to Spurs for a record £125,000 was viewed with gloom by many in Southampton but Ted Bates knew that he had, in the reserves, the ideal replacement in Michael Channon. Martin went on to justify his huge transfer fee at Spurs, eventually winning 24 England caps to augment his 12 Under-23 caps won while he was a Saint. After finishing his playing days at Brighton he flirted with the managerial/coaching side of the game before becoming an hotelier in Hertfordshire.

Appearances:
FL: 174 app. 97 gls.
FAC: 7 app. 4 gls.
LC: 8 app. 6 gls.
Total: *189 app. 107 gls.*

❏ **Saints note** - *During the 1965-66 season Martin scored 30 League goals in the first 29 games but strangely failed to find the net in the remaining 13 fixtures.*

Left: Martin Chivers

CHRISTIE, Alexander Gray

Role: Half-back 1922-23
5' 10" 12st.0lbs.
b. Glasgow 27 June 1896
d. Reading 22 May 1981

CAREER: Royal Navy Barracks/Hamilton Academicals/Reading 1919/Walsall June 1921/SOUTHAMPTON May 1922/Norwich City July 1923/Rochdale July 1924/Exeter City May 1928.

Alex Christie

Debut v Port Vale (a) 17.2.22

Alex Christie had a brief spell at the Dell and, although a contemporary account described him as 'coolness personified', he had limited chances in what was a strong half-back line at that time. On the retained list for the 1923-24 season he was, however, allowed a free transfer in July and moved to Norwich City.

Appearances:
FL: 5 app. 0 gls.
Total: *5 app. 0 gls.*

CHRISTIE, John Alexander

Role: Goalkeeper 1950-59
5' 10" 10st.11lbs.
b. Fraserburgh 26 September 1929

CAREER: Inverness Thistle/Ayr United Jan 1951/SOUTHAMPTON Jan 1951/Walsall June 1959/Burton Albion Aug 1962/Rugby Town July 1963.

Debut v Swansea Town (a) 3.2.51

John Christie came to Southampton's attention whilst serving his national service at Farnborough and Sid Cann was quick to secure his transfer from Ayr United. Agile and brave, John spent long periods in and out of the side. He was transfer listed at the end of the 1955-56 season and yet played 44 games the following year. The close season of 1959 saw him Midlands bound with Walsall and he was to win Fourth and Third Division

Championship medals at Fellows Park before stepping into non-league football with Peter Taylor at Burton Albion. His playing days ended in 1964 and he returned to Southampton working as a representative in the electrical business whilst lending assistance to Pat Parker, his one time team mate, then manager of Cowes.

Appearances:
FL: 192 app. 0 gls.
FAC: 17 app. 0 gls.
Total: *209 app. 0 gls.*

CHRISTMAS, Edwin Cecil Russell

Role: Forward 1911-12
5' 10" 11st.5lbs.
b. Southampton January qtr 1886
d. France, killed in action November 1916

CAREER: Bannister Court/SOUTHAMPTON am. 1908.

Debut v Crystal Palace (a) 16.3.12

Cecil Christmas

Cecil Christmas was a local amateur who first joined Southampton during the 1908-09 season and would possibly have gone far if business claims had not prevented him from devoting much time to soccer. He briefly left the game during 1910 but George Carter, the reserve team manager, aware of Cecil's pace and dribbling skills, persuaded him to return to the Dell in 1911. He was rewarded with two first team outings in March 1912 but his courageous play led him to be injured badly enough to force his permanent retirement.

Appearances;
SL: 2 app. 0 gls.
Total: *2 app. 0 gls.*

John Christie

CLARK, Joseph Walter

Role: Forward 1922-23
5′ 8″ 11st.0lbs.
*b. Willington Quay
15 February 1890*

CAREER: Wallsend
Park Villa/Hebburn
Argyle/Cardiff City
May 1913/Aberaman
Athletic Apr 1921/
SOUTHAMPTON May
1922/Rochdale June
1923.

*Debut v South Shields (a)
26.8.22*

The only newcomer to the Saints' staff at the beginning of the 1922-23 season, Joe Clark had impressed whilst playing for Cardiff in the previous season's replayed cup tie. Unfortunately for Southampton he never reproduced such form in a red and white shirt and was transfer listed at £100. With no takers he was given a free transfer in the summer of 1923 to Rochdale.

Appearances:
*FL: 20 app. 0 gls.
FAC: 1 app. 0 gls.*
Total: *21 app. 0 gls.*

CLARK, Thomas Henry

Role: Forward 1909-11
b. Tilbury 4 June 1887

CAREER: St. Mary's Guild/Shirley
Warren 1908/SOUTHAMPTON am.
Aug 1909, pro. Nov 1909.

*Debut v Southend United (h) 27.12.09 *
(scored on debut)*

Thomas Clark first appeared at the Dell in a trial match in 1907 but did not become a Saint until August 1909. He had the good fortune to score on his debut later that same season but he remained firmly in the shadow of Frank Jefferis throughout the next two years and he was not on Saints' retained list at the end of the 1911-12 season.

Appearances:
SL: 5 app. 1 gl.
Total: *5 app. 1 gl.*

CLARKE, Colin John

Role: Forward 1986-89
5′ 11″ 12st.10lbs.
b. Newry, N. Ireland 30 October 1962

CAREER: Ipswich Town Oct 1980/
Peterborough June 1981 (Gillingham-loan-Mar
1984)/Tranmere Rovers July 1984/A.F.C.
Bournemouth July 1985/SOUTHAMPTON
July 1986 (A.F.C. Bournemouth-loan-Dec
1988)/ Queen's Park Rangers Mar 1989/
Portsmouth May 1990.

*Debut v Queen's Park Rangers (h) 23.8.86 *
(scored on debut)*

It took Colin Clarke some time to launch his career from the obscurity of the lower divisions. Rejection by Bobby Robson at Ipswich Town, followed by a free transfer from Peterborough to Tranmere, did nothing to

Colin Clarke

suggest that the young Irishman had a rosy future in the game, and yet, within two years, he was scoring for his country in the World Cup Finals. Just days after his return from Mexico, Chris Nicholl spent £400,000 to bring him to the Dell and he was an immediate sensation scoring a hat-trick on his debut - the first ever Saint to perform this feat. Twenty League goals in his first season and 16 in the next, established Colin as a striker of international repute but as quickly as he won the fans' praise he fell from grace with a series of transfer requests and talk of a move to a

Graham Clarke

"bigger team". After six months of acrimony, during which he languished in the reserves and was loaned to Bournemouth, he was sold to Queen's Park Rangers for a fee approaching £800,000 and, although at first the sizeable fee looked justified, Colin later struggled to maintain his early Southampton form. Portsmouth broke their transfer record when they paid Q.P.R. £450,000 for him in the close season of 1990.

Appearances;
FL: 82 app. 36 gls.
FAC: 3 app. 1 gl.
LC: 12 app. 2 gls.
Total: *97 app. 39 gls.*

❑ **Saints note** - *Whilst Colin was at Southampton he won a total of 13 Northern Ireland caps.*

CLARKE, Graham Peter

Role: Full-back 1957-59
5' 4" 12st.1lbs.
b. Nottingham 11 August 1935

CAREER: Nottingham Boys/ SOUTHAMPTON June 1953/Ashford Town Aug 1959.

Debut v Shrewsbury Town (h) 19.10.57

Graham Clarke made a name for himself in Nottingham schools football as a wing-half. At 16 he was capped for England in the 1951 youth internationals and the following season skippered the national youth side on two occasions. He signed for Southampton on a part-time professional basis in June 1953 and then did not make his debut in the reserves until 1955. Although he was a regular and consistent member of the combination team, the form of Len Wilkins and then Ron Davies in the first team led to his release into non-league football.

Appearances:
FL: 3 app. 0 gls.
Total: *3 app. 0 gls.*

CLARKE, William Harry

Role: Full-back 1905-07
5' 10" 12st.0lbs.
b. Kettering January qtr. 1880

CAREER: Kettering/Kettering St. Mary's/ Kettering/Sheffield United Sept 1902/ Northampton Town c.s. 1903/ SOUTHAMPTON Apr1905.

Debut v Brentford (h) 2.9.05

Regarded as the club's best capture during the 1905 close season, Bill Clarke had previously played for Northampton Town and was generally considered the most promising left-back in the Southern League. His speed enabled him to overhaul the quickest of forwards but, soon after his move south, he fell ill and although he showed glimpses of the form that brought him into prominence his overall play was disappointing. Bill had the additional misfortune to suffer a serious knee injury in 1907 and after a year struggling to regain fitness he retired in October 1908.

Appearances:
SL: 51 app. 0 gls.
FAC: 4 app. 0 gls.
Total: *55 app. 0 gls.*

Bill (Harry) Clarke

CLARKE, William Henry

Role: Forward 1938-39
5′ 7 ″ 10st.5lbs.
b Leicester July qtr 1916

CAREER: Leicester Nomads/Leicester City
Feb 1936/Exeter June 1937/SOUTHAMPTON
July 1938.

Debut v Blackburn Rovers (a) 15.4.39

Bill Clarke featured in Leicester City's 1937-38
pre-season squad photograph but moved to
Exeter before ever making Leicester's first
team. Within a year he was at the Dell but
played only twice, the final game being the last
competitive fixture on the record books before
World War Two. Given a free transfer, Bill
failed to find another League club and his
professional career came to an end.

> **Appearances:**
> *FL: 2 app. 0 gls.*
> **Total:** *2 app. 0 gls.*

CLAWLEY, George

Role: Goalkeeper 1896-98 & 1903-07
6′ 2″ 12st.7lbs.
b. Scholar Green 10 April 1875
d. Southampton 16 July 1920

CAREER: Crewe Alexandra Aug 1893/
Stoke Sept 1894/
SOUTHAMPTON St.
Mary's c.s. 1896/Stoke
May 1898/Tottenham
Hotspur c.s.1899/
SOUTHAMPTON
c.s.1903.

Debut v Chatham (h)
19.9.96

One of the finest
uncapped goalkeepers
ever to grace the
football fields of
England, George
Clawley possessed the
physical requirements
of height and reach
that were to make him
one of the greats
around the turn of the
century. Within his first

CLARKE'S
Football Series No. 30.

George Clawley.
Photo by Globe Photo Co., Southampton

two seasons as a Saint he helped the club to
their first ever championship and then
captained the team as they not only retained
the title but reached the F.A. Cup semi-final.
He moved back to Stoke in 1898 and a year
later joined Tottenham where he had the
misfortune to break his leg. The injury
sidelined him for a whole season but he
returned to play his part in Spurs' cup-
winning run in 1901. Returning to the Dell in
1903, he replaced Jack Robinson, and straight
away gained his third championship medal.
After a further 121 Southern League games
George decided to retire in 1907 and he
became landlord of the Wareham Arms Hotel
in Southampton.

> **Appearances:**
> *SL: 163 app. 0 gls.*
> *FAC: 28 app. 0 gls.*
> **Total:** *191 app. 0 gls.*

CLEMENTS, Stanley F. T.

Role: Centre-half 1946-55
6′ 2″ 12st.12lbs.
b. Portsmouth 25 June 1923

CAREER: Gosport Borough/(Portsmouth
during World War Two) SOUTHAMPTON
July 1944/ Basingstoke Town Feb 1955 player-
coach.

Debut v Fulham (h) 24.5.47

A big strong centre-half, Stan
arrived at the Dell during
wartime and spent six seasons
playing second fiddle to Eric
Webber in the first team before
eventually becoming captain in
1952. A brief spell as player/coach
at Basingstoke convinced him that
his future lay outside the game and
he reverted to his original trade, that
of surveyor. He emigrated to South
Africa in the late 1950's.

> **Appearances:**
> *FL: 116 app. 1 gl.*
> *FAC: 4 app. 0 gls.*
> **Total:** *120 app. 1 gl.*

Stan Clements

CLIFTON, Brian

Role: Forward 1957-63
5' 11" 11st.4lbs.
b. Whitchurch
15 March 1934

CAREER:
Andover/Whitchurch/
Portals F.C./
SOUTHAMPTON Feb   *Brian Clifton*
1953/Grimsby Town Oct
1962/Boston United1966/ Gainsborough
Trinity 1969/Boston United 1970-73/Ross F.C.
manager 1973-76/Tarten Over 40's (Grimsby)
during 1980's.

Debut v Brighton & Hove Albion (h) 28.9.57

A product of Hampshire schools football,
Brian Clifton was 'discovered' by ex-Saint Stan
Woodhouse whilst turning out in the Hants
League for Whitchurch. His first two years as a
Southampton player were spent in the R.A.F.
doing his National Service but, when he
eventually forced his way into the first team,
he soon displayed his versatility playing either
in the half-back or forward lines. His main
strength was his heading and, after his move
to Grimsby for £8,000 in 1962, he often
appeared in the centre-half position for the
Mariners. Upon finishing with football Brian
took up work as a draughtsman at a frozen
food company in Grimsby. In May 1991 Brian
was living in Cleethorpes and working as the
drawing office manager with the same
company.

> **Appearances;**
> *FL: 111 app. 35 gls.*
> *FAC: 2 app. 0 gls.*
> *LC: 8 app. 1 gl.*
> **Total:** *121 app. 36 gls.*

COAK, Tim David

Role: Full-back 1976-78
5' 5" 10st.4lbs.
b. Southampton
16 January 1958

CAREER: Hampton Park
school and Southampton
schools/SOUTHAMPTON
app. July 1974, pro. Jan
1976/Salisbury 1978/

Gosport Borough Sept 1984/
Waterlooville/Bashley July 1989/Gosport
Borough Oct 1989/Eastleigh Jan 1991.
Debut v Orient (a) 26.4.77

When Tom Parker saw Tim Coak playing for
the Southampton Under-14 Schoolboy team he
had no hesitation in recommending that the
club sign the young full back on associate
schoolboy terms. That was in December 1972
but, despite Tom Parker's confidence, Tim
never quite made the grade in the top flight.
An attacking full-back he had, by 1978, already
embarked on a career with a whole host of
local non-league clubs while still only 20 years
old.

> **Appearances:**
> *FL: 4 app. 0 gls.*
> *FAC: 2 app. 0 gls.*
> **Total:** *6 app. 0 gls.*

COATES, Arthur

Role: Full-back 1912-13
5' 10" 12st.6lbs.
b. Wensleydale, Yorkshire

CAREER: Salford United/Heywood United/
Exeter City 1910/SOUTHAMPTON c.s. 1912/
Heywood United c.s. 1913.
Debut v Northampton Town (h) 4.9.12

Arthur Coates was introduced to senior
football by former Saint,
Arthur Chadwick, at
Exeter City and was
signed by Southampton
in the summer of 1912
as a replacement for
right-back Jack
Eastham. He showed
early promise but, as
the 1912-13 season
unfolded, his form
faded and he was
released to Heywood
United, a former club, in
the close season of 1913.

> **Appearances;**
> *SL: 21 app. 0 gls.*
> **Total:** *21 app. 0 gls.*

Tim Coak

COATES, Herbert James Leopold

Role: Forward 1928-34
5′ 8″ 11st.0lbs.
b. West Ham October qtr. 1901
d. Southsea 25 October 1965

CAREER: Royal Navy/SOUTHAMPTON am.
Oct 1928/Leyton 1934.
Debut v Chelsea (a) 27.10.28

"Rigger" Coates' first taste of League football
came at the relatively late age of 27, having up
to then confined his soccer talents to the Royal
Navy XI. He remained an amateur throughout
his six seasons at Southampton preferring to
remain in service on the Royal Yacht, Victoria
and Albert, to pursue what undoubtedly
would have been a successful professional
career. In 1959 a contemporary reflected that
"Rigger was one of the finest inside lefts that
ever wore an England Amateur jersey, and his
clever dribbling, his brilliant anticipation and
his terrific shots more than compensated for
the fact that his play may have been a bit on
the showy side". Altogether he won eight
England Amateur caps and in 1934 moved to
top amateur side Leyton. He continued to play
for the Royal Navy until 1937. He survived the
war to become the manager of a public house
in Portsmouth in 1945 and later worked for the
Southern Electricity Board.

Appearances;
FL: 99 app. 26 gls.
FAC: 3 app. 0 gls.
Total: *102 app. 26 gls.*

*Left:
Herbert
'Rigger'
Coates*

*Right:
Glenn
Cockerill*

COCKERILL, Glenn

Role: Midfield 1985-
6′ 0″ 12st.4lbs.
b. Grimsby 25 August 1959

CAREER: Louth United/Lincoln City Nov 1976/Swindon Town Dec 1979/Lincoln City Aug 1981/Sheffield United Mar 1984/ SOUTHAMPTON Oct 1985.

Debut v Luton Town (a) 19.10.85

Twenty six year-old Glenn Cockerill was Chris Nicholl's first ever Southampton signing and arrived in the First Division having served a lengthy apprenticeship in the lower leagues. The scorer of some stunning goals for the club, Glenn, alongside Jimmy Case, was the bedrock of the Saints midfield throughout Chris Nicholl's six year tenure of office and his surging runs are a particular feature of his game. His high fitness level often means that he improves as matches unwind and his stamina has frequently stood the team in good stead in the final minutes of vital First Division clashes. Was appointed team captain in August 1991.

Appearances:
FL: 203 (10) app. 28 gls.
FAC: 14 (1) app. 2 gls.
LC: 27 (1) app. 3 gls.
Total: *244 (12) app. 33 gls.*

❏ **Saints note** - *Glenn's younger brother, John, plays for Grimsby while their father, Ron, was on the books of Huddersfield and Grimsby.*

COHAM, John Harding

Role: Forward 1910-11
b. Southampton April qtr 1892

CAREER: St. Mark's School/Freemantle School/St. Paul's Athletic/Eastleigh Athletic/ Bishopstoke/SOUTHAMPTON c.s.1910/ Partick Thistle c.s.1911.

Debut v Exeter City 4.2.11

John Coham was a pupil of St. Mark's Junior School which adjoined the Eastern side of the Dell and graduated to play Hampshire County football with Eastleigh Athletic. Introduced to the Saints in the summer of 1910, he proved to be a fleet-footed left-winger who, although on the light side, was an excellent deputy for Joe Blake. John left the area in 1911 and, moving to Scotland, signed for Partick Thistle to enjoy three seasons at Firhill Park before returning to live in Southampton.

Appearances:
SL: 6 app. 0 gls.
Total: *6 app. 0 gls.*

COLE, Norman Philip

Role: Forward 1933-35
5′ 10″ 12st.0lbs.
b. Woolston, Southampton 7 November 1913
d. Southampton 29 November 1976

CAREER: Sholing School/Taunton School/ Itchen Sports/Thornycrofts/Newport (I.O.W.) /SOUTHAMPTON am. Aug 1932, pro. Oct. 1932/Norwich City May 1935.

Debut v Bradford City (a) 30.12.33

When Ted Drake departed for Arsenal a forlorn gap was created in Southampton's forward line and it was to Norman Cole that the fans, George Kay and the local press turned. The Echo did their best to remain optimistic describing Norman as "big, strong and ruddy of hair" and on another day "vigorous and fast." Initially he lived up to our local reporters' expectations, scoring a hat-trick

Norman Cole

against West Ham United on April 7th but in the following season the whole team, and in particular the forward line, struggled to make any sort of impact. Norman finished top scorer with a paltry eight goals but, within days of the season ending, was transferred to Carrow Road. His stay at Norwich lasted just one season during which he made one League outing and he returned south to work for Southern Railways in Southampton Docks as an engineer. He was later employed at Follands.

Appearances:
FL: 34 app. 13 gls.
FAC:1 app. 0 gls.
Total: *35 app. 13 gls.*

COLLINS, Eamonn Anthony Stephen

Role: Midfield 1984-86
5' 6" 8st. 3lbs.
b. Dublin 22 October 1965

CAREER: Blackpool Apr 1980/ SOUTHAMPTON app. Dec 1981, pro. Oct 1983/Portsmouth May 1986 (Exeter City-loan-Nov 1987) (Gillingham-loan-Nov 1988)/ Colchester United Apr 1989.

Debut v Queen's Park Rangers 29.9.84

It's fair to say that Alan Ball wielded considerable influence on Eamonn Collins' development as a young footballer. They first met at Blackpool, where Alan Ball was having his first taste of management, and decided that he would play the then 14 year-old Eamonn in a Texaco Cup match, making him an overnight celebrity in the national sports pages. Alan Ball obviously believed in the young Irishman's capabilities for, when he returned to the Dell, he persuaded Eamonn to come with him as an apprentice. A light-weight

Eamonn Collins

midfielder, Eamonn played regularly for the reserves but lacked the muscle to force himself into the first team and it was no surprise when he followed his mentor, first to Portsmouth, and then to Colchester.

Appearances:
FL: 1 (2) app. 0 gls.
LC: 1 (1) app. 0 gls.
Total: *2 (3) app. 0 gls.*

CONNOR, Richard John

Role: Half-back 1959-61
5' 8" 11st.0lbs.
b. Jarrow 13 August 1931

CAREER: St. Bedes (Jarrow)/Newcastle United Jan 1950/South Shields c.s. 1951/ Grimsby Town Aug 1952/SOUTHAMPTON July 1959/Tranmere Rovers July 1961/ Aldershot July 1962, asst. trainer 1963/ Rochdale manager Feb 1970/Darlington manager July 1973-May 1974/Grimsby Town coach-asst. manager 1974-1976;/Rochdale asst. manager 1976-80.

Debut v Norwich City (a) 22.8.59

A neat, strong half-back, Dick Connor moved South from Grimsby in the summer of 1959 to strengthen Saints' half-back line, and his constructive influence was immediately felt as the team surged towards promotion. A shrewd player, his acquisition by Ted Bates had been equally shrewd as Dick missed just one game during the whole championship season. He had one season with the Saints in the Second Division before, rather surprisingly, he left for Tranmere, although within a year he was back in Hampshire with Aldershot. In 1980 he left football to become a publican in the Rochdale area. Eight years later he moved back to his home town and worked on a part-time basis assisting Jim Smith at Newcastle. He has fond memories of his time at the Dell and attended the 1985 centenary dinner.

Appearances:
FL: 78 app. 2 gls.
FAC: 8 app. 0 gls.
LC: 5 app. 0 gls.
Total: *91 app. 2 gls.*

COOPER, John

Role: Forward 1921-23
5′ 9″ 11st.0lbs.
b. Wednesbury, Staffs January qtr 1898

CAREER: Darlaston/SOUTHAMPTON Apr 1921

Debut v Brentford (h) 31.12.21

Said by the Football Echo to be "the best inside-right in the Birmingham League" at the time he joined Saints, John Cooper, together with team mate Henry Johnson, topped the goalscoring charts whilst with Darlaston. With Manchester United, Cardiff City and Sunderland all keen on securing their services, it was Saints who moved fast to sign the duo in April 1921. Unlike Johnson, John was unable to live up to expectations and, although he met with some success at Southern League level (16 goals in 34 appearances during his first full season), he found it impossible to push the old war horse Arthur Dominy from the senior side. Placed on the transfer list in May 1923 with a £200 price tag, John left the area and although given a free transfer a year later he was never seen again in League circles.

Appearances:
FL: 5 app. 0 gls.
Total: *5 app. 0 gls.*

Andy Cook

COOK, Andrew Charles

Role: Full-back & Midfield 1987-91
5′ 9″ 10st.12lbs.
b. Romsey 10 August 1969

CAREER: Mountbatten School/Eastleigh & Winchester Schools/Hampshire Schools/SOUTHAMPTON trainee c.s. 1985, pro. July 1987/Exeter City Sept 1991.

Debut v Manchester United (h) 15.8.87

Andy Cook took the place of full-back Mark Dennis for the opening two games of the 1987-88 season and showed much promise before the arrival of Derek Statham heralded a return to the reserves. As a youth player Andy had featured on the left-wing and also appeared at times in midfield but suffered from not truly settling into any one position. His versatility on the left-hand side of the pitch will be a useful asset to his new club Exeter and with Alan Ball as his boss, Andy's career should blossom.

Appearances:
FL: 11 (5) app. 1 gl.
FAC: 1 app. 0 gls.
LC: 4 app. 0 gls.
Total: *16 (5) app. 1 gl.*

John Cooper

COSTELLO, Frederick G.

Role: Forward 1907-09
b. Birmingham 1884
d. France 19 December 1914

CAREER: Soho Villa/West Bromwich Albion
am. Sept 1904/Halesowen/SOUTHAMPTON
May 1907/West Ham United Mar 1909/Bolton
Wanderers June 1909/Nelson 1910/Merthyr
Town/Salisbury City.
*Debut v Luton Town (a) 14.9.07 * (scored on debut)*

An import from the Birmingham area during
the 1907 close season, Frank Costello made a
considerable impact when he gained first team
selection in September. Although a trifle slow
he was clever with the ball and had a habit of
disconcerting opposing defences by making
for goal when he was expected to make a wing
pass. During the 1908-09 campaign Frank was
converted from his usual inside-forward
position to centre-forward but a failure to
maintain form was followed by a transfer to
West Ham. He failed to make the Hammers'
first team and moved to Bolton after only three
months. He later settled to live in
Southampton but lost his life serving his
country in France at the beginning of the war.

Appearances:
SL: 41 app. 10 gls.
FAC: 7 app. 3 gls.
Total: *48 app. 13 gls.*

COUNDON, Cuthbert

Role: Forward 1925-28
5' 7" 11st.0lbs.
b. Sunderland 3 April 1905
d. Sutton 18 December 1978

CAREER: Sunderland Schoolboys/
Mercantile Dock XI/Jarrow 1923/
SOUTHAMPTON Apr 1925/
Wolverhampton Wanderers June
1928/Southend United
May 1929/Guildford City
July 1930/ Sutton United
trainer/coach Sept 1935.
Debut v Swansea (h)
*24.10.25 * (scored on*
debut)

Dubbed "The Kid" by the Saints supporters
when he made his League debut in October
1925, Cuthbert's youthful appearance was
certainly misleading. As a twenty year-old and
still doing an apprenticeship as a joiner, he was
a sturdily built winger brimful with
enthusiasm. With two goals in his first three
games Cuthbert formed an instant
understanding with Arthur Dominy only to be
thwarted by the return of regular winger
Henderson. After three seasons with limited
chances, he was transfer-listed at £300, the
figure Saints had paid Jarrow in April 1925. As
it turned out, Saints received only half that
figure on his transfer to Wolves in June 1928.

Appearances:
FL: 26 app. 3 gls.
FAC: 1 app. 0 gls.
Total: *27 app. 3 gls.*

COWPER, Peter Poole

Role: Forward 1930-32
5' 8" 12st.0 lbs.
b. Tyldesley 1 September 1902
d. Clifton, Cumbria 26 September 1962

Cuthbert Coundon

CAREER: Burns Celtic/Parkside Rangers/Atherton/ Wigan Borough 1923/ Rossendale United 1924/West Ham United June 1924/ Grimsby Town June 1927/Lancaster Town Apr 1928/New Brighton Aug 1928/ SOUTHAMPTON June 1930/Southport Mar 1932/Carlisle July 1932/Wigan Athletic July 1933/Altrincham Sept 1934/Prescot Cables 1936.

Debut v Tottenham Hotspur (h) 26.12.30   *Peter Cowper*

Much travelled by the time of his Dell arrival, Peter Cowper was a prolific goalscorer for the reserves with 33 goals in 50 matches but was never able to reproduce his predatory instincts in the first team. He was soon packing his bags again in a move that took him north to a further five clubs.

Appearances:
FL: 5 app. 0 gls.
Total: *5 app. 0 gls.*

COX, Walter

Role: Goalkeeper 1894-96
b. Southampton

CAREER: SOUTHAMPTON St. Mary's 1892/ Bristol St. Georges c.s.1897/Bedminster May 1898/Millwall Oct 1899/Manchester City May 1900/Bury Mar 1903/Preston North End Jan 1906/Dundee May 1906.

Debut v Reading (h) F.A.C. 3.11.1894

Walter Cox played his first game for the Saints as an outfield player in 1892 but within a couple of years had decided that his future lay between the posts. His first team appearances were limited and he was regularly overlooked by the club's slection committee in favour of Ruffell, Barrett, Williamson and Cain. His most memorable match came in the F.A. Cup against Sheffield Wednesday in February 1896 when, despite conceding three goals, he performed heroically

and consequently won County representation. With the arrival of George Clawley, Walter moved on to Bristol.

Appearances:
SL: 3 app. 0 gls.
FAC: 7 app. 0 gls.
Total: *10 app. 0 gls.*

CRABBE, Stephen Allan John

Role: Midfield 1974-76
5′ 8″ 10st.6lbs.
b. Weymouth 20 October 1954

CAREER: Westham School, Weymouth/ SOUTHAMPTON app. 1970, pro. Oct 1972/(Hellenic (S. Africa) Mar 1976 loan), (Gillingham loan Jan 1977, permanent Feb 1977)/Carlisle United Aug 1981/Hereford United Aug 1982/ Crewe Alexandra Aug 1983/Torquay United Sept 1985/Crawley Town Aug 1986/ Canterbury City Nov 1987/Ashford Town player-coach July 1990.

Debut v West Ham United (FAC) (h) 4.1.75

Predictably nicknamed "Buster", John Crabbe was a tenacious midfielder who graduated through the usual youth channels to make his

John Crabbe

debut when Saints met West Ham in the Third Round of the F.A. Cup. He kept his place to make his League debut at York the following Friday but the arrival of Jim McCalliog was to restrict Buster to a life in the reserves and, after leaving Saints, his career was restricted to the lower divisions.

Appearances:
FL: 8 (4) app. 0 gls.
FAC: 1 app. 0 gls.
Total: *9 (4) app. 0 gls.*

CRABBE, William

Role: Full-back 1899-1900

CAREER: SOUTHAMPTON 1899.

Debut v Swindon Town (a) 13.1.1900

Bill Crabbe's only game for the Saints was an away match with Swindon which was played at Reading due to the fact that Swindon's ground was closed. Reports of the match describe the young right-back's performance as plucky but he was never seen again and, as his origins are also unknown, he remains an anonymous figure in the club's history.

Appearances:
SL: 1 app. 0 gls.
Total: *1 app. 0 gls.*

Stan Cribb and a young mascot

CRIBB, Stanley Roy

Role: Forward 1924-30
5' 8" 11st.0lbs.
b. Gosport 11 May 1905
d. Gosport 13 January 1989

CAREER: Grove Road School, Gosport/Elson St. Thomas/Gosport Athletic 1923/ SOUTHAMPTON Sept 1924/West Ham United May 1930/Queen's Park Rangers June 1931/Cardiff City July 1932/Haslar Sports F.C. coach 1943/Gosport Borough 1944 honorary manager.

Debut v Crystal Palace (h) 24.1.25

Stan was signed from Hampshire League Champions Gosport Athletic in 1924 having already won County representative honours before reaching his seventeenth birthday. He was a quick outside-left who became a dependable penalty-taker for the Saints and he remained at the Dell for six seasons. West Ham paid £500 for him in 1930 but he never made their first team preferring to move to Queen's Park Rangers where he scored 13 times in 28 appearances. A further 11 League goals in 26 League outings at Ninian Park preceded a premature retirement in 1933. He continued to be involved in football helping in the formation of Gosport Borough F.C. and was their manager between 1944 and 1967. He followed football passionately right up to his death, scouting for the Saints in the Portsmouth area and hardly missed a match at his beloved Privett Park.

Appearances:
FL: 70 app. 22 gls.
FAC: 5 app. 0 gls.
Total: *75 app. 22 gls.*

CRICK, George William

Role: Half-back 1914-15
5' 9" 12st.0lbs.
b. Newmarket October qtr. 1891

CAREER: Market Harborough/ SOUTHAMPTON May 1914.

Debut v Millwall (h) 23.1.15

One of two young players signed from Leicestershire side Market Harborough, George Crick joined Saints as a half-back in May 1914. A member of the club's South

George Crick

Lawrence Cumming

Eastern League team, he became adaptable to any of the right-side defensive positions including centre-half and, with eight first team appearances under his belt, appeared to have a rosy future until the suspension of soccer due to the war foreshadowed his retirement from the game.

Appearances:
SL: 8 app. 0 gls.
Total: *8 app. 0 gls.*

CUMMING, Lawrence

Role: Forward 1930-31
5′ 11″ 12st.4lbs.
b. Londonderry 1907

CAREER: Alloa Athletic/Huddersfield Town Mar 1927/Oldham Athletic Oct 1929/ SOUTHAMPTON June 1930/Alloa Athletic 1931/Queen of the South Sept 1933/St. Mirren.

Debut v Preston North End (a) 30.8.30

Lawrence Cumming had won three Northern Irish caps whilst at Huddersfield and Oldham and Saints' management parted with £500 to acquire his services. His debut was far from auspicious as Saints went down 5-0 at Preston on the opening day of the 1930-31 season but

in the next nine games he scored four goals, including two in the away win at Plymouth. His goalscoring dried up completely on the heavier pitches and he was placed on the transfer list at his own request. He moved back to Scotland, at first on a non-contract basis with Alloa, and then on a £100 transfer to Queen of the South. Lawrence later found work in advertising with a Scottish newspaper.

Appearances:
FL: 20 app. 4 gls.
FAC: 1 app. 0 gls.
Total: *21 app. 4 gls.*

CUMMINS, Joseph Henry

Role: Forward 1933-34
5′ 10″ 12st.0lbs.
b. Plympton, Devon 8 April 1910

CAREER: Jersey Wanderers/ SOUTHAMPTON Nov 1933/Sportive Union Tourcoing (France) Sept 1934/Newport (I.O.W.).

Debut v Millwall (a) 9.4.34

Joe Cummins was signed from Channel Island soccer in November 1933 and quickly settled into the combination side. His only League outing came in the inside right position, the day after his 24th birthday at Millwall but he sustained an early injury that resulted in him being a passenger for most of the game. Soon after the start of the following season he moved to the continent, although he later returned to Hampshire to play on the Isle of Wight and work at the Ordnance Survey.

Appearances:
FL: 1 app. 0 gls.
Total: *1 app. 0 gls.*

CUNNINGHAM, Charles A.

Role: Forward 1912-13
b. London

CAREER: London Civil Service/
SOUTHAMPTON trial Dec 1912.

Debut v Millwall (h) 28.12.12

Cunningham, an amateur right-winger from the London Civil Service, arrived at the Dell in December 1912 as a trialist. In what was a struggling side the right-winger failed to impress the selectors and it was not long before he returned to the capital.

Appearances:
SL: 1 app. 0 gls.
Total: *1 app. 0 gls.*

CURRAN, Edward Terence

Role: Forward 1978-79
5' 10" 12st.4lbs.
b. Kinsley 20 March 1955

CAREER: Kinsley/Doncaster Rovers July 1973/ Nottingham Forest Aug1975 (Bury-loan-Oct 1977)/Derby County Nov 1977/ SOUTHAMPTON Aug 1978/Sheffield Wednesday Mar 1979/Sheffield United Aug 1982 (Everton-loan-Dec 1982), perm. Sept 1983/ Huddersfield Town July 1985/Panionios (Greece) July 1986/Hull City trial Oct 1986/ Sunderland Nov 1986/Grantham n/c/ Grimsby Town Oct 1987/Chesterfield Mar 1988/Goole Town manager Nov 1989.

Debut v Norwich City (a) 19.8.78

Lawrie McMenemy spent £60,000 on Terry Curran hoping that his crossing abilities would help Ted MacDougall score the goals vitally

Terry Curran

needed if Saints were to re-establish themselves back in Division One. Terry was tricky but had a maverick streak that could infuriate fans and coaches alike. He did score one priceless goal in the League Cup semi-final against Leeds United and, considering that Saints made a profit of £40,000 when he moved on to join Jack Charlton at Hillsborough, his stay at the Dell was a profitable if not a lengthy one. Terry matured at Sheffield and enjoyed an excellent 1979-80 season during which he scored 22 goals provoking short-lived talk of International Honours.

Appearances:
FL: 25 (1) app. 0 gls.
FAC: 5 app. 0 gls.
LC: 8 app. 1 gl.
Total: *38 (1) app. 1 gl.*

CURRY, Joseph

Role: Half-back 1911-12
5'9" 12st.0lbs.
b. Newcastle January qtr 1887

CAREER: Scotswood/Manchester United Feb 1908/SOUTHAMPTON May 1911.

Debut v Millwall (h) 2.9.11

One of George Swift's first signings as Saints'

manager Joe Curry, a Manchester United reserve, came to the Dell in May 1911. First team opportunities were limited and when there was a chance of inclusion he was more often than not "hors de combat". By the time he regained his fitness the half-back line had found some form and, after a frustrating season, Joe gave up the professional game and returned to live in his native north east.

Appearances:
SL: 7 app. 0 gls.
Total: *7 app. 0 gls.*

CURTIN, Charles

Role: Forward 1913-15
5' 7" 11st.5lbs.
b. Gateshead July qtr 1890
d. Clapham, Bedford 29 July 1967

CAREER: Ryhope Villa/Norwich City July 1911/SOUTHAMPTON Apr 1914/West Stanley/Workington 1921/Caernarvon Athletic 1926-27.

Debut v Northampton Town (h) 18.4.14

A sturdily built outside right, Charles Curtin moved to Southampton from Norwich in 1914 and played in the last two games of the 1913-14 campaign. Exceptionally fast, he could turn and leave many of his

Charles Curtin

opponents floundering. During the following season Charles provided an endless supply of dangerous and accurate crosses which enabled Dominy and Kimpton to become the chief marksmen in the Southern League. As with many of his countrymen he joined the war effort in 1915 and left the area, only to reappear later back in his native north east with West Stanley.

Appearances:
SL: 29 app. 5 gls.
FAC: 4 app. 0 gls.
Total: *33 app. 5 gls.*

CURTIS, Alan Thomas

Role: Forward 1983-86
5' 10" 12st.5lbs.
b. Rhondda 16 April 1954

CAREER: Porth G.S./Swansea City July 1972/Leeds United June 1979/Swansea City Dec 1980/SOUTHAMPTON Nov 1983 (Stoke City-loan-Feb 1986)/Cardiff City Mar 1986/ Swansea City Oct 1989/Barry Town player-coach c.s.1990/Haverford West County July 1991.

Debut v Stoke City (h) 3.12.83

Alan Curtis joined Leeds United for the large fee of £350,000, having risen to prominence and international honours at Swansea. He returned to Swansea for £180,000 after an unhappy 18 months at Elland Road and spent a further three seasons at the Vetch before trying his luck in England again, this time with the Saints. He was a quiet, deceptive and thoughtful player who at times justified his £80,000 transfer fee only to have games in which he would be largely anonymous.

Alan Curtis

Injuries, and the arrival of Jimmy Case, led to a move back to South Wales, firstly with Cardiff and, finally, back again to Swansea.

Appearances:
FL: 43 (7) app. 5 gls.
FAC: 3 app. 1 gl.
LC: 12 app. 1 gl.
Eur: 1 app. 0 gls.
Total: *59 (7) app. 7 gls.*

❏ **Saints note** - *Alan appeared for Wales five times during his spell at the Dell and later won his 35th and final cap during the 1986-87 season against Russia. He was at the time playing his football in the Fourth Division at Swansea. He is a nephew of Roy Paul the former Welsh International.*

CURTIS, George Frederick

Role: Forward 1947-51
5' 8" 11st.4lbs.
b. West Thurrock 3 December1919

CAREER: Anglo (Purfleet)/Margate (loan)/Arsenal am. Dec 1936, pro. Apr 1937/(guest for Swansea Town, Chelsea and Clapton Orient during World war Two) SOUTHAMPTON Aug 1947/Valenciennes (France) Aug 1952/ Chelmsford City player-coach Aug 1953-Aug 1955/ Sunderland coach 1957-62/Brighton manager c.s.1962-Jan 1964/Cambridge University coach/Hastings coach/ Stevenage manager Jan 1964-68/Hull City coach/San Diego Toros coach 1968/Rosenborg (Norway) manager 1968-71/Norway coach-manager 1971-76/Qatar coach 1979-81.

Debut v Doncaster Rovers (a) 23.8.47

George Curtis played 11 League games for Arsenal during the 1946-47 season and had impressed Bill Dodgin, who valued him at £10,000, in an exchange transfer that also saw Rudkin arrive at the Dell and Don Roper move to Highbury. Nicknamed "Twinkletoes" by his team-mates George was a clever, nimble player whose reluctance sometimes to get stuck in was more than compensated for by his artistry and elegance. His feints and tricks might not have endeared him to some of his more rugged team-mates but the fans certainly appreciated his tactical approach to the game. After five memorable seasons he moved into the French Second Division for a fee of £1,500 but was soon embarking on a coaching course at Lilleshall working with Walter Winterbottom. His coaching skills were quickly in demand and were to take him to various parts of the globe over the next quarter of a century, including a long spell in Norway where, as manager of Rosenborg in 1969, he once more renewed his acquaintance with the Saints when the two sides met in the Fairs Cup competition. Today George lives on the Essex coast and still enjoys coaching youngsters in London as part of the F.I.F.A. coaching scheme, remaining as passionate about the game as ever.

Appearances:
FL:. 174 app. 11 gls.
FAC: 9 app. 1 gl.
Total: *183 app. 12 gls.*

George Curtis

CUTTING, Stanley William

Role: Half-back
1938-39
5' 8" 10st.13lbs.
b. St. Faiths,
Norwich 21
September 1914

CAREER:
Norwich & Norfolk
Boys/Norwich City/ SOUTHAMPTON May
1937/Exeter City July 1939/(Blackpool,
Stockport County, Rochdale, Millwall
during World War Two)/ Exeter City Asst.
trainer 1948.

Stanley Cutting

Debut v Chesterfield (h) 8.4.39

Stanley Cutting followed manager Tom Parker
from Norwich City in May 1937 and became a
regular member of the Combination Side over
the following two seasons. After three League
outings he moved to Exeter in the close season
of 1939, a club he returned to serve at the war's
conclusion. During the hostilities Stan joined
the R.A.F. and, whilst posted in Egypt,
represented Suez Canal Zone versus Cairo
Zone. A later posting took him to India where
he played for the R.A.F. against All India at
Lahore. Stan retired from Exeter's coaching
staff in 1953 to become an hotelier.

    Appearances:
    FL: 3 app. 0 gls.
    Total: *3 app. 0 gls.*

DAINTY, Herbert Charles

D

Role: Centre-half
1904-05
5'8" 12st.0lbs.
b. Geddington, Northamptonshire 6 February 1879

CAREER: Kettering/Leicester Fosse Aug
1899/New Brighton Tower May 1900/
Leicester Fosse Aug 1901/Northampton c.s.
1902/Notts County May 1903/
SOUTHAMPTON May 1904/Dundee May
1905/ Bradford Park Avenue May 1911/Ayr
United player-manager Oct 1913/Dundee
Hibernian player-manager Apr 1915, chairman
1922/South America coaching/Ipswich coach
1932-34.

Debut v Luton Town (a) 3.9.04

By the time Bert Dainty joined the Saints in
May 1904 he had already played for five
professional teams and his transient lifestyle
did not,
unfortunately,
terminate with his
move to the Dell.
A worthy
successor to
previous Saints'
centre-halves,
Bowman and
Chadwick, Bert
was coolness
personified and
was at his best
during desperate
pressure around

Bert Dainty

the goal area. He was also a mainspring when
it came to feeding the ball to the forwards and
the announcement of his imminent departure
to Dundee provoked an outcry in the town.
Breaking with his self-imposed tradition of an
annual transfer, Bert found Dundee to his
liking, staying on Tayside for six years, and
was one of four Englishmen in Dundee's 1910
Scottish Cup winning team. Resuming his
itinerant behaviour Bert moved to England
with Bradford and then back to Scotland,
firstly with Ayr and later with Dundee
Hibernian, soon to become Dundee United.
After the war Bert's travelling instincts took on
more epic proportions with a sojourn coaching
in South America before finding himself back

in Ipswich between 1932 and 1934, again in a coaching capacity. His subsequent destination in 1934 is not known unfortunately but his restlessness should not obscure the fact that he was one of the most cultured centre-halves of his generation.

Appearances:
SL: 31 app. 1 gl.
FAC: 3 app. 0 gls.
Total: *34 app. 1 gl.*

❏ **Saints note** - *During the World War One years Bert formed his own side known as Dainty's XI and played regular matches for charity against other Tayside teams.*

DALE, Joseph

Role: Half-back 1895-96

CAREER: Stoke June 1894/SOUTHAMPTON St.Marys Oct 1895

Debut v Clapton (a) 19.10.1895

A Stoke import in October 1895, Joe Dale followed the busy trail of players from the Potteries to Southampton but, unlike many of the others, his inclusion in the First XI was brief. His debut coincided with a 3-7 thrashing at Clapton and before long he trod the well-worn trail back again to the Midlands.

Appearances:
SL: 3 app. 0 gls.
FAC: 2 app. 0 gls.
Total: *5 app. 0 gls.*

Andrew Davidson

displaying a distinct lack of pace. His neat distribution could not compensate for his ponderousness and within three months he was back in Grimsby hoping to rediscover his sprinting boots!

Appearances:
SL: 5 app. 0 gls.
FAC: 2 app. 0 gls.
Total: *7 app. 0 gls.*

DAVIDSON, Andrew Crawford

Role: Centre-half 1909-10
5'10" 12st.7lbs.
b. Auchinleck, Ayrshire 24 February 1878

CAREER: Ayr United/Middlesbrough May 1900/Bury June 1906/Grimsby Town May 1908/SOUTHAMPTON July 1909/Grimsby Town Oct 1909/Grimsby Rovers.

Debut v Plymouth Argyle (h) 1.9.09

Andrew Davidson had been Grimsby's captain during the 1908-09 season and, although he had a reputation for being a quick centre-half, he seemed to have left his sprinting boots behind at Blundell Park because he was soon

DAVIE, Alexander Grimmond

Role: Goalkeeper 1970-71
6'0" 12st.4lbs.
b. Dundee 10 June 1945

CAREER: Dundee United./Luton Town Sept 1968/SOUTHAMPTON May 1970/Dundee United May 1972.

Debut v Manchester United (a) 20.2.71

A former Scottish Under-23 international goalkeeper, Sandy Davie arrived at the Dell primarily as understudy to fellow Scot Eric Martin. In his one outing he had the misfortune to concede five goals and he was soon on his way back to his native Dundee where he enjoyed several good seasons. He also spent some time in New Zealand playing with North Auckland Suburbs during the late Seventies.

Appearances:
FL: 1 app. 0 gls.
FAC: 0 app. 0 gls.
Total: *1 app. 0 gls.*

Sandy Davie

DAVIES, Ronald Thomas

Role: Full-back 1957-64
5'9" 10st.5lbs.
b. Merthyr Tydfil 21 September 1932

CAREER: Merthyr Tydfil am./Cardiff City

Oct 1952/SOUTHAMPTON Mar 1958/Aldershot Aug 1964/Andover June 1967.

Debut v Swindon Town (a) 7.4.58

Ron Davies had spent six seasons at Ninian Park and, although a full back, had at one time featured in Cardiff's forward line. Ted Bates, more mindful of Ron's defensive qualities spent £7,000 to bring him to the Dell and he proved a worthy successor to the recently departed Len Wilkins. He played every game in Saints' championship season of 1959-60 and was unlucky not to gain international recognition during his spell with the club. The arrival of fellow Welshman Stuart Williams signalled an end to his days at the Dell although he enjoyed a couple of seasons at Aldershot. A stalwart of the Ex-Saints XI, Ron still lives locally and maintains an active interest in the game.

Appearances:
FL: 162 app. 0 gls.
FAC: 12 app. 0 gls.
LC: 11 app. 0 gls.
Total: *185 app. 0 gls.*

Ron Davies (below left)

DAVIES, Ronald Tudor

Role: Forward 1966-73
6'0" 12st.6lbs.
b. Ysgol Basing, Holywell 25 May 1942

CAREER: Flint Schools XI/Blackburn Rovers (trial)/Chester July 1959/Luton Town Oct 1962/Norwich City Sept 1963/SOUTHAMPTON Aug 1966/Portsmouth Apr 1973/Manchester United Nov 1974/Arcadia Shepherds(S.Africa) Mar 1975/Millwall Nov 1975/Los Angeles Aztecs Apr 1976/Dorchester Town Sept 1976/Los Angeles Aztecs Apr 1977/Tulsa Roughnecks July 1978/Seattle Sounders Apr 1979/White Horse (Ampfield) Winchester League 1982/Totton Apr 1982.

Debut v Manchester City (h) 20.8.66

Mick Channon was once quoted as saying that Ron Davies was the best header of a ball he had ever seen, let alone played with and there are not many in or out of Southampton who would disagree. At his peak in Saints' first three seasons in Division One he notched 85 goals in 119 League games and, according to Matt Busby, was the best centre-forward in Europe. Ron's early days were spent at Chester where he was made to hurdle

wearing army boots - training, he later claimed, which gave him his strength when jumping for crosses. After spells at Kenilworth Road and Carrow Road Ted Bates spent a record £55,000 to bring the 24 year old centre-forward to Southampton as the club prepared to face their inaugural season in the top flight. It was money wisely spent as Ron's goals prevented certain relegation although his awesome aerial prowess would have been undermined without the vital precision crossing of Terry Paine. No slouch on the ground, Ron topped the Division's scoring charts for two successive seasons and it was a credit to the Dell management that all offers from wealthier clubs were firmly rejected. Inevitably, Ron took a battering from many a desperate defender unable to cope with his mastery of the airways and eventually a series of injuries reduced his effectiveness. It was a sad day when the amiable Welshman left the Dell for Fratton Park but he left behind a generation of local schoolboys uninterested in practising their footwork, preferring instead to emulate their idol, and pursue the art of leaping like a salmon to plant the ball in the back of the net with their heads. After 59 games for Portsmouth, Manchester United finally got their man and Ron, now way past his prime, moved to Old Trafford. He never started a game for United but made eight appearances as substitute before ending his career with three League outings for Millwall. He won 29 caps for Wales, 23 of them whilst at the Dell and his 134 League goals included three four-goal hauls, the most memorable being at Old Trafford in August 1969. Ron was also a talented artist and his caricatures of team-mates often featured in the local press. In recent years he has moved to Los Angeles where he coaches at local schools and colleges, and latterly in Florida.

Appearances:
FL: 239 (1) app. 134 gls.
FAC: 19 (1) app. 9 gls.
LC: 13 app. 6 gls.
Eur: 6 (2) app. 4 gls.
Total: *277 (4) app. 153 gls.*

❑ **Saints note** - *Ron's younger brother, Paul, also a centre-forward, had a brief spell at Arsenal before playing 51 League games at Charlton Athletic.*

DAVIES, Thomas Osborne

Role: Forward 1909-10
5'7" 11st.0lbs.
b. Swindon 27 March 1882

CAREER: Swindon Swifts/Swindon Town 1900/Nottingham Forest Apr 1902/ Reading 1906/ Salisbury City 1908/ SOUTHAMPTON trial Apr 1909.

Debut v Plymouth Argyle (h) 1.9.09

Formerly a football League player with Nottingham Forest, Tom Davies came to Southampton on trial in April 1909 from Salisbury City. A permanent move followed for the dapper little striker who shaped up well whenever called into the first eleven and he became a prime favourite with the crowd. A broken leg,, sustained in a reserve team fixture at Eastleigh in March 1910, ended his playing career with the Saints.

Appearances:
SL: 8 app. 1 gls.
Total: *8 app. 1 gl.*

Tom Davies

DAVIS, Richard Frederick

Role: Full-back 1964-65
5'11" 11st.0lbs.
b. Plymouth 14 November 1943

CAREER: Plymouth Argyle app Aug 1960, pro Nov 1961/SOUTHAMPTON July 1964/Bristol City July 1965/Barrow Mar 1969/Falmouth Town manager.

Debut v Plymouth Argyle (a) 17.2.65

A strongly built left-back, Richard Davis spent a solitary season at the Dell, making his only appearance against his home town team

Plymouth Argyle. He later played seven times for Bristol City and fifty times for Barrow, before returning to the West Country to manage Falmouth Town. Richard later helped with Argyle's School of Excellence for young players.

Appearances:
FL: 1 app. 0 gls.
Total: *1 app. 0 gls.*

DAVIS, Stephen Mark

Role: Centre-half 1989-1991
6'2" 12st.8lbs.
b. Hexham 30 October 1968

CAREER: Ponteland High School/ Northumberland Schools/Montague Boys Club/SOUTHAMPTON trainee Aug 1986, pro. July 1987 (Burnley-loan-Nov 1989- Feb 1990)/(Notts County-loan-Mar 1991)/ Burnley Aug 1991.

Debut v Norwich City (h) 27.2.90

Steve Davis was a young central defender who struggled to break into the first team on a regular basis. His first taste of league soccer came at Turf Moor where he spent three months on loan. His form with Burnley impressed the locals and soon after his return from the Dell he was given his Southampton debut in the role of sweeper. Unfortunately for Steve the sweeper tactic was not one particularly favoured by the Saints management and as a consequence he had few further opportunities to shine. He was placed on the transfer list in 1991 and spent the last two months of the season on loan to Notts County before finally moving, on a permanent basis, to Burnley.

Appearances:
FL: 5 (1) app. 0 gls.
Total: *5 (1) app. 0 gls.*

DAWE, Leonard Sydney

Role: Forward 1911-13
b. Brentford October qtr 1889
d. Acton, London 12 January 1963

CAREER: Portsmouth Grammar School/
Emanuel College, Cambridge/Gosport
United/Dulwich Hamlet/Cambridge
University/SOUTHAMPTON am. Mar 1912
/Ilford Mar 1913.

Debut v Plymouth Argyle (h) 30.3.12

An amateur, 'Cantab', student centre-forward,
L. S. Dawe gave Saints valuable service during
the miserable 1912-13 season and always took
the field wearing spectacles. Sometimes
unavailable due to his studies, he severed his
connection with the club in 1913 when he
became a master at a large school on the
outskirts of London. Nevertheless he
continued playing for Ilford and gained
England Amateur International honours in
October 1912 when he played against Ireland
in Belfast.

L.S. Dawe

> **Appearances:**
> SL: 11 app. 3 gls.
> **Total:** 11 app. 3 gls.

❏ **Saints note** - *A month before becoming a
Southampton player Dawe took part in the annual
Cambridge University versus Oxford University
match and scored in his side's 3-1 victory.*

DAWTRY, Kevin Austin

Role: Midfield 1978-79
5'6" 8st.13lbs.
*b. Hythe, Southampton 15 June
1958*

CAREER: St. Mary's College
and Southampton
Schools/SOUTHAMPTON
app. Oct 1974, pro. June
1976/Crystal Palace May
1980/Bournemouth Mar
1981 (Reading-loan-Sept
1982/ R. S. Southampton
1984/ Salisbury
1985/Fareham Town
Oct 1986/Gosport Borough c.s.
1987/Salisbury Sept 1988/Blackfield &
Langley Apr 1990.

Kevin Dawtry

Debut v Nottingham Forest (a) 2.6.79 (substitute).

Kevin Dawtry was spotted as a schoolboy by
Tom Parker but, despite showing good
dribbling ability and a willingness to take on
opponents, he only made one substitute
appearance replacing an
injured Osher Williams.

> **Appearances:**
> FL: 0 (1) app. 0 gls.
> **Total:** 0 (1) app. 0 gls.

DAY, Alfred

Role: Half-back 1937-38
5'8" 10st.10lbs.
b. Ebbw Vale 2 October 1907

CAREER: Pontygof School,
Ebbw Vale/ Cheshunt/
Northfleet/Tottenham
Hotspur May 1931/Millwall
May 1936/SOUTHAMPTON
May 1937/Tranmere Rovers
May 1938/Swindon Town
June 1939/(Brighton & Hove
Albion, Lincoln City, Ipswich Town, Reading
during World War Two).

*Debut v Aston Villa
(h) 4.9.37*

A former Welsh
international (1
cap awarded in
1934), Alf Day
arrived in
Southampton on a
free transfer from
Millwall. A calm,
neat player who
specialised in the
ground pass rather
than the cleared
high ball, he was
never really
appreciated by the
Dell crowd and
moved on after 12
months. After his retirement from football, Alf
found employment at a North London power
station and in March 1991 still resided in the
capital.

Alfred Day

Appearances:
FL: 22 app. 0 gls.
Total: *22 app. 0 gls.*

DAY, Eric Charles

Role: Forward 1946-57
5'6" 10st.7lbs.
b. Dartford 6 November 1921

CAREER: SOUTHAMPTON Apr
1945/ Gravesend and Northfleet
June 1957.

Debut v Millwall (a) 16.11.46

As a pupil at Watford Grammar
School, Eric Day found himself
playing rugby football, a sport he
pursued in the R.A.F. upon his call
up in 1941. He was posted to
R.A.F. Ford in Sussex and, after
breaking his fingers in a rugby
game, decided to try his luck at
soccer. Coincidentally the physical training
instructor at Ford was Bill Luckett, the old
Saints player and he immediately spotted
Eric's potential as a hard, fast and aggressive
forward. He contacted the Saints who sent
Arthur Dominy to Sussex to offer Eric a
contract. Eric remembers being keen but

Eric Day

Norman Dean (right) in action against Norwich.

shoved the unsigned contract into his pocket, preferring to wait and see. He was involved in the D-Day invasions and it was not until the war showed signs of being over that Eric, mindful of post-war employment, decided to contact the Saints to see if they were still interested. He was given a couple of trial games away to Birmingham and home to Spurs and was offered another contract, which this time was promptly signed. Over the next twelve years Eric gave the Saints sterling service with his terrier-like attitude and cannon-ball shooting causing opposition defenders countless problems. He headed the Division Three scoring charts for three consecutive seasons and, at one time early on in his career, was the target of more than one top London club. In 1956 he became a part-time player devoting a lot of his time to being service manager at a local garage and, when Ted Bates bought Jimmy Shields, Eric reluctantly decided to retire from League soccer. He had two seasons at Gravesend before a cartilage problem effectively ended his playing days. Eric, a keen golfer, now lives in Wiltshire, where he continues to show great interest in the fortunes of the club he served so admirably, and he was present at Saints' Centenary dinner.

Appearances:
FL: 398 app. 145 gls.
FAC: 24 app. 11 gls.
Total: *422 app. 156 gls.*

DEAN, Norman

Role: Forward 1965-66
5'9" 10st.9lbs.
b. Corby, Northants 13 September 1944

CAREER: Corby Town/SOUTHAMPTON am. Sept 1961, pro. Apr 1963/Cardiff City Mar 1967/Barnsley Sept 1968/Bedford Town 1973-74.
Debut v Tranmere Rovers (LC) (a) 25.9.63

Norman Dean first arrived at Southampton in September 1961, signing on as a young amateur. He spent his mornings training at the Dell and then continued a welding apprenticeship in the afternoons with C.P.C. He signed as a professional in April 1963 and, later that same year, made his senior debut when Saints met Tranmere Rovers in the League Cup. Over the next two seasons he built up a reputation in the reserves as something of a sharpshooter and, when given his first League outing at Norwich City in September 1965, he responded with an important goal in a 4-3 victory. Altogether Norman played 18 times in Saints' promotion season scoring some invaluable goals and is still fondly remembered by the fans for a hat-trick he scored in the 5-2 defeat of Portsmouth in February 1966. Never making Southampton's First Division side, he was signed by Jimmy Scoular, Cardiff's manager, for £6,000 prior to the 1967 transfer deadline. He was never a regular at Ninian Park but wrote his name in their record books during their European campaign of 1967-68 by scoring the winner versus Moscow Torpedo and netting in both legs of the semi-final versus Hamburg. A £10,000 transfer took Norman to Oakwell where a broken leg caused him to miss the entire 1971-72 season and, despite fighting his way back to full fitness, he was given a free transfer to Bedford Town. His leg continued to cause him trouble and within a year Norman decided to retire from the game completely. In April 1991 he was living in Corby, Northamptonshire.

Appearances:
FL: 18 app. 11 gls.
FAC: 1 app. 0 gls.
LC: 1 app. 0 gls.
Total: 20 app. 11 gls.

DELAMOTTE, F. A.

Role: Forward 1891-92

CAREER: SOUTHAMPTON St. Mary's 1888, secretary 1889-90.

Debut v Warmley (FC) (a) 3.10.1891
* (scored on debut)

F. A. Delamotte was a popular member of the St. Mary's team in the days when winning the Hampshire Junior Cup was the club's main priority. In those days goalkeepers received nothing like the protection they do today, and Delamotte loved to close in on a custodian who was attempting to catch a shot. "Go for him Delly" was an often-heard cry from the Antelope Ground spectators and Delamotte's aggression earned him plenty of goals. A County representative player he turned out against the Corinthians in April 1892 and Surrey the following November. In 1893 "Delly" left the area to take up the Borough Surveyor's appointment in Conway, North Wales.

Appearances:
FAC: 2 app. 2 gls.
Total: 2 app. 2 gls.

DENBY, John

Role: Half-back 1911-15
5'9" 11st.0lbs.
b. Sutton-in-Ashfield, Nottingham

CAREER: Chesterfield/SOUTHAMPTON Aug 1911.
Debut v Millwall (h) 2.9.11

One of many new players signed during the summer of 1911, Denby followed Saints' new manager, George Swift, from Chesterfield. A strong reliable player, he played in all three half-back positions with equal merit and was the team's defensive pivot. His steady influence was to have a considerable effect on team performances and bring an improvement in defensive play during the last two seasons before the suspension of League action in 1915.

Appearances:
SL: 127 app. 8 gls.
FAC: 7 app. 0 gls.
Total: 134 app. 8 gls.

John Denby

DENNIS, Mark Earl

Role: Full-back 1983-87
5'9" 10st.8lbs.
b. Streatham 2 May 1961

CAREER: Chelsea Boys/Birmingham City app June 1977, pro Aug 1978/SOUTHAMPTON Nov 1983/ Queen's Park Rangers May 1987/Crystal Palace Aug 1989/Brighton & H.A. trial Aug 1991.

Debut v Leicester City (a) 30.11.83

Mark Dennis arrived from Birmingham for a cut price fee of £30,000, due mainly to his reputation of being one of the game's hot-heads with an awful disciplinary record. He quickly settled and got down to the business of playing football, and playing it well. Defensively alert and uncompromising, Mark gave the team an extra cutting edge with his pulsating overlaps down the left touchline and, in his first season, Saints reached the F.A. Cup semi-finals and runners-up spot in Division One. His enthusiasm made him a popular character with the crowd but, sadly, his discipline was again to let him down. A series of run-ins with new manager, Chris Nicholl, resulted in an inevitable transfer and fans rued the departure of one of the most brilliant, but ultimately flawed, defenders ever seen at the Dell.

Appearances:
FL: 95 app. 2 gls.
FAC: 14 app. 0 gls.
LC 16 app. 0 gls.
Eur: 2 app. 0 gls.
Total: *127 app. 2 gls.*

Mark Dennis

DEWAR, George

Role: Half-back 1898-99
b. Dumbarton 20 July 1867
d. 2 September 1915

CAREER: Dumbarton Athletic/Dumbarton Sept 1887/Blackburn Rovers Aug 1889/New Brighton Tower June 1987/SOUTHAMPTON May 1898.

Debut v Sheppey United (h) 12.11.1898

George Dewar served his apprenticeship as a ship's upholsterer before embarking on a full time professional soccer career with Blackburn. The decision to turn his back on a career at sea was a wise one as, by the time Saints competed for his signature, in 1897, he had been capped by Scotland and had gained F.A. Cup Winners' medals with Blackburn Rovers. George who, although a Scot, was inexplicably nicknamed "Geordie", decided to join New Brighton in 1897 but soon regretted the move and after a season organised a transfer to Southampton the following year. He was now into his thirties and, with his best days behind him, was only on the Dell payroll for one year before he moved back to Scotland.

Appearances:
SL: 4 app. 0 gls.
Total: *4 app. 0 gls.*

DIAPER, Albert

Role: Half-back 1912-13
b. Woolston 1893
d. Southampton
4 September 1964

CAREER: Bitterne
Guild/Woolston/
SOUTHAMPTON
1912/ Thornycrofts
1919.

Debut v Brentford (h)
24.3.13

Albert Diaper

A product of local soccer, Albert Diaper joined the club in 1912 and, mainly because he was an adroit passer, was thought to have a promising future. Well built, his only game in the First XI came when he was recalled from Southampton's railway station as a last minute replacement for Denby. Albert remained at the club until 1915 and later appeared in Thornycroft's league team of 1919.

Appearances:
S.L: 1 app. 0 gls.
Total: *1 app. 0 gls.*

DIGBY, Derek Francis

Role: Forward 1953-55
5'6" 10st.4lbs.
b. Teignmouth 14 March 1931

CAREER: Dawlish Town/Exeter City
Aug 1949/ SOUTHAMPTON Sept
1953/Weymouth c.s. 1955.

Debut v Colchester United (h) 23.9.53

Derek Digby spent two seasons at the Dell as cover for both first team wingers, Flood and Hoskins. Although described as "quick on his toes", he never established himself and despite some good performances in the reserves he was released into non-league football.

Appearances:
FL: 15 app. 2 gls.
Total: *15 app. 2 gls.*

DODD, Jason Robert

Role: Full-back 1989-
5'10" 11st.10lbs.
b. Bath 2 November 1970

CAREER: Bath City/SOUTHAMPTON non-contract March 1989, pro. April 1989.

Debut v Queen's Park Rangers (a) 14.10.89

Jason Dodd was signed from Bath as an 18 year-old and joined the second year trainees under the guidance of Dave Merrington. Six months later Saints' fans were given their first glimpse of the young full-back when, making his home debut against Liverpool at the Dell, he had the uneviable task of marking John Barnes. Not only did he completely snuff out the efforts of the dangerous England winger but found enough time and composure to supply a perfect cross for Paul Rideout's opening goal. Saints won the game 4-1 and Jason's popularity, at least with the fans has been in the ascendancy ever since. Showing quite astounding maturity, Jason's signing must rate as Chris Nicholl's finest transfer dealing and yet the former manager often chose to drop Jason when others in the side perhaps seemed more worthy of the axe. Despite losing his place to midfielder Barry Horne at the tail end of the 1990-91 campaign, Jason managed to hold on to his England

Derek Digby

Under-21 place, and Southampton's fans were left to muse why the best young right-back in the country was being kept out of the first team by a man better suited to a midfield position.

Appearances:
FL: 37 (4) app. 0 gls.
FAC: 6 app. 0 gls.
LC: 8 (1) app. 0 gls.
Total: *51 (5) app. 0 gls.*

ason Dodd

DODGIN, William

Role: Centre-half 1945-46
b. Gateshead 17 April 1909

CAREER: Newcastle & Gateshead Schools/ Wallsend 1920/Kirkley and Waveney (Lowestoft)/Huddersfield Town am Oct 1929, pro Nov 1929/Lincoln City Mar 1933/ Charlton Athletic Aug 1934/Bristol Rovers May 1936/Clapton Orient July 1937/ SOUTHAMPTON June 1939, manager January 1946/Fulham manager Aug 1949/Brentford Oct 1953-Apr 1957/Yiewsley manager Mar 1959-Dec 1960/Sampdoria manager-coach May 1957-Feb 1958/Bristol Rovers chief scout, Aug 1961, caretaker-manager July 1969, permanent Nov 1969, chief scout July 1972-1983.

Debut v Newport County (FAC) (h) 5.1.46

Bill Dodgin was a workmanlike, rather than spectacular, wing-half who first showed his leadership qualities when becoming captain of Lincoln. Progressing to the Valley in August 1934 Bill helped Charlton in their rise from the Third to the First Division in consecutive seasons before short spells at Bristol Rovers and Clapton Orient preceded a final playing move to Southampton. Bill played in two of the three League games that were declared null and void with the outbreak of the Second World War but did, over the next six years, make 84 war time appearances. His only senior competitive games for the Saints came in the 1945-46 F.A. Cup competition which was reintroduced a year before league soccer resumed in earnest. That same season Bill took on coaching responsibilities before being handed the managerial reigns in January 1946. His methods immediately made an impact and, building around a strong nucleus of players already on the books, Bill constructed a memorable squad that dominated the Second Division over the next three years.

The extreme disappointment Bill felt when the team failed to gain promotion to the First Division, especially in 1949, manifested itself with a decision to take his organisational skills to Craven Cottage. In an article written in October 1955 Bill described this decision as "the biggest mistake of his career" and indeed, after a three year struggle, Fulham suffered relegation to the Second Division. In 1952 Bill crossed west London to shoulder further managerial responsibilities at Brentford.

Appearances:
FAC: 4 app. 0 gls.
Total: *4 app. 0 gls.*

Bill Dodgin being helped off the pitch by Chelsea centre-forward Tommy Lawton during a wartime match on 29th December 1945.

DOLLIN, Albert Edwin

Role: Forward 1892-93
b. Southampton 1866
d. Southampton 22 April 1955

CAREER: Freemantle/SOUTHAMPTON St Mary's c.s. 1892/Freemantle 1893/Eastleigh Athletic.

Debut v Newbury (FAC) (h) 15.10.1892

"Jack" Dollin was the first Saints player to be financially renumerated for his services and late in life he recalled being paid a "pound a week and given a job in the week". His professional status was kept a secret for a considerable time which later led to some confusion when club historians were attempting to establish just who was the first player to be paid by the board. On the pitch Jack's versatility stood him in good stead throughout the 1892-93 season although he could also be unpredictable in front of goal. By the end of the year Jack had also twisted both his knees and he decided to return to amateur status with his previous team, Freemantle. He later became a stalwart of Eastleigh Athletic remaining with them well into the 1900's.

> **Appearances:**
> *FAC: 2 app. 0 gls.*
> **Total:** *2 app. 0 gls.*

DOMINY, Arthur Albert

Role: Forward 1912-26
5'8" 11st. 6lbs.
b. South Stoneham 11 February 1893
d. Mitcham 23 September 1974

CAREER: Weston Grove/Peartree Athletic/Bitterne Guild Sept 1911/Woolston c.s. 1912/SOUTHAMPTON Mar 1913/ (Guest for Glasgow Rangers, Arsenal and Harland & Wolff during World War One)/ Everton May 1926/Gillingham Mar 1928/Clapton Orient May 1929/Newport (I.O.W.) 1931/SOUTHAMPTON scout 1931/Itchen Sports mid 1930's/SOUTHAMPTON manager June 1943-46, scout 1946.

Debut v Stoke (a) 5.4.13

"Art" Dominy first came to prominence at County level during the 1911-12 season, scoring over 50 goals for Bitterne Guild, and

such prolific scoring naturally aroused the interest of the Southampton directors who secured his transfer in 1913. A boilermaker by trade Arthur made an immediate impact by becoming Saints' top scorer in 1913-14, his first full season, and the following year his 30 goals put him on top of the Southern League goalscoring charts. His ball control was second to none; he always managed to keep the ball near his feet, rarely allowing it to break away, and he also had the priceless ability, for a forward, of being able to beat an opponent at close quarters. During the war he was employed at Harland & Wolff and often played for his works' team against the Saints as well as guesting for Arsenal and Rangers. Returning to a full time soccer career in 1919, Arthur formed a formidable striking partnership with Bill Rawlings and became the first Saints player to be given honours after the war when he was selected to play for the Southern League against the Irish League in Ireland. Although a full International cap eluded him (he appeared in countless England trial matches) he had the privilege of captaining the Saints in their promotion to the Second Division in 1922 and he was duly rewarded with a benefit game against Preston. Arthur's long and meritorious career at the Dell came to an eventual end in 1926 when he was given a free transfer to Everton where he

'Art' Dominy

formed an alliance and friendship with Dixie Dean. (In later years, when Arthur was scouting for the Saints and travelling all over the country, he would often visit Dixie who ran a pub in Chester.) Returning to the Southampton area in 1931 he became 'mine host' at the Mason's Arms in St. Mary's Street and he continued to play for Newport on the Isle of Wight where he once again teamed up with Bill Rawlings. In 1934 he was offered the manager's job at Le Havre but decided to stay in the licensing trade. By now most of his spare time was spent scouting for the Saints although, prior to World War Two, he also helped run a sports stadium in Bournemouth. In 1943, following the sudden resignation of Tom Parker, the Saints asked Arthur to take on the responsibilities of team manager and, although the position was only part-time, Arthur gave valuable assistance right up to the appointment of Bill Dodgin in 1946. A Saints fan, through and through, Arthur never missed a game and after the war took over the stewardship of the Saints Supporters' Club thus maintaining his links with the club he served so well right up to his death in 1974.

Jack Dorkin

Appearances;
SL: 112 app. 65 gls.
FL: 222 app. 68 gls.
FAC: 35 app. 13 gls.
Total: *369 app. 146 gls.*

❏ **Saints note** - *Arthur's younger brother, Tom, was on the Saints' books during the 1914-15 season and, at one time, was considered to be the better player.*

DONNELLY, Anthony

Role: Full-back 1919-20
5'9" 11st.8lbs.
b. Middleton, Manchester Apr qtr 1886

CAREER: Heywood United/Manchester United July 1908/Glentoran/ SOUTHAMPTON Sept 1919.

Debut v Reading (h) 15.9.19

Having gained experience with Manchester United and Glentoran in pre-World War One football, Tony Donnelly arrived at the Dell as a trialist in 1919 after he was demobbed from the Royal Artillery. Playing at left back he enjoyed a sound match against Reading but then decided to leave the area within a week, giving no reason for his departure.

Appearances:
SL: 1 app. 0 gls.
Total: *1 app 0 gls.*

DORKIN, Jack W.

Role: Forward 1893-95
b. At sea aboard the S.S Tamar July 1866

CAREER: Ipswich Rangers 1883/Edinburgh St Bernards/Royal Engineers/ SOUTHAMPTON St Mary's 1892/Basingstoke Nov 1902/ Romsey Town manager-coach 1908.

*Debut v Swindon Town (h) 30.3.95 * (scored on debut)*

Jack Dorkin was playing football before the formation of Southampton St Mary's and became one of the club's first professionals in 1892 when he was "bought out" of the Royal Engineers. A prolific marksman during the pre-Southern League days, he was past his best by 1894, although in his three Southern League outings he scored in each game. Retiring in 1895 he was persuaded two years later to take part in a "Sixes" tournament but broke a leg in an accident that convinced him to hang up his boots. Although making a brief comeback in November 1902, Jack's time was taken up with the sports outfitters business he ran in partnership with England and Hampshire cricketer Victor Barton.

Appearances:
SL: 3 app. 3 gls.
FAC: 3 app. 1 gl.
Total: *6 app. 4 gls.*

❏ **Saints note** - *Whilst in the Royal Engineers, Jack represented the Army in a game against Corinthians.*

DOUGALL, Peter

Role: Forward 1929-32
5'8" 11st. 0lbs.
b. Denny 21 March 1909
d. 12 June 1974

CAREER: Denny Pace Thistle/Burnley Oct 1926/Clyde Feb 1929/SOUTHAMPTON Sept 1929/Arsenal Sept 1933/Everton Aug 1937/ Bury June 1938/ (Manchester Utd during World War Two).

Debut v Stoke City (a) 19.10.29

Saints signed Peter Dougall from Clyde and the fee for his transfer was met by the Saints Supporters' Club. On form he had been described as "in the Alex James' class" and it was true that he combined skill with an ability to beat a man on a sixpence. Unfortunately he had the tendancy to sometimes over-elaborate and the exasperated Dell management transfer-listed him at £500. After a brief spell playing on the continent he surprisingly re-surfaced in Arsenal's first team in February 1934, coincidentally partnering the aforementioned James! The following season, still at Highbury, Peter played alongside Ted Drake before moving on to support Dixie Dean in Everton's 1937-38 forward line.

Appearances:
FL: 29 app. 5 gls.
Total: *29 app. 5 gls.*

Peter Dougall

Dickie Dowsett

DOWSETT, Gilbert James

Role: Forward 1956-57
5'8" 10st. 9lbs.
b. Chelmsford 3 July 1931

CAREER: Sudbury Town/Tottenham Hotspur May 1952/Southend United May 1955/ SOUTHAMPTON July 1956/Bournemouth June 1957/Crystal Palace Nov 1962/ Weymouth June 1965/ Bournemouth commercial manager June 1968-Mar 1983.

Debut v Bournemouth (a) 15.12.56

Despite scoring on his debut for Spurs, Dickie Dowsett never played another game for the London club and joined Southend in May 1955. At Roots Hall he caught the eye of ex-Saint Frank Dudley who passed his recommendations on to Ted Bates. Becoming a Saint in July 1956, Dickie only made two League appearances, one on the left wing and one on the right wing before he was allowed to join Bournemouth for £100. His career blossomed with the Cherries and fast determined running, coupled with a considerable ability in the air, confirmed his popularity with the Dean Court faithful. In the ensuing five seasons Dickie was to top the goalscorers' list on three occasions, a fact

Ted Drake (left) shakes hands with Bill Light

which led to Crystal Palace paying £3,500 for him in 1962. Dickie is now Production Manager at Icarus (Toys) in Bournemouth.

Appearances:
FL: 2 app. 0 gls.
FAC: 1 app. 0 gls.
Total: *3 app. 0 gls.*

DRAKE, Edward Joseph

Role: Forward 1931-34
5'10" 11st. 10lbs.
b. Southampton 16 August 1912

CAREER: Southampton Schools/Winchester City/SOUTHAMPTON am. June 1931, pro. Nov 1931/Arsenal Mar 1934/ (West Ham United, Leicester City and Fulham during World War Two)/ Hendon manager/Reading manager June 1947/Chelsea manager June 1952-Sept 1961/Barcelona asst. manager Jan 1970-June 1970/Fulham director and life president.

Debut v Swansea Town (a) 14.11.31

As a young boy growing up in Southampton, Ted Drake fondly recalls how his idol was Billy Rawlings, the Saints and England centre-forward, and how, kicking a ball around the back streets of the town, he would imagine himself to be the first Southampton-born player to play centre-forward for England. It wasn't too long before his childhood dreams were to be realised as George Kay, encouraged by Ted's form at Winchester, persuaded the youngster to give up his job as a gas-meter inspector and sign for the Saints. After only one complete season his bravery and skills attracted the attention of Arsenal but, content at the Dell, Ted decided to reject a move to Highbury and during 1933-34 blasted his way to the position of top scorer in Division Two. Arsenal, with George Allison recently installed as manager, returned to the Dell, this time determined to acquire Ted's talents and the whole of Southampton went into mourning when he finally decided to join the Gunners for a fee of £6,000. Ted's exploits both in an Arsenal and England shirt have now become part of footballing folklore and, right up to the outbreak of the war, he led both forward lines with an old fashioned cut-and-thrust style now redundant in modern football. During the war Ted joined the R.A.F. but a spinal injury hastened his move into managerial roles, culminating in the guiding of Chelsea to their first Division One title in 1955. An all-round sportsman, Ted made 16 appearances for Hampshire as a middle order batsman between 1931 and 1936 and today lives in South West London where he continues to follow the fortunes of his home-town team with considerable interest.

Appearances:
FL: 71 app. 47 gls.
FAC: 3 app. 1 gl.
Total: *74 app. 48 gls.*

❏ **Saints note** - *Ted became the first man to play in, and then manage a First Division championship team.*

DUDLEY, Frank Ernest

Role: Forward 1950-54
5'10" 12st. 4lbs.
b. Southend 9 May 1925

CAREER: Southend United am. Sept 1945, pro. Oct 1945/Leeds United Aug 1949/ SOUTHAMPTON Feb 1951/Cardiff City Oct 1953/Brentford Dec 1953/Folkestone July 1958-July 1960/Southend United youth manager 1961-65.

Debut v Swansea Town (a) 3.2.51

Frank Dudley signed the forms that made him a Saints player on the Leeds to London train in a transfer that saw Ernie Stevenson move in the opposite direction. A reliable goalscorer, Frank was quicker than most and packed a powerful shot that made him an instant hit with the Dell crowd. A move to Cardiff in the autumn of 1953 did not work out and, within two months, he signed for Brentford with whom he spent five seasons. Qualifying at Lilleshall as a coach in 1952, Frank, to this day, enjoys working with the local schools and only gave up playing himself when reaching his 65th birthday. After leaving the professional game Frank became a local government officer in his native Southend until taking retirement in 1985.

Appearances:
FL: 67 app. 32 gls.
FAC: 6 app. 1 gl.
Total: *73 app. 33 gls.*

❏ **Saints note** - *On Christmas Day 1951 Saints were playing away at Brentford who were enjoying an unbeaten home run in Division Two. Just after half-time with the score at 1-1 Frank collected the*

Frank Dudley scores the first of his three goals against Fulham on 27th December 1952. In goal for Fulham is ex-Saint Ian Black and Jimmy Hill is the Fulham player in the background.

ball on the half-way line and proceeded down the wing. For some unknown reason the Brentford defenders held back and, cutting inside, Frank scored with a cross shot to give the Saints a shock victory. Saints were at home to Brentford the very next day and Frank recalls whilst crossing the Dell car park, prior to the game, being met by two Brentford players who enquired whether Frank had intended to score the previous day's winner in such a manner. Apparently a furious row had developed after the game in Brentford's dressing room with the Bees' manager castigating the two men for lax marking. The two players angrily retorted that the goal had been a fluke and a cross, rather than a shot, had been the intention. The aftermath to this story was that both players were soon to leave Brentford as a indirect result of Frank's goal, and, because the two players were none other than Jimmy Hill and Ron Greenwood, perhaps Frank's strike, intended or not, changed the future of English football.

DUNMORE, Alfred

Role: Forward 1932-33
5'8" 11st. 4lbs.
b. South Shields Jan qtr 1911

CAREER: Stanhope Road School/County Durham School/Simonside F.C. 1928/ Newcastle United Swifts 1929/Newcastle United 1929/Derby County Apr 1930/

SOUTHAMPTON June 1932.
Debut v West Ham United (h) 24.9.32

Fred Dunmore arrived at the Dell from Derby County without a League appearance to his credit. His one game in a red and white shirt came in a 4-3 victory over West Ham United when he replaced the injured Dick Neal on the right wing. In 1932-33, his only season at Southampton, he was a regular in the Combination Side and was joint top scorer with nine goals in 47 games. Fred was released from his contract in May 1933.

Appearances:
FL: 1 app. 0 gls.
Total: *1 app. 0 gls.*

DUNN, William Marshall

Role: Forward 1937-38
5'10" 10st. 4lbs.
b. Lambhill, Glasgow 9 October 1910
d. Glasgow 7 September 1980

CAREER: Glasgow Ashfield/Glasgow Celtic 1932/Newton Villa/Brentford June 1935/SOUTHAMPTON May 1937/Raith Rovers c.s. 1938.
Debut v Norwich City (a) 28.8.37
* *(scored on debut)*

Fred Dunmore   Billy Dunn

Billy Dunn's first taste of professional football came at Park Head where, during 1933-34, he played ten first team games for Celtic and also scored 51 goals for their reserves. Brentford, then a First Division team, brought Billy to London and, although he only made three appearances in the Bees' first team, he did finish as top scorer in their London Combination XI. When he arrived at the Dell the Echo praised his "skilful play and marksmanship" and although he scored on his debut he was destined to spend most of the 1937-38 season again in the reserves. He refused terms in the summer of 1938 and was transfer-listed at £750 before returning to Scotland with Raith Rovers.

James Dunne

returned to Ireland but was not forgotten by the fans for when later passing through the Docks with the Irish National Team en route for an international in Europe, he was given a big cheer by the Southampton Dockers.

Appearances:
FL: 36 app. 14 gls.
FAC: 1 app. 0 gls
Total: *37 app. 14 gls.*

❏ **Saints note** - *Jimmy Dunne's son, James, was a player in the English League between 1967-78, with Torquay United and Fulham, and won one cap for Eire. Jimmy himself won a total of 15 caps, two of them whilst a Saints player.*

Appearances:
FL: 14 app. 3 gls.
FAC: 1 app. 1 gl.
Total: *15 app. 4 gls.*

DUNNE, James

Role: Forward 1936-37
5'10" 11st.3lbs.
b. Ringsend 3 September 1905
d. Dublin 14 November 1949

CAREER: Gaelic football/Shamrock Rovers Nov 1923/New Brighton Oct 1925/Sheffield United Feb 1926/Arsenal Sept 1933/ SOUTHAMPTON July 1936/Shamrock Rovers June 1937/Bohemian coach 1942/Shamrock Rovers player-coach 1947.

Debut v Chesterfield (h) 29.8.36
* (scored on debut)

Jimmy Dunne arrived at the Dell with a fair pedigree behind him as he had been top scorer in the First Division with Sheffield United in 1930-31 and had cost Arsenal £8,000 in 1933. Fair-haired, the Saints' fans nicknamed him 'Snowy'. Jimmy was dangerous in the air and had a short striding run which enabled him to retain his balance in quick moves near the goal. After just one season at the Dell he

DUNNE, Martin

Role: Forward 1910-11
5'7" 11st.6lbs.
b. Padiham 1887

CAREER: East Lancashire Regiment/Oswaldtwistle Rovers/ Accrington Stanley/ SOUTHAMPTON May 1910/Stalybridge Celtic c.s. 1911.

Debut v Luton Town (a) 3.9.10 * (scored on debut)

One of many Northern-born players signed by Saints in the early 1900's, Martin Dunne moved south from Accrington Stanley in May 1910. He immediately created a favourable impression with the fans in pre-season practice matches and progressed to start the 1910-11 campaign brilliantly. Exceptionally quick off the mark, Martin was a champion sprinter and used his speed with admirable effect that year to become top scorer for the club, although his eventual tally of nine goals could have been much more had it not been for a foot injury which hampered his form in the latter stages. Martin left the Dell in 1911 to follow team-mate John Johnston who had become manager of Stalybridge Celtic.

Appearances:
SL: 30 app. 9 gls.
FAC: 1 app. 0 gls.
Total: *31 app. 9 gls.*

DURBER, Peter

Role: Full-back 1898-1900
5' 8" 11st. 7lbs
b. Wood Lane, Stoke-on-Trent April qtr 1873

CAREER: Wood Lane/Audley/Stoke May 1896/SOUTHAMPTON May 1898/Stoke c.s. 1900/Glossop Aug 1901/Northampton Town c.s. 1902.

Debut v Gravesend (a) 24.9.1898

Previously with Stoke, Peter Durber had left the coal mines in 1896 determined to exploit his soccer skills on a professional footing. Soon after his Southampton arrival in 1898, he distinguished himself with a series of polished displays in the full-back position and his strong tackling, coupled with an ability to find a colleague with a pass, earned him respect from opponents and, more importantly, an international trial in 1900. Disappointed not to be awarded a full cap, Peter returned to Stoke and, after retiring from football in 1908, he took over a public house in the Potteries.

Appearances:
SL: 43 app. 0 gls.
FAC: 9 app. 0 gls.
Total: *52 app. 0 gls.*

DYER, Albert Edward

Role: Forward 1906-07
5'10" 11st.4lbs
b. Portsmouth
20 December 1886

CAREER:
SOUTHAMPTON c.s. 1906/ Gainsborough Trinity Sept 1908/ Eastleigh Athletic Sept 1908/Southampton Cambridge c.s. 1909/Woolston 1910/Bitterne Guild Aug 1911/Southampton Cambridge 1912/Romsey Town Sept 1913.

Debut v Northampton Town (a) 6.4.07

A local discovery, Bert Dyer became a second team regular during the 1906-07 season and made his solitary first team jaunt in a 4-2 victory over Northampton Town when Sam Jepp was taken ill shortly before kick-off. His failure to make the grade hastened a transfer to Gainsborough, a Second Division team, but within a month he returned to the Southampton area and won a Hampshire Senior Cup Winners medal with Eastleigh Athletic.

Appearances:
SL: 1 app. 0 gls.
Total: *1 app. 0 gls.*

Peter Durber

EARLES, Patrick

Role: 1974-77
5'7" 10st. 0lbs.
b. Titchfield 22 March 1955

CAREER: St. Mary's College/
SOUTHAMPTON app. Aug 1970, pro. Nov
1972/Reading Jan 1977/Road Sea
Southampton 1983/Bognor Regis c.s. 1987.
Debut v Portsmouth (a) 6.4.76

A small but fast forward, Pat Earles won
England Schoolboy honours prior to appearing
in a Saints shirt during the 1974-75 season
when he came on as a substitute in the home
game with Fulham. A further 16 months were
to pass until his first full game at Fratton Park,
in place of Peter
Osgood, who had
been suspended by
the club for a breach
of discipline
following the F.A.
Cup semi-final. With Channon and Osgood
effectively blocking any progress in the senior
side Pat moved to Reading where he made
over 200 appearances, scoring 68 times. He
retired from League soccer in 1983 to
concentrate on a career in the probation service
although he continued to play for local non-
league sides.

Appearances:
FL: 4 (8) app. 1 gl.
FAC: 0 (1) app. 0 gls.
LC: 1 app. 1 gl.
EUR: 0 (2) app. 0 gls.
Total: *5 (11) app. 2 gls.*

EARLS, Michael Marien

Role: Defender 1973-75
6'0" 11st.10lbs.
b. Limerick 25 March 1954

CAREER: Ballynanty/ SOUTHAMPTON app.
Jan 1971, pro. March 1972/Aldershot June
1975/Woking July 1979/Fleet Town, AFC
Millbrook/Netley Central Sports coach May
1990/Sholing Sports manager May 1991.
Debut v Liverpool (a) 26.2.74

Mick Earls was invited for a trial in 1970 and
signed as a professional in 1972. He made a
sound debut in a 1-0 defeat at Anfield and
looked forward to having a promising future
until a broken leg cut short his progress. He
made a brief comeback at Aldershot in 1975
but retired prematurely in 1978 aged 24.

Appearances:
FL: 8 app. 0 gls.
Total: *8 app. 0 gls.*

EASTHAM, John Bilborough

Role: Full-back 1906-12
5'10" 12st.0lbs.
b. Blackburn
d. Stalybridge 3 May 1932

CAREER: St. Peter's School/Blackburn Rovers
Mar 1900/Glossop Sept 1905/
SOUTHAMPTON May 1906.

Pat Earles

Debut v Luton Town 15.9.06

Plucked from the hot-bed of Northern League football, Jack Eastham made an anonymous start to his Dell career but overcame his early difficulties to develop into one of the club's finest right-backs during the Southern League era. Robust and fearless, he soon became indispensable and, after becoming team captain, provided invaluable guidance to some of the team's younger players. The club recognised his worth by granting him a benefit against Portsmouth in September 1911 and at the end of that season he retired and returned to the Blackburn area.

Appearances:
SL: 161 app. 4 gls.
FAC: 14 app. 0 gls.
Total: *175 app. 4 gls.*

COPE'S
"CLIPS"
CIGARETTES

No. 417.—EASTHAM
Southampton
Noted Footballers

EDMONDS, Thomas

Role: Centre-half 1905-06
b. Edinburgh 6 August 1878

CAREER: Preston Pans Athletic/ Dundee/ Preston North End Oct 1903/Southport Central 1904/ SOUTHAMPTON May1905.

Debut v Brentford (h) 2.9.05

Although a Scot by birth, Tom Edmonds played the bulk of his early football in Lancashire before joining the Saints from Southport in 1905. Slim and wiry, he suffered a succession of injuries which disorientated his play so much that only occasionally did he show glimpses of the form that had gained him a reputation in the north. After one season he returned to live in Lancashire.

Appearances:
SL: 9 app. 0 gls.
Total: *9 app. 0 gls*

Jack Edwards (second left) joins Len Wilkins, Auggie Scott, Eric Day and Charlie Wayman watching Ted Bates play snooker.

EDWARDS, JOHN

Role: Forward 1949-52
5'10"
b. Salford 23 February 1924
d. Nottingham December 1978

CAREER: Adelphi Lads Club/Nottingham Forest May 1944/ SOUTHAMPTON June 1949/Kidderminster Harriers July 1952/Notts County Nov 1952/Kings Lynn c.s. 1954.

*Debut v Grimsby Town (h) 20.8.49 * (scored on debut)*

Jack Edwards played his junior football in Manchester but, because of the confusion of the war, slipped City and United's net and signed for Nottingham Forest. In 1947 his form reputedly attracted bids of £14,000 from Arsenal and Liverpool and two years later, despite competition from West Bromwich Albion, Bill Dodgin splashed out £10,000 on Jack who was later described in the club handbook as "a real box of tricks". He was certainly a clever ball player and popular with the crowd, yet his career took an inexplicable nose-dive which resulted in him going on loan to a non-league team in the summer of 1952. Later the same year he moved to Notts County in a deal that brought Alex Simpson to the Dell, but he never prospered at Meadow Lane and dropped out of league football soon after his 30th birthday. Jack Edwards was later to lose his life in a street mugging in Nottingham in 1978.

Appearance:
FL: 82 app 16 gls.
FAC: 3 app 0 gls.
Total: *85 app. 16 gls.*

EKE, Harry Lenney

Role: Forward 1913-14
5'8" 11st. 0lbs.
b. St. Faith's April qtr 1894

CAREER: St Mary's Cray/SOUTHAMPTON (trial) Oct 1913.

Debut v Queen's Park Rangers 25.10.13

Eke came to the Dell on a trial basis from St Mary's Cray and had represented Kent Juniors against London. He was prematurely given his Southern League debut only a week after his arrival, as an injury to Dominy and the unavailability of anyone else had left the team selectors with no alternative. Not ready for first team football there was to be no fairy tale debut for the young Kent man and after several weeks he returned to local county football.

Appearances:
SL: 1 app. 0 gls.
Total: *1 app. 0 gls.*

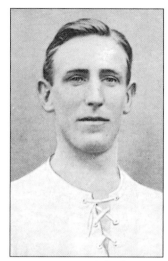
Jack Elkes

ELKES, Albert John

Role: Forward 1921-23
6'0" 11st. 10lbs.
b. Snedshill, Salop
31 December 1894
d. Rayleigh 22 January 1972

CAREER: Wellington St. Georges/Wellington Town 1911/Stalybridge Celtic 1914/ Shifnal Town/ Birmingham Jan 1918/ SOUTHAMPTON Mar 1922/Tottenham Hotspur May 1923/ Middlesbrough Aug 1929/ Watford Aug 1933/ Stafford Rangers Aug 1934/ Oakengates Town 1935-1937.

Debut v Southend United (h)
*4.3.21 * (scored on debut)*

Jack Elkes, an inside-forward, arrived at the Dell as part of a unique four player exchange deal with Birmingham. A dream debut at home to Southend saw him net a couple of goals, only for his dream to turn into a nightmare the following Saturday when, again versus Southend, he broke his collar bone. For a tall man Jack was a clever player and after only one full season with the Saints he moved to Tottenham for a fee of £1000. He was still playing in his late thirties for Watford.

Appearances:
FL: 33 app. 7 gls.
FAC: 9 app. 1 gl.
Total: *42 app. 8 gls.*

ELLERINGTON, William

Role: Full-back: 1946-56
6'0" 12st.4lbs.
b. Southampton 30 June 1923

CAREER: Barnes School/Sunderland Technical School/Fatfield Juniors/Sunderland am. 1939/SOUTHAMPTON am. Sep 1940 (cancelled by league Oct 1940) pro. Sept 1945, player-coach 1956, reserve team trainer 1968, club scout 1973.

Debut v Queen's Park Rangers (FAC) (h) 26.1.46

Southampton born and the son of an old Saints player of First World War days, Bill Ellerington spent his youth in Sunderland and won Schoolboy International honours. He returned to the Solent area in 1940, signing amateur forms for the club but, when it was discovered that Sunderland already held his registration, the League cancelled his Southampton forms. Throughout the war he continued to assist the Saints as a guest until September 1945 when he signed as a professional. During the war-time matches Bill developed into a stylish full back with excellent ball control and penetrative distribution. On the resumption of league football in 1946 Bill deservedly became established as the club's right-back before illness and injury blighted his career. In January 1947, whilst in the North-East for the Newcastle cup-tie, he contracted pneumonia and was side-lined for nearly a year. Fully recovered he found that his place in the team had been taken by Alf Ramsey whose fine form had been recognised by an England call up. Events turned full circle when Alf became injured and Bill reclaimed, not only the Southampton right-back slot, but,within four months, the vacant England right-back

position. It was obvious that Saints could not keep two such talented right-backs and Alf departed to Tottenham leaving Bill to spend loyally the rest of his playing and coaching days at the Dell. As a scout Bill is credited with spotting young Mick Channon and by the time of his premature retirement in 1980 he had clocked up over thirty-five years unstinting service. Today Bill still resides in Southampton and follows the club's fortunes with more than a little enthusiasm. His elegance and sportsmanship are still fondly remembered by those fortunate to see him play.

Appearances:
FL: 227 app. 10 gls.
FAC: 12 app. 1 gl
Total: 239 app. 11 gls.

ELLIOTT, Bernard Harry

Role: Half-back 1949-58
5'7" 9st.12lbs.
b. Beeston, Nottingham 3 May 1925

CAREER: Beeston Fields Senior School/ Beeston Lads Club/Nottingham Forest Oct 1942/Boston United 1948/SOUTHAMPTON Oct 1949/Poole Town July 1959.
Debut v Tottenham Hotspur (a) 25.2.50

'Bryn' Elliott had been in Nottingham Forest's league side of 1947-48 before dropping into non-league soccer with Boston. Saints rescued him, and team-mate Tom Lowder, bringing both men to the Dell in October 1949. Four months later Bryn was given his debut in a vital promotion clash at White Hart Lane in front of a crowd of 70,302 and, although Saints went down 4-0 on the day, Bryn's never-say-die attitude combined with a neat, precise style showed that he had plenty to offer. Bryn went on to become a regular in the Saints half-back line and served the club admirably through their Third Division days before a brief spell at Poole heralded the end of his career. He has since concentrated on the running of his off-licence business not a stone's throw from the Dell, and keeps more than an eye out for the Saints' result on Saturday nights.

Appearances:
FL: 235 app. 2 gls.
FAC: 16 app. 0 gls.
Total: 251 app. 2 gls.

Bill Ellerington

Bryn Elliott

ELLISON, James

Role: Full-back 1927-28
5'11" 12st.0lbs.
b. Manchester 4 February 1906
d. Manchester 1986

CAREER: St Helen's Town/
Tranmere Rovers c.s. 1921/
Rotherham Town Aug 1923/
Rhyl Athletic/
SOUTHAMPTON am May
1927, pro Oct 1927/Rochdale
July 1928/Connahs Quay c.s. 1929.

James Ellison

Debut v Port Vale (h) 10.3.28

Signed from Welsh non-league football, James
Ellison came through a trial period to sign
professional forms in October 1927. He
complemented his one league appearance with
59 games in the reserves before being given a
free transfer in May 1928.

> **Appearances:**
> *FL: 1 app. 0 gls.*
> **Total:** *1 app. 0 gls.*

EMANUEL, Thomas

Role: Full-back 1938-46
5'7" 11st.8lbs.
b. Treboeth 1 August 1915

CAREER: I.C.I. Works XI/
Swansea Town Sept 1935/
SOUTHAMPTON Sept
1938/ (guest for Swindon
Town & Wrexham during
World War two) Battalion
soccer whilst serving in
Africa, India, Burma and
Madagascar)/Llanelly 1946.

Debut v Newcastle United (a) 24.9.38

As rugby
football was the
dominant code
in South Wales,
Tom did not
play much
soccer until he
became
employed at
I.C.I.. Whilst
playing in a
local cup final at
the Vetch Field,
his form was
impressive
enough to
prompt
Swansea into

Tom Emanuel

offering terms to the promising left back. Three
years later Tom Parker splashed out £2,200 to
acquire Tom's talents and the speed with
which he settled into Saints' defence convinced
the fans the money had been well spent. Sadly
the war intervened and although Tom
returned to the Dell to play two F.A. Cup
games against Newport County in January
1946, he was soon to be given a free transfer to
Llanelly in the Welsh League. Retiring from
football in 1948 he became a bus inspector in
Swansea, the town where he still resides.

> **Appearances:**
> *FL: 33 app. 0 gls.*
> *FAC: 3 app. 0 gls.*
> **Total:** *36 app. 0 gls.*

❑ **Saints note** - *Coincidentally, Tom's debuts for
Swansea and Southampton both happened to be
against Newcastle United.*

ENGLEFIELD, Frank

Role: Forward 1899-1900
b. Southampton August 1878

CAREER: Freemantle Mission/Freemantle/
SOUTHAMPTON May 1898/Freemantle c.s.
1900/Southampton Wanderers 1902.
Debut v Bedminster (a) 25.11.1899

Frank Englefield emerged from the thriving
local soccer scene and joined the Saints from
local rivals Freemantle in 1898. An outside-left,
he made two United League appearances
during the 1898-99 season and had the
satisfaction of gaining Hampshire County
honours against Dorset in March 1899. He
made his one and only Southern League
appearance the following season, not as a
winger but in the unaccustomed left-half berth,
and understandably failed to shine. The path
to a steady first team place was effectively
blocked by Alf Milward who was performing
heroics on the left wing and, finding himself
out in the cold, Frank decided to return to the
"Magpies".

Appearances:
SL: 1 app. 0 gls.
Total: *1 app. 0 gls.*

❏ **Saints note** - *Frank's brother-in-law was Phil
Mead who not only made one appearance as a
Saints' goalkeeper in 1901 but was also a famous
Hampshire and England cricketer.*

EPHGRAVE, George Arthur

Role: Goalkeeper 1946-48
6'4" 13st.5lbs.
b. Reading 29 April 1918

CAREER: Guernsey/Tottenham am.
(Northfleet) Oct 1935/Aston Villa Oct 1936/
Swindon Town Mar 1939/SOUTHAMPTON
trial Apr 1946, signed Apr 1946/Norwich City
July 1948/Watford Aug 1951/Deal Town
Aug 1952/March Town June 1954.
Debut v Swansea Town (h) 4.9.46

George Ephgrave, standing 6'4" in height, is
the tallest-ever goalkeeper to appear in
Southampton colours. With a handspan of ten
inches he could pick up an old leather ball one-
handed, reach the cross bar without lifting his

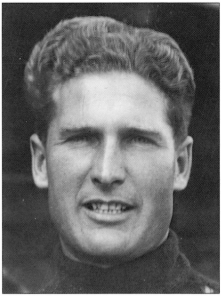
George Ephgrave

heels and, with his arms outstretched, had a
span of six feet eight inches. Prior to joining
the club, George had spent four years as a
P.O.W. in Odessa after being captured at Crete
and, with the resumption of normal football,
had competed with Len Stansbridge for the
Saints' goalkeeping jersey. With the arrival of
Ian Black his chances of regular football
diminished and a £500 transfer to Norwich
was followed by a move to Watford.
Throughout his career he used his height well
to deal with crosses but could be suspect
against low shots. Retiring from the game,
George at first became a publican and then he
later moved to Guernsey specialising in
growing tomatoes in his market garden.

Appearances:
FL: 36 app. 0 gls.
FAC: 2 app. 0 gls.
Total: *38 app 0 gls.*

EVANS, Harry Alfred

Role: Forward 1946-47
b. Lambeth 17 April 1919
d. St. Pancras 22 December 1962

CAREER:
Woking/Fulham/Romford/Aldershot,/
SOUTHAMPTON Oct 1943/Exeter City

June 1947/Aldershot March 1949, secretary 1950, secretary-manager Dec 1950/Tottenham Hotspur asst. manager 1962.

Debut v Newport County (FAC) (h) 5.1.46

Harry Evans became a Southampton player while serving in the R.A.F. in 1943 and made a total of 71 wartime appearances for the club prior to the resumption of normal football in 1946. He only made Saints' league eleven on the one occasion, wearing the centre-forward's shirt in the home game versus Bradford in November 1946 and moved onto Exeter in the summer of 1947. After a spell in charge at Aldershot he became Bill Nicholson's assistant at Tottenham.

Appearances:
FL: 1 app. 0 gls.
FAC: 4 app 0 gls.
Total: *5 app. 0 gls.*

EVANS, Richard

Role: Forward 1902-04
b. Smallthorne 1875
d. Salisbury 13 January 1942

CAREER: Burslem Port Vale May 1898/ Reading c.s. 1900/SOUTHAMPTON c.s. 1902.

Debut v Brentford (h) 6.9.02

Dick Evans was originally from the Potteries and was secured by the club from fellow Southern Leaguers, Reading, in the close season of 1902, arriving with a high reputation. Nicknamed "Jammer" he was the owner of a deadly shot and, as a quick and reliable right winger, rapidly became the idol of the crowd who also loved his never-say-die spirit. He contributed a major part in the two Southern League Championships of 1902-03 and 1903-04 before ill-health unfortunately cut short his career. Dick later became the landlord of the London Arms in the Docks, a position he held until his retirement in 1936.

Appearances:
SL: 41 ap. 16 gls.
Total: *41 app. 16 gls.*

EVERIST, Frank James

Role: Forward 1906-07
5'10" 11st.6lbs.
b. Orpington 1884

CAREER: Grasmere United/Cray Wanderers/ Orpington/SOUTHAMPTON May 1906/ Croydon Common c.s. 1907/Dartford c.s. 1908.

Debut v Brentford (a) 29.9.06

Recommended to Saints by a keen supporter living in Kent, Frank Everist was a splendid runner who had won over forty prizes on the track. His speed meant that he distinguished himself in the reserves but, whenever he moved up a notch to the first team, he found his athletic abilities not good enough to ever establish himself. Unusually, during his one year stint at the Dell, Frank was also employed to look after the maintenance of the ground although this 'extra' job did not prevent him from following a number of Saints players to Croydon Common in 1907.

Appearances:
SL: 8 app. 2 gls.
Total: *8 app. 2 gls.*

Frank Everist

FAIRGRIEVE, Walter Robert

Role: Forward 1898-99
5'7" 10st.4lbs.
b. Edinburgh 30 August 1874

CAREER: Dalry Primrose/Glasgow
Perthshire/Everton (trial) 1898/
SOUTHAMPTON May 1898/Luton Town
June 1899.

Debut v New Brompton (h) 17.9.1898

A former Scottish Junior international, Walter
Fairgrieve had also represented Glasgow in a
game against Lanarkshire and, after a month's
trial period at Goodison, joined Southampton
on a professional contract. One game wearing
the outside right shirt was the sum total of his
twelve months at the Dell, and after a
frustrating period in the reserves, he moved to
Luton.

Appearances:
SL: 1 app. 0 gls.
Total: *1 app. 0 gls.*

FARRELL, John

Role: Forward 1895-98 & 1899-1900
5'9" 11st. 2lbs.
b. Tunstall 1873
d. Stoke 22 February 1947

CAREER: Dresden Utd/Stoke Oct 1894/
SOUTHAMPTON St. Mary's Apr 1895/Stoke
c.s. 1898/SOUTHAMPTON May1899/New
Brighton Tower June 1900/Northampton
Town c.s. 1901/West Ham United c.s. 1902.

Debut v Millwall (a) 14.9.1895

Jack Farrell was considered the greatest
"catch" of all the Stoke imports in April 1895
and had cost the Potteries club £40 the
previous October. Contemporary reports at the
time of his arrival described him as fast, tricky
and reliable and he soon justified his
reputation with a series of impressive displays.
His level headed attitude earned him the team
captaincy for the 1896-97 season and he not
only led the team to its first-ever Southern
League championship but scored thirteen
goals in 20 games from the centre-forward
position. The following year the club again
won the title and reached the last four of the
F.A. Cup but, although Jack played his part, an

injury sustained in the first semi-final side-
lined him for the last six weeks of the season.
After returning to Stoke for a year he again
became a Saint for the 1899-1900 season when
the F.A. Cup Final was reached, although the
game itself was surrounded by controversial
team selection involving Jack being chosen in
preference to Roddy MacLeod, the man in
form. Disillusioned with all the discord, Jack
moved on to New Brighton Tower and then
Northampton Town. After one season at West
Ham, spent entirely in the reserves, Jack
decided to end what had been an eventful
career and in his later years he became a
publican in his native Tunstall.

Appearances:
SL: 73 app. 40 gls.
FAC: 24. app. 14 gls.
Total: *97 app. 54 gls.*

FARWELL, Arthur

Role: Forward 1891-92

CAREER: SOUTHAMPTON St. Mary's 1888

Debut v Warmley (FAC) (a) 3.10.1891

An inside-forward of considerable repute at
county level. Arthur Farwell was a loyal one-
club man who served St. Mary's for a five year
period. Quick and full of tricks, Arthur had the
knack of hitting vital goals in important
games. His last minute equaliser at Cowes in
the County Junior Cup semi-final in 1889 was
the most noteworthy, and his scoring in those
early days did much to establish St. Mary's as
the town's premier club. Active until 1893,
Arthur retired from football with the advent of
professionalism and became a draper in
Havant. He did however maintain a
connection with St. Mary's, not by playing
football but by assisting in the choir!

Appearances:
FAC: 2 app. 0 gls.
Total: *2 app 0 gls.*

FASHANU, Justinus Soni

Role: Forward 1982-83
6'1" 12st. 7lbs.
b. Hackney, London 19 February 1961

CAREER: Shropham/Attleborough/

Peterborough/Norwich City app Sept 1977, pro Dec 1978 (Adelaide City-loan-summer 1980)/ Nottingham Forest Aug 1981 (SOUTHAMPTON-loan-Aug-Oct 1982)/Notts County Dec 1982/Brighton & Hove Albion June 1985/Los Angeles Heat player-manager/ Edmonton Brickmen July 1988/Manchester City Oct 1989/West Ham United Nov 1989/ Leyton Orient Feb 1990/Southall player-coach Mar 1991/ Newcastle United (trial) July 1991/Leatherhead Nov 1991/Torquay United Dec 1991.

Debut v Coventry City (a) 28.8.82

On loan from Nottingham Forest in August 1982 Justin Fashanu quickly rediscovered his old form at the Dell. Although labelled a £1 million misfit following his move from Norwich to Forest, he helped the Saints overcome the sudden departure of Keegan as well as re-kindling his confidence. McMenemy would have liked to have made the move permanent but money was not available and so Justin moved to Notts County. His league career came to an abrupt end at Brighton following a knee injury and he took himself to America where he played for Los Angeles Heat and the Edmonton Brickmen. After receiving further medical treatment in the States Justin returned in 1989 and had a succession of trials with Manchester City and West Ham but was not offered a permanent contract.

Appearances:
FL: 9 app. 3 gls.
Total: *9 app. 3 gls.*

❏ **Saints note** - *Justin is the only 'on-loan' player to score for Saints.*

FENWICK, Herbert

Role: Half-back 1919-20
5'8" 11st. 0lbs.
b. Wallsend-on-Tyne October qtr 1900

CAREER: Harland & Wolff/SOUTHAMPTON May 1919.

Debut v Exeter City (h) 30.8.19

A boilermaker by trade, Bert Fenwick moved from his native north-east to help the war effort in the shipyards of Harland and Wolff. A member of the works team that won the 1918-19 South Hants War League, he was invited to sign for Southampton in May 1919 as a

professional. After starting the 1919-20 season well and becoming a regular in the first two months, he lost his place to Andrews and left the area soon after.

Appearances:
SL: 11 app. 0 gls.
Total: *11 app. 0 gls.*

FISHER, Hugh Donnelly

Role: Midfield 1966-77
5'8" 10st.3lbs.
b. Pollock, Glasgow 9 January 1944

CAREER: Glasgow Roman Catholic Under-15's/Gowan Bank Youth/Glasgow Youth/ Blackpool Aug 1962/SOUTHAMPTON Mar 1967/Denver Dynamos Apr-Aug 1975/ Southport player-manager Mar 1977/ Basingstoke Oct 1978/Andover June 1979/ Waterlooville July 1979.

Debut v Everton (a) 18.3.67

Hughie Fisher's £35,000 arrival at the Dell coincided with the transfer deadline of 1967 and Saints' desperate battle to avoid relegation. His tenacity in midfield paid

Hughie Fisher

immediate dividends as he helped Saints snatch a 1-0 victory at Goodison on his debut and then played a significant role in the following 4-2 home win over Fulham. A cartilage injury and the form of Fred Kemp initially held up his progress but, despite breaking a leg in October 1971, he determinedly fought his way back to full fitness and a regular position in the team. His equalizer at the Dell against Aston Villa in the last minute of the F.A. Cup Third Round in 1976 remains a vivid memory, and he must have considered himself very unlucky not to have played in the final as he sustained a pelvic strain, prior to the semi-final, that resulted in him losing his place to Paul Gilchrist. After a brief sojourn managing Southport, Hughie returned to the Southampton area to become a sales representative for a brewery and is often a visitor to the Dell.

Appearances;
FL: 297 (5) app. 7 gls.
FAC: 22 (2) app. 3 gls.
LC: 17 (1) app. 1 gl.
Eur: 9 (1) app. 0 gls.
Total: *345 (9) app. 11 gls.*

❏ **Saints note** - *Hughie's father, Peter, was a professional with Clyde, Burnley, Watford and Stenhousemuir.*

FISHLOCK, Laurence Barnard

Role: Forward 1934-36
5'9" 11st.10lbs.
b. Battersea, London 2 January 1907
d. Sutton 26 June 1986

CAREER: Battersea Schools/Crusaders (London jnr)/Romford/Dulwich Hamlet Aug 1927/Fulham May 1928/Crystal Palace May 1929/Aldershot July 1932/Millwall June 1933/SOUTHAMPTON Sept 1934/Fulham trial Sept 1937/Gillingham Jan 1938.
*Debut v Port Vale (a) 3.9.34 * (scored on debut)*

Laurie Fishlock, an amateur international soccer inside-left and later England Test cricketer, arrived at the Dell from Millwall in September 1934. At the time the club were short of experienced players and he helped plug the left-wing gap created by the departure to Fulham of Johnny Arnold. After rendering two good seasons' service his Test

Laurie Fishlock

Cricket duties put a temporary halt to his life as a Saint as he toured Australia with the M.C.C. throughout the 1936-37 season. Laurie was eventually transfer-listed in May 1937 at £500 and had a brief trial with Fulham before joining Gillingham. A fine left handed batsman, he continued his cricket career with Surrey for whom he scored over 22,000 runs and later become a top coach. He was also cricket coach to St. Dunstan's College for many years.

Appearances:
FL: 69 app. 14 gls.
FAC: 2 app. 2 gls.
Total: *71 app. 16 gls.*

FITCHETT, John

Role: Half-back 1902-03
5'10" 11st.7lbs.
b. Manchester 1879

CAREER: Talbot/Bolton Wanderers May 1897/Manchester United 1902/SOUTHAMPTON May 1902/Manchester United Mar 1903/Plymouth Argyle c.s. 1903/Manchester United June 1904/Manchester City 1905/Fulham May 1905/Sale Holmfield c.s. 1906/Exeter City Feb 1910.
Debut v Brentford (h) 6.9.02

John Flood
(see overleaf)

A footballing prodigy as a juvenile, John Fitchett had already represented the Football League on three occasions, as well as playing in an unofficial international in Germany in 1901, by the time he became a Southampton player in 1902. He seemed to have a strong tie with his native city for, after only one season at the Dell during which time his energetic tackling and neat passing appealed to the fans, he returned to Manchester, a manoeuvre he repeated in 1904 after a spell at Plymouth. Whilst at the Dell John was sometimes criticised for over-elaboration and it was no surprise when, after hanging up his boots, he became an actor, touring with the Karno Theatrical Company. He later became manager of the Vaudeville Theatre in Exeter, where he came briefly out of retirement to assist the local side.

Appearances;
SL: 8 app. 0 gls.
FAC: 1 app. 0 gls.
Total: *9 app. 0 gls.*

FLEMING, John

Role: Forward 1891-92
b. Leith September 1864
d. Scotland August 1934

CAREER: Vale of Leven/93rd Argyle & Sutherland Highlanders/SOUTHAMPTON St. Mary's Dec 1891/Aston Villa May 1892/Lincoln City Oct 1892/Larkhall Saints (Strathclyde) May 1893.

Debut v Reading (FAC) (h) 24.10.1891
* (scored on debut)

On 10th October 1891 the Saints played an exhibition match against the 93rd Highland Regiment at the County Ground and lost 2-0. The St. Mary's management were so impressed by two of the army players, John Fleming and Sandy McMillan, that they immediately signed them on with a view to the forthcoming important cup-tie with Reading that was due to take place in a fortnight's time. Both men duly made their debuts in the cup-tie and made a huge impact in St. Mary's 7-0 victory. Private "Jock" Fleming featured at centre-forward and his aggressiveness led to him notching a hat-trick. Reading's secretary immediately lodged an appeal to the F.A. (see McMillan) and St. Mary's were expelled from

the competition due to both players not being registered at least 28 days before the game. Jock, unlike Sandy McMillan, did continue to play for St. Mary's until the end of December when he was posted abroad to India with his regiment. He returned to England in May 1892 having left the army and, signing on for Aston Villa, scored twice on his debut.

Appearances:
FAC: 1 app. 3 gls.
Total: *1 app. 3 gls.*

FLOOD, John Ernest

Role: Forward 1952-58
5'6" 10st.8 lbs..
b. Southampton 21 October 1932

CAREER: Pennington St. Marks Lads/SOUTHAMPTON Nov 1949/Bournemouth and B.A. June 1958/Headington United July 1959/Yiewsley Oct 1959/Cowes Nov 1961.

Debut v Blackburn Rovers (h) 25.4.53
* (scored on debut)

One of eight footballing brothers, John Flood played his early football in the New Forest for the successful Pennington St. Marks Youth team and gained county and international schoolboy honours before signing for the Saints as a seventeen year-old. He progressed through the club's junior and reserve teams to make his scoring debut in Saints' last home match as a Second Division club in April 1953. A good club man, whole-hearted and hardworking, John was the backbone of the Saints' forward line as they came to terms with life in the Third Division South. With the emergence of Terry Paine, John crossed the New Forest to join Bournemouth but after only 17 games dropped into non-league football.

Appearances:
FL: 122 app. 28 gls.
FAC: 6 app. 1 gl.
Total: *128 app. 29 gls.*

❑ **Saints note** - *One of John's brothers, Brian, was an aspiring goalkeeper on the Dell staff during the 1957-58 season.*

See previous page for picture of John Flood

FLOWERS, Timothy David

Role: Goalkeeper 1986-
6'2" 13st.4lbs.
b. Kenilworth 3 February 1967

CAREER: Wolverhampton Wanderers app.
Aug 1983, pro. Aug 1984 (SOUTHAMPTON-
loan-Apr 1986, transferred June 1986)/
(Swindon Town-loan-Mar 1987, Swindon
Town-loan-Nov 1987).

Debut v Manchester United (a) 13.9.86

Signed from Wolves while still a teenager, Tim
Flowers cost nearly £100,000 and was regarded
as one of the country's top young 'keepers. His
debut coincided with a 5-0 defeat at Old
Trafford and his first appearance at home was
even more catastrophic when, in the course of
conceding a fourth goal, Tim suffered a severe
facial injury and had to be replaced by Colin
Clarke. Overcoming these early setbacks he
took over the green jersey on a full-time basis
when Peter Shilton departed for Derby County
but lost his place in October 1987 to the
recently-arrived John Burridge. Despite being
capped at Under-21 level, Tim still found it
hard to oust his one time mentor at Wolves
and it wasn't until Burridge left for Newcastle
United that he was able to reclaim the
goalkeeping position with any great
permanence. Very popular with the fans, Tim
is as agile as any of the league's leading goalies
yet, occasionally, does not dominate the
penalty area as much as he should. If he can
perhaps learn to be more positive both with his
commands and actions there is no reason at all
why he should not be the Saints' goalkeeper
for many years to come.

Appearances;
FL: 95 app. 0 gls.
FAC: 8 app. 0 gls.
LC: 15 app. 0 gls.
Total: *118 app. 0 gls.*

Tim Flowers

Gerry Forrest

FORREST, Gerald

Role: Full-back 1985-90
5'10" 10st.11lbs.
b. Stockton 21 January 1957

CAREER: Southbank/Rotherham United Feb 1977/SOUTHAMPTON Dec 1985/ Rotherham United Aug 1990/Gateshead United Aug 1991.

Debut v Arsenal (h) 7.12.85

When Chris Nicholl plucked Gerry Forrest from the relative obscurity of lower division soccer it seemed like a typical Nicholl foray into the transfer market. Gerry was approaching his thirtieth birthday and, while he soon proved to be a steady and reliable full-back, his arrival hardly put thousands into the coffers at the next home gate. Nevertheless he made the transition to top flight football with the minimum of fuss and totally justified the £100,000 fee. 1989-90 proved to be a disastrous season for the popular defender for, when making his first appearance of the season in a home match against Wimbledon in September 1989, he suffered a nasty injury that side-lined

him for nearly six months. By the time he had recovered Gerry found that Jason Dodd and Aleksey Cherednik had leap-frogged ahead of him in the pecking order for the right-back position, and a summer free transfer back to Rotherham seemed to be a wise move especially as he had family commitments in the area.

Appearances;
FL: 112 (3) app. 0 gls.
FAC: 5 app. 1 gl.
LC: 11 app. 0 gls.
Total: *128 (3) app. 1 gl.*

FORSYTH, Robert Campbell

Role: Goalkeeper 1965-68
6'1" 13st.5lbs.
b. Plean, Stirlingshire 5 May 1939

CAREER: Falkirk/ Shettleston Jnrs/ St. Mirren Apr 1955/ Kilmarnock Nov 1960/ SOUTHAMPTON Dec 1965.

Debut v Plymouth Argyle (h) 11.12.65

When Campbell Forsyth joined Saints for a fee

of £10,000 in December 1965 he had just helped Kilmarnock to the Scottish League title and had been awarded his fourth international cap. He quickly settled into English football and his fine displays between the posts played a prominent part in the club's successful push for promotion. Unfortunately, after only eight First Division games, he broke his leg in a match at home to Liverpool and, although he gamely fought a seven-month battle to fitness, he never regained his old form and decided to retire in May 1968. Campbell became a brewery representative soon after and, for a long time, was the club's scout north of the border, recommending, amongst others, Jim Steele and Gerry O'Brien.

Appearances:
FL: 48 app. 0 gls.
FAC: 1 app. 0 gls.
LC: 2 app. 0 gls.
Total: *51 app. 0 gls.*

Campbell Forsyth

FOSTER, John

Role: Forward 1908-09
5'7" 11st.8lbs.
b. Yorkshire

CAREER: Stockport County/Watford 1906/Sunderland Dec 1907/West Ham United May 1908/SOUTHAMPTON Mar 1909/Huddersfield Town May 1909/Castleford Town 1910

Debut v Southend United (h) 6.3.09

Whilst at Watford, John Foster had developed quite a reputation as a dashing leader of attacking football and Sunderland paid £800 for his sharpshooting skills in December 1907. His move to Roker Park coincided with a decline in his health and, not unnaturally, his form slumped. His doctor advised him to move to the milder climate of the south which he did by joining West Ham United, and then Southampton, in an exchange deal that saw Costello make the reverse trip. His career at the Dell started badly when he missed some easy chances and, although he did manage a goal at Queen's Park Rangers in his fifth match, he moved on again at the season's conclusion.

Appearances:
SL: 6 app. 1 gl.
Total: *6 app. 1 gl.*

FOSTER, Robert

Role: Goalkeeper 1932-33
5'10" 11st.lbs.
b. Dean, nr. Bolton April qtr. 1911

CAREER: Farnworth Standard/Accrington Stanley Jan 1932/SOUTHAMPTON June 1932/Wrexham June 1933/Bury Aug 1935/ Oldham Athletic Sept 1936-May 1937/Mossley 1937-38.

Bob Foster

Debut v Port Vale (h) 29.8.32

Bob Foster was signed as cover for Bert Scriven and his stay at the Dell lasted 18 months during which time he had one League appearance and 36 outings for the reserves. In 1936 he was running a newsagent's business in the north-west when Oldham offered him a trial. Bob was on the losing side just once in 11 Latic appearances.

Appearances:
FL: 1 app. 0 gls.
Total: *1 app. 0 gls.*

FOULKES, William Isaiah

Role: Forward 1954-55
5'10" 11st.4lbs.
b. Merthyr Tydfil 29 May 1926
d. Chester 7 February 1979

CAREER: Cardiff City Feb 1945/Winsford United/Chester Apr 1948/Newcastle United Oct 1951/ SOUTHAMPTON Aug 1954/Winsford United Jan 1956/Chester July 1956/Hyde United July 1961.

Debut v Brentford (h) 21.8.54

Welsh international Billy Foulkes was a member of Newcastle's cup winning side of 1952 and joined the Saints, together with Tommy Mulgrew, for a combined fee of £12,000. Due to a back injury his stay with Southampton was far from happy as the club claimed he had been carrying his injury at the time of signing. The Saints sought a reduction in the £5,000 fee paid to Newcastle and, whilst

the F.A. considered the evidence, Billy played for Winsford United in the Cheshire League. With the appeal finally going against the Saints, Billy returned to the League scene with Chester who paid less than £1,000 for his registration. Saints' spectacular loss of over £4,000 was compounded by the fact that he went on to play over 170 games for the Cheshire side. After his retirement from the game Bill had a milk-bar business in Chester.

Appearances:
FL: 23 app. 1 gl.
Total: *23 app. 1 gl.*

FOXALL, Frederick Howard

Role: Forward 1919-1922
5'10" 11st.2lbs.
b. Stourbridge 2 April 1898
d. Smethwick 17 June 1926

CAREER: Aston Villa 1916/Blackheath Town 1916/SOUTHAMPTON May 1919/ Birmingham Mar 1922/Watford June 1923.

Debut v Exeter City (h) 30.8.19

Fred Foxall was spotted by Saints' trainer James McIntyre playing for Blackheath Town

Billy Foulkes

Fred Foxall

at Coventry in 1918 and was immediately invited for a trial. After signing Southern League forms in May 1919 he quickly made the outside-left position his own with some excellent wing play. His well-placed centres from varying angles were a strong feature of his repertoire although invariably his best performances came in away matches. In May 1921 he invoked controversy by signing for Aston Villa without Southampton's permission and, after F.A. intervention, he was ordered to re-sign for the Saints. He continued to give good service up until March 1922 when he moved to Birmingham in the double exchange deal that brought Elkes and Getgood to the Dell. After joining Watford in 1923 Fred unfortunately broke a leg and never kicked a ball again. It is not known whether his death three years later had anything to do with his leg injury but the fact that he was only 25 when he died must create a doubt that he ever made a full recovery.

Appearances:
SL: 38 app. 5 gls.
FL: 67 app. 7 gls.
FAC: 9 app. 0 gls.
Total: *114 app. 12 gls.*

FOYLE, Martin John

Role: Forward 1982-84
5'10" 11st.2lbs.
b. Salisbury 2 May 1963

CAREER: Bemerton/SOUTHAMPTON app. 1980, pro. Aug 1980 (Munkfors (Sweden)-loan-May-Oct 1982) (Blackburn Rovers-loan-Mar 1984) / Aldershot Aug 1984/Oxford United Mar 1987/Port Vale June 1991.

Debut v Coventry City (h) 15.1.83

Spotted by Football League referee, Tony Glasson, Martin Foyle was playing in the Wiltshire League when he was recommended to Lawrie McMenemy in 1980. Spending the summer of 1982 playing in the Swedish League helped with his development and he returned to make his debut in January 1983. A clever and stylish ball player, Martin's finest moment with the club came in October 1983, when, coming on as a second half substitute, he scored two goals to eliminate Carlisle from the Milk Cup. A modest fee took Martin to the Recreation Ground in August 1984 but, when

Martin Foyle

Oxford spent £140,000 on him in March 1987, the Saints received a further £40,000 which was a third of Aldershot's profit.

Appearances:
FL: 7 (6) app. 1 gl.
LC: 0 (2) app. 2 gls.
Total: *7 (8) 3 gls.*

FRASER, John

Role: Forward 1902-05
5'11' 13st.0lbs.
b. Dumbarton 10 November 1876
d. 1 October 1952

CAREER: Dumbarton 1894/Motherwell/ Notts County Jan 1898/Newcastle United June 1899/St. Mirren c.s. 1901/SOUTHAMPTON May 1902/Dundee c.s. 1905, later player-manager/Chelsea scout 1919, later asst. manager until late 1930's.

*Debut v Brentford (h) 6.9.02 * (scored on debut)*

Jack Fraser started his footballing career at the relatively late age of eighteen, although by the time he joined the Saints he had a wealth of League experience under his belt. He was a bulky man and Saints initially played him in the centre-forward position with spectacular success as Jack scored a hat-trick on his debut and, later the same year, four against Watford. Strangely for a big man, he found the wing positions more to his liking and he presented an awesome sight to defending goalkeepers when cutting inside and bearing down on them in full flight. A firm favourite with the Dell faithful, his stay would have been longer had not the purchase of a local tobacconist's shop fallen through. Instead Dundee offered him terms he could not refuse and in 1910 he won a Cup-Winners medal which made up for being on the losing side in the 1897 final with Dumbarton. Jack later moved into managerial positions with Dundee and Chelsea.

John Fraser

Appearances;
SL: 73 app. 25 gls.
FAC: 7 app. 1 gl.
Total: *80 app. 26 gls.*

FRASER, William Cuthbert

Role: Forward 1929-32
5'8" 11st.4lbs.
b. Cowpen Village, Blyth July qtr. 1905

CAREER: Blyth Juniors/New Deleval Temperance/Cowpen Celtic/Royal Tank Corps/East Stirlingshire/ Northampton Town Nov 1926/ Aldershot May 1929/ SOUTHAMPTON June 1929/Fulham July 1932/ Northampton Town June 1933/Salisbury City 1934, player-coach 1935.

Debut v Reading (a) 14.12.29

Bill Fraser cost the Saints £200 when he was signed from Hampshire neighbours, Aldershot, and although he had considerable ability he suffered acutely from nerves in front of crowds. The club would have liked to have held onto him but mounting debts forced Saints to accept a £500 bid from Fulham.

Appearances:
FL: 56 app. 11 gls.
Total: *56 app. 11 gls.*

FREEMAN, Alfred

Role: Forward 1946-47
b. Bethnal Green, London 2 January 1920

CAREER: Tottenham Hotspur, trial 1939/ SOUTHAMPTON Nov 1943/ (Sunderland during World War Two) /Crystal Palace Aug 1948/Reading Aug 1949 /Canterbury City Aug 1954.

Debut v Swansea Town (h) 4.9.46

In 1939 Alf had a trial with Tottenham but the outbreak of war temporarily curtailed any hopes of a professional contract and he joined the Duke of Cornwall's Light Infantry to serve at Normandy. Whilst playing Army soccer during the war Alf played alongside Alf Ramsey and, when the two men signed for the Saints in 1943, they became firm friends and shared digs. In Alf Ramsey's autobiography

Bill Fraser

Alf Freeman

"Talking Football", Alf Freeman is given credit for encouraging the young Ramsey to think tactically, advice that was to pay dividends for Saints, Spurs and later England. Meanwhile Alf Freeman struggled to emulate his friend and a move to Crystal Palace followed in August 1948. At Selhurst Park Alf played just one League game, coincidentally against the club he was next to join, Reading. At present Alf lives in North West London and goes to watch Arsenal or Tottenham whenever he can obtain a ticket.

Appearances;
FL: 7 app. 2 gls.
Total: *7 app. 2 gls.*

FRENCH, Joseph

Role: Centre Half 1899-1901
b. Southampton

CAREER: Clifton/Southampton Oxford/ SOUTHAMPTON 1899/New

Brompton c.s. 1901/Freemantle c.s. 1902.
Debut v Bedminster (h) 31.3.1900

Joe French was playing in the local parks when he caught the eye of Harry Haynes, the then Saints' fullback. Given a trial in the club's reserve side he soon signed a professional contract and became a capable understudy to Arthur Chadwick, although his chances of ousting the England international from the first team were negligible. Joe transferred to New Brompton in the summer of 1901 and made fourteen first team appearances before he returned to Southampton to play for Freemantle.

Appearances:
SL: 6 app. 0 gls.
Total: *6 app. 0 gls.*

FRY, Charles Burgess

Role: Full-back 1900-03
5'10" 11st.13lbs.
b. Croydon 25 April 1872
d. Hampstead 7 September 1956

CAREER: West Kent F.C. 1884/Repton School 1887/Wadham College 1891/Oxford University 1892-95/Old Reptonians/ Corinthians 1892-1903/SOUTHAMPTON Dec 1900/Portsmouth Dec 1902.
Debut v Tottenham Hotspur (h) 26.12.1900

Charles Burgess Fry, or "C.B.", was the complete all round sportsman, excelling at athletics, rugby, football and, in particular, cricket. Possessing the physique of "an Ancient Greek", C. B. Fry, the athlete, equalled the world long jump record while at university, jumping 23'6". He also ran the 100 yds in 10.2 seconds and leaped 5'8" in the high jump. Awarded his Oxford Blue for soccer, he played all his

Joe French

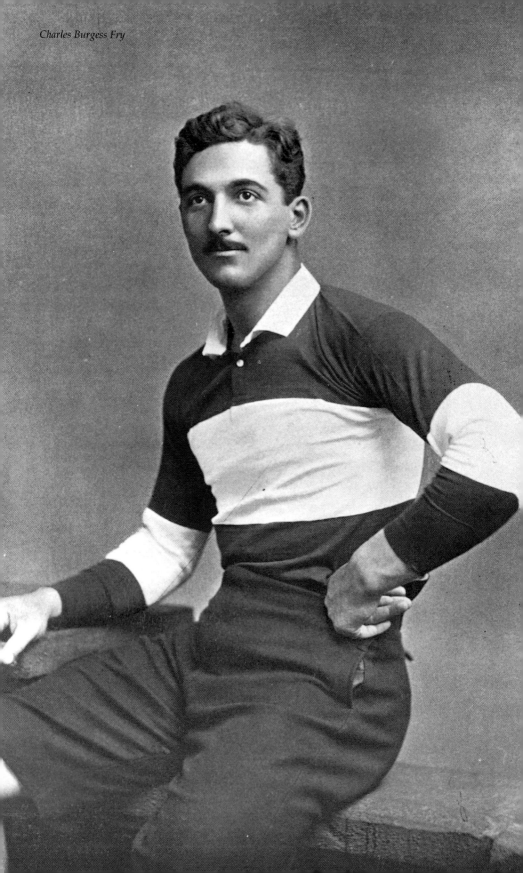

Charles Burgess Fry

early football with the Corinthians and, although extremely proud of his amateur status, decided in 1900, that entering the professional game would enhance the likelihood of international honours. Southampton were chosen as not only were they the leading lights in the Southern League but the Dell was only four miles from his West End home. In December 1900 the Football Echo proudly stated, "A player of Fry's stamp would be a distinct gain for the best club in the kingdom; he is, without doubt, the finest amateur back playing, a player who shines conspicuously in a constellation of football stars." The Football Echo was being a little over-enthusiastic as Fry's game was initially a little refined for the hurly-burly of League football and he never relished the physical excesses of some of the tackles. Nevertheless his debut against Spurs was greeted with wild enthusiasm by the crowd and press alike. The Football Echo, still full of praise, said, "The famous amateur's screw kicking under difficulties was simply astonishing," and apparently when he suffered an attack of cramp in the closing stages of the game, the spectators burst into a spontaneous rendition of "for he's a jolly good fellow." With the press and fans on his side, an England cap became a formality and he was duly picked for the England team to play Ireland, the match taking place at the Dell in March 1901. Local interest was particularly high as not only was this the first international ever staged at Southampton but there were a further two Saints players selected in the shape of Arthur Turner and goalkeeper Jack Robinson. The following years, with C.B. making himself available for important matches, Saints marched to the F. A. Cup Final, a match they were to lose after a replay and, although he had his moments in the cup run, there were times when even the Football Echo questioned his tackling abilities. Perhaps realising his days as a defender were numbered, C.B. did try a couple of games as a centre-forward during the 1902-03 season but, with the club growing impatient with his unavailability, he decided to join Portsmouth where an injury sustained soon afterwards led to his retirement from the game. Fry continued to dominate the English cricketing stage, playing for Hampshire up until 1921. He hit a total of 94 first class centuries with an average of 50.22 and played in 26 Tests for England, captaining them in 1912. In later years C.B. ran a training ship, called the Mercury, for young cadets on the Hamble, whilst dabbling in politics and journalism. His biography, "Life Worth Living" was published in 1939 and in 1955 he appeared on television as the subject of "This Is Your Life". He remained in the public eye right until the end, attending the Second Test between England and Australia at Lord's in June 1956. The "News Chronicle" in its obituary called Fry "the perfect human being" and, undoubtedly, he was the finest all round sportsman this country has ever produced (a legend he himself carefully nurtured) but his personality had its fair share of fallibility. One thing is certain, the chances of the Saints ever again fielding a full-back who is an Oxford triple blue and the holder of the world long-jump record is as likely as the Dell staging another full England International!

Appearances:
SL: 16 app. 0 gls.
FAC: 9 app. 0 gls.
Total: *25 app. 0 gls.*

❑ **Saints note** - *C.B. Fry's world long jump record survived until 1900 when the American, Alvin Kraenzlein won the Olympic title in Paris.*

FRY, Roger Norman

Role: Full-back 1970-72
5'10" 11st.7lbs.
b. Southampton 18 August 1948

CAREER: SOUTHAMPTON am. June 1966, pro. Oct 1967/Walsall July 1973/Salisbury July 1977/North Baddesley Aug 1980.
Debut v Crystal Palace (h) 4.5.71

Locally born, Roger Fry was a product of Southampton Schools soccer and figured regularly in the reserves for three seasons before making his debut in the final League game of the 1970-71 season, a 6-0 defeat of Crystal Palace. The following season saw him in direct competition with Dennis Hollywood for the left-back shirt and, with the young Steve Mills looking promising in the reserves, Roger decided to try his luck at Walsall. He later returned to the Southampton area to live and has turned out for the Ex-Saints from time to time.

Appearances;
FL: 23 app. 0 gls.
FAC: 2 app. 0 gls.
LC: 1 app. 0 gls.
Total: *26 app. 0 gls.*

FUNNELL, Anthony

Role: Forward 1977-79
5'6" 10st.10lbs.
b. Eastbourne 20 August 1957

CAREER: Eastbourne United/
SOUTHAMPTON Jan 1977/Vancouver White
Caps summer 1977/Gillingham Mar 1979/
Brentford Mar 1980/Bournemouth Sept 1981/
Poole Town Oct 1982.

*Debut v Notts County (a) 3.9.77 * (scored on debut)*

Tony Funnell came to the Dell in January 1977
from Sussex side Eastbourne and some
outstanding performances in the reserves saw
rapid promotion to the senior side. After a
spell back in the reserves he returned to score
some valuable goals in the run-up to Division
One promotion, the most vital one being at
Orient in the penultimate game of the season.
The fans' high opinion of the young striker did
not tally with that of the Dell management and
they were dismayed to see him move on the
following season after only two games. He
subsequently failed to set the lower divisions

alight and an injury sustained at Bournemouth
finished his League career. In 1990 he was still
playing for Poole Town while employed as
their commercial manager and in May 1991 the
Saints played Poole in a testimonial game for
Tony.

Appearances:
FL: 13 (4) app. 8 gls.
FAC: 0 (1)app 0 gls.
LC: 1 (1) app. 1 gl.
Total: *14 (6) app. 9 gls.*

FURBY, William

Role: Half-back 1894-95
b. Staffordshire 1871

CAREER: SOUTHAMPTON St. Mary's Mar
1894/Freemantle c.s. 1895.

Debut v Luton Town (a) 27.10.1894

Bill Furby joined the Saints a few months prior
to the club gaining entry into the Southern
League. He was an adaptable half-back who
was a useful crosser of the ball, but the form of
Thomson and Taylor meant that first team
opportunities were limited and he joined arch-
rivals Freemantle. Bill's date of death is not
known but he was still alive in 1969 aged 98.

Appearances:
SL: 5 app. 0 gls.
FAC: 2 app. 0 gls.
Total: *7 app. 0 gls.*

Tony Funnell

GABRIEL, James

Role: Half-back 1967-72
5'10" 12st.11lbs.
b. Dundee 10 October 1940

CAREER: Lawside Academy/Tynecastle Boys Club/Dundee North End/Dundee 1957/Everton Mar 1960/SOUTHAMPTON July 1967/Bournemouth July 1972/(Swindon Town -loan- Oct-Dec 1973)/Brentford Mar 1974/Seattle Sounders c.s. 1974. player-coach Apr 1976/coach in Argentina 1979/Phoenix manager/ San Jose Earthquakes coach 1981, manager/coaching director of Washington State Youth Assoc/National Coach of Coaches /Bournemouth asst. manager Mar 1987/Everton asst. manager June 1990, caretaker-manager Oct 1990, Reserve team coach Nov 1990.

Debut v Newcastle United (a) 19.8.67

Aged 19, Jimmy Gabriel left his home town club Dundee for Everton undaunted by his £30,000 price tag. He quickly made the right-half position his own and, while at Goodison, not only helped Everton win the championship and the F.A. Cup but gained two full Scottish International caps as well. After losing his place to Howard Kendall, Jimmy made a £45,000 move to the Dell where his versatile defensive skills were desperately needed in the club's customary fight to avoid relegation. His competitive influence played a huge part in the

Jimmy Gabriel

Saints eventually establishing themselves in the top flight and, since hanging up his boots, he has, not surprisingly, coached successfully in the States and alongside Harry Redknapp at Dean Court before returning to Goodison Park.

Appearances:
FL: 190 (1) app. 25 gls.
FAC: 17 app. 1 gl.
LC: 9 app. 0 gls.
Eur: 7 app. 1 gl.
Total: *223 (1) app. 27 gls.*

❏ **Saints note** - *Jimmy's father was a professional with East Fife and Forfar.*

GALLEGO, José Augustin

Role: Forward 1948-49
b. Renteria, Spain 8 April 1923

CAREER: Cambridge City 1945/Brentford Jan 1947/SOUTHAMPTON May 1948/Colchester United c.s. 1950/Cambridge United c.s. 1952/Biggleswade 1957/Exning/Camden United Coach/Milton F.C. coach.

Debut v Barnsley (a) 2.10.48

José Gallego came to England as an evacuee from the Spanish Civil War with his three sisters and younger brother Antonio, who himself was to make one appearance as a goalkeeper for Norwich City. Jose and Tony teamed up together for Cambridge City in 1945-46, who, that year, coached by ex-Saint Vic Watson, lifted the East Anglian Cup. An eighteen month stay at Brentford preceded his move to the Dell but, over a similar period with the Saints, he only played one league game in which he had the misfortune to suffer a cracked ankle. He joined Bill Rochford at Colchester in 1950 and then enjoyed six seasons at Cambridge United. Jose played minor league football until well past his fiftieth birthday and spent thirty years working for the Gas Board as a meter inspector. Nowadays he lives in Cambridge and keeps fit with the odd round of golf.

Appearances:
FL: 1 app. 0 gls.
Total: *1 app. 0 gls.* *See overleaf for picture*

José
Gallego

GAUGHRAN, *Bernard Michael*

Role: Forward 1937-38
5'8" 11st.10lbs.
b. Dublin

CAREER: Dublin Bohemians/Glasgow Celtic
c.s. 1936/SOUTHAMPTON June 1937/
Sunderland Nov 1937/Notts County May
1938/Dundalk 1939/Porterdown.
Debut v Sheffield Wednesday (h) 9.10.37
* (scored on debut)

In May 1936, Tom Parker, then still manager at
Norwich City, visited Dublin on a scouting
mission and took note of Benny Gaughran as
one to watch. Shortly afterwards Benny moved
to Celtic, but when he was freed after only one
season Tom Parker did not hesitate to offer
him a contract at the Dell. His spell at the Dell
was brief but spectacular and four goals in
seven games stimulated a bid of £1000 from
Sunderland. The Saints' board, ever alert to a
tidy profit, accepted, and Benny duly swopped
the red and white stripes of Saints for those of
the Wearside club.

    Appearances:
FL: 7 app. 4 gls.
Total: *7 app. 4 gls.*

Benny Gaughran

GAYNOR, Leonard Alfred

Role: Forward 1953-54
5'8" 10st.8lbs.
b. Ollerton 22 September 1925

CAREER: Notts Schools/Giltbrook Villa 1944/
Ilkeston Colliery/Brinsley 1946/Eastwood
Colliery 1947/Hull City Apr 1948/
Bournemouth June 1951/SOUTHAMPTON
Mar 1954/Aldershot Feb 1955/Oldham
Athletic July 1957/Yeovil Town Jan 1958/
Cambridge City.
Debut v Reading (a) 13.3.54

During the 1953-54 season Saints and
Bournemouth encountered each other four
times, twice in the league and twice in the F.A.
Cup - and George Roughton was impressed by
the Cherries' hardworking inside-forward. Len
Gaynor signed for the Saints in March 1954
and played twelve out of the fourteen games
left that season. He lost his place for the 1954-
55 season but his industry and experience
assisted the Reserves to victory in the
Combination Cup Final against Norwich City.
Aldershot became his third Hampshire club in
February 1955 and he captained them up until
his departure to Oldham.

Appearances:
FL: 12 app. 1 gl
Total: *12 app. 1 gl.*

Len Gaynor

Terry Gennoe

GENNOE, Terence William

Role: Goalkeeper 1978-80
6'2" 12st.5lbs.
b. Shrewsbury 16 March 1953

CAREER: Bricklayers Sports/Bury June 1973
(Blackburn Rovers-loan-Apr-May 1974) (Leeds
United-loan-Mar-Apr 1975) /Halifax May
1975/SOUTHAMPTON Feb 1978 (Everton-
loan-Aug-Oct 1980) (Crystal Palace-loan-Jan-
Feb 1981) /Blackburn Rovers Aug 1981.
Debut v Derby County (a) 23.9.78

A qualified teacher, Terry Gennoe joined the
Saints from Halifax Town for a fee of £35,000
and, at the time, he was hailed as one of the
most promising goalkeepers outside the First
Division. He became first choice for the green
jersey in September 1978 and during the
season set a club record by keeping six
consecutive clean sheets. Terry's form helped
Saints to the League Cup Final against
Nottingham Forest but he did not enjoy a
particularly happy game at Wembley and was
dropped the following Wednesday for an F.A.
Cup tie at Highbury. A loss of confidence
followed and, after two loan periods, he made

a permanent move to Ewood Park where he settled down to become a Rovers' regular throughout the eighties, and broke their goalkeeping appearances record.

Appearances:
FL: 36 app. 0 gls.
FAC: 5 app. 0 gls.
LC: 10 app. 0 gls.
Total: *51 app. 0 gls.*

GEORGE, Charles Frederick

Role: Forward 1978-81
5'11" 11st.9lbs.
b. Islington, London 10 October 1950

CAREER: Holloway Comprehensive/ Islington/Middlesex & London Schoolboys/ New Middleton/Arsenal app May 1966, pro Mar 1968/Derby County July 1975 (St. George Budapest (Australia)-loan-May 1977) (Minnesota Kicks (U.S.A.)-loan-May 1978) /SOUTHAMPTON Dec 1978 (Nottingham Forest-loan-Jan 1980)/ Bulova (Hong Kong) Sept 1981/A.F.C. Bournemouth Mar 1982/ Derby County Mar 1982/Dundee United trial Sept 1982/Coventry City Aug 1983.

Debut v Bolton Wanderers (a) 24.3.79

One of Highbury's favourite sons, Charlie George was just 21 when he helped Arsenal win the double in 1971. He took his precocious talents to the Baseball Ground in 1975 and, three years later, became Southampton's record outlay at £400,000 in a transfer deal that took the best part of a month to conclude. His signature was hardly dry on the registration form when his knee gave way and he didn't have his first game at the Dell until eight months after putting pen to paper. This led to some Saints fans sporting lapel badges that said, "I've seen Charlie George play!" Even when he did play he displayed only flashes of the old skill but his career at the Dell was blighted by a glut of niggling injuries, including a lost finger in a bizarre gardening accident. Saints released Charlie from his contract and, after a spell in Hong Kong, he returned for a couple of games with Bournemouth. But his career which had started with so much promise had fizzled out and his one England cap, won whilst with Derby, was a sad testament to his undoubted ability. After running a pub in the New Forest, Charlie returned to London to become a partner in a garage firm.

Appearances:
FL: 44 app. 11 gls.
FAC: 5 app. 0 gls.
LC: 3 app. 3 gls
Total: *52 app. 14 gls.*

Charlie George

GEORGE, W.

Role: Forward: 1901-02
b. Southampton

CAREER: Bitterne Guild/ SOUTHAMPTON
Nov 1901

Debut v Reading (a) 19.3.02

George was a local soccer discovery and a
sturdily-built right-winger who had pace and a
good shot. Despite apparently having all the
necessary attributes he made just one
appearance in the Southern League, played
one game for the club in the Western League
and then, like so many other players from his
generation, left the club after just one season.

Appearances:
SL: 1 app. 0 gls.
Total: 1 app. 0 gls.

GETGOOD, George

Role: Half-back 1921-23
5'8" 11st.2lbs.
b. Coylton 15 November 1892
d. Kidderminster 22 July 1970

CAREER: Ayr United
1912/Reading July 1914/
Birmingham Aug 1921/
SOUTHAMPTON Mar
1922/Wolverhampton
Wanderers Jan 1923/ Kidderminster Harriers
Mar 1925/Aberdare Athletic July
1926/Shrewsbury Town Nov 1926/Bathgate
1927/Bo'ness 1928/Nuneaton Town Feb 1929.

Debut v Southend United (h) 4.3.22

George Getgood came to the Dell with Jack
Elkes in a double transfer deal involving
Birmingham. An accomplished and versatile
player, his best position was at centre-half.
He continued to live in Birmingham
during his spell at the Dell and it
was no surprise when he
transferred back to the Midlands
within a couple of years. In 1925
George became the licensee of the
Great Western Hotel in Bewdley
near Kidderminster.

Appearances:
FL: 35 app. 1 gl.
Total: 35 app. 1 gl.

❏ **Saints note** *- For some inexplicable reason
whilst at Reading, George played under the name of
George Goodman. (Other players have resorted to
adopting an alternative identity - especially in the
early years - and it was, perhaps, so that they could
return as amateurs under these names after their
professional careers were over).*

GIBBINS, William Vivian Talbot

Role: Forward 1933-34
5'11" 11st.6lbs.
b. Forest Gate 10 August 1901
d. Herne Bay 21 November 1979

CAREER: Godwin Rd School/Clapton F.C.
1919/West Ham United Dec 1923/Clapton
F.C. Jan 1932/Brentford Feb 1932/Bristol
Rovers June 1932/SOUTHAMPTON Sept
1933/Leyton 1934/Catford
Wanderers 1934, retired 1939.

*Debut v Manchester United (a)
11.11.33*

Capped at both amateur and
full England levels, Viv Gibbins
was "one of the last great
amateurs imbued with the
Corinthian spirit". He played
simultaneously for Clapton F.C.
and West Ham and, during the
1930-31 season, was the
Hammers' top scorer with 18
goals. Thirty-two years old by the
time he reached the Dell, his
footballing career was in decline and, being a
qualified schoolteacher, he moved back to
London to eventually
become headmaster of
Harold Road School in
West Ham. Viv retired
in the early 1970's but
continued to keep his
interest in the game
alive by watching local
schools football and
making the odd visit to
Upton Park.

Appearances:
FL: 2 app. 0 gls.
Total: 2 app. 0 gls.

Viv Gibbins

GIBSON, Andrew

Role: Forward 1911-12
b. Glasgow

CAREER: Strathclyde/SOUTHAMPTON May 1911/Leeds City Sept 1912.

Debut v Millwall (h) 2.9.11

Andrew Gibson's acquisition from "under the noses of the two Glasgow clubs", provoked much celebration in Southampton and the following month the club's manager, George Swift, claimed at the A.G.M. that "Gibson was the best forward he had seen, and would be a thousand pounds man". Saddled with such high expectations Andrew predictably failed to deliver and in March 1912, along with Hamilton, was involved in a breach of discipline which led to both players being suspended *sine die* by the club. Both men were, at the time of suspension, in the first team having played against Norwich City on March 9th and their crimes were obviously serious as neither player pulled on a red and white shirt again.

> **Appearances:**
> *SL: 18 app. 4 gls.*
> **Total:** *18 app 4 gls.*

GILCHRIST, Paul Anthony

Role: Forward 1971-77
5'11" 12st.4 lbs.
b. Dartford 5 January 1951

CAREER: St. Paul's School/Cannock House/Chelsfield/Swanley Old Boys/Crockenhill/Charlton Athletic app July 1967, pro Mar 1968 (Luton Town-loan) (Cambridge United-loan-Jan 1970) (Fulham-loan-Mar 1971) (Yeovil-loan)/Doncaster Rovers July 1971/SOUTHAMPTON Mar 1972 (Alahfi (Saudi Arabia)-loan-Dec 1976 - Jan 1977)/Portsmouth Mar 1977/Swindon Town Aug 1978/Hereford United Mar 1980/Dunstable.

Debut v Arsenal (a) 28.3.72

Maurice Setters, Doncaster's manager, went on record as saying that Ted Bates had secured a bargain when paying £30,000 for Paul Gilchrist and when Paul forced his way into the first team within a season, the Doncaster manager's judgement seemed fully vindicated. Originally a forward, Paul could also adapt to playing in

Paul Gilchrist

midfield, should the need arise, often displaying a subtle distribution. During the 1976 F.A. Cup run he showed he had not lost his eye for goal when he scored two memorable goals, a spectacular over-the-shoulder shot against West Bromwich Albion and the other a 25 yard strike against Crystal Palace in the semi-final. Only in the team because of an injury to Hugh Fisher, Paul is sometimes the forgotten man when fans recall the Cup-winning side, probably because he only made a further two league appearances before moving to Fratton Park. Later on a serious injury ended his career whilst he was at Hereford. In December 1990 he was a service adviser for BMW in Redhill, Surrey.

> **Appearances:**
> *FL: 96 (11) app. 17 gls.*
> *FAC: 10 app. 2 gls.*
> *LC: 6 (1) app. 1 gl.*
> **Total:** *112 (12) app. 20 gls.*

GILCHRIST, R.

Role: Forward 1892-93

CAREER: SOUTHAMPTON St. Mary's 1892.

Debut v Newbury (h) 15.10.92 FAC.

R. Gilchrist spent only two months with St. Mary's, between September and November

1892, in which time he appeared in two English Cup ties. He never settled, mainly because the side was struggling at the time (one win in eight games) and he departed soon after the club's cup exit against Maidenhead.

Appearances:
FAC: 2 app. 0 gls.
Total: *2 app. 0 gls.*

GILL, Ernest Harry

Role: Full-back 1899-1900
5'9" 11st.3lbs.
b. Mountsorrel, Leicester July qtr 1877
d. Hull April qtr 1950

CAREER: Poole White Star/Bridgewater/ Bristol City/Grimsby Town/ SOUTHAMPTON 1899/Freemantle c.s. 1900/ Leicester Fosse May 1901.

Debut Sheppey United (h) 17.3.1900

An amateur full-back, Ernest Gill had been a Somerset County player before the Saints gave him a trial against Sheppey United in March 1900. Despite having a poor game he was offered a position which he decided to decline. He subsequently turned out for Freemantle in the Southampton Senior League before joining Leicester in 1901. He had one game for Leicester (replacing George Swift, later to become Saints' manager) and then had the misfortune to break a leg in a reserve team fixture.

Appearances:
SL: 1 app. 0 gls.
Total: *1 app. 0 gls.*

❏ **Saints note** - *Ernest played five matches for Leicestershire County Cricket Club in the summer of 1901. His brother George played for Somerset, London County and also Leicestershire.*

GILL, Mervyn John

Role: Goalkeeper 1955-56
5'11" 12st.0lbs.
b. Exeter 13 April 1931

CAREER: Bideford Town 1948/Portsmouth am. Sept 1953/Woking 1955/ SOUTHAMPTON am. Dec 1955, pro. Apr 1956/Torquay United Sept 1956/Bath City July 1962.

Debut v Walsall (a) 28.4.56

Mervyn Gill

Mervyn Gill represented the R.A.F. while doing his National Service at Thorney Island before signing amateur forms with Saints. Demobbed in April 1956, he quickly signed as a professional but a 3-1 victory at Walsall was to be his only game. Eric Webber then signed him for Torquay United and he gave the Devon club five seasons of good service. From December 1962 until retiring in December 1990 Mervyn worked for English China Clay Quarries. He lives in Bridport, Dorset.

Appearances:
FL: 1 app. 0 gls.
Total: *1 app. 0 gls.*

GITTENS, Jon

Role: Centre Half 1985-87 & 1991-
5'11" 12st.6lbs.
b. Moseley 22 January 1964

CAREER: Bromsgrove Brookfield/Paget Rangers/SOUTHAMPTON Oct 1985/ Swindon Town July 1987/SOUTHAMPTON Mar 1991.

Debut v Birmingham City (a) 19.4.86

Jon Gittens was signed from the Midland Combination side Paget Rovers soon after completing a two-year menswear tailoring course in Birmingham. He was a raw but fast centre-half and he learned quickly, playing alongside Kevin Bond or Mark Wright. A free agent in the summer of 1987, he refused a new contract and joined Swindon Town with a tribunal fixing the fee at an unrealistic £40,000. He was a regular in Swindon's first team and played his part in the Wiltshire team's quest for a place in Division One, but Chris Nicholl raised a few eyebrows by spending £400,000 to bring Jon back to the Dell a day before the 1991 transfer deadline.

Appearances:
FL: 25 (1) app. 0 gls.
FAC: 1 app. 0 gls.
LC: 4 app. 0 gls.
Total: *30 (1) app. 0 gls.*

❏ **Saints note** - *Jon Gittens is the first Saints player to have had his transfer fee fixed by an independent tribunal.*

Jon Gittens

GLEN, Alexander

Role: Forward 1906-07
6'1" 13st.4lbs.
b. Kilsyth 11 December 1878

CAREER: Fitzhugh Rovers/ Glasgow Park Head/Grimsby Town July 1902/Notts County May 1903/Tottenham Hotspur May 1904/ SOUTHAMPTON May 1906/Portsmouth c.s. 1907/Brentford c.s. 1908.

Debut v Swindon Town (a) 1.9.06

A former medical student at the Royal Infirmary in Glasgow, Alex Glen had served in the Boer War as a surgical dresser before returning to England to start a professional career with Grimsby Town. He arrived in Southampton in 1906 and the club, recognising his intellect, immediately made him vice-captain. He was a dexterous, elegant dribbler and, being a tall man, swerved and weaved

Alex Glen, pictured in a Cup game with Sheffield Wednesday in 1907.

with devastating effect. He preferred the ground pass and formed a strong partnership with Frank Jefferis on the right hand side of the Saints attack, which worked well until the last two months of the season when, inexplicably, his form deserted him dramatically. He moved along the coast to Fratton Park in the ensuing summer and finished his career in West London with Brentford.

Appearances:
SL: 29 app. 10 gls.
FAC: 3 app. 0 gls.
Total: 32 app. 10 gls.

❏ **Saints note** - *When Saints toured Germany in 1907 Alex's fluent German led to him becoming the Club's official interpreter.*

GLOVER, Horace Victor

Role: Fullback 1906-11
b. Ashford 1883
d. Winchester 28 January 1967

CAREER: Ashford/Hastings & St. Leonards/ SOUTHAMPTON May 1906/West Ham United Sept 1911/Boscombe Dec 1913.

Debut v Swindon Town (a) 1.9.06

Horace Glover was an architect's assistant during his amateur days with Hastings and St. Leonards and came to Southampton on the recommendation of ex-player Jimmy Yates. He built up a very high reputation after immediate inclusion in the club's senior eleven and such was his form that tempting offers from League sides were received. Strong, decisive tackling and excellent distribution were features of his play and his level-headed attitude earned him the team captaincy in 1909. After spells at West Ham and Boscombe, Horace returned to Southampton and lived a stone's throw from the Dell at Milton Road.

Appearances:
SL: 160 app. 4 gls.
FAC: 14 app. 0 gls.
Total: 174 app. 4 gls.

Horace Glover

Tony Godfrey

GODFREY, Tony William

Role: Goalkeeper 1958-66
5'9" 10st.6lbs.
b. Pangbourne 30 April 1939

CAREER: Basingstoke Town/Norwich City am. Jan 1956/SOUTHAMPTON am. May 1956, pro May 1958/Aldershot Dec 1965/Rochdale July 1970/ Aldershot July 1972/ Basingstoke/Andover manager June 1977/ Alton Town manager Feb 1979/Fleet manager-coach/ Basingstoke coach.

Debut v Stockport County (h) 13.12.58

An apprentice bricklayer, Tony Godfrey became the first Basingstoke player to be transferred to a league team when Ted Bates, acting on Stan Clements' advice, paid £500 for the talented young goalkeeper. He was a member of the Saints' Youth side which reached the semi-final of the F.A. Youth Cup in 1957 and, although small for a 'keeper, his anticipatory skills and agility more than compensated. During his National Service he represented the Army whilst jockeying with Bob Charles and Ron Reynolds for the Southampton number one position. Later, when Ted Bates signed Campbell Forsyth, Tony moved to Aldershot but was immediately sidelined for 18 weeks with hepatitis. In 1970 he moved to Rochdale, then managed by ex-Saint Dick Connor, and became their Player of the Year in his second season. Tony returned to the south for another spell with Aldershot and then ended up at his original club, Basingstoke. Aged 45 he answered an injury crisis to become not only Basingstokes's youngest ever goalkeeper, but also their oldest. He was present at Saints' Centenary dinner in 1985 and today lives near Basingstoke where he runs his own building business.

Appearances:
FL: 141 app. 0 gls.
FAC: 4 app. 0 gls.
LC: 4 app. 0 gls.
Total: *149 app. 0 gls.*

GOLAC, Ivan

Role: Full-back 1978-82 & 1983-86
5'10" 13st. 1lbs.
b. Kuprivnica, Yugoslavia 15 June 1950

CAREER: Partizan Belgrade/ SOUTHAMPTON non-contract Aug 1978, pro Sept 1978/Bournemouth Nov 1982/ Manchester City Mar 1983/Bjelasica (Yugoslavia) September 1983/ SOUTHAMPTON Mar 1984 (Portsmouth-loan-Jan-Apr 1985)/Zumen player-coach c.s. 1986/Partizan Belgrade coach Dec 1988-Sept 1990.

Debut v Bolton Wanderers (h) 22.8.78

Lawrie McMenemy took full advantage of the Yugoslavian law that gave their professional footballers freedom of contract once they reach 28 years old and spent £50,000 to bring Ivan Golac to the Dell. He had won four International caps and, once initial work permit problems had been sorted out, thrilled the Dell crowd with his surging, flamboyant style. He tackled with ferocity, loved to overlap and contributed hugely to Saints' positive mode of play in the early 1980's. Realising his dream of playing at Wembley by appearing in the 1979 League Cup Final, arguably he was the most successful European import of his era. Player of the Year in 1981, Ivan fell out with the club over terms and took himself off to Bournemouth, Manchester City and then back to Yugoslavia before he grew 'homesick' for Southampton and re-offered his services to the club in March 1984. Lawrie McMenemy had a reputation for welcoming back prodigal players and Ivan played several more games in the 1985-86 season. Today, he still maintains a home in Chandlers Ford and visits the Dell whenever possible. In June 1991 Ivan applied, and was interviewed for the vacant managerial position at Celtic.

Appearances:
FL: 167 (1) app. 4 gls.
FAC: 12 app. 0 gls.
LC: 13 app. 0 gls.
Eur: 3 app. 0 gls.
Total: *195 (1) app. 4 gls.*

Ivan Golac

GOODCHILD, Andrew James

Role: Goalkeeper 1909-11
5'10" 11st.10lbs.
*b. Southampton
4 April 1892
d. Eastleigh 2 October 1950*

CAREER: Foundry Lane School/St. Pauls Athletic/ SOUTHAMPTON Sept 1909/Manchester City Oct 1911/Guildford City Aug 1927.

Debut v Reading (h) 30.4.10

Jim Goodchild

Jim Goodchild signed for Saints after being given two trial matches and became the understudy to regular custodian Burrows. He made his debut in the very last game of the 1909-10 season and, in the following campaign, made four more appearances before the club decided to release him due to his being "surplus to requirements". He obtained employment in the Docks only to have his career revived by Manchester City who had been alerted to his availability by Saints' scout, Jimmy Yates. Jim became a regular in City's defence over the next sixteen years and, described as "safe rather than brilliant", made over 200 appearances. He turned out on the losing side in the 1926 F.A. Cup final against Bolton Wanderers and a year later returned to Southampton to become licensee of the Royal Albert Hotel, playing two seasons on a part-time basis with Guildford City. In 1941 he took over the Cricketers Arms in Eastleigh where he remained until his death in October 1950.

Appearances:
SL: 5 app. 0 gls.
Total: *5 app. 0 gls.*

GORDON, Daniel

Role: Full-back 1904-05 & 1911-12
5'10" 13st. 0lbs.
b. West Calder, Midlothian 7 January 1881

CAREER: Broxburn/Everton Apr 1903/SOUTHAMPTON c.s. 1904/St. Mirren c.s. 1905/Middlesbrough May 1908/Bradford

Park Avenue Nov 1908/Hull City Apr 1910/SOUTHAMPTON May 1911.
Debut v New Brompton (a) 17.9.04

Previously a member of Everton's Lancashire Combination side, Dan Gordon moved to Southampton in 1904 as understudy to George Molyneux. A capable full-back with the physique of a blacksmith, he also had a deceptive burst of speed which he used to good effect as Southampton reserves won the Hampshire Senior Cup in 1905. Dan left the club for his native Scotland and, after playing for three northern clubs, he returned to the Dell six years later to give valuable experience to a struggling side. He retired from the game in the summer of 1912 and returned to Scotland to live.

Appearances:
SL: 18 app. 0 gls.
Total: *18 app. 0 gls.*

GOTSMANOV, Sergei A. E.

Role: Forward 1990-1991
5'8" 10st. 5lbs.
b. U.S.S.R. 17 March 1959

CAREER: Dynamo Minsk/Brighton non-contract Feb 1990/SOUTHAMPTON Aug 1990/Halle (Germany) Sept 1991.

Debut v Rochdale (h) 9.10.90 R.C.

Sergei Gotsmanov was Chris Nicholl's only signing during the 1990 close season and priced at £150,000 was considered by some to be purchased solely to keep Saints' other Russian player, Alex Cherednik, company. Those fans

Sergei Gotsmanov (right) with fellow Russian Alex Cherednik.

with keener memories, however, recalled a fine goal Sergei scored for Russia against England at Wembley in June 1984 and indeed in his short six month spell at the Goldstone Ground he had become something of a cult figure with the crowd. Unfortunately for the diminutive forward, chances in the Saints' attack were to be few and far between during 1990-91, although his performances in the F.A. Cup matches against Coventry City had hinted at better things to come.

Appearances:
FL: 2 (6) app. 0 gls.
FAC: 2 app. 0 gls.
LC: 2 app. 0 gls.
Total: *6 (6) app. 0 gls.*

Darlington in March 1988 where, in only the second match of the 1988-89 season, a Littlewoods Cup tie at Doncaster, he sustained a serious knee injury. Over the next twenty months Keith underwent six operations in his bid to regain full fitness and, although he did eventually manage one reserve game, in May 1990 his contract expired and he and Darlington parted company. In November 1990 Keith reappeared at the Dell when the Saints, facing a goalkeeping injury crisis, asked Basingstoke if they could borrow their former 'keeper to play in the Reserves.

Appearances:
FL: 2 app. 0 gls.
Total: *2 app. 0 gls.*

GRANGER, Keith William

Role: Goalkeeper 1985-86
5'10" 10st. 0lbs.
b. Southampton 5 October 1968

CAREER: Millbrook School/
SOUTHAMPTON app. July 1985, pro. Oct 1986 (Darlington-loan-Dec 1987-Mar 1988, permanent Mar 1988)
/Basingstoke Town Aug 1990 (SOUTHAMPTON-loan-Nov 1990) /Bashley Feb 1991/Maidstone United non-contract Mar 1991/Newport I.O.W. Sept 1991.

Debut v Everton (a) 3.5.86

Keith Granger became the first Southampton schoolboy goalkeeper since Bob Charles to make it into the first team when he suffered a "baptism of fire" in two away games at Everton and Tottenham in May 1986. He had only just recovered from an injury when he was unexpectedly thrust into the limelight due to the unavailability of Peter Shilton and the recent transfer of Phil Kite. Keith never made it back to the first team and moved to

GRANT, Wilfred

Role: Forward 1946-50
5'7" 11st.0lbs.
b. Bedlington 3 August 1920
d. Worcester 17 July 1990

CAREER: Bedlington Station School/West Sleekton/Morpeth Town/Newcastle United am. 1937/Manchester City am. Jan 1943, pro Feb 1943/SOUTHAMPTON Oct 1946/Cardiff City Mar 1950/Ipswich Town Oct 1954/Llanelly player-manager June 1957/ Cardiff City coaching-training 1958-63/ Worcester City manager Dec 1971.

Debut v West Bromwich Albion (a) 5.10.46

While stationed at Wareham serving with the R.A.F., Wilf Grant wrote a letter to Southampton asking if they would like him to play as a guest. When the chance came for a permanent move from Manchester City to the Dell for a £1,100 fee soon after the resumption of normal football, he jumped at the opportunity

Wilf Grant

and quickly settled on the right-wing. Unfortunately Bill Dodgin preferred him on the left-wing, causing a slump in Wilf's consistency and form and he was transfer-listed in October 1948. The next eighteen months were ones of frustration as he found himself in and out of the team, and it was a relief when he joined Cardiff in an exchange deal that brought Ernie Stevenson to the Dell. Within months of his Ninian Park arrival he was moved to the centre-forward position and, with his devastating turn of speed, found instant goal-scoring form. He ended 1950-51 as top scorer with 14 goals and the following year, with Cardiff gaining promotion to Division One, scored 26 goals in 42 games, prompting a call up into the England 'B' team. After retiring from professional football, Wilf moved to Worcester where he worked as a college sportsmaster.

Appearances:
FL: 61 app. 12 gls.
FAC: 3 app. 1 gl.
Total: *64 app. 13 gls.*

GRAY, William

Role: Half-back 1906-07
5'9" 11st.0lbs.
b. Partick 16 February 1881

CAREER: Inverness Thistle/Partick Thistle 1900/SOUTHAMPTON c.s. 1906/Partick Thistle May 1907.

Debut v Swindon Town (a) 1.9.06

A migrant from Scottish League soccer, Bill Gray had enjoyed five years at Partick Thistle before his Southampton transfer in 1906. Engaged as a left half-back, he showed form during his only season at the Dell, missing just six Southern League games. Unhappy with southern

Bill Gray

Frank Grayer

surroundings he returned to the Highlands in May 1907.

Appearances:
SL: 28 app. 0 gls.
FAC: 3 app. 0 gls.
Total: *31 app. 0 gls.*

GRAYER, Frank

Role: Full-back 1910-12
6'0" 12st.8lbs.
b. Brighton 13 February 1890
d. Southampton 21 January 1961

CAREER: St. Denys School/ St. Mary's Athletic/ SOUTHAMPTON Aug 1908/ Liverpool July 1912.

Debut v Swindon Town (a) 11.2.11

A modest and unassuming youngster, Frank Grayer was selected to join the Saints' professional staff after a successful trial in August 1908. A solid, reliable performer at full-back with a good turn of speed, Frank attracted numerous scouts to the Dell although never winning a regular place in the first team. Liverpool, aware of his potential, offered him tempting terms and Saints duly accepted £100 for his transfer. In his three seasons at Anfield Frank made only one League appearance and, with the outbreak of the Great War joined the Army. He was so badly injured at Ypres that he never played football again and, returning to Southampton at the war's end, he found employment with a furniture company, Shepherd and Hedges, until his retirement in 1955.

Appearances:
SL: 6 app. 0 gls.
Total: *6 app. 0 gls.*

❏ **Saints note** - *Whilst at Anfield, Frank shared accommodation with the famous Liverpool goalkeeper Elisha Scott.*

GREEN, George

Role: Full-back 1913-15
6'0" 12st.0lbs.
b. Crayford, Kent

CAREER: Northfleet
United/
SOUTHAMPTON Apr
1914/Northfleet United
1919.

*Debut v Northampton Town
(h) 18.4.14*

Saints had to beat off the
attentions of Derby,
Brighton and Fulham
before securing the
signature of George Green
in 1914. An outstanding
full-back, neat in style and
quick off the mark, it was thought that George
would have gone far in the game had it not
been for the Great War. He made several
wartime appearances in 1918 but decided to
rejoin Northfleet in 1919 and the club
acquiesced to his request to be released.

George Green

Appearances:
SL: 21 app. 0 gls.
Total: *21 app. 0 gls.*

GREENLEES, Donald

Role: Half-back 1899-00
5'10" 12st.0lbs
b. Bridgeton, Glasgow 14 January 1875

CAREER: St. Mirren/SOUTHAMPTON May.
1899/St. Mirren c.s. 1900/Shirley Warren Nov
1908.

Debut v Queen's Park Rangers (h) 21.10.1899

Rated as one of the best half-backs in Scotland
at the time he joined Saints in 1899, Don
Greenlees was never able to command a
regular senior team place and was regarded as
an understudy to fellow countrymen Meston
and Petrie. He returned home in 1900 and
rejoined the Scottish Saints but eight years
later returned to live in Southampton.

Appearances:
SL: 8 app. 0 gls.
Total: *8 app 0 gls.*

GREGORY, Jack Leslie

Role: Full-back 1946-54
5'8" 10st.12lbs.
*b. Southampton
25 January 1925*

CAREER: Woolston Youth
Club/ SOUTHAMPTON
1943/ (Brighton & Hove
Albion during World War
Two) Leyton Orient June
1955/Bournemouth July
1959/Ashford Town Aug
1960/Hastings United July
1962/ Cowes Mar
1963/Sholing Sports
manager-coach 1965-66.

*Debut v Luton Town (h)
22.2.47*

Jack Gregory was signed by the Saints during
the war and, although at the Dell for more than
a decade, never really established himself as

Jack Gregory

the regular left-back. His most consistent season was 1953-54 when he played 42 out of 46 Division Three (South) fixtures and took over the team captaincy. The arrival of Tommy Traynor precipitated a free transfer to Leyton Orient where Jack enjoyed four seasons and 90 league games. Finishing his career at Dean Court he returned to Southampton to live and, until his retirement, worked as a boilermaker in the Docks.

Appearances:
FL: 66 app. 0 gls.
FAC: 2 app. 0 gls.
Total: *68 app. 0 gls.*

GRIGGS, Philip Ronald

Role: Forward 1938-39
b. Southampton 12 June 1918
d. Southampton 30 June 1980

CAREER: Southampton Schoolboys/ Sholing Boys/Spring Albion/ SOUTHAMPTON am. June 1937, pro Apr 1939.

Debut v Plymouth Argyle (a) 6.5.39

Phil Griggs was a member of the 1932 Southampton Schoolboys' team that reached the national final and he went on to play for the F.A. Amateur XI in 1939 before deciding to turn professional soon after. His one and only senior game for the first team turned out to be the last game before the suspension of league football and any thoughts of a return to professional soccer at the war's conclusion

were shattered when he had the misfortune to lose a leg during the conflict.

Appearances:
FL: 1 app. 0 gls.
Total: *1 app. 0 gls.*

GUMBLEY, Alfred Howard

Role: Half-back 1919-20
b. Birmingham April qtr 1901

CAREER: Birmingham League soccer/ SOUTHAMPTON trial Feb 1920

Debut v Brighton & Hove Albion (h) 14.2.20

Alf Gumbley was an amateur who came south for a trial after recommendations about his form in the Midlands. Although he acquitted himself well on his debut, which Saints won 3-0, he was allowed to return to Birmingham League football.

Appearances:
SL: 1 app. 0 gls.
Total: *1 app. 0 gls.*

GUERAN, Sidney F.

Role: Forward 1936-38
5'9" 10st.3lbs.
b. Grays, Essex 2 October 1916
d. Killed in action 18 September 1944 at Arnhem

CAREER: Ramsgate Schools/Arsenal May 1935/ Margate (SOUTHAMPTON-loan-Mar 1936)/Exeter City July 1938-Oct 1938.

The Southampton Boys team of 1932 with Phil Griggs seated at the left of the front three.

Debut v Nottingham Forest 1.5.37

Tom Parker used his Arsenal connections to sign Sid Gueran on loan from the Gunners' nursery side, Margate, in March 1936. A thoughtful and constructive inside-forward, Arsenal exercised their right to recall him in the close season of 1938 and he made a permanent move to Exeter City later the same summer. A sapper in the Royal Engineers, Sid Gueran lost his life at Arnhem during World War Two.

Sid Gueran

Appearances:
FL: 3 app. 0 gls.
Total: *3 app. 0 gls.*

GUNTER, David Reginald

Role: Full-back 1955-56
5'9" 11st.0lbs.
b. Portsmouth 4 March 1933

CAREER: Portsmouth am./SOUTHAMPTON am. June 1954, pro. May 1955/Sittingbourne July 1956/Guildford City during 1959-60.

Debut v Queen's Park Rangers (a) 27.8.55

The brother of Phil Gunter, the Portsmouth full-back (1951-63), David also started his career at Fratton Park before moving along the south coast to try his luck at the Dell. He played most of his football for the Combination Side, making the odd appearance when Tommy Traynor was absent, before being released in May 1956 to join the non-league circuit.

Appearances:
FL: 7 app. 0 gls.
Total: *7 app. 0 gls.*

GURR, Gerald Robert

Role: Goalkeeper 1966-70
6'1" 12st.8lbs.
b. Brighton 20 October 1946

CAREER: Middlesex Youth/ Arsenal am. 1962/Queen's Park Rangers am./Guildford City 1963/ SOUTHAMPTON Mar 1964/ Aldershot Mar 1971.

Debut v Leicester City (h) 14.1.67

Gerry Gurr started his footballing career as a centre-forward with Middlesex Youth, but soon converted to goalkeeper to take his place as a fifteen year-old playing in Arsenal's South East Counties team. Arriving at the Dell from Guildford, he had to wait patiently behind seven other goalkeepers before his debut in January 1967 when, in a 4-4 draw against Leicester, he saved a penalty. An injured leg sustained in the same game side-lined him for some time and then an accident occurred that was to have later repercussions; he dislocated his shoulder in a reserve fixture against Nottingham Forest. In September 1968 he was recalled to first team duty and played the remaining 34 games of the season with his agility helping Saints attain seventh place in Division One. Tipped for international recognition and with Saints in Europe, Gerry's future looked bright but his old shoulder injury worsened to the extent that it would dislocate at the slightest movement. At this juncture the club and Gerry parted company

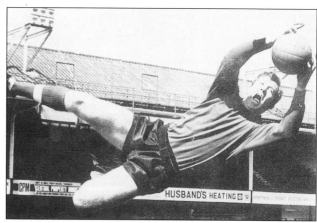

Gerry Gurr

and he was forced to contemplate a life outside football. Happily, after an operation, Gerry was offered a contract by Aldershot manager, ex-Saint Jimmy Melia, who agreed not to stand in his way should a bigger club show any interest. Unfortunately, by the time Portsmouth tabled a bid Jimmy Melia had departed and new manager, Tommy McAnearney, refused to sanction any move. Not wanting to spend any more time in the Fourth Division Gerry decided to quit football and become a professional musician. He still lives in Southampton, plays the odd match for the Ex-Saints and, showing no bitterness toward what might have been, happily strums his guitar for a living.

Appearances:
FL: 42 app. 0 gls.
FAC: 4 app. 0 gls.
LC: 3 app. 0 gls.
Total: *49 app. 0 gls.*

GURRY, John William

Role: Half-back 1935-36
5'9" 11st.4lbs.
b. Barking 17 July 1907
d. Leicester 1 October 1983

CAREER: West Ham United am. Dec 1929/ Barking Town/Leicester City May 1930/ SOUTHAMPTON July 1935/Chester June 1936.

Debut v Swansea Town (h) 31.8.35

Jack Gurry was playing in the Athenian League with Barking when his job in the hosiery trade took him to the Midlands and Leicester offered him the chance of league football. After 23 games he moved to the Dell where, during the 1935-36 season, he played 31 games for the reserves and nine first team matches in four different positions. Placed on the available list in May 1936 for a fee of £250, he eventually joined Chester on a free transfer and tasted brief glory when, in November the same year, he scored a hat-trick against Lincoln in a 7-3 win. He returned to the Leicester area after retiring from the game and once more became involved in the hosiery business.

Appearances:
FL: 9 app. 0 gls.
Total: *9 app. 0 gls.*

HACKETT, Reginald Lawrence

Role: Half-back 1919-20
5'8" 11st.7lbs.
b. Cradley Heath

CAREER: Cradley Heath St. Lukes/ Blackheath Town/SOUTHAMPTON May 1919 /Birmingham League Soccer 1920.

Debut v Exeter City (h) 30.8.19

One of three Blackheath players secured by Saints' trainer, McIntyre, in 1919, Reg Hackett had gained two Junior international caps against Ireland and Scotland before his Southampton move. A consistent performer during the club's first season after the war, he inexplicably left the Dell in April 1920 to return to the Midlands.

Appearances:
SL: 31 app. 0 gls.
Total: *31 app. 0 gls.*

HADDLETON, Arthur

Role: Forward 1930-32
5'10" 11st.10lbs.
b. Chester-le-Street 6 April 1910
d. Eastleigh 5 January 1971

CAREER: Horden Colliery/SOUTHAMPTON Oct 1930/Fulham June 1932/ Swindon June 1933/Walsall July 1934/Pirelli General 1935.

Debut v Bury (a) 18.4.31

After arriving at the Dell from the north-east in 1930, Arthur Haddleton made an immediate impression with eleven goals from seventeen reserve team games. Playing one first team game in 1930-31 he started the 1931-32 campaign in memorable fashion, writing himself into the club's record books by scoring in eight consecutive

Arthur Haddleton

matches. Failure to maintain such a prodigious scoring rate resulted in an eventual return to the reserves and, because of the vagaries of the club's bank balance, Arthur found himself sold to Fulham. He scored two goals on his debut and added a further two goals in three games before he moved on to Swindon. His professional career, which promised much but achieved little, was finally ended by a fractured leg sustained in 1934 while at Walsall and he returned to live in Eastleigh, working and playing for Pirelli General.

Appearances:
FL: 17 app. 10 gls.
Total: *17 app. 10 gls.*

HADLEY, George A.

Role: Half-back 1913-15
5'7" 11st.2lbs.
b. West Bromwich 5 June 1893

CAREER: Willenhall Swifts/ SOUTHAMPTON July 1913/Aston Villa Mar 1919/Coventry City July 1920.

Debut v Reading (a) 1.11.13

A Scottish Junior International, George Hadley left Willenhall Swifts to claim a regular place in the Saints' line-up a year later. A stocky, versatile half-back, he could also play up front and it was a shame that a promising career was interrupted by the war. The Saints held on to his registration until 1919 when he was sold to Aston Villa. After just four games George joined Coventry City but retired in 1921 after sustaining an injury.

Appearances:
SL: 57 app. 4 gls.
FAC: 5 app. 0 gls.
Total: *62 app. 4 gls.*

HADLEY, Harry

Role: Half-back 1907-08
5'8" 11st.4lbs.
b. Barrow in Furness April 1878
d. 1950

CAREER: Cradley Heath Schools/Colley Gate

George Hadley

United/Halesowen/West Bromwich Albion May 1897/Aston Villa Feb 1905/Nottingham Forest Apr 1906/SOUTHAMPTON Apr 1907/Croydon Common 1908/ Halesowen/ Merthyr Town manager May 1919-Oct 1919, & Oct 1921-Apr 1922/ Chesterfield manager Apr 1922-Aug 1922/ Merthyr Town 3 more spells/Aberdare Athletic manager Nov 1927-Apr 1929/ Gillingham manager/Bangor City manager July 1935 to 1936.

Debut v Luton Town (a) 2.9.07

Ripe with experience and hall-marked with ability, Harry Hadley moved south from Nottingham Forest in April 1907. An England International (1903) he was a methodical yet energetic half-back, dedicated to looking after the forwards by supporting, feeding and directing them into advantageous positions. After just the one season, Harry moved to Croydon Common and then later became a successful manager with a host of lower League clubs.

PROMINENT FOOTBALLERS.
H. HADLEY, SOUTHAMPTON.

Appearances:
SL: 29 app. 0 gls.
FAC: 1 app. 0 gls.
Total: *30 app. 0 gls.*

HAINES, Wyndham William Pretoria

Role: Forward 1928-32
5'7" 12st.10lbs.
*b. Warminster Common 14
July 1900
d. Frome
5 November 1974*

Haines
Southampton

CAREER: Sambourne
School/Warminster
Town/Frome Town/
Portsmouth Dec 1922/
SOUTHAMPTON May
1928/Weymouth Sept 1932/Frome Town 1938.

Debut v Hull City (a) 25.8.28

Somerset-born, Willie Haines had become
something of a legend during his spell at
Fratton Park, with the Portsmouth crowd often
voicing their approval of his forward play with
a rendition of the popular refrain "To be a
farmer's boy". "Farmer Haines" was certainly
a centre-forward with a style of his own. You
were never likely to see him dashing around
the field and he seldom, if ever, tried to hit the
ball hard, preferring instead to place it
with tantalising precision. His
admirable tally of 119 goals in 165
games for Pompey was augmented by a
creditable 47 goals in 70 games for the
Saints and, despite being plagued by
injuries during his four-year stint at the
Dell, he still managed to twice top the
club's goalscoring list. In 1932 he signed
on for Weymouth and in 1935 became
the landlord of the Vine Inn, Frome,
which he ran until 1949. During the
fifties "Farmer Haines" moved into the
dry cleaning business and in 1960 he
was president of the Portsmouth
Supporters Club.

Appearances:
FL: 70 app. 47 gls.
FAC: 1 app. 0 gls.
Total: *71 app. 47 gls.*

❏ **Saints note** - *'Farmer Haines' playing
record for Weymouth was remarkable in
that he scored 275 goals in 205
appearances.*

HALL, Harry

Role: Forward 1914-15
5'8" 11st.6lbs.
*b. Fleckney,
Leicestershire*

CAREER: Market
Harborough/
SOUTHAMPTON May
1914.

*Debut v Bristol Rovers (a)
17.3.15*

Harry Hall's arrival at the
Dell in May 1914 coincided with that of fellow
Market Harborough player George Crick, and
both men became regulars in Saints' second
string team competing in the South Eastern
League. He replaced Arthur Dominy for his
one senior outing but, despite making several
wartime appearances, was not retained on the
resumption of normal soccer in 1919.

Appearances:
SL: 1 app. 0 gls.
Total: *1 app. 0 gls.*

Harry Hall

HALL, Richard Anthony

Role: Centre Half 1990-
6'1" 13st.0lbs.
b. Ipswich 14 March 1972

CAREER: Ipswich Town Schoolboys June
1987/Scunthorpe United trainee July 1988,
pro. Mar 1990/SOUTHAMPTON Feb 1991.
Debut v Wimbledon (h) 11.5.91 (sub)

Richard Hall made his Scunthorpe United debut
on Boxing Day 1989 against Grimsby but then
did not feature again until the 1990-91 season.
Within months Richard had begun to attract a
multitude of scouts to Glanford Park and Chris
Nicholl showed commendable foresight in
securing the young defender for a fee of
£200,000 in February 1991. Richard made his
debut at the end of 1990-91 season and is
certainly one for the future.

Appearances:
FL: 0 (1) app. 0 gls.
Total: *0 (1) app. 0 gls.*

Richard Hall

HAMER, David Bowen

Role: Full-back 1894-97
5'8" 13st.4lbs.
b. Rhayader,Wales July qtr 1866

CAREER: Royal Engineers (Aldershot)/
SOUTHAMPTON St. Mary's Dec 1891/
Cowes c.s. 1892/SOUTHAMPTON St.
Mary's 1894/Cowes 1897/
SOUTHAMPTON asst
player-coach 1898.

*Debut v Chatham (h)
6.10.1894*

David Hamer,
familiarly known
as "Taffy", was a
member of the
Royal Engineers'
side that carried off
the Hampshire
Senior Cup twice in
successive years
(1899 & 1890). He
left the Armed
Services in
December 1891 and
soon after joined
the St Mary's

team. After only one season at the Antelope he
migrated to Cowes returning to take part in
the club's first ever match as a Southern
League team in 1894. Possessing a
terrific volley and deceptive
speed for a big man he was in
and out of the senior team over
the next few seasons and won a
total of twenty County caps, at
one time playing thirteen matches
in succession. After becoming
assistant coach at the Dell, Taffy
was recalled to active service in
December 1899 and saw
action in South Africa
during the Boer War. He
left the army in
November 1902 but,
aged 36, he decided
against playing again
and settled in the
Southampton area.

Appearances:
SL: 8 app. 0 gls.
FAC: 4 app. 0 gls.
Total: *12 app. 0 gls.*

'Taffy' Hamer

HAMILTON, Henry Gilhespy

Role: Forward 1911-12
b. South Shields July qtr 1887

CAREER: Craghead United/Sheffield Wednesday Dec 1908/Huddersfield Town Apr 1910/SOUTHAMPTON May 1911/Belfast Celtic Mar 1912/South Shields 1913.

Debut v Millwall (h) 2.9.11

A prolific spell of goalscoring whilst at Huddersfield alerted the attention of Saints' manager, George Swift, who duly made Henry Hamilton one of his first signings. Although he found the net with acceptable regularity during the 1911-12 season, it was said that he never got used to the cramped surroundings of the home ground - certainly something was not right because in March 1912 Henry and Andrew Gibson both received *sine die* suspensions for a serious breach of club discipline. After a spell in Belfast he returned to his native north east to play for South Shields but took no further part in football after World War One.

Appearances:
SL: 23 app. 9 gls.
FAC: 1 app. 0 gls.
Total: *24 app. 9 gls.*

HANDLEY, George Albert

Role: Forward 1911-12
5'7" 11st.0lbs.
b. Totley, Sheffield January qtr 1886

CAREER: Hallam/Chesterfield Jan 1904/Bradford City Oct 1906/SOUTHAMPTON May 1911/Goole Town player-manager Apr 1912/Bradford City Dec 1913/Royal Flying Corps/Bradford City May 1919/Bruhl F.C. /St Gallen coach Apr 1922.

Debut v Millwall (h) 2.9.11

As a youngster George Handley played four times in the annual

Sheffield Schools versus London Schools match and, when he joined the Saints in 1911, renewed his association with George Swift whom he had first met at Chesterfield. He was an orthodox player who depended on team-mates to create openings yet his centres from the outside left berth were invariably well placed. Although one of the club's more successful imports for the 1911-12 season, his leaving to become the player-manager of Goole Town predictably coincided with the departure of George Swift. During World War One George joined the Royal Flying Corps and then returned to Bradford City.

Appearances:
SL: 24 app. 2 gls.
FAC: 1 app. 0 gls.
Total: *25 app. 2 gls.*

HARDY, G.

Role: Forward 1912-13
b. London

CAREER: Leytonstone/SOUTHAMPTON trial Apr 1913/Leytonstone.

Debut v Gillingham (h) 26.4.13

An amateur trialist from East London, Hardy played against Gillingham, replacing Percy Prince at outside-left. Failing to impress he was allowed to return to Leytonstone, his original club.

Appearances:
SL: 1 app. 0 gls.
Total: *1 app. 0 gls.*

HARE, Thomas

Role: Full-back 1965-66
5'7" 10st. 3lbs.
b. Motherwell 1 April 1944

CAREER: Fauldhouse United/
SOUTHAMPTON Apr 1963/Luton Town July
1967/Workington July 1968/Netley Oct
1968/Basingstoke Town May 1972/
Waterlooville 1973/Sholing Sports May 1976/
Swaythling F.C. 1977/West End F.C. 1979/
Colden Common F.C. 1980/Vosper
Thornycrofts 1981.

Debut v Huddersfield Town (h) 13.11.65

Tommy Hare joined the Saints as an 18 year
old wing half from Fauldhouse United, a
Scottish club near Glasgow. Converted to full
back, he performed well in the Combination
League and was elevated to the first team
during Southampton's 1965-66 promotion
season. The arrival of David Webb prevented
any further progress for the young full-back
and, failing to make a single appearance in the
1966-67 season, he agreed to join Luton Town.
In July 1991 Tommy was living in Park Gate
while working for O.P.C.S. in Titchfield.

Appearances:
FL: 13 app. 0 gls.
FAC: 1 app. 0 gls.
Total: *14 app. 0 gls.*

Tommy Hare

HARFIELD, Leslie Philip

Role: Forward 1970-71
5'8" 10st 6lbs
b. Southampton 22 November 1952

CAREER: Deanery School/Southampton &
Hampshire Schools/SOUTHAMPTON app
July 1968, pro Nov 1969/Luton Town Sept
1972/Folkestone July 1973/Sholing Sports Sept
1975/National Docks Labour Board c.s. 1977.

Debut v Nottingham Forest (a) 6.2.71

A former England Schools and Youth
International, Les Harfield signed associate
schoolboy forms in November 1967 and was
regarded as an exciting prospect. Despite
scoring in only his second game (a 6-0 defeat of
Crystal Palace) he failed to capitalise on early
promise and he joined Luton Town where,
after just one appearance as a substitute, his
league career ended.

Appearances:
FL: 2 app. 1 gl.
Total: *2 app. 1 gl.*

HARKUS, George Cecil M.B.E.

Role: Half-back 1923-30 &1931-32
5'9" 11st.6lbs.
b. Newcastle 25 September 1898
d. Southampton 28 September 1950

CAREER: Nunsmoor Edinburgh
Emmet/Scotswood/Aston Villa am May 1921,
pro Feb 1922/SOUTHAMPTON May
1923/Lyon (France) 1930/Oldham Athletic
(trial) Dec 1930/New Milton c.s.
1931/SOUTHAMPTON Feb 1932/Southport
Reserve Team player-coach Sept 1932.

Debut v Barnsley (h) 19.1.24

A £250 transfer in May 1923 initiated the arrival
at the Dell of George Harkus and it was money
well spent as he became one of the most popular
players ever to play for the club. Tremendously
energetic and enthusiastic, he was a natural
captain who put so much into his game that
when the 90 minutes were up he was often "all
in". An inspiration to younger players, George
came close to winning international recognition
(he did tour Canada with the F.A. XI in 1926)
before, in 1930, deciding to move to New Milton to
run the Wheatsheaf Public House. The club were

reluctant to release him, holding on to his registration and putting a price of £750 on his head. Meanwhile George, who had originally intended to retire, changed his mind and turned out for Hampshire League team, New Milton, before an injury crisis at the Dell prompted the club to ask for his services once more. After a further two games he moved to Lancashire to take up a player-coach position at Southport, but was hurt in a game versus Barrow Reserves in October 1932 and never played again. Later employed at the Ministry of Labour in London, George joined the R.A.F. upon the outbreak of World War Two and went on to attain the rank of Flight Lieutenant. Awarded the M.B.E. in the King's birthday honours list of 1949 for "keeping up morale in the forces whilst stationed in the Middle East", he maintained his links with soccer throughout his R.A.F. career and he had been appointed to serve on their selection committee just before his untimely death, in September 1950, after an illness.

Appearances:
FL: 220 app. 3 gls.
FAC: 15 app. 2 gls.
Total: *235 app. 5 gls.*

HARRIS, George

GEORGE C. HARKUS
SOUTHAMPTON

Role: Forward 1905-07
5'10" 12st.0lbs.
b. Rocester, Staffordshire

CAREER: Uttoxeter Town/Stoke Nov 1900/ Reading 1904/SOUTHAMPTON May 1905/ Tutbury Town 1908.
Debut v Brentford (h) 2.9.05

Having only made ten appearances in four years at Stoke, George Harris blossomed at Reading where eleven goals in 28 games led to an international trial. The Saints were eager to sign him and, once settled, he soon developed into a consistent striker with a powerful and accurate shot. After forming an effective striking partnership with Fred Harrison he inexplicably retired from the professional game in April 1907 and became a landlord at a hostelry in Tutbury, a village near Burton upon Trent. After a year out of the game he turned out for the town side in the Burton & District League.

Appearances:
SL: 48 app. 9 gls.
Total: *48 app. 9 gls.*

HARRIS, James William

Role: Forward 1932-33
5'8" 11st.3lbs.
b. Tunbridge Wells, Kent April qtr 1907

CAREER: Folkestone/West Ham United Dec 1929/SOUTHAMPTON July 1932.
Debut v Millwall (a) 27.8.32

Jimmy Harris had played seven games in West

George Harris on the ball in a 2-1 defeat by Brentford in the Southern League in 1906.

Ham's First Division side between 1930 and 1932 before his summer signing at the Dell in 1932. A left-winger, he played in the first two games of the 1932-33 campaign deputising for the cricketing Johnny Arnold, and then spent the rest of the season playing in the reserves. After 44 Combination games and eight goals he was released from his contract.

Appearances:
FL: 2 app. 0 gls.
Total: 2 app 0 gls.

HARRIS, Joseph W.

Role: Half-back 1906-07
b. Eastleigh

CAREER: Eastleigh Athletic/
SOUTHAMPTON Mar 1907.

Debut v Watford (h) 30.3.07

Introduced to the Saints half-back line in March 1907, Joe Harris came from the obscurity of local parks' soccer. A bustling type of player, he also distributed the ball well but was unable to do himself justice in what was then a struggling side. He left the Dell in 1908 for unknown pastures.

Appearances:
SL: 3 app. 0 gls.
Total: 3 app. 0 gls.

HARRISON, Bernard Reginald Stanhope

Role: Forward 1959-60
5'8" 10st.4lbs.
b. Worcester 28 September 1934

CAREER: Portsmouth am./Crystal Palace Oct 1955/SOUTHAMPTON Aug 1959/Exeter City July 1960/Poole Town Aug 1961/Dorchester Town June 1962/Portals/Winchester City Feb 1968.

Debut v Barnsley (a) 7.10.59

An England Schoolboy International, Bernard Harrison is probably better remembered for his Hampshire County Cricket exploits than his three league games in October 1959 for the Saints. He was, nonetheless, a useful right-

winger who acted as cover for Terry Paine in Southampton's Division Three championship season of 1959-60.

Appearances:
FL: 3 app. 0 gls.
Total: 3 app. 0 gls.

❏ **Saints note** - *Bernard played 14 matches for Hampshire County Cricket Club between 1957 and 1962 and scored one century.*

HARRISON, Frederick

Role: Forward 1900-08
5'10" 11st.10lbs.
b. Winchester 2 July 1880
d. Swaythling, Southampton 21 November 1969

CAREER: Fitzhugh Rovers/Bitterne Guild/SOUTHAMPTON Sept 1900/Fulham Nov 1907/West Ham United Apr 1911/Bristol City Aug 1913.

Debut v Reading (h) 8.4.01

Joe Turner, a famous Saints player, was taking a walk on Southampton Common when he noticed Fred Harrison, "a fast goal-getter with a deadly shot" and before long, "Buzzy", as he was known, was introduced to the Dell public as a forward of outstanding promise. During 1902-03 he hit five league goals in consecutive home games against Wellingborough and Northampton Town to finish the season with an aggregate of 17 goals in just 13 games. The following year he notched 27 goals in 32 matches as Saints romped to the Southern League title and he was deservedly given an international trial. Described in the Athletic News as a player "modelled on George Hedley with the cunning of Harry Wood", it was undoubtedly the influence of these two players that helped Fred to his outstanding scoring exploits. Despite no shortage of offers from northern clubs, he continued to win the praise of the Dell faithful by knocking in the goals at regular intervals and became the top scorer in the club's Southern League days. Eventually Fulham offered the, then, gigantic sum of £1,000 for both him and Fred Mouncher and, with the club in a state of financial crisis, the offer was too big to decline. He never repeated

Fred Harrison

his spectacular scoring feats at any of his subsequent clubs although his popularity with each team's fans was never in doubt. After being gassed during action in the Great War he returned to Southampton where he set up a master plasterers business. He celebrated his golden wedding anniversary in 1954 and died in 1969 aged 89. He was, up until the arrival of Bill Rawlings, the finest centre-forward the club had produced and with a little more luck in his trial match he might have enjoyed a long career in an England shirt.

Appearances:
SL: 153 app. 83 app.
FAC: 13 app. 5 gls.
Total: *166 app. 88 gls.*

❏ **Saints note** - *Fred once scored seven goals for Southampton reserves and, whilst at Fulham, netted five in a League game.*

HARTLEY, Abraham

Role: Forward 1898-1899
5'7" 12st. 0lbs
b. Dumbarton 8 February 1872
d. Southampton 9 October 1909

CAREER: Artizan Thistle/Dumbarton/ Everton Dec 1892/Liverpool Dec 1897/ SOUTHAMPTON May 1898/Woolwich Arsenal July 1899/Burnley Dec 1899.

Debut v Brighton United (h) 3.9.1898
* (scored on debut)

Successfully converted from right-back to centre-forward during his days at Everton, Abe Hartley moved to Southampton from Liverpool for whom he scored one goal in seven matches. The son of a tailor and one of three brothers who had played for Dumbarton, he had the unorthodox habit of placing a rolled up cigarette behind his ear prior to the kick off and then smoking it in the dressing room at half-time. The fear of losing his cigarette did not prevent Abe from scoring a creditable 14 goals in 21 games as the Saints celebrated their first season at the Dell by winning the Southern League championship for the third consecutive time. After a brief spell at Arsenal during which time he scored one goal in five games, he returned to live in Southampton and, whilst employed with the London and South Western Railway, collapsed and died

outside the pay office in Southampton Docks aged only 37.

Appearances:
SL: 21 app. 14 gls.
FAC: 3 app. 2 gls.
Total: *24 app. 16 gls.*

HARTSHORNE, Arthur

Role: Full-back 1905-06
5'8" 12st.0lbs.
b. Darlaston 1881

CAREER: Moxley White Star/Wolverhampton Wanderers Dec 1900/Burslem Port Vale/Stoke Apr 1902/SOUTHAMPTON May 1905/ Northampton Town May 1906.

Debut v Northampton Town (a) 23.9.05

Arthur Hartshorne arrived at the Dell with a wealth of league experience behind him and, billed as a "well-built full-back", was, at first glance, viewed by the more critical of Saints' fans to be a little overweight. Displaying a nice line in ball control, he was, at times, brilliant and belied his bulk showing good pace during opponents' attacks. Arthur never quite settled in the south and as soon as the curtain fell on the 1905-06 season took himself to the Midlands by way of Northampton Town.

Appearances:
SL: 25 app. 0 gls
FAC: 5 app. 0 gls.
Total: *30 app. 0 gls.*

HAXTON, Frederick Robert

Role: Half-back 1904-06
b. St. Olave, London October qtr 1879

CAREER: Chandlers Ford Star 1898/Eastleigh Athletic Sept 1899/Chandlers Ford United 1900/Eastleigh Athletic Jan 1901(assisted SOUTHAMPTON Reserves during Jan 1904/ SOUTHAMPTON c.s. 1904/Eastleigh Athletic c.s. 1906.

Debut v Brighton & Hove Albion (h) 1.10.04

Fred Haxton was one of the many young men to reach professional football with Southampton courtesy of Eastleigh Athletic and was regarded as a keen, untiring fellow with a reputation of being "hard as nails". His two seasons as a Saint were spent mainly as cover for Bert Houlker and, whilst playing for the reserves, he won a Hampshire Senior Cup Winners' medal. In 1906 he returned to Eastleigh Athletic but in March 1909 went to Manchester to take up an appointment in the commercial world.

Appearances:
SL: 3 app. 0 gls.
Total: *3 app. 0 gls.*

HAYES, Austin William Patrick

Role: Forward 1976-80
5'5" 9st.13lbs.
b. Hammersmith, London 15 July 1958
d. London 3 December 1986

CAREER: Ealing & District Schools/Middlesex Schools/SOUTHAMPTON app. Sept 1974, pro July 1976/Los Angeles Aztecs May-Aug 1978/Millwall Feb 1981/Northampton Town Aug 1983/Swedish soccer Apr 1986.

Debut v Carrick Rangers (E.C.W.C.) (h) 3.11.76
* (scored on debut)

A product of Southampton's London Selection Centre, Austin Hayes was a neat, darting forward who, making his first team debut in the European Cup Winners' Cup match against Carrick Rangers, scored twice. He made his full league debut in April 1977 at Blackburn Rovers and two years later, although still not a regular in the first team, was chosen to play for the Republic of Ireland in an international against Denmark. Austin played at Wembley in the 1979 League Cup Final against Nottingham Forest but, with the likes of Keegan, George and Boyer blocking his path to a regular selection, he accepted a £50,000 transfer to Millwall. After a spell at Northampton Town he moved to Sweden but tragically his life was cut short by cancer in December 1986. As a tribute, the Austin Hayes Memorial Trophy has been inaugurated and is played for annually between a Saints associate schoolboy team and a select eleven.

Appearances:
FL: 22 (10) app. 5 gls.
FAC: 4 app. 1 gl.
LC: 2 (1) app. 1 gl.
Eur: 1 (1) app. 2 gls.
Total: *29 (12) app. 9 gls.*

HAYNES, Harry

Role; Full-back 1896-1900
5'11" 11st.6lbs.
b. Walsall 21 April 1873
d. Southampton 29 May 1902

CAREER: Walsall Unity/Wolverhampton Wanderers Feb 1893/Small Heath July 1895/SOUTHAMPTON St Mary's c.s. 1896.

Debut v Chatham (h) 19.9.96

A stable-fitter by trade, Harry Haynes learnt his soccer in the Walsall district and, after spells at Wolves and Small Heath, was signed on Birmingham Railway Station with a pen borrowed from the booking office. Initially a half-back he successfully converted to the left-back position and also had the odd game on the left wing. In September 1898 he combined his football duties with that of landlord, pulling the pints at the Turks Head and, two years later, gave up playing altogether, concentrating on spotting new talent for the club (notably Joe French). In 1902, whilst mine host at the Edinburgh Castle, he collapsed and died suddenly at the premature age of 28.

Appearances:
SL: 63 app. 4 gls.
FAC: 13 app. 1 gl.
Total: *76 app. 5 gls.*

HAYTER, Frederick

Role: Forward 1896-97
b. Southampton

CAREER: SOUTHAMPTON St Mary's 1895/Southampton Oxford 1897.

Debut v Swindon Town (h) 27.2.1897

Fred Hayter was the regular second string inside-left between 1895 and 1897 and made his debut at the County Ground in February 1897 replacing the injured Watty Keay. A Hampshire County player on numerous occasions, Fred disappeared from view in 1898.

Appearances:
SL: 2 app. 0 gls
Total: *2 app. 0 gls.*

HEANEY, Anthony James

Role: Full-back 1960-61
5'7" 10st.2lbs.
b. Plymouth 9 May 1940

CAREER: Netley Methodists: Lymington (Saints nursery)/SOUTHAMPTON am. May 1958, pro. June 1958/Poole Town Aug 1961/Dorchester Town June 1962/Salisbury June 1963/Netley Central Sports c.s. 1964.

Debut v Brighton & Hove Albion (h) 17.9.60

An apprentice motor mechanic at the time of his addition to the Saints' staff in May 1958, Tony Heaney showed enough early promise to gain England Youth International honours but was given a free transfer after making only one first team appearance. Signing for Netley in 1964 and still playing for them in 1990, Tony originally took a job at Fords but after two years moved to the Docks where he has remained ever since.

Appearances:
FL: 1 app. 0 gls.
Total: *1 app. 0 gls.*

Bill Heaton

HEATON, William Henry

Role: Forward 1948-49
5'6" 10st.0lbs.
b. Holbeck, Leeds 26 August 1918
d. Leeds 16 January 1990

CAREER: Ingram Road Schools/Leeds City Boys/Yorkshire Schools/Huddersfield Town trial/Whitkirk/Leeds United am. Nov 1937, pro. Aug 1938/SOUTHAMPTON Feb 1949/ Stalybridge Celtic Sept 1949/Rochdale Nov 1950.

Debut v Lincoln City (h) 12.2.49

Bill Heaton was known as "the wizard of the dodge" and moved to Southampton for a fee of £7,000 to replace the recently departed Wilf Grant. He had won Amateur International and FA honours at Leeds and was an immediate success on the left-wing but soon fell out of favour with the club when he refused to move home to the south. The row brewed throughout the summer of 1949 and Bill decided to play for Stalybridge Celtic in the Cheshire League while Saints held onto his registration. He was eventually allowed to return to the Football League with Rochdale but after only four games he retired from the professional scene to become a tradesman for a Leeds slating and roofing company.

Appearances:
FL: 15 app. 0 gls.
Total: *15 app. 0 gls.*

Tony Heaney

Trevor Hebberd

HEBBERD, Trevor Neal

Role: Midfield 1976-82
5'11" 11st.1lb.
b. Alresford 19 June 1958

CAREER: Alresford/SOUTHAMPTON app.
Sept 1974, pro. July 1976/Washington
Diplomats Mar - Aug 1981 (Bolton Wanderers
loan Sept - Oct 1981) (Leicester City loan Nov -
Dec 1981)/ Oxford United Mar 1982/Derby
County Aug 1988/Portsmouth Sept 1991.
Debut v Hull City (h) 5.2.77

Trevor Hebberd first appeared in the
Southampton Reserve team aged 16 and had a
nonchalant, unhurried style that was not only
deceptive but disguised an effective versatility.
"Smiler", as he was popularly known,
appeared in a variety of positions and was a
valuable member of the club's squad without
really ever truly asserting himself. At Oxford
he won a Milk Cup Winners' Medal in 1986
and at long last matured into a forceful
midfield player of some repute.

Appearances:
FL: 69 (27) app. 8 gls.
FAC: 4 (3) app. 0 gls.
LC: 9 (1) app. 3 gls.
Total: *82 (31) app. 11 gls.*

HEDLEY, George Albert

Role: Forward 1903-06
5'9" 12st.0lbs.
b. Southbank 20 July 1876
d. Wolverhampton 16 August 1942

CAREER: Southbank/Sheffield United May
1898/SOUTHAMPTON May 1903/
Wolverhampton Wanderers May 1906/Bristol
City manager April 1913-1915.
Debut v Millwall (h) 10.10.03

Considered something of a veteran at the time
of his joining Southampton, George Hedley
had gained two F.A. Cup Winners' medals and
an international cap while with Sheffield
United. It was through an accident that he
came to leave the Blades. Having torn heart
muscles, it was thought that his footballing
days were numbered. However, with no
transfer fees between the Football and
Southern leagues he accepted an invitation to
join the Saints. Once at the Dell he moved from
his usual centre-forward position to inside-
right and quickly formed a robust and
opportunist partnership with Fred Harrison
which was to yield more than seventy goals
over a three-year period. Popular with team-
mates and spectators alike, it was surprising
that the club sanctioned his departure in 1906
to Wolverhampton Wanderers where he
added a further F.A. Cup Winners' medal to
his collection. He remained at Molineux for six
years before a brief managerial flirtation with
Bristol City. George later took charge of a
boarding house in Wolverhampton.

Appearances:
SL: 70 app. 30 gls.
FAC: 10 app. 4 gls.
Total: *80 app. 34 gls.*

*George
Hedley*

HENDERSON, Douglas

Role: Full-back 1935-39
5'9" 11st.8lbs.
b. Southampton 6 March 1913

CAREER: St. Denys School/Park Avenue/
SOUTHAMPTON am. Sept 1934, pro. Sept
1934/Bristol City June 1939/Southampton
Police.

Debut v Bury (a) 1.1.36

Discovered by Saints' trainer, Bert Shelley,
while playing on Southampton Common,
Doug Henderson was a reliable full-back who
was equally at home in the half-back line.
Never a regular, he joined Bristol City on a free
transfer in the summer of 1939 but, with the
outbreak of war, returned to Southampton to
become a policeman. Doug enjoyed a long

Doug Henderson

career in the force and continues to reside in
Southampton in his retirement (1991).

Appearances:
FL: 22 app. 0 gls.
FAC: 2 app. 0 gls.
Total: *24 app. 0 gls.*

HENDERSON, William James

Role: Forward 1923-28
5'9" 11st.8lbs.
b. Carlisle 11 January 1899

CAREER: Carlisle United/Arsenal Oct 1921/Luton
Town Mar 1923/SOUTHAMPTON Nov 1923 Coventry
City June 1928/Carlisle United Oct 1929.

Debut v Fulham (a) 10.11.23

The club's difficulties with wingers during the 1923-24
season prompted Saints to pay a £500 transfer fee to
Luton Town for the services of Bill Henderson. A
puzzling player, not only to the opposition but often to
his own team-mates, he could make the most amazing
runs, dribbling the ball through places where it did not
seem possible. His footwork was so convoluted that he
was dubbed "Tishy" by the crowd, after a famous race
horse of the day which was supposed to cross its legs
as it ran. He was certainly the most unconventional
right-winger who played for Saints during the 1920's
with his play shifting unaccountably from the exquisite
to "sheer vaudeville". After entertaining the Dell
crowd for five years "Tishy" moved to Coventry for
£200 and when he finally retired from soccer was to be
found running a tobacconists in his native Carlisle.

Appearances:
FL: 152 app. 10 gls.
FAC: 16 app. 0 gls.
Total: *168 app. 10 gls.*

HENDERSON, William

Role: Full-back 1901-02
5'8" 11st.10lbs.
b. Broxburn circa 1878

CAREER: Broxburn Athletic/
Everton Nov 1896/Reading
1897/SOUTHAMPTON c.s.
1901/Everton c.s. 1902/Reading
c.s. 1904/ Clapton Orient Aug
1906/New Brompton 1908.

Debut v New Brompton (h) 7.9.01

Southampton director Mr. E. C.
Jarvis was instrumental in
securing the services of Bill
Henderson from Reading in
1901. His arrival, however,
coincided with that of C. B. Fry, the
famous amateur right-back, and resulted in
Bill standing down when the Corinthian was
able to play. A capable defender, he tackled
strongly and was quick to the ball with his
only fault being, possibly, his over-
zealousness. He left the club after one season
determined to obtain a position in regular first
team football but, had he waited a month or
two, his wishes could have been fulfilled at the
Dell as C. B. Fry, in the meantime, had also
departed.

> F 368 **W. Henderson**
> Southampton
> **OGDEN'S**
> **CIGARETTES**

Appearances:
SL: 21 app. 0 gls.
Total: *21 app. 0 gls.*

HENNIGAN, Michael

Role: Centre-half 1963-64
5'11" 11st.6lbs.
b. Thyburgh 20 December 1942

CAREER: St. Gerards RC School, Rotherham/
Huddersfield Town am. Dec 1957/Rotherham
United am./Sheffield Wednesday May 1961/
SOUTHAMPTON June 1962/Brighton & Hove
Albion July 1964/Bloemfontein (South Africa)
1965-68/Stevenage July 1968-69/Marconi
Fairfield (Australia) 1970/Coached local &
semi pro. soccer in Sheffield area 1971-84/
Sheffield Wednesday Youth team coach 1984-
88/Leeds United coach 1988.

Debut v Newcastle United (a) 11.9.63

Mike Hennigan spent two seasons at the Dell

acting as cover for
Tony Knapp and, after
a short period at
Brighton, was one of
the first British players
to try his luck in South
Africa. In 1990 Mike
was first team coach at
Elland Road and, as
right-hand man to
manager Howard
Wilkinson, was a major
force behind Leeds'
successful charge to the
Second Division
Championship and
subsequent consolidation
in the top half of Division
One the following season.

Appearances:
FL: 3 app. 0 gls.
Total: *3 app. 0 gls.*

HILL, Frank Robert

Role: Half-back 1937-39
5'8" 11st.0lbs.
b. Forfar 21 May 1906

CAREER: Forfar Athletic 1924/Aberdeen Sept
1928/Arsenal May 1932/Blackpool June 1936/

Frank Hill

SOUTHAMPTON Sept 1937/Preston North End asst. trainer-coach 1938-39/Crewe Alexandra player-manager July 1944-Sept 1948/Burnley manager Sept 1948/Preston North End manager Aug 1954/Coached in Iraq 1956/Notts County manager Oct 1958/Charlton Athletic manager Nov 1961-Aug 1965/Manchester City scout 1965.

Debut v Manchester United (a) 25.9.37

Frank Hill was a Scottish international and the holder of a 1933 League Championship medal by the time he became a Saint in 1937. The club paid £2,200 for his services and they had signed a strong personality with considerable abilities as a ball-winning half-back. Nicknamed "Tiger", Frank's resolve and leadership helped steer the club away from relegation during 1937-38 only for him to suffer a series of injuries the following season that side-lined him for long periods. He subsequently fell out with certain sections of the crowd and finally upset the board when it was revealed that he had secretly made several applications for managerial positions. Leaving the club to take up a position as assistant trainer at Preston, the Saints, anxious to recoup some of their outlay, held on to his playing registration. In 1943 he embarked on a long and meritorious managerial career and, despite his previous acrimonious exodus, applied for the vacancy at the Dell in 1952.

Appearances;
FL: 51 app. 3 gls.
FAC: 2 app. 0 gls.
Total: *53 app. 3 gls.*

HILL, Leonard George

Role: Goalkeeper
1925-26
5'11" 12st.0lbs.
b. Islington
15 February 1899
d. Southend
October qtr 1979

CAREER: Cranley Rovers/Southend am. 1919/Queen's Park Rangers Aug 1920/ SOUTHAMPTON June 1925/Rochdale June 1926/Lincoln City July 1927/Grays Thurrock July 1929.

Len Hill

Debut v Blackpool (a) 29.8.25

Barry Hillier

A survivor of the Great War, Len Hill had cheated death on a couple of occasions before embarking on the somewhat safer occupation of a professional goalkeeper. In his one season at the Dell he proved to be an able understudy to Tommy Allen but moved on in search of more regular first team football.

Appearances:
FL: 10 app. 0 gls.
FAC: 1 app. 0 gls.
Total: *11 app. 0 gls.*

HILLIER, Barry Guy

Role: Full-back 1957-59
5'8" 10st.4lbs.
b. Redcar, Yorkshire 8 April 1936

CAREER: Gosport Secondary School/ SOUTHAMPTON April 1953 (Chester-loan-July 1954)/Poole Town July 1959/Dorchester Town July 1960/Andover Apr 1963.

Debut v Queen's Park Rangers (h) 14.9.57

Barry Hillier signed professional forms in

April 1953 but, after 20 reserve team matches, he was called up for National Service in the army, based at Rhyl. At this point Barry was allowed to join Chester on loan and assisted them for the remainder of his service. Returning to the Dell in 1956, he captained the reserve team between 1958 and 1959 as well as making nine senior outings. In 1959 Barry gave up football for a career in business although he played on a part-time basis for Mike Keeping's Poole Town. Today he is the sales and marketing director of a consumer goods company in East Hampshire and maintains an interest in most sports.

Appearances:
FL: 9 app. 0 gls.
Total: *9 app. 0 gls.*

❏ **Saints note** - *Barry's father, Joe, was a goalkeeper for Cardiff, Middlesbrough and Newport County.*

HINTON, John

Role: Forward 1914-15
5'10" 11st.4lbs.
b. Southampton

CAREER: Sholing Athletic/SOUTHAMPTON 1912/R.A.F. Farnborough/Thornycrofts 1919/ Barnstaple Feb 1921/Exeter City Mar 1921/ Thornycrofts 1922.

Debut v Queen's Park Rangers (a) 16.1.15

A joiner by trade, John Hinton was discovered in Hampshire League football and, after joining Saints in 1912, showed his potential by scoring a hat-trick in a Southern Alliance match the following year. He was never really given an extended run in the first eleven and in 1915 severed his connections with the club by joining the R.A.F. Stationed at Farnborough, John was selected to play in an Air Force International at Stamford Bridge when the England team met their Scottish rivals. After demobilisation he threw in his lot with Thornycrofts and, as captain, led them in their famous F.A. Cup match against Burnley at Fratton Park in 1919.

Appearances:
SL: 2 app. 0 gls.
Total: *2 app. 0 gls.*

HOARE, Joseph Henry

Role: Full-back 1902-03 & 1904-05
b. Southampton October qtr 1881
d. West End, Southampton 24 March 1947

CAREER: Southampton Oxford 1897/ SOUTHAMPTON 1902/Liverpool May 1903/ SOUTHAMPTON c.s. 1904/Bitterne Guild c.s. 1905/SOUTHAMPTON Mar 1907/Salisbury City c.s. 1908/Bitterne Guild 1909/Woolston 1912.

Debut v Luton Town (h) 25.10.02

John Hinton

Joe Hoare

A carpenter and joiner by trade, Joe Hoare became understudy to Southampton's international full-back, George Molyneux, in 1902 and, although considered to be handicapped by a lack of weight, more than compensated with his pluck and endurance. Reading and Liverpool were both keen to sign him in 1903 and, after choosing the latter, Joe became a regular in the Reds' defence for a time. After losing his place in the side due to an accident he decided to return to the town of his birth where he became the proprietor of a flourishing tobacconists' shop in Woolston. He did play three more times for the Saints during 1904-05 but decided to retire from professional soccer before the season's end, although he did once re-appear in a striped shirt for the 1907 Southern Charity Cup Final.

Appearances:
SL: 8 app. 0 gls.
Total: *8 app. 0 gls.*

HOBSON, *Gordon*

Role: Forward 1986-89
5'9" 10st.7lbs.
b. Sheffield 27 November 1957

CAREER: Winterton Rangers/Lincoln City Dec 1977/Grimsby Town June 1985/ SOUTHAMPTON Nov 1986/Lincoln City Sept 1988/Exeter City Aug 1990.

*Debut v Watford (h) 29.11.86 * (scored on debut)*

Gordon Hobson was a former Sheffield plumber who was given his chance in professional football by Lincoln City and had come to the attention of Chris Nicholl while the Southampton manager had been on the coaching staff at Grimsby. Costing the Saints £120,000

Gordon Hobson

and arriving in the First Division at a relatively late age, Gordon proved to be a diminutive forward with a nice sense of balance. He scored a hat-trick at Maine Road in April 1987 becoming the first Saint to score three away goals in the First Division since Ron Davies in 1969. An ankle injury plus the emerging talents of youngsters Alan Shearer and Matthew le Tissier brought an end to his two years at the Dell and Gordon rejoined his first League club for a fee of £60,000.

Appearances:
FL: 32 (1) app. 8 gls.
FAC: 2 app. 1 gl.
LC: 1 app. 0 gls.
Total: *35 (1) app. 9 gls.*

HODGKINSON, *Albert Victor*

PROMINENT FOOTBALLERS.

A. HODGKINSON, SOUTHAMPTON.

Role: Forward
1907-09
5'7" 11st.0lbs.
*b. Pembroke Dock
10 August 1884
d. Shilton Lock,
Shardlow
25 November 1939*

CAREER: Old Normanton/ Hinckley Town 1902/Derby County May 1903/Grimsby Town Oct 1903/Plymouth Argyle May 1904/Leicester Fosse May 1905/ Bury June 1906/ SOUTHAMPTON May 1907/ Croydon Common Aug 1909/ Southend United Mar 1911/Ilkeston United Nov 1911.

Debut v Crystal Palace (h) 7.9.07
* (scored on debut)

A sound and consistent performer with all his previous clubs, Bert Hodgkinson was still developing as a dashing outside-left when he came to Southampton in 1907. A mercurial player, who would suddenly achieve the sensational only to, just as suddenly, disappear from prominence, he also rarely did what his opponents expected of him. His reputation grew during his spell at the Dell and he was rewarded with a Welsh Cap against Ireland in

April 1908. Bert was also a baseball player of some repute and had won two gold medals at the National Baseball Association's annual tournament. From 1911-32 he was the owner of the Rose & Crown Inn at Chellaston, Derby.

Appearances:
SL: 57 app. 18 gls.
FAC: 6 app. 0 gls.
Total: *63 app. 18 gls.*

❏ **Saints note** - *Bert's brother Bill was a centre-forward with Derby County.*

HODGKINSON, John

Role: Half-back 1895-97
b. Tunstall

CAREER: Tunstall/SOUTHAMPTON St. Mary's Dec 1895/New Brompton c.s. 1897.

Debut v Chatham (h) 18.1.1897

An export from the Potteries, John Hodgkinson arrived at the Antelope as a trialist but quickly settled and strengthened the left-half position in the first team. Saints' trainer, Dawson, nicknamed him "Ironside" as his short cropped hair and rolled up sleeves gave him a tough image which he maintained throughout his two years at the Dell.

Appearances:
SL: 20 app. 3 gls.
FAC: 8 app. 1 gl.
Total: *28 app. 4 gls.*

HOGG, John

Role: Half-back 1905-06
5'8" 11st.0lbs.
b. Sunderland 22 May 1881
d. Newcastle upon Tyne 2 August 1944

CAREER: Chillingham Schools/Newcastle Schools/Sunderland/ Morpeth Harriers/ Sheffield United May 1903 /SOUTHAMPTON May 1905/West Stanley c.s. 1907/Hartlepool United Nov 1909.

Debut v Watford (h) 7.10.05

John Hogg

John Hogg came from a famous family of North Eastern footballers, (one brother William played for Sunderland and England and another, Robert, played for Grimsby) and although he had the occasional game at centre-half he was more at home at right-half. He was primarily a destructive, rather than constructive, player and although he appeared at time to be slow he had an easy stride. Reliable and a great trier, John did have a tendency to be overawed in important matches and, after a bad game in the cup replay at Sheffield Wednesday in February 1907, never again appeared in a Saints shirt.

Appearances:
SL: 43 app. 1 gl.
FAC: 7 app. 0 gls.
Total: *50 app. 5 gls.*

HOLLANDS, Frederick George

Role: Forward 1894-95
b. Poplar, London October qtr. 1870

CAREER: Millwall Athletic c.s. 1890/ SOUTHAMPTON St. Mary's c.s. 1894/ Millwall July 1895, re-instated amateur 1896.

*Debut v Chatham (h) 6.10.1894 * (scored on debut)*

One of the first professional imports to arrive at the Antelope Ground ready for the first season of Southern League football in 1894, Fred Hollands was a small, fair-haired left-winger. A smart, nimble dribbler he featured in all but one fixture throughout that inaugural Southern League season and then returned to his native South East London to play for Millwall once more.

Appearances:
SL: 15 app. 3 gls.
FAC: 5 app. 2 gls.
Total: *20 app. 5 gls.*

HOLLINS, Arthur

Role: Forward 1913-15
5'10" 11st.7lbs.
b. Wolverhampton

CAREER: Wolverhampton Early Closers/ Walsall/Wellington Town/SOUTHAMPTON Feb 1914.

Debut v Queen's Park Rangers (h) 28.2.14

Arthur Hollins chose Southampton in preference to Wolverhampton when he signed from Birmingham League side Wellington Town and his speed in the centre-forward position produced an impressive ratio of ten goals in 18 League appearances. A cigarette card issued in 1917 of Arthur pictured in Saints strip reveals that he was O.H.M.S. but thereafter his fate is unknown.

F. & J. SMITH'S CIGARETTES

SOUTHAMPTON.
A. HOLLINS,
O.H.M.S.

Appearances:
SL: 18 app. 10 gls.
Total: *18 app. 10 gls.*

HOLLOWBREAD, John Frederick

Role: Goalkeeper 1964-66
5'11" 12st.6lbs.
b. Enfield, Middlesex 2 January 1934

CAREER: Enfield Town/Tottenham Hotspur Jan 1952/SOUTHAMPTON May 1964/ Mullard Sports.

Debut v Middlesbrough (h) 22.8.64

John Hollowbread was signed within hours of being placed on Tottenham's transfer list and cost Southampton £3,000. He made his debut in the first match of the following season and played thirty consecutive games before losing his place to Tony Godfrey. Regaining the goalkeeping jersey for the first game of the 1965-1966 season, John was in fine form until a serious knee injury in only the sixth match, against Coventry City, not only forced his substitution but ended his career. After a testimonial against Portsmouth, John settled in Hampshire and became landlord of a pub in Romsey.

Appearances:
FL: 36 app. 0 gls.
FAC: 2 app. 0 gls.
LC: 2 app. 0 gls.
Total: *40 app. 0 gls.*

HOLLYWOOD, Denis Fallen

Role: Full-back 1962-72
5'6" 10st.12lbs.
b. Govan 3 November 1944

CAREER: SOUTHAMPTON app. Oct 1960, pro. Dec 1961/Blackpool July 1972/Bath City Oct 1972/Basingstoke Town Jan 1973.

Debut v Preston North End (h) 6.10.62

Denis Hollywood had the distinction of being the first ever club apprentice to graduate into

John Hollowbread

Denis Hollywood

HOLMES, Colin Albert

Role: Centre-half 1959-60
6'0" 12st.1lb.
b. Winchester 28 March 1939

CAREER: Romsey Road School/Winchester Schools/King Alfred Old Boys/Winchester City 1954/SOUTHAMPTON am. Jan 1956, pro. Feb 1957/Winchester City c.s. 1961/ Salisbury Aug 1963.

Debut v Wrexham (a) 9.4.60

Colin Holmes was born in Winchester in the same week as Terry Paine and both men, playing for Winchester in 1955, were invited to Arsenal for a trial. Like Terry, Colin was invited back to Highbury but decided instead, with a little persuasion from Ted Bates, to sign for the Saints. He won an England Youth Cap against Luxembourg in 1956 and was a member of the club's successful F.A. Youth Cup team of 1956-57 but here the similarity between his and Terry Paine's career ended as Colin only played one senior game for the Saints before being released in May 1961. He took up a job in the Post Office and turned out once more for Winchester and later Salisbury.

Appearances:
FL: 1 app. 0 gls.
Total: *1 app. 0 gls.*

CAP THAT!
*Back (left to right): Bob Charles, John Bailey, Bill Ellerington, **Colin Holmes**.*
Front: Tony Heany, Terry Paine, Peter Vine, John Sydenham.

the League side and although in his first game he played in the number 4 shirt it was in the right back position that he excelled. A Scottish Youth international and the winner of one Scottish Under-23 cap (versus England in February 1965), Denis was a ferocious tackler who never took any prisoners. His name on the team sheet sent a chill up many an opposing winger's spine and he was the cornerstone of a Southampton defence that gained a notorious reputation in the late sixties. Denis served the club well for the best part of a decade and it was a surprise that after moving to Blackpool he failed to make their first team and dropped out of League football soon after. He returned to live just outside Southampton and accepted the offer of a job in the Docks.

Appearances:
FL: 234 app. 4 gls.
FAC: 15 app. 0 gls.
LC: 13 app. 0 gls.
Eur: 4 (1) app. 0 gls.
Total: *266 (1) app. 4 gls.*

HOLMES, Nicholas Charles

Role: Midfield 1973-87
5'11" 11st.11lbs.
b. Woolston 11 November 1954

CAREER: St. Mary's College/Southampton
Schools/SOUTHAMPTON app. Aug 1970,
pro. Nov 1972/East Cowes Vics Nov 1987/
SOUTHAMPTON coach May 1988-May 1989.
Debut v Arsenal (a) 2.3.74

A loyal, one club man (and a rarity in modern
mercenary football), Nick Holmes spent
fourteen years at the Dell and, along with
David Peach, remains one of only two men
who played in two Wembley finals for the
club. Naturally left-sided, Nick could play
left-back or in midfield and was a thoughtful,
yet thrustful, player who could always be
relied on. An urbane man, he was a natural
choice to be club captain in March 1980 and
with the captaincy came a tribute from
manager Lawrie McMenemy; "When you talk
of bread and butter players he is top of the
tree." International honours eluded Nick
although he was once selected for the England
Under-23's only for an injury to rule him out
and, when he was forced to retire from the
game in May 1987 with a pelvic injury, only
Mick Channon and Terry Paine had made
more appearances. After a brief spell playing
on the Isle of Wight, Nick returned to the Dell
in a coaching capacity but, after a year,
decided to quit football to purchase a general
store near Salisbury.

Appearances:
FL: 437 (7) app. 56 gls.
FAC: 45 app. 2 gls.
LC: 38 app. 6 gls.
Eur: 12 app. 0 gls.
Total: *532 (7) app. 64 gls.*

HOLT, Arthur George

Role: Forward 1932-39
5'9" 11st.7lbs.
b. Southampton 8 April 1911

CAREER: Southampton Schools/Bitterne Park
Congregationals/Totton/SOUTHAMPTON
am. Sept 1931, pro. Oct 1932/ (Cunliffe Owen
during World War Two).
Debut v Manchester United (a) 7.1.33

Arthur Holt

Arthur Holt had won Hampshire County
honours before becoming a Saint and on his
debut he took the centre-forward place of
influenza victim Ted Drake. A punchy,
enterprising player, Arthur settled into the
inside-forward role and was reputed to be one
of the hardest kickers of a dead ball in the
Football League. He was a stalwart in the
forward line throughout the troublesome
thirties and also had a successful cricketing
career with Hampshire C.C.C. that continued
into the post-war period. Arthur joined the
police at the outbreak of hostilities and, later
on, became cricket coach at the County ground
as well as opening a sports shop in the city. He
is still very much involved in local sport and
remains as animated as ever when talking
about his life as a professional sportsman.

Appearances:
FL: 206 app. 46 gls.
FAC: 8 app. 1 gl.
Total: *214 app. 47 gls.*

❏ Saints note - *Often, in Arthur's 79 matches for
Hampshire, he would open the batting with fellow
Saint Johnny Arnold.*

Nick Holmes

HOOPER, Harold

Role: Full-back 1921-24
5'9" 12st.0lbs.
b. Brierley Hill July qtr 1900

CAREER: Brierley Hill Alliance/
SOUTHAMPTON May 1921/Leicester City
May 1924/Queen's Park Rangers May 1926.
Debut v Watford (a) 22.10.21

Harry Hooper provided cover for full-backs
Tom Parker and Fred Titmuss during his
three-year spell at the Dell but obviously
found a permanent place in the first team
difficult to attain. Eventually "Rufus", as he
was dubbed by the fans, moved to Filbert
Street in an exchange transfer that took Fred
Price and Dennis Jones in the opposite
direction. At Leicester he was regarded as
"dour and resolute", and played in 33 League
games.

Appearances:
FL: 19 app. 0 gls.
FAC: 1 app. 0 gls.
Total: *20 app. 0 gls.*

❑ **Saints note** - *Harold Hooper's cousin, Charlie
Roberts, played for Manchester United and
England.*

Harry Hooper

Barry Horne signs for the Saints and Chris Nicholl.

HORNE, Barry

Role: Midfield 1988-
5'10" 11st.6lbs.
b. St. Asaph, Denbighshire 18 May 1962

CAREER: Flint Town United/Rhyl F.C./
Wrexham June 1984/ Portsmouth July 1987/
SOUTHAMPTON Mar 1989.
Debut v Arsenal (h) 25.3.89

Barry Horne was a relative late-comer to the
ranks of professional football having first
completed chemistry and then engineering
degrees at Liverpool University. Playing part-
time football at Rhyl he was persuaded to sign
for Wrexham after the two clubs had met in
the Welsh Cup and, three years later, he
moved south to join Alan Ball's Portsmouth for
£60,000. When Barry signed for the Saints
twenty months later he not only became their
most expensive player at £700,000 but became
the first player to move from Fratton Park to
the Dell since Bill Rochford made the same
journey in 1946. Initially slow to settle, Barry
showed that his main strengths lay in his
combative style and steady work-rate. 1990-91
was undoubtedly the Welsh international's
best season, winning over many of the fans
with his determined tackling. He also
displayed a certain amount of versatility by

playing the final couple of months in the right-back position and as a new era dawns at the Dell a large amount of responsibility will rest on Barry's shoulders.

Appearances:
FL: 77 (1) app. 5 gls.
FAC: 8 app. 1 gl.
LC: 10 (1) app. 2 gls.
Total: *95 (2) app. 8 gls.*

HORSFALL, Frank George

Role: Half-back 1946-47
b. Perth, Australia 19 September 1924

CAREER: Newcastle Schools 1938/ SOUTHAMPTON am. 1943, pro. Dec 1944/ Southend United July 1949/Guildford City Aug 1950/SOUTHAMPTON asst. trainer Sept 1955, coach 1968, reserve team coach 1975, youth team coach 1983, first team coach 1985, reserve team coach Feb 1987, retired June 1989, but continued as coaching assistant to reserve team.

Debut v Chesterfield (a) 3.5.47

Born in Australia, George Horsfall returned with his family to the north-east when he was only two-years-old and, during the war, serving in the Royal Navy, he found himself stationed at Southampton. In 1943 he played in the reserves whenever on leave and so began a long association with the club. In 1944 George was serving in the North Sea and the Saints were so keen to sign him on a professional footing that the forms were sent to Devonport to await his return. In 1949 he joined Southend United for a fee of £1,000 and then spent five years as a semi-professional in the Southern League with Guildford before Ted Bates, recently installed as Saints' boss, brought him back to the Dell to assist with coaching. Fully qualified as an F.A. coach George spent the next 34 years giving tuition at all levels and also, in 1963, became a qualified physiotherapist.

Appearances:
FL: 2 app. 0 gls.
Total: *2 app. 0 gls.*

HORTON, Henry

Role: Half-back 1951-54
5'11" 12st.0lbs.
b. Malvern, Worcester 18 April 1923

CAREER: Worcester City/Blackburn Rovers Jan 1947/SOUTHAMPTON June 1951/ Bradford Park Avenue May 1954/Hereford United Sept 1955.

Debut v Barnsley (a) 25.8.51

George Horsfall

Henry Horton

£10,000 was spent to bring Henry Horton to the Dell and he proved to be a brave, reliable half-back who became immensely popular with the fans. (He once suffered a serious jaw injury at Rotherham yet insisted on remaining on the pitch until the completion of the match). A brilliant all-round sportsman, he had previously played cricket for Worcestershire but joined Hampshire soon after moving to Southampton. Henry joined ex-Saint Norman Kirkman at Bradford Park Avenue in 1954 but continued to play for Hampshire C.C.C. until 1967. He scored 21,000 runs in 405 matches for the county, and later was placed on the first class umpires list. Today he lives in Worcester.

Appearances:
FL: 75 app. 12 gls.
FAC: 5 app. 1 gl.
Total: *80 app. 13 gls.*

HORTON, John Wooldridge

Role: Forward 1921-22
5'9" 11st.4lbs.
b. Thurnscoe October qtr 1902

CAREER: Wombwell Town/
SOUTHAMPTON May 1921.

Debut v Watford (h) 29.10.21

While playing in the Midlands League with Wombwell Town John Horton won a reputation as a prolific scorer and in the 1920-21 season netted 40 goals. Once at the Dell he scored steadily for the reserves playing in the Southern League but, after making his debut in the first team, had the misfortune to break his leg in a reserve game at Bristol City which effectively terminated his career.

Appearances:
FL: 1 app. 0 gls.
Total: *1 app. 0 gls.*

HORTON, James William George

Role: Forward 1934-35
5'10" 11st.0lbs.
b. Farnham 6 January 1907
d. Aldershot July 1972

CAREER: Royal Engineers/Wellington Works/Aldershot Traction/Aldershot Town/ Woking Town Oct 1928/Aldershot Nov 1928/ Millwall Jan 1930/SOUTHAMPTON Sept 1934/Aldershot Oct 1935.

Debut v Port Vale (a) 3.9.34

Signing for Woking in the autumn of 1928, Sonny Horton's form was so impressive (five

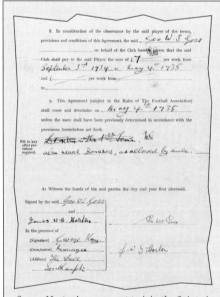

Sonny Horton's agreement to join the Saints in September 1934 for £7 a week plus bonuses.

goals on his debut and a hat-trick in the next game) that Aldershot offered him a contract within a month. Barely a year later he was signed by Millwall for a not inconsiderable fee rumoured to be in the region of £3,500. In and out of Millwall's side over the next four and a half years, Sonny was signed by Saints for £500 at a time when the club were short of experienced players. A bit of a character off the field, he would change into his playing kit keeping his bowler hat on until leaving the dressing room! An electrician by trade and a top class tennis player, Sonny wound up his career at Aldershot where a leg injury forced him to give up playing. After the war he worked as a groundsman at the Recreation Ground.

Appearances:
FL: 4 app. 1 gl.
FAC: 1 app. 0 gls.
Total: *5 app. 1 gl.*

❏ **Saints note** - *Sonny's son, Billy, was a player for Aldershot in the early 1960's while his son James is currently on the books of Farnborough Town.*

HOSKINS, Albert Herbert

Role: Forward 1906-08
5'9" 10st.6lbs.
b. Southampton 1885
d. Southampton 19 February 1968

CAREER: St. Mary's Guild/Freemantle/ SOUTHAMPTON 1904/ Shrewsbury Town/ Wolverhampton Wanderers May 1908/ Dudley Town/ Wellington Town, later secretary/ Wolverhampton Wanderers asst. secretary Aug 1919, secretary 1922-24, manager June 1924-Mar 1926/Gillingham manager 1926-Aug 1930.

Debut v West Ham United (a) 25.12.06

Bert Hoskins first attracted the attention of the Southampton scouts while giving an impressive display for Freemantle against Saints reserves at the Dell in 1904. He made his debut on Christmas Day 1906 but always remained just on the brink of establishing himself properly in the first eleven. Strangely he never scored a League goal despite playing 21 times but did score in each of his three F.A. Cup outings. Joining Wolves in 1908 Bert played 13 games and then later managed the same club for a period in the mid-twenties.

Appearances:
SL: 21 app. 0 gls.
FAC: 3 app. 3 gls.
Total: *24 app. 3 gls.*

HOSKINS, John Frederick

Role: Forward 1952-59
5'10" 10st.7lbs.
b. Southampton 10 May 1931

Bert Hoskins

CAREER: Millbrook Rangers/Winchester City/SOUTHAMPTON July 1952/Swindon Town July 1959/ Cambridge United.

Debut v Blackburn Rovers (a) 6.12.52

A great-nephew of former Saints' player Bert Hoskins who played in the early 1900's, John Hoskins came to local prominence as a prolific goalscorer with Winchester. After joining the Saints in the summer of 1952 he soon became a regular feature in the outside-left berth and gave a series of impressive, if languid, performances that led to his selection for the F.A. touring team of the West Indies in 1955. A successful tour (6 goals in 11 games) left John on the threshold of major success but in 1956 he was side-lined by two

John Hoskins

Ted Hough

cartilage operations which curtailed his progress. Bouncing back to form in 1957 he gained further recognition, representing the Southern Section of the Third Division against the North in March 1958. Moving to Swindon in August 1959, John surprisingly dropped out of League football after only ten games and, although he was an admirable servant for the Saints, more ambition could have perhaps taken his career further. John still lives in Southampton and is a bus driver.

Appearances:
FL: 220 app. 64 gls.
FAC: 15 app. 3 gls.
Total: *235 app. 67 gls.*

HOUGH, Edward

Role: Full-back 1921-31
5'10" 11st.8lbs.
b. Walsall 4 December 1899
d. Birmingham 3 September 1978

CAREER: Talbot Stead Works / SOUTHAMPTON Oct 1921 / Portsmouth May 1931 / Bristol Rovers Dec 1932 / Portsmouth Electricity F.C.

Debut v Aberdare (h) 17.4.22

It was fortunate that the Southampton director who was dispatched to a Walsall Works team to secure the services of Ted Hough had his wallet with him, as Talbot Stead agreed to release their promising full-back if the director stood a round of drinks! This unusual transfer fee, which ended up as 52 pints-worth, was beer money well spent as Ted remained with the Saints for a decade, originally as a centre-half and converting to full-back when Tom Parker transferred to Arsenal. Moving to near neighbours Portsmouth for a fee of £200 he only played one game before a transfer to Bristol Rovers. Ted later returned to Portsmouth to work at the local power station as a fitters mate.

Appearances:
FL: 175 app. 0 gls.
FAC: 9 app. 0 gls.
Total: *184 app. 0 gls.*

HOULKER, Albert Edward

Role: Half-back 1903-06
5'6" 10st.5lbs.
b. Blackburn 27 April 1872
d. Blackburn 27 May 1962

CAREER: Blackburn Hornets / Oswaldtwistle Rovers / Cobwall / Park Road / Blackburn Rovers Aug 1894 / Portsmouth May 1902 / SOUTHAMPTON May 1903 / Blackburn Rovers May 1906, (retired 1907) / Colne c.s. 1909 / Blackburn Rovers Jan 1918.

Debut v Kettering Town (h)
19.9.03

Bert Houlker, or "Kelly" as he was more frequently known, was already an England international by the time of his Dell arrival and, while with the Saints, he not only won a further two caps but a Southern League Championship medal as well. Tenacious and strong, rather than clever, he was immensely popular at all his clubs and, although he intended to retire from the game in 1906, his old club, Blackburn Rovers, tempted him to sign on for one more season. He later settled in Blackburn, played one wartime game for them in 1918 when aged 45, and worked as an overseer at Golden Street Mill. In the 1930's Bert ran a coal and haulage firm and, retiring in 1947, lived a month past his ninetieth birthday.

Appearances:
SL: 59 app. 3 gls.
FAC: 8 app. 0 gls.
Total: *67 app.*
3 gls.

plays a hard individual game. Is a strong, rather than clever, left half-back, who has seen service in Blackburn Rovers and Portsmouth. Stands 5 ft. 6½ in., and weighs 10 st. 5 lbs.

A. E. HOULKER, Southampton,

HOWLAND, Claude Allen S.

Role: Full-back 1901-02
b. Fulham October qtr. 1880

CAREER: London amateur soccer/
SOUTHAMPTON trial Mar 1902.

Debut v Bristol Rovers (a) 5.3.02

Given a trial at Bristol Rovers, Howland was a young London lad and he was not at the Dell more than a fortnight before he decided to return to the capital.

Appearances:
SL: 1 app. 0 gls.
Total: *1 app. 0 gls.*

HUGHES, Arthur

Role: Forward 1908-09
5'9" 12st.0lbs.
b. Birkenhead January qtr. 1883
d. Birkenhead 18 December 1962

CAREER: Birkenhead/Tranmere Rovers/
Bolton Wanderers May 1907/
SOUTHAMPTON c.s. 1908/Manchester City
July 1909.

Debut v Brighton & Hove Albion (a) 2.9.08

Arthur Hughes signed for the Saints in the summer of 1908 to act as cover for George

Smith but, within a few weeks, Smith was to die tragically and Arthur took his place on a pre-season European tour. A series of outstanding games including a hat-trick against The Hague convinced the club's executive that Arthur was the man to spearhead the Saints attack and indeed, using his fine ball control, he started the season in spectacular fashion notching 12 goals in 14 games. Equally happy using either foot, Arthur distributed the ball with panache and it was a considerable blow when a serious leg injury incurred at Watford in November resulted in an untimely and lengthy spell on the treatment table. Disillusioned at losing the momentum of his early season form he left the club for Manchester City the following summer but never registered a first team appearance. Arthur found later employment as a bricklayer in the municipal corporation building department back in his native Birkenhead.

Appearances:
SL: 21 app. 15 gls.
FAC: 1 app. 0 gls.
Total: *22 app. 15 gls.*

HUXFORD, Clifford George

Role: Half-back 1959-66
5'9" 11st.0lbs.
b. Stroud 8 June 1937

CAREER: Chelsea junior 1953, Feb 1955 pro/ SOUTHAMPTON May 1959/Exeter City May 1967/Worcester City July 1968/Basingstoke Town player-coach May 1969/Stevenage 1970/Aldershot player-coach May 1971/ Basingstoke Town player-coach Feb 1974/ A.C. Delco Sept 1976/Bashley coach 1988/ Totton coach July 1989/Fareham manager Nov 1989, resigned April 1991.
Debut v Norwich City (h) 22.8.59

Cliff Huxford played ten First Division games for Chelsea before joining Saints in a part-exchange deal that involved Charlie Livesey moving to Stamford Bridge. He played every game in Southampton's memorable Division Three Championship season of 1959-60 and was a tower of strength in the heart of the defence. A forceful, indomitable player, Cliff became Saints' captain and stayed with the club long enough to make one appearance in their Division One campaign of 1966-67. He has since been involved with a whole host of non-league Hampshire sides, most recently at Fareham where his son is a player.

Appearances:
FL: 276 (2) app. 4 gls.
FAC: 22 (1) app. 0 gls.
LC: 15 app. 0 gls
Total: *313 (3) app. 4 gls.*

❏ **Saints note** - *Cliff's brother, Derek, had one game for Swindon Town.*

Left: Arthur Hughes

Right: Cliff Huxford

INGLIS, Sergt.

Role: Half-back
1895-96
b. Scotland

CAREER: Argyle & Sutherland Highlanders/
SOUTHAMPTON St. Mary's loan April 1896.

Debut v Ilford (h) 4.4.1896

An army player, Inglis was loaned to the
Saints for the final game of the 1895-96 season.

Appearances:
SL: 1 app. 0 gls.
Total: *1 app. 0 gls.*

IRELAND, Sidney

Role: Full-back 1911-15
5'8" 12st.0lbs.
b. Tamworth 1889

CAREER: Kingsbury
Colliery/SOUTHAMPTON
c.s. 1911 (Manchester United
during World War One)/
Merthyr Town June 1919.

Sid Ireland

Debut v Northampton Town (h) 30.9.11

Sid Ireland was only 22 when he arrived in
Southampton but he had already spent several
years as a coal-miner and initially he found it
hard to settle in the south. However, once
acclimatised he became a regular left-back,
being an ever-present in 1912-13 and missing
only two matches the following season.
Regarded as the best left-back in the Southern
League, he was awarded representative
honours against the Scottish and Irish Leagues
and continued to play for the Saints until his
capture by the Germans in 1918. After a year as
a prisoner of war Sid returned to Southampton
but, in the summer of 1919, in a move which
was described by the Athletic News as "an
outstanding capture", joined Merthyr Town.

Appearances:
SL: 120 app. 0 gls.
FAC: 7 app. 0 gls
Total: *127 app. 0 gls.*

❏ **Saints note** - *Sid played several representative
matches during the first World War, for the
Midlands against the Rest of England in 1916 and
for an England XI in the same year.*

JACQUES

Role: Forward 1907-08
b. Southampton

CAREER: Rushden United/SOUTHAMPTON
Dec 1907.

Debut v Plymouth Argyle (a) 14.12.07

Although a Sotonian by birth, Jacques played
all his early football in the Midlands before
being offered a trial by his home team in
December 1907. He was immediately plunged
into the first team for a match at Plymouth and
his inclusion was seen as too hasty by a critical
local press. Unfortunately for Jacques the local
newspaper's fears were well-founded, as he
had a nightmare game wearing the centre-
forward's shirt against much more
experienced opposition and, after one more
appearance in a Western League game he
departed.

Appearances:
SL: 1 app. 0 gls.
Total: *1 app. 0 gls.*

JEFFERIS, Frank

Role: Forward 1905-11
5'10" 11st.8lbs.
b. Fordingbridge
3 July 1884
d. New Cross
21 May 1938

CAREER:
Fordingbridge
Turks/
SOUTHAMPTON
Apr 1905/Everton
Mar 1911/Preston
North End Jan 1920,
player-coach c.s. 1922/ Southport player-coach
June 1923/Preston North End reserve coach
Oct 1925/Southport coach May 1926/Millwall
trainer May 1936.

Debut v New Brompton (h) 18.11.05

Frank Jefferis was born in Fordingbridge on
the edge of the New Forest and, although the
area was not famous as a hot bed of soccer
talent, they did have a fine non-league team in
the shape of the Fordingbridge Turks. Whilst
with the Turks Frank blossomed into an

CHURCHMAN'S
CIGARETTES

F.JEFFERIS

elegant, clever forward and in March 1905 he
was invited to the Dell for a trial. He scored
two hat-tricks, one in a first team friendly
against the Corinthians, the other in a reserve
fixture and the Saints were quick to offer him
terms as well as placating Fordingbridge Turks
by dispatching a £5 note! Frank was a real find.
He brought out the best in his team-mates and
combined a tidy approach with some deft ball
play. A firm favourite with the crowd, he was
awarded a benefit in October 1910 against
Manchester City but was suddenly transferred
to Everton for £1,500 in the following March.
The size of Everton's offer proved too
irresistible to the Southampton board but they
must have felt a twinge of remorse when Frank
won two England caps within a year of his
transfer and a championship medal in 1915.
Incredibly fit, Frank was still playing after the
war and in 1927, aged 43, turned out twice for
Southport during an injury crisis. He became
trainer at Millwall in May 1936 and remained
at New Cross until his death at the
ground in 1938.

Appearances:
SL: 170 app. 48 gls.
FAC: 14 app. 0 gls.
Total: *184 app. 48 gls.*

JEFFERY William Walls

Role: Full-back 1894-95
5'9" 11st.9lbs.
b. Dalderby, Lincolnshire 1868

CAREER: West Manchester/Lincoln
City/ Grimsby Town/Gainsborough
Trinity/ Burnley Aug 1891/Woolwich
Arsenal June 1893/SOUTHAMPTON St
Mary's Nov 1894.

Debut v Millwall (h) 17.11.1894

Bill Jeffrey signed for St. Mary's just after
the start of the initial Southern League season
of 1894-95 and strengthened a weak left-back
position, forming a strong partnership with
Marshall. Remaining at Southampton long
enough to win a Hampshire Senior Cup
Winners' medal Jeffery then disappeared from
public notice.

Appearances:
SL: 13 app. 0 gls.
FAC: 2 app. 0 gls.
Total: *15 app. 0 gls.*

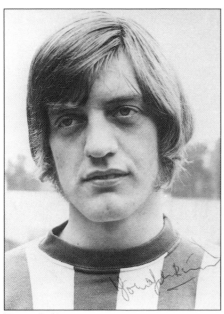

Tommy Jenkins

JENKINS, Thomas Ernest

Role: Forward 1969-73
5'9" 10st.8lbs.
b. Bethnal Green, London 2 December 1947

CAREER: East London Schoolboys/Leyton Orient Jan 1966/West Ham United Dec 1967/Margate/ Reading July 1969/SOUTHAMPTON Dec 1969/Swindon Town Nov 1972/Seattle Sounders Mar 1976 and manager 1987.

Debut v Nottingham Forest (h) 13.12.69

Rejected by two London clubs, Tommy Jenkins eventually made his league bow at Reading and such was his form in the early months of the 1969-70 season that Ted Bates splashed out £60,000 to bring him to the Dell. A jinking left-winger, Tommy was the master of the feint but he would often run up a blind alley rather than release the ball and, like many wingers, could infuriate as much as he could excite. Never a prolific goal scorer, he did once have the satisfaction of striking a wonder goal at Upton Park when he left half the West Ham team (including Bobby Moore) on their bottoms in a mazy run that culminated with a fine shot into the Hammers' net. He joined Swindon late in 1972 without ever realising his true potential

and dropped out of league football three years later to try his luck in the States with the Seattle Sounders, a team he later managed.

Appearances:
FL: 84 app. 4 gls.
FAC: 3 app. 0 gls.
LC: 4 (1) app. 1 gl.
Eur: 4 app. 1 gl.
Total: *95 (1) app. 6 gls.*

JEPP, Samuel Richard

Role: Half-back 1907-11
5'9" 11st.8lbs.
b. Northtown, Aldershot 22 February 1887

CAREER: Aldershot Athletic/Royal Army Medical Corps/Aldershot Athletic/SOUTHAMPTON 1907/South Farnborough c.s. 1911/Swansea Town c.s. 1912/Wellington Works (Aldershot) 1919.

Debut v Brentford (a) 15.2.08

If Sam Jepp was playing today he would be known as a utility player due to his ability to slot into virtually any position and, while his versatility was very useful to the club, Sam suffered from being "Jack of all trades but master of none". In 1912 he became one of Swansea Town's first professionals but his spell in South Wales did not last long as he was working back in his native Aldershot when the war broke out.

Appearances:
SL: 70 app. 2 gls.
FAC: 2 app. 0 gls.
Total: *72 app. 2 gls.*

Sam Jepp

JEPSON, Albert Edward

Role: Forward 1928-32
5'8" 11st.0lbs.
b. Castleford, Yorkshire 9 May 1902
d. Binfield, Berkshire 18 December 1981

CAREER: Frickley Colliery/Huddersfield
Town May 1927/SOUTHAMPTON Aug 1928/
Fulham June 1932/Brighton & Hove Albion
May 1933/ (Port Vale & Swansea during
World War Two) Hove player-coach 1948.
Debut v Hull City (a) 25.8.28

Bert Jepson was a right-winger who, after
fighting off initial competition from Robert
Weale, made the position his own for a couple
of seasons until the arrival of Dick Neal. A
neat, consistent performer, Bert was happy to
stay at the Dell but, with the club sinking into
debt, he was put on the list for £500 although
he eventually joined Fulham on a free transfer.
After hanging up his boots Bert became
manager of a Brighton dairy but, in 1948 at the
age of 46 and with a special F.A. permit, he
was again playing when Sussex League team
Hove enlisted him as their player-coach.

Appearances:
FL: 92 app. 18 gls.
FAC: 3 app. 0 gls.
Total: *95 app. 18 gls.*

JOHNSON, Henry Edward

Role: Forward 1921-24
5'7" 11st.9lbs.
b. Birmingham January qtr 1897

CAREER: Coventry City Sept 1919/Darlaston
loan 1921/SOUTHAMPTON Apr 1921/
Queen's Park Rangers Feb 1924.
Debut v Bristol Rovers (h) 10.12.21

A former junior international, Henry Johnson
first came to prominence playing for the
British Army in 1919 and Saints considered
themselves fortunate to sign him on a free
transfer. In only his second game he scored
twice in a memorable 8-0 thrashing of
Northampton Town but, despite this
promising beginning, Henry found difficulty
in maintaining any consistent form and was in
and out of the side. In February 1924 Queen's
Park Rangers sought, and gained, his transfer
and he left for a more productive career at
Loftus Road.

Appearances:
FL: 38 app. 8 gls.
FAC: 2 app. 1 gl.
Total: *40 app. 9 gls.*

Bert Jepson

Henry Johnson

JOHNSTON, John Shand

Role: Half-back 1907-11
5'8" 11st.0lbs.
b. Lennoxtown 1880

CAREER: Stalybridge Rovers
1898/Bury May 1901/
SOUTHAMPTON May 1907/
Stalybridge Celtic player-
manager c.s. 1911.

Debut v Luton Town (h) 2.9.07

John Johnston was a member of
Bury's 1903 F.A. Cup winning
team and made an immediate
impact in Southampton's half
back line when he arrived at the
Dell in 1907. A distinct
individual, through all the heat and
bustle of the game he was never seen without a
blade of grass or some convenient substitute
protruding from his mouth. His gait was another
distinguishing characteristic of his play but his
main feature was the way in which he would
coach the forwards. John's leadership qualities
were to stand him in good stead as he later
guided Stalybridge Celtic to the Lancashire
Combination title and was also in charge when
they entered the Southern League in 1914.

Appearances:
SL: 110 app. 2 gls
FAC: 9 app. 0 gls.
Total: *119 app. 2 gls.*

PROMINENT FOOTBALLERS.

J. JOHNSON,
SOUTHAMPTON.

moving to Leicester as part
of the deal, but found it
awkward to break into the
senior side due to the
reliable form of Shelley,
Campbell and Harkus. In
1925 he joined non-league
Mansfield, a club he was still
serving in the late 1940's.

Appearances:
FL: 7 app. 0 gls.
Total: *7 app. 0 gls.*

JONES, Frederick

Role: Forward 1914-15
5'10" 11st.6lbs.
b. Hucknall, Derbyshire

CAREER: Notts County c.s. 1912/Coventry
City c.s. 1913/SOUTHAMPTON Apr 1914/
Coventry City c.s. 1919/Pembroke Dock.

*Debut v Luton Town (h) 2.9.14 * (scored on debut)*

Not a proven goalscorer with his previous clubs,
Fred Jones nonetheless formed a potent partnership
with Arthur Dominy and Sid Kimpton. A burly,
bustling inside left, Fred's promising career was to
be a short one due to the outbreak of the Great War.

Appearances:
SL: 31 app. 13 gls.
FAC: 4 app. 1 gl.
Total: *35 app. 14 gls.*

JONES, Dennis

Role: Half-back 1924-25
5'7" 10st.0lbs.
b. Shirebrook 14 May 1894
d. Bolsover, Derbyshire 7 September 1961

CAREER: Shirebrook/Leicester City June 1921/
SOUTHAMPTON May 1924/Mansfield Town
1925/Shirebrook 1926/Sutton Town Aug 1927/
Wombwell Aug 1928/Leicester City & Mansfield
Town, scouting/Mansfield Town asst. trainer 1949.

Debut v Sheffield Wednesday (a) 6.9.24

Starting off as centre-half in the Central
Alliance League with his home town team,
Dennis Jones switched to right-half for
Leicester and carried on in the same position
when he joined the Saints. Dennis cost the
Saints a fee of £200 with Harold Hooper

Dennis
Jones

JONES, George Edwin

Role: Forward 1919-20
5'10" 11st.6lbs.
b. Earlestown

CAREER: Elston Rovers 1912/Crewe Alexandra 1914/Bury Mar 1918/ SOUTHAMPTON May 1919/Goole Town c.s. 1920.

Debut v Exeter City (h) 30.8.19

A member of Bury's Lancashire War League XI in 1918, George Jones had also gained representative honours with the Northern Command before being invited to join the Saints. As understudy to Bill Rawlings his first team chances were rationed but in his seven games during 1919-20 he found the net five times. Before he left Southampton he also won yet more representative honours, this time gaining selection for the South Eastern League XI and scoring twice against London Combination.

Appearances:
SL: 7 app. 5 gls.
Total: *7 app. 5 gls.*

JONES, Kenneth

Role: Full-back 1965-70
5'10" 11st.6lbs.
b. Havercroft 26 June 1944

CAREER: Monkton Colliery/Bradford Park Avenue Sept 1961/SOUTHAMPTON June 1965/Cardiff City July 1971/Bath City July 1973/Basingstoke Town c.s. 1974.

Debut v Coventry City (a) 14.9.65

A trialist with Arsenal and Aston Villa, Ken Jones was regarded as the best full back in the 4th Division when Saints paid £15,000 to Bradford to acquire his services. Initially troubled by injury, Ken only played eight games in the promotion year of 1965-66 but gradually settled and the fact that he could adapt to either left or right-back made him a more than useful player to have on the books. Ken stayed long enough at the Dell to taste European football before linking up with his former Bradford manager, Jimmy Scoular, at Cardiff City. Injuries again hampered his career at Ninian Park and

after only six games he returned to live in the Southampton area.

Appearances:
FL: 79 app. 0 gls.
FAC: 7 app. 0 gls.
LC: 5 app. 0 gls.
Eur: 1 app. 0 gls.
Total: *92 app. 0 gls.*

JONES, William Ernest Arthur

Role: Forward 1949-52
5'11"
b. Cwmbwrla, Swansea 12 November 1920

CAREER: Cwmbwrla Jnrs/Manselton School/ Swansea Schools/Swansea Town am. Aug 1937/Bolton Wanderers Aug 1938/ (Bury and Chester during World War Two)/Swansea Town 1946/Tottenham Hotspur May 1947/ SOUTHAMPTON May 1949/Bristol City player-coach Nov 1951/Rhyl F.C. Apr 1954, manager Aug 1954/Poole Town Jan 1956/SOUTHAMPTON Youth coach 1956-58/Horwick RMI chairman 1961.

Debut v Grimsby Town (h) 20.8.49

Ernie Jones attended the same Welsh school that later spawned the Charles brothers, Mel

Ken Jones
FULL BACK

Ernie Jones

JORDAN, Frank

Role: Forward 1908-10
5'10" 11st.2lbs.
b. Southampton 1883
d. Bitterne, Southampton 28 March 1938

CAREER: Bevois Town School/
SOUTHAMPTON 1905-1906, resigned 1908/
Reading c.s. 1910/Stoke c.s. 1911/
Merthyr Town c.s. 1912/Abertillery.
Debut v Crystal Palace (a) 16.9.08

Frank Jordan was a reserve player in 1905-06
who disappointed the club's management
when he decided to move to South Africa in
the summer. His move to the Cape did not
work out and when he returned to the area in
1908 the Saints re-engaged him and before
long he became a regular inside-left. Fleet of
foot and an agile dribbler, Frank always gave
his best and he went on to serve his
subsequent clubs with equal endeavour.
Returning to live in Southampton, he was
employed by Southampton Gas and Coke
Company for over twenty years and was a
prominent member of their cricket eleven as
well as Secretary of the whist team.

Appearances:
SL: 42 app. 5 gls.
FAC: 2 app. 1 gl.
Total: *44 app. 6 gls.*

Nurse and Gary Sprake, and joined the Saints
as part of the transfer deal that took Alf
Ramsey to White Hart Lane. Capped four times
by Wales, Ernie was a clever outside-left who
had the misfortune to fracture his ankle in
January 1950. After a spell at Bristol City he
moved to Rhyl and there not only managed the
team but helped design and erect the
floodlights. He returned to the Dell for two
years in 1956, after one game for Poole Town,
to help with the youngsters and then returned
to live in Bolton where he was employed as an
engineer at Hawker Siddeley. Retiring in 1980,
he became a member of the National
Association of Inventors and Innovators and,
still active, now designs water leisure products.

Appearances:
FL: 44 app. 4 gls.
FAC: 1 app. 0 gls.
Total: *45 app. 4 gls.*

Frank Jordan

JORDAN, Joseph

Role: Forward 1984-87
6'1" 12st.1lb.
b. Carluke 15 December 1951

CAREER: Blantyre Victoria/Greenock Morton Oct 1968/Leeds United Oct 1970/Manchester United Jan 1978/A. C. Milan 1981/Verona 1983/SOUTHAMPTON Aug 1984/Bristol City Feb 1987, asst. player-manager Nov 1987, manager Mar 1988/Hearts, manager Sept 1990.

Debut v Sunderland (a) 25.8.84

Scottish international Joe Jordan had been exiled in Italian football for three years when Lawrie McMenemy brought him to the Dell for a £150,000 fee. Aggressive and fearless, Joe would launch himself into places angels would fear to tread, sometimes losing a few teeth in the process! Although in the autumn of a robust career he gave everything to Southampton's cause but, with Colin Clarke's arrival, he took a free transfer to Bristol City. Becoming their manager Joe enjoyed a fine Littlewoods Cup run and, in 1990, guided City to promotion to Division Two before he was tempted back to his native Scotland to manage Hearts.

Appearances:
FL: 48 app. 12 gls.
FAC: 3 app. 2 gls.
LC: 10 app. 3 gls.
Total: *61 app. 17 gls.*

❏ **Saints note** - *Joe Jordan is the only Scottish player to have scored in three World Cup tournaments.*

Joe Jordan

JOYCE, John William

Role: Goalkeeper 1899-1900
6'0" 14st.0lbs.
b. Burton upon Trent, 26 June 1877
d. Greenwich June 1956

CAREER: Burton Pioneers 1895/Woodville
1896/Overseal Town 1897/SOUTHAMPTON
May 1898/Millwall May 1900/Burton United
Aug 1901/Blackburn Rovers May 1902/
Tottenham Hotspur 1903/Millwall c.s. 1903/
Tottenham Hotspur mid. 1909-1910/Millwall
1915, asst. trainer 1919-May 1938.
Debut v Queen's Park Rangers (h) 21.10.1899

John Joyce cost the Saints £80 and was
purchased as cover for England International
Jack Robinson. A useful goalkeeper to have in
reserve, "Tiny" as he became euphemistically
known by Saints' fans, was anything but and
often used his bulk to punt the ball up field
further than any other contemporary
goalkeeper. He made his debut in December
1898 against Warmley but when they
withdrew from the League the game became
null and void leaving Tiny to wait another ten
months before his official debut. In search of
regular first-team football he went to Millwall,
where he later helped with work on the
construction of the ground and he even briefly
held the managerial reins when Bob Hunter
became ill in the early thirties.

> **Appearances:**
> *SL: 7 app. 0 gls.*
> **Total:** *7 app. 0 gls.*

JUDD, Michael David

Role: Forward 1967-70
5'7" 9st.8lbs.
b. Southampton 18 June 1948

CAREER: Harefield Juniors/Merry Oak
School/Thornhill Sports/Bitterne United/
SOUTHAMPTON app. July 1964, pro. Aug
1965/Old Simmarians/Cowes/Newport
County Aug 1975/Cowes Dec 1975.
*Debut v Arsenal (a) 15.4.68 * (scored on debut)*

Mick Judd was a lively young forward who,
having been given trials with the England
Youth Squad in 1965, graduated to First
Division soccer in January 1967 when he
appeared as a substitute against Chelsea at the
Dell. His full debut a few months later was
most memorable as, on Easter Monday at
Highbury, he scored one of the goals in a 3-0
victory. Mick appeared in the last ten games of
the successful 1968-69 season and deemed to
stand on the threshold of an auspicious future
only for fate to deal a cruel blow in the shape
of a serious knee injury sustained in October
1969. An attempt to fight his way back to
fitness proved fruitless and Mick was forced to
quit the professional game aged only 22.
Today he combines his job as a brewery
representative with the running of a New
Forest guest house.

> **Appearances:**
> *FL: 14 (1) app. 3 gls.*
> **Total:** *14 (1) app. 3 gls.*

JUDD, Walter James

Role: Forward 1950-53
b. Salisbury 25 October 1926
d. Nomansland, New Forest 18 December 1964

CAREER: Downton/Nomansland/
SOUTHAMPTON Aug 1949/Nomansland Feb
1957 (F.A. permit).
Debut v Leicester City (a) 21.4.51

Walter Judd

Walter Judd was a "Bevin Boy" in a South Wales coal mine prior to becoming a professional with the Saints and, after 27 goals in 34 reserve games, was promoted to the first team. In 1951-52 he scored nine goals in 19 games and his excellent form led to selection for the England 'B' team against the British Olympic XI. Misfortune struck in October 1952, however, when Walter snapped ligaments in his leg and although he bravely fought his way back to play a few reserve matches, medical advice given at the time confirmed a premature retirement. He later worked for the Forestry Commission in the New Forest.

Appearances:
FL: 34 app. 13 gls.
FAC: 1 app. 0 gls.
Total: *35 app. 13 gls.*

JURYEFF, Ian Martin

Role: Forward 1983-84
5'11' 12st.0lbs.
b. Gosport 24 November 1962

CAREER: SOUTHAMPTON app. Aug 1979, pro. Jan 1980 (Munkfurs (Sweden)-loan-Mar-May 1984) (Mansfield Town-loan 1984) (Reading-loan-Nov 1984 -Jan 1985)/Orient Feb 1985 (Ipswich Town-loan-Feb 1989) / Halifax Town Aug 1989/ Hereford United Dec 1989/Halifax Town Sept 1990.

Debut v Coventry City (a) 26.11.83 (as sub)

Ian Juryeff never played a full game for the Saints, but did make two appearances as a substitute, both of them away from home. A versatile player, basically a forward but able to play in the back four if required, Ian made a permanent move to Orient after spending loan spells in Sweden and Reading.

Appearances:
FL: 0 (2) app. 0 gls.
Total: *0 (2) app. 0 gls.*

KATALINIC, Ivan

Role: Goalkeeper 1979-82
6'0" 12st.13lbs.
b. Yugoslavia 17 May 1951

CAREER: Hadjuk Split/SOUTHAMPTON Feb 1980/Hadjuk Split coach c.s. 1982.
Debut v Norwich City (h) 29.3.80

Ivan Katalinic was a Yugoslavian international goalkeeper who failed to fully adjust to the English game. He did show some flashes of ability, most notably in November 1981 when, keeping a clean sheet in four matches, he won a national newspaper's monthly Golden Gloves award and earned the dubious nickname from some of the Saints' younger, more impressionable fans, of the "Kat".

> **Appearances:**
> *FL: 48 app. 0 gls.*
> *FAC: 1 app. 0 gls.*
> *LC: 3 app. 0 gls.*
> *Eur: 2 app. 0 gls,.*
> **Total:** *54 app. 0 gls.*

Ivan Katalinic

KEAY, Walter

Role: Forward
1895-1900
*b. Whiteinch,
Scotland August 1871
d. Winchester 16 January 1943*

CAREER: Brookland/Whitfield/Whiteinch/ Partick Thistle/Darlington/Derby County July 1893/SOUTHAMPTON St. Mary's Apr 1895/ SOUTHAMPTON reserve coach 1923.
Debut v Millwall (a) 14.9.1895

Enticed to the Antelope from Derby County, Watty Keay was a masterly inside-forward who was very much instrumental in the club's success story in the years leading up to 1900. Watty was often the catalyst that knitted together the forward line and his partnership with Joe Turner in particular was regarded as the finest during the Southern League era with Watty creating the chances on which Joe capitalised. He scored Saints' first ever goal at the Dell in 1898 which was the same year as Turner's departure and the subsequent decline in his own form. When he retired in 1900 grateful fans presented him with an inscribed pocket watch and he became a local publican for several years. Later employed as a shipwright at Shamrock Quay by Camper and Nicholson, Watty also found time in 1923 to coach Southampton reserves.

> **Appearances:**
> *SL: 60 app. 22 gls.*
> *FAC: 23 app. 6 gls.*
> **Total:** *83 app. 28 gls.*

KEEGAN, Joseph Kevin

Role: Forward 1980-82
5'8" 11st.7lbs.
b. Armthorpe 14 February 1951

CAREER: St. Peter's School/Peglers Brassworks Reserves/Enfield House Youth Club/Lonsdale Hotel/Scunthorpe United app Jan 1967, pro Dec 1968/Liverpool May 1971/ S. V. Hamburg June 1977/SOUTHAMPTON July 1980/Newcastle United Aug 1982.
Debut v Manchester City (h) 16.8.80

Most Southampton fans over the age of consent can remember exactly where they

Kevin Keegan

were and what they were doing when Lawrie McMenemy made not only local but national headlines with the revelation of Kevin Keegan's intention to join the Saints. The date was February 10th 1980 and, allowing for the 1976 Cup triumph, it was McMenemy's finest hour as Kevin was arguably the most celebrated player in Europe at that time. (Kevin later admitted that apart from the obvious challenge of joining a lesser First Division club it was the manipulative and persuasive charms of McMenemy that influenced his decision the most). No season could be more eagerly awaited by Saints fans than 1980-81 and, although it was a little anti-climatic due to a series of niggling injuries to the England international, the team did at least qualify for Europe. Kevin would be the first to admit to not being the most naturally gifted of players yet his determination, speed, fitness and intelligence gave him the indelible hallmark of an all-time great and in 1981-82 he possibly experienced his finest-ever season culminating in being voted the P.F.A. player of the year. A proud man, Kevin had however by this stage clashed with the manager and, unable to forgive remarks made in the heat of a dressing room row, vowed to move on in the close season. His intention to leave, whether known or not by the club, was not disclosed to the public until a week before the start of the new season when a move to St. James Park

prompted an outcry from disgruntled season-ticket holders. Inevitably becoming a folk hero at Newcastle, Kevin helped them to regain their Division One status and then decided to retire to live in Spain whilst still at the top.

Appearances:
FL: 68 app. 37 gls.
FAC: 5 app. 2 gls.
LC: 3 app. 1 gl.
Eur: 4 app. 2 gls.
Total: *80 app. 42 gls.*

Gallaher's Cigarettes.

ALEXANDER E. M. KEEPING
SOUTHAMPTON

KEEPING, Alexander Edwin Michael

Role: Full-back
1924-33
6'0" 12st.0lbs.
b. Milford 22 August 1902
d. Milford 28 March 1984

CAREER: Ringwood Collegiate/Milford/ SOUTHAMPTON am. 1919, pro. Dec 1920/ Fulham Feb 1933/Real Madrid coach Feb 1949/H.B.S. (Holland) manager/Ermelo (Holland) manager/Poole Town manager 1959.

Debut v Hull City (a) 25.10.24

Signed from his home town club for a bargain £25 in 1919, Michael Keeping, then only 16, was given ten shillings a week to cover travelling expenses. His rise to first team status took some time - four years were to elapse before his debut - but, with the departure of Fred Titmuss, he blossomed into an

Kevin Keegan exchanges pennants before a UEFA Cup tie in Ireland.

outstanding left-back. He oozed class and being fleet of foot could turn on the run to sweep the ball straight up the touchline to the waiting winger. Selected for an international trial in February 1926 he joined an F.A. XI touring party to Canada in the summer and continued to display his formidable skills on the Second Division stage without once being tempted to the premier league. In September 1931 he turned out for the Football League against Ireland and looked all set for his international call when he was struck down with appendicitis and lost the chance. A debonair man, contemporaries recall him as being equally stylish off the pitch and, much to the amusement of his team-mates, he would take hours over his appearance. In 1933, with the club entering into a state of financial decline Mike, along with John Arnold, was sold to Fulham for a combined fee of £5,100 with the Fulham manager and ex-Saints' boss, Jimmy McIntyre, boasting that it was "the best deal I ever brought off". Mike served the Cottagers in his usual immaculate manner up until 1941 when he returned to Milford and the family's motor car business. Later, after a spell abroad Mike took over the reins at Poole Town and often returned to his old club in search of players.

Appearances:
FL: 265 app. 10 gls.
FAC: 16 app. 2 gls.
Total: *281 app. 12 gls.*

KELLY, Gerard Michael

Role: Forward 1937-39
5'7" 11st.4lbs.
b. Hylton, Sunderland
18 September 1908
d. Luton January qtr. 1983

CAREER: Hylton Colliery/ Sunderland Nov 1927/Nelson June 1928/Huddersfield Town Oct 1929/Charlton Athletic. Mar 1932/Chester Dec 1932/ Port Vale June 1936/ SOUTHAMPTON Sept 1937.

Debut v Burnley (a) 20.11.37

Gerard Kelly arrived at the Dell to add depth to the Southampton forward line and, having previously been on the books of six League clubs, had a

wealth of experience behind him. A very quick right-winger who could also play in the centre-forward position, he featured more in the reserves than in the first team and terminated his professional career with the outbreak of World War Two.

Appearances:
FL: 19 app. 2 gls.
Total: *19 app. 2 gls.*

KELLY, Hugh Redmond

Role: Goalkeeper 1950-51
6'0" 13st.8lbs.
b. Lurgan 17 August 1919
d. Belfast 30 September 1977

CAREER: Glenavon/Belfast Celtic/Fulham Mar 1949/SOUTHAMPTON July 1950/Exeter City June 1952/Weymouth July 1956.

Debut v Barnsley (a) 19.8.50

Hugh Kelly started his footballing career as an inside-forward with Glenavon but was forced into goal one day when the regular Glenavon goalkeeper failed to show. Two Irish Cup-winners' medals were won following a move to Belfast Celtic and, when they disbanded following crowd disturbances, Hugh and three team-mates joined Fulham in a £25,000 transfer. While at Craven Cottage he won the first of four Irish caps, overcoming the humiliation of conceding nine goals on his debut against England. Arriving at the Dell as a straight swap for Ian Black, Hugh was perceived as a colourful character who would often gather the ball one-handed, something inherited from his Gaelic Football days. His popularity with the crowd did not, however, extend as far as manager Sid Cann's office

Gerard Kelly

Hugh Kelly

KEMP, Frederick George

Role: Half-back 1965-70
5'8" 11st.0lbs.
b. Salerno, Italy 27 February 1946

CAREER: Wolverhampton Wanderers app Apr 1961, pro May 1963/SOUTHAMPTON June 1965/Blackpool Nov 1970 /Halifax Town Dec 1971/Hereford United July 1974/Durban City (South Africa) 1975 (Weymouth-loan-Feb-June 1976/Telford United June 1976 - c.s. 1977.

*Debut v Preston North End (h) 27.11.65 * (scored on debut)*

Fred Kemp arrived at the Dell, aged 19, at a cost of £5,000 and immediately impressed all and sundry with his flamboyant explosiveness. "Fiery" Fred was busy to the point of being dynamic and, ever the crowd-pleaser, his name always provoked a cheer when appearing on the match programme. For some unknown reason his ebullient persona did not trigger equal enthusiasm from the board-room and his departure to Blackpool for a fee of £35,000 still puzzles the fans. He dropped out of league football before his thirtieth birthday and in 1976 he was captaining Telford United whilst working as an office furniture salesman in the Midlands. In February 1991 Fred was still in the same business and living in Wolverhampton. He still plays charity football with other ex-Wolves players including Derek Dougan.

and Hugh, after being transfer-listed in the summer of 1951 spent the following season entirely playing in the reserves. Eventually Exeter City rescued his career and the big, burly Irishman enjoyed four seasons in Devon before winding down at Weymouth.

Appearances:
FL: 28 app. 0 gls.
FAC: 2 app. 0 gls.
Total: *30 app. 0gls.*

❏ **Saints note** - *Hugh represented County Armagh in the popular Irish sport of handball.*

Appearances:
FL: 58 (3) app.
10 gls.
FAC: 3 (1) app.
0 gls.
LC: 6 app. 1 gl.
Eur: 1 app. 0 gls.
Total: *68 (4) app.*
11 gls.

Fred Kemp

KENNA, Jeffery Jude

Role: Full-back 1990-
5'11" 11st.9lbs.
b. Dublin 27 August 1970

CAREER: SOUTHAMPTON non-contract
Jan 1987, trainee July 1987, pro. Apr 1989.

Debut v Wimbledon (h) 11.5.91

Given his debut in the final league fixture of
the 1990-91 season Jeff Kenna had already
played for the Republic of Ireland's Under-21
side and marked England's Rodney Wallace in
the match between the two teams in April
1991. A left-back by choice, Jeff played his first
game in the number two shirt but this change
of position did not seem to hinder his
performance. With a new manager at the helm
Jeff has nothing to lose and will be hoping for
more chances in the near future.

Appearances:
FL: 1 (1) app. 0 gls.
Total: *1 (1) app. 0 gls.*

KENNEDY, Patrick Antony

Role: Full-back 1959-60
5'11" 12st.0lbs.
b. Dublin 9 October 1934

CAREER: Johnville (Dublin)/Republic of
Ireland Schoolboys/Manchester United Feb
1953/Blackburn Rovers Aug 1956/
SOUTHAMPTON July 1959/Oldham Athletic
July 1960.

Debut v Norwich City (h) 22.8.59

A former "Busby Babe", Pat Kennedy was a
tallish left back who played in the opening two
games of the 59-60 season before losing his
place to Tommy Traynor. A free transfer took
him back to the Manchester area with Oldham
but he never made the Latics' first team due to
an injury. In 1991 Pat was managing a local
amateur side in Urmston, Manchester.

Appearances:
FL: 2 app. 0 gls.
Total: *2 app. 0 gls.*

❏ **Saints note** - *Pat played for Manchester United
Youth Team in the 1951 F.A. Youth Cup Final
when they beat Wolverhampton Wanderers 9-3
over two legs.*

KENNEDY, William

Role: Half-back 1936-38
5'10" 12st.0lbs.
b. Saltcoats, Strathclyde 2 February 1912
d. Southampton 12 December, 1989

CAREER: Royal Albert/Portsmouth Mar
1932/Carlisle United July 1933/Crewe
Alexandra Sept 1935/SOUTHAMPTON Aug
1936/Hamilton Academicals June 1938.

Debut v Bradford City (h) 12.9.36

Although born in Scotland Bill Kennedy was
no stranger to the south coast when he signed
for the Saints, having previously been a junior
at Fratton Park in 1932. A reliable centre-half,
Bill initially combined well with Kingdon and
King during the 1936-37 season but fell from
grace the following year when he spent much
of his time in the reserves. He refused terms in
May 1938 and moved north of the border to
Hamilton but, after the war, returned to
Southampton to serve aboard the Queen Mary.
When he retired from the sea in 1962 he
worked at Mullards while continuing to live in
the city.

Appearances:
FL: 43 app. 0 gls.
Total: *43 app. 0 gls.*

Bill Kennedy

KIDDLE, Robert Sherren

Role: Forward 1891-96
*b. Southampton April qtr.
1869*

CAREER: Southampton
Harriers/
SOUTHAMPTON St.
Mary's 1889.
*Debut v Warmley (a) FAC:
3.10.1891*

Bob Kiddle had already
achieved distinction on the
running track before his
recruitment to the playing
ranks of St Mary's and was
a prominent member of
the club's pre-Southern
League sides. He appeared
in the club's first foray into
the English Cup in 1891
and made good use of his
athletic skills to outpace
his opponents. By 1894
Bob was past his prime but
he did at least make one
Southern League
appearance in an exciting
3-7 defeat at Clapton. An
amateur throughout his
career Bob, was employed
as a clerk in the town and
in 1919 his son, Russell
Sherren Kiddle, featured
in the Southampton
Reserve side.

Appearances:
*SL: 1 app. 0 gls.
FAC: 5 app. 3 gls.
Total: 6 app. 3 gls.*

KIERNAN, Frederick William

Role: Goalkeeper 1951-56
5'8" 10st.2lbs.
*b. Dublin 7 July 1919
d. Southampton
October/November 1981*

Bob Kiddle

Fred Kiernan

CAREER: Shelbourne
Rovers/Dundalk/
Shamrock Rovers Apr
1951/ SOUTHAMPTON
Oct 1951/Yeovil July
1956.
*Debut v Hull City (h)
6.10.51*

Fred Kiernan was
unusually small for a
goalkeeper but
compensated for his lack
of height with his
tremendous agility.
Always dependable, Fred
was awarded his first Eire
cap versus West Germany
soon after his arrival at
the Dell and over the next
five seasons competed
with John Christie for the
right to be Southampton's
premier custodian.

Appearances:
*FL: 132 app. 0 gls.
FAC: 4 app. 0 gls.
Total: 136 app. 0 gls.*

KILLEAN, Edward

Role: Half-back 1900-01
5'10" 12st.6lbs.
b. Blackburn 1874

CAREER: 3rd Coldstream
Guards/Blackburn
Rovers Aug 1894/Glossop
Nov 1898/
SOUTHAMPTON c.s.
1900/New Brompton c.s.
1901/Blackpool Dec 1903.
*Debut Queen's Park
Rangers (h) 2.3.01*

A former Coldstream
Guardsman, Ted Killean
was signed to provide
cover for Arthur
Chadwick in the centre
half position and proved
to a sturdy, diligent
reserve. He distributed

the ball with precision but, being a trifle slow, was unable to gain a place in a very strong Southampton side and moved on to find regular first team football at New Brompton.

Appearances:
SL: 2 app. 0 gls.
FAC: 1 app. 0 gls.
Total: *3 app. 0 gls.*

KIMPTON, Gabriel Sibley

Role: Forward 1910-20
5'10" 12st.0lbs.
b. Leavesden 1888
d. Leavesden 15th Feb 1968

CAREER: Leavesden/ Watford trial 1909/ SOUTHAMPTON Sept 1910/Thornycrofts 1920/Prague (Czechoslovakia) player-coach 1924/ French National Team coach/Coventry City trainer 1928/ Czechoslovakia coaching 1930's/Coached in France 1936-1940/Le Havre Ath (France) manager 1945.

Debut v Crystal Palace (h) 22.10.10

Sid Kimpton

Sibley or "Sid" Kimpton gained a place in Saints first eleven after only one preliminary trial match with the reserves but his main value was his reliability and versatility. Never thought of as a great player Sid had plenty of pluck and bustle which made him hugely popular and, before he left the Saints, he was rewarded with a well-earned benefit match. In the thirties he was part of the Czechoslovakian coaching set-up and was given a medal when the national side reached the World Cup Final against Italy in 1934. Sid Kimpton was captured by the Germans in 1940 and spent the next five years as a prisoner of war.

Appearances:
SL: 141 app. 27 gls.
FAC: 8 app. 3 gls.
Total: *149 app. 30 gls.*

KING, Cyril William

Role: Half-back 1934-39
5'11" 12st.2lbs.
b. Plymouth July qtr. 1915

CAREER: Plymouth & Devon Schools/ Plymouth United/SOUTHAMPTON am. Nov 1932, pro. Apr 1933 (Darlington loan July 1939).

Debut v Newcastle United (a) 1.12.34

A footballing child prodigy, Cyril King had been capped by his county, Devon, when only a fifteen year old and after joining the staff at the Dell forced his way into the first team before his twentieth birthday. He used his sturdy build to good effect and served the club well for five years before returning to Plymouth to work in the Devonport Dockyards. However, during the summer of 1939 Darlington, discovering his availability, signed him on loan from Southampton who had retained his registration. Cyril never kicked a ball for the north-eastern side due to the outbreak of the war and he then joined the R.A.F. serving in North Africa. He later returned to live in Hampshire and joined the prison service.

Appearances:
FL: 93 app. 2 gls.
FAC: 4 app. 0 gls.
Total:
97 app. 3 gls.

Cyril King

Fred Kiernan
(see page 197)

KING, Ernest Stanley

Role: Half-back 1925-27
5'7" 11st.5lbs.
b. Southampton January qtr 1903

CAREER: 5th Territorials/Hamilton House/
Boscombe Feb 1923/Bournemouth/
SOUTHAMPTON am. Oct 1924, pro. Jan 1925/
Guildford City c.s. 1927.
Debut v Sheffield Wednesday (a) 12.12.25

An Evening Echo employee before joining
Saints, Ernie King had played all his early
football in local junior leagues. He played over
a hundred games for the reserves but made
only two first team appearances, one at right-
half and one at right-back.

> **Appearances:**
> *FL: 2 app. 0 gls.*
> **Total:** *2 app. 0 gls.*

Ernie King

KINGDON, William Issacher Garfield

Role: Half-back 1936-38
5'9" 11st.10lbs.
b. Worcester 25 June 1905
d. Weymouth 18 March 1977

CAREER: Kepex F.C. (Worcester Junior
League)/Kidderminster Harriers Aug
1924/Aston Villa am. Aug 1925, pro. Mar
1926/SOUTHAMPTON June 1936/Yeovil &
Petters United player-manager Jan
1938/Weymouth manager 1950.
Debut v Chesterfield (h) 29.8.36

An England junior international, Bill Kingdon
made over 240 appearances for Aston Villa
before he de-camped to the Dell and,
displaying a nice line in distribution, looked to
be an asset. He briefly became team captain
before the arrival of Frank Hill who not only
took over the captaincy but Bill's number six
shirt. A carpenter by trade, Bill accepted the
manager's job at Weymouth in 1950 combining
this position with running the Fountain Hotel
in the town.

> **Appearances:**
> *FL: 48 app. 1 gl.*
> *FAC: 1 app. 0 gls.*
> **Total:** *49 app. 1 gl.*

Bill Kingdon

KIRBY, George

Role: Forward 1962-64
6'0" 11st.10lbs.
b. Liverpool 20 December 1933

CAREER: Longwen Juniors/
Everton June 1952/Sheffield
Wednesday Mar 1959/Plymouth
Argyle Jan 1960/
SOUTHAMPTON Sept 1962/
Coventry City Mar 1964/Swansea
Town Oct 1964/Walsall May
1965/New York Generals 1967/
Brentford Oct 1968/Worcester
City June 1969/Halifax manager
July 1970-71/Watford manager
1971-73/Halifax manager 1979-81.

Debut v Chelsea (h) 19.9.62
* (scored on debut)

George Kirby

City. He later was one of the
pioneer footballers to explore the
lucrative U.S. soccer scene
although eventually he returned
to this country to manage
Watford and Halifax.

Appearances:
FL: 63 app. 28 gls.
FAC: 8 app. 3 gls.
LC: 2 app. 0 gls.
Total: *73 app. 31 gls.*

❏ **Saints note** - *During
Southampton's 6-0 win over
Middlesbrough in November 1962,
George Kirby scored a hat-trick in
just four minutes.*

George Kirby was an experienced, robust
centre-forward who relished the physical
contact his job entailed. Hard working, he
loved to harass opponents and, using his
exceptional heading ability, forged an
immediate partnership with George O'Brien
which struck no small amount of trepidation
into opposing defences. After featuring
strongly in Saints' progress to the 1963 F.A.
Cup semi-finals, George resumed his nomadic
lifestyle with a £12,000 transfer to Coventry

Norman Kirkman

KIRKMAN, Norman

Role: Full-back 1950-52
5'11" 12st.0lbs.
b. Bolton 6 June 1920

CAREER: Folds Road School/Burnley May
1939/(Brighton & Hove Albion and Fulham
during World War Two)/Rochdale Oct 1946/
Chesterfield Nov 1947/Leicester City Aug
1949/SOUTHAMPTON July 1950/Exeter City
player-manager Mar 1952/Bradford Park
Avenue manager Mar 1953-Feb 1955/
Northwich Victoria manager mid-60's/
SOUTHAMPTON scout/Newcastle scout.

Debut v Barnsley (a) 19.8.50

Originally a schoolboy inside-left playing
alongside Tommy Lawton, Norman Kirkman
progressed to become, in 1939, a full-back with
Burnley but, with his call-up, was posted to
Canada to train as an R.A.F. navigator. During
the war he represented the Royal Air Force in
games against the Army and, after his demobilisation, joined Rochdale. He arrived at the
Dell for a "four figure sum" and was described
in the Echo as a "cool professional player".
Norman initially competed with Edgar Ballard
for the left-back berth but, with up and coming
Peter Sillett also pushing hard, he had to settle
for reserve team football until March 1952
when he became player-manager at Exeter.

Appearances:
FL: 20 app. 0 gls.
FAC: 2 app. 0 gls.
Total: *22 app. 0 gls.*

KIRKUP, Joseph Robert

Role: Full-back 1967-74
5'11" 12st.11lbs.
b. Sunderland 17 December 1939

CAREER: Hickley Juniors/West Ham United
Sept 1956/Chelsea Mar1966/
SOUTHAMPTON Feb 1968/Durban City
(S. Africa) player-coach Feb 1974.
Debut v Everton (h) 26.2.68

Although, as a youngster, Joe Kirkup excelled
at rugby and represented Northumberland
County Schools, it was to be in the code of
association football that he was to make his
mark. Capped at Under-23 level and the
holder of a European Cup-Winners' Cup
medal, he joined Saints in an exchange deal
that sent David Webb to Stamford Bridge.
"Gentleman Joe" was unflappable and,
although not particularly fast, compensated
with his positional play to bring a much-
needed sense of maturity to the Saints'
defence. After returning from South Africa Joe
settled in Hampshire and is running a public
house in Alton.

Appearances:
FL: 169 app. 3 gls.
FAC: 10 (1) app. 1 gl.
LC: 6 app. 0 gls.
Eur: 7 app. 0 gls.
Total: 192 (1) app. 4 gls.

Joe Kirkup

PROMINENT FOOTBALLERS.
G. KITCHEN.

KITCHEN, George William

Role: Goalkeeper
1912-14
6'1" 13st.0lbs.
*b. Buxton,
Derbyshire April qtr.
1876*

CAREER: Buxton/
Stockport County
1897/Everton
1902/West Ham
United 1905/
SOUTHAMPTON
Oct 1912/
Boscombe c.s. 1914.
Debut v Coventry City (h) 26.10.12

A former England trialist, George Kitchen was
perfectly built for goalkeeping duties although
he was past his prime by the time he became a
Southampton player. Nevertheless he instilled
a sense of confidence into a struggling defence
and stayed long enough to see the club's
fortunes change for the better. While at the
Dell he secured the position of golf
professional at Bournemouth Golf Course and
when he retired from soccer fully he was able
to make a living out of his second sport. In
1969 George was known to be still alive and
working as a doorman at Lee Green Working
Mens Club.

Appearances:
SL: 37 app. 0 gls.
FAC: 2 app. 0 gls.
Total: 39 app. 0 gls.

KITE, Phil David

Role: Goalkeeper 1984-86
6'11" 14st.7lbs.
b. Bristol 26 October 1962

CAREER: Bristol Rovers Oct 1980 (Tottenham-
loan-Jan-Feb 1984)/SOUTHAMPTON Aug

Phil Kite

1984 (Middlesbrough-loan March-May 1986)
(Gillingham-loan-Jan 1987, transferred May
1987)/Bournemouth Aug 1989/Sheffield
United Aug 1990.

Debut v Aston Villa (a) 17.11.84

Signed for £50,000 as understudy to Peter
Shilton, Phil Kite had been capped at England
Youth level and made over 100 appearances
for Bristol Rovers. After leaving the Saints for
Gillingham, Phil later reappeared in the First
Division when, in August 1990, having just
signed for newly promoted Sheffield United,
he was thrust into their first team due to an
injury to regular goalkeeper Simon Tracey.

Appearances:
FL: 4 app. 0 gls.
Total: *4 app. 0 gls.*

KNAPP, Anthony

Role: Centre-half 1961-67
5'11" 12st.0lbs.
b. Newstead 13 October 1936

CAREER: Newstead Colliery/Nottingham
Forest am./Leicester City Dec 1953/
SOUTHAMPTON Aug 1961/Coventry City
Aug 1967/Los Angeles Wolves Mar
1968/Bristol City Mar 1969/Tranmere Rovers
Nov 1969/ Poole Town player-manager July
1971/Norwich City reserve team manager
May 1972/Iceland national team manager
1974/Viking Stavanger manager
1978/Fredrikstad manager 1981/Vidar
Stavanger manager 1983/Brann Bergen
manager 1985/Ulf Sandnes manager 1991.

Debut v Plymouth Argyle (h) 19.8.61

At Leicester Tony Knapp had been on the
fringe of an England call-up, having played for

the Football League against the Scottish
League in March 1960 and travelled as reserve
on a tour of Hungary. Owing to an injury he
had failed to win back his place in Leicester's
1961 F.A. Cup Final run. Ted Bates was aware
of Tony's restlessness and more than doubled
the Southampton transfer record to bring the
classy centre-half to the Dell. His signing was
regarded as proof of the club's serious intent to
push hard for promotion and, although it was
to take another five years, Tony Knapp as
captain was one of the main reasons Saints
eventually found themselves in the top flight.
An extremely safe player both in the air and on
the ground, he also had the power to recover
quickly. After six years as a Saint he joined
Coventry City when their regular centre-half
George Curtis broke a leg. Later, Tony
transformed the Icelandic football scene by
some astute management and he went on to
take charge of four top Norwegian teams. He
still lives in Southampton and visits the Dell
whenever possible.

Appearances:
FL: 233 app. 2 gls.
FAC: 16 app. 0 gls.
LC: 11 app. 0 gls.
Total: *260 app. 2 gls.*

Tony Knapp

KNIGHT, William

Role: Goalkeeper 1911-13
b. Toogates

CAREER: Walsall/Aston Villa am. Apr 1907/
Stourbridge (Villa nursery)/
SOUTHAMPTON May 1911.

Debut v Luton Town (a) 18.11.11

Bill Knight shaped up well in the club's trial
matches of 1911 and was regarded as an agile
and vigilant custodian who, if he had a fault,
was inclined to come off his line too hurriedly.
He was the team's regular goalkeeper for a
year but was ousted by the arrival of George
Kitchen.

Appearances:
SL: 38 app. 0 gls.
Total: *38 app. 0 gls.*

Bill Knight

LAWRENCE, George Randolph

Role: Forward 1981-83 & 1984-87
5'10" 12st.2lbs.
b. Kensington, London 14 September1962

CAREER: Christopher Wren Comprehensive School/SOUTHAMPTON app. Aug 1979, pro. Sept 1980 (Oxford United-loan-Mar-May 1982, perm. Nov 1982)/SOUTHAMPTON Jan 1985/ Millwall July 1987/A.F.C. Bournemouth Aug 1989.

Debut v Notts County (h) 17.10.81

Initially recommended by a London schoolmaster, George Lawrence made his Southampton debut replacing Mike Channon and soon brought added meaning to the word unpredictable. Full of strong surging runs

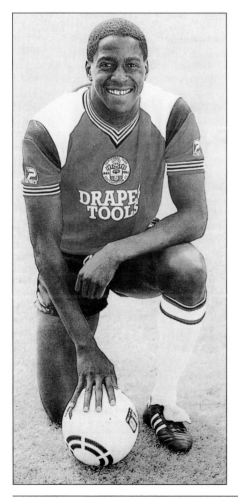

George Lawrence

George would, when remembering to take the ball with him, completely perplex opposing defenders and cause havoc in the penalty area. Definitely entertaining, he was affectionately nicknamed "Chicken George" and although his form could swing from the sublime to the ridiculous, there was never a dull moment when he was around. After moving to Oxford United he surprisingly rejoined the Saints in January 1985 for another two and a half seasons before a £160,000 transfer took him to Cold Blow Lane.

Appearances:
FL: 65 (15) app. 12 gls.
FAC: 5 (1) app. 0 gls.
LC: 9 (3) app. 3 gls.
Eur: 1 (1) app. 0 gls.
Total: *80 (20) app. 15 gls.*

LE TISSIER, Matthew Paul

Role: Forward 1986-
6'0" 11st.6lbs.
b. St. Peter Port, Guernsey 14 October 1968

CAREER: Guernsey Schools/Vale Recreation/ SOUTHAMPTON app. May 1985, pro. October 1986.

Debut v Tottenham Hotspur (h) 2.9.86

Discovered while touring Hampshire with the Guernsey Under-15 XI and one of the very few Channel Islanders to enter professional football ranks, Matthew Le Tissier comes from a large footballing family. Unlike his brothers, however, he managed to overcome initial homesickness to become not only one of the most skilful players ever seen at the Dell but also one of the most talked about forwards of his generation. His three memorable goals against Leicester on a snowbound pitch in March 1987 were an early indication of his prodigious talents and also made him, at the time, the youngest Saint to score a hat-trick. His subsequent path to prominence has not been smooth for, in the true tradition of gifted British wingers, Matthew has added another dimension to the word enigmatic with his confident and apparently casual manner provoking accusations of not caring or not trying. Nevertheless his imperious control of a football and the sublime ease with which he rounds an opponent imparts a Brazilian flavour to his game which thrills the fans, stimulates the journalistic pen and, most importantly, fills football stadiums. His nonchalance, so infuriating to some, conceals a cool-headed composure which is so vital in front of goal and in 1989-90 he became the club's penalty-taker. That same season he notched 20 league goals and was courted by the French manager Michel Platini before Bobby Robson hastily confirmed Matthew's English status by awarding him an England 'B' cap. Voted P.F.A. Young Player of the Year in 1990 he received his award from a previous Dell favourite, Terry Paine, and put an end to rumours linking him to Liverpool by signing a new three-year contract. After a slow start to the 1990-91 season Matthew once more started to find the net with regularity and his increasing value to the team was emphasised when an injury sustained in January sidelined him for a month. If his ability to turn a match with a flash of brilliance could be matched by greater consistency he could become one of the all-time Dell greats but the next year or two will be crucial.

Appearances:
FL: 112 (20) app. 54 gls.
FAC: 8 (1) app. 4 gls.
LC: 14 (6) app. 10 gls.
Total: *134 (27) app. 68 gls.*

LEE, Ernest Albert

Role: Half-back 1900-06 & 1911-15
5'11" 12st.9lbs.
b. Bridport, Dorset August 1879
d. Southampton 14 January 1958

CAREER: Brewery Rovers 1894/Hamworthy St. Michaels 1895/Poole F.C./ SOUTHAMPTON trial Apr 1900, pro. c.s. 1900/Dundee May 1906/SOUTHAMPTON May 1911, player-trainer May 1914, trainer 1919-May 1935.

Debut v Reading (h) 13.10.00

Bert Lee

A raw country lad, Bert Lee's career nearly took another direction when Bristol Rovers sought his signature early in 1900 but Poole's secretary persuaded him that a move to the Dell would be more beneficial. A man with inexhaustible energy, Bert was to play more Southern League games than any other player, albeit over two separate periods, and reached the height of his career in February 1904 when he was awarded his England cap in an international at Wrexham against Wales. By then he had already helped Saints to three championships as well as runners-up spot in the 1902 F.A. Cup Final, and was rewarded with a £125 benefit in November 1905. He moved to Dundee six months later and in his five years north of the border he played in every defensive position including goalkeeper. He became the first Englishman to captain a Scottish cup-winning side when Dundee beat Clyde in the 1910 final and then returned to the Dell in the close season of 1911 to bolster a struggling team. He was given the trainer's job in May 1914 and during the war he served with the 3rd Hampshires and 17th Fusiliers while maintaining an active involvement in army soccer. Keeping an eye open for promising players he noticed Fred Titmuss and was instrumental in bringing the young full-back to the Dell. Resuming his training duties in 1919 he became known as "Gypsy Lee" by the players, some of whom were a little in awe of his tough no-nonsense approach. Bert was awarded a second benefit in December 1923 against the Corinthians and, when he retired in 1935 to become a salesman in his son's radio business, he severed the club's last link with their golden Edwardian era.

Appearances:
SL: 251 app. 13 gls.
FAC: 24 app. 1 gl.
Total: *275 app. 14 gls.*

Lee
Southampton
OGDEN'S
CIGARETTES

Matthew Le Tissier

LEE, Samuel

Role: Midfield 1989-90
5'7" 10st.0lbs.
b. Liverpool 7 February 1959

CAREER: Liverpool app. 1975, pro. Apr 1976/
Queen's Park Rangers Aug 1986/Osasuna
(Spain) July 1987/SOUTHAMPTON Jan 1990/
Bolton Wanderers Oct 1990.

Debut v Chelsea (h) 3.3.90 (as sub)

Sammy Lee came to prominence playing in
Liverpool's midfield and his honours at
Anfield included four Division One
championship medals, a European Cup-
winners' medal and fourteen England caps
won between 1982 and June 1984. A £225,000
transfer to Queen's Park Rangers lasted just a
year before Sammy made a move to Spanish
football for a similar fee. His sojourn with
Osasuna was marred by a knee injury which
eventually led to him being granted a free
transfer to the Saints in January 1990. Sammy
was never given a full game in Southampton
colours but he did at least have the satisfaction
of making a sentimental return to Anfield
when he came on as a substitute in the 5th
round F.A. Cup game in February 1990.
Disenchanted with the lack of regular first
team football Sammy and the club agreed to
cancel their agreement in October 1990 and the
little midfielder moved, on a free transfer, to
Bolton Wanderers.

Appearances:
FL: 0 (2) app. 0 gls.
FAC: 0 (1) app. 0 gls.
Total: *0 (3) app. 0 gls.*

LEWIS, John Richard

Role: Forward 1907-08
5'8" 11st.0lbs.
b. Aberystwyth August 1881
d. Burton upon Trent 12 September 1954

CAREER: Bristol Rovers Sept 1899/
Portsmouth May 1900/Burton United Aug
1901/Bristol Rovers Aug 1904/Brighton &
Hove Albion 1906/SOUTHAMPTON Apr
1907/Croydon Common May 1908/Burton
United Sept 1909.

*Debut v Luton Town (h) 2.9.07 * (scored on debut)*

A Welsh international (versus England in 1906)

John Lewis was a
clever little
forward who
sometimes
found his size a
handicap
against burly
opponents.
Southampton
was his third
south coast
team and he
formed a
useful
partnership
with Fred
Harrison in
his one
season as a
Saint.

PROMINENT FOOTBALLERS.

J. LEWIS,
SOUTHAMPTON.

Appearances:
SL: 24 app. 10 gls.
FAC: 1 app. 0 gls.
Total: *25 app. 10 gls.*

LEWIS, Thomas George

Role: Forward 1946-48
6'0" 12st.0lbs.
b. Troedyrhiw 20 October 1913

CAREER: Troedyrhiw/New Tredegar/
Watford May 1934/SOUTHAMPTON July
1946/Brighton June 1948/Dartford August
1949.

Debut v Swansea (a) 3.10.46

Tom Lewis originally joined Watford as a
seventeen-year-old amateur and remained at
Vicarage Road up until the outbreak of World
War Two. He was a P.T. instructor in the Army
throughout the hostilities and then joined the
Saints for a "four figure fee" in time for the
1946-47 season. A well-built centre-forward,
Tom enjoyed a successful first year at the Dell
with his sporting and never-say-die attitude
endearing him to the fans. His finest moment
was the scoring of a memorable hat-trick
against Bury in the F.A. Cup but
unfortunately, with age catching up on him,
Tom could not reproduce his form in the 1947-
48 campaign and, with Charlie Wayman's
arrival, his days at Southampton were
inevitably numbered.

Tom Lewis

Appearances:
FL: 43 app. 12 gls.
FAC: 2 app. 3 gls.
Total: *45 app. 15 gls.*

LIDDLE, Edward

Role: Centre-half 1905-06
6'0" 12st.6lbs.
b. Sunderland 27 May 1878
d. Redbridge, London October qtr 1968

CAREER: East End Blackwatch/Whitburn/
Seaham White Star/Sunderland/
SOUTHAMPTON Aug 1905/Gainsborough
Trinity Aug 1906/Clapton Orient Aug 1907/
Southend United Oct 1913/Arsenal Sept 1914/
Southend United manager 1919/Queen's Park
Rangers manager 1920/Fulham scout 1922/
manager 1929/West Ham United scout 1931/
Luton Town manager/Chelsea scout/
Portsmouth scout/Brentford scout/Tottenham
Hotspur scout 1953-Jan 1966.

Debut v Northampton Town (h) 27.1.06

Ned Liddle worked in the Wearside shipyards
while playing local soccer and was about to
sign for Lincoln City when he heard
Southampton were prepared to give him a
trial. Taken on to the staff for thirty shillings a
week, he had an excellent physique but his

lack of pace undermined his undoubted
ability. His one outing in the Southern League
came in a memorable 9-1 defeat of
Northampton Town but with the rest of his
season being spent in the reserves a close
season transfer was inevitable. His career
blossomed after leaving the Dell as he became
a first team regular with all his future clubs
and he went on to become a much sought after
manager. Ned eventually retired from the
game aged 88 having spent the previous 13
years scouting for Spurs.

Appearances:
SL: 1 app. 0 gls.
Total: *1 app. 0 gls.*

LINDSAY, Hugh M.

Role: Forward 1960-61
b. Ickenham 23 August 1938

CAREER: St. Clement Danes Grammar
School/London University/Kingstonian/
SOUTHAMPTON am. July 1960/Wealdstone
c.s. 1962/Hampton F.C. 1970-73/Kingstonian
asst. coach/Hampton F.C. asst. manager/
Polytechnic (Southern Amateur League)
manager/Lensbury Veterans.

Debut v Leyton Orient (h) 3.4.61

Hugh Lindsay will, in all probability, be the
last amateur to play for Southampton as such
players in professional football are now
virtually an extinct breed. Capped by England,
Hugh was also a member of the British
Olympic team at Rome in 1960 and returned
from Italy to sign amateur forms at the Dell.
His many commitments prevented him from
being a regular for any Saints team as, being a
member of the Kingstonian club, he was
required to turn out for them on most
Saturdays. Southampton did their best to
persuade Hugh to turn professional but he
always refused the offers because of his
teaching studies. He eventually disappeared
from the League scene but Saints retained his
registration up to and including the 1964-65
season. Today Hugh is a lecturer at Richmond
upon Thames college in Twickenham and
keeps fit by playing for Lensbury Veterans on
a Sunday afternoon.

Appearances:
FL: 2 app. 0 gls.
Total: *2 app. 0 gls.*

LIGHT, William Henry

Role: Goalkeeper
1933-36
5'11" 12st.0lbs.
*b. Woolston,
Southampton 11 June
1913*

CAREER: Woolston
School/Thornycrofts/
Harland & Wolff 1931
/SOUTHAMPTON
Am. May 1932, pro.
Sept 1933/West
Bromwich Albion Mar
1936/Colchester
United 1938, coach and
trainer, retired 1968.

*Debut v Swansea Town
(h) 5.2.34*

Bill Light had the
misfortune to displace
his left knee cap after
only four games in
Southampton's first

Bill Light

team but bounced back to become one of the
country's most promising goalkeepers. His
transfer to West Bromwich Albion for a fee of
£2,000 caused a storm of protest but, with the
Southampton board pleading poverty, his
departure had a ring of inevitability about it.
Strangely, Bill did not take to life at the
Hawthorns - he once let in ten goals in a game
at Stoke - and after thirty appearances joined
Colchester where he lives to this day.

Appearances:
*FL: 45 app. 0 gls.
FAC: 1 app. 0 gls.*
Total: *46 app. 0 gls.*

LITTLEHALES, Alfred

Role: Centre-half 1894-98
*b. Wellington January qtr. 1867
d. Southampton 18 November 1942*

CAREER: Wolverhampton Wanderers/Stoke
Aug 1892/SOUTHAMPTON St. Mary's c.s. 1894.
Debut v Chatham (h) 6.10.94

Alf Littlehales was a member of the Stoke team
which visited the County Ground in 1893 and

doled out an 8-0
footballing lesson to
St. Mary's. Along with
Charlie Baker he was
invited to join the
Saints in time for their
entrance into the
Southern League and
he missed just one
game over the next
two seasons. Clever
on the ball and the
owner of a hard shot,
Alf was given a
benefit match against
Eastleigh in January
1898 and hung up his
boots soon after,
settling down to live
in the Bevois Town
area.

Appearances:
*SL: 51 app. 9 gls.
FAC: 17 app. 3 gls.*
Total: *68 app. 12 gls.*

LITTLER, Oswald

Role: Forward 1929-30
5'9" 11st.7lbs.
*b. Billinge, Manchester
15 February 1907
d. Billinge, Manchester
21 January 1970*

CAREER:
Billinge/Northwich
Victoria/Skelmersdale/Rochdale July 1928/
SOUTHAMPTON Aug 1929/Southport June
1930/Barrow Aug 1931/Winsford c.s. 1933.

Oswald Littler

Debut v Chelsea (h) 21.9.29

A wages clerk at a Lancashire colliery, Oswald
Littler came to the Dell initially on trial in
August 1929 but was given a contract later the
same month. He played twelve consecutive
matches in the autumn of the same year but
then faded from contention and was given a
free transfer in the ensuing close season.

Appearances:
FL: 12 app. 3 gls.
Total: *12 app. 3 gls.*

LIVESEY, Charles Edward

Role: Forward 1958-59
5'10" 11st.8lbs.
b. West Ham, London 6 February 1938

CAREER: Shipman Road School/West Ham Boys/Bata Club/Wolverhampton Wanderers trial/Custom House/SOUTHAMPTON trial Mar 1956, pro. Apr 1956/Chelsea May 1959/Gillingham Aug 1961 /Watford Oct 1962/Northampton Town Aug 1964/Brighton & Hove Albion Sept 1965/Crawley Town June 1969.
Debut v Swindon Town (h) 30.8.58

Charlie Livesey developed into a promising centre-forward in the club's combination side and took his chance in the first team well when replacing the injured Derek Reeves. He certainly had an eye for goal and his sudden rise to fame attracted the attention of several First Division clubs. Eventually Chelsea offered a player (Cliff Huxford) plus cash in a deal that valued Charlie at £20,000 and he moved to Stamford Bridge. He never quite adjusted to First Division football, however, although his goal-scoring record of 17 goals from 39 matches was perfectly acceptable, and he finished his career in the lower divisions.

Charlie Livesey

> **Appearances:**
> *FL: 25 app. 14 gls.*
> *FAC: 3 app. 1 gl.*
> **Total:** *28 app. 15 gls.*

LOASBY, Frank Thomas H.

Role: Full-back 1914-15
5'10' 11st.10lbs.
b. Kettering, Northamptonshire October qtr 1885

CAREER: Desborough/SOUTHAMPTON May 1914
Debut v Exeter City (h) 24.4.15

Arriving from the Midlands, Frank Loasby spent most of the 1914-15 season assisting the club's South Eastern League side and his consistent form finally earned him elevation to the senior team. Unfortunately his big chance coincided with the last fixture played before the outbreak of the Great War and his career was swallowed up in the resulting turmoil.

> **Appearances:**
> *SL: 1 app. 0 gls.*
> **Total:** *1 app. 0 gls.*

Frank Loasby

LOCK, Herbert

Role: Goalkeeper 1907-09 &1922-23
5'8" 12st.0lbs.
b. Southampton 21 January 1887
d. Southampton 16 March 1957

CAREER: St. Mary's Guild/
SOUTHAMPTON c.s. 1907/
Glasgow Rangers c.s. 1909/
Queen's Park Rangers Aug 1921/
SOUTHAMPTON Sept 1922/
Bournemouth & Boscombe
Albion Jan 1924.

Debut v Luton Town (a) 14.9.07

Herbert Lock was a daring and
acrobatic goalkeeper who was
also noted for his uncanny
anticipation when facing penalty kicks. In
the days before a goalkeeper had to stand still
on the goal-line Herbert would pace up and
down rather like a caged lion and eventually
position himself slightly off-centre. The
penalty taker would invariably shoot towards
the larger target and of course Herbert,
anticipating correctly, would make the save.
During the 1908-09 campaign he saved eight
out of twelve penalties awarded against the
Saints. Perhaps a little reckless, Herbert
sustained more than his share of injuries and,
when he met with mishaps on two successive
visits to Watford's Cassio Road, he swore
never to play there again. He kept his vow by
moving to Glasgow Rangers in 1909 and, voted
one season the most popular player in the
Scottish League, he remained at Ibrox until the
outbreak of war when he took work in the
Glasgow shipyards. After a spell with
London's Rangers Herbert returned "home" to
act as cover for Tommy Allen and showed,
when called upon, that he had lost none of his
skill. After a few games at Bournemouth he
settled to live and work in Southampton as a
carpenter and joiner with South Western
Railways.

Appearances:
SL: 55 app. 0 gls.
FL: 11 app. 0 gls.
FAC: 9 app. 0 gls.
Total: 75 app. 0 gls.

H. LOCK

LOGAN, Douglas

Role: Half-back 1955-58
5'8" 10st.5lbs.
b. Aberdeen 30 August 1933
d. Gravesend 1984

CAREER: Aberdeen
Schools/North of Scotland
Schools/Lewis United/
R.A.F. Amport/R.A.F.
Maintenance Command/
SOUTHAMPTON am. Aug
1952, pro. Jan 1954/
Weymouth July 1958/Poole
Town Apr 1960/Tunbridge
Wells June 1960.

*Debut v Norwich City (h)
21.4.56*

A native of Aberdeen, Doug Logan moved to
Hampshire to serve his national service with
the Royal Air Force at Amport, near Andover,
and was recommended to the Saints by Peter
Sillett who was serving at the same airbase. He
progressed to sign professional terms on
completion of his two years in January 1954
and was regarded as a reliable, thoughtful type
of player. Never an automatic first team
choice, he was an excellent asset to have in
reserve.

Appearances:
FL: 21 app. 0 gls.
FAC: 2 app. 0 gls.
Total: 23 app. 0 gls.

LONG, Henry Robert

Role: Forward 1936-38
5'9" 11st.0lbs.
b. Southampton 15 October 1914
d. Southampton 11 May 1989

CAREER: Northam School/Southampton
Schools/Harland & Wolff/Ryde Sports/
SOUTHAMPTON am. Sept 1933, pro. Oct
1934/Newport (I.O.W.) c.s. 1938.

Debut v Doncaster Rovers (h) 7.9.36

Henry Long, a member of the Southampton
Schools' team that reached the final of the
English Schools Shield in 1929, graduated into
the professional ranks in October 1934. He was

Henry Long

a regular in the reserves before moving to the Isle of Wight to play in the Hampshire League with Newport.

Appearances:
FL: 5 app. 0 gls.
Total: *5 app. 0 gls.*

LOVETT, Graham John

Role: Half Back 1971-72
5'10" 10st.4lbs.
b. Sheldon 5 August 1947

CAREER: Cockshutt Hill/Sheldon Heath/Camp Lane Schools/Sheldon/Birmingham & County Schools/West Bromwich Albion am. Feb 1964, pro. Nov 1964 (SOUTHAMPTON-loan-Nov 1971)/Worcester City June 1972/ Solihull Borough/Greaves F.C. retired 1977.

Debut v Leeds United (h) 13.11.71

Graham Lovett arrived at the Dell on loan from West Bromwich Albion in an effort to rebuild what had been a highly promising career. He was

attempting to overcome the effects of two serious motor accidents but, unfortunately, his trial / loan spell at Southampton did not work out and he was forced to retire from the game at the early age of 26.

Appearances;
FL: 3 app. 0 gls.
Total: *3 app. 0 gls.*

❏ **Saints note** - *In 1973 at Birmingham Crown Court Lovett was awarded £14,000 damages against the West Midlands Transport Executive as a result of one of his accidents in Quinton, Birmingham.*

LOWDER, Thomas William

Role: Forward 1949-53
b. Worksop 24 October 1924

CAREER: Crystal Palace am. Sept 1946/ Rotherham United Aug 1947/Boston United c.s. 1949/SOUTHAMPTON Oct 1949/ Southend United May 1953/Boston United June 1954/Skegness 1959-60.

Debut v Chesterfield (a) 26.11.49

Saints' manager, Sid Cann, went to Boston United to watch Bryn Elliott play in a Midland League match and was so impressed with the fast wing play of Tom Lowder that he signed both players. However, Tom never really established himself in the Saints team although he proved to be an able deputy for Ernie Jones and Jack Edwards. While at Southampton, Tom contracted peritonitis which further affected his form and in 1953 he moved to Southend. After just one season he returned to Boston where he took his place in the team which created a sensation by knocking Derby County out of the F.A. Cup in 1955-56. After one final term at Skegness, where he played alongside Charlie Williams, the comedian, Tom returned to Boston to run an off-license & grocery business. He retired in June 1990.

Tom Lowder

Appearances
FL: 39 app. 2 gls.
Total: *39 app. 2 gls.*

LUCKETT, William

Role: Half-back 1927-37
5′ 9″ 11st. 0lbs.
b. *St. Helens, Lancashire 6 September 1903*
d. *Shirley, Southampton 5 July 1985*

CAREER: Skelmersdale/Liverpool trial/
SOUTHAMPTON Aug 1927/Cowes c.s. 1937/
SOUTHAMPTON Reserve & 'A' team trainer
1946-53/O.S.O. F.C. manager 1953/Andover
manager Sept 1954/Southampton Post Office
Jan 1955/Ordnance Survey 'A' 1964.

Debut v Notts County (h) 21.2.28
* *(scored on debut)*

Bill Luckett had a spectacular Southampton
debut scoring two goals from the left-wing
position. He had only been at the club five
months, having arrived at the age of 19 from
the north-western side Skelmersdale and,
while he was not a particularly skilful player,
he had a voracious appetite for work and
would chase around the pitch like a terrier.
Over his decade in the red and white stripes
Bill made the left-half position his own and,
when an ankle injury finally ended his playing
career, his love of the game led to him into a
variety of coaching appointments. During the
war he was a Physical Training Instructor at
R.A.F. Ford and was instrumental in
persuading Eric Day to join the Dell staff. He
also found time to become the landlord of the
Salisbury Arms at Christchurch and later, after
the war, took over the Juniper Berry in
Southampton. In 1964 aged 61, Bill was still
playing in Sunday League soccer for the
Ordnance Survey.

Appearances:
FL: 211 app. 10 gls.
FAC: 8 app. 0 gls.
Total: *219 app. 10 gls.*

Bill Luckett

McALPINE, James Walker

Role: Half-back 1911-15
5'7" 11st.8lbs.
b. Coatbridge, Scotland 5 February 1887

CAREER: Strathclyde Juniors/Craigneuk
Heatherbell 1907/Dalziel Rovers 1908/Vale of
Clyde 1909/Strathclyde Juniors
1910/SOUTHAMPTON May 1911/(Harland
and Wolff during World War One)/Millwall
Mar 1919/Gillingham July 1921.

Debut v Swindon Town (a) 23.9.11

Jim McAlpine was one of the club's best
Southern League signings for, arriving in 1911,
he was a virtual ever-present up until the
suspension of football four years later. Rather
small for a left-half he made up for his lack of
stature with a determined and forceful
temperament that made him a firm favourite
with the Saints crowd. Although he remained
on Saints books throughout the hostilities he
was involved in war work with Harland and
Wolff and turned out for the works eleven,
often against the Saints. Moving to Millwall in
1919, Jim represented the Southern League
versus the Irish League in the October and
then, the following
year, was a member
in the Lions' first
ever League side.

Appearances:
SL: 132 app. 2 gls.
FAC: 8 app. 0 gls.
Total: *140 app. 2 gls.*

McCALL, William

Role: Forward 1922-23
5'9" 11st.0lbs.
b. Maxwelltown circa 1898

CAREER: Queen of the South Wanderers/
Blackburn Rovers Dec 1920/Wolverhampton
Wanderers June 1922/SOUTHAMPTON Jan
1923/Queen of the South Sept 1925.

Debut v Coventry City (h) 10.2.23
* (scored on debut)

Bill McCall came to the Dell in an exchange
deal that saw George Getgood move to Wolves
in January 1923. Reputedly quick he started
auspiciously by scoring on his debut from the
left-wing position but, after losing his place to
Len Andrews, grew steadily disillusioned. He
left the Dell in May 1923 after refusing a
retaining fee. He was transfer-listed at £500
although, by the time he eventually found
another club, that fee had been reduced to
£250.

Appearances:
FL: 8 app. 2 gls.
Total: *8 app. 2 gls.*

McCALLIOG, James

Role: Midfield 1974-77
5'9" 10st.5lbs.
b. Glasgow 23 September 1946

CAREER: Glasgow Schools/Leeds United am
May-Sept 1963/Chelsea Sept 1963/Sheffield
Wednesday Oct 1965/Wolverhampton
Wanderers Aug 1969/Manchester United Mar
1974/SOUTHAMPTON Feb 1975/Chicago
Sting summer 1977/Norwegian soccer
1977/1978 season/Lincoln City player-coach
Sept 1978/Runcorn player-manager c.s.
1979/Halifax Town caretaker-manager Mar
1990, permanent May 1990.

Jim McAlpine

Wembley '76: Jim McCalliog drives a shot past Manchester United's Martin Buchan and Lou Macari.

Debut v Oldham Athletic (a) 15.2.75

Once the most expensive teenager (£37,500) in British football, Jim McCalliog was an experienced midfield player who had played five times for Scotland. He had tremendous vision and will be fondly remembered not only for supplying the through ball for Bobby Stokes to hit the winner in the 1976 F.A. Cup Final but also for the vital goals he scored at Villa and Bradford in the preceding rounds. In 1990 Jim was combining the job of publican with that of community officer in North Yorkshire when Halifax Town parted company with their manager, Bill Ayre, and he was asked to step into the breach.

Appearances:
FL: 70 (2) app. 8 gls.
FAC: 10 app. 3 gls.
LC: 2 app. 0 gls.
Eur: 4 app. 1 gl.
Total: *86 (2) app. 12 gls.*

McCARTHY, Robert Zepp

Role: Full-back 1967-75
5'10" 10st.11lbs.
b. Lyndhurst 21 November 1948

CAREER: Abbotswood Primary/Testwood & Southampton Schools/SOUTHAMPTON am. Oct 1963, pro. Nov 1965/Poole Town July 1975/Cowes Aug 1976/Andover June 1977.

Debut v Fulham (a) 4.5.68

Bob McCarthy came through the club's 'A' and 'B' sides to lead the youth team to the semi-final of the F.A. Youth Cup in 1967. His debut took place at the tail-end of the 1967-68 season but he had to wait another four years, playing in the reserves, until he was given a lengthy spell in the side. Often called into the team when the defence was struggling, Bob had a topsy-turvy career although he possessed a strong tackle and no small amount of enthusiasm. In November 1990 Bob was helping Southampton F.C.'s School of Excellence in a coaching capacity.

Appearances:
FL: 112 app. 2 gls.
FAC: 7 app. 0 gls.
LC: 11 app. 0 gls.
Total: *130 app. 2 gls.*

Bob McCarthy

McCARTNEY, Michael

Role: Full-back 1980-81
5'7" 10st.12lbs.
b. Edinburgh 28 September 1954

CAREER: Scotland
Schools/West Bromwich
Albion app July 1970, pro Dec
1971/Carlisle United May
1973/SOUTHAMPTON July
1980/Plymouth Argyle Aug
1981/Carlisle United Mar
1983/Gretna manager 1988.

Mike McCartney

Debut v Manchester City (h) 16.8.80

A former Scottish Schoolboy international,
Mike made his Southampton debut almost
unnoticed as it coincided with that of Kevin
Keegan's. Rated as one of the best left-backs in
the lower divisions, Mike struggled to adapt
satisfactorily to the top echelons and after one
season at the Dell moved to Plymouth Argyle.
After returning to Carlisle, Mike later crossed
the border to his native Scotland and in
December 1990 was managing Gretna.

Appearances:
FL: 22 app. 1 gl.
LC: 2 app. 0 gls.
Total: *24 app. 1 gl.*

McDONALD, Alexander

Role: Forward 1901-02
5'10" 11st.8lbs.
b. Greenock 12 April 1878

CAREER: Jarrow/Everton Feb
1900/SOUTHAMPTON May
1901/West Ham United Dec
1901/Portsmouth Mar 1902/
Wellingborough 1903/Luton
Town 1905/Croydon Common
1907/Luton Town 1910.

Debut v New Brompton (h) 7.9.01

A first rate marksman, Alex McDonald had
scored one of the Everton goals that eliminated
Saints from the 1901 F.A. Cup competition
and, joining Southampton several months
later, made an explosive start by scoring five
goals in five games. At that time the club had a
wealth of excellent forwards on their books
and despite this sensational start Alex was
thrust into the background which did not suit
his ambitious temperament. In December he
asked for and was granted a move.

Appearances:
SL: 5 app. 5 gls.
Total: *5 app. 5 gls.*

Croydon Common 1907-08 with Alex McDonald seated second from the right on the third row (from the rear). Also in the photo is stalwart Saint Sammy Meston (second from left in second row from the back).

MacDONALD, Elias

Role: Forward 1923-24
5'8" 11st. 0lbs.
b. Beswick, Manchester 11 April 1898
d. Rochester 4 April 1978

CAREER: Manchester Schools/Ancoats Lads Club/Derby County Feb 1920/Caerau 1920/ Derby County Aug 1921/Burton All Saints 1921/SOUTHAMPTON May 1923/Southend United June 1924/Southport May 1925/ Doncaster Rovers June 1926/Barrow Dec 1926 /Chorley Sept 1929/Ulverston Town Sept 1930 /Chorley.

Debut v Barnsley (h) 19.1.24

A former worker for Rolls-Royce, Elias MacDonald was described by the Sports Echo as a"fine winger" at the time of his move to the town, but while he was an ever-present in the remaining games of the 1923-24 season he failed to score a goal. Transfer-listed at £250 in the May he subsequently chose to move to Southend with the fee eventually waived.

    Appearances:
FL: 18 app. 0 gls.
Total: *18 app. 0 gls.*

McDONALD, John Christopher

Role: Forward 1952-53
5'9" 12st.0lbs.
b. Maltby 27 August 1921

CAREER: Wolverhampton Wanderers am May 1937, pro. Sept 1938/Bournemouth May 1939/(Bristol City, Cardiff City, Chelsea, Manchester United, Wolverhampton Wanderers, West Bromwich Albion, York City, SOUTHAMPTON, Bournemouth during World War Two)/Fulham June 1948/ SOUTHAMPTON Aug 1952/Southend United June 1953/Weymouth July 1955/Poole Town August 1957.

Debut v West Ham United (a) 23.8.52

Jack McDonald was a goalscoring left-winger who, having made his name at Dean Court immediately after the war, had joined Fulham for a fee of £12,000 and helped them to the Second Division Championship in 1949. Joining the Saints three years later, he started well, scoring four goals in eight games but, with a sudden loss of form, found himself relegated to reserve-team soccer. Jack later returned to the side at centre-forward but

Elias MacDonald

Jack McDonald

without any success and, after being transfer-listed, moved to Southend for £800. He retired a year later from league soccer to concentrate on his sports teacher's job in Bournemouth but was seen again at the Dell when Weymouth visited in an F.A. Cup match in December 1956. Today Jack lives in Elgin, Scotland.

Appearances:
FL: 16 app. 4 gls.
FAC: 0 app. 0 gls.
Total: *16 app. 4 gls.*

MacDOUGALL, Edward John

Role: Forward 1976-79
5'10"11st.11lbs.
b. Inverness 8 January 1947

CAREER: I.C.I. Recs (Widnes)/Liverpool am 1964, pro. Jan 1966/York City July 1967/ Bournemouth July 1969/Manchester United Sept 1972/West Ham United Mar 1973/ Norwich City Dec 1973/South African soccer June-July 1975/SOUTHAMPTON Sept 1976/ AFC Bournemouth Nov 1978/Detroit Express May 1979/Blackpool player-coach & asst. manager Feb-Oct 1980/Salisbury Aug 1981/ Poole Town Dec 1981/Totton January 1982/ Gosport Borough 1982/Athena (Perth, Australia) summer 1982/Totton Oct-Dec 1982/ Andover coach Oct-Dec 1983.

Debut v Nottingham Forest (h) 18.9.76

Ted MacDougall (right) celebrates a goal for the Saints with Peter Osgood.

A proven and prolific goalscorer, Ted MacDougall was the idol of Dean Court where he became the scourge of Third Division defences and once scored nine goals in an F.A. Cup match versus Margate. An obvious target for bigger clubs, Ted's £200,000 move to Old Trafford broke the Third Division transfer record and playing in the top flight he was capped on seven occasions for Scotland. In 1976 Lawrie McMenemy brought him to the Dell for £50,000 thus re-kindling, for the fourth time, a partnership with Phil Boyer that had originated at York and flourished at Dean Court and Carrow Road. Ted was still a deadly marksman in and around the six yard box and, with Phil Boyer doing the fetching and carrying, he scored an impressive 23 goals from 36 games in his first season. A sensitive soul, Ted's talents always needed careful nurturing from the able McMenemy but with Saints now back in the First Division and time no longer on his side he crossed the New Forest to once more become a crowd favourite at Dean Court. In 1991 Ted was believed to be living in Vancouver, Canada.

Appearances:
FL: 86 app. 42 gls.
FAC: 10 app. 3 gls.
LC: 5 app. 2 gls.
Eur: 2 app. 1 gl.
Total: *103 app. 48 gls.*

McGARRITY, Thomas Welsh

Role: Forward 1952-53
b. Scotstown 24 November 1922

CAREER: Arthurlie (nr. Paisley)/Greenock Morton 1943/SOUTHAMPTON Nov 1952/ Headington United August 1953/Banbury Spencer June 1954.

*Debut v Hull City (h) 29.11.52 * (scored on debut)*

Considering Tom McGarrity made only five appearances and cost the club £4,500 his signing could, with hindsight, be regarded as a costly mistake. Tom scored on his debut but quickly fell from favour and when the 1953-54 season came round he refused to sign on owing to a row about his benefit. The dispute was resolved when Tom decided to retire from soccer. After leaving the Saints he briefly become a physiotherapist at Maidenhead, but soon moved to Oxford where he worked at a succession of local hospitals. He played for

Tom McGarrity

Headington United and then Banbury Spencer and also acted as part-time physio for Oxford United up until the late 1980's.

Appearances:
FL: 5 app. 1 gl.
Total: *5 app. 1 gl.*

McGHEE, George Dilworth

Role: Forward 1908-09
b. Southwell, Notts July qtr. 1883
d. Weston, Notts 9 October 1944

CAREER: Bitterne Guild/SOUTHAMPTON 1908/Bitterne Guild 1909/Vampires/Pirates/Southampton Cambridge 1911.

Debut v Reading (h) 5.12.08

G. D. McGhee was a schoolteacher who moved from Ipswich Municipal Secondary School to King Edward's in Southampton in time for the Christmas term of 1907. Very much an all-round sportsman McGhee quickly made a name for himself in local circles and the school magazine of June 1908 eulogised: "Our success is due chiefly to the very excellent form shown by Mr. McGhee, both with the cricket bat and football. Never has a school had so brilliant a sportsman and popular a master as Mr. McGhee. In football last season he often won games outright by his individual prowess . . ."

It seems Southampton were also alerted to Mr. McGhee's talents and after being given a few games in the reserves he was blooded, in the first team, at centre-forward for a game against Reading in December 1908. A couple of months later he was given another chance in a match at Millwall but sustained an injury which prevented him from ever featuring in the Saints' line-up again. McGhee was also a member of a local amateur team called the Pirates and in the summer of 1909 he led a tour to Europe along with former King Edward's pupil and Saints player, Alec Campbell. McGhee continued teaching until the summer of 1915 when, after receiving permission from the school governors, he enlisted. He was expected to "return shortly" according to the school magazine but this was not to be and his fate thereafter remains unclear.

Appearances:
SL: 2 app. 0 gls.
Total: *2 app. 0 gls.*

McGIBBON, Charles Edward

Role: Forward 1909-1910
6'0" 12st.7lbs.
b. Portsea April qtr. 1880
d. Netley 2nd May 1954

CAREER: Royal Artillery (Portsmouth)/Arsenal Aug 1905/Eltham 1906/New Brompton 1907/Crystal Palace 1908/SOUTHAMPTON May 1909/Arsenal Mar 1910/Leyton Aug 1910/Reading c.s. 1911/SOUTHAMPTON Nov 1911.

Debut v Plymouth (h) 1.9.09

A sergeant in the Royal Artillery based at the Personal Ordnance College, Woolwich, Charlie McGibbon first attracted the attention of the Saints in 1908 when he scored a hat-trick

Charlie McGibbon

at the Dell while playing for Crystal Palace. An amateur throughout his career, Charlie was physically well-suited for the role of centre-forward possessing not only a powerful shot but influential leadership qualities. 19 goals in 28 League games during the 1909-10 season were ample proof of his opportunism in front of goal and it was a blow to the Saints' faithful when his army duties took him back to Woolwich. He immediately found a place in a struggling Arsenal team and his three goals in four games saved the Gunners from relegation. At the beginning of the 1910-11 season Charlie moved on to join Leyton where he teamed up with Charlie Buchan. He returned to Southampton in November 1911 without ever winning a first team place. After surviving the war he found employment as Chief Clerk in the Statistical Offices at Netley Hospital and later worked at Supermarine in Woolston.

Appearances:
FL: 28 app. 19 gls.
FAC: 2 app. 1 gl.
Total: *30 app. 20 gls.*

❑ **Saints note** - *Charlie's son Doug also played for the Saints and, strangely, both men made their debuts against the same club - Plymouth. Charlie played one game for Hampshire County cricket Club in 1919, scored 0 & 1 not out and took 0 wickets for 10 runs.*

McGIBBON, Douglas

Role: Forward 1938-1947
5'10" 11st.7lbs.
b. Netley 24 February 1919

CAREER: Air Service Training (Hamble)/SOUTHAMPTON am. Aug 1938, pro. Dec 1938/Fulham Jan 1947/Bournemouth Sept 1948 /Lovells Athletic Aug 51/Air Service Training (Hamble) manager Aug 1955.

Debut v Plymouth (a) 6.5.39

Son of Charles McGibbon, the Saints' forward of 1909-10, Douglas followed in his father's footsteps as a goal-getter. Asking

Tom Parker for a trial during a charity cricket game, Douglas was given a game with the 'A' team versus Lymington during which he scored a hat-trick. He made his debut in the last game played before the war, and the suspension of League football. Being a skilled aircraft mechanic Doug moved to the Swindon area where he undertook aircraft work for the war effort. In 1944 he played for Swindon Railway and Swindon Town who approached Southampton with a view to signing him on a full-time basis. The Saints' directors refused to release Doug and he returned to the south coast in 1945. He played in the opening game of the 1946-47 season at home to Swansea, thereby waiting seven years between his away and home debut! A hat-trick in that opening game was followed by a further six goals in his next eleven appearances and it was somewhat of a surprise when Bill Dodgin sold him to Fulham for a fee of £4,250. He became only the

Doug McGibbon

second Fulham player to score a hat-trick on his debut when Plymouth were the unlucky victims. A transfer to Bournemouth in September 1948 was followed three years later by a move to Welsh non-league club Lovells Athletic, and there Doug's footballing days came to an abrupt end when he smashed his head against a cross bar bursting a blood vessel. After a spell in hospital he returned to Hamble to work as an aircraft engineer and then as a sports officer. A keen gardener he now lives in Isleworth taking more than a passing interest in the fortunes of the Saints and periodically visiting Craven Cottage.

Appearances:
FL: 13 app. 9 gls.
FAC: 4 app. 2 gls.
Total: *17 app. 11 gls.*

❏ **Saints note** - *During the 1945-46 wartime season Saints beat Chelsea 7-0 at the Dell with Doug scoring no fewer than six times. His third goal was timed by the referee at an incredible four and three fifths seconds after the start of the second half. Doug kicked off to Ted Bates and then sprinted towards the Chelsea goal. Bates then passed to Bill Stroud who hit an immediate long ball to Doug which was firmly volleyed into the back of the net. He recalls that Bill Dodgin was frequently planning such moves and remembers the referee actually showing him his stopwatch as he ran back to the centre-circle. Doug also recalls that the Dell pitch had been shortened slightly due to bomb damage at the Milton Road end, a fact which makes the time taken for the goal a little more plausible.*

McGOWAN, James

Role: Half-back 1949-58
5'7" 10st.10lbs.
b. Cambuslang 12 January 1924
d. Southampton 28 March 1984

CAREER: Fallin Youth club/Armadale Thistle/Celtic 1942/Clyde 1944/Dumbarton 1945/Grimsby Town July 1946/SOUTHAMPTON Mar 1950/Salisbury City Aug 1958.

*Debut v Cardiff City (h) 4.3.50 * (scored on debut)*

Having won Scottish Schoolboy honours in 1938, Jimmy McGowan signed for Celtic during the war and then experienced life in the English First Division with Grimsby. Sid Cann was delighted to capture him for a fee of £8,000 and plunged him straight away into the first team when Jimmy responded with a goal in the 3-1 victory over Cardiff. Showing typical Scottish craft, he was a forager and provider who served the club loyally for nine years although one whole season was lost due to a lung infection. Jimmy later became the licensee at the Drummond Arms in Portswood, Southampton.

Appearances:
FL: 78 app. 9 gls.
FAC: 4 app. 0 gls.
Total: *82 app. 9 gls.*

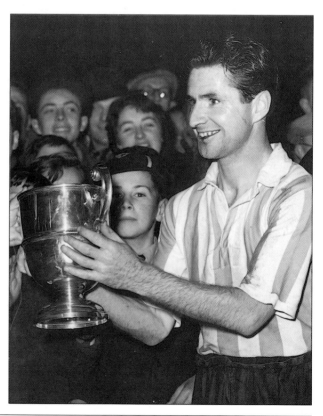

Jimmy McGowan

John McGrath

McGRATH, John Thomas

Role: Centre Half 1967-74
6'0" 12st.7lbs.
b. Manchester 23 August 1938

CAREER: Bolton Wanderers am June 1953/ Miles Plating Swifts/Bury Oct 1955/Newcastle United Feb 1961/SOUTHAMPTON Feb 1968 (Brighton-loan-Dec 1972)/SOUTHAMPTON youth team coach Sept 1973, reserve team coach Sept 1978/Port Vale manager Dec 1979/ Chester City manager 1984/Preston North End manager June 1986, resigned Feb 1990/Halifax Town manager Oct 1991.

Debut v Everton (h) 26.2.68

A £30,000 signing just before the transfer deadline of 1968, John McGrath's acquisition proved to be very astute as the no-nonsense centre-half added grit, determination and presence to a shell-shocked Saints defence. Built like a barn door but fortunately, more mobile, 'Big Jake' developed a fearsome reputation and although he could be alarmingly tough into the tackle he was rarely malicious. He was equally combative in the air and formed the foundation around which Ted Bates constructed most of the team's defensive formations. A "gentle giant" off the pitch, John later won praise for his youth team coaching at the Dell and went on to guide first Port Vale, and then Preston, out of the Fourth Division.

Appearances:
FL: 167 (1) app. 1 gl.
FAC: 8 app. 1 gl.
LC: 13 app. 0 gls.
Eur: 6 app. 0 gls.
Total: *194 (1) app. 2 gls.*

McGRATH, Martin L.

Role: Midfield 1979-80
5'10" 11st.11lbs.
b. Hendon, London 15 October 1960

CAREER: St. Mary's College/ SOUTHAMPTON app. Aug 1977, pro. Oct 1978/Bournemouth June 1980/Oxford City Mar 1981.

Debut v Leeds United (as sub) (a) 8.3.80

England Schoolboy international Martin McGrath's brief taste of first team football came at Elland Road when he replaced Trevor

Hebberd as a second-half substitute. After seventeen games for the Cherries he dropped into non-league football and then, giving up soccer altogether, he found employment in a London casino.

Appearances:
FL: 0 (1) app. 0 gls.
Total: 0 (1) app. 0 gls.

McGUIGAN, John Joseph

Role: Forward 1963-65
5'7" 10st.4lbs.
b. Motherwell 29 October 1932

CAREER: Muirkirk Juniors/Bo'ness Juniors/ St. Mirren Nov 1953/Southend United May 1955/Newcastle United June 1958/Scunthorpe United Jan 1962/SOUTHAMPTON Aug 1963/ Swansea Town Mar 1965.

Debut v Swansea Town (h) 21.9.63
* *(scored on debut)*

A £10,000 addition to the Southampton forward line, John McGuigan scored twice on his debut and was viewed as a tricky, versatile inside-forward who was, unfortunately, the wrong side of thirty. All his goals for the club came in the 1963-64 campaign and when he failed to find the net in any of his 12 games in the subsequent season, Saints accepted a £6,500 bid from Swansea. A year later John had returned to Southampton and was licensee of the Swan Hotel in Portsmouth Road, Woolston. After three years in the pub trade, John decided to go back to Scotland and sent off applications in an attempt to secure a job back in football. After hearing nothing, he turned his back on the game completely and to this day has not been inside

John McGuigan

a football ground in twenty years. In August 1991 John was working in the tool-room of Glagow's Rolls-Royce plant at Hillington.

Appearances:
FL: 33 app. 8 gls.
FAC: 1 app. 0 gls.
LC: 1 app. 0 gls.
Total: 35 app. 8 gls.

❏ **Saints Note** - *John's father had been a pre-war player with Motherwell.*

McILWARNE, John

Role: Centre-half
1930-32, 1933-37
5'9" 12st.4lbs.
b. Irvine 12 June 1904
d. Grimsby 24 April 1980

CAREER: Falkirk/ Portsmouth Feb 1928/ SOUTHAMPTON June 1930/Llanelli c.s. 1932/ SOUTHAMPTON Aug 1933, asst. manager-coach c.s. 1936/Grimsby Town asst. manager July 1937, retired 1948.

Debut v Preston North End (a) 30.8.30

Portsmouth splashed out £4,500 to introduce Johnny McIlwarne to English football and he went some way to repaying some of Pompey's record outlay when he captained them during their F.A. Cup run to Wembley in 1929. Brought to the Dell for £2,650 - another club record - he had the misfortune to suffer an injury in the first month of the 1930-31 season and, strangely, could only get back into the side in the centre-forward position. An unhappy 1931-32 term spent in and out of the team ended in a refusal to sign a new contract and Johnny found his name circulated to other clubs on offer for £2,500. With no takers and the dispute unsettled he could only play for a non-league club and so he turned out for Llanelli, helping them to win the Welsh League. With the restoration of diplomatic relations he returned to the Dell in 1933 but found the year spent in Wales had not sharpened his game. Gradually his confidence improved and in November 1935 Johnny captained the team in their Golden Jubilee match against Tottenham Hotspur. In the summer of 1936, following the reorganisation of the Saints management, he was appointed assistant manager as well as undertaking the duties of coach and team captain. This new role proved far too much and in July 1937 he became the assistant manager at Grimsby, a post he held for eleven years. He maintained a cordial relationship with the Saints and whenever the team played at Blundell Park Johnny would always take time to visit the Saints' dressing room. In 1948 he opened up a private masseur practice in Cleethorpes.

Appearances:
FL: 117 app. 18 gls.
FAC: 4 app. 0 gls.
Total: *121 app. 18 gls.*

McKAY, Donald

Role: Full-back 1896-97
b. Scotland

CAREER: Woolston Works/SOUTHAMPTON St. Mary's 1896.

Debut v Chatham (h) 19.9.96

One of many Scotsmen who migrated to Southampton looking for work in the Woolston shipyards, Don McKay had been a prominent member of the works team for several years. His stay at the Antelope lasted just one year and although he started as the regular right-back in the first team he lost his place to Sammy Meston and finished the season in the reserves.

Appearances:
SL: 8 app. 0 gls.
FAC: 1 app. 0 gls.
Total: *9 app. 0 gls.*

McKEER, Charles Walter

Role: Half-back 1909-11
b. Farnham January qtr 1883
d. Aldershot 2 March 1957

CAREER: SOUTHAMPTON am 1904/Royal Army Medical Corps/SOUTHAMPTON Apr 1910.

Debut v Reading (h) 30.4.10

Originally signed on amateur terms in 1904, McKeer subsequently joined the R.A.M.C. to play in their soccer eleven in the Hampshire League. He rejoined Saints on the completion of his term of service but injuries and a couple of weak performances led to him being freed in the close season of 1911.

Appearances:
SL: 4 app. 0 gls.
Total: *4 app. 0 gls.*

McKENZIE, James R.

Role: Forward 1898-99
5'6" 10st.10lbs.
b. Glasgow November 1877

CAREER: Gatmore/Possil Park/East Stirlingshire/Cowlairs/Burton Swifts Sept 1896/Clyde 1897/SOUTHAMPTON c.s. 1898.

Debut v Brighton United (h) 3.9.1898

An upholsterer by trade Jim McKenzie had played most of his early soccer as an amateur in Glasgow before a successful season in England with Burton Swifts. A lightweight, diminutive winger Jim played in the first-ever game at the Dell but after only five further outings he grew homesick and moved back to Scotland.

Appearances:
SL: 6 app. 3 gls.
Total: *6 app. 3 gls.*

MACKIE, James

Role: Forward 1927-31
5'9" 12st.4lbs.
b. Motherwell 1 January 1894
d. Chichester 5 January 1959

CAREER:
Motherwell/
Blantyre Celtic/
Portsmouth May
1920/
SOUTHAMPTON
Mar 1928.

*Debut v South
Shields (a) 17.3.28*

Jerry Mackie

Signed from Portsmouth Jerry Mackie was seen as Bill Rawlings' replacement and, scoring a hat-trick on his home debut, quickly enhanced his popularity with the paying public. Shrewdly creating chance after chance for Willie Haines, the two ex-Pompey forwards enjoyed a 'swansong' couple of seasons at the Dell. Jerry reached a personal milestone in his career on March 14th 1931 when he scored his one hundredth league goal in a match against Bristol City and, soon after, he retired to become licensee at the Regents Park Hotel in Shirley, Southampton, Remaining a publican for twenty-four years he spent the last few years of his life residing in Bognor Regis.

Appearances:
FL: 81 app. 24 gls.
FAC: 3 app. 0 gls.
Total: *84 app. 24 gls.*

McKIE, James

Role: Full-back 1896-97
b. Scotland

CAREER: 15th Company Royal Artillery/ Freemantle/SOUTHAMPTON 1896/ Chatham c.s. 1897/Dartford Aug 1899

Debut v Chatham (h) 19.9.96

A former soldier and Hampshire County player James McKie was one of the large number of Scotsmen to appear in the cherry stripes during the late nineties. Tough and rugged but never a first team regular he made as many cup appearances as league games and then departed for Kent after just one season.

Appearances:
SL: 6 app. 0 gls.
FAC: 6 app. 0 gls.
Total: *12 app. 0 gls.*

MacLAREN, David

Role: Goalkeepr 1966-67
6'1" 13st.11lbs.
b. Auchterader, Scotland 12 June 1934

CAREER: Comrie Athletic 1948/St Johnstone Y.M. 1950/R.A.F. 1952/Hong Kong 1953/ Malaya

1954/Penang State 1954/Chelsea am 1955/ Dundee Feb 1956/Leicester City Jan 1957/ Plymouth Argyle May 1960/ Wolverhampton Wanderers Jan 1965/ SOUTHAMPTON Sept 1966/Worcester City July 1967/Malaysian National Team Coach 1972/Hakoah (N.S.W. Australia) manager-coach 1972.

Debut v West Ham United (a) 24.9.66

The much-quoted fact that Dave MacLaren was the man who once conceded nine goals while playing in goal for Wolves against Saints only to join the Southampton playing staff within a year, obscures a lively and interesting career. Dave became a radar fitter with the R.A.F. and, serving in the Far East, played for the Malayan and Hong Kong national teams. His spectacular form won him the Scotsman of the Year award and prompted Portsmouth, Leeds, Newcastle and Chelsea to contact him to offer him terms. Eventually signing for Dundee in 1956 he later came to the attention of Saints fans on Boxing Day 1964 when, in goal for Plymouth, he had five goals knocked past him. Within a month he had signed for Wolves and when in September 1966, Saints

Dave MacLaren

lost goalkeeper Campbell Forsyth, Ted Bates, ignoring Dave's previous unhappy Dell experiences, signed him for £5,000. Never seen as a long term investment, Dave and the rest of the defence struggled through the club's inaugural Division One season and when Ted Bates decided to bring Eric Martin to the club in March 1967 Dave's day's were numbered. Returning to the Orient, Dave steered the Malaysian national team to the finals of the Munich Olympic games in 1972 and then twice guided Hakoah to the New South Wales Federation Championship in Australia. He was still living in Australia in 1991.

Appearances:
FL: 22 app. 0 gls
FAC: 2 app. 0 gls.
LC: 2 app. 0 gls.
Total: *26 app. 0 gls.*

❑ **Saints note** - *Dave MacLaren had three brothers who became professional goalkeepers - Jimmy with Chester and Carlisle, Roy with St. Johnstone, Bury and Sheffield Wednesday and Monty who was a reserve with Liverpool.*

McLAUGHLIN, Robert

Role: Half-back 1953-59
5'6" 10st.7 lbs.
b. Belfast 6 December 1925

CAREER: St Martins. Belfast/Distillery/ Wrexham Jan 1950/Cardiff City May 1950/ SOUTHAMPTON Oct 1953/Yeovil Town July 1959/ Salisbury June 1963.

Debut v Torquay United (h) 24.10.53

Having joined Cardiff for £5,000 Bobby McLaughlin had a brief taste of First Division football before becoming part of Southampton's Third Division team. Small but tenacious, he became very popular with the players and fans alike and

served the club admirably over a six-year period. Once Bobby finished playing he returned to the Southampton area to take on a job with Union Castle in the Docks and to this day is only too happy to spend his spare time coaching youth teams.

Appearances:
FL: 169 app. 5 gls.
FAC: 8 app. 0 gls.
Total: *177 app. 5 gls.*

McLEAN, Duncan

Role: Forward 1898-99
5'7" 10st.2lbs.
b. Govan 30 June 1874

CAREER: Summerton/Moor Park/Elderpark Rangers/Partick Thistle/Cowes/ SOUTHAMPTON 1899/Derby County May 1900/Cowes 1902.

Debut v Bristol City (h) 11.3.1899

An engineer employed in the Cowes shipyards, Duncan McLean arrived at the Dell with the approval of Saints director, George Thomas, who had noted the Scot whilst watching him play for Cowes. He made a vital contribution to the run-in of the 1898-99 season when, playing alongside Roddy McLeod, he helped the team retain the Southern League Championship. Extremely versatile, he played in four different positions in his eight outings but, with the arrival of several internationals to the Dell, took a transfer to Derby. Duncan failed to appear in the Rams' senior side and moved back to

R. McLAUGHLIN *(Southampton)*

NEWS CHRONICLE POCKET PORTRAIT

Scotland where he reverted to his earlier trade. He was soon back on the Isle of Wight, assisting the Cowes XI and in 1906 won a County Cup winners' medal. His date of death is unknown but he was last heard of in Southampton in 1952.

Appearances:
SL: 8 app. 3 gls.
Total: *8 app. 3 gls.*

McLEAN, Robert

Role: Half-back 1906-07
5'9" 12st.0lbs.
b. Alexandria, Scotland 26 April 1884

CAREER: Rutherglencairn/Vale of Leven/ Millwall Aug 1904/Newcastle United June 1905/SOUTHAMPTON c.s. 1906.

Debut v Luton Town (a) 15.9.06

Robert McLean found his progress hampered at Newcastle and, being way down the selection pecking order, was grateful for a move to Southampton. A bustling, vigorous type he would have made an ideal addition to the present day Wimbledon squad as he was a great believer in launching the ball to land as near to the opposing goal as quickly as possible. The form of Gray and Robertson meant that, after only a year at the Dell, he departed northwards.

Appearances:
SL: 4 app. 0 gls.
Total: *4 app. 0 gls.*

MacLEOD, Alistair H. M.

Role: Forward 1973-74
5'10" 11st 9lbs
b. Glasgow 1 January 1951

CAREER: Renfrew Juniors/St Mirren/ SOUTHAMPTON May 1973 (Huddersfield Town-loan-Oct 1974)/Hibernian Dec 1974.

Debut v Leeds United (a) 12.1.74

A prolific goalscorer for St Mirren in the 1972-73 season, Ally MacLeod was signed for £25,000 but never reproduced his flair for finding the net whilst at

the Dell. Hibernian rescued his career when they signed him for £20,000 and back in Scotland his career once more flourished.

Appearances:
FL: 2 (1) app. 0 gls.
LC: 1 (1) app. 0 gls.
Total: *3 (2) app. 0 gls.*

McLEOD, Roderick

Role: Forward 1898-00
b. Kilsyth February 1872
d. Lambeth December 1931

CAREER: Kilsyth School/Westburn/Partick Thistle/West Bromwich Albion Jan 1891/ Leicester Fosse Aug 1897/Brighton United May 1898/SOUTHAMPTON April 1899/ Brentford Aug 1900.

Debut v Chatham (a) 22.4.1899

A veteran of two F.A. Cup Finals (1892 &1895) when with West Bromwich, Roddy McLeod was a splendid forward who had the ability to turn a game by using his deft footwork. Baby-faced and small in stature, his finest moments for Southampton came in the 1899-1900 run-up to the final when he scored three goals in two games against Newcastle United and West Bromwich Albion. Dropped for the semi-final in preference to the out-of-touch Jack Farrell, Roddy left the club for Brentford in an understandable fit of pique and, with the Bees, won a Southern League Second Division title in 1901. He retired from professional soccer in 1906 and then fell on hard times, as an appeal was made on his behalf in March 1911 to find employment as a warehouseman or storeman.

Appearances:
SL: 20 app. 6 gls.
FAC: 2 app. 3 gls.
Total:
22 app. 9 gls.

Left: Ally MacLeod

Right: Roddy McLeod

McLOUGHLIN, Alan Francis

Alan McLoughlin

Role: Midfield 1990-
5'8" 10st.11lbs.
b. Manchester 20 April 1967

CAREER: Manchester United
Apr 1985/Stoke City trial
1986/Swindon Town Aug 1986
(Torquay United-loan-Mar
1987)/ SOUTHAMPTON
December 1990/(Aston Villa-
loan-Oct 1991).
Debut v Aston Villa (h) 15.12.90

When Swindon's Alan
McLoughlin shimmied his way
past two Saints defenders and
then slid the ball into the net to
give his club a 1-0 lead in the
Littlewoods Cup match back in
January 1990, Chris Nicholl
made a mental note. His
inclusion in the Republic of
Ireland's World Cup Squad the
following summer enhanced
Alan's blossoming reputation
and further strengthened
Nicholl's determination to sign
the young midfielder at any
price. Arriving at the Dell in
December 1990 his club,
Swindon, duly banked a million
pounds for a man they had
signed on a free transfer from
Manchester United - good business by any
standards. With Southampton's previous
highest transfer shattered by £300,000 the fans
were keen to witness Alan's undoubted talents
but as often happens in football, were to be
disappointed by the initial exploits of their
record signing.   It is fair to say that he has
since struggled to reproduce anything like
million pound form and has at times looked
out of depth in the top flight. With patience
and support it is to be hoped that Chris
Nicholl's judgment will yet be vindicated or it
may be quite a few years before the
Southampton board entrust a manager with
another seven figure cheque.

Appearances:
FL: 22 app. 1 gl.
FAC: 4 app. 0 gls.
Total: *26 app. 1 gl.*

McMANUS, Stuart Joseph

Role: Forward 1985-86
5'11" 12st.7lbs.
b. Falkirk 19 March 1965

CAREER: Surrey Schools/Tottenham Hotspur
assoc schoolboy/SOUTHAMPTON non-
contract Aug 1983, pro July 1984 (Newport
County-loan-Sept 1985)/Orgiyte.IS. June 1986.
Debut v Queen's Park Rangers (a) 11.3.86
* (scored on debut)

Stuart McManus became a non-contract player
for the Saints in August 1983 while doing a
Diploma Course in Physical Education at
Farnham. He scored regularly in the reserves,
notching 30 goals in his first season as a

professional, and returned from a loan spell at Newport to score on his debut. Given a free transfer Stuart took himself to Scandinavia in an attempt to relaunch his footballing career.

Appearances:
FL: 2 app. 1 gl.
Total: *2 app. 1 gl.*

McMILLAN, Alexander

Role: Centre-half 1891-92
b. Scotland
d. Umballa, India 1892

CAREER: 93rd Argyle & Sutherland Highlanders/SOUTHAMPTON St. Mary's Oct 1891.

Debut v Reading (h) 24.10.1891 FAC

Sandy McMillan was added to St. Mary's squad of players just fourteen days before the club's important cup tie against Reading on October 24th 1891. A sergeant in the army, Sandy enjoyed a fine debut and played a significant part in St. Mary's emphatic 7-0 victory. After the match Reading decided to lodge a protest on the grounds that McMillan and one other Southampton player, Fleming, had signed too late (14 days instead of 28 days) to be eligible for the game. The Football Assocation upheld Reading's appeal to

Neil Maddison

disqualify St. Mary's from the competition and Sgt. McMillan returned to his regiment. Within weeks he had been posted to India, where before long he had the misfortune to contract a fatal dose of enteric fever.

Appearances:
FAC: 1 app. 0 gls.
Total: *1 app. 0 gls.*

❏ **Saints note** - *When Reading's secretary, Mr H. Walker, telegraphed the F.A. soon after the game's final whistle to complain, he was told that any official's protest would have to be backed with a sum of money which would be used as a deposit towards the cost of the hearing. Mr Walker cheekily asked his Southampton counterpart, Mr Hendin, if he could advance Reading a share of the game's receipts. Mr Hendin obliged and, so doing, unwittingly helped finance St. Mary's expulsion!*

McMILLAN, John

Role: Half-back 1895-98
b. Glasgow circa 1865

CAREER: Heart of Midlothian/ SOUTHAMPTON St. Mary's Mar 1896.

Debut v Millwall (h) 21.3.1896

John McMillan was a Scottish import to the Antelope in 1896 and he earned the nickname of "Punt" due to his expert kicking action. Along with George Clawley and Bob Buchanan he was an ever-present during the 1896-97 season when the club won their first Southern League Championship, but lost his place the following year when the Southampton squad became stronger and more competitive.

Appearances:
SL: 31 app. 3 gls.
FAC: 7 app. 0 gls.
Total: *38 app. 3 gls.*

MADDISON, Neil Stanley

Role: Midfield 1988-
5' 9" 11st. 8lbs.
b. Darlington 2 October 1969

CAREER: Darlington Schools/ SOUTHAMPTON trainee July 1986, pro. April 1988

*Debut v Wimbledon (a) 3.12.88 * (scored on debut)*

Neil Maddison graduated to the professional ranks alongside the Wallace brothers and Alan Shearer to make 1988 a vintage year for Dave Merrington's youth team set-up. He scored in his first game at Wimbledon and then notched another goal on his home debut against Nottingham Forest. Unfortunately after such a promising start Neil's progress fell behind his contemporaries when a series of injuries sidelined him for some considerable time including a six month spell at the beginning of the 1990-91 season. Showing the courage that once caused Dave Merrington to compare him with Bryan Robson, Neil has fought his way back from these adversities and by April 1991 was again knocking hard on the first team door.

Appearances:
FL: 4 (7) app. 2 gls.
FAC: 0 (2) app. 0 gls.
LC: 0 (2) app. 0 gls.
Total: *4 (11) app. 2 gls.*

MALLETT, Joseph

Role: Half-back 1946-53
5' 7" 11st. 0lbs.
b. Gateshead 8 January 1916

CAREER: St. Cuthbert's school/Dunston C.W.S./Charlton Athletic Nov 1935 (Queen's Park Rangers loan-Apr 1937-May 1938, transferred Feb 1939)/(West Ham United during World War Two)/SOUTHAMPTON Feb 1947/Leyton Orient player-coach July 1953/Nottingham Forest reserve player-coach July 1959/Birmingham City coach June 1964, manager May 1965, asst. manager Dec 1965/Panionios (Greece) coach 1970/New York Cosmos coach Aug 1975/Washington Diplomats coach 1979/San Jose Earthquakes coach 1982/SOUTHAMPTON Scout in Midlands and South East 1983.

Debut v Plymouth Argyle (a) 1.3.47
* (scored on debut)

A bargain purchase from Queen's Park Rangers, Joe Mallett cost £5,000 and, although he was 31-years-old, the club was to reap the reward for the next six seasons. Joe was a strong link between the defence and attack and was particularly sound in his positional play. He became a keen student of football and, as team captain, possessed strong views on how the game should be played. Bill Dodgin's departure in August 1949 caused Joe to become restless at the Dell and five months later he put in a transfer request in the hope of receiving a coaching position. In the event he was to stay loyal to Southampton until the summer of 1953 and when, on 29 April 1953, he played his last game, he was aged 37 years and three months. Joe's coaching abilities took him to Greece where, although successful, the changing political situation forced him to resign and try his luck in the States. More recently, living in East Sussex, Joe has scouted for Saints in the South Eastern area.

Appearances:
FL: 215 app. 3 gls.
FAC: 8 app. 0 gls.
Total: *223 app. 3 gls.*

Joe Mallett

MARSHALL, George

Role: Half-back 1891-96
b. Southampton 8 July 1869
d. Southampton December 1938

CAREER: SOUTHAMPTON St. Mary's 1888.
Debut v Warmley (a) 3.10.1891 FAC

George Marshall is unique in the history of
Southampton Football Club due to the fact that
he is the only man to play in the club's first-
ever F.A. Cup match and their first-ever
League game. He was a convert from the
rugby football code and gained two
Hampshire Senior Cup Winners' medals and
County representative honours before St.
Mary's joined the Southern League in 1894. An
amateur throughout his career, he was a
sturdy, reliable defender equally at home in
the full or half-back positions. George hung up
his boots in 1896 to continue working for the
Ordnance Survey and spent much of his time
at the County Ground, either umpiring or
watching Hampshire.

Appearances:
SL: 22 app. 0 gls.
FAC: 14 app. 0 gls.
Total: *36 app. 0 gls.*

MARTIN, Eric

Role: Goalkeeper 1966-75
5'11" 11st. 8lbs.
b. Perth 31 March 1946

CAREER: Blair/St. Johnstone/Cowdenbeath/
Dunfermline Athletic/SOUTHAMPTON Mar
1967/Washington Diplomats c.s. 1975.
Debut v Everton (a) 18.3.67

A former dust-sampler in a coal mine, Eric
Martin was a Scottish Under-23
international and joined Saints for £25,000 as
the club fought a desperate battle to avoid
relegation in their first season in Division
One. Pitch-forked immediately into the fray,
Eric gave a magnificent display on his debut
and kept a clean sheet in a memorable 1-0
victory at Goodison Park. A popular and
colourful character Eric was, because of his
tousled hairstyle, nicknamed "Harpo" by his
team-mates and there were times in the
early seventies when he was being widely
tipped for full international honours. After
suffering a serious leg fracture in the States
he gave up playing to work for an American
television network.

Appearances:
FL: 248 app. 0 gls.
FAC: 19 app. 0 gls.
LC: 13 app. 0 gls.
Eur: 8 app. 0 gls.
Total: *288 app. 0 gls.*

Eric Martin

MASKELL, Craig Dell

Role: Forward 1985-87
5' 9" 10st. 5lbs.
b. Aldershot 10 April 1968

CAREER: Andover Schools/
SOUTHAMPTON app. July 1984,
pro. Apr 1986 (Swindon Town-
loan Mar 1987)/ Huddersfield
Town May 1988/Reading Aug
1990.
*Debut v Nottingham Forest (h)
6.9.86*

Craig Maskell

Craig Maskell had his name on the scoresheet before making his full debut, having notched up a goal at Spurs in May 1986 when coming on as a substitute. He was a composed, stylish forward who scored regularly for the reserves but found his lack of pace a hindrance in his efforts to secure regular first team football. After joining Huddersfield for £50,000 Craig's career flourished, hitting 43 goals in 87 games. He then joined Reading for £250,000 with Saints receiving a further £100,000 from the deal.

Appearances:
FL: 2 (4) app. 1 gl.
Total: *2 (4) app. 1 gl.*

MATSON, Francis Robert

Role: Forward 1931-32
5'8" 11st. 4lbs.
b. Cardiff 21 November 1905

CAREER: Cardiff Corinthians/Cardiff City Dec 1926/Newport County Aug 1930/SOUTHAMPTON Sept 1930.

Debut v Leeds United (h) 19.12.31

Frank Matson was at Ninian Park during Cardiff City's golden era making twenty-seven appearances and scoring three goals for the Bluebirds. A hard working right-winger Frank's stay at the Dell lasted two years, most of which was spent in the reserves.

Appearances:
FL: 2 app. 0 gls.
Total: *2 app. 0 gls.*

MATTHEWS, Frank

Role: Forward 1925-27
5'8" 11st. 0lbs.
b. Wallsend 26 December 1902
d. North Cleveland April qtr. 1981

CAREER: Blackpool May 1922/Barnsley May 1923/SOUTHAMPTON May 1925/Chesterfield June 1927.

Debut v Sheffield Wednesday (a) 12.12.25

Frank Matthews scored on his home debut against Stoke and for a brief period during 1925-26 made the inside-left berth his own. Limited to just three outings in the following campaign he was listed at £50 and joined non-league Chesterfield who were being managed by ex-Saint Alec Campbell.

Appearances:
FL: 19 app. 6 gls.
Total: *19 app. 6 gls.*

Frank Matthews

MAUGHAN, Wesley James

Role: Forward 1958-62
5'9" 10st.11lbs.
b. Sholing, Southampton 17 February 1939

CAREER: Cowes Secondary Modern/Cowes/
SOUTHAMPTON am June 1956, pro. May
1957/Reading Mar 1962/Chelmsford City/
Cambridge United/Brentwood Town
(Margate-loan-Jan 1968)/Chelmsford City
(Brentwood & Chelmsford combined during
c.s. 1969)/ Bexley United Sept 1969/
Basingstoke Town Nov 1972/Fleet Jan 1973/
Bexley United Aug 1974.

Debut v Reading (a) 21.2.59

Discovered by Ted Bates while playing in a
Hampshire Youth Cup tie on the Isle of Wight,
Wes Maughan was a trainee accountant. He
became a notable figure in the club's successful
youth team of 1957 when he netted eleven
times in nine F.A. Youth cup-ties including
two splendidly taken goals at Old Trafford in
the semi-final. A real ninety-minute player,
Wes was a stalwart in the reserves scoring 47
goals in 101 appearances but, after featuring in
the first team only randomly, sought a transfer.
He moved to Elm Park for a £4,000 fee but
soon after his arrival was found to have a
problem with his eyesight and Reading,
unsuccessfully, sought a reduction in his fee.

Appearances:
FL: 6 app. 1 gl.
FAC: 1 app. 0 gls.
Total: *7 app. 1 gl.*

MAYER, Wilfred

Role: Forward 1936-38
5'6" 10st.6lbs.
b. Stoke-on-Trent 18 February 1912
d. Stoke-on-Trent April 1979

CAREER: Newcastle P.S.A./Downings
Tileries/Stoke City Aug 1932/
SOUTHAMPTON Mar 1937/Wellington
Town.

Debut v Leicester City (h) 20.3.37

One of Tom Parker's first acquisitions, Wilf
Mayer cost the Saints £650 and was a nippy
forward, at home both on the wing or at
inside-forward. He never really met the club's

Wilf Mayer

expectations of him and, transfer-listed at £500
in May 1938, he failed to attract any offers
from a League team, even though that fee was
halved the following month. Eventually Wilf
moved to Wellington and with them in 1940 he
won a Welsh Cup Winners' medal.

Appearances:
FL: 14 app. 0 gls.
Total: *14 app. 0 gls.*

MEAD, Charles Philip

Role: Goalkeeper 1907-08
b. Battersea, London 9 March 1887
d. Bournemouth 26 March 1958

CAREER: SOUTHAMPTON 1907

Debut v West Ham United (h) 21.12.07

A sporting legend in Hampshire, Phil Mead
made his name not on the soccer field but as a
first-class batsman for Hampshire C.C.C. and
England. He had decided to sign on for the
Saints for one season to assist the club's
reserve eleven as a useful inside-forward but
never had any intention of taking up football

full-time. His one senior outing was a fluke as he had been on his way to Fratton Park with the reserves when he was recalled to the Dell where the directors faced a dilemma. No experienced goalkeepers were available for a game against West Ham and Phil was asked if he would oblige. He shaped up well but was only required to save two shots and kept a blank sheet in a 0-0 draw. He returned to cricket the following summer and spent twenty-seven years as a professional with Hampshire scoring 55,061 first class runs at an average of 47.67. Although blind for the last ten years of his life Phil still took great pleasure in continuing to attend matches at the County Ground.

Appearances:
SL: 1 app. 0 gls.
Total: *1 app. 0 gls.*

C. P. MEAD

MEASURES, C. William

Role: Centre-half 1891-92

CAREER: Geneva Cross/SOUTHAMPTON St. Mary's 1890.

Debut v Warmley (a) 3.10.1891 FAC

Bill Measures was an army man, attached to Netley Hospital, who played regularly for the Geneva Cross team which was based at the hospital. With no binding registrations in those days Bill was able to assist the Saints on several occasions in friendlies, the first of which was against the famous London Caledonians at the Antelope in September 1890. Although his loyalties remained with the hospital side for the county competitions he was added to the list of members of the St. Mary's club when they entered the F.A. Cup for the first time in 1891. After that his footballing career took a back seat to his army

service and he featured in only one other game wearing a Cherry squares shirt.

Appearances:
FAC: 1 app. 0 gls.
Total: *1 app. 0 gls.*

MEEHAN, Peter

Role: Full-back 1898-1900
5'9" 13st.13lbs.
b. Broxburn 28 February 1872
d. 1915

CAREER: Broxburn Shamrock/Hibernian Feb 1892/Sunderland June 1893/Glasgow Celtic May 1895/Everton Jan 1896/SOUTHAMPTON Aug 1898/Manchester City Sept 1900/Barrow c.s. 1901/Clyde c.s. 1903/Broxburn Athletic 1904.

Debut v Royal Artillery (h) 8.10.1898

Originally employed in the Linlithgowshire coal mines Peter Meehan joined the club for a record fee of £200 and he helped Saints win the Southern League Championship for the third time. He was a Scottish international (v Ireland 1896) and while at the Dell gave some formidable performances in the right-back position. Peter's final game for the club came in the ill-fated F.A. Cup Final at Crystal Palace in 1900 and, after a short, unhappy spell in the north-west of England, he returned to Scotland.

Appearances:
SL: 36 app. 1 gl.
FAC: 9 app. 0 gls.
Total: *45 app. 1 gl.*

MELIA, James

Role: Forward 1964-69
5'7" 11st.2lbs.
b. Liverpool 1 November 1937

CAREER: Liverpool Schools/Liverpool am. May 1954, pro. Nov 1954/Wolverhampton Wanderers Mar 1964/SOUTHAMPTON Dec 1964/Aldershot player-coach Nov 1968, player-manager Apr 1969-Jan 1972/Crewe Alexandra player-coach, manager Feb 1972/Southport manager July 1975, resigned Sept 1975/Brighton manager Mar 1983-Oct 1983/Belenenses (Portugal) coach May 1983-Nov

Jimmy Melia

1985/Stockport manager July 1986-Nov 1986/
Kuwait coaching/Dallas, Texas coaching 1991.

Debut v Newcastle United (h) 19.12.64

A player who had spent eight seasons at
Liverpool, Jimmy Melia was a creative inside-
forward whose availability at Wolves
prompted Ted Bates to part with a record
£30,000. Capped for England, Jimmy was a real
schemer whose finesse and vision was not
always appreciated by the Dell crowd. A vital
ingredient in the recipe for the club's survival
during the period following promotion to the
top flight, Jimmy's guile and experience
proved invaluable. A colourful extrovert he
joined the managerial roundabout in 1972 and
surfaced to national media attention when
finding himself in charge of Brighton's
unlikely run to Wembley in 1983. In March
1991 Jimmy was coaching indoor league soccer
in Dallas, Texas.

Appearances:
FL: 139 app. 11 gls.
FAC: 6 app. 0 gls.
LC: 7 app. 1 gl.
Total: *152 app. 12 gls.*

MESTON, Samuel

Role: Half-back 1895-1906
5'10" 11st.13lbs.
b. Arbroath 16 January 1872
d. Ashurst, Hampshire 14 August 1948

CAREER: Arbroath Victoria/Stoke Jan 1894/
SOUTHAMPTON St. Mary's Apr 1895/
Salisbury City c.s. 1906/Croydon Common
player-trainer c.s. 1907/Salisbury City 1909/
Chandlers Ford/Eastleigh Athletic 1913/
Bishopstoke W.M.S.C. trainer 1923.

Debut v Millwall (a) 14.9.1895

A gargantuan figure in the club's Southern
League era, Sammy Meston arrived in
Southampton as part of the "Stoke invasion"
and went on to win six championship medals
(a record) and two F.A. Cup runners-up
medals. Bert Lee alone played more Southern
League games and only Terry Paine and Nick
Holmes made more F.A. Cup appearances
which, in an age when professionals were loyal
only to the wage packet, shows Sam Meston's
massive contribution to the growth of the club.
He could play in most positions but was
happiest in the right-half role and his "long
toms", a reference to his cannon-like shots
which became his trademark, were sorely
missed when he cast off the red and white for

Sammy Meston

the last time in May 1906. His love of the game kept him playing way into his forties while he continued to earn a living as a brake-fitter's mate at Eastleigh Railway Works. Sam turned out for the ex-Saints XI during the 1920's, a period which coincided with his son's arrival as a professional at the Dell.

Appearances:
SL: 246 app. 18 gls.
FAC: 42 app. 2 gls.
Total: *288 app. 20 gls.*

MESTON, Samuel William

Role: Forward 1921-26
5'8" 11st.0lbs.
b. Southampton 30 May 1902
d. Woolston 12 October 1953

CAREER: Sholing Athletic Aug 1921/ SOUTHAMPTON Jan 1922/Gillingham Aug 1926/Everton Mar 1928/Tranmere Rovers July 1929/Newport (I.O.W.) c.s. 1931.

Debut v Merthyr Town (h) 8.4.22

The son of former Saint, Sammy Meston (1895-1906), Sam junior started life as a centre-forward, converting later to the right-wing position and looked to have a chance of emulating his famous father's career. A

Sam Meston Jnr

coppersmith by trade, Sam was just beginning to establish himself in the first team when he broke a leg in a game against Bristol City in October 1923 and the injury side-lined him for a year. When attempting a come-back he had the misfortune to break the same leg and, although he made a full recovery, he was never the same player again. After a move to Gillingham he surprisingly went on to join Everton where he played one game alongside Dixie Dean (who that season was to score sixty League goals). Returning to Southampton, Sam became a "bookie's runner" in the town and died prematurely of a heart attack in 1953.

Appearances:
FL: 10 app. 2 gls.
Total: *10 app. 2 gls.*

METCALF, Thomas Clark

Role: Half-back 1905-06
b. Burton-on-Trent October qtr. 1878
d. Burton-on-Trent May 1938

CAREER: Burton United Jan 1903/ SOUTHAMPTON Mar 1904/Salisbury City c.s. 1906/Wolverhampton Wanderers Feb 1908.

Debut v Northampton Town (a) 23.9.05

Plucked from the obscurity of the Midlands League, Tom Metcalf was the reserve team pivot throughout his fifteen months as a Saints player and had won a Hampshire Senior Cup Winners' medal within a month of his arrival. Wolves resurrected his career in 1908 but soon after his move back to the Midlands he retired from the game and worked for the brewers Ind Coope and Alsopps Ltd.

Appearances:
SL: 1 app. 0 gls.
Total: *1 app. 0 gls.*

MIDDLETON, Stephen Roy

Role: Goalkeepr 1973-77
6'0" 12st.7lbs.
b. Portsmouth 28 March 1953

CAREER: Gosport & Fareham Schools/ SOUTHAMPTON app. Oct 1969, pro. July 1970 (Torquay-loan Mar-Apr 1975)/ Portsmouth June 1977.

Debut v Queen's Park Rangers (a) 25.8.73

Steve Middleton

Steve Middleton enjoyed only one lengthy run in the Southampton first team, that being in the first few months of the 1975-76 season. However, he suffered a loss of confidence in the November and he missed out on what could have been an F.A. Cup Winners' medal. Released from his contract in May 1977 he joined his home town team but after only 26 games decided to quit football to run a pub in Portsmouth.

Appearances:
FL: 24 app. 0 gls.
LC: 3 app. 0 gls.
Eur: 2 app. 0 gls.
Total: *29 app. 0 gls.*

MILLS, Michael Denis M.B.E.

Role: Full-back 1982-85
5'7" 11st.11lbs.
b. Godalming, Surrey 4 January 1949

CAREER: Portsmouth app. May 1964/Ipswich Town Feb 1966/ SOUTHAMPTON Nov 1982/ Stoke City player-manager June 1985/ Colchester United manager Jan-May 1990/ Middlesbrough scout 1990/Coventry City asst. manager Nov 1990-Nov 1991.

Debut v Nottingham Forest (h) 13.11.82

During a 17 year playing career at Ipswich, Mick Mills had won most of the honours the game has to offer and had captained his country in the 1982 World Cup Finals. Although nearly 34 at the time, his career was far from over and, joining Southampton for £50,000, he immediately instilled a sense of unflappability and panache to the defence. Never satisfied with playing the easy ball, Mick became team captain in March 1984 when Steve Williams was injured and successfully guided the team to runners-up position. Awarded the M.B.E. the same year, Mick was a model professional and in his final season at the Dell was, despite being in his thirty-seventh year, ever present in the side.

Unhappy managerial experiences in 1989-90 saw both teams with which he was involved relegated, and later the same summer hopes of a new job coaching in Kuwait were dashed by the Iraqi invasion.

Appearances:
FL: 103 app. 3 gls.
FAC: 10 app. 0 gls.
LC: 8 app. 0 gls.
Eur: 2 app. 0 gls.
Total: *123 app. 3 gls.*

Mick Mills

MILLS, Stephen John

Role: Full-back 1972-77
5'7" 10st.2lbs.
b. Portsmouth 9 December 1953
d. Southampton 1 August 1988

CAREER: Gosport Grammar School/Gosport
Schools/Hampshire Boys Capt/
SOUTHAMPTON app. Aug 1969, pro. July
1971/Miami Toros May-Aug 1976/Weymouth
Dec 1977.

Debut v Notts County (h) 3.10.72 LC

Steve Mills was the grandson of Portsmouth's
1934 F.A. Cup goalkeeper, Jock Gilfillan, and
originally came to the Dell on a week's trial.
Extremely quick and a fierce tackler, Steve was
a natural left-back and was soon rewarded,
after a series of impressive Southampton
appearances, with England Under-23
recognition. On the brink of an illustrious
career, fate was to deal Steve the first of two
cruel blows and the biography of a precocious
and prodigious talent becomes the story of a
brave young man, uncomplainingly coming to
terms with that fate. Firstly, in February 1975
Steve was involved in a serious road crash and
suffered severe injuries as a result of which he
was forced, after a few come-back matches, to
give up the game. He moved back to Gosport
and took over his parents' newsagents
business before, in 1986, he discovered he was
suffering from leukaemia. It was at this point
that the courage that was to later be such an
inspiration took over and Steve not only
decided to fight the disease but to become
involved in charity work by creating a fund for
leukaemia research. Despite being hospitalised
by the side-effects of subsequent treatment,
Steve organised the biggest charity match ever
seen in the south, with an all-time Saints XI
playing the current team at the Dell. With such
names as Keegan, Chivers and Channon
present, the game was watched by a 20,000
crowd and the evening, highly emotional,
became a few months later a moving tribute to
Steve's memory. Although Steve eventually
lost his battle against his illness in August
1988, the charity and fund-raising goes on in
his name.

Appearances:
FL: 57 (4) app. 0 gls.
FAC: 5 app. 0 gls.
LC: 8 app. 0 gls.
Total: *70 (4) app. 0 gls.*

Steve Mills

MILWARD, Alfred

Role: Forward 1899-1901
5'7" 11st.9lbs.
b. Great Marlow, Bucks 12 September 1870
d. Winchester 1 June 1941

CAREER: Sir William Borlase's Grammar
School/Old Borlasians/Marlow/Everton
1888/New Brighton Tower c.s. 1897/
SOUTHAMPTON May 1899/New Brompton
c.s. 1901/Southampton Cambridge c.s. 1903.

Debut v New Brompton (h) 2.9.1899
* *(scored on debut)*

The son of a Marlow tradesman, Alf Milward
had reached the peak of his career with
Everton where, gaining League Championship
and F.A. Cup Winners' medals, he was
regarded as a hard-working and technically
superior left-winger. Very determined, he
never accepted defeat until the final whistle
but he fell out with the Goodison Park
management and was forced to drop out of the
League to join Cheshire League side, New
Brighton Tower. In 1898 Southampton began
negotiations for his transfer but were deterred
by the £200 fee that Everton wanted for their
England International. The following year Alf
did become a Saint, with no fee attached, and
he quickly settled to embark on another
chapter of a distinguished career. Although

weighty for a left-winger, he remained full of pace and his partnership with Edgar Chadwick, renewed from their Everton days, was recognised as the most devastating in the game. Alf possessed the ability to deliver beautifully angled cross-field passes but it was more for his wonderful shooting from the wing that he was respected and his goal-scoring record was remarkable considering the position in which he played. Finishing his career in Kent, he returned to live in Southampton becoming landlord at the Diamond Jubilee in Orchard Lane. He also qualified as a referee in charge of Southampton F.A. fixtures in 1909.

Appearances:
SL: 56 app. 36 gls.
FAC: 7 app. 4 gls.
Total: *63 app. 40 gls.*

MITCHELL, John Desmond

John Mitchell

Role: Forward 1950-51
b. Sarisbury Green
19 January 1928

CAREER: St. Mary's School/Sarisbury Green/Gosport Athletic/ SOUTHAMPTON Mar 1949/ Newport (Isle of Wight) c.s. 1951.
Debut v Luton Town (a) 2.9.50

A left-winger, John Mitchell was demobbed in March 1949 and joined the Saints later the same month. On his home debut he played well enough to suggest a promising future, with one national newspaper enthusing "Mitchell uses the ball with real purpose". After deciding against a proposed transfer to Barnsley, John turned his back on football to follow a career in accountancy and, later, worked for the National Westminster Bank in Southampton.

Appearances:
FL: 7 app. 0 gls.
Total: *7 app. 0 gls.*

Alf Milward

MITTON, John

Role: Half-back 1927-28
5'11" 12st.0lbs.
b. Todmorden, Yorks. 7 November 1895
d. Kings Lynn, Norfolk November 1981

CAREER: Brierfield FC/Burnley 1914 am./
Bury 1916/Exeter City June 1919/ Sunderland
Oct 1920/Wolverhampton Wanderers May
1923/SOUTHAMPTON June 1927.

Debut v Leeds United (a) 3.9.27

John Mitton had been captain of
Wolverhampton Wanderers before his £150
transfer to Southampton and although he
never established himself in the senior side he
provided adequate cover for all three half-back
positions.

> **Appearances:**
> *FL: 8 app. 0 gls.*
> **Total:** *8 app. 0 gls.*

❑ **Saints note** - *John was also a professional
cricketer and in 1920 played two games for
Somerset C.C.C.*

John Mitton

MOGER, Henry Herbert

Role: Goalkeeper
1900-03
6'2" 12st.6lbs.
*b. Southampton
September 1879
d. Manchester circa
1930*

CAREER:
Forest Swifts/
Freemantle
1898/
SOUTHAMPTON
c.s. 1900/
Manchester
United May 1903.

Debut v Bristol City (h) 24.11.1900

"COPE'S "CLIPS" CIGARETTES

No. 121—MOGER
Manchester United
Noted Footballers

Harry Moger was a local goalkeeper who,
during his time at the Dell, was a worthy
understudy to England International Jack
Robinson. Tall and lean, Harry was
particularly useful in high-ball situations when
he would come off his goal line to punch the
ball out from a scrimmage, and Manchester
United were quick to spot his undoubted
potential. At United, well away from
Robinson's shadow, Harry gained a
commendable reputation and helped United to
win two League championships and the F.A.
Cup, narrowly failing to attract the England
selectors' eye.

> **Appearances:**
> *SL: 14 app. 0 gls.*
> **Total:** *14 app. 0 gls.*

❑ **Saints note** - *In 1899 Harry was suspended for
two months due to his having played amateur
football for Forest Swifts whilst registered as a
professional with Freemantle.*

MOLLOY, William George

Role: Forward 1949-50
5'7" 10st.0lbs.
b. Coventry 28 August 1929

CAREER: St. Osburgs Youth Club 1940-45/
Coventry City am. Mar 1945/Coventry Works
Team/SOUTHAMPTON Oct 1949/Lockheed
Leamington/Newport County Nov 1950/

Millwall Mar 1952/Rugby Town July 1952/
Snowdon Colliery July 1953/Canterbury City
June 1954/Dover 1955/Nuneaton Borough
July 1956/Bedworth United July 1957-1958.
Debut v Blackburn Rovers (h) 22.10.49

Bill signed for Coventry City as an amateur in
March 1945 but resisted an offer to turn
professional and joined the army instead.
Based near Andover at Lugershall, Bill came to
the attention of Saints' scouts and was invited
for a trial and this time accepted the offer of a
professional contract. Arriving at the Dell in
October 1949 Bill Molloy shaped up well in his
first game for the reserves, stylishly scoring
two goals and being rewarded soon after with
the inside-left role on his first team debut.
Although he had the pleasure of starting the
move that led to Ted Bates scoring the first
goal for Southampton, it was reported that he
lacked the necessary pace. Bill was put on the
free transfer list and nearly joined Aston Villa
but the deal collapsed when Sid Cann
suddenly decided to ask Villa for £750.
Disheartened, Bill decided to play for
Leamington Lockheed while working for them
in the maintenance department. After playing
for a succession of non-league sides Bill
became a painter and decorator in Coventry
and still lives there and watches their home
games.

Appearances:
FL: 1 app. 0 gls.
Total: *1 app. 0 gls.*

Bill Molloy

MOLYNEUX, George

Role: Full-back 1900-05
5'10" 12st.6lbs.
b. Liverpool July qtr. 1875
d. Rochford, Essex 14 April 1942

CAREER: South Shore/Kirkdale 1894/Everton
Mar 1896/Wigan County 1897/Everton May
1898/SOUTHAMPTON May 1900/
Portsmouth May 1905/Southend United c.s.
1906, player-manager 1910/Colchester Town.
Debut v Luton Town (a) 1.9.1900

Having been secured on a free transfer in 1900,
George Molyneux swiftly developed into a top
class left-back with all-round ability. Regarded
as the best exponent of the art of heading in
the country it was no surprise when he was
selected for the ill-fated Ibrox match between
Scotland and England. Although the game was
deleted from the records George did win a
total of four international caps while a
Southampton player and also gained three
Southern League championship medals during
his five years at the Dell.

Appearances:
SL: 142 app. 0 gls.
FAC: 17 app. 0 gls.
Total: *159 app. 0 gls.*

MONK, Frank Vivian

Frank Monk

Role: Centre-half 1910-12
5'10" 11st.10lbs.
b. Salisbury July qtr 1886
*d. Salisbury 15 November
1962*

CAREER: Queens Road
School, Wimbledon/ St. Marks
College, Chelsea/ Salisbury
City/ SOUTHAMPTON
1910/ Glossop Sept 1911/ Fulham Oct
1911/SOUTHAMPTON 1911/ Fulham Mar
1912/Salisbury City 1912.
Debut v Crystal Palace (h) 22.10.10

Frank Monk was an outstanding all-round
amateur sportsman who gained honours at
swimming, cricket and athletics (St. Martins
Harriers) as well as being the 1909 Salisbury
marathon champion. His teaching studies
meant he could only make intermittent

George Molyneux

appearances for the Saints but when he did play he used his athleticism to good effect and was a very sure tackler. Selected for an amateur international in January 1911, Frank successfully came through the match to win four caps before the end of the season. 1911-12 was Frank's last season in league football and, after brief spells with several clubs, he hung up his boots and moved to teach in the west country.

Appearances:
SL: 20 app. 0 gls.
FAC: 1 app. 0 gls.
Total: *21 app. 0 gls.*

MONTGOMERY, James

Role: Goalkeepr 1976-77
5'10" 11st.9lbs.
b. Sunderland 9 October1943

CAREER: St. Hilda's School/Sunderland Boys /Sunderland Oct 1960 (SOUTHAMPTON-loan-Oct 1976)/Birmingham City Feb 1977/ Nottingham Forest Aug 1979/Sunderland Aug 1980.

Debut v Luton Town (a) 23.10.76

The hero of Sunderland's 1973 F.A. Cup Final victory over Leeds United, Jim Montgomery was one of the country's top goalkeepers in the sixties and came to the Dell on loan in October 1976. Saints were experiencing traumas as far as goalkeepers were concerned and Jim was to be one of five custodians used during the 1976-77 season. He later admitted that his period at the Dell was the worst in his career.

Appearances:
FL: 5 app. 0 gls.
Total: *5 app. 0 gls.*

Jim Montgomery

MOON, Charles H.

Role: Forward 1909-10
b. Southampton

CAREER: Bannister Court School/ SOUTHAMPTON 1909.
Debut v Swindon Town (h) 4.4.10

Charles Moon grew up and went to school in the Bannister area which borders the Dell, and joined the playing staff in 1909. In his one game at centre-forward he struggled to make much of an impression and, as he was the butt of some barracking from the crowd, was never given another chance. A second Lieutenant in the county of London Territorials during the Great War.

Appearances:
SL: 1 app. 0 gls.
Total: *1 app. 0 gls.*

MOORE, James

Role: Forward 1919-21
5'8" 10st.4lbs.
b. Felling-on-Tyne 1 September 1891

CAREER: Barnsley Aug 1911/

Jimmy Moore

SOUTHAMPTON May 1919/Leeds United
May 1921/Brighton & Hove Albion June
1922/Halifax Town Sept 1923/Queen's Park
Rangers Nov 1924/Crewe Alexandra July
1925/N.A.C. Breda (Holland) coach Mar 1927.

*Debut v Exeter City (h) 30.8.19 * (scored on debut)*

A carpenter by trade, Jimmy Moore was a
member of Barnsley's 1912 Cup-winning team
and was discovered by the Saints in 1916
whilst helping to construct aeroplanes in
Saunders & Co. boatyard in Cowes on the Isle
of Wight. He guested in several wartime
games and was then persuaded to sign on a
permanent basis in May 1919. Neat in his
footwork, he was also a particularly clever
header of the ball as he seemed to be able to
glide it to the feet of his wing partner with un-
nerving accuracy. Notorious for his unhappy
expression Jimmy also had the unfortunate
distinction of being the first Saints player to be
sent off in a Football League fixture (versus
Grimsby December 1920). Because of family
reasons he was granted a transfer to Leeds in
1921 and eventually, after a spell coaching in
Holland, he returned to live in Barnsley where
he purchased a greengrocer's business and
also later became a director of Barnsley F.C.

Appearances:
SL: 41 app. 10 gls.
FL: 42 app. 12 gls.
FAC: 6 app. 0 gls.
Total: *89 app. 22 gls.*

MOORE, Kevin Thomas

Role: Centre-half 1987-
5'11" 12st.2lbs.
b. Grimsby 29 April 1958

CAREER: England Schools/Grimsby Town
June 1976/Oldham Athletic Feb 1987/
SOUTHAMPTON July 1987.

Debut v Manchester United (h) 15.8.87

Kevin Moore is a member of a well-known
Grimsby footballing family. His father Roy and
his Uncle Norman were often in Grimsby
Town's half-back line in the 1940's while his
two younger brothers David and Andrew have
also featured in more recent Mariners'
defensive line-ups. Kevin initially started his
footballing career as a full-back but, converting
into a centre-half early in 1980, soon developed

into one of the best central defenders in the
lower divisions. Joe Royle, Oldham's manager,
paid £100,000 for him in February 1987 but
written into Kevin's contract was a clause that
allowed him to move on to any First Division
club if Oldham failed to win promotion. Chris
Nicholl, a team-mate of Kevin's during their
Blundell Park days saw him as a cheap
(£150,000) replacement for the transfer-seeking
Mark Wright and made his move a few weeks
before the start of the 1987-88 season. Kevin
soon showed sterling defensive qualities which
went some considerable way to easing the
blow of Wright's departure. His
wholeheartedness made him an ideal reserve
captain whenever Jimmy Case was absent and
the last four years spent playing in the top
flight has been a just reward for one of the
game's unsung heroes. In the last couple of

Kevin Moore

seasons Kevin has remained good in the air but, losing a little of his pace, has often been blamed for some of the team's defensive ineptitude. He has always taken this criticism squarely on the chin and, when recalled to first-team duty, has continued to perform with impressive commitment. One of Chris Nicholl's last acts as Southampton's manager was to offer Kevin a free transfer in May 1991, but in July Ian Branfoot offered him a one year contract in the hope that his experience and whole-heartedness would rub off on the youngsters in the Reserves.

Appearances:
FL: 97 (3) app. 8 gls.
FAC: 10 app. 0 gls.
LC: 13 (1) app. 1 gl.
Total: *120 (4) app. 9 gls.*

MOORHEAD, George

Role: Centre-half 1920-21
b. Lurgan, Co. Armagh

CAREER: SOUTHAMPTON Aug 1920/ Brighton Aug 1922/Linfield Dec 1922/ Glenavon 1924/Linfield 1925.

Debut v Reading (a) 18.12.20

George Moorhead joined the Saints upon leaving the army and with his talent for giving precise passes looked to have an outstanding future as a centre-half. Unfortunately, due to an infringement of technicalities when signing for Saints, he had his registration cancelled and was suspended for twelve months by the Football Association. Picking up the threads, he later registered with Brighton and then, moving back to his native country, enjoyed eight seasons during which time he was awarded three Northern Ireland caps.

Appearances:
FL: 9 app. 0 gls.
FAC: 5 app. 0 gls.
Total: *14 app. 0 gls.*

MORAN, Steven James

Role: Forward 1979-86
5'8" 10st.11lbs.
b. Croydon 10 January 1961

CAREER: Sarisbury Sparks /Price's College, Fareham/SOUTHAMPTON Aug 1979/ Leicester City Sept 1986/Reading Nov 1987/ Exeter City Aug 1991.

Debut v Middlesbrough (a) 18.10.80

A late arrival on the professional scene, Steve Moran completed his studies before embarking on his footballing career but wasted little time in displaying an insatiable appetite for scoring. Refreshingly eager, he scored with his first kick when coming on as a substitute against Manchester City and then notched another in his next appearance from the bench. Profiting from having Kevin Keegan and Mike

Steve Moran

Channon amongst his team-mates, Steve frequently gave the impression of having a fanatical obsession with hitting the net and finished his debut season with an impressive 18 goals from 30 games. Closer marking, coupled with a serious back injury that sidelined him for nine months, temporarily brought a decline in his strike rate but not before he was voted P.F.A. Young Player of the Year in 1982. When Saints finished the 1983-84 season in runners-up position it was Steve's 21 goal tally that made the headlines and heightened the possibilities of inclusion in England's forthcoming tour of South America. As events turned out Steve was not given the chance to add to his two Under-21 caps and the following year suffered a loss of form and confidence which was not helped when his mentor and manager Lawrie McMenemy departed for Wearside. With the arrival of a new broom, Steve's fortunes slumped further, but when Chris Nicholl sanctioned a £300,000 transfer to Filbert Street he hoped to rediscover his opportunistic skills. Unfortunately the Leicester fans witnessed only occasional flashes of the old Steve Moran and when his indifferent form continued after a move to Elm Park it seemed that one of the game's most promising forwards would end up prematurely on the scrap-heap. However, Ian Porterfield, Reading's new manager, instilled a sense of discipline and new-found confidence into Steve's game and, looking fitter, he at last rediscovered some of the form that made him such a Dell favourite. Unfortunately, with Porterfield's sacking, Steve suffered another dip in form and in the close season of 1991 was given a free transfer to eventually join old team-mates Alan Ball and Steve Williams at Exeter.

Appearances:
FL: 173 (7) app. 78 gls.
FAC: 18 app. 12 gls.
LC: 16 (3) app. 6 gls.
Eur: 7 (1) app. 2 gls.
Total: 214 (11) app. 98 gls.

PROMINENT FOOTBALLERS.

F. MOUNCHER,
SOUTHAMPTON.

MOUNCHER, Frederick William

Role: Forward 1903-08
5'10" 12st.0lbs.
b. Southampton October qtr 1883

CAREER: Fitzhugh Rovers/ Southampton Cambridge/ SOUTHAMPTON 1903/Fulham Nov 1907.

Debut v Swindon Town (a) 26.9.03

At home on either wing, Fred Mouncher's other main asset was his phenomenal bursts of speed and, once at the Dell, he re-acquainted himself with Fred Harrison, a team-mate from his Fitzhugh Rovers days. Too inconsistent for some fans' liking, Fred often performed better in away matches and nearly joined Dundee in 1906 when flattering terms were offered. He remained in his home town until the November of the following year when Saints, in financial trouble, sold him and Fred Harrison to Fulham for a combined fee of £800. Fred was selected for an international trial at Manchester in January 1908 but his career was soon blighted by ill-health and he eventually had to retire due to consumption in 1911. He later became the licensee of the Railway Hotel in St. Denys.

Appearances:
SL: 99 app. 14 gls.
FAC: 9 app. 2 gls.
Total: 108 app. 16 gls.

MOUNSEY, George Frederick

Role: Centre-half 1914-15
5'8" 11st.10lbs.
b. South Queensferry 19 December 1889
d. Southampton 3 November 1914

CAREER: Willington Athletic/ SOUTHAMPTON May 1914.

Debut v Crystal Palace (h) 17.10.14

Signed from a County Durham side, George Mounsey was a fair-haired reserve centre-half who was to die just three weeks after his first team debut. Playing in a South-East Counties fixture at Watford he was knocked unconscious although he recovered to complete the match. However, after returning to Southampton, he collapsed and died two days later. The coroner, at the ensuing inquest, recorded heart failure as the cause of his death.

Appearances:
SL: 1 app. 0 gls.
Total: *1 app. 0 gls.*

MULFORD, Arthur Henry

Role: Forward 1891-93
b. Southampton January qtr 1871

CAREER: SOUTHAMPTON St. Mary's 1890.

Debut v Warmley (a) 3.10.1891 FAC

Arthur Mulford originally featured in Southampton St. Mary's first team in a friendly at the Antelope against Reading in September 1891. A month later he and the club had their first taste of F. A. Cup action in the successful defeat of Warmley. Mulford made just one more cup appearance the following year against Newbury but despite scoring he failed to ever appear for the first team again.

Appearances:
FAC: 2 app. 1 gl.
Total: *2 app. 1 gl.*

MULGREW, Thomas

Role: Forward 1954-62
5'8" 11st.10lbs.
b. Motherwell 13 April 1929

CAREER: Cleland Juniors/ Morton/ Northampton Town July 1949/Newcastle United Oct 1952/ SOUTHAMPTON Aug 1954/Aldershot Aug 1962/ Andover Aug 1965.

Debut v Brentford (h) 21.8.54
* (scored on debut)

Valued at £7,000 in a £12,000 transfer deal that also

brought Billy Foulkes to Southampton, Tommy Mulgrew scored after only fifteen seconds of his debut and the goal remains the fastest ever scored by a Saints player at the Dell. Tommy had a long innings in a red and white shirt and, always in the thick of things, became the first player in nearly twenty-one years to be sent off when a brush with authority saw him dismissed in a home match with Coventry at Christmas 1954. A regular scorer and a crowd favourite, Tommy left the club for Aldershot after a disagreement over re-engagement terms. A brief spell at Andover preceded a move to Northampton where he found employment at a local factory while also turning out for the works team. In 1991 Tommy was still living in Northampton.

Appearances:
FL: 293 app. 90 gls.
FAC: 23 app. 10 gls.
LC: 9 app. 0 gls.
Total: *325 app. 100 gls.*

Tommy Mulgrew

MURPHY, William

Role: Forward 1926-29
5'6" 10st.7lbs.
b. St. Helens 23 March 1895
d. Liverpool 7 January 1962

CAREER: Peasley Cross Juniors/Alexandra
Victoria/Liverpool/ Manchester City Feb
1918, pro. May 1919/SOUTHAMPTON Aug
1926/Oldham Athletic June 1929/Tranmere
Rovers Aug 1930/Ellesmere Port Town Sept.
1932.
Debut v Portsmouth (a) 28.8.26

Bill Murphy

As a schoolboy Bill Murphy was a brilliant
cross-country runner and was reputed to be so
fast that he was in great demand by pigeon
fanciers for conveying the time of arrival of
birds to headquarters. Bill, or "Spud" as he
was known, only took up football when his
athletics club disbanded, but after joining
Manchester City during World War One he
became a permanent fixture on their left wing
for eight years. Saints paid £350 to bring
Spud's wing skills to the Dell and he soon
showed why a local reporter had described his
play as "cute, quick and clever". His sojourn at
Southampton spanned three seasons, the first
two of which were outstanding, but a dramatic
loss of form during 1928-29 precipitated a £100
transfer to Oldham.

Appearances:
FL: 74 app. 9 gls.
FAC: 7 app. 0 gls.
Total: *81 app. 9 gls.*

NAUGHTON, William A.

Role: Forward 1895-98
b. Scotland

CAREER: Stoke July 1891/SOUTHAMPTON
St. Mary's Apr. 1895/Hibernian c.s. 1898.

Debut v Millwall (a) 14.9.1895

Described as an "inveterate practical joker" by
Saints' trainer, Billy Dawson, Will Naughton
was a member of the "Stoke Invasion" that
arrived in Southampton in April 1895.
"Chippy", as he was commonly known, had
been suspended in 1891 for playing as an
amateur while receiving payments but once at
the Antelope found form after switching from
inside to outside-right. An elusive winger, he
could pin-point his centres to perfection, and

during 1897-98, his crosses to Jack Farrell and
Bob Buchanan were partly instrumental in the
Southern League Shield being won for the first
time.

Appearances:
SL: 36 app. 15 gls.
FAC: 11 app. 3 gls.
Total: *47 app. 18 gls.*

NEVILLE, Stephen Francis

Role: Forward 1974-78
5'9" 10st.3lbs.
b. Walthamstow 18 September 1957

CAREER: Walthamstow Schools/
SOUTHAMPTON app. July 1974, pro. Oct
1975/Exeter City Sept 1978/Sheffield United

NEAL, Richard Marshall

Role: Forward 1931-37
5'9" 11st.0lbs.
b. Rotherham 14 January 1906
d. Fence 26 December 1986

CAREER: Dinnington Main/ Blackpool am.
Jan 1926, pro. Feb 1926/ Derby County May
1931/ SOUTHAMPTON Feb 1932/Bristol
City May 1937/Accrington Stanley June
1938.

Debut v Bradford (h) 20.2.32

Arriving from Derby, Dick Neal's transfer
fee was generously met by the Supporters'
Club and he was immediately plunged into
the first team. Rarely out of the side over the
next few seasons, Dick hogged the number
seven shirt and, during a period when the
team and club suffered a slump in their
fortunes, he was a model of consistency.
Clever and industrious, Bristol City sought
and succeeded in obtaining his services in 1937.

Appearances:
FL: 170 app. 17 gls.
FAC: 7 app. 0 gls.
Total: *177 app. 17 gls.*

❏ **Saints note** - *Dick came from a real footballing family as his father played for Mexborough
Athletic, his brother for Liverpool and Darlington and his brother-in-law was Hull City's Frederick
Gibson. For good measure, his son Richard won four England Under-23 caps whilst turning out for
Lincoln, Birmingham and Middlesbrough.*

Steve Neville

Oct 1980 (Exeter City-loan-Oct 1982, perm. Aug 1983)/Bristol City Nov 1984/Exeter City July 1988, player-coach c.s. 1989/South China F.C. (Hong Kong) Aug 1991.

Debut v Blackpool (h) 12.11.77

Having originally written to the club asking for a trial, Steve Neville developed into a skilful darting forward who made a fleeting substitute appearance against Millwall at the end of the 1974-75 season. Perhaps becoming a little over-confident, Steve then spent the next two and a half seasons kicking his heels in the reserves until he was given a five match stint in the 1978-79 season. Chasing first team football and moving to the lower divisions, Steve has since scored well over a hundred goals for his various clubs.

Appearances:
FL: 5 (1) app. 1 gl.
FAC: 1 (1) app. 0 gls.
Total: *6 (2) app. 1 gl.*

NICHOLL, Christopher John

Role: Centre-half 1977-83
6'11" 12st.13lbs.
b. Wilmslow 12 October 1946

CAREER: Macclesfield Schools/Burnley app. June 1963/Burnley pro. Apr 1965/Witton Albion 1966/Halifax Town June 1968/Luton Town Aug 1969/Aston Villa Mar 1972/ SOUTH-AMPTON June 1977/Grimsby Town player-asst. manager Aug 1983/ SOUTHAMPTON manager Aug 1985-June 1991/Wigan Athletic scout c.s. 1991.

Debut v Brighton & Hove Albion (h) 20.8.77

Statistically unique, Chris Nicholl is the only player who, in the same match, has scored two goals (from open play) for both sides. This dubious and unlikely feat, achieved when on the books of Aston Villa, did not inhibit Chris' development into one of the country's finest centre-halves. Lawrie McMenemy paid £80,000 to bring the Northern Irish international to the Dell when it was common knowledge that every team Chris had previously joined had won immediate promotion. This record was maintained at Southampton and, with the club back in the top flight, Chris helped to ensure they remained there with a succession of "rock like" performances in the heart of the defence. He played in Northern Ireland's memorable 1982 World Cup campaign and, winning an eventual total of 51 caps, moved on, in 1983, to Blundell Park to start his managerial appren- ticeship. Two years later the Southampton directors, left rudderless by the untimely departure of Lawrie McMenemy, took a gamble by appointing the unproven assistant manager at Grimsby as the Saints' new boss. Totally different in style and personality to Lawrie McMenemy, Chris' cautious approach kept Southampton afloat in the First Division but, under his guidance, the club never re- scaled the heady heights achieved by his predecessor. In June 1991 the directors, deeply disappointed with a poor 1990-91 season, decided to break with tradition and sack Chris who still had a year to run on his contract.

Appearances:
FL: 228 app. 8 gls.
FAC: 17 app. 0 gls.
L.C. 21 app. 1 gl.
Eur: 2 app. 0 gls.
Total: *268 app. 9 gls.*

❑ **Saints note** - *Chris' brother, Terry, was a professional with Crewe, Southend and Gillingham.*

Chris Nicholl

NICHOLLS, Ernest Frederick

Role: Forward 1891-94
b. Southampton 21 November 1871
d. Southampton February 1971

CAREER: SOUTHAMPTON St. Mary's 1888.
Debut v Warmley (a) 3.10.1891 FAC
* (scored on debut)

Ernie Nicholls was probably the club's most consistent goalscorer prior to the advent of professionalism in October 1892. Introduced as a sixteen year old to the side in October 1888, Ernie scored the club's first ever goal in the F.A. Cup at Warmley in 1891 and he proceeded to notch up over forty goals in all fixtures up until his first team retirement in 1894. A fine all-round cricketer, Ernie was a member of the Deanery Club and became their captain in 1902. Living until 1971 Ernie was approaching his hundredth year when he passed away and, remaining a keen Saints fan throughout his life, held a season ticket at the Dell for over sixty years.

Appearances:
FAC: 5 app. 4 gls.
Total: *5 app. 4 gls.*

NICOL, Thomas

Role: Full-back 1897-99
b. Whitburn, Scotland 24 February 1870.

CAREER: Carpross Swifts/Broxburn/ Burnley Feb 1891/ Mossend Swifts Mar 1891/ Blackburn Rovers Nov 1896/ SOUTHAMPTON St. Mary's c.s. 1897/ Southampton Wanderers 1902.

Debut v Sheppey United (a) 2.10.1897

Originally a forward Tom Nicol had scored four goals on his Burnley debut but, upon joining Southampton, converted into the full-back role, a position he

Tom Nicol

had always fancied himself in. Tom was a good judge of his own prowess for he became overnight one of the finest backs ever to don the cherry and white shirt. Completely fearless, even reckless, he usually won the ball irrespective of obstacles. He retired in 1899 to become the landlord of the Kingsland Tavern in St. Mary's Street and then later took over a pub in the Portsmouth area.

Appearances:
SL: 25 app. 1 gl.
FAC: 12 app. 1 gl.
Total: *37 app. 2 gls.*

❏ **Saints note** - *A bowls player of some repute, Tom became a knight in 1907 winning the 133rd Championship of the Southampton Bowling Green Club, one of the world's oldest clubs.*

NIHAN, M.

Role: Forward 1911-12

CAREER: 4th Royal Fusiliers/ SOUTHAMPTON 1911.

Debut v West Ham United (h) 6.1.12

A young army footballer, Nihan was tried at centre-forward in a game against West Ham United, after which the local press commented he "conveyed the impression of being a very serviceable player". This cursory description belied the fact that Nihan was playing out of position much preferring the right wing and, not being offered that role in his second and final game, he rejoined his regiment.

Appearances:
SL: 2 app. 0 gls.
Total: *2 app. 0 gls.*

NINEHAM, George Arthur

Role: Forward 1894-95
b. Southampton January qtr 1873
d. Bitterne Park 8 May 1950

CAREER: SOUTHAMPTON St. Mary's 1892/ Freemantle 1895.

Debut v Uxbridge (h) 4.11.1893 FAC

One of the few local players to make the transition from the friendly era to the more competitive Southern League scene, Arthur Nineham joined St. Mary's in 1892 and remained an amateur throughout his stay with the club. Arthur enjoyed taking on, and beating, defenders and his scoring record reveals an eye for goal. Employed at Southampton Docks throughout his working life, he committed suicide during old age in May 1950.

Appearances:
SL: 7 app. 4 gls.
FAC: 3 app. 5 gls.
Total: 10 app. 9 gls.

NIXON, Eric Walter

Role: Goalkeeper 1986-87
6'2" 14st.3lbs.
b. Manchester 4 October 1962

CAREER: Curzon Ashton/Manchester City app. Oct 1983, pro. Dec 1983 (Wolverhampton Wanderers-loan-Aug 1986) (Bradford City-loan-Nov 1986) (SOUTHAMPTON -loan Dec-Jan 1986-87) (Carlisle United-loan-Jan 1987) (Tranmere Rovers-loan-Mar 1988, perm. July 1988).

Debut v Chelsea (h) 26.12.86

With Tim Flowers and Peter Shilton injured, Eric Nixon came to the Dell for a loan period over Christmas 1986 and did all that was asked of him. Spending other loan spells at Bradford and Wolves and moving on to Carlisle after leaving the Dell, Eric had the unusual distinction of playing in all four divisions in the same season.

Appearances:
FL: 4 app. 0 gls.
Total: 4 app. 0 gls.

Eric Nixon

NORBURY, Duncan Victor

Role: Full-back
1906-07
5'10" 11st.8lbs.
b. Bartley
3 August 1887
d. Sutton
23 October 1972

CAREER:
Bartley/Brockenhurst/ SOUTHAMPTON 1905/Bartley Cross 1907.

Debut v Brentford (a) 29.9.06

All-round sportsman, Victor Norbury was a better cricketer than footballer but, nevertheless, was a handy full-back to have in the reserves. He showed maturity and confidence in his three outings but eventually his love for cricket took him away from full-time soccer in 1907. While trying to gain a regular position with Hampshire County Cricket Club he decided to keep fit by playing in New Forest football but broke his leg in his first game for Bartley Cross.

Appearances:
SL: 3 app. 0 gls.
Total: 3 app. 0 gls.

❏ **Saints note** - *Victor played eleven matches for Hampshire C.C.C. between 1905 and 1906 and 14 matches for Lancashire C.C.C. between 1919 and 1922.*

NORTHEY, George

Role: Forward 1901-02
b. Launceston, Devon October qtr 1883

CAREER: SOUTHAMPTON trial Apr 1902.
Debut v Luton Town (h) 9.4.02

A young Devonian, Northey was given a trial and, partnering Arthur Turner on the right wing, showed considerable knowledge of the game and some neat touches. The opinion of the local press was that the Saints should offer him a contract but, for reasons unknown, he was never heard of again.

Appearances:
SL: 1 app. 0 gls.
Total: 1 app. 0 gls.

Roy Oakley

O'BRIEN, George

Role: Forward
1959-66
5'6" 10st.11lbs.
b. Dunfermline 22 November 1935

CAREER: Blairhall Colliery/Dunfermline Athletic 1952/Leeds United Mar 1957/SOUTHAMPTON July 1959/Leyton Orient Mar 1966/Aldershot Dec 1966.

Debut v Norwich City (h) 22.8.59

In Dumfermline's first team when only 16, George O'Brien made his name as a sharp-shooting inside-right at Elland Road before Ted Bates spent £10,000 to bring him to the Dell. He immediately forged a devastating partnership with Derek Reeves that propelled the Saints to the Division Three championship in 1960. On his day George was a lethal finisher and although sometimes erratic he topped the scoring lists on four occasions and scored a total of ten hat-tricks in the League and Cup. His goalscoring rate for the club is second only to Charlie Wayman's and a return of 19 goals from 18 F.A. Cup games is fully indicative of George's predatory prowess in and around the penalty area. In November 1965 he was taken ill with jaundice and this set-back precipitated a short-lived move to Leyton Orient the following March. After an equally brief spell at Aldershot, George decided to retire and, never kicking a ball again, he became the landlord of the Waterloo Arms in Shirley. In 1990 George moved to Edinburgh to become a sub-postmaster,

George O'Brien

although within a year he had returned to Southampton and taken over another pub, the Star & Garter in Freemantle. His son played for Dunfermline (1979-81).

Appearances:
FL: 244 app. 154 gls.
FAC: 18 app. 19 gls.
LC: 15 app. 5 gls.
Total: *277 app. 178 gls.*

OAKLEY, Royston James

Role: Centre-half 1953-56
6'0" 13st.1lb.
b. Tipton, Staffs 5 January 1928

CAREER: Wolverhampton Wanderers am. May 1944/Aston Villa am. June 1946/Guernsey Rangers 1949/SOUTHAMPTON am. May 1950, pro. Nov 1950/Bath City July 1957.

Debut v Torquay United (h) 24.10.53

An engineer by trade, Roy Oakley aroused Southampton's interest when playing for Guernsey Rangers in a friendly at the Dell in April 1950 and he signed amateur forms the following month while working at Vickers Armstrong. Eventually relinquishing his amateur status to become a fully fledged professional, Roy spent most of his seven years at the Dell playing for the reserves and, being freed at the conclusion of the 1956-57 season, he moved on to taste Southern League football. He later worked for the Ministry of Defence in Bath and today lives in Wiltshire.

Appearances:
FL: 6 app. 0 gls.
Total: *6 app. 0 gls.*

O'BRIEN, Gerry

Role: Midfield
1969-76
5'6" 9st.9lbs.
b. Glasgow
10 November 1949

CAREER:
Glasgow Schools/
Drumchapel/
Clydebank 1968/
SOUTHAMPTON
Mar 1970 (Bristol
Rovers-loan Mar-
Apr 1974)/Swindon
Town Mar 1976/
Clydebank Aug
1977.

Debut v Liverpool (h)
11.3.70

A bricklayer and a
part-time
professional with
Clydebank, Gerry
O'Brien was spotted
by Saints' scout and
former goalkeeper Campbell Forsyth. Aware
that Coventry City and Nottingham Forest
were also interested, Ted Bates made the long
trek to Glasgow to watch Gerry partake in a
one-all draw with East Fife and that very
evening signed the young Scot for £22,500 - a
record for the Scottish Second Division. A
delightfully artistic player, Gerry possessed all
the necessary skills but, being small in stature,
sometimes struggled to overcome the physical
rigours of life in the First Division. In and out
of the side over a seven-year period, Gerry
broke his leg during the 1975-76 season and
transferred to Swindon in the hope of regular
first-team football. The move did not suit him
and after returning to Glasgow he was once
again playing for Clydebank when a hip injury
that necessitated an operation led to his
premature retirement and a return to
bricklaying.

Appearances:
FL: 66 (12) app. 2 gls.
FAC: 6 (4) app. 0 gls.
LC: 2 (1) app. 0 gls.
Eur: 0 (1) app. 0 gls.
Total: *74 (18) app. 2 gls.*

Gerry O'Brien

OFFER, Henry Thomas

Role: Forward
1894-95
b. Devizes 1871
d. Newport, I.O.W.
12 January 1947

CAREER: Swindon
Town/Woolwich
Arsenal Sept 1889/
Burnley Feb 1891/
SOUTHAMPTON
St. Mary's c.s. 1893.

Debut v Uxbridge
(h) 4.11.1893 FAC

A member of the
first ever Arsenal
team to appear in
the F.A. Cup, Harry
Offer also played
Cup football for St.
Mary's before
appearing in their
first ever Southern
League eleven at
home to Chatham in 1894. An aggressive
player, Harry's enthusiasm sometimes
overtook him in efforts to obtain the ball and
he found greater success after converting from
a full-back to a forward. He had the distinction
of scoring St. Mary's first ever Southern
League goal in October 1894 before he retired
to resume his profession as a joiner in 1895.

Appearances:
SL: 13 app. 4 gls.
FAC: 7 app. 6 gls.
Total: *20 app. 10 gls.*

O'GRADY, Harry

Role: Forward 1931-32
5'8" 11st.4lbs.
b. Tunstall 16 March 1907

CAREER: Church Football/Nantwich trial
1929/Witton Albion 1929/Port Vale Nov
1929/SOUTHAMPTON Aug 1931/Leeds
United Aug 1932/ Burnley May 1933/Bury
May 1934/Millwall June 1935/Carlisle Aug
1936/Accrington Stanley May 1937/Tunbridge
Wells Rangers Oct 1938.

*Debut v Burnley (h) 29.8.31 * (scored on debut)*

An inexperienced inside-right at the time of his joining Southampton, Harry O'Grady's only previous taste of League soccer had been one game for Port Vale in the 1930-31 season. Despite a scoring debut Harry spent much of his season at the Dell in the reserves and when Leeds sought his transfer he was quick to seize his chance. His stay at Elland Road was also to last just a season and mirrored his period at the Dell in that he made eight appearances for Leeds and scored twice, compared to his seven games and two goals for the Saints.

Appearances:
FL: 7 app. 2 gls.
Total: *7 app. 2 gls.*

O'NEIL, Brian

Role: Midfield 1970-75
5'7" 11st.8lbs.
b. Bedlington 4 January 1944

CAREER: Bedlington School/Burnley Jan 1961/SOUTHAMPTON May 1970/ Huddersfield Town Oct 1974/Bideford Town player-manager Sept 1976/Taunton Town 1977/Salisbury Dec 1977/Bishops Waltham Town Oct 1982.

Debut v Manchester City (h) 15.8.70

Brian O'Neil

Brian O'Neil was the club's record signing at £75,000 when he joined Southampton in the summer of 1970 and his ebullient character and terrier-like midfield play soon won approval from the terraces. Nicknamed "Buddah", Brian was frequently in trouble with referees for his over-zealousness and he was suspended on several occasions, including one spell of nine weeks. Nevertheless his resilience and energy were an inspiration to others and, a real character on or off the pitch, he once aroused the mirth of this team-mates when he took to the field of play wearing odd boots. Brian also had the ability to let fly with the ball from about thirty-five yards and, when he moved on, his spectacular shots and effervescent personality were sorely missed. Memorably scruffy, Brian was once perfectly characterised in one of Ron Davies' famous cartoons by being drawn with his socks rolled down and with a baggy shirt hanging to his knees. Nowadays he lives just outside Southampton and works in the building trade.

Appearances:
FL: 148 (1) app. 16 gls.
FAC: 7 app. 2 gls.
LC: 9 (1) app. 0 gls.
Eur: 2 app. 0 gls.
Total: *166 (2) app. 18 gls.*

OSBORNE, Frank Raymond

Role: Forward 1931-33
5'11" 10st.7lbs.
b. Wynberg, South Africa 14 October 1896
d. Epsom 7 March 1988

CAREER: Gymnasium School, S. Africa/ Netley 1911/Bromley 1919/Fulham Nov 1921/ Tottenham Hotspur Jan 1924/ SOUTHAMPTON June 1931/Fulham director Mar 1935, manager Sept 1948, general manager 1950, retired Oct 1964.

Debut v Port Vale (a) 17.10.31

South African born, Frank Osborne moved to England in 1911 and at Fulham, and particularly Tottenham, emerged to become one of the top forwards of the 1920's. Southampton paid £450 to bring the England International to the Dell which was a sizeable fee considering Frank, approaching his 35th

259

birthday, was in the autumn of his career. In May 1932, because of the club's worsening financial situation, Frank was placed on the transfer list as his wages of £8 in the winter and £6 in the summer were considered to be too extravagant. Contemplating retirement, Frank actually remained at the Dell for one more season and five more games before he returned to London to start work as a sales representative. Before long he was invited to join the board at Fulham and he remained connected with the Cottagers in varying capacities right up to his death in 1988.

Appearances:
FL: 17 app. 0 gls.
FAC: 3 app. 0 gls.
Total: 20 app. 0 gls.

❏ **Saints note** - *Frank had a younger brother, Harold, who, as an amateur, made one appearance for Norwich City. Another brother, Reg, was a left-back with Leicester City. Reg also won an England cap against Wales in 1927.*

OSGOOD, Peter Leslie

Role: Forward 1973-78
6'1" 12st.6lbs.
b. Windsor 20 February 1947

CAREER: Spital Old Boys/Windsor & Eton/ Chelsea am. Mar 1964, pro. Aug 1964/ SOUTHAMPTON Mar 1974(Norwich City-loan-Nov 1976)/Philadelphia Fury Dec 1977/ Chelsea Dec 1978-Sept 1979/Spitals & Aldwyk Bay Rowdies/Portsmouth Youth Coach June 1986-June 1988.

Debut v Stoke City (a) 16.3.74

When Lawrie McMenemy surprisingly splashed out a record £275,000 to bring Peter Osgood to the Dell he was giving Saints' fans a foretaste of his predilection for bringing high profile, senior and even wayward "stars" to the Dell. His signing coincided with the club's unsuccessful battle to avoid relegation and, in hindsight, although his arrival galvanised the city and put thousands on the gates, it did relatively little to help keep the club in the top flight. Blessed with profligate talent, Peter was a natural crowd pleaser who could control the ball and deliver a pass - seemingly in one movement. His skills were ultimately wasted in the Second Division although he showed powers of commitment and concentration that, had they been displayed earlier on in his Chelsea career, would have inevitably led to more England caps. After being released from his contract in December 1977 Peter flirted with American soccer but in December 1978 returned, rather like the prodigal son, to Stamford Bridge where he had once been so idolised. Unfortunately the magic was no longer evident and, growing disillusioned, he quit the game in September 1979 to embark on a nomadic coaching career in such diverse places as The Gambia, the Far East and Butlin's. Alan Ball appointed him Youth team coach at Fratton Park in the summer of 1986 but when the club was taken over by a new chairman in June 1988 he lost his job. In November 1990, Peter working as a sports promotions manager, organised a reunion dinner for the 1976 F.A. Cup Final team.

Appearances:
FL: 122 (4) app. 28 gls.
FAC: 12 app. 1 gl.
LC: 9 app. 2 gls.
Eur: 6 app. 2 gls.
Total: 149 (4) app. 33 gls.

Peter Osgood

OSMAN, Harry James

Harry Osman

Role: Forward
1937-39
5'7" 9st.6lbs.
b. Bentworth,
Alton 29 January
1911.

CAREER:
Okeford United/
Poole Town 1930
/Dorset County
XI 1931/
Plymouth Argyle
am. Dec 1935/
pro. Dec 1935/
SOUTHAMPTON June 1937/Millwall Mar
1939/(Southampton and British Army during
World War Two) Bristol City Oct 1947/
Dartford July 1948/ Canterbury City player-
manager 1951/ Winchester City permit-player
1952, manager 1953-Oct 1957.

Debut v Norwich City (a) 28.8.37
* (scored on debut)

Harry Osman had first caught the eye when
Tom Parker was manager of Norwich City and
later, when installed as Saints' boss, Parker
moved with alacrity to bring the Hampshire-
born forward to the Dell on a free transfer.
Harry made an immediate impact and his
twenty-two goals scored in 1937-38 from the
outside-left berth was the most ever recorded
from that position for the club. The following
season Harry continued to play well but was
less prolific and Millwall persuaded Saints to
release him for £2,000, a transfer which came
as a shock to most of the fans. Harry
returned to the Dell several times during
the war playing as a guest but was later
wounded while serving with the Tank
Corps in Italy. In the fifties he combined
the running of the Wyke-ham Arms in
Winchester with the task of running the
city's Football Club and was instrumental
in recommending Terry Paine to his ex-
Saint colleague, Ted Bates. Today Harry
lives in Florida but avidly continues to
follow the Saints' fortunes.

Appearances:
FL: 70 app. 31 gls.
FAC: 1 app. 0 gls.
Total: *71 app. 31 gls.*

OSMAN, Russell Charles

Role: Centre-half 1988-1991
6'0" 11st.10lbs.
b. Repton 14 February 1959

CAREER: Ipswich Town app July 1975, pro
Mar 1976/Leicester City July 1985/
SOUTHAMPTON June 1988/Bristol City Dec
1991.

Debut v West Ham United 27.8.88

Russell Osman's career as a stylish central
defender blossomed under the astute guidance
of Bobby Robson at Portman Road and when
the Ipswich manager took charge of England
he rewarded Russell by picking him eleven
times for the national side. A decline, however,
in the fortunes of Ipswich seemed to coincide
with stagnation in Russell's own career and
Gordon Milne, Leicester's manager decided to
invest £240,000 to bring the elegant
international to Filbert Street. Unfortunately
Leicester quickly followed Ipswich into the
Second Division and it was left to Chris
Nicholl to resurrect Russell's flagging
prospects. During his spell at the Dell he
played some good games and even scored
several spectacular goals but by and large
flattered to deceive. Certainly he never
displayed the qualities that made him first
choice for England although he could at times
still adopt a composed air. During 1990-91 his
form varied dramatically and after a series of
public disagreements with the manager
Russell decided, in the close season of 1991, to
refuse a new contract and seek another club.
However, in the wake of Nicholl's departure,
new boss Ian Branfoot persuaded the defender
to accept a further year's
terms, but he still moved
on to Bristol City before
the year end.

Appearances:
FL: 87 (4) app. 6 gls.
FAC: 7 app. 0 gls.
LC: 18 app. 0 gls.
Total: *112 (4) app. 6 gls.*

❏ **Saints note** - *Russell's
father, Rex, made two
appearances for Derby
County in the 1953-54
season.*

Russell Osman

PADDINGTON, Albert Hillman

Role: Half-back 1900-03
5'5" 11st.10lbs.
b. Bishopstoke 30 June 1881

CAREER: Bishopstoke 1895/Chandlers Ford 1897 /Eastleigh Athletic 1898/ SOUTHAMPTON Sept 1899/Brighton & Hove Albion c.s. 1903/Eastleigh Athletic 1906.

Debut v Reading (h) 13.10.1900

Bert Paddington

One of the rare breed of local players to make the grade at the turn of the century, Bert Paddington or "Paddy" as he was more popularly known, became captain of the reserves soon after joining the club. He was an able deputy either at left or right-half and in February 1902 had his finest game for the club when, in a cup replay against Spurs, he completely shackled Cameron and Gilhooley two of Tottenham's strikers. Never rewarded with an extended run in the first team he moved along the south coast to Brighton before rejoining Eastleigh Athletic.

Appearances:
SL: 12 app. 0 gls.
FAC: 2 app. 0 gls.
Total: *14 app. 0 gls.*

PAGE, John

Role: Half-back 1952-61
5'10" 13st.2lbs.
b. Frimley Green 21 October 1934

CAREER: Mytchett Boys/Surrey Schools/ SOUTHAMPTON Oct 1951/Hastings United June 1962.

Debut v Sheffield United. (a) 8.11.52

John Page was discovered playing for Surrey Schools by Saints' trainer, Jimmy Easson, and had his first game in a red and white shirt while still a schoolboy. John made his league bow playing on the left-wing but, once he had filled out, converted into a natural half-back

particularly at home in the number five shirt. He was a model of consistency and also became the club's penalty taker with all but three of his goals coming from the spot. During the 1961-62 season John suffered a slipped disc which, together with the arrival of Tony Knapp, heralded an end to his innings at the Dell and, turning down the chance to join Eric Webber's Torquay United, he eventually ended his playing days at Hastings. Today John lives in Camberley, Surrey.

Appearances:
FL: 190 app. 24 gls.
FAC: 12 app. 1 gl.
LC: 7 app. 1 gl.
Total: *209 app. 26 gls.*

John Page

PAINE, Terence Lionel M.B.E.

Role: Forward 1956-74
5'7" 10st.8lbs.
b. Winchester 23 March 1939

CAREER: All Saints School/Highcliffe Corinthians/Winchester City 1954/ SOUTHAMPTON am. Aug 1956, pro. Feb 1957/Hereford United player-coach Aug 1974 /Kazma (Kuwait) coach 1977/Coventry City scout 1980/Cheltenham Town manager Nov 1980/Wits University, South Africa 1983/ Coventry City Youth team coach May 1988/ Wits University Apr 1991.

Debut v Brentford (h) 16.3.57

A member of Winchester City's first team while still a fifteen year-old schoolboy, it was obvious that Terry Paine had the talent to go all the way and it was fortunate for Southampton that he chose to join them in preference to Portsmouth or Arsenal, both of which had given him a trial. After giving up his job as a coach-builder at Eastleigh's British Rail Depot Terry's rise to stardom was guaranteed to be meteoric and after just one outing in the reserves he was given his first team debut. The following week, on his 18th birthday, he scored in an away fixture at Aldershot and over the next 17 years hardly missed a game. Oozing confidence, the young winger initially infuriated the seasoned Dell professionals but, to a man, they all recall being impressed by his undoubted ability, if not enchanted by his brashness. With maturity, Terry gained not only respect from his colleagues but international recognition when he played and scored in an England Under-23 match against Holland in March 1960. Possessing superb ball-crossing skills, Terry could land a ball on a sixpence and Derek Reeves and George O'Brien were the first of many forwards to capitalise on the expertise of the canny winger, as Saints marched to the 1960 Division Three Championship. As Saints' fortunes prospered so did Terry's and, after being made team captain in August 1961, he won the first of 19 full England caps in May 1963. Becoming an integral part of Alf Ramsey's build-up plans for the 1966 World Cup, Terry made the 22-man squad and played in one game (versus Mexico) in the finals themselves. Unfortunately that game was to be his last in an England shirt as Alf Ramsey chose to discard wing-men, but on the club front Terry's career was entering a more promising era. He had just scored the vital goal at Leyton Orient that confirmed Saints' promotion to the First Division and his visionary skills were about to be needed more than ever. Over the next few seasons Terry, with help from fellow winger John Sydenham, provided the pin-point crosses on which forwards such as Ron Davies and Martin Chivers were to thrive. Gradually, with the almost total demise of wingers, Terry took his passing proficiencies into midfield and his dexterous distribution was partially instrumental in the launching of Mike Channon's spectacular rise to prominence. Steering clear of serious injury in a remarkable way, Terry often was guilty of committing petty fouls and any games missed were usually the result of suspensions arising from such indiscretions. After breaking both goalscoring and appearances records, Terry's long and meritorious career in the red and white stripes finally ended in August 1974 and, moving to Hereford, he participated in a further 106 games to establish an all-time league record of 819 appearances. Goalkeeper Peter Shilton has since beaten this figure but the record for an outfield player remains intact

Terry Paine

Terry Paine

and looks unlikely to be beaten. Awarded the M.B.E. for his services to football Terry had indulged in various business interests while at the Dell and had also been a Southampton Borough Councillor for three years but, upon retirement, decided to remain in football, concentrating on coaching. Much of the eighties were spent in Johannesburg where he was the manager of a multi-racial club but in 1988 he returned to live in the Midlands to work with John Sillett, a colleague from his Hereford United days, as Coventry City's Youth team coach. In 1990 he was invited to present Matthew Le Tissier with his Young Player of the Year award and became involved in the World Cup by working for the South African media. No other player has served Southampton so admirably and only Ted Bates (significantly in charge throughout Terry's life as a Saint) has made a larger contribution to the club's fortunes.

Appearances:
FL: 709 (4) app. 160 gls.
FAC: 50 app. 11 gls.
LC: 37 app. 12 gls.
Eur: 8 app. 2 gls.
Total: *804 (4) app. 185 gls.*

❑ **Saints note** - *It is believed that Terry Paine is the only player wearing the number seven shirt to have scored a hat-trick at Wembley.*

Pat Parker

PARKER, Patrick John

Role: Centre-half 1951-59
6'1" 11st.5lbs.
b. Bow, Devon 15 July 1929

CAREER: Bere Alston/R.A.F. Chilmark/ Plymouth Argyle am. 1949/Newton Abbott 1950/SOUTHAMPTON Aug 1951/Poole Town July 1959/Cowes July 1960, manager June 1961, general manager Apr. 1975.
Debut v Leicester City (a) 3.9.51

A part-time professional with Newton Abbott, Pat Parker had been overlooked by local sides Torquay United and Plymouth Argyle before Sid Cann spotted his talents in a friendly match against the Saints. His early years at the Dell were marred by injury - at the end of his first season in a friendly game against his old club he broke a leg and then twelve months later, in another friendly against R.A.F.

Maintenance Command, he fractured the same limb. Pat fought back from these setbacks and some sterling performances in the heart of the Southampton defence received recognition when he was selected to play for the Third Division South v Third Division North at Coventry in November 1956. Transfer-listed in May 1959 he joined Poole Town on a free transfer the following month and then, in 1961, began a long association with Cowes on the Isle of Wight. Pat played frequently for the Yachtsmen until his 49th birthday and today he continues to live in Southampton.

Appearances:
FL: 132 app. 0 gls.
FAC: 10 app. 0 gls.
Total: *142 app. 0 gls.*

PARKER, Thomas Robert

Role: Full-back 1919-26
5'10" 12st.0lbs.
*b. Peartree Green, Southampton
19 November 1897
d. Southampton
1 November 1987*

CAREER: St. Marks
(Woolston)/Sholing
Rangers/Sholing
Athletic/SOUTHAMPTON am. 1918, pro.
May 1919/Arsenal Mar 1926/ Norwich City
manager Mar 1933/ SOUTHAMPTON
manager Feb 1937-June 1943/Norwich City
manager Apr 1955-Mar. 1957/
SOUTHAMPTON scout 1962, chief scout Aug
1963-July 1975.

Debut v Exeter City (h) 30.8.19

Without doubt one of the greatest full-backs to
ever grace the Dell, Tom Parker won every
honour the game had to offer during a long
and distinguished career. He served his
apprenticeship playing in minor war league
football and first appeared in a Saints shirt in
1918. A renowned penalty-taker, Tom scored
ten out of ten during the 1918-19 season which,
added to the two goals scored from open play,
made him the club's second highest scorer
behind Bill Rawlings. Such form warranted his
engagement for the more strenuous Southern
League programme which was due to restart
in 1919 and he began a long full-back
partnership with Fred Titmuss which became
famed throughout the land. Never the fastest
of players, he had wonderful positional sense
and his tackling was always well-timed. He
won his one and only England cap in May
1925 in Paris against France and, thrust into
the international limelight, became the subject
of many big offers from the top glamour clubs.
Initially Southampton resisted such overtures
but with money needed to finance the
purchase of the Dell they reluctantly accepted
an Arsenal offer of £3,250 and he moved on to
Highbury. Arsenal, under Herbert Chapman,
were about to enter a golden era and Tom was
immediately made captain, a position he held
for six seasons. The undoubted highlight of his
career came in the 1930 F.A. Cup Final when
he received the trophy from King George V
after the 2-0 win against Huddersfield. (This

was the second of his three Cup Final
appearances, for he was in the Arsenal
side that lost to Cardiff in 1927 and
Newcastle in 1932). After 258 League
games and League Championship
success in 1930-31 he gave up playing in
1933 to become manager of Norwich
City. At the Nest he led Norwich to
promotion in 1934 and first engaged the
young Ted Bates who was to follow Tom
to the Dell when he became Saints'
manager in 1937. The war interrupted his
attempts to rebuild a decent Southampton
side and after a row with the Saints board
in June 1943, he resigned to pursue a
career with the Ministry of Transport as a
ship's surveyor in Southampton Docks. Apart
from a two-year spell back in soccer
management with Norwich, between 1955 and
1957 Tom remained in this job until his
retirement in 1962. Soon after he was
approached by Saints' manager, Ted Bates, to
become a part-time scout, later chief scout, and
by the time of his final retirement from this
position in 1975 he had introduced many fine
young players to the club. He died just weeks
before his 90th birthday but remained
sprightly and interested in Southampton's
fortunes right up until the end.

Appearances:
SL: 40 app. 4 gls.
FL: 206 app. 7 gls.
FAC: 29 app. 1 gl.
Total: *275 app. 12 gls.*

❑ **Saints note** - *Southampton reached the semi-
final of the 1924-25 F.A. Cup but were eliminated
when Tom scored an own goal, missed a penalty
and was then involved in a mix-up which resulted
in Sheffield United's second goal.*

PARKIN, Raymond

Role: Forward 1937-39
5'10" 12st.0lbs.
*b. Crook, Co. Durham 28 January 1911
d. Market Bosworth, Leics 18 July 1971*

CAREER: Esh Winning/Newcastle United am.
Oct 1926/Arsenal Feb 1928/Middlesbrough
Jan 1936/SOUTHAMPTON Sept 1937.

Debut v West Ham United (h) 18.9.37
* (scored on debut)

A former team-mate of Southampton manager

Ray Parkin

Tom Parker at Arsenal, Ray Parkin was purchased for a fee of £1,500 from Middlesbrough and when he scored on his debut his goal ended a club drought that had endured 524 minutes. Very versatile, he operated in the half-back, inside and centre-forward positions but, with the outbreak of war, joined up and never played professionally again.

Appearances:
FL: 57 app. 10 gls.
FAC: 1 app. 0 gls.
Total: *58 app. 10 gls.*

PATON, David Samuel Craig

Role: Centre-half 1963-68
6'0" 11st.0lbs.
b. Saltcoats 13 December 1943

CAREER: Saltcoats Junior School/
Saxone 1959 /St. Mirren 1962/
SOUTHAMPTON July 1963/

Aldershot Nov 1969 (Margate-loan-Jan-Mar 1971, transferred July 1971)/ Irvine Meadow 1972/Irvine New Town coaching.
Debut v Northampton Town (a) 4.4.64

Given a free transfer by St. Mirren in May 1963, David Paton was invited to the Dell for a trial and after playing in the final Combination game of the season was signed on a professional footing. Considered to be the "automatic reserve team centre-half" throughout his life as a Saint, his first team appearances were few and far between. Wallowing in the reserves for six seasons, Dave's defensive qualities could have been put to better use elsewhere but he remained loyal until November 1969 when a £5,000 transfer took him to Jimmy Melia's Aldershot. In 1972 Dave returned to Scotland where he has since worked as fork-lift driver and storeman in Irvine and he maintains an interest in the game by coaching a youth side called Irvine New Town.

Appearances:
FL: 13 app. 0 gls.
LC: 2 app. 0 gls.
Total: *15 app. 0 gls.*

David Paton

PATRICK, Roy

Role: Full-back 1961-63
5'11" 12st.9lbs.
b. Overseal 4 December 1935

CAREER: Derby County
Feb 1952/Nottingham
Forest May 1959/
SOUTHAMPTON June
1961/Exeter City Mar
1963/Burton Albion Aug
1965.

*Debut v Plymouth Argyle
(h) 19.8.61*

Roy Patrick made his
debut for Derby aged 16
years 277 days and was
their youngest post-war
player until Steve Powell's
debut in 1971. After a spell
at Nottingham Forest he
was recommended to Ted
Bates by Joe Mallett and duly arrived at the
Dell in the summer of 1961. He failed to hold
down a regular place and was put on the
transfer list at his own request in September
1962, eventually moving to Exeter City six
months later. Soon after Roy suffered a back
injury which persuaded him to seek
employment outside the game and he joined
Rolls-Royce in the Midlands. Still employed
with the same company Roy now lives near
Glasgow where he is a season ticket holder at
Ibrox.

Roy Patrick

    Appearances:
FL: 31 app. 0 gls.
FAC: 2 app. 0 gls.
Total: *33 app. 0 gls.*

PATTEN, J.

Role: Forward 1906-07

CAREER: Shrewsbury/SOUTHAMPTON trial
Mar 1907.
Debut v Watford (h) 30.3.07

On trial, Patten arrived at the Dell having been
told he was due to play for the reserves at
Ryde but, because of an injury crisis, was
shocked to find himself included in the senior
eleven against Watford at the Dell. The local
press, describing his
performance, commented:
"His policy of parting
before an opponent can
get to him is to be
commended", and in his
four games he managed to
use this elusiveness to
have his name written on
the score sheet twice. It is
unknown whether it was
the club's decision or his
not to prolong his career
in a red and white shirt,
for in the summer Patten
moved back to
Shrewsbury.

    Appearances:
SL: 4 app. 2 gls.
Total: *4 app. 2 gls.*

PEACH, David Sidney

Role: Full-back 1973-80
5'9" 10st.13lbs.
b. Bedford 21 January 1951

CAREER: Chelsea ass. schoolboy Oct 1965/
Gillingham app May 1966/pro with F.A. Feb
1969/Bedford Town/Gillingham pro Sept
1969/SOUTHAMPTON Jan 1974/Swindon
Town Mar 1980/Orient Mar 1982/Andover
Aug 1983/Wellworthy Athletic player-
manager June 1986/Christchurch manager
Apr 1990, resigned July 1991/AFC Lymington
Sept 1991.

Debut v Ipswich Town (a) 2.2.74

A former Huntingdonshire cricketer, David
Peach was rated as the best player in the
Fourth Division by Lawrie McMenemy when
he made him his first signing in January 1974.
His full debut came in a disastrous 7-0 defeat
at Ipswich but, after a few games in midfield,
David settled to become an accomplished,
attacking left-back. He became the club's
regular penalty-taker and, while the whole of
Southampton held their breath, he coolly
stroked home the second goal in the F.A. Cup
semi-final against Crystal Palace. One of only
two players (the other being Nick Holmes) to
have played in two Wembley finals for the
club, David added to his F.A. Cup winners'
medal by collecting England Under-21 caps

David Peach

and a call-up to the full England squad when they toured South America in 1977. Unlucky not to get a game, he nevertheless made national headlines when, netting from the spot against Manchester United on August 18th 1979, he became the highest scoring full-back in the Football League's history. Transferred to Swindon Town for £150,000, David later had a spell with Orient where he became the only player in the Football League at that time to have played on every ground. Today David lives in the New Forest where he runs his own building and decorating business.

Appearances:
FL: 221 (3) app. 34 gls.
FAC: 21 (1) app. 6 gls.
LC: 20 app. 2 gls.
Eur: 5 app. 2 gls.
Total: *267 (4) app. 44 gls.*

PEARSON, Harold

Role: Forward 1923-24
5'8" 11st.4lbs.
b. Brierley Hill 7 January 1901
d. Dudley, W.Midlands October qtr. 1972

CAREER: Brierley Hill/SOUTHAMPTON May 1923.

Debut v Sheffield Wednesday (h) 14.9.23
*(scored on debut)

An import from Birmingham League football, Harold Pearson was brought to the Dell to act as cover for Bill Rawlings. Scoring twice on his debut, he was quick and determined and many fans felt he wasn't given enough chances to establish himself properly. Transfer-listed in May 1924 for £250, Harold gave up full-time soccer and returned to the Midlands.

Appearances:
FL: 8 app. 4 gls.
Total: *8 app. 4 gls.*

PECK, W. S.

Role: Forward 1892-93
CAREER: SOUTHAMPTON St. Mary's Sept 1892.
Debut v Newbury (h) 15.10.1892 FAC

W. S. Peck's origin and fate is unclear but it is known he first appeared in St. Mary's team at the beginning of the 1892-93 season and played in the first seven games which included the F.A. Cup victory over Newbury. At home on the left or in the centre-forward role he was dropped following a 5-0 defeat at the hands of Swindon in November 1892 and then disappeared from contemporary records.

Appearances:
FAC: 1 app. 0 gls.
Total: *1 app. 0 gls.*

PENK, Henry

Role: Forward 1960-64
5'4" 10st.3lbs.
b. Wigan 19 July 1934

CAREER: Wigan Athletic/Portsmouth Sept 1955/Plymouth Argyle June 1957/ SOUTHAMPTON July 1960/Salisbury July 1964/Basingstoke Town June 1965/New Milton Jan 1971.

Debut v Middlesbrough (a) 10.9.60

An experienced winger, Harry cost the Saints £1,500 and was regarded as a plucky player who used the ball intelligently. At home on either wing he found the competition for a first team place stiff as Paine and Sydenham had

Harry Penk

PENTON, Harry Baven

Role: Forward 1910-12 & 1912-13
5'11" 10st.12lbs.
b. Boscombe January qtr. 1890

CAREER: Pokesdown St.James/Pokesdown/
Boscombe/SOUTHAMPTON Feb 1911/
Boscombe Jan 1912/SOUTHAMPTON c.s.
1912/Boscombe 1913/Eastleigh Athletic 1914
retired 1928.
Debut v Crystal Palace (a) 25.2.11

A prolific marksman in his minor league days,
registering 60 in one season with Pokesdown
and 26 in another with Boscombe, Baven
Penton made his debut for the Saints within
two days of his arrival. He became a regular
feature in the forward line in the latter half of
the 1910-11 season but, after struggling to
reproduce his shooting skills the following
year, he joined Boscombe for a fee of £10 and
became their first ever professional at 30
shillings a week. Six months later he moved
back to the Dell but, with a new manager in
charge, he made only one appearance before
again crossing the New Forest to rejoin the
Cherries. After the Great War Baven
reappeared playing in goal for Eastleigh
Athletic.

Appearances:
SL: 14 app. 3 gls.
Total: *14 app. 3 gls.*

made the numbers seven and eleven shirts
their own during the 1959-60 championship
season. However, with the latter called up for
National Service, Harry took his chance and
enjoyed two fairly consistent seasons before
the return of John Sydenham finally brought
the curtain down on his league career.
Employed ever since at Husband's Shipyard in
Southampton, Harry, apart from being an
enthusiastic member of the Ex-Saints XI, has
played amateur cricket with Hursley Park and
was with them when they went all the way to
the Lord's final in the 1984 village knockout
competition.

Appearances:
FL: 52 app. 6 gls.
FAC: 4 app. 1 gl.
LC: 4 app. 0 gls.
Total: *60 app. 7 gls.*

Baven Penton

PERFECT, Frank Thomas

Role: Full-back 1938-39
5'9" 12st.2lbs.
b. Gorleston 9 March 1915
d. Guiseley 17 July 1977

CAREER: Stradbroke Road/Yarmouth Town
Boys/Gorleston am./ Norfolk County
1932/Norwich City Mar 1933 am /Mansfield
Town June 1936/Wolverhampton Wanderers
Dec 1936/Tranmere Rovers Feb 1938/
SOUTHAMPTON Jan 1939.

Debut v Newcastle United (h) 28.1.39

In January 1939 Southampton crashed out of
the F.A. Cup at the hands of non-League side
Chelmsford and Tom Parker, angry at the
team's humiliating performance, was anxious
to sign new players. Having been previously
acquainted with Frank Perfect's talents when
both men were at Norwich City he moved
swiftly to bring the bulky full-back to the Dell
for a fee of £2,500. In his fifteen league
appearances Frank did all that was asked of
him and also displayed a liking for hitting
good long through passes. Like so many of his
contemporaries Frank terminated his
professional career at the outbreak of the
Second World War.

Appearances:
FL: 15 app. 0 gls.
Total: *15 app. 0 gls.*

PETRIE, Charles

Role: Forward 1927-29
5'8" 11st.0lbs.
b. Chorlton July qtr. 1895

CAREER: Openshaw/
Manchester City am.
Sept 1918/Stalybridge
Celtic c.s. 1919/
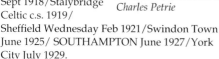
Charles Petrie
Sheffield Wednesday Feb 1921/Swindon Town
June 1925/ SOUTHAMPTON June 1927/York
City July 1929.

Debut v Leeds United (a) 3.9.27

Transfer-listed by Swindon Town in the
summer of 1927, Charles Petrie's signature was
secured for a £150 transfer fee. An experienced
inside-forward, although past his prime,
Charles provided extra competition for first
team places and scored some vital goals
during his stay at the Dell. After moving to

York City on a free transfer he failed to make
their league side and retired soon after.

Appearances:
FL: 24 app. 7 gls.
Total: *24 app. 7 gls.*

PETRIE, Robert

Role: Half-back 1897-1900
5'7" 11st.0lbs.
b. Dundee 25 October 1874

CAREER: Arbroath/Dundee East End/
Dundee/Sheffield Wednesday Apr 1893/
SOUTHAMPTON May 1897/New Brighton
Tower Oct 1900/Arbroath 1905/Dundee
Wanderers 1908.

Debut v Tottenham Hotspur (a) 18.9.1897

Familiar to Southampton fans due to his
contribution to Sheffield Wednesday's F.A.
Cup victory at the Antelope in 1896, Bob Petrie
arrived in the town in May 1897 and made no
little contribution to his new club's impressive
showing in the same competition over the next
three years. Very much a team player, Bob was
never showy but always reliable and at his best
when the chips were down. He made his last
appearance for the Saints in the 1900 Cup Final
against Bury.

Appearances:
SL: 50 app. 6 gls.
FAC: 18 app. 0 gls.
Total: *68 app. 6 gls.*

PHILLIPS, 'Gunner'

Role: Full-back 1895-96

CAREER: Royal Artillery (Portsmouth)/
SOUTHAMPTON St. Mary's-loan- Apr
1896/R.G.A. Portsmouth.

Debut v Clapton (h) 3.4.96

Phillips was a member of the Royal Artillery
team that won the Army and Hampshire Cups
and was loaned to the Saints when regular
full-back, Hamer, was injured. After returning
to the Artillery side he played in their F.A.
Amateur Cup Final defeat by Bishop Auckland
and was still a regular when the side gained
promotion to the Southern League in 1898.

Appearances:
SL: 1 app. 0 gls.
Total: *1 app. 0 gls.*

PHILLIPSON-MASTERS, Forbes E.

Role: Centre-half 1976-78
6'1" 12st.10lbs.
b. Bournemouth 14 November 1955

CAREER: Bournemouth Schools/Wimborne Youth Club/SOUTHAMPTON app. Aug 1972, pro. June 1974(Exeter City-loan Sept-Oct 1976) (Bournemouth-loan Sept-Oct 1977)(Luton Town -loan Mar-May 1979)/Plymouth Argyle Aug 1979(Bristol City-loan-Nov 1982, transferred Jan 1983 (Exeter City loan-Mar-Apr) /Yeovil Town Aug 1985/Weston-Super-Mare coach 1987/Poole Town Aug 1987 (Registered but never played).

Debut v Bristol Rovers (a) 9.4.77

Forbes Phillipson-Masters, a name that reads like a half-back line, served his Southampton apprenticeship as a goalkeeper only to be given a free transfer in 1974 by Lawrie McMenemy. John McGrath, then Saints youth team coach, persuaded the youngster to try his luck in the centre-half position and, working hard to perfect his game, Forbes soon showed an aptitude for playing out on the field. Bill Stroud, another back-room coach at the Dell, once described Forbes as the only "manufactured" player he had ever seen, but an eventual £50,000 transfer to Plymouth where he was to make over a hundred league appearances proved the worth of John McGrath's conversion techniques.

Appearances:
FL: 9 app. 0 gls.
Total: *9 app. 0 gls.*

PICKERING, Michael John

Role: Centre-half 1977-79
5'11" 12st.6lbs.
b. Huddersfield 29 September 1956

CAREER: Heckmondwyke Grammar School/ Spen Valley Boys/Barnsley Oct 1974/ SOUTHAMPTON June 1977/Sheffield Wednesday Oct 1978(Norwich City-loan Sept-Oct 1983)/San Diego Sockers May-July 1981 (Bradford City-loan Nov-Dec 1983)(Barnsley-loan Dec 1983)/Rotherham United Jan 1984/ York City July 1986/Stockport County July 1987/Hallam/Goole Town 1989/Frickley Athletic Aug 1991.

Debut v Brighton & Hove Albion (h) 10.8.77

Forbes Phillipson-Masters

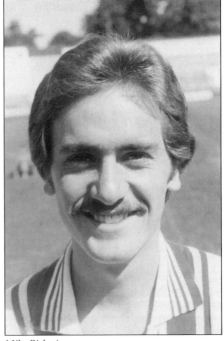

Mike Pickering

Signed from Barnsley for £35,000, Mike Pickering made the transition from Fourth to Second Division football with the greatest of ease and, playing alongside another newcomer Chris Nicholl, missed just one game in the promotion season of 1977-78. Strong and quick into the tackle his future looked assured but Lawrie McMenemy decided that he was not up to life in the top flight and, much to the surprise of the fans, he was allowed to move to Hillsborough. Having made 100 appearances for his previous club Barnsley, Mike went on to also play over 100 games for two of his subsequent teams, Sheffield Wednesday and Rotherham.

Appearances:
FL: 44 app. 0 gls.
FAC: 4 app. 0 gls.
LC: 3 app. 0 gls.
Total: *51 app. 0 gls.*

❏ **Saints note** - *By the time he was 22 years old Mike had already played in all four divisions.*

PIKE, Ernest Harry

Role: Full-back 1902-03
b. Southampton July qtr. 1880
d. Westend, Southampton 18 January 1960

CAREER: SOUTHAMPTON 1902, re-instated am. May 1905.
Debut v Reading (h) 14.2.03

Not a lot is known about this young full-back except that he was plucked from the reserves to replace Molyneux, who was away on international duty, and performed well in a makeshift team that beat Reading 4-1.

Appearances:
SL: 1 app. 0 gls.
Total: *1 app. 0 gls.*

POLLARD, Walter

Role: Forward 1934-36
5'9" 11st.2lbs.
b. Burnley 26 September 1906
d. Burnley 16 April 1945

CAREER: Burnley Sunday School League/ Burnley Sept 1924/West Ham United June 1929/Soucaux (France) player-coach 1933/ Fulham July 1934/SOUTHAMPTON Dec 1934 /Brighton June 1936.

Walter Pollard

Debut v Bradford City (h) 9.2.35

Having initially exchanged the claret and blue of his home town club, Burnley, for that of West Ham, Walter Pollard next tried his luck in France. His stay as player-coach was brief as he failed to get on with the Gallic temperament of some of his colleagues and preferred a return to English soccer, firstly with Fulham and then Southampton. He was an industrious inside-forward whose experience as a coach was of particular benefit to younger players at the Dell. After serving Brighton equally well, Walter found employment in the Electricity Department of Ilford Borough Council and coached the works' side until a heart attack took his life at the very young age of 38.

Appearances:
FL: 23 app. 3 gls.
Total: *23 app. 3 gls.*

PONTING, William Robert

Role: Half-back 1896-97
b. Andover 1872
d. Whetstone, Middlesex 21 March 1952

CAREER: Andover/Ryde/SOUTHAMPTON St. Mary's Mar 1897/Andover 1897.
Debut v Reading (a) 31.3.1897

An Andover schoolmaster, Billy Ponting was a leading amateur player in Hampshire football circles and he had been captain of the County Junior eleven in 1893. He was given a spell in the St. Mary's team in April 1896 when Hodgkinson was injured, and played his part in the run-in to the club's first Southern League title. He retired from serious football that summer and continued with his teaching career although he was later to become an influential insurance broker in London during the 1930's.

Appearances:
SL: 5 app. 0 gls.
Total: *5 app. 0 gls.*

POWELL, Lee

Role: Forward 1990-
5'8" 8st.10lbs
b. Newport, Gwent 2 June 1973

CAREER: SOUTHAMPTON trainee August 1989, pro. May 1991.
Debut v Rochdale (h) 9.10.90 (as sub) LC

Lee Powell had the unusual distinction of playing for the Welsh Under-21 side before he had made his full first team debut for Southampton or indeed even signed professional terms. Saints' fans had seen him fleetingly in the Rumbelows League Cup match against Rochdale when he showed a clean pair of heels to the Rochdale full-backs on a couple of occasions and he reminded many of John Sydenham.

Appearances:
LC: 0 (1) app. 0 gls.
Total: *0 (1) app. 0 gls.*

PRATT, Wayne

Role: Midfield 1980-81
5'8" 9st.9lbs.
*b. Southampton
1 March 1960*

CAREER:
Price's College/
SOUTHAMPTON app.
July 1976, pro. Mar 1978
/Waterlooville c.s.
1981/Portsmouth trial

Wayne Pratt

Apr 1982/F.C. Mein Munkfors (Sweden) summer 1982/ Reading trial Oct 1982/Waterlooville Oct 1982/Gosport Borough Aug 1984/Andover Apr 1985/Road Sea, Southampton Mar 1987/Weymouth/ Poole Town/Netley Central July 1989.
Debut v Leeds United. (h) 22.11.80

A product of the club's youth policy, Wayne Pratt was skipper of the reserves in the 1980-81 season and was thrust into his Division One debut when the club was in the middle of an injury crisis. Not retained in the ensuing close season Wayne embarked on the non-league trail and also enjoyed a summer playing in Sweden.

Appearances;
FL: 1 app. 0 gls.
Total: *1 app. 0 gls.*

PRICE, Ernest Clifford

Role: Forward 1923-26
5'9" 11st.0lbs.
b. Market Bosworth, Leics 13 June 1900

CAREER: Coalville Swifts/Leicester Fosse am. Jan 1917, pro. Oct 1920/(Coalville Swifts-loan-Nov 1919)/Halifax Town June 1922/ SOUTHAMPTON Dec 1923/Nottingham Forest June 1926/Loughborough Corinthians Oct 1928.
Debut v South Shields (a) 22.12.23

Described as "an inside-left of the studious type" by the local press of the day, Cliff Price formed an immediate understanding with James Carr and his debut coincided with the club's first away win of the season. His passes were usually well-judged and after giving good service for three seasons he returned to the Midlands.

Appearances:
FL: 59 app. 16 gls.
FAC: 6 app. 2 gls.
Total: *65 app. 18 gls.*

❏ **Saints note** - *Cliff was the uncle of Fred Price (1924-25) and the two relatives appeared together in the same team on six occasions.*

Cliff Price

Fred Price

PRICE, Frederick Thomas

Role: Forward 1924-25
5'6" 9st.9lbs.
b. Ibstock, Leics 24 October 1901

CAREER: Whitwick Imperial/Leicester City
Nov 1920/SOUTHAMPTON May 1924/
Wolverhampton Wanderers May 1925/
Chesterfield c.s. 1927.
Debut v Coventry City (a) 20.9.24

The nephew of Cliff Price (1923-26), Fred Price
arrived at the Dell with Denis Jones from
Leicester City as part of an exchange deal that
saw Harry Hooper move to Filbert Street.
At Leicester he was considered to be a clever
player but first team opportunities were few,
which was also to be the case at the Dell. He
did form a brief partnership on the left-wing
with his uncle but in May 1925 he asked for a
transfer and moved for £250 to Wolverhampton Wanderers.

Appearances:
FL: 9 app. 0 gls.
Total: *9 app. 0 gls.*

❑ **Saints Note** - *Fred's brother, Jack, played for
Leicester Reserves, Bristol Rovers, Swindon Town
and Torquay United.*

PRICE, T.

Role: Full-back 1893-94

CAREER: Geneva Cross/SOUTHAMPTON St.
Mary's 1891.
Debut v Reading (a) 25.11.1893 FAC

"Ginger" Price was recruited from Netley
side Geneva Cross in 1891 but took some time
to figure regularly in the first team. He was a
hard-tackling full-back whose speed and
finesse won him plenty of admirers and it
was a shame that a serious leg injury
sustained in January 1894 was to end a
promising career.

Appearances:
FAC: 1 app. 0 gls.
Total: *1 app. 0 gls.*

PRINCE, Percy

Role: Forward 1908-14 & 1919-1920
5'10" 12st.0lbs.
b. Liverpool 15 August 1887
d. Rutherford, New Jersey U.S.A. December 1973

CAREER: Cranbury Avenue/Southampton
Oxford/SOUTHAMPTON 1907/Boscombe c.s.
1914/SOUTHAMPTON Aug 1919/Boscombe
Nov 1920/Harland and Wolff Aug 1921/
Cunard Sports manager 1923.

Debut v New Brompton (a) 17.10.08

Although born in Liverpool, Percy Prince was
raised in Southampton and played all his early
football on the local Common. He was signed
by Saints as an amateur in 1907 and, although
making his first team debut in October 1908, he
had to wait patiently for three years before
claiming a regular senior place. A sharp
shooting centre-forward, keen and
enthusiastic, there was "none more zealous in
the interests of his team", whilst his genial
nature gained him a host of friends.
Nicknamed "Peewee" by his team-mates,
Percy became the club's leading scorer with
eleven league goals during the 1912-13
campaign but, then in a more supporting role,
his scoring ability faded to just four the
following season. Discarded by Saints in 1914
Percy moved briefly to Boscombe in the
Hampshire League and assisted them
throughout the wartime period. He returned
to Southampton in 1917 and was re-signed for
the Southern League programme in August
1919. Although only making four senior
appearances, all at half-back, Percy gained
Hampshire League and Senior Cup medals
while a member of the reserves and also
gained County representative honours before
semi-retirement in May 1920. A Cunard
employee for 32 years, he moved to their New
York office in 1930 as Assistant Catering
Officer and worked on calls dealing with the
Queen Mary, Queen Elizabeth, Mauritania and
Aquitania. He retired in 1952 and continued to
live in New Jersey up to his death in 1973.

Appearances:
SL: 83 app. 25 gls.
FAC: 2 app. 0 gls.
Total: *85 app. 25 gls.*

PRING, Denis Frederick

Role: Forward 1958-59
5'6" 10st.10lbs.
b. Newport, Monmouthshire 8 November 1940

CAREER: Bryglass Secondary School/
Newport Y.M.C.A. Youth/Newport County
am./SOUTHAMPTON am. Sept 1958, pro. Feb
1959/Poole Town Aug 1961/Basingstoke
Town May 1971/Fleet Town June 1973/Cowes
1973, player-manager Aug 1976/West End
1976.

Debut v Norwich City (a) 7.3.59

Discovered at Newport County by Bill Stroud,
Denis Pring made a promising start to his Dell
career and appeared in the first team when
only 18 years old. A regular member of the
Combination Side for the next two seasons, he
suffered severe ligament damage in a game at
Charlton in February 1961 and this injury
brought a premature end to a promising
professional career.

Appearances:
FL: 4 app. 0 gls.
Total: *4 app. 0 gls.*

Percy Prince

PUCKETT, David Charles

Role: Forward 1980-86
5'7" 10st.5lbs.
b. Southampton
29 October 1960

CAREER:
Merry Oak School/
SOUTHAMPTON app.
Mar 1977, pro. Nov 1978
(Nottingham Forest-loan
Oct-Nov 1983)/ A.F.C.
Bournemouth July 1986
(Stoke City-loan-Mar
1988)(Swansea City-
loan-Nov 1988)
(Aldershot-loan-Jan
1989, transferred Apr
1989).

*Debut v West Ham
United (a) 22.9.81*

David Puckett

PURVES, Charles Ruben

Role: Forward 1951-54
5'6" 10st.6lbs.
b. High Spen
17 February 1921

CAREER: Shilton FC/
Walker Celtic /
Spennymoor United/
Charlton Athletic Oct
1946/SOUTHAMPTON
June 1951/
Sittingbourne July
1954/Margate June
1956/Dorchester Town
June 1957/Ford Sports
1961/ Basingstoke
Town player-manager
c.s. 1964.

*Debut v Doncaster
Rovers (h) 12.9.51*

Dave Puckett eventually made his full debut after nine appearances in the number twelve shirt and over his six seasons as a Southampton player much of his time was to be spent warming the substitutes' bench. A deceptively strong-running forward, Dave was never given more than seven consecutive games in the first team and, predictably, struggled to maintain any consistency. Nevertheless he was highly regarded and, at one time, Brian Clough took him on trial to Nottingham Forest to have a closer look at his skills. Eventually moving to Dean Court on a free transfer - a perhaps overly generous gesture by the club - Dave immediately found form but then had the misfortune to suffer a serious ligament injury. He has recently rebuilt his career at Aldershot where he has also become something of a penalty expert, at one time scoring 19 penalties on the trot.

Appearances:
FL: 51 (43) app. 14 gls.
FAC: 2 (1) app. 0 gls.
LC: 5 (7) app. 2 gls.
Total: *58 (51) app. 16 gls.*

❏ **Saints note** - *David Puckett is the first Saint to reach 50 appearances as a substitute.*

Having tasted First Division football with Charlton Athletic, Charlie Purves came to the Dell in June 1951 with the Saints about to enter a period of decline. On his day a constructive inside-right, he enjoyed one good season as a first-teamer but, unfortunately for the Saints, it proved to be the relegation season of 1952-53. Charlie continued to live in Southampton after quitting the professional soccer scene and worked at Vosper Thornycrofts.

Appearances:
FL: 30 app. 2 gls.
FAC: 6 app. 2 gls.
Total: *36 app. 4 gls.*

❏ **Saints note -**
While a Charlton player, Charlie turned up for a match against Newcastle United wearing a black and white Magpies' rosette. He was immediately reprimanded by the Charlton management, for wearing the colours of the team he had supported since his childhood.

Charlie Purves

RADFORD, Walter Robert

Role: Forward 1906-07
5'8" 10st.11lbs.
b. Pinxton, Notts January qtr. 1881

CAREER: Derbyshire Junior Football/
Wolverhampton Wanderers Jan 1906/
SOUTHAMPTON May 1906/Wolverhampton
Wanderers May 1907.
Debut v Swindon Town (a) 1.9.06

Having made two
appearances in the First
Division with Wolves,
Walter Radford
experienced an indifferent
1906-07 season in the
Southern League with
Southampton. He was
dropped after four games
but re-introduced with
some success at the end of
March when he scored
two goals against
Northampton Town.
Rejoining his old club,
Walter's career blossomed
in the familiar
surroundings of Molineux
and he was a scoring
member of the Wolves
side that defeated the
Saints in the 1908 F.A.

Walter Radford

Cup semi-final at
Stamford Bridge. In 1919
he became a referee in the Erewash Amateur
League, from where he progressed to the
Football League list of referees.

Appearances:
SL: 9 app. 2 gls.
Total: *9 app. 2 gls.*

RAMSEY, Sir Alfred Ernest

Role: Full-back 1946-48
5'8" 11st.0lbs.
b. Dagenham 22 January 1920

CAREER: Beacontree Heath School/
Dagenham & Essex Schools/Five Elms/
Portsmouth am. Jan 1940/SOUTHAMPTON
am. Oct 1943, pro. Apr 1944/Tottenham
Hotspur May 1949/Eton Manor part-time

manager Feb 1954/Ipswich Town manager
Aug 1955/England manager Apr 1963 to
1974/Birmingham City caretaker-manager
Sept 1977-78.
Debut v Plymouth Argyle (h) 26.10.46

Although enjoying a distinguished playing
career that encompassed thirty-two
international caps, Alf Ramsey's finest hour
was as England's manager when, in 1966, the
World Cup was won for the first and only
time. Born in Dagenham, he was based in
Hampshire with the army during the war and
originally signed for Portsmouth as an
amateur before attracting Southampton's
attention whilst playing in a friendly match
against them. He signed a professional
contract in April 1944 and, when on leave,
would appear for the Saints either in the
centre-half or centre-forward positions before

Alf Ramsey

converting to the right-back position in time for the resumption of normal soccer in 1946. At first Bill Ellerington kept him from gaining a regular place in the team but after Bill was sidelined with pneumonia in January 1947 Alf made the most of his rival's misfortune. He was strong, positive and meticulous with his distribution and in no time was attracting enough favourable comments from the international selectors to win his first cap against Switzerland in December 1948. An ironic twist in fortunes was to follow however, when, sustaining an injury in a friendly at Plymouth the following month, he lost not only his club place to Bill Ellerington but his international position as well. Alf's failure to regain immediately the number two shirt prompted a transfer request which led to his joining Tottenham with a price tag of £21,000 around his neck. A fine career at Spurs ensued and, nicknamed "The General", he resumed his England career and gained a reputation as a formidable penalty-taker. Moving inevitably into management in 1955, Alf took Ipswich from Division Three South to the First Division Championship in 1962 and it was no surprise to those who knew him when he succeeded Walter Winterbottom as the new manager of England in 1963. He was knighted in January 1967 following the 1966 triumph but was later sacked after the national side's failure to qualify for the 1974 World Cup. Today Alf lives in Ipswich and keeps busy watching and writing about football. In January 1991 he was asked by England's manager, Graham Taylor, to be a member of his advisory panel.

Appearances:
FL: 90 app. 8 gls.
FAC: 6 app. 0 gls.
Total: *96 app. 8 gls.*

RAWLINGS, William Ernest

Role: Forward 1919-28
5'9" 11st.0lbs.
b. Andover
3 January 1896
d. Chandlers Ford
25 September 1972

CAREER: Andover/ SOUTHAMPTON am. 1918, pro. May 1919/Manchester

United Mar 1928/ Port Vale Nov 1929/New Milton c.s. 1930/Newport, I.O.W. 1930.

*Debut v Swansea Town (h) 1.9.19 *(scored on debut)*

Bill Rawlings joined the British Army at the outbreak of the Great War and served with the 2nd/3rd Wessex Field Ambulance to be awarded the 1914 Star. In 1918 Saints discovered his talents and promptly signed him as an amateur. Bill immediately gave notice of his gift for goalscoring with a tally of 16 goals in 15 appearances. Turning professional to coincide with the first proper season after the war, Bill forged a lethal partnership with Arthur Dominy that was to pay dividends in the years ahead. Powerful, both on the ground and in the air, he was a centre-forward in the traditional mould and his right-foot was as lethal as any in the land. In 1921-22 Bill jumped to the forefront of centre-forwards in the country by scoring 29 league goals (a Southampton record until 1949) and despite performing this feat in the Third Division he was selected to lead the country's forward line against Wales in March 1922. An idol amongst the town's young schoolboys, (Ted Drake amongst them), Bill maintained his prolific scoring record throughout his career and, although the Saints' directors turned a deaf ear to inquiries from Everton and Newcastle, it was an offer of £3,860 from Manchester United that eventually proved too tempting. Bill, now in his thirty second year, did not stay long at Old Trafford and, after a move to Port Vale, a serious injury effectively brought his league career to a conclusion. In 1932 Bill, once more in harness with his old hunting partner Arthur Dominy, helped Newport win the Hampshire Senior Cup and then, making a clean break from football, he spent ten years running a pub followed by twenty-five years as a civil servant with the Admiralty.

WM. E. RAWLINGS SOUTHAMPTON

Appearances:
SL: 33 app. 19 gls.
FL: 294 app. 156 gls.
FAC: 37 app. 18 gls.
Total: *364 app. 193 gls.*

READER, George

Role: Forward 1920-21
5'8" 11st.10lbs.
b. Nuneaton 22 November 1896
d. Southampton 13 July 1978

CAREER: St. Luke's College to Exeter City Aug 1919/ SOUTHAMPTON Sept 1920/ Harland & Wolff 1921/Cowes 1922/as referee, SOUTHAMPTON F.A. list 1931/Hampshire F.A. list/ Football League list as linesman 1936, as referee 1939/International List of Referees 1943/Referee for the 1950 World Cup Final Brazil v Uruguay/retired July 1950/ SOUTHAMPTON Director 1952, Vice-chairman Oct 1961,Chairman Nov 1963.

Debut v Queen's Park Rangers (a) 13.11.20

George Reader

George Reader was initially an amateur with Exeter City in their Southern League team and moved to Southampton for a £50 fee as understudy to Bill Rawlings. Although then a professional footballer, George continued with his studies to become a schoolmaster, qualifying a year after joining the Saints. When he was transfer-listed in May 1921 due to the club deciding to reduce the size of their squad, he settled into his original chosen profession, while satisfying his playing urge by representing Cowes until 1930. However, it was to be his career as a referee which gave him a distinctive niche in the game's history as he graduated from taking charge of matches on Southampton Common to refereeing the 1950 World Cup Final in Rio. (Along the way he officiated in the Rest of Europe versus Great Britain game at Hampden Park in May 1947). Soon after packing away his whistle George joined the Southampton board and, becoming Chairman in 1963, proudly sat next to the Queen as his team won the F.A. Cup in 1976.

Appearances:
FL: 3 app. 0 gls
Total: 3 app. 0 gls.

❏ **Saints note** -*George played one game for Exeter City and scored - versus Southampton on 3 January 1920.*

REEVES, Derek Brian

Role: Forward 1954-63
5'8" 11st.8lbs.
b. Parkstone 27 August 1934

CAREER: Poole & Dorset Schools/Bournemouth Gasworks/SOUTHAMPTON Dec 1954/Bournemouth Nov 1962/Worcester City June 1965.

*Debut v Bournemouth (a) 20.4.55 *(scored on debut)*

A private in the Dorset Regiment during his National Service, Derek Reeves joined the Saints in December 1954 - two months after being demobbed. Starting as an inside-forward and then moving to centre-forward, he scored on his debut against his home town club, Bournemouth, and quickly became the scourge of Third Division defences throughout the late 1950's. A quick, bustling player with explosive finishing he was able to capitalise on any half-chance inside the penalty area and his lack of height certainly did not interfere with his heading capabilities. Derek was Southampton's top goalscorer for four

Derek Reeves

consecutive seasons, culminating in 1959-60 when his 39 League goals created not only a Saints' but a Division Three record, both of which remain unbeaten to this day. Finding Second Division defences a lot less generous, Derek struggled to maintain his prodigious scoring and moved to Bournemouth for a fee believed to be around £8,000, although, surprisingly, he only managed eight goals in 35 games before moving on to Worcester. He later found employment as a representative for a building firm and continues to live on the outskirts of Bournemouth. In 1990 Derek was working for Dorset Social Services as an ambulance driver.

Appearances:
FL: 273 app. 145 gls.
FAC: 21 app. 14 gls.
LC: 10 app. 9 gls.
Total: 304 app. 168 gls.

❏ **Saints note** - *In October 1960 Derek netted all five goals as Saints beat Leeds United 5-4 in the, then, recently introduced League Cup. Although this record remained until 1967, when Alan Wilkes scored five for Queen's Park Rangers against Oxford United, it was not actually beaten until October 1989 when Oldham's Frank Bunn scored six against Scarborough.*

REID, Robert Collinson

Role: Forward 1934-35
b. Hove January qtr. 1914

CAREER: Brighton Schools/Southwick (Sussex League)/Sussex/SOUTHAMPTON am. Jan 1935/Newport (I.O.W.) c.s. 1936/Bitterne Nomads.

Debut v Birmingham (h) 26.1.35 FAC

Robert Reid was a young amateur forward who found himself suddenly propelled into the first team for an important fourth round cup-tie at home to Birmingham. The Saints had to rush his registration off to the Football Association when they realised that their regular left-winger, Laurie Fishlock, who had scored the two goals to eliminate Watford in the previous round, was unlikely to be fit and no other winger was available. However, Robert's fairy tale elevation to the big time did not have a happy ending and he appeared to be overawed as the team crashed to a 3-0

defeat. In his eighteen months at the Dell Robert featured in 33 games for the reserves, scoring six goals, before he signed on for Newport on the Isle of Wight.

Appearances:
FAC: 1 app. 0 gls.
Total: 1 app. 0 gls.

❏ **Saints note** - *Robert is the only Saints' player this century to have played in an F.A. Cup match never having made an appearance in the League.*

REILLY, Matthew Michael

Role: Goalkeeper 1895-96
5'11' 13st.6lbs.
b. Donnybrook 22 March 1874
d. Dublin 9 December 1954

CAREER: Benburb (Gaelic Football)/Royal Artillery (Portsmouth) 1893 (SOUTHAMPTON St. Mary's-loan -Dec 1895) (Freemantle-loan)/Portsmouth 1899/Dundee 1904/Notts County Oct 1905/Tottenham Hotspur Oct 1906/Shelbourne c.s. 1906.

Debut v Reading (h) 21.12.1895

'Ginger' Reilly

281

A member of the Royal Artillery side that reached two Army Cup Finals, Gunner "Ginger" Reilly was a convert from Gaelic Football. Loaned to Saints, with the permission of the Army authorities, he kept clean sheets in his two games, both of which ended in 5-0 victories. The local press thought him "brilliant" and it was true that he was both quick and sure in his handling and kicking. Matt was a key member of the Artillery's rise to Southern League membership and, with their demise in 1899, went on to achieve Irish international recognition whilst on the books of Portsmouth. He later became a publican in Southsea.

Appearances:
SL: 2 app. 0 gls.
Total: *2 app. 0 gls.*

❏ **Saints note -**
Matthew Reilly was a team-mate of 'Gunner' Phillips (1895-96) in the 1896 F.A. Amateur Cup Final against Bishop Auckland and was voted Man of the Match when he kept the score down to a 1-0 defeat.

REYNOLDS, John

Role: Half-back
1897-98
*b. Blackburn
21 February 1869
d. Blackburn
12 March 1917*

CAREER: Park Road/Witton/ Blackburn Rovers/ Park Road/East Lancashire Regiment 1886/ Distillery c.s. 1890/ Ulster/West Bromwich Albion

John Reynolds

Mar 1891/Aston Villa Apr 1893/ Glasgow Celtic Aug 1897/ SOUTHAMPTON Feb 1898/Bristol St. George July 1898/Coached in New Zealand 1902/ Stockport County c.s. 1903/Willesden Town 1904/Cardiff City coach 1907-08

Debut v Chatham (a) 5.2.1898

John Reynolds played five times for Ireland before his Lancashire birth was discovered, and he then went on to win a further eight English Caps as well as three Championship medals with Aston Villa. Nicknamed "Baldy" by some of the more irreverent Southampton fans, by 1898 his best days were behind him and he only stayed long enough to make two appearances for the club, both in the right-half position. In 1902 he made the long trek out to New Zealand to do some coaching but soon returned, initially to Stockport County and finally Willesden Town. Retiring in 1905, John later took up residence in Sheffield where he worked as a collier until his death in 1917.

Appearances:
SL: 2 app. 0 gls.
Total: *2 app. 0 gls.*

❏ **Saints note -**
John Reynolds scored West Bromwich Albion's first ever penalty in a Division One game against Nottingham Forest on 3rd April 1893.

REYNOLDS, Ronald Sidney Maurice

Ron Reynolds

Role: Goalkeeper
1959-64
6'0" 12st.0lbs.
b. Haslemere 2 June 1928

CAREER: Aldershot am. June 1945, pro. Dec 1945/Tottenham Hotspur July 1950/SOUTHAMPTON Mar 1960.

Debut v Tranmere Rovers (h) 19.3.60

Ted Bates beat the transfer deadline by twenty-four hours when be brought Ron Reynolds to the Dell and the experienced goalkeeper repaid the £10,000 fee by adding the necessary composure required in the team's run-up to the Division Three championship. He broke his ankle at the onset of the 1961-62 season but fought his way back into the first team only to have his career finally brought to an end by a dislocated shoulder sustained at Fratton Park in September 1963. After his injury Ron scouted briefly for Saints and Crystal Palace but later in 1964 joined a firm of insurance brokers. He set up his own business four years later although today he has virtually retired while continuing to live in Haslemere.

Appearances:
FL: 90 app. 0 gls.
FAC: 9 app. 0 gls.
LC: 11 app. 0 gls.
Total: *110 app. 0 gls.*

RICHARDS, L.

Role: Forward 1912-13
b. Devon

CAREER: SOUTHAMPTON trialist Feb 1913

Debut v Exeter City (h) 3.2.13

A west country amateur, Richards was invited to the Dell for a trial after impressing a Southampton scout in the area. After his only game for the club, a 2-2 draw against Exeter, a local reporter offered the following description, "a fine, strapping fellow with a good shot".

Appearances:
SL: 1 app. 0 gls.
Total: *1 app. 0 gls.*

RIDEOUT, Paul David

Role: Forward 1988-91
5'11' 12st.1lbs.
b. Bournemouth 14 August 1964

CAREER: Priestlands School/Southampton & Hampshire Schools/Lawrence Boys Club/ Lymington/Swindon Town app. June 1980, pro Aug 1981/Aston Villa June 1983/Bari (Italy) July 1985/SOUTHAMPTON July 1988 (Swindon Town-loan-Mar 1991)/Notts County Sept 1991/Glasgow Rangers Jan 1992.

Debut v West Ham United (h) 27.8.88
* (scored on debut)

Paul Rideout achieved footballing fame as a young England schoolboy when he scored a memorable Wembley goal in a televised match against Scotland. Despite being on Southampton's books at the time he was allowed to join Swindon as a seventeen year old and, after a spell at Villa Park and three years playing in Italy, it took a £350,000 fee for the Saints and Paul to become re-acquainted. His fortunes fluctuated, with some outstanding games being followed by many indifferent ones. With the rise to prominence of Alan Shearer, Paul found himself increasingly in the shadows and during the 1990-91 season made no secret of his

Paul Rideout (left) and manager Chris Nicholl.

restlessness. When Chris Nicholl signed Jon Gittens from Swindon Town in March 1991 he made the reverse move, on a loan basis, in the hope that Ossie Ardiles, the Swindon manager, would make the transfer permanent in the ensuing close season. With Ardiles moving to manage Newcastle and then the sacking of Chris Nicholl, Paul's future at the Dell was in the balance, and he moved on to newly promoted Notts County for £300,000.

Appearances:
FL: 64 (7) app. 19 gls.
FAC: 5 (2) app. 0 gls.
LC: 13 app. 2 gls.
Total: *82 (9) 21 gls.*

RIDGES, George

Role: Forward 1892-93
b. Freemantle, Southampton 1867
d. Southampton 7 April 1940

CAREER: Southampton Harriers/Freemantle/ SOUTHAMPTON St. Mary's loan Oct 1892.

Debut v Maidenhead (h) 29.10.1892 FAC

George Ridges was described as a strong, active and brainy inside-right when St. Mary's borrowed him from Freemantle. In his only appearance, a disastrous 4-0 home defeat to Maidenhead in the second qualifying round of the F.A. Cup, George failed to shine and swiftly returned to Freemantle. The following March he captained the Magpies when they defeated St. Mary's 2-1 in the Hampshire Senior Cup Final played at the County Ground.

Appearances:
FAC: 1 app. 0 gls.
Total: *1 app. 0 gls.*

ROBERTS, Albert

Role: Full-back 1930-38
5'9" 11st.4lbs.
b. Goldthorpe 27 January 1907
d. Elsecar 27 January 1957

CAREER: Ardsley Athletic/SOUTHAMPTON Aug 1929/Swansea Town Aug 1938.

Debut v Swansea Town (h) 28.2.31

Signed from Yorkshire non-league side

Albert Roberts

Ardsley Athletic in August 1929, Albert Roberts joined the Saints as an understudy to Mike Keeping. He made only a handful of appearances in his first four seasons at the Dell and it was not until the transfer of Keeping to Fulham in March 1933 that he began to establish himself in the side. A reliable full-back, he played consistently until 1938 when in May he refused terms and was transfer-listed at £500. After the war Bert settled in Doncaster but sadly died on his fiftieth birthday.

Appearances:
FL: 156 app. 0 gls.
FAC: 5 app. 0 gls.
Total: *161 app. 0 gls.*

ROBERTSON, John Nicol

Role: Half-back 1906-12
5'8" 11st.4lbs.
b. Coylton 1884
d. Glasgow

CAREER: Drogan/Glasgow Rangers/Bolton Wanderers Apr 1902/SOUTHAMPTON May 1906/Glasgow Rangers Mar 1912.

Debut v Norwich City (h) 8.9.06

Described as "a really classy half-back and an exceedingly capable player" by the local Sports Echo, John Robertson joined the Saints after being unable to command a regular spot in Bolton Wanderers' league side. Intermittently "in the wars" throughout his relatively long career in the red and white stripes, he received a serious knee injury after only two appearances and this set the pattern for his six seasons at the Dell. A utility player, he turned out in all half and full-back positions as well as having several games in the forward line and always showed enterprise. He was rewarded, in 1911, with selection to the Southern League representative eleven which played the Irish League in Belfast and then had a second game against the Football League at Stoke. His departure for Glasgow Rangers caused no little dismay in local circles, for the club were struggling and needed to hang on to players such as John Robertson.

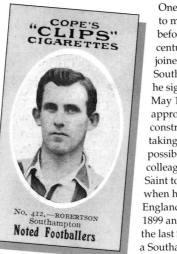

COPE'S "CLIPS" CIGARETTES

No. 412.—ROBERTSON
Southampton
Noted Footballers

Appearances:
SL: 153 app. 1 gl.
FAC: 11 app. 1 gl.
Total: *164 app. 2 gls.*

ROBERTSON, John Tait

Role: Half-back 1898-99
5'8" 11st.6lbs.
b. Dumbarton 25 February 1877
d. Milton 24 January 1935

CAREER: Poinfield/Sinclair Swifts/Greenock Morton/Everton Oct 1895/SOUTHAMPTON May 1898/Glasgow Rangers Aug 1899/ Chelsea player-manager Aug 1905/Glossop player-manager Jan 1907/Manchester United reserve team-manager c.s. 1909/later coached on the continent.

Debut v Brighton United (h) 3.9.1898

Jock Robertson

One of the finest half-backs to move south of the border before the turn of the century, Jock Robertson joined eleven fellow Scots on Southampton's books when he signed from Everton in May 1898. Tough in his approach, Jock could also be constructive and favoured taking the ball as far upfield as possible before releasing it to a colleague. He became the first Saint to be capped for Scotland when he led his country against England at Birmingham in April 1899 and, incredibly, it is also the last Scottish cap to be won by a Southampton outfield player. Soon after the game against England Jock moved back to Scotland and, with Glasgow Rangers, won a further fourteen caps to earn a glowing reputation. Jock became Chelsea's first-ever manager on their formation in 1905 and guided them to third position in their first season in Division Two. He surprisingly left Stamford Bridge in January 1907 to take charge of Glossop who were in the lower depths of the same division.

Appearances:
SL: 19 app. 0 gls.
FAC: 3 app. 0 gls.
Total: *22 app. 0 gls.*

ROBERTSON, Thomas

Role: Full-back 1902-04
5'8" 12st.0lbs.
b. Newton Mearns, Renfrewshire c. 1877

CAREER: Newton Thistle/Edinburgh St. Bernards/Stoke May 1894/Hibernian 1896/Stoke May 1897/Liverpool Apr 1900/SOUTHAMPTON May 1902/Brighton & Hove Albion c.s. 1904.

Debut v Brentford (h) 6.9.02

A member of Liverpool's League Championship team of 1901, Tom Robertson was also in the Liverpool side that was astonishingly beaten at Anfield 4-1 by Southampton on their way to the F.A. Cup Final. When he joined the Saints a few months later he did so much against the wishes of the

Liverpool management and their reluctance to release him was vindicated as Tom played his part in Southampton's two Southern League Championships of 1903 and 1904. He was a reliable full-back who possessed a powerful kick and the ability to time his tackles with perfection and yet, off the pitch, he was known as a retiring fellow. Tom had a "holy horror" of being interviewed and was always elusive when a reporter was after a story. After moving along the south coast to join Brighton in 1904, he retired a year later to take over a public house in Hove.

Tom Robertson

Appearances:
SL: 45 app. 1 gl.
FAC: 5 app. 0 gls.
Total: *50 app. 1 gl.*

Ted Robinson moved to Southampton from Lancashire in time for the opening of the 1927-28 campaign and, over the season, he made 67 reserve appearances. His only taste of first team soccer came on New Year's Eve at Stoke and at the end of the year the Saints management decided to give him a free transfer back to his native Lancashire. Finishing his career with a fourteen-year stretch at Wigan's Springfield Park, Ted retired from playing in 1947 and then became a member of the Hindley Fire Service.

Appearances:
FL: 1 app. 0 gls.
Total: *1 app. 0 gls.*

ROBINSON, John William

Role: Goalkeeper 1898-1903
5'11" 12st.6lbs.
b. Derby 22 April 1870
d. Derby 28 October 1931

ROBINSON, Edward

Role: Full-back 1927-28
5'8" 12st.0lbs.
b. Hindley 27 September 1903
d. Hindley 28 July 1972

CAREER: Hindley St. Benedicts 1916/Castle Hill 1919/Hindley Rovers 1922/Hindley St. Benedicts 1923/ Hindley Green 1924/ Chorley 1925/ SOUTHAMPTON Aug 1927/Southport May 1928/Wigan Athletic June 1933/ player-trainer 1946.

Debut v Stoke City (a) 31.12.27

CAREER: Derby Midland/Lincoln City Jan 1889/Derby County June 1891/ New Brighton Tower Aug 1897/ SOUTHAMPTON May. 1898/Plymouth Argyle May 1903/ Exeter City Oct 1905/ Millwall Dec 1905/ Green Waves (Plymouth) c.s. 1907/ Devon County XI 1907-08/Exeter City Sept 1908/Stoke City May 1909/Rochester (New York) Oct 1912.

Debut v Brighton United (h) 3.9.1898

Ted Robinson

Considered to be the country's premier goalkeeper at the turn of the century, John Robinson cost Saints £400, a small fortune in those days. Spectacular and of unquestionable brilliance, fast and agile, he made crowds gasp at his daring and bravery. His first season with Saints was climaxed by a courageous display at Bristol City, when Southampton needed a win to retain their championship. Spraining the muscles of his hand during the first-half, he left the field but returned because of the vast importance of the game, and suffered intense pain as Saints fought back from being 2-0 down to win 4-3. During his five-year stay at the Dell John won four Southern League Championship medals, appeared in both the 1900 and 1902 F.A. Cup Finals and gained six England International caps. In 1903 he moved to Plymouth and went on to assist several clubs before ending his outstanding and sometimes controversial career in America in 1912. A wayward character, John was involved in several unsavoury incidents over the years. In 1900 he was reported to the F.A. for allegedly trying to poach Steve Bloomer from Derby for Southampton. Two years later, in October 1902, he was suspended after an incident at New Brompton when he struck a spectator in the face, and two months after that, he was cautioned by the F.A. for an article in the local press about the incident. In November 1910 he was again suspended, this time by the Stoke directors for alleged insubordination after a Birmingham league match. An insurance salesman after the war in his native Derby, John was seriously injured after falling from an upstairs window in December 1922 and suffered, as a result of the fall, from epilepsy.

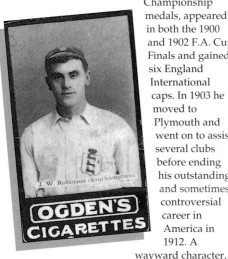

Appearances:
SL: 116 app. 0 gls.
FAC: 21 app. 0 gls.
Total: *137 app. 0 gls.*

ROCHFORD, William

Role: Full-back 1946-50
5'10" 12st.0lbs.
b. Newhouse 27 May 1913
d. East Hedleyhope, Bishop Auckland 9 December 1984

CAREER: Esh Winning Juniors/Cuckfield/ Portsmouth am. July 1931, pro. Aug 1931/ SOUTHAMPTON July 1946, player-coach Aug 1949/Colchester July 1950.

Debut v Swansea Town (h) 4.9.46

A Portsmouth player for 15 years and the captain of their F.A. Cup-winning side of 1939, Bill Rochford or "Rocky", joined the Saints for £550 and took his place in the team in the first League game after the Second World War. Robust, and a stern challenger for the ball, he became automatic choice for captain and was a father figure to many of the younger and less experienced players of the club. Up and coming defenders such as Ramsey and Ellerington certainly benefited from his professional expertise and, with his career drawing to a close, in August 1949 he applied for the vacant managerial position at the Dell. Strongly tipped for the job and the players' choice, Bill was overlooked in preference to

Bill Rochford

Peter Rodrigues skippered the Saints to FA Cup success in 1976.

Sid Cann although he was appointed player-coach. Naturally disappointed, Bill remained just one more year before moving briefly to Colchester who were about to embark on their debut season in the Football League. Upon retirement from football Bill returned to the north-east to take up farming in the Gateshead area.

Appearances:
FL: 128 app. 8 gls.
FAC: 6 app. 0 gls.
Total: *134 app. 8 gls.*

RODRIGUES, Peter Joseph

Role: Full-back 1975-77
5'9" 11st.11lbs.
b. Cardiff 21 January 1944

CAREER: Cardiff City am. June 1959, pro May 1961/Leicester City Dec 1965/Sheffield Wednesday Oct 1970/SOUTHAMPTON July 1975/Romsey Town 1977/Coaching in San Diego/Telephone Sports 1987.

Debut v West Bromwich Albion (h) 16.8.75

If any proof is needed about the unpredictability of football then a study of Peter Rodrigues' year between July 1975 and May 1976 would confirm the vagaries of life as a professional footballer. In the summer of 1975 Peter was given a free transfer by Sheffield Wednesday and was considering a life outside the game that had earned him forty Welsh caps. Eventually Southampton, worried about the progress of Steve Mills, who had still not recovered from a car accident, decided to bring Peter to the Dell as cover and within nine months he was being handed the F.A. Cup from Her Majesty the Queen. Peter was a fine overlapping full-back who, at Leicester, had lost out in the 1969 F.A. Cup Final against Manchester City when he missed arguably their best chance on the day. Renowned for his sliding tackles, his experience was a stabilising influence throughout the 1975-76 season and only a knee injury sustained during the following year prevented him from enjoying a longer career as the club's right-back. After his retirement he took over the King Rufus pub at Eling where a big painting behind the bar reminded the locals just who the landlord was. In 1987 Peter went to live in Wales where he ran the White Mill Inn near Carmarthen, but in

Dennis Rofe

December 1990 he returned to Hampshire and bought a restaurant in Hythe.

Appearances:
FL: 59 app. 3 gls.
FAC: 8 app. 0 gls.
LC: 3 app. 0 gls.
Total: *70 app. 3 gls.*

ROFE, Dennis

Role: Full-back 1982-84
5'7" 11st.7lbs.
b. Epping 1 June 1950

CAREER: East London Schools/Orient app Sept 1965, pro Feb 1968/Leicester City Aug 1972/Chelsea Feb 1980/SOUTHAMPTON July 1982, reserve team coach 1984, first team coach Feb 1987/Bristol Rovers coach July 1991/Caretaker manager Oct 1991, manager Dec 1991.

Debut v Coventry City (a) 28.8.82

Dennis Rofe originally joined the Saints on a six-month trial period after being freed by Chelsea but quickly persuaded manager, Lawrie McMenemy, that he was worth keeping. When he had joined Leicester in August 1972 the fee was £112,000 which was then a record for a full-back (the record was broken within 24 hours when Leicester sold David Nish to Derby) and his vigorous play earned him one England Under-23 cap. An effervescent character and something of a dressing room joker, Dennis' main contribution to Southampton was off the pitch as an enthusiastic assistant to Chris Nicholl but unfortunately the Saints' directors decided he should accept some of the responsibility for the team's poor showing during the 1990-91 season. Within a month of his dismissal, Dennis joined the recently-installed manager of Bristol Rovers, Martin Dobson, and then, following Dobson's hasty departure, was in charge at Twerton Park before the end of 1991.

Appearances:
FL: 18 (2) app. 0 gls.
LC: 6 app. 0 gls.
Eur: 1 app. 0 gls.
Total: *25 (2) app. 0 gls.*

ROGERS, Andrew

Role: Forward 1979-82
5'8" 10st.0lbs.
b. Chatteris 1 December 1956

CAREER: Chatteris Town/Peterborough July 1976/Hampton 1978/SOUTHAMPTON Feb 1980 (Plymouth Argyle-loan-Sept-Nov 1981, transferred Nov 1981)/Reading July 1985 (Southend United-loan-Oct-Dec 1986, transferred Dec 1986)/Carshalton Athletic July 1987/Farnborough Town July 1989.

Debut v Ipswich Town (h) 19.4.80 (as sub)

Andy Rogers' first taste of league football came at Peterborough where after 29 matches and one goal he dropped into non-league football in south-west London. The Saints revived his flagging fortunes and although Andy only made five appearances as a substitute during his eighteen month stay he eventually commanded a £50,000 fee when he moved to Home Park. After appearing in the 1983 F.A. Cup semi-final for Plymouth against Watford and making 163 appearances for the Devon club Andy had further spells at Reading and Southend before once more dropping into non-league soccer.

Appearances:
FL: 0 (5) app. 0 gls.
Total: *0 (5) app. 0 gls.*

ROGERS, Joseph

Role: Full-back/Forward 1894-96
5'10" 12st.6lbs.
b. Macclesfield 5 November 1874

CAREER: Stoke United/Macclesfield/ SOUTHAMPTON St. Mary's Dec 1894/ Grimsby Town May 1896/Newcastle United Apr 1898/Preston North End Jan 1901/ Coaching in Germany/Grimsby Town 1906/ Tivoli (Grimsby Thursday League).

Debut v Reading (h) 5.1.1895

Joe Rogers was signed from his home town club and soon after his arrival caused a local sensation when, in an exhibition match at the Antelope in January 1895, he scored ten goals in a game against the Wiltshire Regiment on a quagmire pitch. Despite an obvious aptitude for beating goalkeepers the Saints coaching staff converted Joe into the full-back position where, although his speed, control and kicking ability came in useful, he became unsettled. Joe joined Grimsby in May 1896 and, given a free hand in the Mariners' attack, repaid them with some prolific scoring. After a move to Newcastle Joe continued to show form and, in 1899 as a member of the first England team to tour Germany, won three unofficial caps, scoring five goals in one of the games.

Appearances:
SL: 15 app. 2 gls.
FAC: 1 app. 0 gls.
Total: *16 app. 2 gls.*

ROLES, Albert G.

Role: Full-back 1945-49
5'7"10st. 2lbs.
b. Southampton 29 September 1921

CAREER: Deanery School/Southampton & Hampshire Schools/Albion Boys/ SOUTHAMPTON am. 1938, pro. Oct 1940 (West Ham United during World War Two) Gloucester City June 1949/Cowes player-manager 1949-52/C.P.C. Sports scout.

Debut v Newport County (FAC) (h) 5.1.46

Albie Roles was discovered playing in local Southampton Junior league soccer and became a regular member of the club's 'B' side before being promoted to the reserve team just as war brought the curtain down on league soccer.

An apprentice engineer, Albie made over 180 war-time appearances for the club and gave good service as a mobile left-back. He was called for his National Service in 1946 and, demobbed in 1948, he found himself immediately placed on the transfer list only to be eventually re-engaged for the 1948-49 season. His one league game (at Bradford) took place in the April which was followed the next month by his release into non-league football for a short spell at Gloucester followed by acceptance of the manager's job at Cowes. His playing days ended abruptly when he caught tuberculosis and he was hospitalised for two years. With recovery came employment at Harland and Wolff and the last sixteen years have been spent working as a technician at the Institute of Higher Education.

Appearances:
FL: 1 app. 0 gls.
FAC: 4 app. 0 gls.
Total: *5 app. 0 gls.*

❏ **Saints note** - *A keen cricketer, Albie played for Hampshire Second XI as well as Deanery C.C.*

Don Roper

ROPER, Donald George Beaumont

Role: Forward 1945-47 & 1956-58
5'9" 10st.12lbs.
b. Botley 14 December 1922

CAREER: Meon Valley Boys/Hedge End Boys /Bitterne Nomads/Eastleigh/ SOUTHAMPTON June 1940/Arsenal Aug 1947/SOUTHAMPTON Jan 1957/Weymouth June 1959/Dorchester Town July 1960.

Debut v Newport (h) 5.1.46 FAC
*(scored on debut)

A prolific schoolboy goalscorer, Don Roper was spotted by Toby Keleher, assistant to Tom Parker, playing in parks' football, but it took some persuasion before he agreed to sign professional forms. Plunged straight into Southampton's first team in the War League, Don was pitted against many of the country's top centre-halves but emerged with flying colours. The club's principal goalscorer throughout the duration of the hostilities, "The Don", nicknamed after the famous Australian cricketer, converted to the outside-right position and continued to impress as a dashing two-footed winger. With the war's end Don's form soon had the big clubs sniffing around

and his departure to Arsenal in return for George Curtis and Tommy Rudkin plus cash, had an air of inevitability about it. Arsenal had been so desperate to sign Don that manager Tom Whittaker had made eleven visits to the Dell and, over the next nine and a half years, he more than justified Arsenal's £20,000 valuation. Don had the pleasure of scoring the equalising goal at Huddersfield which brought Highbury their first post war championship in 1948 and added to this early success by picking up a further championship medal in 1953. In January 1957 Don returned to the Dell and, becoming captain, gave the club a further two seasons service before moving to finish a fine career in Dorset with Weymouth and finally Dorchester.

Appearances;
FL: 120 app. 40 gls.
FAC: 11 app. 2 gls.
Total: *131 app. 42 gls.*

❏ **Saints note** - *Don was an all-round sportsman and played one match as a middle-order batsman for Hampshire C.C.C. His pedigree, however, had its roots in football as his grandfather had played for Chesterfield and his father was an amateur with the Royal Marines and Huddersfield.*

ROWE, Douglas Heath

Role: Forward 1934-35
5'9" 11st.10lbs.
b. Nottingham July qtr. 1909

CAREER: Sneinton/Luton Town am. Mar 1932, pro. Mar 1932/Lincoln City Aug 1933/ SOUTHAMPTON Aug 1934/Union Sportif Tourcoing (France) Oct 1934.

Debut v Burnley (a) 25.8.34

Initially signed in the hope that he would solve the club's problem on the left-wing, Douglas Rowe did not really stay long enough to show his true form. He scored on his home debut but soon after lost his position to Laurie Fishlock and sought a move. His spell in France did not last much longer than his period at the Dell for he returned to England in 1935 but did not appear in League football again. He had a brother who achieved some fame as an Olympic wrestler.

Appearances;
FL: 2 app. 1 gl.
Total: *2 app. 1 gl.*

❏ **Saints note** - *Douglas himself was a top-class wrestler, winning the England Amateur Welterweight Championship. He also won many prizes for weight-lifting.*

ROWLEY, Richard William Morris

Role: Forward 1926-30
6'0" 12st.0lbs.
b. Enniskillen 13 January 1904
d. Southampton 18 April. 1984

CAREER: Fulwood Barracks/ Taunton College Grammar /Tidworth United/ Andover Sept 1922/ Swindon Town Nov 1924/Casuals 1925 /SOUTHAMPTON am. May 1926, pro. Nov 1926/ Tottenham Hotspur Feb 1930/Preston North End Dec 1931, retired 1934.

Debut v Portsmouth (a) 28.8.26

Dick Rowley

The son of a major in the army, Dick Rowley was a Wiltshire County player and originally joined Southampton as an amateur to replace the recently departed Arthur Dominy. A gangly inside-forward, he soon struck up an understanding with Bill Rawlings and, after scoring five goals in the club's run up to the 1927 F.A. Cup semi-final, attracted scouts from all over the country. His best season came in 1929-30 when he became the first Saint to score four goals in an away game (versus Bradford) and, by the February, he had scored 25 goals in as many games. Recognised at international level by Northern Ireland, he had won four caps when Spurs, mindful of his predatory instincts, made an irresistible offer of £3,750 for his services and Saints had lost yet another star forward to a richer London club.

Appearances;
FL: 104 app. 52 gls.
FAC: 9 app. 6 gls.
Total: *113 app. 58 gls.*

RUDDOCK, Neil

Role: Centre-half 1988-
6'2" 12st.6lbs.
b. London 9 May 1968

CAREER: Millwall Mar 1986/Tottenham Hotspur Apr 1986/Millwall June 1988/ SOUTHAMPTON February 1989.

Debut v Sheffield Wednesday (a) 18.2.89

Neil Ruddock was only 20 years old when he was recruited to Southampton's battle against relegation in February 1989 but he had already been the subject of two £200,000 plus transfers between Millwall and Tottenham Hotspur. He immediately slotted into the heart of a struggling Saints' defence and promptly displayed his confidence when he volunteered to take a crucial penalty in the final minutes of a vital match against fellow strugglers, Newcastle. While the crowd held their breath Neil ran up and smashed the ball into the back of the net to signal not only one of the biggest roars ever heard at the Dell but more significantly the team's first League win in eighteen matches. As the club climbed away from the danger area the fans quickly warmed to the combative defender but Neil's ruggedness, while making him popular with Southampton's paying public did not impress some of the game's officials. Some fine displays were often marred by an alarming lack of discipline and his subsequent frequent suspensions gave him a tag of unreliability which his undoubted talents did not deserve. Happily, during the 1990-91 season Neil showed a huge improvement in his self-control and has at times looked to be the finished article. Neil occasionally played on the left-

wing at Millwall and, despite his size, can often look elegant on the ball whilst his distribution with his left foot can be, for a centre-half, thoughtful and accurate. He won England Under-21 honours in the close season of 1989 and with further maturity can look forward to a long career in the top flight.

Appearances;
FL: 70 (7) app. 9 gls.
FAC: 4 app. 2 gls.
LC: 9 (1) app. 1 gl.
Total: *83 (8) app. 12 gls.*

RUDDY, Thomas

Role: Forward 1932-34
5'8" 11st.6lbs.
b. Stockton-on-Tees 1 March 1902
d. Cleveland 11 November 1979

CAREER: Stockton Shamrocks/Darlington am. Oct 1924, pro. 1925/Derby County May 1928/Chesterfield Dec 1931/SOUTHAMPTON Sept 1932/Spennymoor c.s. 1934.

Debut v Preston North End (h) 24.12.32

Considerably experienced at the time of his Dell arrival, Tom Ruddy had played alongside Dick Neal while at Derby and his transfer was partly met by the Supporters Club. He had been a quick forward with a hard shot but, with age

Tom Ruddy

creeping up on him, lost a bit of pace during his stay at Southampton and decided to try his luck in the North-Eastern League with Spennymoor.

Appearances:
FL: 24 app. 3gls.
FAC: 1 app. 0gls.
Total: *25 app. 3 gls.*

RUDKIN, Thomas William

Role: Forward 1947-49
5'8" 10st.7lbs.
b. Peterborough 17 June 1919

CAREER: Wolverhampton Wanderers am. Feb 1938, pro. Feb 1938/Lincoln City May 1938/ (Darlington, Hartlepool United, Middlesbrough, SOUTHAMPTON during World War Two) Peterborough 1945/Arsenal Jan 1947/SOUTHAMPTON Aug 1947/Bristol City May 1949/Weston player-manager May 1952.
Debut v Doncaster Rovers (a) 23.8.47

Tom Rudkin first wore the red and white of Southampton as a guest in the 1942-43 wartime season and rejoined the club in the summer of 1947 as part of the Don Roper transfer. Valued at £3,000, Tom could play on either wing but only made sporadic first team appearances before moving to Ashton Gate in 1949.

Appearances;
FL: 9 app. 0 gls.
FAC: 1 app. 0 gls.
Total: *10 app. 0 gls.*

RUFFELL, Daniel Ralph

Role: Goalkeeper 1891-94
b. Southampton 3 October 1867
d. Southampton 3 October 1940

CAREER: SOUTHAMPTON St. Mary's Nov 1885.
Debut v Warmley (a) 3.10.1891 FAC

Ralph Ruffell was Southampton St. Mary's first ever goalkeeper and played in the club's inaugural fixture in November 1885. Over the next six seasons Ralph was more responsible than any other man for the rapid growth made as the team progressed - from friendlies to triumphant participation in the Hampshire Junior and then Senior Cups. He played in the first ever F.A. Cup tie in 1891 by which time he had won numerous Hampshire Senior Caps. Regarded as totally fearless, Ralph sustained a dislocated knee cap in the Hampshire Senior Cup final against the Royal Engineers in March 1894 which effectively ended his career although he did make the odd appearance for the club's reserve eleven when required. Ralph had an important appointment as an engineer in Southampton Docks for many years.

Appearances:
FAC: 6 app. 0 gls.
Total: *6 app. 0 gls*

Tom Rudkin

SALTER, John Macgregor

Role: Forward 1923-24
*b. Bitterne,
Southampton
3 August 1898
d. Bitterne,
Southampton
21 June 1982*

CAREER:
Bitterne Sports/
SOUTHAMPTON Oct
1923/Thornycrofts
1924/Southampton
Civil Service 1925.

*Debut v Fulham (a)
10.11.23*

A product of local
junior football Jock
Salter managed just
one appearance in
Southampton's Division Two team before ill-
health ended his professional ambitions.
During World War One he had been gassed
and, never making a complete recovery, found
day to day training too exhausting. Returning
to local soccer he found employment at, and
played for, Thornycrofts.

Jock Salter

Appearances:
FL: 1 app. 0 gls.
Total: *1 app. 0 gls.*

SALWAY, Edward Elijah

Role: Half-back 1912-13
5'11" 12st.4lbs.
*b. Nursling, Southampton April qtr. 1891
d. Southampton October qtr. 1950*

CAREER: Romsey/Nursling United/
SOUTHAMPTON 1911.

Debut v Exeter City (a) 5.10.12

Ted Salway was a young gardener hailing
from rural Hampshire who, after successfully
coming through a trial match, was regarded as
'a rough diamond with plenty of potential'.
After a year in the club's reserve team he was
polished into a fine half-back and had gained
County representative honours with
Hampshire. Ted's pace and inexhaustible
energy soon earned him his call-up into the

first eleven where,
during the 1912-13
season, he was tried
in various positions
including a couple
of games at inside-
left. He spent the period between 1913 and
1915 back in the reserves without ever being
selected again for the first team, although he
did make
spasmodic
appearances in the
first war-time
season of 1915-16.
Ted joined up in
October 1915 and
was sent to the
Western Front in
1916 where, at the
Battle of Ypres in
July 1917, he was
severely wounded.
Losing an eye and a
leg he was invalided
home to Southampton later that same month.
In May 1920 he was granted a benefit game at
the Dell when Portsmouth Amateurs played a
fixture against a Southampton Reserve eleven.

Ted Salway

Appearances:
SL: 10 app. 0 gls.
Total: *10 app. 0 gls.*

SANDERS, William Isaac

Role: Forward 1912-13
b. Holsworthy July qtr. 1885

CAREER: R.G.A. Portsmouth/
SOUTHAMPTON Mar 1913.

Debut v Brentford (h) 24.3.13

A stalwart gunner from Gosport, Bill Sanders
made a favourable impression when
introduced into the Saints' first team and he
played a significant part in a creditable 3-1
victory over Brentford. However, the club
were enduring a miserable season, (Bill was
one of thirty-four players used that year) and
in his next game at Plymouth, the team
reverted to form and were soundly beaten 6-1.
This hefty defeat ensured Bill's early return to
his army unit in Portsmouth.

Appearances:
SL: 2 app. 0 gls.
Total: *2 app. 0 gls.*

SAUL, Frank Lander

Role: Forward 1967-70
5'9" 11st.12lbs.
*b. Benfleet, Essex
23 August 1943*

CAREER: Canvey Island
School/Tottenham
Hotspur am. Aug 1958,
pro. Aug 1960/
SOUTHAMPTON Jan
1968/Queen's Park
Rangers May 1970/
Millwall Mar 1972/
Dagenham Mar 1976.
*Debut v Leeds United (a)
13.1.68*

Frank Saul was an
England Youth
International who had
scored one of
Tottenham's two goals
against Chelsea in the 1967 F.A. Cup final. He
came to Southampton as part of the record
breaking £125,000 transfer deal involving
Spurs and Martin Chivers in January 1968,
with his valuation set at £40,000. Not really the
ideal replacement for Chivers, Frank struggled
to settle alongside Ron Davies although he did
manage to score some vital cup goals. (In a
quarter of the games, Frank scored five times
as many cup goals as he did in the League).
Frank returned to the capital in 1970 and,
finishing his league career in 1976, he was, in
1990, running a small fashion emporium and
knitwear business in the East End.

1954-1960/
Wycombe
Wanderers 1960/
Hedge End
(Southampton)
manager July 1971.

*Debut v Chesterfield
(h) 20.9.47*

Auggie Scott played
his early football for
Hylton Colliery in
the North-East and
the Colliery side
were famous for
producing league
players as, along with
Auggie, eight other
men from the same
side graduated into
professional football.
When war broke out
Auggie was on the
books of Luton but,
posted with the British
Army to Burma between 1943 and 1946, his
career took a back seat and was only
resurrected when the Saints paid a small fee to

Appearances:
*FL: 49 (3) app. 2 gls.
FAC: 8 app. 6 gls.
LC: 4 (2) app. 4 gls.
Eur: 0 (2) app. 0 gls.*
Total: *61 (7) app. 12 gls.*

SCOTT, August Fisher

Role: Forward 1947-50
5'5" 9st.3lbs.
b. Sunderland 19 February 1921

CAREER: Hylton Colliery/Luton Town 1938/
SOUTHAMPTON July 1947/Colchester Aug
1951/Cheltenham Town player-manager c.s.

Auggie Scott

bring him to the Dell. He made up for his lack of inches and poundage by his cleverness with the ball and played in a variety of forward positions for the club before Bill Rochford persuaded him to join him at Colchester. After finishing his career at Cheltenham he stayed in the town to work in the building trade although in 1969 he returned to follow the same trade in Southampton. A brother-in-law to fellow ex-Saint, Wilf Grant, Auggie continues to live on the outskirts of the city.

Appearances:
FL: 45 app. 9 gls.
FAC: 3 app. 1 gl.
Total: *48 app. 10 gls.*

SCOTT, John Redvers

Role: Centre-half 1937-38
5'10" 12st.0lbs.
b. Grimethorpe 4 December 1905
d. Shirley, Southampton 9 March 1976

CAREER: Featherstone Rovers (Rugby League)/Pilkington's Recreationals/Doncaster Rovers am. Mar 1929, pro. Aug 1929/Norwich City July 1931/SOUTHAMPTON player-coach

Jack Scott

& asst. trainer May 1937/St. Nicholas (Southampton Senior League) coach 1948.
Debut v Swansea (a) 27.12.37

Released by Norwich City in May 1937, Jack Scott followed Tom Parker from Carrow Road to join the Saints training staff and was given responsibility for the club's nursery side. Extremely fit and "as tough as old boots" he regularly played in the "A" team in the Hampshire League to be suddenly called upon to fill the number nine shirt when, at Christmas 1937, the club suffered an abundance of injuries. As strong as an ox, Jack had played rugby league back in his native Yorkshire and had dabbled at all-in wrestling as well as boxing. (He had trained with Harold Angus, an Olympic Games wrestling champion, and sparred with George Slack, the Doncaster heavyweight boxer). He played a few wartime matches for the club and worked at Follands but, when peace returned, he found employment with the local council and, rather curiously, considering his robust and flamboyant sporting career, worked quietly in the city library.

Appearances:
FL: 1 app. 0 gls.
Total: *1 app. 0 gls.*

❏ **Saints note** - *Jack had a brother, William, who was on the books at Bournemouth.*

SCOTT, Mr.

Role: Forward 1899-1900
b. Surrey

CAREER: SOUTHAMPTON trial April 1900.
Debut v Millwall (h) 25.4.1900

Scott was an amateur right winger who was given a trial in an academic Southern League fixture which occurred four days after the disastrous F.A. Cup Final defeat against Bury. Billed as the "Surrey flier", Scott was given scant service from his demoralised team-mates and predictably failed to impress enough to be engaged on a permanent footing.

Appearances:
SL: 1 app. 0 gls.
Total: *1 app. 0 gls.*

SCRIVEN, Herbert Richard

Role: Goalkeeper 1930-37
5'10" 11st.12lbs.
b. Winsor, New Forest 2 February 1908

CAREER: Andover/Totton/
SOUTHAMPTON Dec 1929/Salisbury
City April 1938.
Debut v Oldham Athletic (a) 8.9.30

Bert Scriven was plucked from the
obscurity of Hampshire League football
and, once he had established himself
between the posts, he was regarded as
having the safest pair of hands in the
Second Division. Bert spent seven years
as the club's premier goalkeeper and was
awarded a benefit match as a reward for
his loyalty. After retiring from football in
1937 Bert became "mine host" at the Bear
and Ragged Staff at Michelmarsh and
turned out in a few games for Salisbury.
After the war he moved to a farm just
outside Marlow where, now aged 83, he
still follows the progress of the Saints
with a critical eye.

Appearances:
FL: 225 app. 0 gls.
FAC: 8 app. 0 gls.
Total: *233 app. 0 gls.*

SCURR, David William

Role: Full-back 1959-61
5'8" 10st.12lbs.
b. Bursledon 25 September 1939
d. Southampton 26 July 1991

CAREER: Hamble School/Southampton &
Hampshire Schools/C.P.C. Sports &
Lymington (Saints nursery)/SOUTHAMPTON
May 1957/Andover Sept 1963.
Debut v Coventry City (a) 12.3.60

A local discovery, David Scurr's two years at
the Dell were spent almost entirely in the
reserves where he provided cover for regular
left back, Tommy Traynor. David was a
cricketer of some note; he once took 7-21 for
Hampshire Second XI against the Royal Navy
and later played for the Deanery Club.

Appearances:
FL: 2 app. 0 gls.
FAC: 1 app. 0 gls.
Total: *3 app. 0 gls.*

SEALY, Anthony John

Role: Forward 1977-79
5'6" 10st.12lbs.
b. Hackney, London 7 May 1959

CAREER: Wallsend Schools/Wallsend Boys
Club/SOUTHAMPTON app. Aug 1975, pro.
May 1977/Crystal Palace Mar 1979 (Port Vale-
loan-Feb-May 1980)/Queen's Park Rangers
Mar 1981(Port Vale-loan-Feb 1982)/Fulham
Dec 1983/Leicester City Sept 1985 (Bourne-
mouth-loan Mar-May 1987)/Sporting Braga
c.s. 1987/Brentford non-contract Mar 1988-
Sept 1989/Swindon non-contract Sept
1989/Bristol Rovers Sept 1989/Finland cs 1991.
Debut v Sheffield United (h) 25.2.78

Spotted by Saints' North Eastern scout, Jack
Hixon, while scoring 224 goals in schools and
boys club soccer during the 1973-74 season,
Tony Sealy made his reserve team debut at the
age of 16 and looked to have quite a future in
the game. Blessed with plenty of confidence
and bravado, Tony continued to score goals
with apparent ease for the second string and,
given his league debut in the latter half of the
1977-78 season, was unlucky to sustain an
injury in only his second game. Although he

Tony Sealy

Rovers/SOUTHAMPTON 1898/New
Brompton 1899/Queen's Park Rangers c.s.
1901/Southampton Wanderers 1902/Clapton
Orient 1903/Leyton 1905.
Debut v Tottenham Hotspur (h) 29.3.1896

George Seeley, nicknamed "The Lion Tamer"
due to his once entering a lion's cage in a
circus that was visiting Southampton, was
recruited from local minor soccer in 1896. An
understudy to Joe Turner, he only made one
appearance before he tried his luck in Bristol in
an effort to win more regular first team soccer.
His game improved with experience and, after
a couple of years, he returned to Southampton
a better player. Speedy, versatile and a real
trier, he was however prone to inconsistency
and for that reason was allowed to move on.

Appearances:
SL: 9 app. 1 gl.
Total: *9 app. 1 gl.*

came on as a substitute in the 1979 League Cup
Final his career at the Dell died an inexplicable
death and, soon after his Wembley run-out, he
was sold, somewhat reluctantly, to Crystal
Palace for £50,000. Ever since he has scored
goals for his various clubs without quite living
up to the early promise shown as a youth. He
made an unlikely move in 1987 to Portugal
where Keith Burkinshaw, manager of Sporting
Braga, used Tony's energy and thrust as a
perfect foil for the skilful Brazilian, Cascavel.

Appearances:
FL: 2 (5) app. 0 gls.
LC: 0 (1) app. 0 gls.
Total: *2 (6) app. 0 gls.*

❏ **Saints note** - *Soon after leaving Southampton
for Selhurst Park, Tony returned to the Dell to
spectate at a reserve match but found himself taking
over a linesman's job when one of the match
officials became ill.*

SEELEY, George Alfred

Role: Forward 1896-97 & 1898-99
5'6" 11st.7lbs.
b. Risbridge July qtr. 1877
d. Ventnor, Isle of Wight 15 October 1921

CAREER: Gordon Avenue/SOUTHAMPTON
St. Mary's 1896/Bristol St. Georges/Eastville

SELSTON, Sidney Charles

Role: Forward 1912-13
b. Farnham January qtr. 1888

CAREER: R.G.A. Sheerness/
SOUTHAMPTON Feb 1912.
Debut v Brighton & Hove Albion (h) 22.2.13

An army representative player, Selston was
one of many new players tried by the club
during the troublesome 1912-13 campaign. The
team's general lack of confidence seemed to
convey itself directly to the youngster for,
playing on the right wing, he tended to part
with the ball either hurriedly or prematurely.
Although his nervousness diminished with
each game, the club decided he was still
surplus to requirements and he rejoined his
army unit in Kent.

Appearances:
SL: 4 app. 0 gls.
Total: *4 app. 0 gls.*

SHAND, Hector MacKenzie

Role: Forward 1904-05
5'8" 11st.7lbs.
b. Inverness 1 May 1879

CAREER: Citadel F.C./Inverness Thistle/

SOUTHAMPTON 1905/ Inverness Thistle c.s. 1905/ Middlesbrough Aug 1906/Millwall May 1907.

Debut v Queen's Park Rangers (h) 29.4.04

PROMINENT FOOTBALLERS.

H. SHAND.

Hector Shand made the long journey south to join the Saints at the tail end of the 1904-05 season and was given the right-wing position for the last game. He had a steady afternoon but was unable to acclimatise and returned to Scotland within weeks. Saints' fans were re-acquainted with him in February 1908 when he returned to the Dell wearing the colours of Millwall.

Appearances:
SL: 1 app. 0 gls.
Total: *1 app. 0 gls.*

SHARP, Alexander

Role: Centre-half 1929-30
5'10" 11st.11lbs.
b. Prestonpans, Lothian

CAREER: Ayr United/SOUTHAMPTON Mar 1930.

Debut v West Bromwich Albion (a) 3.5.30

On trial from Ayr United, Alex Sharp journeyed south in March 1930 and played seven times for the reserves before being given his first team chance in the final league game of the season. With the side going down 5-1 to West Bromwich Albion it can be safely assumed that Alex did not enjoy a comfortable afternoon and he was not engaged for the 1930-31 season.

Appearances:
FL: 1 app. 0 gls.
Total: *1 app. 0 gls.*

SHARP, Bertram

Role: Full/Half-back 1900-01
b. Hereford January 1876
d. Liverpool c. 1941

CAREER: Hereford Thistle/Hereford Town/Hereford Thistle/Aston Villa June 1897/Everton Apr 1899/SOUTHAMPTON May 1900/Everton May 1901/Reinstated as amateur Aug 1904/ Kirkdale am Aug 1904/Southport Central Jan 1905.

Debut v Luton Town (a) 1.9.00

Bertram Sharp was the younger brother of the famous Everton and England international Jack Sharp and, although never attaining the fame achieved by his elder brother, he was known as an honest, hardworking defender. Versatile and a good athlete, he performed consistently in his one season as a Saint before he returned to Goodison where, some years later along with Jack, he was appointed to the board. In 1904 Bertram became the landlord of a flourishing hostelry business which was situated opposite Goodison Park.

Bertram Sharp

Appearances:
SL: 22 app. 1 gl.
Total: *22 app. 1 gl.*

❏ **Saints note** - *Bertram was a good cricketer and, in the summer of 1900, he averaged over 40 with the bat for Herefordshire.*

SHARPE, John William Henry

Role: Full-back 1976-78
5'10" 10st.12lbs.
b. Portsmouth 9 October 1957

CAREER: Portsmouth Schools/ SOUTHAMPTON app. Oct 1974, pro. Oct 1975/Gillingham Sept 1978/SOUTHAMPTON Mar 1985 non-contract/Swansea City Sept 1985 non-contract.

Debut v Bristol Rovers (a) 9.4.77

John Sharpe

A former Portsmouth Schools captain, John Sharpe was recommended to the Dell by Saints' scout and former player, Stan Cribb. A well-balanced full-back who tackled well, John had to wait patiently for his debut but took his chance when Peter Rodrigues became injured at the tail end of the 1976-77 season. Sent off in a pre-season tournament in Scotland, John lost his place for the opening of the 1977-78 campaign and thereafter struggled to build on the promising form shown in the previous year. The arrival of Ivan Golac was the final nail in the coffin of John's Southampton career and he duly moved to Gillingham for £50,000. He briefly reappeared at the Dell in March 1985 when Lawrie McMenemy, mindful of the shortage of cover, engaged him on a non-contract basis until the end of the season.

Appearances:
FL: 21 app. 0 gls.
FAC: 1 app. 0 gls.
Total: *22 app. 0 gls.*

SHEARER, Alan

Role: Forward 1987-
5'11" 11st.3lbs.
b. Newcastle 13 August 1970

CAREER: Newcastle & Northumberland Schools/SOUTHAMPTON trainee July 1986, pro. April 1988.
*Debut v Arsenal (h) 9.4.88 *(scored on debut)*

Alan Shearer could never have envisaged a more spectacular full league debut when, in a game at home to Arsenal, he hit a hat-trick and thus replaced Jimmy Greaves in the record books as the youngest ever player to score three goals in a First Division match. Strangely Alan then struggled to find First Division nets with any regularity but as compensation developed into a perfect target man for the more predatory skills of Rodney Wallace and Matthew Le Tissier. Despite possessing a comparatively small stature for a centre-forward, Alan often dominates in the air and his strength and aggression have triggered more than a hint of panic from some of the league's finest defenders. 1990-91 was an excellent season for the young Geordie as not only did he become a fixture in the Saints number nine shirt but also a regular in the England Under-21 team. In particular, May 1991 was a spectacular month for Alan as not only did he win the Saints Player of the Year award but he also played a massive part in the England Under-21 success in Toulon. He scored seven goals in four games, including a hat-trick against Mexico plus a brilliant winner against France in the final and also had the honour of captaining the side in the game against Russia. That took Alan's goal tally for the Under-21's to 11 goals in nine matches and he is being touted as a certainty for full England honours before too long.

Appearances:
FL: 64 (12) app. 10 gls.
FAC: 4 (2) app. 2 gls.
LC: 10 (2) app. 8 gls.
Total: *78 (16) app. 20 gls.*

See over for picture

Alan Shearer

SHEARER, Samuel

Role: Forward 1908-10
b. Coylton 29 December 1883

CAREER: Trabboch/SOUTHAMPTON Aug
1908/ Nithsdale Wanderers (Dumfries) 1910/
Bradford Park Avenue Dec 1912.
Debut v Brighton & Hove Albion (a) 2.9.08

A product of Scottish junior football, Sam
Shearer showed considerable promise in the
early trial matches and was included in the
senior side at the outset of the 1908-09 season.
Naturally skilful, he always managed to keep
the ball close to his feet which ultimately led to
him incurring plenty of kicks and bruises on
his ankles. His individuality, although baffling
opponents, was never properly exploited or
harnessed by his team-mates and Sam
eventually lost his first team place to Frank
Jordan.

Appearances:
SL: 17 app. 0 gls.
Total: *17 app. 0 gls.*

Sam Shearer

SHEERAN, Charles

Role: Forward 1911-12
5'9" 11st.5lbs.

CAREER: 4th Royal Fusiliers/
SOUTHAMPTON c.s. 1911/Woolston c.s.
1912/Dartford c.s. 1913.
Debut v Millwall (a) 30.12.11

A Hampshire County representative player,
Charlie Sheeran joined the Saints after
completing his army service and showed such
form in the reserves that he was eventually
given two first team outings in the right-wing
position. He was fast and could centre well
although he particularly relished cutting in
and making for goal rather than taking the ball
towards the corner flag. He scored twelve
goals in the reserves during the 1911-12 season
but confounded the local paper's forecast that
"he looks like building a very creditable
reputation" by dropping out of professional
soccer and playing in the Hampshire League
with Woolston.

Appearances:
SL: 2 app. 0 gls.
Total: *2 app. 0 gls.*

SHELLEY, Frederick Albert

Role: Half-back 1919-32
5'9" 11st.8lbs.
b. Romsey 11 August 1899
d. Anfield 29 December 1971

CAREER: Romsey Comrades/Eastleigh
Athletic Nov 1919/SOUTHAMPTON Dec
1919, nursery trainer 1932, first team coach
1935/ Liverpool coach Mar 1937.
Debut v Cardiff City (h) 17.1.20

Previously in local soccer, Bert Shelley
achieved some outstanding performances in
wartime football abroad. Serving with the
2nd/5th Hampshire Territorials in 1915, he
was a member of the Battalion side that
reached the semi-finals of the Calcutta Cup in
India and, three years later as a member of the
1st/4th Wiltshires, he gained Divisional Cup
Winners honours in Egypt. Following his
demobilisation Bert signed for Eastleigh
Athletic and before long attracted the attention
of Southampton who were eager to sign young
players in preparation for their transition from
membership of the Southern League to the
Football League. Bert settled into the reserves

"Come on then!" - Bert Shelley clowns with fellow Saint Arthur Dominy (above), while (below), seated front left, Bert is pictured in India during his time with the 2nd/5th Hampshire Territorials. Pictured (right) in later years is Bert in his Liverpool blazer.

and was given his big chance in the first team when an injury to Arthur Andrews, sustained in a cup match at West Ham, left the team without a recognised right-half. This produced a dilemma for the directors. Pondering a foray into the transfer market they were instead persuaded by trainer, Bert Lee, to "give the young Shelley a chance" and so was launched a career that eventually encompassed 448 games, a club record which lasted until Tommy Traynor overhauled it in the mid-1960's. Bert soon gained considerable repute as a half-back of the "stopper mould", having the knack of smothering opposing forwards by his ability to anticipate and intercept through-balls. Consistency was his middle name and, not missing a match between 1921 and 1924, Bert was unfortunate not to win full England honours, although he did tour South Africa with an F.A. XI in 1929. With his long career drawing to a close Bert was, in 1932, appointed coach to the club's very first nursery team competing in the Hampshire League, and so successful was he that, in 1935 with the retirement of Bert Lee, he was rewarded with his former mentor's position of first team trainer. Serving under George Kay, Bert eventually followed the Saints' boss to Anfield where he was the Reds' coach between 1937 and 1956. Remaining on Merseyside until his death in 1971 Bert still helped in the development of the youngsters and had a hand in laying the foundations of what is today the impressive coaching set-up at Liverpool.

Appearances:
SL: 18 app. 1 gl.
FL: 392 app. 8 gls.
FAC: 38 app. 0 gls.
Total: *448 app. 9 gls.*

SHENTON, George P.

Role: Forward 1896-97

CAREER: SOUTHAMPTON St. Mary's 1896.

Debut v New Brompton (a) 6.2.1897
*(scored on debut)

George, although marking his debut by scoring, was unable to oust regular right-winger Naughton from the first team on a permanent basis. He was outstanding at County level, however, and was picked to play for Hampshire against Dorset in March 1897.

Appearances:
SL: 1 app. 1 gl.
Total: *1 app. 1 gl.*

Jimmy Shields

SHIELDS, Robert James

Role: Forward 1956-59
5'8" 11st.4lbs.
b. Londonderry
26 September 1931

CAREER:
Londonderry Boys Club/Belfast Crusaders/ Sunderland Mar 1954/ SOUTHAMPTON July 1956/Headington United Mar 1959/South Shields 1961.

Debut v Bournemouth (h) 18.8.56
*(scored on debut)

A former Irish Youth and amateur international, Jimmy Shields' transfer fee of £1,000 was generously met by the Southampton Supporters Club. A strong, forceful forward, Jimmy quickly gained further international honours when he was picked for the Northern Ireland team for a match against Scotland at Hampden Park in November 1956. Unfortunately he had the misfortune to break his left leg in the first minute of a reserve fixture in September 1957 and never made a complete recovery. After just three games in the 1958-59 season Jimmy accepted his league career was over and made a move to Headington United. A joiner by trade, he is now working in Sunderland.

Appearances:
FL: 38 app. 20 gls.
FAC: 4 app. 1 gl.
Total: *42 app. 21 gls.*

SHILTON, Peter Leslie O.B.E.

Role: Goalkeeper 1982-87
6'0" 14st.0lbs.
b. Leicester 18 September 1949

CAREER: Leicester Schools/Leicester Boys/
Leicester City app June 1965, pro. Sept 1966/
Stoke City Nov 1974/Nottingham Forest Sept
1977/SOUTHAMPTON Aug 1982/Derby
County June 1987.

Debut v Coventry City (a) 28.8.82

Peter Shilton first made his mark at the Dell
when, in goal for Leicester during a match in
October 1967, he scored with a drop kick
against Campbell Forsyth! He had been
Leicester's youngest-ever debutant and at
Filbert Street had been Gordon Banks'
understudy before first taking Banks' Leicester
place and then his England position. At Stoke,
and particularly Nottingham Forest, Peter
became known as simply the best goalkeeper
in the world, with his almost fanatical
dedication to fitness and training becoming
legendary. After winning European Cup
honours at the City Ground, Southampton
enticed him to the Dell for a fee of £325,000
and the Saints fans wallowed in the hitherto
unprecedented luxury of watching the
country's finest first line of defence in action.
Positionally faultless, and possessing
impeccable handling, Peter captained his
country for the 1986 World Cup Finals and,
during his five years in Saints' colours,
overtook Mike Channon as Southampton's
most capped player of all time. Losing none of
his agility as he moved towards his forties
Peter's reputation was often quite enough to
unnerve opposing forwards in one-to-one
situations, and his dominating presence did
much to help the burgeoning career of the
young Mark Wright. In June 1987 he decided
he had had enough of life at the Dell and the
club, happy to trim an excessive wage bill, sold
him to Derby for a giveaway £100,000.
Maintaining his immaculate standards at the
Baseball Ground, Peter overhauled Terry
Paine's all-time league appearance record and
then overtook Bobby Moore's number of
England games, gaining his 109th cap against
Denmark in June 1989. The following summer
Peter played his part in England's surprise run

to the 1990 World Cup semi-final before wisely
deciding to retire from international football
while still at the top of the nation's
goalkeeping pyramid. An inspiration to two
generations of aspiring custodians, Peter
entered his forties as a First Division player,
having made his league bow for Leicester back
in May 1966, which, incredibly, was before
many of today's top strikers were born!

Appearances:
FL: 188 app. 0 gls.
FAC: 17 app. 0 gls.
LC: 28 app. 0 gls.
Eur: 4 app. 0 gls.
Total: *237 app. 0 gls.*

Peter Shilton

SHIPLEY, George Michael

Role: Midfield 1979-80
5'8" 10st.8lbs.
b. Newcastle 7 March 1959

CAREER: St. Mary's Boys Club (Newcastle)/
Newcastle Schools/ Northumberland
County/SOUTHAMPTON app. Aug 1975,
pro. Mar 1977(Reading-loan-Mar-May 1979)(
Blackpool-loan-Oct-Nov 1979)/ Lincoln City
Jan 1980/Luton Town (trial) May
1983/Charlton Athletic July 1985/Gillingham
July 1987/Walsall trial June 1989/Lincoln City
non-contract Aug-Dec 1989/Maidstone United
scout 1990/Gillingham youth team manager
July 1991/Middlesbrough youth team
manager Aug 1991.

Debut v Bolton Wanderers (a) 25.8.79

Playing in the same boys club league as Tony
Sealy, George Shipley was discovered by the
Saints' north-eastern scout, Jack Hixon. George
had his first taste of league soccer on loan with
Reading before returning to Southampton to
force his way into the team at the beginning of
the 1979-80 season. Despite a memorable Dell
debut when Liverpool were beaten 3-2, George
was never given another run-out and he made
a £38,000 move to Lincoln within a few
months. A tenacious midfielder, George made

223 appearances for the Imps and then must
have felt great satisfaction in lining up for
Charlton Athletic against Southampton for a
Division One match in November 1986. In 1990
George returned to the Dell to help coach part-
time at the club's School of Excellence but
returned to his native north-east in August
1991 to run Middlesbrough's Youth team.

Appearances:
FL: 2 (1) app. 0 gls.
Total: *2 (1) app. 0 gls.*

SILLETT, Charles Thomas

Role: Full-back 1931-38
5'8" 11st.7lbs.
b. Plumstead October 29th 1906
d. At sea 7 March 1945

CAREER: 60th Kings Royal Rifles Corps
(Tidworth) 1926/Barking Town 1931/
SOUTHAMPTON am. Oct 1931, pro. Nov
1931/Guildford City July 1938.

*Debut v Burnley (a) 2.1.32 *(scored on debut)*

Sergeant Charlie Sillett was a physical training
instructor based at Tidworth whose skill on the
football field won him a variety of army
representative honours. He gained further
experience playing in the Athenian League for

George Shipley

Charlie Sillett

Barking before joining Saints on the expiry of his term of army service at the end of 1931. After only two games in the reserves he was given his league baptism at Burnley and responded superbly with a couple of goals from the centre-forward position. A versatile player, Charlie eventually settled into the full-back position, equally at home on either side of the pitch. Very popular with fans and colleagues alike, Charlie became team captain in 1937 and led the side with distinction before retiring from league soccer in 1938. After a brief swansong at Guildford he settled in the New Forest to become mine host at 'The Lamb' at Nomansland. Tragically though, he lost his life at sea when the S.S. Corvus was sunk off the Isle of Wight coast in March 1945. Charlie was the father of Peter and John Sillett, both players themselves, the former with Saints, Chelsea and England, the latter with Chelsea, Coventry and Plymouth.

Appearances:
FL: 175 app. 9 gls.
FAC: 8 app. 1 gl.
Total: 183 app. 10 gls.

Peter Sillett

Peter Sillett was the son of Charles Sillett (1931-38) and inherited his father's skills and more besides. He joined the Saints in January 1949 and soon afterwards gained England Youth recognition. Extremely well built, he weighed over 13 stone when only 18. Peter matured quickly into a left-back of some distinction and the Echo, during the 1950-51 season, said that "he kicks a very nice ball". Unfortunately the Saints were facing mounting debts and, with this fact known to many of the country's top clubs, it wasn't too long before Peter was "induced" to join Ted Drake's Chelsea. Playing in the capital, Peter continued to attract rave notices and England Under-23 caps were followed by his first full international against France in May 1955. Peter remained at Stamford Bridge until 1962 when, after a spell at Guildford, he took over the manager's position at Ashford Town. In December 1990 he was still living in Ashford but running Hastings Town.

Appearances:
FL: 59 app. 4 gls.
FAC: 5 app. 0 gls.
Total: 64 app. 4 gls.

SILLETT, Richard Peter Tudor

Role: Full-back 1951-53
6'0" 13st.4lbs.
b. Southampton 1 February 1933

CAREER: South Wiltshire Schools/ Nomansland/ SOUTHAMPTON am. Jan 1949, pro. June 1950/Chelsea May 1953/Guildford City June 1962/Ashford United player-manager July 1965-Dec 1973 (played until 1970)/Folkestone manager 1974-75/Ashford United manager Jan 1976-Feb 1976/Hereford Scout 1975-78/Hastings United manager 1978-83/Coventry City scout/Asford United manager Apr 1985-May 1987/Poole Town appointed manager June 1987 (unable to take up position due to poor health)/Hastings Town manager 1987.

Debut v Cardiff (h) 22.9.51

SIMPSON, Alexander

Role: Half-back 1952-55
5'10" 11st.11lbs.
b. Glasgow 24 November 1924

CAREER: Benburb/Wolverhampton Wanderers Jan 1947/Notts County Oct 1949/ SOUTHAMPTON Nov 1952/ Shrewsbury Town June 1955/Nuneaton Borough July 1958.

Debut v Lincoln City (a) 22.11.52

Transferred to Southampton as part of the exchange deal that saw Jack Edwards move to Notts County, Alex Simpson had an excellent temperament and was handed the team captaincy a month after his arrival. A fractured ankle suffered in February 1953 was a cruel blow to both him and the club, having an obvious detrimental effect on the struggle to avoid relegation. Recovering in time for Saints' first season outside Division Two for over thirty years, Alex played a further fifty-five Division Three South games before being freed to join Shrewsbury in the summer of 1955.

Appearances:
FL: 68 app. 1 gl.
FAC: 7 app. 0 gls.
Total: 75 app. 1 gl.

SIMPSON, Terence John Norman

Terry Simpson

Role: Half-back
1958-62
5'11" 11st.6lbs.
b. Southampton
8 October 1938

CAREER: Ludlow School/Merry Oak School/ Southampton Schools/SOUTHAMPTON am. July 1954, pro. June 1956/Peterborough United June 1962/ West Bromwich Albion May 1963/Walsall Mar 1967/Gillingham July 1968, trainer and asst. coach June 1970/Swaythling Athletic Jan 1972 /N.D.L.B. (Southampton Senior League) 1973.

Debut v Bury (h) 1.11.58

A member of the town's team that reached the final of the English Schools Trophy in 1954, Terry Simpson made his debut for the reserves in March 1956. He could play up front or in the half-back line but found his versatility a hindrance in his efforts to secure a settled place at the Dell. After moving to Peterborough for a £5,000 fee Terry joined First Division side West Bromwich Albion in 1963 and, in the left-half position, was an ever-present during 1963-64. His career ended with a broken leg sustained whilst with Gillingham and Terry returned to live in Southampton, taking up a job at Swaythling's Ford Transit plant.

Appearances:
FL: 22 app. 1 gl.
FAC: 3 app. 2 gls.
Total: 25 app. 3 gls.

SLADE, Donald

Role: Forward 1910-12
5'8" 11st.2lbs.
b. Southampton 26 November 1888
d. West End 24 March 1980

CAREER: Foundry Lane School/ Southampton Ramblers 1908/ SOUTHAMPTON 1910/Lincoln City Aug 1912/Woolwich Arsenal Dec 1913/Fulham May 1914/(Guested for Southampton and Harland & Wolff during World War One) Dumbarton 1919/Ayr United 1920/Dundee United 1922-23.

Debut v Norwich City (a) 1.4.11

A bricklayer by trade, Donald Slade became a prolific goalscorer at reserve team level after joining the Saints but, although equally at home in the three inside-forward positions, had to wait a considerable time before given his first team opportunity. After just three games he found himself back in the reserves and, scoring on 23 occasions during the 1911-12 season, became frustrated at seemingly being ignored by the first team selection committee. Donald predictably sought a transfer but the Southampton board turned down the request and only relented when he

Donald Slade

successfully appealed to the F.A. Allowed to join Lincoln City on a free transfer, Donald made twenty-three appearances, scoring nine goals, and was snapped up by Arsenal for the sizeable fee of £1,000. Despite costing the Gunners a small fortune his stay at Highbury was brief and within months Donald was allowed to move to Craven Cottage where he remained until the suspension of normal football in 1915. Returning to Southampton he worked for the duration of the war in Harland and Wolff's rolling mills, maintaining the brick linings of the furnaces. With the arrival of peace, Don tried his luck with a succession of Scottish clubs and gained considerable popularity amongst the partisan Scots supporters. Becoming a pub manager in Troon, Donald remained north of the border until 1927 when he returned to England to run public houses in Reading, Flackwell Heath and Beaconsfield. He initially retired to live in Marlow but eventually returned to West End in Southampton where, at the grand old age of 91, he died in 1980.

Appearances:
SL: 3 app. 0 gls.
Total: 3 app. 0 gls.

SLADE, Reginald Edward J.

Role: Full-back 1914-15
5'11" 12st.4lbs.
b. Southampton January qtr. 1892

CAREER: Foundry Lane School/Malmesbury United/Southampton Cambridge/SOUTHAMPTON 1912/Mid Rhondda player-manager 1923.
Debut v Queen's Park Rangers (a) 16.1.15

Reg Slade, the younger brother of Donald Slade (1910-12), first appeared at the Dell in a junior trial match in August 1910 while a member of Malmesbury United eleven. Signed by Saints in 1912, he also simultaneously assisted Southampton Cambridge in the Southampton Senior League and it wasn't until 1913 that he became a full-time professional. Basically the reserve left-back in the years immediately prior to the Great War, Reg made the same number of Southern League appearances as his brother and stayed at the Dell until 1916 when he joined up. He was next heard of playing in Wales in the

1920's while working as a cinema manager. Reg lost his life during the Second World War in an air raid.

Appearances:
SL: 3 app. 0 gls.
Total: 3 app. 0 gls.

SLOAN, Thomas

Role: Forward 1928-29
b. Craghead 11 September 1905
d. 25 September 1987

CAREER: Craghead United/SOUTHAMPTON Aug 1928.
Debut v Port Vale (h) 27.8.28

Tom Sloan came to the Dell on trial from the north east and made his league bow just three days after being registered as a Southampton player. He replaced the injured Bert Jepson in the right-wing position but did nothing extraordinary in the game, which Saints lost 2-1. Tom remained at the Dell for several months, playing seven reserve games, before returning to local soccer in the north east.

Appearances:
FL: 1 app. 0 gls.
Total: 1 app. 0 gls.

SMALL, Archibald Rammell

Role: Forward 1911-13
5' 10" 12st.4lbs
b. Droitwich April qtr. 1889

CAREER: Royal Engineers/SOUTHAMPTON am. 1911/Royal Engineers (Ordnance Survey Office).
Debut v West Ham United (a) 9.9.11
*(scored on debut)

A gifted local amateur, Archie Small was a prominent member of the Royal Engineers side based at the Ordnance Survey Office before signing for the Saints. At home in the inside-right position he made his debut in the second game of the 1911-12 season but, after six games, was dropped as the team began to struggle. In the reserves Archie found the net with consistency and his 19 goals earned him a County Cap for Hampshire. He was recalled to

Archie Small

Jack Small

the first team along with several others in March 1912 as a desperate and ultimately successful measure to avoid relegation. He featured only briefly in the following season and later returned to the Engineers' side. Still actively playing after the war in 1919 he went on to gain further County caps while remaining employed throughout his working life at the Ordnance Survey.

Appearances:
SL: 20 app. 3 gls.
Total: *20 app. 3 gls.*

SMALL, Henry John

Role: Forward 1901-02
b. Southampton circa 1881
d. Southampton 5 June 1946

CAREER: Freemantle/SOUTHAMPTON 1900/Manchester United am. 1902, pro. May 1904/Salisbury City c.s. 1905.

Debut v Millwall (a) 1.3.02

Henry Small was an amateur inside-forward, known to his team-mates as Ranji, who, having joined the club from their local rivals Freemantle, spent two years as understudy to the great Edgar Chadwick. He made his debut

in the Western League in December 1900 and scored, but had to wait another fifteen months for his senior bow. He left the Southampton area in 1902 and, moving to Manchester, joined United, originally as an amateur and later as a professional. Henry failed to make a senior appearance in his three years at Old Trafford and returned south in 1905.

Appearances:
SL: 4 app. 0 gls.
Total: *4 app. 0 gls.*

SMALL, John

Role: Half-back 1913-15
5'10" 12st.8lbs.
b. South Bank 29 October 1889

CAREER: St. Peters School, South Bank/ Craghead United/Sunderland Aug 1912/ SOUTHAMPTON Aug 1913/(Royal Army Medical Corps and Harland and Wolff during World War One)/Thornycrofts 1919/Mid Rhonda 1920/Harland & Wolff Dec 1920.

Debut v Brighton & Hove Albion (a) 3.9.13

Plucked from Sunderland Reserves, Jack Small became a popular player at the Dell, admired not only by the crowd but also by his colleagues. The sort of player whose influence on team spirit was always positive, Jack relished a challenge and his sturdy half-back play was an inspiration. After joining the R.A.M.C. in 1915 he spent sixteen months in Salonika, but was invalided back to Southampton when he suffered a serious bout of malaria. After the war Jack became a member of the famous Thornycrofts team that drew with Burnley in the F.A. Cup before hanging up his boots in 1921. He later joined the Merchant Navy.

Appearances:
SL: 47 app. 2 gls.
FAC: 4 app. 0 gls.
Total: *51 app. 2 gls.*

SMALLWOOD, Frederick

Role: Forward 1936-38
5'5" 10st.0lbs.
b. Wrexham October qtr. 1910

CAREER: Llanerch Celts/Wrexham am. Sept 1933/Chester am. Sept 1934, pro. Oct 1934/ Macclesfield Town 1935/SOUTHAMPTON June 1936/Reading June 1938/(Wrexham, Newcastle United, Sunderland & Hartlepool United during World War Two).

*Debut v Chesterfield (h) 29.8.36 *(scored on debut)*

Fred Smallwood was a former coal-miner from the Gresford Colliery in Wales and had gained Welsh amateur caps before his transfer from non-league soccer to Southampton. A small but nippy left-winger Fred would, on match days, carry a lucky rabbit's foot in the pocket of his shorts and in his first season at the Dell it certainly brought him plenty of success. Luck then deserted him, however, as he was injured in a pre-season practice match in 1937, lost his first team place to the up-and-coming Harry Osman and only featured in another eight games for the club. He refused terms in May 1938 and chose to join Reading for a £500 fee before retiring from professional soccer during the war years. A joker by reputation Fred was also a good musician and after settling in the Sunderland area played in a small dance band.

Appearances:
FL: 48 app. 10 gls.
FAC: 1 app. 0 gls.
Total: *49 app. 10 gls.*

SMITH, Eugene Victor Charles

Role: Half-back 1899-1902
b. Bitterne, Southampton 1878
d. Southampton 29 December 1951

CAREER: Bitterne/SOUTHAMPTON 1899.
Debut v Swindon Town (a) 13.1.1900

Vic Smith was a local amateur who was employed in the town's Ordnance Survey Office. He was noted for the prodigious distance he was able to kick the ball and often won bets on his ability to dispatch it the complete length of the pitch. Most of his period at the Dell was spent as captain of the reserves, a position he continued to hold after becoming a full-time police officer in 1903. In the force for twenty-eight years, Vic reached the rank of Sergeant and remained a keen supporter of the Saints. It was said that he never missed a home game and indeed when he died in 1951 it was on his way home from a match at the Dell.

Appearances:
SL: 4 app. 0 gls.
Total: *4 app. 0 gls.*

Fred Smallwood

SMITH, Frederick

Role: Full-back 1913-14
5'10" 12st.0lbs.
b. Buxton

CAREER: Buxton 1904/
Stockport County Sept 1906/
Derby County Sept 1909/
Macclesfield 1910/
SOUTHAMPTON May 1913.
Debut v Reading (a) 1.11.13

Fred Smith

When Fred Smith was signed
by Southampton he was at
the veteran stage of his career
and had already given up
playing full-time to
concentrate on his job as a
motor mechanic in Macclesfield. He
commenced his short Dell stay by captaining
the reserves where his clean cut, up-standing
image had a beneficial effect on the
youngsters. Given his senior debut as part of
eight team changes brought on by three
successive defeats, Fred's determination and
speed stood him in good stead but with age
creeping up on him and struggling to maintain
full fitness, he decided to call it a day in 1914
and returned to the Macclesfield area.

Appearances:
SL: 16 app. 0 gls.
FAC: 1 app. 0 gls.
Total: *17 app. 0 gls.*

SMITH, George Clarence Bassett

Role: Half-back 1938-49
5'8" 11st.8lbs.
b. Portsmouth 24 March 1919

CAREER: Amherst Schools/Guernsey
Schools/Guernsey Rangers/Huddersfield
Town trial 1937/SOUTHAMPTON am. Oct
1937, pro. July 1938/Crystal Palace May 1950.
Debut v West Bromwich Albion (a) 4.2.39

Although born in Portsmouth, George Smith
grew up in the Channel Islands where he
played junior football. After becoming a
professional at the Dell in time for the 1938-39
season he gave a series of tenacious wing-half
displays in the reserves and became known to
his team mates as the "Guernsey Terrier".

George's persistent, hardworking style eventually led
to his introduction into the
first team and he had made
nine appearances when the
outbreak of war caused the
suspension of the normal
league programme. He saw
active service with the R.A.F.
as an air gunner before
resuming his Dell career
following his demobilisation
in 1946. At ease in either the
right or left-half positions he
enjoyed a couple of seasons
as a regular until, in October
1948, he lost his place to the
young Len Wilkins and
never appeared in the first
team again. After just seven games at Selhurst
Park he retired from professional soccer and
later emigrated to Australia.

Appearances:
FL: 95 app. 1 gl.
FAC: 6 app. 0 gls.
Total: *101 app. 1 gl.*

❏ **Saints note** - *Christened G.C. Bassett - the
'Smith' was a cognomen added later - George is,
even so, the only player with the surname of Smith
to have played for Saints in the Football League.*

George Clarence Bassett Smith

SMITH, George

Role: Forward 1907-08
b. Preston 1879
d. Southampton 3 July 1908

CAREER: Leyland/Preston North End July 1899/Aston Villa June 1901/Blackburn Rovers May 1903/Plymouth Argyle 1906/ SOUTHAMPTON 1907.

George Smith

Debut v Bradford (h) 5.10.07

George Smith was originally a half-back during his Blackburn and Plymouth days and although he started his time at Southampton in that same position he quickly moved into his more favoured role of inside-forward. A direct player George was not given to over elaboration and shot with tremendous power. He certainly looked to be a promising acquisition and everyone at the club was greatly shocked when he suddenly collapsed and died in the summer of 1908.

Appearances:
SL: 21 app. 5 gls.
FAC: 6 app. 0 gls.
Total: *27 app. 5 gls.*

SMITH, Stanley

Role: Forward 1908-11
5'5" 11st.0lbs.
b. Southampton 1887

CAREER: Southampton Cambridge/Ryde/ Bitterne Guild/SOUTHAMPTON 1908.
Debut v West Ham United (a) 25.12.08

Having represented Hampshire at County level prior to enlisting as a Southampton player, Stan was a small but plucky winger. His three years at the Dell were spent mainly in the reserves where he displayed a particular talent for accurately crossing the ball from awkward and seemingly impossible positions. Choosing to give up soccer in 1911 Stan joined the 18th Hussars to serve his country during the Great War.

Appearances:
SL: 9 app. 0 gls.
Total: *9 app. 0 gls.*

SMITH, Tom

Role: Forward 1898-99
5'9" 11st.6lbs.
b. Ashton-in-Makerfield 1877

CAREER: Ashton Athletic 1893/Ashton Town 1895/Preston North End May 1897 /SOUTHAMPTON c.s.1898/Queen's Park Rangers 1899.

Debut v Brighton United (h) 3.9.1898
(scored on debut)

Signing for Southampton in the close season of 1898, Tom Smith was one of two men with the same name made available by Preston North End. One of the Tom's had a reputation for being a "star" player while the other was purported to be of only mediocre ability. When Tom won the 100 yards race in the club annual sports day and scored on his debut Saints believed they had signed the "star" but subsequent events i.e. indifferent form, confirmed that Tottenham Hotspur, who had prudently acquired the other Tom Smith, were in fact the proud employers of the more outstanding player. Meanwhile Southampton's Tom Smith, by now presumably rather hurt by the real reasoning behind his acquisition had lost not only confidence but his first team place to Jimmy Yates and in the ensuing summer he joined Southern League newcomers Queen's Park Rangers.

Appearances:
SL: 14 app. 1 gl.
Total: *14 app. 1 gl.*

SMITH, William

Role: Forward
1913-14
5'10" 12st.0lbs.
b. Denaby

CAREER: Hickleton Main Colliery/ Brentford Oct 1912/ SOUTHAMPTON c.s. 1913/Halifax Town c.s. 1914.

Debut v Brighton & Hove Albion (a) 3.9.13

Bill Smith

Bill Smith played his early football in the

315

Sheffield League before gaining something of a goalscoring reputation at Griffin Park. When he signed for the Saints his ten goals in twenty-seven outings for Brentford raised the expectations of the fans but, despite showing persistence and industry, he struggled to find his scoring touch. After losing his place to another newcomer, Arthur Hollins, Bill remained in the reserves until returning to his native Yorkshire.

Appearances:
SL: 20 app. 4 gls.
Total: *20 app. 4 gls.*

although, while in the reserves, he did win eight medals including two for the Hampshire Senior Cup, two for the Hampshire County League and two for the Southampton Senior Cup. A versatile and useful player to have in the background George was rewarded in 1912 with a benefit match against Woolston which realised £23 13s 3d. In November 1912 he left the Dell and very soon after emigrated to Australia.

Appearances:
SL: 13 app. 0 gls.
Total: *13 app. 0 gls.*

SMITH, William George

Role: Full/Half-back 1907-11
b. Peartree Green, Southampton December 1886

CAREER: Peartree Green/SOUTHAMPTON c.s. 1907.

Debut v Norwich City (h) 21.3.08

George Smith found first team opportunities rationed during his five years at the Dell

SMOKER, Henry George

Role: Forward 1900-04
b. Arlesford, Hampshire, 1 March 1881
d. Wallasey, Cheshire 7 September 1966

CAREER: SOUTHAMPTON c.s. 1900.

Debut v Wellingborough Town (h) 7.11.03

Henry Smoker was a speedy left-winger who favoured taking on the full-back rather than

William George Smith (second from the left, back row) with Walter Toomer, Frank Grayer, Jim Goodchild, Percy Prince, H. Rainsley and Harry Bamford.

delivering the early cross. He was the son of George Smoker, who was a cricketer with Hampshire C.C.C. in 1885, and he left the Dell himself in 1904 to concentrate on a professional career at the County Ground. Henry played thirty-one matches for Hampshire between 1901 and 1907 mainly as a right-handed bowler although he was also a useful lower order left-handed batsman. He later played cricket for Cheshire and the Lancashire league. He was brother-in-law to another footballer and cricketer Victor Norbury.

Appearances:
SL: 2 app. 0 gls.
Total: *2 app. 0 gls.*

SOUTHERN, A.

Role: Forward 1910-11

CAREER: Loyal North Lancashire Regiment/ SOUTHAMPTON trial Apr 1911.
Debut v Southend United (h) 8.4.11

Southern came to the Dell on trial in April 1911 having just helped his regiment secure the Army Cup. He was given his Southern League debut within a week of his arrival and was perceived to be able to run intelligently with the ball. He scored a goal in his second match but his three outings for the club came in the middle of a depressing month when, out of seven games, six were lost and he was duly allowed to return to his regiment at Tidworth.

Appearances:
SL: 3 app. 1 gl.
Total: *3 app. 1 gl.*

SOYE, James

Role: Forward 1905-06
5'8" 10st.5lbs.
b. Govan 14 April 1885

CAREER: Rutherglen Glencairn/Belfast Celtic & Hibernian trials/Belfast Distillery/ SOUTHAMPTON c.s. 1905/Newcastle United May 1906/Aberdeen May 1909-15.
Debut v Norwich City (a) 9.9.05

Although born in Scotland it was while playing in Ireland that Jimmy Soye first

discovered the knack of goalscoring and, crossing the Irish Sea to join the Saints in 1905, he continued to indulge his scoring appetite. Small but muscular, Jim was clever enough to avoid the more robust challenges and although his form trailed off in the latter half of the season Newcastle had seen enough of his potential to offer terms. At St. James Park his career did not take off as predicted and after just seven games over a three-year spell Jim took himself back to his native Scotland. His career finally flourished north of the border and, justifying his early promise, he became a regular in Aberdeen's first team making over 200 league and cup appearances. An electrical engineer by trade, Jim also won a Scottish League Cup medal while at Aberdeen.

Appearances:
SL: 18 app. 5 gls.
Total: *18 app. 5 gls.*

SPELLACY, James Joseph

Role: Forward 1896-97

CAREER: SOUTHAMPTON St. Mary's 1896/ Cowes.
Debut v Newton Heath (a) 13.2.1897 FAC

James was a reserve forward who replaced "Chippy" Naughton in an important F.A. Cup replay against Newton Heath (later Manchester United). He never made a league line-up for the Saints but was a member of the Cowes team that briefly played in the Southern League in 1899-1900. He also represented Hampshire in a game against Dorset on the 20th March 1897.

Appearances:
FAC: 1 app. 0 gls.
Total: *1 app. 0 gls.*

SPENCE, George

Role: Half-back/ Forward 1903-04
5'10" 12st.0lbs.
b. Rothersay, Bute 27 September 1877

George Spence

CAREER: St. Mirren/Derby County Apr 1898/Reading 1900/Preston North End May 1901/Reading 1902/SOUTHAMPTON c.s. 1903/Hull City 1904/Clyde c.s. 1906/ Cowdenbeath c.s. 1907.

Debut v New Brompton (a) 12.9.03

Classified very much as a utility player George Spence won a Southern League Championship medal in his one season as a Saint and was described in the local press as "fast, tricky, clever and a glutton for work". George never settled in the south and after moving to Humberside registered Hull's first ever goal in the Football League.

Appearances:
SL: 14 app. 3 gls.
Total: *14 app. 3 gls.*

SPENCER, Thomas Hannah

Role: Forward 1965-66
5'10" 12st.11lbs.
b. Glasgow 28 November 1945

CAREER: Glasgow Celtic/SOUTHAMPTON July 1965/York City June 1966/Workington Mar 1968/Lincoln City Jan 1972/ Rotherham United July 1974/Worksop Town.

Debut v Middlesbrough (h) 2.4.66

Tommy Spencer was a strongly-built centre-forward who made three consecutive appearances in April 1966. Saints were pushing hard for promotion and although Tommy did not score the team picked up five valuable points. He lost his place when Norman Dean recovered from injury and, with the club finally winning their place in the First Division, his services were dispensed with. At York, he scored twenty goals in fifty-seven games but, moving to Workington, converted into a defender before finishing his career at Rotherham in 1977.

Appearances:
FL: 3 app. 0 gls.
Total: *3 app. 0 gls.*

SPERRING, Alistair

Role: Goalkeeper 1983-84
6'2" 13st.3lbs.
b. Hayling Island 26 October 1963

Alistair Sperring

CAREER: SOUTHAMPTON app. July 1980, pro. Aug 1983 (Swindon Town-loan Aug-Sept 1984)/Reading trial Jan 1985/Bognor Regis Town.

Debut v Rotherham United (a) 8.11.83 LC

Alistair Sperring was a tall young goalkeeper who became Peter Shilton's understudy for the 1983-84 season. He failed to play league football for Southampton but was called upon for a League Cup tie at Rotherham when Shilton was injured. With the arrival of Phil Kite, Alistair was released into non-league soccer.

Appearances:
LC: 1 app. 0 gls.
Total: *1 app. 0 gls.*

SPINNER, Terry James

Role: Forward 1972-74
5'9" 10st.4lbs.
b. Woking 6 November 1953

CAREER: Cove Grammar School/London & Hampshire Schools/SOUTHAMPTON app. Aug 1969, pro. July 1971/Walsall July 1974/ Burton Albion Aug 1976.

Terry Spinner

Debut v Chelsea (a) 21.8.73

An outstanding youth player, Terry Spinner represented England at schoolboy level before becoming a Southampton apprentice. Despite topping the reserve goalscoring charts for two successive seasons Terry failed to capitalise on his early promise and after just one full game in the first team was given a free transfer. Disappointingly he failed to establish himself with Third Division Walsall and left them for non-league soccer before he had made twenty appearances.

Appearances:
FL: 1 (1) app. 0 gls.
Total: 1 (1) app. 0 gls.

STAGE, William

Role: Forward 1930-31
5'7" 11st.0lbs.
b. Whitby 22 March 1893
d. Blackley 12 May 1957

CAREER: Middlesbrough am.
Aug 1913, pro. Dec 1913/
Hibernian 1919/St. Bernards/

Bury Oct 1921/Burnley June 1928/
SOUTHAMPTON July 1930.
Debut v Nottingham Forest (h) 1.9.30

Bill Stage was signed by manager Arthur Chadwick and, aged 37, was at the end of a long and distinguished career that had started before the Great War. A fetcher and forager on the field, Bill's experience was put to good use assisting the club's second string. Making just four first team appearances Bill had the satisfaction of scoring in his very last league game which came in November 1930 at Charlton. He retired from professional soccer in May 1931.
Appearances:
FL: 4 app. 1 gl.
Total: 4 app. 1 gl.

STANSBRIDGE,
Leonard Edward Charles

Role: Goalkeeper 1937-52
5'11" 12st.4lbs.
b. Southampton 19 February 1919
d. Southampton 19 May 1986

CAREER: Regents Park School/Southampton Schools/Bitterne Boys/SOUTHAMPTON am. May 1936, pro. Aug 1936/(Rotherham & Swansea during World War Two)/Basingstoke Town 1953.
Debut v Plymouth Argyle (a) 7.5.38

WILLIAM STAGE
BURY

Len Stansbridge was the Southampton goalkeeper in the successful 1932 English Schools Trophy team and graduated to professional status in August 1936. He developed into a strong, reliable, deputy custodian, a tag he loyally accepted throughout his long years of service to the club. Len made his league bow in the last game of the 1937-38 season and let in four goals as the team lost to Plymouth. He had a further five outings the following year before joining the Royal Army Medical Corps upon the outbreak of war. At Dunkirk Len courageously stayed behind to tend the injured and, captured by the enemy, was to spend the next four years as a prisoner of war in Poland. Len kept fit during his captivity by playing in a series of "P.O.W. Internationals" and, returning to Southampton in 1945, was re-engaged at the Dell. Over the next seven years Len was the regular "back up" goalkeeper, ably deputising for Ian Black, Hugh Kelly, Fred Kiernan and John Christie whenever required. After hanging up his gloves Len became groundsman at the Southampton Sports Centre and then in 1962 returned to the Dell under a similar guise. Often seen prodding the penalty areas at half-time with his pitch-fork, Len lovingly cared for the playing-field at the Dell for twenty-two years before his retirement in the summer of 1984.

Len
Stansbridge

Appearances:
FL: 48 app. 0 gls.
FAC: 4 app. 0 gls.
Total: *52 app. 0 gls.*

into one of the best young defenders in the county and only the form of Kenny Sansom prevented him from winning more than three England caps. A fierce tackler who loved to make forward runs, Derek was about to move to Liverpool for £250,000 during the 1986-87 season but the deal fell through on medical grounds at the last moment. Chris Nicholl, however, anxious to replace Mark Dennis, had no such qualms about bringing him to the Dell for a knock down fee of £100,000 soon after the start of the 1987-88 season. He settled quickly and not only proved his fitness by playing 38 games but was named by the fans as their Player of the Season. The following year was less successful and an injury, coupled with the arrival of Micky Adams from Leeds, led to Derek asking for a transfer. He joined Alan Ball at Stoke for a fee based on his number of appearances, but could not prevent the Potteries club sliding into Division Three in 1990.

Appearances:
FL: 64 app. 2 gls.
FAC: 4 app. 1 gl.
LC: 7 app. 1 gl.
Total: *75 app. 4 gls.*

STATHAM, Derek James

Role: Full-back 1987-89
5'5" 11st.0lbs.
b. Wolverhampton 24 March 1959

CAREER: St. Mary's Primary/St. Edmunds Junior School/West Bromwich Albion app. July 1975, pro. April 1976/SOUTHAMPTON Aug 1987/Stoke City July 1989/Aston Villa trial July 1991/Walsall Aug 1991.

Debut v Portsmouth (a) 22.8.87

Derek Statham made his debut in 1976 for West Bromwich Albion and, despite playing at left-back, scored a goal. He quickly developed

Derek Statham

STEAD, William Alexander George

Role: Goalkeeper
1905-06
b. Portsea July qtr. 1887
d. Southampton
5 June 1939

CAREER:
SOUTHAMPTON
1905/Salisbury City
1906/Aberdeen 1906/
Salisbury City 1906/
Clapton Orient 1907/
Salisbury City 1908.

Debut v Brentford (a)
30.12.05

Bill Stead

Bill Stead started the 1905-06 campaign as Southampton's third choice goalkeeper but, due to injuries sustained by Clawley and Burrows, he was propelled into the first eleven for two Southern League matches. His third appearance came in the eagerly awaited F.A. Cup clash with local rivals Portsmouth and for 18 year-old Bill the game had the added significance of being against his home town club. The match kicked off in front of 14,000 noisy fans and Portsmouth did their best to unsettle the rookie goalkeeper in the early stages of the contest. Bill, showing little signs of nerves, produced a phlegmatic performance which completely belied his youth and inexperience, as the Saints romped to a satisfying 5-1 victory over their south coast neighbours. Realising there was little likelihood of ousting George Clawley on a permanent basis Bill left the Dell for Salisbury just six months after the Portsmouth game, and was connected with the Wiltshire club up until 1920 when he became a seaman aboard the Mauritania. He later also sailed on the Durban Castle while working for the Union Castle line.

Appearances:
SL: 2 app. 0 gls.
FAC: 1 app. 0 gls.
Total: *3 app. 0 gls.*

STEELE, James

Role: Defender 1971-77
6'0" 12st.2lbs.
b. Edinburgh 11 March 1950

CAREER: Dundee Apr 1967/
SOUTHAMPTON Jan 1972 (Glasgow Rangers-loan-Nov 1976)/Washington Diplomats c.s. 1977/Memphis/Memphis Rogues 1980/Chicago/Pittsburg.

Debut v Nottingham Forest (h) 29.1.72

Jim Steele's signing was shrouded in secrecy as Ted Bates moved swiftly to acquire the services of the tall defender from under the noses of many big clubs. Jim had a cultured left foot and an aggressive, no-holds-barred attitude which won him admiration on the terraces but not many friends among the men in black. Able to play at full-back or in the centre of the defence, Jim's finest game for the club was in the 1976 F.A. Cup final against Manchester United when he was voted Man of the Match. Aged 26, Jim should soon have been at his peak but, perversely, his career plummeted to the extent that in the close season of 1977 he moved to the States and never appeared on a British soccer pitch again. Jim's maverick character and his disciplinary problems are two possible reasons for his apparent demise but, nevertheless, it remains something of a mystery that Lawrie McMenemy, the master of player-management, could not satisfactorily harness such undoubted talent. In November 1990 Jim, a foreman at an electrical plant in Washington, flew home to attend the reunion dinner held for the 1976 F.A. Cup squad.

Appearances:
FL: 160 (1) app. 2 gls.
FAC: 16 app. 0 gls.
LC: 12 app. 0 gls.
Eur: 4 app. 0 gls.
Total: *192 (1) app. 2 gls.*

Jim Steele

STEVEN, David

Role: Forward 1897-99
5'6" 11st.2lbs.
b. Dundee 16 March 1878
d. Dundee 28 April 1903

CAREER: Dundee Violet/Dundee/Bury Aug 1896/Dundee 1897/SOUTHAMPTON c.s. 1897/Dundee 1899.

Debut v Reading (h) 19.2.1898

David Steven was introduced to English soccer by the famous Scottish agent Peter Allen who initially induced him to Bury in 1896. A player of above average ability, David moved to Southampton after a dispute with The Shakers prevented him joining any other Football League team. The fans enjoyed his fearless, dashing forward play for two seasons before he decided to return to his home town to continue his career. Tragically he suffered a fatal heart attack in April 1903 which was just one month after his twenty-fifth birthday.

Appearances:
SL: 17 app. 6 gls.
FAC: 2 app. 0 gls.
Total: *19 app. 6 gls.*

David Steven

STEVENS, Brian Edward

Role: Goalkeeper 1956-58
6'3" 13st.0lbs.
b. Andover 13 November 1933
d. Hursley 10 May 1980

CAREER: Andover Old Boys/ SOUTHAMPTON Sept 1956/Southport Feb 1959/Salisbury Dec 1959.

Debut v Ipswich Town (h) 1.5.57

An exceptionally tall goalkeeper, Brian Stevens was signed as cover for John Christie. Making his debut in the penultimate game of the 1956-57 season against champions, Ipswich Town, Brian only enjoyed one lengthy run in the first team when he played ten consecutive games the following year. The arrival of Tony Godfrey diminished his hopes of a regular place and he was released to join Southport a month before the 1959 transfer deadline.

Appearances:
FL: 12 app. 0 gls.
Total: *12 app. 0 gls.*

STEVENS, Samuel Batson

Role: Half-back 1958-59
6'0" 12st.3lbs.
b. Rutherglen 2 December 1935

CAREER: Rutherglen Academy/Glasgow Schools/Queen's Park/Airdrieonians 1956/ SOUTHAMPTON June 1957/Poole Town Aug 1959/Andover Aug 1961/Portals/ Swaythling Athletic player-manager.

Debut v Chesterfield (a) 25.8.58

Sam Stevens was a physical training instructor in the Army Signal Corps and attracted the attention of Southampton when guesting for them in a friendly in April 1956. Finishing his national service, Sam initially joined Airdrie but in June 1957 signed professionally for the Saints and took his place in the reserve eleven. A good sportsman and wholehearted half-back Sam surprisingly remained in league soccer for only one season before signing for Mike Keeping's Poole Town in 1959. A teacher by profession, Sam still lives near Southampton and in 1990 was helping Lew Chatterley coach the club's younger players.

Appearances:
FL: 14 app. 0 gls.
Total: *14 app. 0 gls.*

STEVENSON, Ernest

Role: Forward 1949-51
5'8"11st.6lbs.
b. Rotherham 28 December 1923
d. St. Helens 15 October 1970

CAREER: Wath Wanderers/Wolverhampton
Wanderers 1943/Cardiff City Nov 1948/
SOUTHAMPTON Mar 1950/Leeds United Feb
1951/Wisbech July 1952.
Debut v Blackburn Rovers (a) 11.3.50

Ernie Stevenson was Cardiff's top scorer
during the 1948-49 season and at Ninian Park
had been described as "competitive, a strong
dribbler and difficult to dispossess". His
arrival at Southampton was a surprise as he
had played for Cardiff at the Dell only the
previous Saturday and had been the pick of
their forwards. Fulham had also been keen to
acquire his services but, with Southampton
offering a "five figure fee" and Wilf Grant,
Ernie was persuaded to become a Saint.
Despite scoring five goals in the twelve games
remaining in the 1949-50 programme, Ernie
failed to truly settle in the south and eleven
months later took part in another player-
exchange transfer when he swopped places
with Frank Dudley of Leeds United. Sixteen
games and five goals later Ernie found himself
surplus to Elland Road requirements and freed
into non-league football.

Ernie Stevenson

Appearances:
FL: 23 app. 8 gls.
Total: *23 app. 8 gls.*

STEVENTON, Ernest

Role: Goalkeeper 1913-15
5'11" 12st.0lbs.
b. Walsall July qtr. 1888
d. Walsall 23 November 1950

CAREER:
Walsall/Wednesday Old
Athletic/ SOUTHAMPTON
May 1913/Blackpool 1917/
Later director of Walsall.

Debut v Crystal Palace (h)
8.11.13

Ernie Steventon was
considered to be the best
young goalkeeper in the

Black Country and once established between
the posts at the Dell was soon demonstrating
his agility. He was briefly in the shadow of
veteran goalkeeper George Kitchen but,
showing an extremely safe pair of hands,
quickly made the first team
green jersey his own during
the 1913-14 season. The
following year he shared the
goalkeeping duties with
Arthur Wood but the
outbreak of the Great War
signalled an abrupt end to
Ernie's career although he
did have a few wartime
games with Blackpool.

Appearances:
SL: 44 app. 0 gls.
FAC: 1 app. 0 gls.
Total: *45 app. 0 gls.*

Ernie Steventon

STODDART, William Michael

Role: Centre-half 1928-30
5'9" 11st.10lbs.
b. Lanchester October qtr. 1907

CAREER: West Stanley/Manchester City
Mar 1926/ Coventry City May
1927/SOUTHAMPTON June 1928/Bristol
Rovers July 1931/Accrington Stanley July
1933-May 1934.
Debut v Reading (a) 14.12.29

Bill Stoddart was part of the exchange deal
that saw Tommy Allen and Bill Henderson
move in the opposite direction to Coventry
City. Never fulfilling the club's expectations of
him, Bill became a regular in the reserves for
whom he made over a hundred appearances.
Transfer-listed in May 1930, he moved to
Bristol Rovers two months later for a £200 fee.

Appearances:
FL: 12 app. 0 gls.
FAC: 1 app. 0 gls.
Total: *13 app. 0 gls.*

Bill Stoddart

STOKES, Robert William

Role: Forward 1968-77
5'7" 10st.2lbs.
b. Portsmouth 20 January 1951

CAREER: Hillside School/Paulsgrove
School/Portsmouth Schools/
SOUTHAMPTON app. Sept 1966, pro. Feb
1968/Washington Diplomats May 1977/
Portsmouth Aug 1977/Washington Diplomats
c.s. 1978/Cheltenham Town/Dartford Oct
1978/Chichester City/Waterlooville Mar
1981/Whitchurch/Petersfield United Aug
1985/Old Simmarians manager Apr 1988.
*Debut v Burnley (h) 7.4.69 *(scored on debut)*

Rejected by Portsmouth, Bobby Stokes had
been monitored by Saints scout Tom Parker
and on completion of his schooling was invited
to join the apprentices at the Dell. Soon after
signing professional forms Bobby won an
England Youth Cap when coming on as a
substitute in a match against Russia. His free
scoring in the reserves won him a call-up to
the senior eleven at Easter 1969 and he
responded with a brace of goals in a 5-1 victory
over Burnley. Despite this early success Bobby

had to wait until the 1971-72 season before he
appeared in the first team with any great
regularity but it was said of him that "you
could wind him up in August and he would
still be running in May", such was his stamina.
Small for a striker, Bobby had the compen-
satory knack of being able to hang in the air
and was the perfect foil for some of his more
famous forward colleagues. Fame was,
however, to come his way on May Day 1976.
With a simple swing of his less favoured left
leg Bobby scored the most vital goal in the
club's history and etched his name indelibly
into F.A. Cup Final folklore. The goal that
brought the cup to Southampton for the first
and only time could not have been scored by a
more modest or likeable man but, proving
there's little sentiment in football, Bobby was
to start only a further eight domestic games in
Saints' colours. The team were to lose the
opening match of the 1976-77 season at home
to Carlisle and Bobby was immediately
dropped with the result that, not for the first
time, he became unsettled. (He had nearly left
the Dell six months before the final when an
exchange deal with Paul Went of Portsmouth
had been considered only for the transfer to be
called off at the last minute when Bobby
declined terms). This time there was to be no
happy end to the season and, when Ted

MacDougall was signed, Bobby was given a free transfer to American soccer a mere 12 months after his Wembley triumph. Returning to England for the opening of the 1977-78 season Bobby finally agreed to join his home town club but his stay at Fratton Park was far from spectacular and one sensed that his appetite for the game had evaporated. Nevertheless he did continue to play non-league soccer while running a public house and later a cafeteria business in the Portsmouth area.

Appearances:
FL: 194 (22) app. 40 gls.
FAC: 17 app. 7 gls.
LC: 11 (1) app. 5 gls.
Eur: 8 (3) app. 2 gls.
Total: *230 (26) app. 54 gls.*

STRIDE, William Francis

Role: Half-back 1891-93
b. Southampton 1865
d. Southampton 21 February 1942

CAREER: Freemantle/Southampton Harriers/ SOUTHAMPTON St. Mary's 1888.

Debut v Warmley (a) 3.10.1891 FAC

William 'Banquo' Stride was an athlete "par excellence" who won many prizes as a runner with the Athletic Association. He joined St.

Mary's when Southampton Harriers disbanded following their defeat by St. Mary's in the 1888 Hampshire Junior Cup Final and became known as a formidable half-back. Bill clocked up over a hundred appearances over the next six years and participated in the club's first foray into the F.A. Cup. After gaining County representative honours several times, he decided to retire when the club gained admittance into the Southern League but he continued to live locally and worked for the Southampton Borough Engineers department.

Appearances:
FAC: 4 app. 0 gls.
Total: *4 app. 0 gls.*

STROUD, William James Alfred

Role: Half-back 1945-47
5'9" 10st.12lbs.
b. Hammersmith 7 July 1919

CAREER: Regents Park School/Highbury Sports/SOUTHAMPTON am. May 1938, pro. Feb 1940/Leyton Orient June 1947/Newport County June 1950/Hastings United Aug 1953/Newport County reserve team player-coach Nov 1954/SOUTHAMPTON Youth Team coach 1963-Jan 1987/Hampshire Intermediate XI coach 1987.

Debut v Newport City (h) 5.1.46 FAC

Bobby Stokes and his historic F.A. Cup-winning goal.

Bill Stroud

converted into a half-back and, with the resumption of first class soccer, he found himself the automatic choice for the right-half position. After one season Bill joined Leyton Orient in a deal worth £3,000 plus Edgar Ballard, and stayed at Brisbane Road long enough to make sixty-five appearances. After playing a similar number of games for Newport Bill moved into coaching only to develop tuberculosis which forced him into retirement. Reverting to his original trade, Bill was later tempted back into soccer in 1963 when his old team mate, Ted Bates, offered him a coaching position at the Dell. Over the next fourteen years a multitude of Saints youngsters were to reap the benefit of Bill's enthusiasm and commitment to the game.

Appearances:
FL: 29 app. 4 gls.
FAC: 6 app. 0 gls.
Total: *35 app. 4 gls.*

SUMMERS, John Lawrence

Role: Forward 1936-38
5'9" 11st.9lbs.
b. Chorlton, Manchester 8 February 1915
d. Southampton 12 April 1991

CAREER: Manchester Schools 1928/ Lancashire Schools 1929/ Manchester North End 1931/ Burnley Feb 1932(Fleetwood-loan) /Preston North End 1932/ Tunbridge Wells Rangers 1933/ Leicester City April 1934/Derby County May 1935/ SOUTHAMPTON Oct 1936/ Southampton Police 1938.

Debut v Fulham (a) 10.10.36

An electrician by trade, Bill Stroud was a product of local junior league soccer and was introduced to Southampton by Toby Keleher who had been appointed coach of the newly formed 'B' team in the summer of 1938. As captain, Bill was an ever-present in their first season of 1938-39 and showed considerable promise as a goalscorer by netting 36 times. With the outbreak of war Bill's development was put on hold although over the next six years he was to make more than 175 wartime appearances. During these years Bill

Originally on the books of Burnley at the age of 17, John Summers had the chance to join Manchester United but was denied permission by the Turf Moor management. Joining Preston instead, his career seemed still-born when he was freed within a year but,

John Summers

regaining his confidence in the Southern League with Tunbridge, his career flickered back to life. At Leicester John scored on his debut and then, moving to the Baseball Ground, he became understudy to the England International Sammy Crooks. Arriving at the Dell for a fee of £250, which was partly met by the Southampton Supporters Club, John formed an encouraging partnership with fellow ex-County player, Dick Neal, and the fans could feel pleased with their investment. Sustaining an injury at the beginning of the 1937-38 season Johnny lost his place to the up-and-coming Billy Bevis and, unable to impress new manager Tom Parker, decided to quit football to join the local constabulary. John was a Southampton policeman for thirty years and, after retiring in 1968, continued to live in the city. He played for the successful Southampton Police team that shared the Police Cup with Sheffield in 1948 and won it outright in 1951. He stopped playing in 1954 and was chairman of the Southampton forces football section until 1990.

Appearances:
FL: 31 app. 7 gls.
FAC: 1 app. 1 gl.
Total: *32 app. 8 gls.*

Jim Swinden

SWINDEN, James Frederick

Role: Forward 1926-28
5'5" 11st.0lbs.
b. Fulham 30 January 1905
d. Eastleigh March 1971

CAREER: Eastleigh Athletic c.s. 1922/ Winchester City Apr 1923/Salisbury 1924/ SOUTHAMPTON trial Nov 1925, pro. Dec 1925/Newport I.O.W. 1929/Pirelli General.
Debut v Swansea Town (a) 23.4.27

Jim Swinden was a fitter at Eastleigh Locomotive Works who, given a trial in a reserve match versus Folkestone in November 1925, responded with a brace of goals. He was small for a forward but compensated with his tremendous speed and no little skill. Limited to only three appearances in his four seasons at the Dell, Jimmy returned to Hampshire League soccer and was re-employed on the railways. He remained active in local football circles for a lengthy time, running and coaching the county's representative sides.

Appearances:
FL: 3 app. 0 gls.
Total: *3 app. 0 gls.*

SYDENHAM, John

Role: Forward 1956-70
5'6" 9st.6lbs.
b. Southampton 15 September 1939

CAREER: St. Mary's College/Southampton & Hampshire Schools/C.P.C. Sports (Saints nursery) 1955/SOUTHAMPTON am. Aug 1955, pro. Apr 1957/Aldershot Mar 1970/Bath City Aug 1972/ Athena (Western Australia) player-manager Apr 1974/Newport (I.O.W.) player-manager Aug 1975-Nov 1975/ Dorchester Town Dec 1975/A.C. Delco May 1976/Athena player-coach 1980.
Debut v Newport County (h) 4.5.57

John Sydenham first burst onto the soccer scene as a 13 year-old schoolboy when he brought honour to St. Mary's College by being their first pupil to play for the Southampton Schools XI. By playing his part in the side that reached the final of the 1954 English Schools trophy he came to the notice of the Saints and in due course became part of the successful 1956-57 Southampton Youth Side which did so well in the F.A. Youth Cup. At this time John first joined forces with another young winger, Terry Paine, and before long both players were in the first team tearing Third Division defences to shreds. Whereas Paine was the more skilful John was devastatingly fast

John Sydenham (left) with Ted Bates (centre) and Terry Paine.

and would simply knock the ball past his opponent and, giving him a yard or two, would still reach the ball first. England Under-23 honours arrived during the promotion season of 1959-60 before John's career was interrupted by National Service in July 1960 which put a brake on his progress. Happily, John regained his place on the left-wing and, as much as any, played his part in the club finally reaching the top flight in 1966. Unfortunately Saints' arrival in the First Division coincided with the advent of wingers dropping out of fashion and John was often not selected for away games in preference to an extra defender. Uncomplainingly he remained loyal to the club and in 1969 enjoyed a spectacular afternoon at Old Trafford when he laid on all four of Ron Davies' goals to set up a memorable 4-1 victory. With age inevitably slowing him down a little John lost

much of his effectiveness and after a testimonial against Portsmouth he saw out the remainder of his league career with Aldershot. In the mid-eighties, John emigrated to Perth in Western Australia to run an insurance consultancy but every two years he returns to take in a couple of matches at the Dell and still relishes a kick around in the local parks. To Saints fans the words Paine and Sydenham roll off the tongue as effortlessly as peaches and cream and the two of them will always be remembered as the club's finest-ever pair of wingers.

Appearances:
FL: 341 (1) app. 36 gls.
FAC: 31 app. 1 gl.
LC: 21 app. 2 gls.
Eur: 4 app. 0 gls.
Total: *397 (2) app. 39 gls.*

TALKES, Wayne Anthony Norman

Role: Midfield 1971-74
5'8" 11st.12lbs.
b. Ealing, London 2 June 1952

CAREER: Fairway School (I.O.W.)/Bembridge
Youth Club/SOUTHAMPTON app. July 1967,
pro. July 1969(Doncaster Rovers-loan-Dec
1973-Jan 74)/Bournemouth July 1974/Totton
Aug 1975/Brockenhurst player-coach Apr
1976, manager July 1976/Basingstoke Town
Mar 1977/Midanbury 1979/Eastleigh coach
Aug 1986/Midanbury 1986-1989.

Debut v West Ham United (a) 1.5.72

Wayne Talkes

Although born in
London, Wayne Talkes
grew up on the Isle of
Wight and was spotted
and signed on associate
schoolboy forms in
September 1965. Wayne
was a fixture in the
reserve eleven for five
seasons but made only
limited progress in his
quest for first team action.
He did, however, provide excellent cover for
the regular midfielders throughout his stay at
the Dell which ended in 1974 when he crossed
the New Forest to try his luck at Dean Court.
However, a serious ankle injury forced an
early retirement from the professional game
within a year of his leaving the Dell although
he continued to play non-league football up
until 1989.

Appearances:
FL: 7 (2) app. 0 gls.
LC: 0 (1) app. 0 gls.
Total: *7 (3) app. 0 gls.*

TANKARD, Allen John

Role: Full-back 1985-87
5'10" 11st.7lbs.
b. Fleet, Hampshire 21 May 1969

CAREER: Aldershot Schools/Hampshire
Schools/SOUTHAMPTON yts June 1985, pro.
May 1987/Wigan Athletic July 1988.

Debut v Sheffield Wednesday (h) 26.4.86

Allen Tankard initially appeared in the first
team in a friendly
against Brentford
when aged only 16
years 2 months. He
became a reserve
regular during the
1985-86 season and won England Under-17
honours before making his league debut a
month before his seventeenth birthday. Mature
beyond his years, Allen looked to have a bright
future in the game but, like so many young
hopefuls, failed to build on his early promise
and was released in the close season of 1988 on
a free transfer.

Appearances:
FL: 5 app. 0 gls.
Total: *5 app. 0 gls.*

TAYLOR, Ernest James

Role: Half-back 1893-96
5'7" 11st.0lbs.
b. Liverpool 1869
d. Southampton 13 November 1944

CAREER: St. Cuthberts/Stanley/
SOUTHAMPTON St. Mary's c.s. 1893/
Freemantle 1896.

Debut v Uxbridge (h) 4.11.1893 FAC

An outstanding amateur sportsman, Ernie
Taylor came to Southampton from Liverpool
in 1893 with the American Shipping Line. He
became a member of the St. Mary's team and
for three seasons was more than skilful enough
to hold his
own with the
best of the
professionals.
Ernie was a
reliable half-
back who was
described at
the time as
being: "a
versatile player
with ample
resource and a
great variety of
methods; he
plays a

Ernie Taylor

defensive as well as offensive game with equal success." After winning several County caps and being a member of St. Mary's first-ever League team Ernie continued his amateur career with Freemantle in 1896. He was also involved with many other sporting bodies: a cricketer with Deanery, a committee member of Stoneham Golf Club and active with the Hampshire Rugby Union. As chairman of White Star Line Sports Association he was one of the founders of the annual football match to raise funds for the Seamen's Orphanage (1899 to 1934). Ernie remained with the American and White Star Lines throughout his working life, was appointed chief cashier in 1922 and held this post until 1934 when, on the merger with Cunard, he retired.

Appearances:
SL: 19 app. 1 gl.
FAC: 6 app. 3 gls.
Total: 25 app. 4 gls.

TAYLOR, Fred

Role: Forward 1912-13
5'8" 11st.6lbs.
b. Halesowen

CAREER: Stourbridge Jan 1910/Hull City c.s. 1910/Wellington Town c.s. 1911/ SOUTHAMPTON c.s. 1912/Barrow-in-Furness c.s. 1913.

Debut v Northampton Town (h) 4.9.12

Signed specifically on the recommendation of Saints' trainer, Jimmy McIntyre, Fred Taylor arrived with the reputation of being a prolific scorer. He had netted 27 goals in the previous season with Wellington but was to find the pace much faster at first class level. Eventually losing his place to Fred Turnbull, he saw out the rest of the season in South- ampton's Southern All- iance team where he scored four goals in 12 games.

Appearances:
SL: 13 app. 2 gls.
FAC: 1 app. 0 gls.
Total: 14 app. 2 gls.

TAYLOR, Samuel James

Role: Forward
1926-28
5'8" 11st.7lbs.
b. Sheffield
17 September 1893
d. Sheffield January
qtr. 1973

Sam Taylor

CAREER: Atlas and Norfolk Ironworks/ Silverwood Colliery/(Rotherham County & Bradford Park Avenue during World War One) Huddersfield Town May 1919/Sheffield Wednesday June 1921/Mansfield Town May 1925/ SOUTHAMPTON June 1926/Halifax Town June 1928/Grantham/Chesterfield May 1929/Llanelly Aug 1930.

Debut v Portsmouth (a) 28.8.26 *(scored on debut)

A member of Huddersfield Town's 1920 F.A. Cup Final side, Sam Taylor joined Southampton from non-league team Mansfield but the £300 fee was paid to Sheffield Wednesday who still retained his registration. A thoughtful and intelligent inside-forward, Sam formed part of the fine Taylor, Murphy, Woodhouse triangle which was probably the best Southampton left-wing combination in pre-World War One soccer. Simple, planned moves often allowed Sam a free run at goal or, alternatively, he would act as a decoy allowing "Spud" Murphy an uninhibited surge down the flank. Although thirty-three years old at the time of his arrival Sam remained a regular over his two years at the Dell before moving back to the north to join Halifax. A "red hot billiards player," Sam was also an accomplished pianist, playing anything from classical to jazz.

Appearances:
FL: 69 app. 17 gls.
FAC: 7 app. 0 gls.
Total: 76 app. 17 gls.

Fred Taylor

TAYLOR, Thomas

Role: Forward 1927-29
5'7" 11st.7lbs.
b. St. Helens 1901

CAREER:
Rhos Sept 1925 am.
(Welsh National
League
North)/Manchester
City July 1926/
SOUTHAMPTON Aug
1927.

*Debut v Grimsby Town (a)
24.9.27*

Tommy Taylor

Tommy Taylor had been on
Manchester City's books for
one year before joining Southampton but at
Maine Road had failed to make the first team.
Faring little better at the Dell he did at least
enjoy some sort of consistency when he netted
in his third, fourth, fifth and sixth games for
the club. Unfortunately his seventh and eighth
games were not so fruitful and he was given a
free transfer in November 1929.

Appearances:
FL: 8 app. 4 gls.
Total: *8 app. 4 gls.*

❏ **Saints Note** - *In March 1926 Tommy
represented the Welsh League in a game against
Cheshire played at Chester.*

Eddie Thomas

THOMAS, Edwin Henry Charles

Role: Goalkeeper
1950-51
*b. Swindon
9 November 1932*

CAREER: Swindon
Railway Works XI/
SOUTHAMPTON
am. May 1950, pro.
May 1951/
Salisbury Jan 1956.

*Debut v
Birmingham City (h)
7.10.50*

Eddie Thomas was serving an
apprenticeship as a British Railways
engineer and, playing in his local works
eleven, was spotted by a Southampton
scout. Still an amateur, he became the
club's regular reserve team goalkeeper
for the beginning of the 1950-51
season only to be suddenly given his
first team debut in October when
Hugh Kelly was called away on
international duty. Eddie was only 17
years and 329 days old when he took
the field against Birmingham and thus
was the youngest-ever Southampton
goalkeeper until the arrival of Bob Charles
in September 1959. He was beaten on two
occasions as Saints lost the match but both
Birmingham's goals were not considered to be
his fault. Eddie soon earned an England Youth
call-up and won caps against the three home
countries before taking the decision to sign a
professional contract in May 1951. His career
was, however, still-born as he was never
selected for another first team game and, with
John Christie sharing the goalkeeper's jersey
with Fred Kiernan, an exciting future
gradually took on a bleak outlook. Eddie left
the club in 1953 and was next heard of playing
for Salisbury during the 1955-56 season.

Appearances:
FL: 8 app. 0 gls.
Total: *8 app. 0 gls.*

THOMAS, Reginald G.

Role: Full-back
1931-32
5'10" 11st.6lbs.
*b. Weymouth
2 January 1915*

CAREER:
Weymouth
Central School/
Dorset Schools/
Weymouth Wolves/
Weymouth/ SOUTHAMPTON am. Sept 1930,
pro. Dec 1930/Folkestone June
1934/Guildford City/ Sittingbourne/Margate.

Reg Thomas

Debut v Bradford City (h) 12.3.32

Reg Thomas was a hard-tackling full-back who
acted as cover for regular right-back Bill
Adams throughout his career at the Dell. His

stay encompassed four years and, after playing eight consecutive games in the latter half of the 1931-32 season, his contribution to the club's fortunes was confined to 83 reserve team appearances. He turned his back on a professional career in 1934 and, soon after, joined the Metropolitan Police Force.

Appearances:
FL: 8 app. 0 gls.
Total: *8 app. 0 gls.*

THOMPSON, David Stanley

Role: Forward 1966-71
5'7" 10st.10lbs.
b. Scotton 12 March 1945

CAREER: Otley School/Yorkshire Schools/ Dawson, Paine & Elliott F.C./Wolverhampton Wanderers Apr 1962/SOUTHAMPTON Aug 1966/Mansfield Town Oct 1970/Chesterfield Dec 1973.

Debut v Everton (h) 25.10.66

Dave Thompson was signed for £7,500 to act as an understudy for both Terry Paine and John Sydenham. Predictably, openings were few and far between but when he did have an outing it was usually in the left-wing position.

*David
Thompson*

A key member of the reserve eleven for four years Dave only found regular first-team football after leaving the Dell in October 1970. A bad knee injury brought the curtain down on Dave's career while at Chesterfield, although in June 1991, and living in Otley, he confessed to having enjoyed every moment of his footballing life.

Appearances:
FL: 21 (2) app. 0 gls.
FAC: 3 (1) app. 0 gls.
Total: *24 (3) app. 0 gls.*

THOMPSON, George Herbert

Role: Goalkeeper 1927-30
6'0" 11st.7lbs.
b. Treeton October qtr. 1900
d. Preston 6 June 1968

CAREER: Treeton R.R./York City/ SOUTHAMPTON Aug 1927/ Dinnington Miners' Welfare.

Debut v Notts County (a) 10.9.27

Signed from non-league York City George Thompson provided goal-

George Thompson

keeping cover, initially for Tommy Allen and then Willie White. He kept a clean sheet on his debut but only made sporadic appearances between the first team posts although playing 159 times for the reserve eleven. Transfer-listed for £250 at the end of the 1929-30 season he eventually returned to his native Yorkshire. A joiner by trade, George later became a foreman in Dinnington coalmines.

Appearances:
FL: 14 app. 0 gls.
FAC: 2 app. 0 gls.
Total: *16 app. 0 gls.*

❏ **Saints note** - *He had two sons, both of whom became professional goalkeepers - George Jnr. with Preston and Carlisle, and Desmond with Burnley, York City and Sheffield United.*

THOMSON, W. J. G.

Role: Half-back/Full-back 1894-96

CAREER: Stoke July 1892/SOUTHAMPTON
St. Mary's Mar1894/Cowes 1896.
Debut v Chatham (h) 6.10.1894

"Lachie" Thomson was one of the most
popular players during the initial professional
era and, coming from the "Stoke", was the
forerunner of the "Stoke invasion" of a few
years later. Initially a full-back, Lachie played
in the centre-half position in the club's first
game in the Southern League and a
contemporary description of him said, "strong
and with plenty of pluck, he plays the game
with judgement as well as energy". In 1896 he
moved to the Isle of Wight to assist Cowes and
helped them to their brief Southern League
status in 1899.

Appearances:
SL: 27 app. 1 gl.
FAC: 10 app. 1 gl.
Total: *37 app. 2 gls.*

THORPE, Frank

Role: Centre-half 1906-09
6'0" 11st.8lbs.
b. Hayfield October qtr. 1879
d. Blackpool 17 April 1928

CAREER: Newton Heath Feb 1897/
Stalybridge
Rovers/Bury June
1901/Plymouth
Argyle 1906/
SOUTHAMPTON
Mar 1907/Bury
May 1909.

Debut v
Northampton Town
(a) 6.4.07

Frank Thorpe
was the owner of
an F.A. Cup-
winners' medal,
gained in Bury's
6-0 victory over
Derby in 1903
and was a
welcome

"Lachie" Thomson

addition, strengthening Southampton's
defence. An intelligent centre-half, Frank
quickly gained the captaincy of the side and
over the next couple of seasons the club's
league placing improved. He rejoined Bury in
1909 to assist the Shakers' second eleven.

Appearances:
SL: 65 app. 5 gls.
FAC: 6 app. 0 gls.
Total: *71 app. 5 gls.*

TILFORD, Arthur

Role: Full-back 1932-33
5'10" 11st.10lbs.
b. Ilkeston 14 May 1903

CAREER: Trowell St. Helens/Nottingham
Forest May 1924/Blackpool May 1926/
Coventry City May 1929/Fulham Feb 1932/

SOUTHAMPTON Feb 1933/Fulham c.s. 1933/ Walsall June 1934.

Debut v Bradford City (h) 25.2.33

A left-back, Arthur Tilford's arrival at the Dell from Craven Cottage came about due to some sad personal circumstances. Arthur had just suffered a family bereavement with the death of his young son and a temporary move to Southampton was suggested to help him recover from his loss. Loan transfers were not then known in the Football League but Arthur was allowed to do his training at Craven Cottage and duly returned there at the end of the 1932-33 season.

Appearances:
FL: 10 app. 0 gls.
Total: *10 app. 0 gls.*

TITMUSS, Frederick

Role: Full-back 1919-26
5'9" 11st. 6lbs.
b. Pirton April qtr. 1895
d. Plymouth 2 October 1966

CAREER: Pirton United/Luton Alliance 1914/Hitchin Town/SOUTHAMPTON May 1919/Plymouth Argyle Feb 1926/St. Austell 1932.

Fred Titmuss

Debut v Exeter City (h) 30.8.19

Serving with the Lancashire Fusiliers during the Great War, Fred Titmuss played football with Bert Lee who soon formed a high opinion of his soccer abilities. Fred fancied himself as an inside-left but after being persuaded to join the ranks at the Dell was converted into an outstanding left-back. Taking his place in Saints' first competitive line-up immediately after the war, Fred formed a partnership with Tom Parker that was, in the mind of many, the finest full-back coupling in the country. Certainly both men earned England call-ups with Fred winning his "colours" in a match against Wales in March 1922. His speciality was the slide tackle although his perfect positional play often meant that such 'last-ditch' defending was hardly ever needed. Fred was the subject of large bids from some of the country's top clubs but preferred to remain and play his part in the highly entertaining Saints team of the early 1920's. His career almost came to an abrupt end in February 1924 when it was feared that the sight of his eye had been damaged after being struck by the lace of the ball. Fortunately Fred recovered completely and continued to serve the club well until February 1926 when he was suddenly.... and surprisingly, sold to Plymouth for a £1,750 fee. Fred gave six years good service to the Devon club and then settled in the area to become a licensee.

Appearances:
SL: 22 app. 0 gls.
FL: 188 app. 0 gls.
FAC: 27 app. 0 gls.
Total: *237 app. 0 gls.*

❏ **Saints note** - *Fred won two England caps, both against Wales. His debut came with Bill Rawlings - the first time two players from Division Three had appeared in the England side, and the only time two have turned out at this level from the same club.*

TOMAN, Wilfred

Role: Forward 1900-01
5'8" 10st.7lbs.
b. Bishop Auckland

CAREER: Victoria Athletic (Aberdeen)/ Dundee/Victoria United/Burnley Nov 1896/ Everton Apr 1899/SOUTHAMPTON c.s. 1900/Everton c.s. 1901/Stockport County Jan

1904/Newcastle United am. Aug 1906/ Scottish Junior Soccer 1909.

Debut v Portsmouth (a) 22.9.1900

Wilf Toman was a clever centre-forward who came to the Dell backed with a goal aggregate of 37 from just 88 games for Burnley and Everton. Rather prone to accidents, Wilf was a game player who often turned out despite his injuries, and his *forte* was his ability to support his fellow forwards. After helping Saints to retain the Southern League Championship in 1901 he returned to Everton who still held his football league registration. Scoring on his debut for them, Wilf sustained a serious injury in only his second game which sidelined him for two and a half seasons. Beginning his comeback with Stockport, Wilf later moved to Newcastle but never made the Magpies' first eleven and returned to live in Scotland in 1909.

Appearances:
SL: 19 app. 7 gls.
FAC: 1 app. 0 gls.
Total: *20 app. 7 gls.*

TOMLINSON, Isaac

Role: Forward 1905-06
b. Chesterfield 16 April 1880
d. Bournemouth 24 August 1970

CAREER: North Wingfield 1899/Chesterfield Apr 1900/Woolwich Arsenal Apr 1903/ Chesterfield June 1904/SOUTHAMPTON May 1905/Portsmouth c.s. 1906/Heart of Midlothian Apr 1907/Bournemouth & Boscombe Albion scout 1929.

Debut v Brentford (h) 2.9.05

"Ike" Tomlinson had created a big impression in a cup-tie played by Chesterfield at Portsmouth in January 1905 and there were quite a few clubs keen to secure his services. The Saints' secretary, Ernest Arnfield, stubbornly refused to take no for an answer and Chesterfield's top goal-scorer became a Saint in the close season of 1905. Ike was an extremely speedy winger and with his accurate shooting was considered to be the double of a former Saint, Joe Turner, in his style. Unfortunately, he had an excitable temperament and, suffering from nerves,

particularly in away matches, often failed to deliver the goods on opponents' pitches. His nerves were sometimes so bad that before important games he preferred to walk around the ground rather than sit in the dressing room. A move to Fratton Park did not improve this problem and after only five games in Pompey's Southern League XI during the 1906-07 season, he moved to Scotland. Ike later became a licensee in his home town of Chesterfield before returning to the south coast in 1929, where he combined his job of running an hotel with that of scouting for Bournemouth & Boscombe.

Appearances:
SL: 29 app. 8 gls.
FAC: 5 app. 3 gls.
Total: *34 app. 11 gls.*

TOMLINSON, Reginald William

R. TOMLINSON (SOUTHAMPTON)

Role: Forward 1938-39
6'0" 13st.0lbs.
b. Sleaford 2 July 1914
d. Bitterne 16 May 1971

CAREER: Horncastle Town/Grimsby Town Aug 1935/SOUTHAMPTON May 1938/ Southampton War Police Reserve/ Portsmouth during World War Two/ Southampton Police 1946/South of England Police XI.

Debut v Coventry City (a) 10.9.38

With no chances of first team football at Grimsby, Reg Tomlinson moved to Southampton for a substantial fee and was the club's centre-forward in the last season before the outbreak of war. He added considerable height and weight to the Saints' attack and formed a useful partnership with Fred Briggs. Reg was quick for a big man and, possessing a good shot, scored at a respectable rate throughout the year. Like many other Saints players, he joined the local police upon the suspension of normal peacetime soccer and from then on his football was confined to wartime guest matches. After the war Reg was a member of the Southampton Police side that reached two national Police Cup finals as well as winning a Hampshire League Division Two championship in 1947. He retired from the force in 1970 after 30 years service.

Appearances:
FL: 36 app. 12 gls.
FAC: 1 app. 1 gl.
Total: *37 app. 13 gls.*

TOOMER, Walter Edward

Role: Half-back 1906-13
b. Southampton 9 February 1883
d. Southampton 28 December 1962

CAREER: St.Johns College,Battersea/Fulham/Chelsea 1905/SOUTHAMPTON 1906, Director May 1950.

Debut v Norwich City (a) 5.1.07

Walter Toomer was the son of a cricket bat maker and played all his early football in London where he was studying to become a teacher. An amateur throughout his career Walter took up a school appointment in Southampton soon after joining the Saints in 1906 and combined both activities with

Walter Toomer

helping to run his father's sports outfitters in London Road. Walter remained at the Dell for eight years mainly as captain of the reserves but, when called upon by the first team, performed competently. In 1914 he joined the Royal Artillery and spent most of the Great War serving in France. After returning to Southampton in 1919 he resumed teaching but could not settle and instead turned full-time to the family business which still exists to this day. In May 1950 Walter was made a director at the Dell and, very much a fan, regularly travelled to away matches.

Appearances:
SL: 10 app. 0 gls.
Total: *10 app. 0 gls.*

TOWNSEND, Andrew David

Role: Midfield
1984-88
5'11" 12st.7lbs.
b. Maidstone
23 July 1963

CAREER:
Welling United Aug 1980/ Weymouth Mar 1984/ SOUTHAMPTON Jan 1985/Norwich City Aug 1988/ Chelsea July 1990.

Debut v Aston Villa (h) 20.4.84

Andy Townsend

Signed from Weymouth in a £35,000 deal, Andy Townsend gave up his job as a computer operator with Greenwich Council to become a full-time professional. Although making his debut in Mark Dennis' left-back position it was on the left side of midfield that Andy was to display his flair. His career was, in August 1986, interrupted by a broken leg sustained, coincidentally, in a friendly against his previous club but, within six months, he fought his way back into first team contention. Surprisingly sold to Norwich for a £300,000 fee, Andy blossomed into a constructive, penetrative performer and before long had staked a place in the Republic of Ireland's midfield. After enjoying a successful 1990

World Cup, Chelsea parted with a million pounds to bring him to Stamford Bridge with Norwich enjoying a profit of £700,000 at Southampton's expense.

Appearances:
FL: 77 (6) app. 5 gls.
FAC: 2 (3) app. 0 gls.
LC: 7 (1) app. 0 gls.
Total: *86 (10) app. 5 gls.*

❏ **Saints note** - *Andy's father, Don, was a full-back with Charlton Athletic.*

TRAYNOR, Thomas Joseph

Role: Full-back 1952-66
5'8" 12st.7lbs.
b. Dundalk 22 July 1933

CAREER: Dundalk/SOUTHAMPTON June 1952 retired 1966.

Debut v Brentford (a) 11.10.52

Tommy Traynor

Tommy Traynor had the chance to join Manchester City or Chelsea but chose instead to become a Saint after listening to Fred Kiernan praise the Dell set-up. An Eire amateur international, Tommy was blooded during the Saints' relegation season of 1952-53 and became the club's regular left-back the next year. An ebullient Irishman, Tommy had not only a merciless sliding tackle but a deceptive turn of pace which often surprised opposing wingers. Over a distinguished fourteen year career at the Dell, Tommy won eight full caps for Eire and in February 1964 passed Bert Shelley's appearance record for the club. His presence and influence, especially in the latter years, were an inspiration to the younger players and, after retiring in 1966, he was given a testimonial against the Dutch side, Twente Enschede. Tommy became a checker in Southampton Docks but still remains active in youth soccer by helping organise the Tyro Under-15 League.

Appearances:
FL: 433 app. 7 gls.
FAC: 34 app. 0 gls.
LC: 13 app. 1 gl.
Total: *480 app. 8 gls.*

TRIGGS, Walter Henry

Role: Full-back 1901-02
b. Southampton January qtr. 1880

CAREER: Freemantle 1897/SOUTHAMPTON 1900.

Debut v Kettering Town (a) 2.4.02

Walter Triggs had the unenviable task of having to oust the outstanding international George Molyneux from the left-back position if he wanted to make a mark in the first team. Given his chance in April 1902 in two consecutive away matches, (George Molyneux was playing at Ibrox Park in the fateful England v Scotland fixture in which 25 people died following the collapse of a stand), Walter did his best but with the return of Molyneux he once more returned to the reserves and left the club for pastures unknown soon afterwards.

Appearances:
SL: 2 app. 0 gls.
Total: *2 app. 0 gls.*

TRUEMAN, Albert Harry

Role: Half-back 1908-11
5'6" 11st.0lbs.
b. Leicester April qtr. 1882

CAREER: Holy Trinity School/Leicestershire Schools/Leicester Fosse Aug 1899/Grasmere Swifts/Hinckley Town/Coalville Town/ Leicester Fosse Aug 1905/ SOUTHAMPTON May 1908/ Sheffield United Mar 1911/ Darlington c.s. 1913/(Leicester during World War One).

Debut v Brighton & Hove Albion (h) 7.9.08

Albert Trueman

Albert Trueman had been regarded as a brilliant juvenile footballer and had signed for his home town club soon after leaving school. Standing at just 5'6" he was regarded by many to be too small to be a half-back but soon proved that his judgement and skill made up for his lack of inches. Bert was also quick, resourceful and decisive in action and overall was a most difficult obstacle for opposing forwards. His consistency made him an important ingredient in the Saints line-up for three seasons during which time he was selected to represent the Southern League on four occasions and given an international trial match in 1911. Soon after, he grew restless at the Dell and was allowed a transfer to Sheffield United before finishing his professional career at Darlington. In September 1916, at Filbert Street, he was persuaded, somewhat reluctantly, to once more don a Leicester shirt in a war-time game against Grimsby when the home team were short of players.

Appearances:
SL: 87 app. 4 gls.
FAC: 5 app. 0 gls.
Total: 92 app. 4 gls.

❏ **Saints note** - *Albert scored the winning goal for the Southern League against the Football League in November 1910, which gave them a clean sweep in that season's Inter-League tournament.*

TULLY, Frederick Charles

Role: Forward 1933-37
5'6" 11st.0lbs.
b. St. Pancras, London July qtr. 1907

CAREER: Priory School/Tynemouth Schools/ Rosehill Villa/Preston Colliery/Chaddleton/ Aston Villa Oct 1926/SOUTHAMPTON June 1933/Clapton Orient June 1937.

Debut v Bradford City (h) 26.8.33

Signed as Johnny Arnold's replacement, Fred Tully was described in the Sports Echo as "a winger of thrust and enterprise". Short but stocky he was definitely a busy sort of player who could play anywhere in the forward line except centre-forward. Forming a useful partnership with Dick Neal, Fred gave four years of good service before moving back to his native East London in 1937. He retired from the game during the war and joined his father's carpentry business although, later on, he worked as an attendant at Cheddeston Mental Hospital in North Staffs.

Appearances:
FL: 97 app. 9 gls.
FAC: 4 app. 0 gls.
Total: *101 app. 9 gls.*

TURNBULL, Frederick Stephen

Role: Forward 1912-13
5'7" 11st.6lbs.
b. Wallsend October qtr. 1888

CAREER: Newcastle United/Coventry City 1911/SOUTHAMPTON Oct 1912/North Shields c.s. 1913.

Debut v Brighton & Hove Albion (h) 19.10.12
*(scored on debut)

Fred Turnbull followed Saints' trainer Jim McIntyre to the Dell from Coventry having previously spent a couple of years playing for Newcastle reserves. Although scoring on his debut Fred only found the net on two other occasions in 24 games and with the club going through a transitionary period he was allowed to leave in 1913.

Appearances:
SL: 23 app. 2 gls.
FAC: 2 app. 1 gl.
Total: *25 app. 3 gls.*

TURNER, Arthur D.

Role: Forward 1899-02 & 1904-05
5'8" 11st.4lbs.
b. Farnborough June 1877
d. Farnborough 4 April 1925

CAREER: Aldershot North End/South Farnborough/Camberley St. Michaels/ Brentford (trial)/Reading (trial)/ SOUTHAMPTON May 1899/Derby County May 1902/Newcastle United Jan 1903/ Tottenham Hotspur Feb 1904/ SOUTHAMPTON c.s. 1904/South Farnborough Athletic.

Debut v Millwall (a) 14.10.1899

The only Hampshire-born player to appear in the Saints F.A. Cup Final sides of 1900 and 1902, 'Archie' Turner was also the first man from the county to be capped by England.

A clever outside-right, he achieved the then unique distinction of receiving his international call-up in his debut season in first-class football. Archie's somewhat rapid rise to fame had the effect of making him a marked man with opposing full-backs but, despite being on the wrong end of some tough treatment, he continued to produce some exciting wing-play. A master of delivering accurate centres, if he had a fault it was a reluctance to shoot, preferring instead to find a colleague who perhaps would not be in such a promising position. Tempted to join Derby County by a sizeable financial inducement and the opportunity of playing alongside the famous England inside-right Steve Bloomer, Archie failed to shine in such illustrious company and, never adding to his two England caps, later regretted leaving the Dell. He returned in 1904 but his day had already passed and his early form had evaporated to such an extent that he quit the professional game a year later to join his father's business in Farnborough.

Appearances:
SL: 78 app. 24 gls.
FAC: 20 app. 6 gls.
Total: *98 app. 30 gls.*

'Archie' Turner

TURNER, Ernest

Role: Forward 1925-26
5'7" 11st.0lbs.
b. Brithdir, Wales 1898
d. Merthyr, 7 December 1951

CAREER:
Bargoed/Caerphilly/
Merthyr Town May 1922/
SOUTHAMPTON May 1925.

Debut v Hull City (a) 31.8.25

A regular in Merthyr's
league side for three seasons
Ernest Turner had
represented the Welsh F.A.
on several occasions before his transfer to
Southampton. Equally at home at inside or
centre-forward, Ernest featured regularly in
the first team during the 1925-26 season but
unexpectedly left the Dell and the country in
May 1926 to emigrate to Canada.

Ernest Turner

Appearances:
FL: 16 app. 3 gls.
Total: *16 app. 3 gls.*

❏ **Saints note** - *Ernest's brother Bert played for
Charlton Athletic and scored for both sides in the
1946 FA Cup final against Derby County.*

Fred Turner

TURNER, Frederick Arthur

Role: Full-back 1953-55
b. Southampton
28 February 1930
d. Southampton 9 July 1955

CAREER: Bitterne Nomads
/SOUTHAMPTON am July
1948, pro. Feb 1950/
Torquay United Aug 1951/
SOUTHAMPTON Mar
1953.

Debut v Watford (a) 31.10.53

The son of Saints' director,
Mr. W. Turner, Fred progressed through junior
local soccer to become a fully-fledged
professional in February 1950. Called upon to
do his National Service in Devon Fred sought,
and was granted, a transfer to Torquay but
only made one appearance before his
demobilisation in 1953. After re-signing for the
Saints, he developed quickly into an
outstanding full-back with a fine sense of
positional play. A quiet, thoughtful player
Fred had just established himself in the first
team when illness forced him to quit playing
in February 1955. The illness, which was
diagnosed as leukaemia, sadly claimed
his life six months later.

Appearances:
FL: 19 app. 0 gls.
FAC: 2 app. 0 gls.
Total: *21 app. 0 gls.*

TURNER, Harry

Role: Forward 1903-05
b. Farnborough

CAREER: South Farnborough/
SOUTHAMPTON trial Apr
1900/South Farnborough/
SOUTHAMPTON 1903/ Farnborough
1905/Reading Feb 1908/South
Farnborough 1908.

Debut v Tottenham Hotspur (h) 26.12.03

Harry Turner followed in his elder
brother's footsteps by becoming a
Saints player in 1903, three years after
coming to the Dell for a trial in April

1900. Although lacking the skills of 'Archie', Harry certainly had an eye for goal, scoring six times in fifteen Southern League outings. After gaining a Hampshire Senior Cup winners medal in April 1905 with the reserves Harry returned to the Aldershot District League with Farnborough, although his career did enjoy a brief renaissance in 1908 at Reading.

Appearances:
SL: 15 app. 6 gls.
Total: *15 app. 6 gls.*

TURNER, Ian

Role: Goalkeeper 1973-78
6'0" 12st.5lbs.
b. Middlesbrough 17 January 1953

CAREER: Eston School/North Riding Schools /Southbank/Huddersfield Town Oct 1970 (Grimsby Town-loan-Feb 1972)/transferred March 1972) (Walsall-loan-Feb 1973)/ SOUTHAMPTON March 1974 (Newport County-loan-Mar-Apr 1978)/Fort Lauderdale summer 1978 (Lincoln City-loan Oct-Dec 1978)/Walsall Jan 1979 (Luton Town-loan-Feb 1980)(Halifax Town-loan-Jan-Feb 1981)/ Witney Town 1982/Salisbury July 1984/Totton Mar 1985/Road Sea Mar 1985/Waterlooville Apr 1985/Romsey Town c.s. 1986/Caretaker manager Jan 1987/Brockenhurst manager Mar 1987/Newport (I.O.W.) c.s. 1988/Totton Feb 1989.

Debut v Tottenham Hotspur (a) 13.4.74

One of ten children, Ian Turner was originally a centre-half for his home village side, South Bank, and only went in goal as a stand-in in a game against Huddersfield Reserves. His form was duly reported to Ian Greaves, manager of Huddersfield, and after a two-week trial Ian's professional career was underway. Arriving at the Dell during the latter stages of Southampton's battle to avoid relegation in 1974 he was pitched almost immediately into the fray, replacing the veteran Eric Martin. Lawrie McMenemy had become acquainted with Ian's goalkeeping at Grimsby but his signing did not prevent the drop into the Second Division. Nevertheless, he soon showed he was a brave and dependable cust-odian and played a significant part in Saints' F.A. Cup triumph in 1976. (In the final itself he overcame a nervous start to finish the game full of confidence). He had the misfortune to

Ian Turner

injure himself in the first game of the 1976-77 campaign and thereafter, although making a full recovery, struggled to reproduce his earlier verve and assurance. After a succession of loan transfers he finished his league career at Fellows Park in 1982 and since then has contented himself with local non-league soccer. In 1990 Ian, a commissioning engineer at B.P.'s Wytch Farm oilfield in Dorset, attended a reunion dinner of the 1976 F.A. Cup Final side.

Appearances:
FL: 77 app. 0 gls.
FAC: 12 app. 0 gls.
LC: 6 app. 0 gls.
Eur: 2 app. 0 gls.
Total: *97 app. 0 gls.*

TURNER, Joseph

Role: Forward 1895-98 & 1901-04
5'8" 11st.9lbs.
b. Burslem March 1872
d. Southampton 20 November 1950

CAREER: Newcastle Swifts 1893/Dresden United 1894/SOUTHAMPTON St. Mary's Apr 1895/Stoke May 1898/Everton Apr 1900/ SOUTHAMPTON c.s. 1901/New Brompton c.s. 1904/Northampton Town c.s. 1906/ Eastleigh Athletic/South Farnborough Athletic.

Debut v Millwall (a) 14.9.1895

Joe Turner was secured by Saints' secretary Charles Robson during "a raid" on the Potteries district and joined the Saints for thirty shillings a week. His runs down the left-wing were of electrifying speed and his early partnership with Wattie Keay shone with brilliance. Despite being a winger, Joe scored an unusually high number of goals and, although Keay was the ideal provider, many of his tally were of his own making. In 1898 Joe returned to the Potteries for a couple of seasons before moving to Everton. While at Goodison he visited Southampton for a cup-tie and reminded the Dell public of his vast array of skills by capping an impressive performance with Everton's third goal. Within months, however, he was once more wearing the red and white stripes and in his second term as a Saint helped the club to the final of the 1902 F.A. Cup and was a virtual ever-present in the two championship winning sides of 1903 and 1904. After giving up playing football for a living in 1908 Joe was employed at a Stoke brewery, although later he returned to Southampton to live until his death, aged 78, in 1950.

Appearances:
SL: 124 app. 56 gls.
FAC: 29 app. 18 gls.
Total: *153 app. 74 gls.*

J. Turner
Southampton

OGDEN'S CIGARETTES

north-eastern side Leadgate Park and cost a £200 transfer fee. Originally signed as a full-back, Bill quickly transferred to the left-half position during an injury crisis and from then on hardly ever had a poor game. He was the only man to have cost a fee in the club's 1921 promotion side but was worth every penny as the half-back line of Shelley, Campbell and Turner did so much to cement Saints existence as a top Second Division club in the early 1920's. After five seasons of dependable service Bill moved to Bury in exchange for Woodhouse and Callagher.

Appearances:
SL: 17 app. 0 gls.
FL: 149 app. 1 gl.
FAC: 20 app. 0 gls.
Total: *186 app. 1 gl.*

❏ **Saints note** - *Bill was selected to play for an F.A. XI versus The Army at Fratton Park on 12th October 1921.*

TYSON, Charles F.

Role: Centre-half 1912-13
6'0" 12st.6lbs.
b. Yorkshire

CAREER: Dulwich Hamlet/SOUTHAMPTON 1912.

Debut v Portsmouth (h) 28.9.12

Registered with both Saints and Dulwich Hamlet, Charles Tyson was a student studying to be a teacher. More robust than the average amateur he was most useful in close quarter tussles and could be trusted to keep a tight grip on opposing forwards. Why his career at the Dell ended in 1913 is not known but it is presumed that his teaching duties took him away from the area.

Appearances:
SL: 14 app. 0 gls.
FAC: 2 app. 0 gls.
Total: *16 app. 0 gls.*

❏ **Saints note** - *Charles won an England amateur cap in March 1911 for a game versus France.*

TURNER, William

Role: Half-back 1919-24
5'10" 12st.0lbs.
b. Southmoor,
Nr. Durham 1896

CAREER: Dipton United 1913/ Scotswood/Leadgate Park/ SOUTHAMPTON Sept 1919/ Bury Apr 1924/Queen's Park Rangers July 1927.

Bill Turner

Debut v Southend United (h) 8.11.19

Bill Turner joined Southampton from the

VECK, Robert

Role: Forward 1945-50
5'7" 10st.4lbs.
b. Titchfield 1 April 1920

CAREER: SOUTHAMPTON am. Sept 1938/ (Leeds United, Bradford P.A., St. Johnstone, York City, Yeaden, R.A.F. Church Fenton, United Services Egypt, Egyptian Railways during World War Two)/SOUTHAMPTON pro. Sept 1945/Gillingham July 1950/ Chelmsford City Aug 1951.

Debut v Newport County (h) 5.1.46 FAC

Before the war Bobby Veck had shown much promise and as a youngster in the club's nursery eleven netted 14 goals in 11 Southampton Junior League and Cup games. The war put a temporary halt to his career although while serving with the R.A.F. in Egypt he represented the United Services. Returning to the Dell to sign professional forms at the end of the hostilities Bobby played and scored in the first League game of the post war season at home to Swansea. Losing his left-wing place to Eric Day and then Bill Wrigglesworth he spent much of the next five years in the reserves although he was called upon to play in the centre-forward position when Charlie Wayman was injured in April! 1949.

Appearances:
FL: 23 app. 2 gls.
FAC: 3 app. 1 gl.
Total: *26 app. 3 gls.*

Bobby Veck

VERNEY, George W.

Role: Half-back 1891-94

CAREER: SOUTHAMPTON St. Mary's 1888/ Cranbury Avenue 1898.

Debut v Warmley (a) 3.10.1891 FAC

George Verney was a tenacious half-back whose persistence in his efforts to challenge for any loose ball won him plenty of admirers at the Antelope Ground. Combining excellently with 'Banquo' Stride, George featured in Saints' first ever F.A. Cup match and remained at the club until 1896 although for the last couple of seasons he contented himself by assisting the reserves. He ended his footballing career by turning out for minor local side Cranbury Avenue.

Appearances:
FAC: 6 app. 1 gl.
Total: *6 app. 1 gl.*

VERNON, Douglas Sydney

Role: Forward 1928-29
5'10" 12st.0lbs.
b. Devonport 19 May 1905
d. Morden 26 March 1979

CAREER: Royal Air Force/SOUTHAMPTON am. Feb1929/Wycombe Wanderers 1930/ Leyton 1931/Metropolitan Police Force.

Debut v Oldham Athletic (a) 9.2.29

Douglas Vernon

A leading aircraftsman, Douglas Vernon was an amateur centre-forward who had played for the R.A.F. representative XI before joining the Saints playing staff in February 1929. He was immediately given his first team chance and played five consecutive matches before he was recalled by the R.A.F. and posted to the Far East during the crisis with China. When he returned from active duty Southampton retained his registration but allowed him to play for Wycombe with whom he gained an Amateur Cup-Winners' Medal in 1931. After a spell at Leyton, Doug left the R.A.F. to join the Metropolitan Police Force for whom he turned out over a seven year period.

Appearances:
FL: 5 app. 0 gls.
Total: *5 app. 0 gls.*

VINE, Peter William

Role: Forward 1958-59
5'7" 10st.8lbs.
b. Southampton 11 December 1940

CAREER: Itchen Grammar School/

SOUTHAMPTON am. Apr 1956, pro. Dec 1957 /Poole Town Aug 1959-1960/Hastings United/Andover Sept 1962.
Debut v Bury (a) 21.3.59

Peter Vine was signed as an amateur as soon as he left school in April 1956 and made rapid progress in the Saints' nursery team. He made several reserve team appearances before his seventeenth birthday and his goalscoring ability won him England Youth honours in 1958. Peter was given his first team debut in March 1959, replacing the injured Don Roper, but his first game was also to be the last as his youthful promise evaporated into thin air. After a season playing for Mike Keeping's Poole Town, Peter retired from serious football to concentrate on a career with Thames Waste Paper Company. In 1977 he became manager of a Southampton waste paper business and in 1990 was still involved with the same company.

Appearances:
FL: 1 app. 0 gls.
Total: *1 app. 0 gls.*

Peter Vine

WALDRON, Malcolm

Role: Defender 1974-83
6'0" 12st.6lbs.
b. Emsworth 6 September 1956

CAREER: Warblington School/Havant & Hampshire Schools/SOUTHAMPTON app. July 1973, pro. Sept 1974/Washington Diplomats May 1981/SOUTHAMPTON Aug 1981/Burnley Sept 1983/Portsmouth Mar 1984/Road Sea Feb 1987.

Debut v Nottingham Forest (a) 12.4.75

Malcolm Waldron's talents were spotted by Saints' scout, Stan Cribb, while he was playing for Havant and Hampshire School teams and after Pompey dallied over offering terms Southampton stepped smartly in. He established himself at the beginning of the 1976-77 season and, although he could play anywhere in the back four, his best position was probably sweeper where his speed and heading ability often paid dividends. Saints' Player of the Year in 1979 Malcolm gained England international honours when selected for a "B" international against New Zealand the same year. Extremely agile and lithe for a big man, he also packed a thunderbolt of a shot and scored some memorable goals for the club. In May 1981 he moved to the States to spend the summer with the Washington Diplomats but, after his return to the Dell, embarked on an unhappy period when a loss of form and a succession of injuries eventually led to a £90,000 transfer to Burnley. A personality clash with manager John Bond resulted in a return south and a move to Fratton Park but, again, injuries blighted his progress. He decided to retire from the professional game in December 1986.

Appearances:
FL: 177 (1) app. 10 gls.
FAC: 15 app. 0 gls.
LC: 19 app. 0 gls.
Eur: 4 app. 1 gl.
Total: *215 (1) app. 11 gls.*

Malcolm Waldron

WALKER, David

Role: Half-back 1965-74
5'11" 11st.10lbs.
b. Colne 15 October 1941

CAREER: Burnley am. May 1958, pro. May 1959/SOUTHAMPTON May 1965/Cape Town City Feb 1974.

Debut v Derby County (a) 21.8.65

David Walker was on the verge of signing a new two-year contract with Burnley when Ted Bates persuaded him to move south in a deal that cost Southampton £20,000. "Docker", as he became known, was a tough no-nonsense defender and what he lacked in speed he made up for in determination. A cool unemotional player, he took his place amongst the likes of Hollywood, Webb, McGrath and Gabriel in a Saints' defence of the late 1960's which earned the disapproval of more than one opposition manager. Uncompromising is a word that Saints' fans would prefer to use and Dave, as much as any of the others, helped Saints maintain their hard-won place in the First Division. His last two years at the Dell were spent mainly in the reserves and the fact that

David Walker

his departure in 1974, along with John McGrath, coincided with relegation to Division Two illustrates both players' value. Finishing his career in South Africa, he later returned to Southampton and today runs a successful antiques business.

Appearances:
FL: 189 (8) app. 1 gl.
FAC: 19 app. 0 gls.
LC: 9 app. 0 gls.
Eur: 6 app. 0 gls.
Total: *223 (8) app. 1 gl.*

WALKER, John Young Hilley

Role: Forward 1952-58
5'8" 10st.11lbs.
b. Glasgow 17 December 1928

CAREER: Campsie Black Watch/ Wolverhampton Wanderers Aug 1947/ SOUTHAMPTON Oct 1952/Reading Dec 1957/Reading Youth & Reserve Coach 1974-1979.

Debut v Luton Town (h) 4.10.52
*(scored on debut)

Johnny Walker

Johnny Walker was purchased for £12,000 and, playing in the inside-left position, scored within eight minutes of his debut. Building on this auspicious beginning he went on to give five good years service to the club. He had the curious habit of whirling his arms when in pursuit of the ball, but he was a neat, constructive forward. Johnny loved the game and was always ready to throw his jacket down in the street to join in an impromptu kick-about with schoolboys. It was a shock when he asked for a transfer in January 1957 but with the return of Don Roper his first team place was not assured and he was duly allowed to move to Elm Park for a £2,500 fee in the following December. Johnny enjoyed seven successful years at Reading and after playing 286 league games retired in 1964. In March 1991 Johnny was living in Theale while working as a maintenance engineer at the Royal Mail, Reading. He still keeps an avid interest in football and coaches his local works side.

Appearances:
FL: 172 app. 48 gls.
FAC: 14 app. 4 gls.
Total: *186 app. 52 gls.*

WALLACE, David Lloyd

Role: Forward 1980-90
5'5" 9st.12lbs.
b. Greenwich, London 21 January 1964

CAREER: West Greenwich School/ SOUTHAMPTON app. July 1980, pro. Jan 1982 /Manchester United Sept 1989.

Debut v Manchester United (a) 29.11.80

Spotted by Saints' Youth Development Officer Bob Higgins during a school coaching day at West Greenwich, Danny Wallace, aged 16 years 314 days, became the youngest ever Saint to play in the first team when making his debut at Old Trafford in November 1980. Southampton had signed the young forward from under the noses of Millwall and Arsenal and throughout the eighties Danny delighted the Dell crowds with his explosive pace and individual goals. Small but compact, and highly competitive, Danny scored on his England Under-21 debut against Greece at Fratton Park and in January 1986 did the same when awarded his full cap against Egypt in Cairo. His England call-up was a just reward for his committed attitude and, while he could frustrate the crowds with his erratic crossing, who could ever forget the sensational brace of goals he scored in a live televised match against Liverpool in March 1984? Soon after his full England appearance

Danny began to suffer a series of niggling injuries and, putting on a little weight, struggled to maintain the elusiveness which made him such a nightmare to defenders. He also grew unsettled and, despite being joined in the first team by his younger twin brothers, (the first trio of brothers in the First Division since 1919), he decided to seek a change of clubs. It was a sorry day when he was allowed to move to Old Trafford for a then club record of £1.2 million, but with brother Rodney being seen as an ideal replacement and the fee far above anything previously received, the club could ill-afford to turn down the move. Since his transfer Danny has continued to struggle with injury problems but he did have the satisfaction of picking up a 1990 F.A. Cup-Winners' medal when United beat Crystal Palace after a replay.

Appearances:
FL: 233 (15) app. 64 gls.
FAC: 21 (2) app. 4 gls.
LC: 36 app. 6 gls.
Eur: 2 (1) app. 0 gls.
Total: *292 (18) app. 74 gls.*

Danny Wallace

WALLACE, Lawrence Michael

Role: Forward 1938-39
b. Sandown, I.O.W. April qtr. 1917

CAREER: University College, Southampton/
SOUTHAMPTON am. Feb 1939.
Debut v Manchester City (a) 18.3.39

A student at Southampton's University
College, Lawrence Wallace was a sprinter in
England's athletic team in the 1938 Empire
Games in Australia. Selected to play for the
Universities Athletic Union XI against an
Amateur XI at the Dell in February 1939,
Lawrence attracted so much attention during
the match that the club immediately signed
him on amateur terms. Not surprisingly, he
was a fast left-winger who could use either
foot but he found his debut at Manchester's
Maine Road somewhat overwhelming and
struggled to find any rhythm. He continued
his degree course at college and represented
the A.A.A. throughout the summer of 1939.
He also appeared in the club's reserve eleven
during the early years of the War.

Appearances:
FL: 1 app. 0 gls.
Total: *1 app. 0 gls.*

*Ray Wallace's
sending off at York
was to have lasting
repercussions.*

WALLACE, Raymond George

Role: Full-back 1989-1991
5'6" 10st.2lbs.
b. Lewisham 2 October 1969

CAREER: SOUTHAMPTON trainee July 1986,
pro. Apr 1988/Leeds United May 1991.
Debut v Sheffield Wednesday (h) 22.10.89

Raymond Wallace is probably the least gifted
of the three brothers but makes up for his lack
of skill with an intense determination.
Replacing the injured Gerry Forrest at the
right-back position Ray's tenaciousness
overshadowed his lack of experience but when
he was sent off in a Littlewoods League Cup
fixture at York, his robustness was to have
long lasting repercussions. Banned for the next
two League games, Jason Dodd was given his
number two shirt and Saints rattled off two
memorable 4-1 victories against Queen's Park
Rangers and Liverpool. Incredibly in the next
twenty months, up until his transfer to Leeds,
Raymond did not start another League match
for the Saints with first Dodd and later Alex
Cherednik barring the path to a first team
recall. His simultaneous transfer to Elland
Road alongside twin Rodney, was a wise move
by Leeds' boss, Howard Wilkinson, for
although Ray will find it hard to break into the
Leeds first team his presence will no doubt
help his brother settle.

Appearances:
FL: 33 (2) app. 0 gls.
FAC: 2 app. 0 gls.
LC: 7 app. 0 gls.
Total: *42 (2) app. 0 gls.*

❏ **Saints note** - *There is a fourth Wallace brother
named Clive who, at the age of 15, was offered a
trial by Saints.*

WALLACE, Rodney Seymour

Role: Forward 1988-91
5'7" 10st.1lb.
b. Lewisham 2 October 1969

CAREER: SOUTHAMPTON trainee July 1986,
pro. Apr 1988/Leeds United May 1991.
Debut v West Ham United (h) 30.4.89

Rodney and Raymond Wallace are the

younger twin brothers of Danny, and all three made history in October 1989 when they played together in the same team in a match against Sheffield Wednesday. Rodney has yet to emulate his elder brother in terms of England recognition but many Saints' fans regarded Rod as the better player. His goal scoring ratio was certainly higher than Danny's and his crossing and team-work were probably more consistent. Unfortunately for the Southampton public Rod fell out with the club, mainly miffed over the way he believed they treated Danny's transfer and the initially modest new terms offered to himself. He asked for a move and steadfastly refused to sign a series of improved offers from a management who became belatedly aware of his value to the team. His departure, in May 1991, had a sad inevitablity about it and the £1,600,000 fee was a small consolation to the fans who regarded the little forward's darting skills as irreplaceable. A member of the England Under-21 eleven for two seasons, Rod will be hoping that his move to Leeds can perhaps enhance his chances of a full international cap.

Appearances:
FL: 101 (17) app. 45 gls.
FAC: 10 app. 3 gls.
LC: 18 (1) app. 6 gls.
Total: *129 (18) app. 54 gls.*

❏ **Saints note** - *The last three brothers to play in the First Division were the Carrs who played for Middlesbrough in 1919-20. However, no set of twins and an elder brother have ever before featured in a Division One side. The £1.6 million fee which the independent tribunal ordered Leeds to pay Saints in July 1991 was the highest valuation ever handed out by the body.*

WALLER, Wilfred Hugh

Role: Goalkeeper 1900-01
5'11" 12st.10lbs.
b. 1877

CAREER: Queen's Park/Bolton Wanderers/ Corinthians/Tottenham Hotspur Jan 1899/Richmond Association 1900/ Bournemouth & District League XI 1900/ SOUTHAMPTON Sept 1900/Watford.
Debut v Luton Town (a) 1.9.1900

Wilf Waller was an amateur custodian who had won representative honours for the Bournemouth and District League before joining the Saints at the start of the 1900-01 season. He made his debut in the opening game as Jack Robinson was serving a one-match suspension but, with the return of the club's volatile but brilliant regular goalkeeper, Wilf only managed one further senior outing. In April 1903 he and his family moved to South Africa.

Appearances:
SL: 2 app. 0 gls.
Total: *2 app. 0 gls.*

Rod Wallace

WARD, A.

Role: Forward 1894-95

CAREER: Lancaster Regiment/
SOUTHAMPTON St. Mary's Mar 1895/
Lancaster Regiment.

Debut v Millwall (a) 23.3.1895

An army amateur centre-forward, Ward came
to the notice of the St. Mary's officials when he
exhibited outstanding skills in the Lancaster
Regiment's 3-0 friendly victory over Saints in
February 1895. The club secured his services
for the visit to Millwall the following month
but the occasion proved too much and he
struggled to combat the quicker Lions'
defenders. This game was to be his only
venture into senior soccer and he returned to
Army service.

    Appearances:
SL: 1 app. 0 gls.
Total: *1 app. 0 gls.*

Frank Ward

WARD, Alfred

Role: Forward 1908-09
5'10" 12st.6lbs.
b. Eastwood 1885

CAREER: Clowne White Star/Notts County
Oct 1903/Brighton & Hove Albion May 1904/
Aberdeen 1905/Bradford Park Avenue 1907/
SOUTHAMPTON May 1908.

*Debut v Brentford (h) 2.1.09 *(scored on debut)*

Recognised as a
forward of
considerable ability
before he joined the
Saints in May 1908,
Alf Ward's career at
the Dell practically
ended before it had
started. A member of
the club's
touring party
on the
Continent in
May 1908, he
displaced the
cartilage of

Alf Ward

his right knee in the final match in Leipzig and
returned to Southampton where he underwent
three operations in an effort to put it right.
Alf's recovery was not complete until January
1909 when, on his debut, he did at least have
the satisfaction of scoring the only goal of the
game against Brentford. Although Alf did
have a few more outings the knee continued to
give trouble and he took the decision to retire
at the season's end.

    Appearances:
SL: 4 app. 2 gls.
Total: *4 app. 2 gls.*

WARD, Frank

Role: Half-back 1933-35
5'9" 12st.0lbs.
b. Leigh 21 January 1903

CAREER: Walshaw United/Bury Oct
1923/ Preston North End June 1927/
SOUTHAMPTON July
1933/Folkestone c.s. 1935.

Debut v Bradford City (h) 26.8.33

Frank Ward joined the Saints in the
summer of 1933 and brought with him

a wealth of experience gained while on the books of Bury and Preston. A versatile defender, Frank could play either at full or half-back and, at the beginning of the 1934-35 season, also had a couple of games in the inside-left berth. He was given a free transfer in the summer of 1935 and moved to Kent to play for Folkestone.

Appearances:
FL: 27 app. 0 gls.
Total: *27 app. 0 gls.*

WARD, Herbert Foster

Role: Forward 1893-95
5'10" 12st.4lbs.
b. Hammersmith 24 March 1873
d. Winchester 6 June 1897

CAREER: Bruce Castle School (Tottenham)/ SOUTHAMPTON St. Mary's 1893.

Debut v Uxbridge (h) 4.11.1893 FAC
*(scored on debut)

Herbert Ward

Herbert Ward's career as a schoolmaster led him to Southampton when he accepted a teaching post at Handel College. A fine all-round sportsman, Herbert joined St. Mary's as a left-winger in 1893 but the following year, with the team entering the Southern League, he was asked to take over the centre-forward role. He was a tireless worker at all times and his goalscoring prowess was rewarded with five Hampshire County Caps, two of them as captain. In 1895 Herbert decided to quit football to concentrate on cricket and over the next two years he played thirty-three games for Hampshire as a stylish middle order, right-handed batsman. In June 1897 while actually playing in a match Herbert suddenly collapsed and died. At first the case of death was presumed to be sunstroke but a later diagnosis revealed that typhoid fever was responsible.

Appearances:
SL: 9 app. 6 gls.
FAC: 6 app. 6 gls.
Total: *15 app. 12 gls.*

❏ **Saints note** - *Herbert's brother, the Reverend Charles Gordon Ward, also played cricket for Hampshire C.C.C. between 1897 and 1901.*

WARHURST, Sam Lee

Role: Goalkeeper 1937-39
5'10" 11st.6lbs.
b. Nelson 29 December 1907
d. Southampton 17 February 1981

CAREER: Stalybridge Celtic/Nelson June 1928/Bradford City June 1932/ SOUTHAMPTON May 1937, trainer-coach Mar 1946-52.
Debut v Norwich City (a) 28.8.37

Sam Warhurst joined Southampton in the twilight of his career but in the two seasons prior to the outbreak of war became the club's regular custodian. On the small side, Sam nevertheless proved to be a sound 'keeper with a fine reputation for sportsmanship and comradeship. He played for the Saints during the Second World War and also had the odd game for Cunliffe Owen before, with the resumption of normal football, he was appointed team coach. When the club were relegated in 1953 Sam decided it was time to move on and he became mine host at the St.

One of his main assets was his speed and he was regarded as more than a match for any forward. He could also use the ball well and would have probably remained at the Dell for some considerable time had it not been for the directors' mistaken impression that one of his knees was unsound. Jack was allowed to move to Fratton Park where he made 227 Southern League appearances to prove beyond doubt that the Southampton board had made a grave error. After the Great War Jack became Portsmouth's trainer, a position he held until just after the Second World War.

Appearances:
SL: 17 app. 0 gls.
FAC: 1 app. 0 gls.
Total: *18 app. 0 gls.*

Sam Warhurst (second left) in the dugout with Charlie Wayman (left)

Mary's Hotel in East Street. When the pub was demolished to make way for a shopping centre in 1972 Sam decided to retire.

Appearances:
FL: 78 app. 0 gls.
FAC: 2 app. 0 gls.
Total: *80 app. 0 gls.*

WARNER, John

Role: Full-back 1905-06
5'10" 12st.4lbs.
b. Preston 1883
d. Preston 16 May 1948

CAREER: St. Michaels (Preston)/Preston North End Sept 1902/ SOUTHAMPTON May 1905/ Portsmouth c.s. 1906, later trainer.

Debut v Brentford (h)
2.9.05

Jack Warner was a bricklayer by trade who had made eleven appearances with Preston over a three-year period.

WARREN, Ernest Thorne

Role: Forward
1929-30
5'10" 11st.0lbs.
b. Sunderland January qtr. 1909

CAREER: Usworth Colliery/ SOUTHAMPTON Mar 1929/Burton Town c.s. 1931/ Northampton Town July 1933/Hartlepool United Aug 1934.

Ernie Warren

Debut v West Bromwich Albion (a)
3.5.29

Ernie Warren arrived at the Dell fresh from representing his colliery side and his form in Southampton's reserve side (8 goals in 12 games) prompted his inclusion in the forward line for the last game of the 1929-30 season. The game was a disaster with Saints going down 1-5 at the Hawthorns and although Ernie remained "on the books" for another twelve months he was never given another chance.

Appearances:
FL: 1 app. 0 gls.
Total: *1 app. 0 gls.*

WATERSTON, Archibald Rutherford

Role: Forward 1928-29
5'10" 11st.7lbs.
b. Musselburgh 13 October 1902
d. Edinburgh 13 May 1982

CAREER: Musselburgh Brutonians 1922/
Leicester City July 1923/Cowdenbeath 1926/
Newport County July 1927/SOUTHAMPTON
Dec 1928/Tranmere Rovers July 1929/
Southport Oct 1930/Doncaster Rovers July
1932/Aldershot July 1934/Edinburgh City.

Debut v Clapton Orient (a) 8.12.28

Having scored 35 goals for Newport County in
a season and a half, Archie Waterston's £300
transfer fee was considered a snip by Saints
fans. Unable to reproduce such prodigious
scoring in the Second Division, however,
Archie was sold to Tranmere Rovers within
seven months and it was not until joining
Southport that he was to rediscover his goal
touch. (During the 1930-31 season he hit 30
goals which established a club record that
lasted until their League demise in 1978). After
ending his soccer career in 1935 Archie
returned to his native Musselburgh where he
worked at Brunton's Wool Mills as a foreman
in the dye department.

Appearances:
FL: 6 app. 1 gl.
FAC: 1 app. 0 gls.
Total: *7 app. 1 gl.*

WATSON, David Vernon

Role: Centre-half 1979-82
5'11" 11st.7lbs.
b. Stapleford 5 October 1946

CAREER: Stapleford Old Boys/Notts County
Jan 1967/Rotherham United Jan 1968/
Sunderland Dec 1970/Manchester City June
1975/Werder Bremen, West Germany June
1978/SOUTHAMPTON Oct 1979/Stoke City
Jan 1982/Vancouver Whitecaps Apr 1983/
Derby County Sept 1983/Fort Lauderdale Sun
May 1984/Notts County player-coach Sept
1984/Kettering Town Aug 1985.

Debut v West Bromwich Albion (a) 20.10.79

Dave Watson, England's premier central

defender, arrived at the Dell for £200,000
having just endured a miserable year playing
in the German Bundesliga. Very strong and
masterful in the air, Dave won a further
eighteen England caps while at the Dell and
his imperious presence was a major stabilising
influence in Saints' defence for a couple of
years. At the start of the 1981-82 season he lost
his position to the younger Malcolm Waldron
and with his international place in jeopardy he
was forced to seek a move. Playing in a further
two England internationals while at Stoke, he
set a record (later equalled by Peter Shilton), of
being capped while on the books of five
different clubs. In 1989 he returned to the Dell
to play in the Steve Mills Charity Match for the
ex-Saints but by then he had retired from the
game to concentrate on running a successful
business.

Appearances:
FL: 73 app. 8 gls.
FAC: 5 app. 0 gls.
LC: 3 app. 0 gls.
Eur: 2 app. 0 gls.
Total: *83 app. 8 gls.*

Dave Watson

WATSON, Reginald Herbert

Role: Forward 1929-31
5'9" 12st.6lbs.
b. Thelwall 26 August 1900
d. Thelwall January qtr. 1971

CAREER: Thelwall/Arpley Street/Grappon Hall F.C./Fairfield United/Monkshall F.C./Witton Albion/Manchester United (trial)/Oldham Dec 1921/SOUTHAMPTON June 1929/Rochdale Sept 1931, retired Feb 1932.
Debut v Barnsley (a) 31.8.29

Makeweight in the deal that sent "Spud" Murphy to Oldham, Reg Watson had spent most of the 1920's playing in Lancashire and struggled to acclimatise to the south. A great "trier", he played the first six games of the 1929-30 campaign in the left-wing position but then lost his place to the up-and-coming Johnny Arnold. Finding his feet in the reserves Reg netted 36 times in 63 reserve games before being placed on the transfer list at £200 in May 1931. He subsequently received a "free" the following August and returned to Lancashire.

Appearances:
FL: 19 app. 5 gls.
Total: *19 app. 5 gls.*

WATSON, Victor Martin

Role: Forward 1935-36
5'10" 12st.4lbs.
b. Girton 10 November 1897
d. Girton 3 August 1988

CAREER: Girton/Cambridge Town/Peterborough & Fletton United/Brotherhood Engineering Works/Wellingborough Town/West Ham United Mar 1920/SOUTHAMPTON June 1935/Cambridge City trainer-coach c. 1946.

Debut v Swansea Town (h) 31.8.36
(scored on debut)

A giant in pre-war footballing circles, Vic Watson's arrival at the Dell caused quite a stir. At Upton Park he had been an absolute institution, making 505 league and cup appearances and scoring 326 goals along the way. Capped five times by England, Vic had been persuaded to forsake the Hammers for the Saints by George Kay, who had once been a team-mate at Upton Park. Although 37, Vic top-scored in his one season at Southampton and when he scored a hat-trick against Nottingham Forest in February 1936 he was, and still is, at 38 years and 3 months the oldest player ever to perform such a feat for the club. He retired the following May to grow tomatoes and cucumbers in his native Cambridgeshire and lived to the ripe old age of 90.

Appearances:
FL: 36 app. 14 gls.
FAC: 1 app. 0 gls.
Total: *37 app. 14 gls.*

Reg Watson

Vic Watson

WAYMAN, Charles

Role: Forward 1947-50
5'8" 9st.7lbs.
b. Bishop Auckland 16 May 1921

CAREER: Chilton Colliery/Spennymoor
United/Newcastle United Sept 1941/
(Portsmouth during World War Two)/
SOUTHAMPTON Oct 1947/Preston North
End Sept 1950/Middlesbrough Sept 1954/
Darlington Dec 1956.
Debut v Birmingham City (h) 1.11.47

It's forty years since Charlie Wayman packed
his bags and took the train to Preston North
End but in his comparatively short stay at the
Dell he had become a goalscoring legend and
is still much revered by Saints' older fans. Bill
Dodgin and his Southampton side were first
acquainted with Charlie's instinctive,
predatory abilities when he notched a hat-trick
against them to give Newcastle a 3-1 victory in
the third round of the F.A. Cup in January
1947. Within a few months, Charlie had fallen
out with the St. James Park management when
omitted from the Magpies' semi-final team and
Bill Dodgin left no time in making contact. Bill
had a persuasive personality, and when he
offered Charlie, an ex-miner, "a strawberries
and cream lifestyle" the little Geordie put pen
to paper costing Southampton a record
£10,000. Over the next two and a half seasons
he treated the terraces to an unforgettable

*Charlie Wayman (above) and below in action
scoring one of his 77 League and Cup goals in just
107 Saints appearances.*

exhibition of finishing skills that gave him a
higher goal ratio per game than any other
Southampton striker. Fast, brave and
uncannily perceptive he intuitively seemed to
know where the wingers would place the ball
and was invariably prepared for its arrival. He
remains the only man to hit five goals in a

league match (v Leicester City 23.10.48) and, the same season, scored 32 times in 37 games to finish as the League's top marksman. "Up the middle for Charlie" was the crowd's usual urgent instruction when the team was struggling and, more often than not, with a swing of his deadly left foot the ball would be despatched to the back of the net. Unfortunately for the fans Charlie's wife grew homesick in the south which forced him to seek a transfer and, in September1950, he moved to Preston for £10,000 plus Eddie Brown. Proving that he was no "flash in the pan" Charlie's goals helped Preston to promotion in 1951 and three years later he scored in every F.A. Cup round up to, and including, the final itself. Returning to the north east with Middlesbrough, he played with the young Brian Clough and then finished his career at Darlington. After hanging up his boots he became a brewery representative with Scottish and Newcastle and today lives in happy retirement in Coundon near Bishop Auckland. In 1989 he appeared on television in a "This Is Your Life" programme that featured his ex-Preston colleague, Tom Finney. He still remembers his spell at the Dell with affection and has been known to try and catch a Saints game whenever they visit the north east.

Appearances:
FL: 100 app. 73 gls.
FAC: 7 app. 4 gls.
Total: 107 app. 77 gls.

WEALE, Robert Henry

Role: Forward 1928-30
5'7" 11st.4lbs.
b. Troed y Rhiw 9 November 1903
d. Merthyr Tydfil January qtr. 1970

CAREER: Ebbw Vale Schoolboys/Merthyr Tydfil/Luton Town (trial)/West Ham United Mar 1925/Swindon Town June 1927/ SOUTHAMPTON Dec 1928/Cardiff City Aug 1930/Boston Town/Guildford City 1931/ Newport County Aug 1932/Wrexham Mar 1933/Glentoran Aug 1935/Bath City 1936.
Debut v Clapton Orient (a) 8.12.28

A former Welsh Schoolboy international, Bobby Weale was watched several times by the Saints before a club record of £1,000 was paid

to bring him to the Dell. A fast, clever right-winger, Bobby settled quickly and scored a hat-trick against Notts County within a few weeks of his arrival. Unfortunately this promising start was not maintained and his form became erratic, especially in the second half of the 1929-30 season. In May 1930 terms of £5 per week (both winter and summer), rising to £8 if in the first team were offered, but Bobby declined and moved back to his native Wales. After only five games at Cardiff, he had spells at Newport and Wrexham with whom he made 26 and 23 appearances respectively.

Appearances:
FL: 45 app. 10 gls.
FAC: 3 app. 0 gls.
Total: 48 app. 10 gls.

❑ **Saints note** - *Bobby's younger brother, Tom, came to the Dell as a trialist in 1929 and appeared in one London Combination match. Although never signing for the Saints, he went on to make a name for himself at Folkestone, Cardiff City and Crewe Alexandra.*

Bobby Weale

WEBB, Charles

Role: Forward 1904-05
5'8" 11st.4lbs.
*b. Higham Ferrers, Northamptonshire,
4 March 1879
d. Wellingborough January 1939*

CAREER: Chesham Grenadiers/Higham
Ferrers/Rushden 1898/Kettering 1900/
Leicester Fosse May 1901/Wellingborough c.s.
1902/Kettering 1903/SOUTHAMPTON May
1904/Dundee June 1905/Manchester City Mar
1908/Airdrie June 1909.
Debut v Luton Town (a) 3.9.04

Charles Webb was a harness-maker by trade
who came to Southampton with the reputation
of being a brilliant wing-man. He certainly had
a fine turn of speed with his centres and long
shots being particular features of his play.
Charles' form over his twelve month term at
the Dell alerted the attention of Dundee who
made him an irresistible offer to move north of
the border. With the simultaneous arrival in
Dundee from the Saints of Bert Dainty, the two
men now teamed up together for the third
time, both having played for Leicester Fosse
during 1901-02. After his retirement from
active playing, Charles managed a large
baking concern in Rushden,
Northamptonshire.

Appearances:
SL: 16 app. 5 gls.
FAC: 3 app. 0 gls.
Total: *19 app. 5 gls.*

WEBB, David James

Role: Full-back 1965-68
5'11" 12st.11lbs.
b. Stratford 9 April 1946

CAREER: West Ham United am./Leyton
Orient May 1963/SOUTHAMPTON Mar 1966
/Chelsea Feb 1968/Queen's Park Rangers July
1974/Leicester City Sept 1977/Derby County
Dec 1978/Bournemouth May 1980, player-
coach, manager Dec 1980-Dec 1982/Torquay
United manager Feb 1984-Aug 1985 and
manager-director to June 1986/Southend
United manager June 1986-Mar 1987/Milford
(Bournemouth league) 1988/re-appointed
Southend United manager Dec 1988.

David Webb

*Debut v Wolverhampton Wanderers (a) 12.3.66
(scored on debut)

Dave Webb was signed during Southampton's
final push towards First Division promotion
and his transfer triggered the departure from
the Dell of George O'Brien who made the
reverse move to Leyton Orient. With his
unfashionable crew-cut and swashbuckling
style Dave enjoyed a high profile in the team
and, within a year, he had developed into one
of the country's top defenders. Initially a
robust full back, he could also play in the
centre of defence and after his move to
Stamford Bridge (in another exchange transfer)
he settled to give the London club stalwart
service in this position. He scored in Chelsea's
defeat of Leeds United in the 1970 F.A. Cup
final replay and could count himself unlucky
never to receive "the call" from his country.
His enthusiasm led to a career in management
once he had stopped playing and, in 1990/91,
having led Southend United to Division Three
promotion, he was building one of the most
promising sides seen at Roots Hall for some
time.

Appearances:
FL: 75 app. 2 gls.
FAC: 7 app. 0 gls.
LC: 4 app. 0 gls.
Total: *86 app. 2 gls.*

WEBBER, Eric Victor

Role: Centre-half 1938-51
6'1" 12st.0lbs.
b. Shoreham 22 December 1919

CAREER: Fareham Senior
School/Fareham
Brotherhood/Fareham
Town/Gosport/ SOUTHAMPTON
am. Sept 1938, pro. Mar 1939/
(Mansfield Town and Derby
County during World War Two)
Torquay United player-manager Oct 1951,
manager May 1956/ Poole Town manager Aug
1965-Mar 1970.

Debut v Blackburn Rovers (a) 15.4.39

Eric Webber

Eric Webber was a member of the club's
fledgling nursery side that played in the
Hampshire League in 1938. Showing
considerable promise Eric was quickly
promoted to the ranks of the reserves where in
March 1938 his endeavours were rewarded
with a professional contract. He was given his
debut almost immediately, playing in the
right-half position but, before he had a chance
to consolidate, war had caused the suspension
of normal football. During the
hostilities Eric served in the R.A.F.
and not only managed to have odd
wartime game for the Saints but
also a loan spell as a guest player
for Mansfield. Returning to the Dell
in 1945 he immediately became the
regular centre-half and was an
ever-present in 1948-49 and
1949-50, two seasons when the club
came so desperately close to
promotion. An effective blocker of
anything that came his way he
became team captain in 1950, succeeding Bill
Rochford, and his leadership qualities were
soon to stand him in good stead for in October
1951 he moved to Torquay as their
player/manager. After 14 years at Plainmoor,
Eric had another five years in the "hot seat" at
Poole Town before returning to Southampton
in August 1970 to run the Manor House pub in
Woolston. Retiring in April 1984 he has
remained in Southampton and attended the
club's centenary dinner in 1985.

Appearances:
FL: 182 app. 0 gls.
FAC: 10 app. 0 gls.
Total: 192 app. 0 gls.

Peter Wells

WELLS, Peter Arthur

Role: Goalkeeper 1976-83
6'1" 13st.0lbs.
b. Nottingham 13 August 1956

CAREER: Nottingham Forest app. Aug 1971, pro. Oct 1974/SOUTHAMPTON Dec 1976 (Millwall-loan-Feb-May 1983, transferred May 1983)/Orient July 1985/Fisher Athletic c.s. 1989.
Debut v Blackpool (h) 18.12.76

Peter Wells was signed from Nottingham Forest's reserves for the paltry fee of £8,000 and became the fifth goalkeeper employed between the Southampton posts during the 1976-77 season. A bargain, he proved to be agile, brave and the owner of a safe pair of hands which were put to good use in Saints' promotion season of 1977-78. During his seven years at the Dell, Peter had to compete with the likes of Turner, Gennoe, Middleton and Katalinic but it wasn't until the arrival in 1982 of Peter Shilton that Peter finally relinquished the green jersey permanently.

Appearances:
FL: 141 app. 0 gls.
FAC: 12 app. 0 gls.
LC: 3 app. 0 gls.
Eur: 4 app. 0 gls.
Total: *160 app. 0 gls.*

WHEATLEY, Roland

Role: Forward 1948-51
5'9" 11st.6lbs.
b. Radford 20 June 1924

CAREER: Beeston Boys Club/Nottingham Forest June 1946/SOUTHAMPTON Jan 1949/Grimsby Town June 1951/Halifax Town Jan 1952/Workington Mar 1952/Corby Town July 1952/Stamford June 1953/SOUTHAMPTON scout 1955-73.
Debut v Bradford Park Avenue (a) 4.4.49

Roland Wheatley originally earned his living down a Nottinghamshire coal mine and then during the war enlisted as a paratrooper. Wounded during active service, Roland subsequently struggled to regain fitness and was on the brink of quitting the game for good when Southampton contacted Forest to offer him a life-line. At first things went well, he showed neat control and a formidable left foot but in September 1949 doctors diagnosed a heart defect and the beginnings of arthritis. Advised to retire from playing, Roland was placed in charge of the club's 'A' team but confounded the medical experts by returning to the first team during the 1949-50 season to play eight games and score a valuable goal that gave Saints two precious points against promotion rivals Sheffield United. Anxious for regular first-class football, he asked for

Roland Wheatley

a transfer in February 1951 and had his wish granted four months later with a move to Blundell Park. Still regarded as a skilful forward it was only his lack of pace that prevented him from making more than five outings in Grimsby's first team. Roland returned to the Southampton payroll in 1955 when Ted Bates placed him in charge of the Midlands' scouting network and he remained in this position until 1973.

Appearances:
FL: 10 app. 1 gl.
FAC: 2 app. 0 gls.
Total: *12 app. 1 gl.*

WHEELER, Alfred James

Role: Forward 1934-35
5'9" 11st.6lbs.
b. Bilston April qtr 1910

CAREER: Mossley/SOUTHAMPTON July 1934/Barnsley Aug 1935/Norwich City Oct 1935.
Debut v Port Vale (h) 27.8.34

Alf Wheeler came to the Dell in the summer of 1934 arriving well-recommended by his previous club, Mossley. Perfectly built for an inside-forward role, Alf initially settled well and in November 1934 scored an outstanding hat-trick within the first 27 minutes of a game against Bradford at the Dell. Finding consistency a problem, Alf lost his place to Arthur Holt and his short Southampton career was terminated by a £100 transfer to the Oakwell Ground, Barnsley in the summer of 1935.

Appearances:
FL: 11 app. 6 gls.
Total: *11 app. 6 gls.*

WHEELER, Frederick

Role: Forward 1910-11

CAREER: Colne/SOUTHAMPTON Aug 1910 /Eastleigh Athletic Aug 1911/Woolston 1913.
Debut v Southend United (a) 7.2.10

Fred Wheeler signed for Southampton after successfully coming through several trial matches. His early football had been as an inside-left in the Lancashire League but although he played well enough for the club's second string he was never considered good enough to permanently oust Harry Brown from the senior eleven. Released in May 1911 Fred remained in the locality and played for several years in the Hampshire League.

Appearances:
SL: 3 app. 0 gls.
Total: *3 app. 0 gls.*

WHEELER, Leonard Charles

Role: Forward 1914-15
b. Southampton October qtr 1888
d. Southampton 1 February 1963

CAREER: Bitterne 1910/Bournemouth Sept 1911/SOUTHAMPTON 1912/Bournemouth 1919.
Debut v Northampton Town (a) 24.10.14

A product of local football, Len Wheeler made a spectacular start to his brief professional career by scoring a hat-trick in a practice match prior to the start of the 1914-15 season. Despite this early burst of form Len was only given one senior game during the ensuing twelve months but with the suspension of league soccer in 1915 he remained at the club and, with Dominy and Blake, formed the main nucleus of the attack over the 1915-16 wartime season. Indeed, his goalscoring was impressive, 28 goals in 30 games to be followed by a further six goals in nine games the next year. At this point Len was called up to serve his King and country but, surviving the fighting, he returned to play for Bournemouth (Poppies) and gain Hampshire County honours.

Appearances:
SL: 1 app. 0 gls.
Total: *1 app. 0 gls.*

WHITE, Ian Samuel

Role: Half-back 1962-67
5'8" 11st.8lbs.
b. Glasgow 20 December 1935

CAREER: Port Glasgow Hibs/St. Anthony's/ Petershill/Glasgow Celtic Apr 1956/Leicester City May 1958/ SOUTHAMPTON June 1962/Hillingdon Borough July 1967/Portals player-manager June 1968, to c.s. 1972, general manager 1973 /Swaythling manager Aug 1975.

Debut v Scunthorpe United (a) 18.8.62

Ian White

A former Scotland Junior International, Ian White was on Celtic's books for two years without ever breaking into the senior team and moved to Filbert Street in an attempt to further his football ambitions. At Leicester, first team opportunities were also limited mainly due to the blossoming talents of Frank McLintock and Ian had to content himself with winning the 1959 Combination League with Leicester Reserves. Brought to the Dell for £15,000 in 1962 he became a very useful 'squad' player and teamed up once more with fellow ex-Leicester player Tony Knapp. He did play in the vital last ten games of the 1965-66 promotion year and the opening five games of

the club's inaugural Division One season but, with Hugh Fisher's arrival in March 1967, his days were numbered. Joining Southern League team Hillingdon in July 1967, his professional career came to a sudden end with a shattered ankle which forced him into retirement. He returned to the Southampton area to run a sports shop and in 1991 was still involved in the same business.

Appearances:
FL: 60 (1) app. 5 gls.
FAC: 1 app. 0 gls.
LC: 2 app. 0 gls.
Total: *63 (1) app. 5 gls.*

WHITE, William Collins

Role: Goalkeeper 1928-32
5'10" 11st.7lbs.
b. Kerry Cowdie 5 March 1895

CAREER: Hamilton/Heart of Midlothian/SOUTHAMPTON July 1928/Aldershot July 1932.
Debut v Hull City (a) 25.8.28

Idolised at Tynecastle, Willie White's sudden departure south infuriated the Hearts' fans who were not placated by the sizeable £800 transfer fee. The Southampton Supporters Club kindly donated £375 towards Willie's arrival costs and their contribution helped bring to the Dell a goalkeeper who was very much a student of the game. His 90 minute concentration had the immediate effect of installing confidence in a defence that had leaked 77 goals the previous season and the team ended 1928-29 in fourth position, their best inter-war placing. Willie's tenure of the Southampton goal lasted until September 1930 when he handed the jersey over to a young Bert Scriven only to win it back for the last eight matches of the season. The following year a more mature Scriven finally laid claim to the number one slot on a permanent basis with Willie choosing to finish his career with a short spell at Aldershot. In the mid-thirties Willie returned to Southampton to take over the "Greyhound Inn" in Cossack Street before moving back to his native Scotland to live.

Appearances:
FL: 101 app. 0 gls.
FAC: 2 app. 0 gls.
Total: *103 app. 0 gls.*

❏ **Saints note** - *Willie was one of four brothers who played top class football - John (Leeds United), Thomas (Motherwell) and James (Alloa) were the others..*

WHITELAW, Robert

Role: Half-back 1936-37
5'8" 10st.8lbs.
b. Stonehouse, Falkirk 2 November 1907

CAREER: Larkhill Thistle/Doncaster Rovers July 1926/Glasgow Celtic Aug 1930/Albion Rovers 1931/Bournemouth June 1932/Belfast Glentoran July 1933/Glasgow Celtic/ SOUTHAMPTON May 1936/Kidderminster c.s. 1937.

Debut v Aston Villa (a) 5.9.36

Bobby Whitelaw, an experienced half-back at the time of his Dell arrival, had perfected his trade in such diverse locations as Belfast, Glasgow and Bournemouth. He made his Southampton debut in the very first Second Division match ever played at Villa Park and, during the 1936-37 season, combined well with fellow half-backs Kennedy and Kingdon. Despite playing in nearly half of the club's fixtures that season, Bobby was not offered a new contract in May 1937 and he drifted into non-league football with Kidderminster.

Appearances:
FL: 20 app. 1 gl.
Total: *20 app. 1 gl.*

WHITING, William

Role: Half-back 1901-05

CAREER: Fitzhugh Rovers/SOUTHAMPTON 1901/Salisbury City 1907/Eastleigh Athletic c.s. 1908/Southampton Wanderers 1910.

Debut v Kettering Town (h) 15.2.02

William Whiting was a loyal member of the Southampton club for six years during which time he made only four appearances for the senior XI but well over 200 appearances for the reserves. He won a Hampshire Senior Cup-Winners' medal in 1905 before joining Salisbury in 1907. Whiting later "took up the whistle" and after becoming a member of the Southampton list of referees was promoted to the Southern League list in Sept 1921.

Appearances:
SL: 4 app. 0 gls.
Total: *4 app. 0 gls*

Southampton Referees F.C. 15th April 1921. William Whiting is the centre player in the middle row. The picture was taken prior to his promotion to the Southern League list in September 1921.

Mark Whitlock

WHITLOCK, Mark

Role: Centre-half 1981-86
6'0" 12st.3lbs.
b. Portsmouth 14 March 1961

CAREER: Sarisbury Sparks/SOUTHAMPTON app. Aug 1977, pro. Mar 1979 (Grimsby Town-loan Oct-Dec 1982) (Aldershot-loan Mar-May 1983)/A.F.C. Bournemouth June 1986/ Reading Dec 1988/Aldershot Aug 1990.

Debut v Wolverhampton Wanderers (h) 1.9.81

Mark Whitlock was a quiet, effective central defender who struggled to ever command a regular position in the first team. Whenever called upon Mark was always reliable and his career at the Dell could have perhaps been more successful had the management given him an extended run in the team. After a move to Dean Court Mark returned to the Dell in October 1987 as a member of the Bournemouth side which eliminated the Saints from the Littlewoods Cup.

Appearances:
FL: 55 (6) app. 1 gl.
LC: 5 app. 0 gls.
Eur: 3 app. 1 gl.
Total: *63 (6) app. 2 gls.*

WHITTLE, James Archibald

Role: Forward 1953-54
5'11" 11st.10lbs.
b. Hamilton 5 September 1929

CAREER: Heart of Midlothian (SOUTHAMPTON-loan-Jan 1954)/Heart of Midlothian Aug 1954.

Debut v Swindon Town (a) 23.1.54

A chartered accountant by profession, Jim Whittle joined the Saints on loan from Hearts while doing his National Service at Devizes in the Royal Army Pay Corps. Jim was immediately drafted into the side, wearing the centre-forward shirt, for two games in January 1954 but as both matches were away from home the Dell fans were denied the chance to reach an opinion. The Echo however, informed them that he "was an accurate passer if a little over-deliberate with some of his play". With Eric Day once more wearing the number nine shirt Jim was not selected again and he duly returned to Hearts upon completion of his National Service.

Appearances:
FL: 2 app. 0 gls.
Total: *2 app. 0 gls.*

Jim Whittle

WILCOCK. George Harrie

*Debut v Millwall (h) 2.9.11 *(scored on debut)*

Role: Goalkeeper 1919-20
5'9" 11st.0lbs.
b. Edinburgh 24 January 1890

CAREER: Barnsley Jan 1910/Goole Town
1912/Brighton & Hove Albion 1913/
SOUTHAMPTON 1919/Preston North End
May 1920.
Debut v Bristol Rovers (a) 13.12.19

George Wilcock left the Army in 1910 to
commence his footballing career and was with
Brighton in 1914 when the Great War broke
out. He rejoined his original unit, the Royal
Field Artillery and, being wounded at Loos in
October 1915, was invalided back to England.
He became an Army schoolmaster and
represented the Land Forces in a game against
the Navy at Plymouth which
was being watched by
members of the Southampton
board. His subsequent signing
was a good investment for,
during the 1919-20 season, he
proved to be a very able
custodian and the club were
approached by many of the
country's top teams anxious to
acquire George's services. In
May 1920 the Saints
reluctantly sold him to First
Division Preston but his
experiences at Deepdale were
unhappy and, after just seven
league appearances, he
dropped out of the
professional scene.

Appearances:
SL: 20 app. 0 gls.
FAC: 2 app. 0 gls.
Total: 22 app. 0 gls.

WILCOX, James

Role: Forward 1911-12
5'6" 11st.4lbs.
b. Stourbridge 1887

CAREER: Dudley Town/Aston Villa am. Mar
1906/Birmingham Nov 1908/
SOUTHAMPTON May 1911/Wellington
Town c.s. 1912.

With new Saints' manager George Swift
spending a total of £1,200 on transfers during
May and June 1911, James Wilcox was probably
the only "new man" to do himself any real
justice in a very disappointing season. As an
outside-right he possessed speed, a variety of
crosses and an ability to "manoeuvre astutely"
when beating his full-back. The lack of a
competent partner affected his form later in the
season and for a while he was relegated to the
reserves. Like so many of the new players that
year, James decided his career would prosper
better elsewhere and, soon after the season's
final whistle, he joined Wellington Town.

Appearances:
SL: 27 app. 5 gls.
FAC: 1 app. 0 gls.
Total: 28 app. 5 gls.

WILKINS, Kenneth

Role: Forward 1950-53
b. Salford 24 October 1928

CAREER: Sunderland am.
June 1947/ SOUTHAMPTON
Oct 1949 (Exeter City-loan-Oct
1951)/SOUTHAMPTON July
1952/ Fulham July 1953.
*Debut v Birmingham City (a)
28.2.51 *(scored on debut)*

Ken Wilkins was capped at
County Youth level for
Durham and joined
Southampton following his
demobilisation from the Army
in October1949. Despite
scoring on his debut Ken
found his route to regular
first-team football effectively
blocked by the likes of Ted Bates and Eddy
Brown and accepted a loan spell at Exeter.
Returning to the Dell he made just one further
appearance, replacing the injured Frank
Dudley at Bury in February 1953, before
joining his old manager Bill Dodgin at Craven
Cottage where he failed to make any
impression.

Ken Wilkins

Appearances:
FL: 3 app. 1 gl.
Total: 3 app. 1 gl.

WILKINS, Leonard

Role: Half-back 1948-58
5'10" 12st.0lbs.
b. Southampton 20 September 1925

CAREER: Shirley Warren School/Cunliffe Owen/SOUTHAMPTON Oct 1945/Ontario All Stars (Canada) Apr 1958/San Pedro Canvasbacks (Los Angeles) Apr 1959/Los Angeles All Stars 1959/California All Stars 1960/British Columbia All Stars 1961/ Vancouver assistant coach 1965/Richmond Over 40's.

Debut v Leicester City (h) 23.10.48

Len Wilkins was recruited to the Dell staff after being discovered by Arthur Holt playing for Cunliffe Owen's works' team. His debut at home to Leicester was completely overshadowed by Charlie Wayman's feat of scoring five goals, but Len was in the team to stay and over the next decade was to give the club sterling service. Whole-hearted, Len never spared himself on the field and became an invaluable link in the heart of the defence. Nicknamed "Spud" due to his vegetarian diet and a fondness for potatoes, he was able to play equally well in any of the defender's positions and became the natural choice for the team captaincy in 1954. An example of determination and effort, Len became very popular with the fans and when he left the pitch for the last time after the game against Watford in April 1958 he was given a rousing ovation. He had decided to emigrate and, once in Canada, lost no time signing on for his local team. Soccer, as a sport, was very much in the embryonic stage in North America at this time, but thanks to the sponsorship of a few committed individuals,

Len was able to be a member of various sides which often entertained visiting British clubs. In 1958 he played for the Ontario All Stars in games against Don Revie's Manchester City and the Mexican national side on their way to the 1958 World Cup. After moving to Los Angeles Len was selected in 1960 to represent California in a game against Manchester United played in San Francisco. In 1965 he and his family returned to Canada to settle in Vancouver and, ever since, he has coached a variety of local teams while continuing to play, up until 1990 aged 65, in an over-40's league. In October 1990 Len returned to Southampton for a holiday, visited the Dell, and found time to attend a nostalgic reunion with some of his ex-team mates.

Appearances:
FL: 260 app. 2 gls.
FAC: 14 app. 1 gl.
Total: *274 app. 3 gls.*

WILKINSON, Charles Edward

Role: Full-back 1938-39
5'10" 11st.10lbs.
b. Medomsley, Consett
7 May 1907
d. Medomsley, Consett
October qtr. 1975

CAREER: Consett/Leeds
United Sept 1928/ Sheffield
United Oct 1933/
SOUTHAMPTON July 1938/
Bournemouth player-coach Aug 1939.

Debut v Tottenham Hotspur (h) 27.8.38

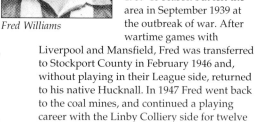
Charles Wilkinson

A member of Sheffield United's 1936 F.A. Cup
final side, Charles Wilkinson
exchanged the red and white stripes of
Sheffield for those of Southampton in
the summer of 1938. Unfortunately,
Charles sustained a serious knee injury
in only his second appearance which
required a cartilage removal and, by
the time he had recovered, the club had
signed Tom Emanuel as a replacement.

Appearances:
FL: 3 app. 0 gls.
Total: *3 app. 0 gls.*

WILLIAMS, Ernest W.

Role: Forward 1912-13
b. Ryde, Isle of Wight

CAREER: Ryde/Portsmouth Dec 1906/
Chelsea Dec 1909/SOUTHAMPTON 1912.

Debut v Brighton & Hove Albion (a) 19.10.12

Capped twice for England at amateur level in
1909, Ernest Williams came to the Dell towards
the end of an illustrious sporting career. He
played one senior match on the left-wing,
replacing the injured Len Andrews, before
calling it a day soon after.

Appearances:
SL: 1 app. 0 gls.
Total: *1 app. 0 gls.*

❑ **Saints note** - *Ernest played one match for
Hampshire County Cricket Club in 1904 when he
scored 15 and 1 in his two innings.*

WILLIAMS, Frederick Arthur

Role: Full-back 1938-39
5'8" 11st.10lbs.
b. Hucknall, Derbyshire 15 April 1918

CAREER: Hucknall Colts/
SOUTHAMPTON am. 1937, pro. May
1938/(Mansfield and Liverpool
during World War Two)/Stockport
County Feb 1946/Linby Colliery
1947-59.

Debut v Tottenham Hotspur (h) 27.8.38

Fred Williams had started his working life as a
Nottinghamshire coalminer in 1932, but came
south to join Southampton's nursery side as an
amateur in 1937. He made
rapid progress through the
ranks to become a regular
first-teamer at the outset of
the 1938-39 season. A tough
tackling defender, Fred
damaged an ankle in
January 1939 which
sidelined him for the rest of
the season. He played two
games in the aborted
1939-40 season but left the
area in September 1939 at
the outbreak of war. After
wartime games with
Liverpool and Mansfield, Fred was transferred
to Stockport County in February 1946 and,
without playing in their League side, returned
to his native Hucknall. In 1947 Fred went back
to the coal mines, and continued a playing
career with the Linby Colliery side for twelve
years.

Fred Williams

Appearances:
FL: 22 app. 0 gls.
Total: *22 app. 0 gls.*

WILLIAMS, George Henry

Role: Forward 1920-21
5'7" 10st.6lbs.
b. Ventnor, Isle of Wight 10 October 1897
d. Southampton 22 February 1957

CAREER: Pear Tree Congregationals/2nd/4th
Hampshire Regiment/SOUTHAMPTON am.
1919, pro. Oct 1920/Exeter City June 1921/

George Williams

Netley Sports Sept 1922/Cowes c.s. 1925/
Salisbury 1926.

Debut v Swindon Town (a) 6.9.20
*(scored on debut)

A local discovery, George Williams joined the
Saints upon leaving the army and, replacing
the injured Arthur Dominy, scored on his
debut. Finding his size a handicap, George
struggled to stamp his authority on the game
although, after a move to Exeter, he found
some success. A leg injury, however, wrecked
further progress and he had returned to
Hampshire League Football within a year of
leaving the Dell. A painter and decorator by
trade, George reverted to this after his
retirement from soccer.

Appearances:
FL: 2 app. 1 gl.
Total: 2 app. 1 gl.

WILLIAMS, Osher Joseph

Role: Forward 1978-79
5'10" 11st.3lbs.
b. Stockton-on-Tees 21 April 1958

CAREER: Middlesbrough app. July 1974/
Manchester United Aug 1976/Gateshead United/

SOUTHAMPTON
Mar 1978 (Exeter City-
loan-Aug-Sept 1979)/
Stockport County Aug
1979/Port Vale Nov
1984/Preston North
End Aug 1986/Cape
Town Spurs (South
Africa) c.s. 1988/
Winsford United/
Lancaster City/
Halifax Town Ass.
Manager Oct 1991.

Osher Williams

Debut v Arsenal (h) 3.3.79

Once on the books of both Middlesbrough and
Manchester United, Osher Williams had his
career resurrected by Lawrie McMenemy's
decision to sign him from non-league
Gateshead United: An orthodox winger, Osher
had plenty of natural ball-control and speed but
his final touch was sometimes lacking. After
leaving the Dell in the summer of 1979 Osher
became a first team regular for Stockport,
Port Vale and, finally, Preston. In 1988 after
spending the summer playing in Cape Town he
was heavily censored by the F.A. who objected
to his involvement in South African soccer.

Appearances:
FL: 4 (1) app. 0 gls.
Total: 4 (1) app. 0 gls.

WILLIAMS, Royston Brian

Role: Forward 1952-55
5'4" 10st.5lbs.
b. Hereford 3 March 1932

CAREER: Hereford Lads Club/Hereford
United Aug 1947/SOUTHAMPTON Nov 1952
/Hereford United July 1955.

Debut v Fulham (a) 26.12.52

Roy Williams was an inside-forward in
Hereford United's Southern League team
before his £4,000 transfer to the Dell. Standing
at five foot four and a half inches he was
possibly the smallest forward ever to be on the
club's books but he had a stocky build and
could "mix it" with the brawniest of defenders.
Referred to as the "little un" by the local press,
Roy scored on his home debut and was a first
team regular for two seasons. Returning to
Edgar Street in 1955, he went on to notch 123
goals in 260 Southern League games before

Roy Williams

strength, becoming the club's Player of the Year in 1977 and winning England Under-21 recognition. Blessed with an abundance of natural skill, Steve, with the ball at this feet, cut an assured figure and an instinctive vision usually led to his domination of midfield. A self-confessed bad loser, he was temperamentally similar to Alan Ball and playing alongside the 1966 World Cup star did much to further his development. One of few players who managed to combine skill with plenty of aggression he made the predicted transition into the full England team in 1983 and only an occasional petulance prevented his gaining more than five caps. He succeeded Alan Ball as team captain and, maturing in this new role, Steve led the side to Division One runners-up position in 1984, playing some outstanding football. The following year was to be a traumatic one for Southampton, with Lawrie McMenemy's disillusionment having a detrimental effect on the likes of Steve and

Steve William

receiving a benefit match (against Southampton) in April 1961. After retiring from football Roy ran his own window cleaning business in Hereford.

Appearances:
FL: 41 app. 7 gls.
FAC: 2 app. 0 gls.
Total: *43 app. 7 gls.*

WILLIAMS, Steven Charles

Role: Midfield 1975-85
5'11" 10st.11lbs.
b. Romford 12 July 1958

CAREER: St. Edwards School, Chadwell Heath/Havering Schools/SOUTHAMPTON app. Sept 1974, pro. July 1976/Arsenal Dec 1984/Luton Town July 1988/ SOUTHAMPTON trial July 1991/Exeter City asst. manager Aug 1991.

Debut v Portsmouth (a) 6.4.76

A product of the Saints' London Selection Centre, Steve Williams joined Southampton straight from school and stepped out of the youth team to make his senior debut a few days after the club had reached the F.A. Cup final in April 1976. He established himself the following season and went from strength to

Mark Wright and, in December, he was granted a transfer to Arsenal for a club record of £550,000. Over three and a half years at Highbury, Steve had some good, bad and indifferent games but never quite captured the magic or the enthusiasm he had shown as a youngster. He never really hit it off with Arsenal's manager George Graham and was allowed to move to Luton for £300,000 in July 1988. Many fans in Southampton had hoped Steve would return to the Dell but, with time running out, Steve's career seemed to be drawing to a quiet and somewhat unfulfilled conclusion. In July 1991 Ian Branfoot offered him a trial with Saints and for a brief spell supporters dreamt of past glories being resurrected; but it was not to be and Steve joined up with former team-mate Alan Ball, recently installed as Exeter's manager.

Appearances:
FL: 277 (2) app. 18 gls.
FAC: 27 app. 3 gls.
LC: 28 (1) app. 3 gls.
Eur: 12 (2) app. 24 gls.
Total: *344 (5) app. 48 gls.*

WILLIAMS, Stuart Grenville

Role: Full-back 1962-66
5'10" 12st.8lbs.
b. Wrexham 9 July 1930

CAREER: Acton Park & Grove Park Grammar Schools/Victoria Youth Club/Wrexham am. Aug 1949/West Bromwich Albion Nov 1950/ SOUTHAMPTON Sept 1962/West Bromwich Albion trainer July 1966/Aston Villa trainer 1970/Payhaan (Tehran) manager 1970-71/ Morton trainer July 1971/SOUTHAMPTON asst. manager-coach Aug 1971/Stavanger (coach) (Norway) c.s. 1973 - c.s. 1974/ Carlisle scout 1974-75.

Debut v Chelsea (h) 19.9.62

Stuart Williams' first taste of league action came as an amateur inside-forward with Wrexham where his father was a director. Against his father's wishes Stuart turned his back on a job in insurance for a living within the game, and his decision was vindicated by a sixteen-year career, which spanned over 400 games for his three clubs, plus 43 Welsh caps. After making his West Bromwich Albion debut

Stuart Williams

in the centre-forward position, Stuart switched to wing-half before settling into the full-back role. The highlight of his career came in the 1958 World Cup when Wales reached the quarter-finals only to lose by one goal (scored by Pele) to the eventual winners, Brazil. In 1962 Ted Bates paid £15,000 to bring the cultured full-back to the Dell and his experience over the next four years was to pay dividends as the club reached out for the First Division. Still good enough to win ten Welsh caps while at the Dell, Stuart retired from the game a few months short of his 36th birthday to return to the Hawthorns in a coaching capacity. Five years later he was back at the Dell as Ted Bates' assistant and kept this position until Ted himself retired in 1973. He quit football in 1975 and, settling in Southampton, became a representative with two tyre companies. In 1987 Stuart, who manages the ex-Saints XI, became the manager of a transport company.

Appearances:
FL: 148 (2) app. 3 gls.
FAC: 10 app. 0 gls.
LC: 7 app. 0 gls.
Total: *165 (2) app. 3 gls.*

❏ **Saints note** - *Winning 33 Welsh caps whilst at The Hawthorns, Stuart remains Albion's most-capped player.*

Stuart Williams with a couple of his Welsh caps

WILLIAMSON, H.

Role: Goalkeeper 1894-95

CAREER: SOUTHAMPTON St. Mary's Nov 1894/Royal Ordnance Factories 1896.
Debut v Millwall (h) 17.11.1894

Despite conceding a goal within three minutes of his St. Mary's debut, Williamson soon settled and helped the club through their inaugural season as a Southern League team. He left the Southampton area in 1895, moving to London to find employment. While in the capital Williamson assisted the Royal Ordnance at Maze Hill, Greenwich who, at the time, played in the same Southern League as St. Mary's. An ever-present in their disbanded side of 1896, Williamson was on the receiving end of a 10-0 defeat at the Antelope in October 1896.

Appearances:
SL: 12 app. 0 gls.
FAC: 2 app. 0 gls.
Total: *14 app. 0 gls.*

WILSON, Arthur

Role: Half-back 1929-32
6'0" 11st.7lbs.
b. Newcastle 6 October 1908

CAREER: Newcastle & Northumberland Schools/Newcastle United Swifts Nov 1926/ Scotswood/SOUTHAMPTON Aug 1927/West Ham United June 1932/Chester Mar 1934/ Wolverhampton Wanderers Nov 1937/ Torquay United Jan 1939.
Debut v Reading (a) 14.12.29

A talented schoolboy footballer, Arthur Wilson represented Newcastle and Northumberland Schools before he signed for the Magpies and played in Newcastle United's third team. He was allowed to leave for Scotswood from where Saints acted quickly to bring the teenager to the Dell. Showing admirable skill in his early reserve appearances Arthur was soon elevated into the first team and, over the next three years, featured regularly either as a half-back or an attacking inside-forward. Surprisingly to almost everyone in the town, Arthur was unexpectedly transfer-listed in May 1932 due to the club's worsening financial situation, and within a couple of months he

Arthur Wilson

had moved to Upton Park in exchange for a £500 cheque. A successful 1932-33 season in the Hammers' colours saw Arthur score a creditable 15 league and cup goals in thirty-three games.

Appearances:
FL: 62 app. 12 gls.
FAC: 3 app. 0 gls.
Total: 65 app. 12 gls.

❏ **Saints note** - *Arthur was also a talented sketch artist and a creditable billiards player.*

WILSON, Geoffrey Plumpton

Role: Forward 1901-02
b. Bourne 21 February 1878
d. Rutland 30 July 1934

CAREER: Rossall School/Corinthians 1898-1902/Casuals/SOUTHAMPTON Oct 1901/London Hospital.
Debut v Swindon Town (h) 19.10.01

Geoffrey Wilson was a member of the famed Corinthians amateur side and had the pleasure of scoring on his England debut against Wales in March 1900. A colleague of C. B. Fry, Geoffrey was a member of the Southampton forward line for three consecutive games in October 1901 replacing the injured Albert Brown. After showing flashes of his international quality Geoffrey left the Dell in November 1901 to concentrate on completing

his medical studies and became a qualified physician and surgeon a year later.

Appearances:
SL: 3 app. 0 gls.
Total: 3 app. 0 gls.

WIMSHURST, Kenneth Pinkney

Role: Half-back 1961-67
5'10" 11st.3lbs.
b. South Shields 23 March 1938

CAREER: South Shields/Newcastle United May 1957/Gateshead Nov 1958/Wolverhampton Wanderers Nov 1960/SOUTHAMPTON July 1961/Bristol City Oct 1967, coach c.s. 1972, joint caretaker-manager Sept 1980 (8.9.80 - 29.9.80) coaching in Egypt 1986/SOUTHAMPTON scout 1989, School of Excellence 1990.
Debut v Swansea Town (h) 2.9.61

Ken Wimshurst was signed for a modest £1,500 fee having been recommended to the club by former player Bill Rochford. Originally an inside-forward Ken switched to the right-half position and was soon regarded as a suave, confident player who liked to join in attacks as well as provide his forwards with a stylish and subtle service. Ken's form peaked during the 1963 F.A. Cup run when his

Ken Wimshurst

prompting and clever passing helped take the club to the semi-finals and there were whispers of some possible international recognition. Although England honours never materialised Ken played a significant part in Southampton's rise to First Division soccer before he was allowed to move to Ashton Gate in October 1967. In the late 1980's he became a shop manager in Bristol and in October 1990 was operating Southampton's School of Excellence in Bath.

Appearances:
FL: 148 (4) app. 9 gls.
FAC: 10 app. 2 gls.
LC: 9 app. 1 gl.
Total: *167 (4) app. 12 gls.*

❏ **Saints note** - *In September 1965 Ken became Southampton's first-ever substitute when, in a match at home against Coventry City, John Hollowbread was injured and had to leave the pitch. Cliff Huxford went into goal and Ken took over at left-half.*

WITHERS, Edward Peter

Role: Forward 1936-37
5'10" 10st.10lbs.
b. Ower, Hampshire 8 September 1915

CAREER: Stanley's Own Rover Scouts/ Clarke's College/SOUTHAMPTON am. Aug 1933, pro. Oct 1934/Bristol Rovers Dec 1937/ Bramtoco Sports c.s. 1938.
Debut v Swansea Town (a) 19.9.36

Ted Withers was a product of New Forest League football who initially joined the Saints ground staff as a amateur in the summer of 1933. Showing an eye for goal at county league level Ted was soon rewarded with a professional contract and established himself in the Combination side. During the 1936-37 season he appeared in four of the five forward positions without making any lasting impression and in December 1937 moved to Bristol Rovers. At Eastville Ted acquired the nickname "Tosh" but after a brief stay lasting just six months he was back in Southampton playing local soccer. He later moved to London where he took up work as a masseur.

Appearances:
FL: 6 app. 0 gls.
Total: *6 app. 0 gls.*

WOOD, Arthur

Role: Goalkeeper
1914-21
5'10" 12st.6lbs.
b. Walsall
14 January 1894
d. Portsmouth
8 April 1941

CAREER:
Portsmouth
Amateurs/
SOUTHAMPTON
am. 1914, pro.
1915/Clapton
Orient May 1921
/Ryde Sports c.s. 1931.
Debut v Luton Town (a) 9.9.14

Son of the great Southampton stalwart Harry Wood, Arthur followed in his father's footsteps, not as a goalgetter but as a goalstopper. As a youngster he had been taken to the Dell to watch his father but had been inspired by the exploits of two great Southampton 'keepers, Clawley and Robinson. Given a trial in April 1913 Arthur was duly taken onto the Dell staff and realised his boyhood ambitions by making his debut between the posts in September 1914. Sharing the goalkeeping duties with Ernie Steventon

Ted Withers

Arthur Wood

throughout the 1914-15 season, Arthur had his career interrupted by the Great War although, after enlisting in the Royal Engineers, he still managed to make regular appearances in Saints' wartime line-ups. Resuming his professional career in May 1919 following his demobilisation, Arthur's nerve, coolness and judgement seemed to ensure a long future at the Dell. However, with the arrival of Tommy Allen, Arthur lost his place and, not content with reserve football he moved to Clapton Orient where he became something of an institution with 374 league outings over a ten year period.

Appearances:
SL: 41 app. 0 gls.
FL: 2 app. 0 gls.
FAC: 4 app. 0 gls.
Total: *47 app. 0 gls.*

WOOD, Harry

Role: Forward
1898-1905
5'9" 13st.3lbs.
b. Walsall 26 June 1868
d. Portsmouth
5 July 1951

CAREER: Walsall Town Swifts/ Wolverhampton Wanderers 1887/ Walsall c.s. 1891/ Wolverhampton Wanderers Nov 1891/ SOUTHAMPTON May 1898/ Portsmouth trainer 1905-12.

Debut v Brighton United (h) 3.9.1898

Harry Wood stands out as probably the most popular footballer to wear the Saints' colours during the Southern League era. It was the Saints' trainer, Billy Dawson, who the club had

to thank for Harry's signature. Billy had been on a short holiday in Stoke and noticed in a daily newspaper that Wood had not yet renewed terms with his club, Wolves. After eventually locating Harry in a Walsall pub, Billy set abut persuading the talented forward to sign for the Saints and duly secured his man the next day, completing the formalities in the waiting room of Birmingham Railway station. Harry was immediately made team captain and with his vast experience and wonderful resourcefulness, was football wisdom personified. While at Wolves Harry had won two England caps and an F.A. Cup-Winners' medal and, at the Dell, complimented these achievements by adding four Southern League Championships. His cunning passing and influence on younger colleagues earned him the nickname of "the wolff" and for seven years he presided over one of the most successful periods in the club's history. After spending another seven years as Pompey's trainer, Harry settled in the Portsmouth area to become licensee of the Milton Arms, a stone's throw from Fratton Park.

Appearances:
SL: 158 app. 62 gls.
FAC: 22 app. 3 gls.
Total: *180 app. 65 gls.*

WOODFORD, George Arthur

Role: Full-back 1937-39
5'10" 11st.10lbs.
b. Lymington 22 April 1915
d. Lymington 21 April 1966

CAREER: Lymington/Norwich City am. Oct 1934, pro. Sept 1935/SOUTHAMPTON June 1937/Lymington c.s. 1939.

Debut v Norwich City (h) 1.1.38

Although born in Hampshire, George Woodford's footballing career commenced under Tom Parker's guidance at Norwich. He made ten appearances for the Canaries before following his manager to the Dell and for two years became a useful deputy for either Sillett or Roberts. Able to use both feet with equal facility, George's play was summed up by one Southampton onlooker as "the outstanding

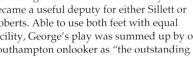

George Woodford

Stan Woodhouse

traits of his game are industry and mobility". After just one outing during the 1938-39 season George joined his home town club, Lymington, on a free transfer.

Appearances:
FL: 7 app. 0 gls.
Total: *7 app. 0 gls.*

WOODHOUSE, Stanley

Role: Half-back 1924-36
5'9" 11st.7lbs.
b. Warrington 20 February 1899
d. Southampton 18 March 1977

CAREER: Monkshill/Bury May 1921/ SOUTHAMPTON May 1924/Basingstoke c.s. 1936/SOUTHAMPTON A & B team trainer 1951-52.

Debut v Oldham Athletic (h) 30.8.24

Arriving at the Dell in 1924 as part of an exchange deal that saw Bill Turner move to Bury, Stan Woodhouse became a fixture at left-half and was, besides Bert Shelley, to make more appearances than any other Saint. An

unsung player during his twelve years at the Dell, Stan was nevertheless a vital cog in the team and his probing passes were a special feature of his game. After leaving the playing staff in 1936 Stan had a brief sojourn at Basingstoke before returning to Southampton to become licensee of the 'Bricklayers Arms' in Warren Avenue.

Appearances:
FL: 351 app. 5 gls.
FAC: 15 app. 0 gls.
Total: *366 app. 5 gls.*

WOOLF, Len James

Role: Forward 1937-38
5'8" 10st.7lbs.
b. Johannesburg, South Africa 1916

CAREER: J.R.A.S. Johannesburg/ SOUTHAMPTON Sept 1937/Guildford City Aug 1938.

Debut v Tottenham Hotspur (h) 11.12.37

Growing up in South Africa, Jimmy Woolf was determined to become a professional footballer in England and in September 1937 he paid for his own passage to Britain in an effort to achieve his ambition. It was a steward on board the Union Castle liner, Balmoral Castle, who, learning of Jimmy's intentions, decided to cable Southampton's manager, Tom Parker. The Southampton management must have had a high regard for the steward's judgement for Jimmy was met at Southampton Docks and signed after a trial match. He figured regularly at inside-right for the combination side and his consistent scoring led to him being given his first team chance in December 1937. Unable to make much of an impression, Jimmy was allowed to move to Guildford in the summer of 1938 where it was hoped he would gain experience playing in the Southern League. The war interrupted any further progress and Jimmy, after seeing active service in Burma, decided to return to South Africa with the resumption of peace.

Appearances:
FL: 1 app. 0 gls.
Total: *1 app. 0 gls.*

WORTHINGTON,
Frank Stewart

Role: Forward 1983-84
5'11" 11st.9lbs.
b. Halifax 23 November 1948

CAREER: Huddersfield Town app. Apr 1964, pro. Nov 1966/Leicester City Aug 1972/Bolton Wanderers Sept 1977 (Philadelphia Fury-loan May 1979)/Birmingham City Nov 1979 (Tampa Bay Rowdies-loan-Apr 1981)/ Leeds United Mar 1982/ Sunderland Dec 1982/ SOUTHAMPTON June 1983/Brighton May 1984/ Tranmere Rovers player-manager July 1985/Preston North End Feb 1987/ Stockport County Nov 1987/Cape Town Spurs Apr 1988 /Chorley Oct 1988 /Stalybridge Celtic Dec 1988/Galway United Feb

Frank Worthington

1989/Weymouth Sept 1989/Guiseley Nov 1989/Hinckley Town player-manager Sept 1990 - Apr 1991/Cemaes Bay c.s. 1991/ Halifax Town player-asst. coach Aug 1991.

Debut v Nottingham Forest (a) 27.8.83

A soccer gypsy and a flamboyant personality on and off the pitch, Frank Worthington made Southampton his seventh league club in the summer of 1983. Frank's stay was short, just a year, but in that time his extravagant ball skills and close control thrilled the fans especially as the club finished runners-up in Division One. Although his scoring ratio as a Saint was poor, his cunning flicks and subtle distribution were the ideal foil for his younger forward colleagues Moran and Wallace. His maverick attitude to the game stirred the man on the terraces but did not always endear him to the authorities and Frank's skill should have been rewarded with more than eight England caps. He left the Dell in May 1984 after failing to agree terms and then, within a year, had shouldered managerial responsibility at Tranmere. From then on Frank has continued to "live out of his suitcase" displaying, it seems, a horror of ever remaining at one club for too long. When he left Stockport for South Africa in April 1988 Frank had set a record of scoring league goals in each of twenty-one successive seasons but was far from ready to exchange his football boots for carpet slippers. He has since hit the non-league trail while also taking part in the over-35's World Cup which took place in South America in January 1989.

Appearances:
FL: 34 app. 4 gls.
FAC: 6 app. 0 gls.
LC: 2 app. 0 gls.
Total: *42 app. 4 gls.*

❏ **Saints note** - *Frank has two brothers, Dave and Bob, who have also been professional footballers. Both men started at Halifax Town. Dave went on to play over 300 games for Grimsby Town and Bob made over 200 appearances for Notts County.*

WRIGGLESWORTH, William Herbert

Role: Forward 1947-48
5′4″ 9st. 4lbs.
b. South Elmsall 12 November 1912

CAREER: Frickley Colliery/Chesterfield May 1932/Wolverhampton Wanderers Dec 1934/ Manchester United Jan 1937/(Walsall, Chelsea and Arsenal during World War Two) Bolton Wanderers Jan 1947/SOUTHAMPTON Oct 1947/Reading June 1948/Burton Albion player-manager 1949/Scarborough Dec 1949/ Accrington Stanley coach.

Debut v Coventry City (h) 18.10.47
*(scored on debut)

A diminutive left-winger Billy Wrigglesworth was very much at the veteran stage by the time of his arrival at the Dell and his transfer was part of an exchange deal that saw Jack Bradley move to Burnden Park. "Wriggy" as he was soon christened, had the unusual and crowd-pleasing habit of trapping the ball with his backside, a feat that won him notoriety amongst the fans. He had the misfortune to suffer an ankle injury in January 1948 and from then on found it impossible to win back his

Billy Wrigglesworth

place from Wilf Grant. After declining proposed moves to York City and Hull, Billy chose to move to Elm Park where, after just five games, he retired from the professional scene.

Appearances:
FL: 12 app. 4 gls.
FAC: 2 app. 0 gls.
Total: 14 app. 4 gls.

WRIGHT, Frank

Role: Forward 1920-21
5′10″ 11st.6lbs.
b. Birmingham October qtr. 1898

CAREER: Hampstead Colliery/ SOUTHAMPTON Oct 1920.

Debut v Grimsby Town (a) 11.12.20

A Birmingham Association representative player while with Hampstead Colliery, Frank Wright was a right-winger who arrived at the Dell soon after the club's entry into the Football League. He showed early promise but, on his debut, the team was soundly beaten 3-0 at Grimsby and he made a swift return to the reserves. Unfortunately his brief experience in the first team seemed to dent his confidence for, in twenty-six subsequent combination games, he found the net just once - form which led to his release in May 1921.

Appearances:
FL: 1 app. 0 gls.
Total: 1 app. 0 gls.

WRIGHT, Mark

Role: Centre-half 1981-87
6′2″ 11st.6lbs.
b. Dorchester-on-Thames 1 August 1963

CAREER: Oxford United Aug 1980/ SOUTHAMPTON Mar 1982/Derby County Aug 1987/Liverpool July 1991.

Debut v Leeds United (a) 17.4.82

Although Mark Wright had only made nine full appearances in Oxford United's first team, his form and promise had been noted by Joe Mallett who, as a Saints' scout, wasted little time in passing on his recommendations. Mark arrived at the Dell in March 1982 along with

Mark Wright

fellow Oxford team-mate, Keith Cassells, and was given his debut the following month in the number nine shirt. His tall but slight build made him an obvious candidate for a central defender's role but initially in this position he appeared gangly and even awkward. As the 1982-83 season unwound however, Mark matured into a graceful and poised defender, a phenomenon hitherto unknown in post-war Southampton defences. The calm but purposeful way he brought the ball forward in preference to the usual belted clearance was an early indication of Mark's potential and, once he had refined his occasionally impetuous tackling, his England call-up was inevitable. Capped at Under-21 level within a year, Mark won his full colours against Wales at Wrexham in May 1984 and the 1986 World Cup beckoned. Fate delivered a cruel blow to both him and the club when, a few months before the tournament, Mark sustained a broken leg in the F.A. Cup semi-final against Liverpool which not only ended Southampton's aspirations of a trip to Wembley but Mark's ambitions of appearing for his country in Mexico. His recovery was complete but with it came an unsettled period which culminated in a transfer request. In the past Mark had gained the reputation of being determined, almost headstrong, but Lawrie McMenemy had always managed to soothe, guide and cajole him. Unfortunately in 1987 McMenemy was no longer at the Dell and Mark's strong determination to leave was not matched by the club's ability to hold on to him and Derby County acquired his skills for a bargain £760,000. Since then, while Southampton have vainly searched for a comparable replacement, Mark's career has gone from strength to strength and in the 1990 World Cup he emerged as one of the tournament's finest players. Following the Rams' relegation back to Division Two, Mark moved to Anfield in July 1991 with Graeme Souness splashing out a hefty £2.2 million fee to acquire his considerable defensive talents.

Jimmy Yates

Appearances:
FL: 170 app. 7 gls.
FAC: 17 app. 1 gl.
LC: 25 app. 2 gls.
Eur: 4 app. 1 gl.
Total: *216 app. 11 gls.*

"Tiny" Yeomans

YATES, James

Role: Forward 1897-98, 1898-1901 & 1904-1905
5' 6" 11st.12lbs.
b. Sheffield 1871
d. Southampton 5 September 1922

CAREER: Ardwick Nov 1892/Sheffield United
Dec 1893/SOUTHAMPTON St. Mary's c.s.
1897/Gravesend c.s. 1898/ SOUTHAMPTON
Mar 1899/Hastings & St. Leonards United c.s.
1901/Copenhagen F.C. coach
1903/SOUTHAMPTON 1905/ Gravesend
1905/Hastings & St. Leonards United during
1905-06/Coach in Brazil and U.S.A. in
1906/Salisbury City 1908-09.

Debut v Tottenham Hotspur (a) 18.9.1897

Experienced in the very best class of football,
Jimmy Yates had been Sheffield United's
outside-right for the previous four seasons
before joining Saints in 1897. A dapper, clever
forward, Jimmy, when at his best, was
virtually unstoppable but his first season with
the club was dogged by ill-health. For that
reason he did not re-sign and instead moved to
the Kent coast to play for Gravesend. He was
back again within a year and this time
rediscovered his true form to play a significant
part in the 1899 and 1901 Southern League
Championships. Jimmy left the Saints for a
second time in the summer of 1901 to play in
Sussex but he kept in touch by scouting for his
old club. In March 1905 he marked his third
spell at Southampton by making one
appearance at home to Northampton Town
and thus became the only player in the club's
history to have signed on for three separate
periods. The next year Jimmy coached both in
South and North America before, in 1907,
returning to Southampton to take up an offer
of a stevedore's job in the Docks. Life was not
too good for Jimmy in his later years, for ill-
health led to unemployment and sadly he was
to commit suicide in September 1922.

Appearances:
SL: 63 app. 16 gls.
FAC: 14 app. 6 gls.
Total: *77 app. 22 gls.*

YEOMANS, Harry Arthur

Role: Goalkeeper
1924-26
6'4" 12st.0lbs.
b. Farnborough 11 April 1901
d. Lavendon 25 February 1965

CAREER: Camberley & Yorktown/
SOUTHAMPTON am.1922, pro. Dec 1922/
Southampton Police 1926.

Debut v Leicester City (a) 14.4.25

A Hampshire County goalkeeper, "Tiny"
Yeomans signed amateur forms in December
1922 and professional forms fifteen days later.
The tallest goalkeeper (along with George
Ephgrave) ever to play for Saints, "Tiny" was
Tommy Allen's understudy and, as a
consequence, never enjoyed a lengthy run in
the first team. In 1926 he decided to abandon
his footballing career to join the Southampton
Police Force although he continued to keep
goal for his new employees.

Appearances:
FL: 12 app. 0 gls.
Total: *12 app. 0 gls.*

Saints players pictured at the Clump Inn, Chilworth prior to the 1902 FA Cup Final

Appearances & Goalscorers for the minor first team competitions during the club's Southern League era 1894-1919.

Abbreviations:
UL: United League 1897-99.
SDC: Southern District Combination 1899-1900
WL: Western League 1900-09
SA: Southern Alliance 1912-14

In 1897 the Saints entered the United League to augment their Southern League matches which, at the time, were too infrequent to bring in a regular income at the turnstiles. After two seasons they entered the Southern District Combination and followed this by entering the Western League. All these matches were regarded as first team fixtures and not only provided much needed revenue, but also enabled the club to give trials to up-and-coming youngsters. In 1912 the Saints also entered a mid-week league known as the Southern Alliance League and this gave the opportunity to people who worked on Saturdays to view matches on a midweek afternoon.

	Appearances					Goals				
	UL	SDC	WL	SA	Total	UL	SDC	WL	SA	Total
Andrews, L.T.	-	-	-	24	24	-	-	-	11	11
Angell, J.W.	-	-	1	-	1	-	-	-	-	-
Bainbridge, J.	-	-	13	-	13	-	-	1	-	1
Ball	-	-	3	-	3	-	-	-	-	-
Baringer, J.	-	-	-	1	1	-	-	-	-	-
Barlow, T.	-	-	12	-	12	-	-	5	-	5
Bell, E.I.	-	-	2	-	2	-	-	1	-	1
Bell, M.	-	-	10	-	10	-	-	2	-	2
Benson, R.	-	-	9	-	9	-	-	-	-	-
Bickell	1	-	-	-	1	-	-	-	-	-
Binder, T.	-	-	-	12	12	-	-	-	1	1
Blackburn, A.	-	-	6	-	6	-	-	-	-	-
Blackmore, W.	-	-	-	3	3	-	-	-	-	-
Blacktin, J.	-	-	2	-	2	-	-	-	-	-
Blair	1	-	-	-	1	-	-	-	-	-
Blake, J.J.	-	-	2	17	19	-	-	-	1	1
Bluff, E.U.	-	-	9	-	9	-	-	3	-	3
Bowden, T.	-	-	7	-	7	-	-	-	-	-
Bowman, T.	-	-	43	-	43	-	-	2	-	2
Bradley, J.W.	-	-	-	4	4	-	-	-	3	3
Bright	-	-	-	3	3	-	-	-	-	-
Brooks, R.	-	-	-	15	15	-	-	-	-	-
Brown, A.	-	-	12	-	12	-	-	6	-	6
Brown, H.	-	-	14	1	15	-	-	8	-	8
Brown, R.	12	-	-	-	12	2	-	-	-	2
Buchanan, R.	13	-	-	-	13	4	-	-	-	4
Buckley, A.	-	-	-	4	4	-	-	-	-	-
Bundy, W.	-	-	1	-	1	-	-	-	-	-
Burrows, T.	-	-	17	-	17	-	-	-	-	-
Butt, L.G.	-	-	-	5	5	-	-	-	-	-

	Appearances					Goals				
	UL	SDC	WL	SA	Total	UL	SDC	WL	SA	Total
Byrne, M.	-	-	1	-	1	-	-	-	-	-
Campbell, A.K.	-	-	1	1	2	-	-	-	-	-
Cavendish, S.	-	4	6	-	10	-	2	1	-	3
Chadwick, A.	26	9	6	-	41	3	1	-	-	4
Chadwick, E.	-	-	26	-	26	-	-	7	-	7
Clarke	-	-	-	1	1	-	-	-	-	-
Clarke, W.	-	-	20	-	20	-	-	-	-	-
Clawley, G.	15	-	51	-	66	-	-	-	-	-
Click, F.	-	-	2	-	2	-	-	-	-	-
Coates, A.	-	-	-	12	12	-	-	-	-	-
Coham, J.H.	-	-	1	-	1	-	-	-	-	-
Coleman	-	-	1	-	1	-	-	-	-	-
Costello, F.	-	-	13	-	13	-	-	5	-	5
Cotton, J.	-	-	1	-	1	-	-	-	-	-
Crabbe, W.	-	2	-	-	2	-	-	-	-	-
Cust, J.	3	-	-	-	3	-	-	-	-	-
Dainty, H.	-	-	11	-	11	-	-	3	-	3
Dawe, L.S.	-	-	-	1	1	-	-	-	1	1
Dawson, H.	-	-	2	-	2	-	-	-	-	-
Denby, J.	-	-	-	17	17	-	-	-	2	2
Desbrow	-	-	1	-	1	-	-	-	-	-
Dewar, G.	5	-	-	-	5	-	-	-	-	-
Diaper, A.	-	-	-	5	5	-	-	-	-	-
Dobson, W.	-	-	-	3	3	-	-	-	-	-
Dominy, A.A.	-	-	-	6	6	-	-	-	1	1
Durber, P.	13	11	-	-	24	-	-	-	-	-
Eastham, J.	-	-	20	-	20	-	-	-	-	-
Edmonds, T.	-	-	5	-	5	-	-	-	-	-
Englefield, F.	2	4	-	-	6	1	-	-	-	1
Evans, R.	-	-	18	-	18	-	-	4	-	4
Everist, F..	-	-	1	-	1	-	-	-	-	-
Fairgrieve, W.	1	-	-	-	1	-	-	-	-	-
Farrell, J.	7	12	-	-	19	1	2	-	-	3
Fitchett, J.	-	-	10	-	10	-	-	3	-	3
Fraser, J.	-	-	28	-	28	-	-	9	-	9
French, J.	-	3	2	-	5	-	-	-	-	-
Fry, C.B.	-	-	4	-	4	-	-	-	-	-
George, W.	-	-	2	-	2	-	-	-	-	-
Glen, A.	-	-	7	-	7	-	-	3	-	3
Glover, H.V.	-	-	24	-	24	-	-	3	-	3
Gordon, D.	-	-	6	-	6	-	-	-	-	-
Gray, W.	-	-	8	-	8	-	-	-	-	-
Greenhalgh, S.	-	-	1	-	1	-	-	-	-	-
Greenlees, D.	-	10	-	-	10	-	-	-	-	-
Hadley, G.A.	-	-	-	6	6	-	-	-	-	-
Hadley, H.	-	-	7	-	7	-	-	-	-	-
Harmsworth, C.	-	1	-	-	1	-	-	-	-	-
Harris, G.	-	-	19	-	19	-	-	5	-	5
Harrison, F.	-	-	76	-	76	-	-	62	-	62

	Appearances					Goals				
	UL	SDC	WL	SA	Total	UL	SDC	WL	SA	Total
Hartley, A.	17	-	-	-	17	21	-	-	-	21
Harthshorne, A.	-	-	17	-	17	-	-	-	-	-
Haxton, F.	-	-	5	-	5	-	-	-	-	-
Haynes, H.	26	6	-	-	32	1	-	-	-	1
Hedley, G.	-	-	30	-	30	-	-	18	-	18
Henderson, W.	-	-	12	-	12	-	-	-	-	-
Hinton, J.	-	-	-	3	3	-	-	-	3	3
Hoare, J.	-	-	7	-	7	-	-	-	-	-
Hodgkinson, A.	-	-	21	-	21	-	-	5	-	5
Hogg, J.	-	-	20	-	20	-	-	1	-	1
Hoskins, A.	-	-	5	-	5	-	-	2	-	2
Houlker, A.	-	-	26	-	26	-	-	1	-	1
Howland, C.	-	-	1	-	1	-	-	-	-	-
Hughes, A.	-	-	4	-	4	-	-	3	-	3
Hunter	-	-	-	1	1	-	-	-	-	-
Ireland, G.	-	-	1	-	1	-	-	-	-	-
Ireland, S.	-	-	-	19	19	-	-	-	2	2
Jacques	1	-	-	-	1	-	-	-	-	-
Jacques	-	-	1	-	1	-	-	-	-	-
Jefferis, F.	-	-	29	-	29	-	-	9	-	9
Jepp, S.	-	-	12	-	12	-	-	1	-	1
Johnston, J.S.	-	-	16	-	16	-	-	-	-	-
Johnston, A.	-	-	1	-	1	-	-	-	-	-
Jordan, F.	-	-	6	-	6	-	-	3	-	3
Joyce, J.	2	6	-	-	8	-	-	-	-	-
Joyce, W.	1	1	-	-	2	-	-	-	-	-
Keay, W.	22	5	-	-	27	5	-	-	-	5
Killean, E.	-	-	11	-	11	-	-	1	-	1
Kimpton, G.S.	-	-	-	14	14	-	-	-	4	4
Kitchen, G.	-	-	-	13	13	-	-	-	-	-
Knight, W.	-	-	-	8	8	-	-	-	-	-
Lee, A.	-	1	69	12	82	-	-	4	-	4
Lewis, J.	-	-	8	-	8	-	-	2	-	2
Liddell, E.	-	-	5	-	5	-	-	-	-	-
Littlehales, A.	3	-	-	-	3	-	-	-	-	-
Lock, H.	-	-	19	-	19	-	-	-	-	-
McAlpine, J.	-	-	-	21	21	-	-	-	1	1
McConnichie, J.	-	-	1	-	1	-	-	-	-	-
McDonald, A.	-	-	7	-	7	-	-	3	-	3
McGhee, G.	-	-	2	-	2	-	-	2	-	2
McGuigan	-	-	1	-	1	-	-	-	-	-
McKenzie, J.	8	-	-	-	8	1	-	-	-	1
McLean, D.	9	-	-	-	9	3	-	-	-	3
McLean, R.	-	-	3	-	3	-	-	-	-	-
McLeod, R.	-	12	-	-	12	-	3	-	-	3
McMillan, J.	9	-	-	-	9	-	-	-	-	-
McNee	-	-	1	-	1	-	-	-	-	-
McPherson, W.	-	-	1	-	1	-	-	1	-	1
Martin, H.	-	-	1	-	1	-	-	-	-	-

	Appearances					Goals				
	UL	SDC	WL	SA	Total	UL	SDC	WL	SA	Total
Meehan, P.	13	12	-	-	25	-	-	-	-	-
Meston, S.	31	12	73	-	116	3	-	3	-	6
Metcalf, T.	-	-	9	-	9	-	-	1	-	1
Milward, A.	-	13	10	-	23	-	4	1	-	5
Moger, H.	-	-	14	-	14	-	-	-	-	-
Molyneux, G.	-	-	67	-	67	-	-	-	-	-
Moore, F.	-	-	1	-	1	-	-	-	-	-
Mouncher, F.	-	-	49	-	49	-	-	5	-	5
Naughton, W.	3	-	-	-	3	2	-	-	-	2
Nicol, T.	19	-	-	-	19	2	-	-	-	2
Norbury, D.V.	-	-	2	-	2	-	-	-	-	-
Norris, T.	-	-	-	1	1	-	-	-	-	-
Northey, G.	-	-	1	-	1	-	-	-	-	-
Oatley	-	-	-	1	1	-	-	-	-	-
Paddington, A.	-	2	15	-	17	-	-	-	-	-
Parsons	-	-	-	2	2	-	-	-	-	-
Penton, B.	-	-	-	3	3	-	-	-	1	1
Petrie, R.	18	8	-	-	26	-	-	-	-	-
Phillips	-	-	-	1	1	-	-	-	-	-
Ponting, W.	3	-	-	-	3	-	-	-	-	-
Porter, N.	-	-	-	2	2	-	-	-	-	-
Pothercary	-	-	-	4	4	-	-	-	-	-
Prince, P.	-	-	1	14	15	-	-	-	4	4
Radford, W.	-	-	3	-	3	-	-	2	-	2
Reynolds, J.	5	-	-	-	5	-	-	-	-	-
Richman	-	-	1	-	1	-	-	1	-	1
Robertson, J.N.	-	-	18	-	18	-	-	-	-	-
Robertson, J.T.	12	-	-	-	12	5	-	-	-	5
Robertson, T.	-	-	25	-	25	-	-	-	-	-
Robinson, J.	18	10	30	-	58	-	-	-	-	-
Salmon	-	1	-	-	1	-	-	-	-	-
Salway, E.E.	-	-	-	19	19	-	-	-	1	1
Sanders, W.	-	-	-	1	1	-	-	-	-	-
Seeley, G.	8	-	-	-	8	-	-	-	-	-
Shand, H.	-	-	1	-	1	-	-	-	-	-
Sharp, B.	-	-	10	-	10	-	-	-	-	-
Shearer, S.	-	-	5	-	5	-	-	-	-	-
Slade, R.	-	-	-	4	4	-	-	-	-	-
Small, A.	-	-	-	4	4	-	-	-	2	2
Small, H.	-	-	12	-	12	-	-	4	-	4
Small, J.	-	-	-	11	11	-	-	-	3	3
Smith, E.	-	1	4	-	5	-	-	-	-	-
Smith, F.	-	-	-	3	3	-	-	-	-	-
Smith, G.	-	-	10	-	10	-	-	3	-	3
Smith, S.	-	-	6	-	6	-	-	1	-	1
Smith, T.	10	-	-	-	10	5	-	-	-	5
Smith, W.	-	-	-	10	10	-	-	-	3	3
Smith, W.G.	-	-	4	1	5	-	-	-	-	-
Smoker, H.	-	1	-	-	1	-	-	-	-	-

	Appearances					Goals				
	UL	SDC	WL	SA	Total	UL	SDC	WL	SA	Total
Soye, J.	-	-	15	-	15	-	-	7	-	7
Spence, G.	-	-	9	-	9	-	-	2	-	2
Stead, W.	-	-	3	-	3	-	-	-	-	-
Steele	1	-	-	-	1	-	-	-	-	-
Steven, D.	15	-	-	-	15	3	-	-	-	3
Steventon, E.	-	-	-	9	9	-	-	-	-	-
Taylor, F.	-	-	-	12	12	-	-	-	4	4
Taylor	2	-	-	-	2	1	-	-	-	1
Thomas	2	-	-	-	2	1	-	-	-	1
Thorpe, F.	-	-	17	-	17	-	-	-	-	-
Toman, W.	-	-	9	-	9	-	-	3	-	3
Tomlinson, I.	-	-	15	-	15	-	-	3	-	3
Toomer, W.	-	-	2	3	5	-	-	-	-	-
Travers	-	-	2	-	2	-	-	-	-	-
Triggs, W.	-	-	3	-	3	-	-	-	-	-
Triggs	1	-	-	-	1	-	-	-	-	-
Trueman, A.	-	-	10	-	10	-	-	1	-	1
Turnbull, F.	-	-	-	10	10	-	-	-	2	2
Turner, A.	-	11	21	-	32	-	1	10	-	11
Turner, H.	-	1	17	-	18	-	-	1	-	1
Turner, J.	13	-	34	-	47	3	-	10	-	13
Waller, W.	-	-	2	-	2	-	-	-	-	-
Ward, A.	-	-	3	-	3	-	-	-	-	-
Warner, J.	-	-	7	-	7	-	-	-	-	-
Webb, C.	-	-	9	-	9	-	-	1	-	1
Welsh, S.F.	-	-	1	-	1	-	-	-	-	-
Whiting, W.	-	-	12	-	12	-	-	-	-	-
Wiggins	-	-	-	1	1	-	-	-	-	-
Wildig	-	-	2	-	2	-	-	-	-	-
Wilson, G.	-	-	1	-	1	-	-	-	-	-
Wood, A.	-	-	-	1	1	-	-	-	-	-
Wood, H.	18	9	58	-	85	6	5	8	-	19
Usher	-	-	1	-	1	-	-	-	-	-
Yates, J.	6	9	14	-	29	-	4	4	-	8
Young	-	-	-	2	2	-	-	-	-	-
Youtman, B.A.	-	-	-	1	1	-	-	-	-	-
Yorke, C	-	-	3	-	3	-	-	-	-	-

Harland & Wolff 1918-19 with South Hants Championship Trophy

(Players only)   Unknown   T. Hogg

Tom Dominy (SFC Reserves)   J. Small (SFC)   Unknown

Unknown   Unknown   A. Andrews (SFC)   McAlpine (SFC)

S. Charcraft (Ex SFC Reserves)   A Dominy (SFC)   W. Rawlings (SFC)   D. Slade (Ex SFC)   H. Burnham

Appearances & Goalscorers for the First World War period 1915-1919.

Competitive matches only

Abbreviations:
SWC: South Western Combination 1915-16
LC: London Combination 1916-17
SHWL: South Hants War League 1917-19

In July 1915 representatives of all the major league competitions, including the Southern League, decided at a meeting in Blackpool that, although strictly competitive football should be suspended, it was in the interest of public morale that the game should be kept going in some form. Southampton, being a port employing thousands on vital war work in the docks (for the majority of whom the Saturday match at the Dell was their only entertainment), endeavoured to comply with the decision, despite a working loss of £1,991 on the previous season. Initially the fixture list consisted of friendlies but, with many teams dropping out, the season looked a thin one. Luckily the South Western League was formed in January 1916 and provided excellent sporting football with Saints just finishing behind Portsmouth. Season 1916-17 saw entry into a strong London Combination with games against some of the country's top clubs such as Arsenal and Tottenham. Unfortunately many of the London clubs found it difficult to travel outside the capital, and so at a meeting of the Combination in July 1917 Southampton, together with Portsmouth, Luton and Watford, were omitted from the 1917-18 fixture list. The prospect of league football now looked bleak, especially when the proposal of a United Services League fell through in September 1917, and it looked as if the club would have to manage with just another series of friendlies. A special meeting at the Dell in November 1917, at the request of Saints, saw the formation of the South Hants War League, and, together with Portsmouth, Cowes, Thornycrofts, Harland & Wolff and two military sides, the league kicked off in January 1918. Saints covered themselves with no glory in this League's two seasons before the normal league programme resumed in 1919, finding it nearly impossible to field a regular eleven. Things were so bad at times that the directors did not know who were to don the boots and jerseys until a few minutes before the kick-off. To make matters worse, a number of the club's old players such as Dominy, Kimpton, McAlpine, Small and Slade were to be found in their opponents' line-ups. Indeed in one match nine out the eleven players opposed to them were old Saints.

THE PLAYERS
For the duration of the war Saints enlisted the services of many local amateurs, servicemen stationed in the area, guest players and several of the club's pre-war professionals. **William Ellerington**, a Middlesbrough player and father of Bill (1945-1956), assisted the club while employed in war work at Harland & Wolff Shipyards, as did **Donald Slade**, a former player, who had played for Fulham prior to the outbreak of war. Of the servicemen who assisted Saints there were Corporal **John Quinn**, a Clyde forward previously with Manchester United, Manchester City and Grimsby; **Eric Tomkins** of Northampton, a member of the Royal Flying Corps and a county player at both hockey and cricket; Sergeant **John Milne**, a Clydebank player who served Saints for three years, netting twelve league goals in forty games; and Corporal **William Henry**, a Manchester City stalwart who was stationed at Aldershot in 1916.

Guest players included **John Moore** who won a cup winners medal while with Barnsley in 1912, together with **Fred Foxall, Fred Titmuss, Reg Hackett, Jos Barratt, H. Fenwick** and **George Bradburn** who all arrived from other clubs during the war and found themselves employed by Saints on the resumption of league soccer in 1919.

Local players discovered by the club in the later years of the war included **Tom Parker, Bill Rawlings** and **Arthur Andrews**.

Alfred Jewett and **Charles Bosbury** also met with some success after wartime action with Saints. Alfred was a member of the famous Thornycroft's side that met Burnley in 1920 and later joined Arsenal before finding regular league action with Lincoln City. Bosbury, although signed by Saints and released in 1921, joined Birmingham where he had a brief spell of fifteen league appearances.

		Appearances				Goals			
	Seasons	SWC	LC	SHWL	Total	SWC	LC	SHWL	Total
Andrews, A.	1918-19	-	-	5	5	-	-	-	-
Andrews, D.	1917-18	-	-	2	2	-	-	-	-
Andrews, L.A.	1915-16	2	-	-	2	2	-	-	2
Atkinson, H.	1916-17	-	6	-	6	-	-	-	-
Bailey, T.H.	1917-18	-	-	1	1	-	-	1	1
Betteridge, A.	1918-19	-	-	3	3	-	-	-	-
Blackmore, W.	1915-19	2	19	23	44	-	4	3	7
Blake, J.J.	1915-17	8	24	-	32	1	1	-	2
Blight, E.B.	1917-19	-	-	11	11	-	-	-	-
Bosbury, C.	1918-19	-	-	2	2	-	-	-	-
Bourne, J.W.	1915-17	1	1	-	2	-	-	-	-
Bown, A.	1917-18	-	-	3	3	-	-	2	2
Boynton, J. (Clyde)	1916-17	-	3	-	3	-	-	-	-
Bradley, J.W.	1917-18	-	-	10	10	-	-	3	3
Broderick, M.A.	1916-17	-	7	-	7	-	-	-	-
Brown, J.C.	1916-17	-	1	-	1	-	-	-	-
Buchan, A.	1917-18	-	-	1	1	-	-	-	-
Burt, J.	1916-17	-	7	-	7	-	1	-	1
Burt, S.F. (Brighton)	1918-19	-	-	1	1	-	-	-	-
Butt, J.	1918-19	-	-	1	1	-	-	-	-
Campbell, A.K.	1915-19	8	26	2	36	-	1	1	2
Colar, C.E.	1918-19	-	-	2	2	-	-	-	-
Cooper, H..J.	1916-19	-	4	5	9	-	-	-	-
Dawson, H.	1916-17	-	1	-	1	-	-	-	-
Denham, W.	1915-16	1	-	-	1	-	-	-	-
Diaper, A.	1918-19	-	-	8	8	-	-	-	-
Dominy, A.A.	1915-17	8	25	-	33	12	15	-	27
Donaldson, S.A.	1916-17	-	7	-	7	-	1	-	1
Duncan, G.A.	1916-17	-	1	-	1	-	-	-	-
Dunford, E.	1917-19	-	-	4	4	-	-	1	1
Duxbury, D.E.	1916-17	-	3	-	3	-	-	-	-
Edey, G.	1918-19	-	-	1	1	-	-	-	-
Eglin, J.F.	1915-16	8	-	-	8	-	-	-	-
Ellerington, W.(M'boro)	1915-17	9	19	-	28	1	-	-	1
Elliott, C.	1916-17	-	2	-	2	-	-	-	-
Evans, R.	1915-16	2	-	-	2	-	-	-	-
Farwell, J.	1916-17	-	1	-	1	-	-	-	-
Figgins, W.	1918-19	-	-	3	3	-	-	1	1
Foxall, F.	1918-19	-	-	2	2	-	-	2	2
Frisby, W.	1915-17	2	3	-	5	-	-	-	-
Gibbon, L.T.(MerthyrT.)	1915-16	3	-	-	3	-	-	-	-
Gilboy, B.E.	1918-19	-	-	3	3	-	-	-	-
Giles, C.	1916-17	-	16	-	16	-	-	-	-
Goode, B.	1918-19	-	-	4	4	-	-	2	2
Gowers, W.	1916-17	-	7	-	7	-	-	-	-
Green, G.	1918-19	-	-	1	1	-	-	-	-
Greer, A.	1916-17	-	1	-	1	-	-	-	-
Hackett, L.R.	1918-19	-	-	2	2	-	-	-	-
Hadley, G.A.	1915-16	1	-	-	1	-	-	-	-

		Appearances				Goals			
	Seasons	SWC	LC	SHWL	Total	SWC	LC	SHWL	Total
Hadfield, P.	1917-19	-	-	13	13	-	-	-	-
Hall, H.	1917-18	-	-	2	2	-	-	-	-
Hartnell, S.	1915-16	2	-	-	2	3	-	-	3
Hayward, A.	1915-17	1	1	-	2	-	-	-	-
Heath, A.	1917-18	-	-	1	1	-	-	-	-
Henry, W. (Man.City)	1916-17	-	17	-	17	-	-	-	-
Hood, W.	1915-16	3	-	-	3	-	-	-	-
Hughes, T.	1916-17	-	1	-	1	-	-	-	-
Hunter, G.	1916-17	-	17	-	17	-	-	-	-
Ireland, S.	1916-17	-	17	-	17	-	-	-	-
Jewett, A.W.	1918-19	-	-	14	14	-	-	-	-
Jobbins, B.	1916-17	-	6	-	6	-	-	-	-
Johnson, B.	1916-19	-	3	3	6	-	-	-	-
Johnston, D.	1918-19	-	-	2	2	-	-	-	-
Jones, T.	1916-17	-	1	-	1	-	-	-	-
Kiddle, R.S.	1916-17	-	2	-	2	-	-	-	-
Kimpton, G.S.	1915-17	9	17	-	26	4	-	-	4
Lacy, A.	1918-19	-	-	4	4	-	-	2	2
Lavenby, A.	1918-19	-	-	1	1	-	-	-	-
Lee, A.	1915-17	8	13	-	21	-	1	-	1
Lee, J.L.	1917-18	-	-	4	4	-	-	-	-
Lewis, L.R.	1916-17	-	2	-	2	-	-	-	-
Lovell, E.	1916-17	-	1	-	1	-	1	-	1
McClure, A. (B'ham)	1917-18	-	-	5	5	-	-	-	-
Millar, J.	1917-18	-	-	1	1	-	-	-	-
Milne, J.	1915-18	3	27	10	40	1	7	4	12
Mitton, J.	1916-17	-	2	-	2	-	-	-	-
Moore, J..	1916-19	-	3	3	6	-	-	10	10
Morris, A.	1915-16	1	-	-	1	-	-	-	-
Orbell, G.	1916-17	-	5	-	5	-	-	-	-
Page, P.	1916-19	-	1	4	5	-	-	4	4
Parker, T.R.	1917-19	-	-	18	18	-	-	7	7
Passmore, A.	1915-16	4	-	-	4	-	-	-	-
Payne, A.	1918-19	-	-	1	1	-	-	-	-
Pearce, J.	1916-18	-	5	5	10	-	2	1	3
Pearson, R.C.	1915-17	1	16	-	17	1	-	-	1
Pepper, H.	1917-19	-	-	3	3	-	-	1	1
Phillips, H.J.	1918-19	-	-	6	6	-	-	1	1
Pickup, F.	1916-17	-	1	-	1	-	-	-	-
Piggin, L.	1917-19	-	-	9	9	-	-	-	-
Porter, R.F.	1915-18	1	-	6	7	-	-	-	-
Price, A.B.	1916-17	-	1	-	1	-	-	-	-
Prince, P.	1918-19	-	-	10	10	-	-	5	5
Pritchard, F.	1918-19	-	-	2	2	-	-	1	1
Quinn, J.J. (Clyde)	1916-18	-	20	-	20	-	11	-	11
Rawlings, W.E.	1918-19	-	-	6	6	-	-	8	8
Roots, H.G.	1918-19	-	-	1	1	-	-	-	-
Roots, P.S.	1917-19	-	-	16	16	-	-	1	1
Rose, F.W.	1916-17	-	1	-	1	-	-	-	-

		Appearances				Goals			
	Seasons	SWC	LC	SHWL	Total	SWC	LC	SHWL	Total
Rose, L.A.	1917-18	-	-	2	2	-	-	-	-
Ryder, J.K.	1917-18	-	-	1	1	-	-	1	1
Salway, E.E.	1915-16	3	-	-	3	-	-	-	-
Simmonds, F.	1917-19	-	-	7	7	-	-	2	2
Skiller, L. (Swindon T.)	1916-17	-	4	-	4	-	-	-	-
Slade, D. (Fulham)	1916-18	-	5	2	7	-	1	1	2
Slade, R.	1915-16	5	-	-	5	-	-	-	-
Small, J.	1915-16	6	-	-	6	-	-	-	-
Smethurst, E.(D'cstr R)	1917-19	-	-	7	7	-	-	4	4
Stemp, F.	1918-19	-	-	2	2	-	-	-	-
Steventon, E.	1916-17	-	1	-	1	-	-	-	-
Swift, H.	1916-17	-	1	-	1	-	-	-	-
Taylor, A.J.	1916-17	-	1	-	1	-	-	-	-
Thwaites, A.W.	1916-17	-	1	-	1	-	-	-	-
Tomkins, E.F. (N'pton)	1915-17	3	24	-	27	-	1	-	1
Townsend, W.	1917-18	-	-	3	3	-	-	-	-
Walker, J.	1916-17	-	1	-	1	-	-	-	-
Webb, J.	1915-16	3	-	-	3	-	-	-	-
Webb, W.J.	1918-19	-	-	2	2	-	-	-	-
Wheeler, L.C.	1915-17	9	9	-	18	12	6	-	18
White, H.W.	1916-18	-	1	1	2	-	-	-	-
Whiterow, F.T.	1918-19	-	-	2	2	-	-	-	-
Wilcox, J.	1915-16	9	-	-	9	1	-	-	1
Willis, E.	1916-17	-	2	-	2	-	-	-	-
Williams, J.	1918-19	-	-	1	1	-	-	-	-
Wood, A.	1915-19	6	11	2	19	-	-	-	-
Worcester, D.	1917-19	-	-	3	3	-	-	-	-
Wright, C.	1915-19	1	4	10	15	-	-	5	5
Youtman, B.A.	1915-19	1	-	4	5	-	-	-	-

Appearances & Goalscorers for the
Second World War period 1939-46.

No sooner had the 1939-40 season started than the outbreak of war forced its abandonment. Saints had played three league games against Swansea, Bury and Newport County when the competition was suspended. No further matches were seen at the Dell for almost two months because Southampton was designated an 'unsafe area' due to the production of armaments.

Several new faces were added to the club's professional staff during the summer of 1939: Higham, Perrett and Dodgin, who were all to make their league debuts before the abandonment. Only Dodgin returned after the war, albeit briefly, and his biography appears in earlier pages. **Norman Higham** (b. Chorley 14.2.12) had previously assisted Bolton Wanderers, Everton and Middlesbrough and, a proven goalscorer, had found the net twice at Newport. Norman assisted Saints briefly during the war and when peace returned to Europe in 1945 he moved to Belgium to take up a brief appointment before returning to play for Horwich R.M.I.

Robert F. Perrett (b. Kenilworth 2.5.15, d. 8.9.52), a winger signed from Huddersfield Town in May 1939, featured at regular intervals during wartime soccer with Saints until 1942 when he left the area to serve in the armed forces. Robert resumed his playing career in 1946 with Ipswich Town and clocked up 115 appearances before retiring in 1949.

Appearances and goals during those three games were:
D. Affleck 3
F. Briggs 3 & 1 gl
T. Emanuel 3
R. Perrett 3
S. Warhurst 3
W. Bevis 2
W. Dodgin 2
N. Higham 2 & 2 gls
R. Parkin 2
F. Perfect 2
R. Tomlinson 2
E. Bates 1
H. Brophy 1
A. Holt 1 & 2 gls
G. Kelly 1
G. Smith 1
F. Williams 1

The immediate effect of the war was not too drastic as far as the club's playing staff was concerned. Only about half the full-time professionals left Southampton and, as in World War One, there were plenty of guest players stationed in the area only too willing to take their places. **John Harris** of Wolves became the club's first guest when the League South competition started in late October 1939. He was later joined by several players with league experience including no less than five Arsenal 'stars' in the Saints side that beat Fulham at Craven Cottage in June 1940: **Compton, Collett, Hapgood, Joy** and **Jones**. In goal for that game was a young Basque refugee, **Raimundo Perez**, who had arrived in England in 1938 together with **Sabin Barinaga** (later to play for Real Madrid and Spain) who had both progressed from the club's 'B' team. After a few games in Saints senior side Raimundo left for home and gained international honours while playing for Bilbao.

It was from that 'B' team in 1938 that the main nucleus of the 1940-41 side was formed. Barry, Stroud, Roles, Salter and locals Creecy and Messom were joined by other young locals Roper, Hassell and Laney to give the side a distinctly youthful look. Bill Ellerington, another youngster, joined the club during the war as his father had done a generation before, and young Bertie Mee, later to manage Arsenal during their league and cup double in 1970-71, served the Saints while stationed nearby. Although results did not go their way, just eight league wins in two seasons (partly because of having to play most of their fixtures away owing to bomb damage to the Dell) the club continued to function in the early years of the war.

The turning point came in 1942 when a large number of guest players arrived to join the maturing young side. **Alf Whittingham** of Bradford City brought a new dimension to goalscoring over the next three years, netting over eighty goals, including eight against Luton Town in January 1943. **Jackie Stamps** of Derby County partnered Alf in the Saints attack for a while together with **Charlie Mitten** of Manchester United, while **Tom Finney**, the famous Preston and England international, made a single appearance against Arsenal at the Dell in December 1942. **Wally Barnes**, at the time an amateur on Portsmouth's books, was another welcome addition to the side during the 1942-43 season. Playing at inside-forward, he was regarded as a star of the future but not with Saints as it turned out. After Tom Parker, the Saints manager, resigned in 1943 the young Barnes was persuaded to join Arsenal and after conversion to full-back, went on to play for Wales many times.

By 1945, with the war nearing its end, the Saints set about preparing for the return of peace-time league action. Many of the pre-war youngsters, such as Bill Stroud, Albie Roles and Bobby Veck, returned to take their places alongside a number of wartime discoveries such as Alf Ramsey, Bill Ellerington, Don Roper and Eric Day. As after the First World War, Saints emerged with a stronger and more promising side than when war broke out.

A Group of players from 1940-41 - (left to right) Cyril Smith, George Messom, Albert Roles, Alf Creecy, Pat Barry, Bill Stroud, Jock Salter, Robert Noss, Alf Bennett, Gordon Fox.

			Appearances			Goals		
			War Lge	War Cup	Tot	War Lge	War Cup	Tot
Abbott, David	am. Dec 1941	1941-42	1	-	1	-	-	-
Affleck, David	pro. May 1937	1941-43	3	2	5	-	-	-
Allen, James	Aston Villa	1939-44	6	2	8	-	-	-
Almond, Kenneth	Burnley	1943-44	1	1	2	-	-	-
Anderson, John	Portsmouth	1943-44	3	-	3	-	-	-
Angell, Raymond	am. June 1937	1940-41	4	-	4	-	-	-
Arnold, John	Fulham	1943-44	1	-	1	-	-	-
Barnes, Wally	Portsmouth	1941-43	22	10	32	12	2	14
Barry, Patrick	pro. Feb 1940	1939-41	30	2	32	-	-	-
Bates, Edric	pro. May 1937	1939-46	163	20	183	59	7	66
Bernard, Eugene	am. 1939	1939-42	7	2	9	-	-	-
Bevis, William	pro. June 1937	1939-46	13	-	13	2	-	2
Bewley, David	Bournemouth & Bos.	1939-40	1	-	1	-	-	-
Bidewell, S.	Chelsea	1941-42	1	6	7	-	1	1
Black, Ian	Aberdeen	1945-46	5	-	5	-	-	-
Bonass, A.	Queen's Park Rangers	1943-44	3	-	3	-	-	-
Bradley, John	pro. May 1939	1939-46	60	2	62	42	-	42
Briggs, Fred	pro May 1938	1939-40	27	1	28	10	-	10
Brooks, W.	Burnley	1945-46	1	-	1	-	-	-
Brophy, Harry	pro. May 1938	1940-41	1	-	1	-	-	-
Bryant, S.	Oct 1941	1941-42	1	-	1	-	-	-
Buchanan, Peter	Chelsea	1942-46	11	-	11	2	-	2
Buckley, Ambrose	Fulham	1939-40	7	-	7	-	-	-
Burgess, Harry	Chelsea	1939-40	1	-	1	-	-	-
Bushby, Thomas	Portsmouth	1942-43	1	-	1	-	-	-
Carter, Victor	am. Mar 1942	1943-44	1	-	1	-	-	-
Clements,Stanley	pro. July 1944	1943-46	4	-	4	-	-	-
Collett, Ernest	Arsenal	1939-40	1	-	1	-	-	-
Compton, Leslie	Arsenal	1939-40	1	-	1	-	-	-
Corbett, Norman	West Ham United	1943-45	5	-	5	-	-	-
Corbett, William	Glasgow Celtic	1943-44	1	-	1	-	-	-
Coupland, J.	Sunderland	1943-44	3	-	3	-	-	-
Creecy, Alfred	am.'39 pro.Oct'40	1939-43	43	8	51	-	1	1
Crossland, B.	Burnley	1943-44	1	-	1	-	-	-
Cruckshank, Jack	pro. Aug 1942	1942-46	6	-	6	-	-	-
Cummins, Alfred	am. July 1937	1940-41	2	-	2	-	-	-
Davie, John	Brighton	1942-44	7	2	9	4	2	6
Davies, Maldwyn	June 1945	1945-46	2	-	2	-	-	-
Day, Eric	pro. Apr 1945	1945-46	2	-	2	1	-	1
Dean, Cyril	pro. July 1939	1939-41	3	-	3	2	-	2
Dempsey, A.	am. Dec 1944	1944-45	1	-	1	-	-	-
Dodgin, William	pro. June 1939	1939-46	72	12	84	2	-	2
Dorsett, Richard	Wolverhampton W.	1944-45	13	3	16	16	7	23
Drinkwater, James	St. Mirren	1943-44	19	2	21	-	-	-
Eckford, James	am. Apr 1941	1941-42	2	-	2	-	-	-
Egglestone, Tom	Derby County	1944-46	14	1	15	-	-	-
Ellerington, William	pro. Sept 1945	1940-46	45	14	59	-	-	-
Ellis, Edwin	am. Apr 1942	1941-42	-	1	1	-	-	-

			Appearances			Goals		
			War Lge	War Cup	Tot	War Lge	War Cup	Tot
Emanuel, Thomas	pro. Sept 1938	1945-46	5	-	5	-	-	-
Ephgrave, George	pro. Apr 1946	1945-46	6	-	6	-	-	-
Evans, Harry	pro. Oct 1943	1943-46	61	10	71	9	-	9
Evans, R.	1944.	1944-45	11	-	11	-	-	-
Ferrier, Ron	Oldham Athletic	1942-43	2	-	2	-	-	-
Finney, Tom	Preston North End	1942-43	1	-	1	-	-	-
Fisher, Fred	Swansea Town	1943-44	1	-	1	-	-	-
Fisher, Kenneth	am. Sept 1940	1940-42	13	1	14	-	1	1
Fox, Gordon	am. Sept 1940	1940-42	10	-	10	1	-	1
Freeman, Alfred	pro. Nov 1943	1943-44	1	-	1	-	-	-
Gilmour, George	Heart of Midlothian	1939-40	3	-	3	1	-	1
Grant, Wilfred	Manchester City	1943-45	13	4	17	7	2	9
Gregory, Jack	pro. 1943	1945-46	3	-	3	-	-	-
Griffiths, Mal	Leicester City	1942-43	-	2	2	-	-	-
Halton, Reginald	Bury	1943-44	6	-	6	-	-	-
Hancon, W.	Clyde	1945-46	1	-	1	-	-	-
Hankey, Albert	Southend United	1941-42	5	-	5	-	-	-
Hamilton, D.	Newcastle United	1943-44	5	5	10	-	-	-
Hapgood, Eddie	Arsenal	1939-40	2	-	2	-	-	-
Harris, John	Wolverhampton W.	1939-43	99	22	121	12	3	15
Harris, Neil	pro. Feb 1941	1940-43	5	1	6	1	1	2
Hayhurst, Albert	Reading	1939-40	1	-	1	-	-	-
Hassell, Thomas	pro. Feb 1940	1939-46	92	20	112	24	2	26
Heathcote, Wilf	Queen's Park Rangers	1945-46	1	-	1	1	-	1
Higham, Norman	pro. May 1939	1939-41	4	7	11	2	-	2
Holt, Arthur	pro. Oct 1932	1939-40	30	2	32	1	-	1
Hooper, Stanley	am. 1940	1940-41	2	-	2	-	-	-
Hopper, Leslie	am. 1939	1939-40	2	-	2	-	-	-
Houldsworth, F.	Reading	1941-44	12	9	21	-	-	-
House, Arthur	am. Sept 1940	1940-42	6	1	7	-	-	-
Howard, Bruce	am. Dec 1941	1941-42	2	-	2	4	-	4
Jones, Charles	Wrexham	1944-45	1	-	1	-	-	-
Jones, John	Northampton Town	1942-46	17	12	29	-	-	-
Jones, Leslie	Arsenal	1939-40	2	-	2	-	-	-
Joy, Bernard	Arsenal	1939-40	1	-	1	-	-	-
Kiernan, T.	Albion Rovers	1939-40	1	-	1	-	-	-
Kingston, Douglas	am. Mar. 1943	1942-43	1	-	1	-	-	-
Kington, Alan	am. Nov 1945	1945-46	1	-	1	-	-	-
Lanham, Harry	Feb 1941	1940-42	4	-	4	-	-	-
Laney, Leslie	am. Apr 1940	1939-44	43	12	55	10	1	11
Lewis, Douglas	pro. Apr 1944	1943-44	1	-	1	-	-	-
Lewis, James	Apr 1941	1940-41	1	-	1	-	-	-
Light, Walter	am. Oct 42 pro Dec 42	1942-43	12	-	12	-	-	-
Logie. James	Arsenal	1939-40	1	-	1	1	-	1
Lonnon. Charles	am. May 1945	1944-45	1	-	1	-	-	-
Malpass, Sam	Fulham	1941-42	1	-	1	-	-	-
McDonald, John	Bournemouth & Bos.	1944-46	2	-	2	-	-	-
McGibbon, Douglas	pro. Dec 1938	1939-46	46	2	48	34	-	34

			Appearances			Goals		
			War Lge	War Cup	Tot	War Lge	War Cup	Tot
McSweeney, Terry	am. Mar 1938	1940-41	4	-	4	-	-	-
Mee, Bertie	Oct 1940	1940-41	14	2	16	2	-	2
Messom, George	am. Aug 1940	1940-43	24	-	24	1	-	1
Middleton, Allan	am. Dec 1941	1941-42	1	-	1	-	-	-
Miles, Arthur	pro. Apr 1944	1943-45	2	-	2	-	-	-
Mills, George	Chelsea	1944-45	7	-	7	5	-	5
Mitten, Charles	Manchester United	1942-44	18	4	22	5	-	5
Mordey, Harry	Charlton Athletic	1939-40	7	2	9	-	-	-
Moss, Frank	Aston Villa	1944-45	11	4	15	-	-	-
Mountford, Reg	Huddersfield Town	1945-46	1	-	1	-	-	-
Noss, Robert	Aug 1940	1940-41	3	-	3	-	-	-
Noyce, Leonard	May 1938	1939-40	1	-	1	-	-	-
Osman, Harry	Millwall	1939-40	10	1	11	2	1	3
Perez, Raimundo	June 1940	1939-40	3	-	3	-	-	-
Permain, Alfred	1939	1940-41	9	-	9	-	-	-
Perrett, Robert	pro. May 1939	1939-42	17	1	18	3	-	3
Pitts, Harold	Fulham	1939-40	1	-	1	-	-	-
Pond, Harold	Carlisle United	1942-45	26	8	34	1	-	1
Powell, Stanley	Oct 1945	1945-46	1	-	1	-	-	-
Ramsbottom, E.	Manchester City	1943-44	-	1	1	-	-	-
Ramsey, Alfred	am. Oct 43 pro Apr 44	1943-46	27	2	29	7	4	11
Rigg, Thomas	Middlesbrough	1942-43	2	-	2	-	-	-
Roberts, E.	Aug 1944	1944-45	6	-	6	-	-	-
Rolfe, A.	Arsenal	1941-42	-	1	1	-	-	-
Roles, Albert	pro. Oct 1940	1939-46	163	25	188	1	-	1
Roper, Donald	pro. June 1940	1939-46	140	26	166	71	15	86
Rothery, G.	Bournemouth & Bos.	1942-45	10	1	11	-	-	-
Roy, John	Norwich City	1939-40	2	-	2	2	-	2
Rudkin, Thomas	Lincoln City	1942-43	2	1	3	-	-	-
Salter, Roland	1939	1939-41	3	-	3	-	-	-
Sanders, J.	1939	1939-40	1	-	1	-	-	-
Scott, John	pro. May 1937	1939-40	1	-	1	-	-	-
Seddon, E.	Everton	1943-44	3	-	3	1	-	1
Sheppard, Donald	am. Dec 1943	1943-45	3	-	3	1	-	1
Shimwell, Eddie	Sheffield United	1943-44	10	5	15	-	-	-
Sibley, Eric	Blackpool	1945-46	6	-	6	-	-	-
Smith, Cyril	am. Apr 1940	1940-41	1	-	1	-	-	-
Smith, George	pro. July 1938	1939-46	36	-	36	3	-	3
Smith, Fred	am. Apr 1940	1941-42	-	1	1	-	-	-
Smith, John	Leicester City	1943-44	1	-	1	1	-	1
Smith, Victor	pro. Sept 1941	1941-42	3	1	4	-	-	-
Smyth, C.	Aberdeen	1939-40	1	-	1	-	-	-
Sneddon, Tom	Rochdale	1943-44	3	-	3	-	-	-
Southern, Leslie	Feb 1941	1940-41	-	1	1	-	-	-
Spence, R.	1939	1939-40	1	-	1	-	-	-
Stansbridge, Len	pro. Aug 1936	1943-45	12	6	18	-	-	-
Staton, Norman	pro. Nov 1943	1943-44	5	-	5	-	-	-
Stamps, Jack	Derby County	1942-43	11	3	14	8	3	11

			Appearances			Goals		
			War Lge	War Cup	Tot	War Lge	War Cup	Tot
Stear, James	pro. Nov 1943	1944-46	9	1	10	-	-	-
Stout, Leonard	Apr 1946	1945-46	1	-	1	-	-	-
Stroud, William	pro. Feb 1940	1939-46	146	29	175	20	3	23
Summerbee, George	Preston North End	1944-45	1	-	1	-	-	-
Swinden, George	Arsenal	1944-45	1	-	1	-	-	-
Sykes, Jack	Millwall	1939-40	1	-	1	-	-	-
Tait, Thomas	Reading	1941-42	5	5	10	-	4	4
Tann, Bertram	Charlton Athletic	1942-45	27	9	36	-	-	-
Targett, Alfred	am. 1939	1939-40	4	-	4	-	-	-
Taylor, Richard	Grimsby Town	1944-45	2	-	2	-	-	-
Tennant, Albert	Chelsea	1939-40	1	-	1	-	-	-
Thomas, Reginald	1943	1943-44	1	-	1	-	-	-
Tomlinson, Reginald	pro. May 1938	1942-43	-	2	2	-	-	-
Tweedy, George	Grimsby Town	1942-43	8	-	8	-	-	-
Vaux, Edward	Chelsea	1939-40	1	-	1	-	-	-
Veck, Roberts	pro. Sept 1945	1945-46	28	-	28	5	-	5
Walsh, Wilf	Derby County	1939-40	1	1	2	-	-	-
Walker, Steve	Exeter City	1944-45	13	-	13	7	-	7
Wardle, William	Grimsby Town	1942-43	14	2	16	5	-	5
Warhurst, Sam	pro. May 1937	1939-46	76	2	78	-	-	-
Weaver, Sam	Chelsea	1939-40	1	-	1	-	-	-
Webber, Eric	pro. Mar. 1939	1939-46	52	2	54	2	-	2
West, Harry	pro. Feb 1940	1939-40	2	-	2	-	-	-
White, Charles	Aug 1940	1940-41	21	2	23	-	-	-
White, Lyle	am. Aug 1938	1940-41	1	-	1	-	-	-
Whitworth, H.	Bury	1943-44	1	-	1	-	-	-
Whittingham Alfred	Bradford City	1942-46	63	15	78	65	19	84
Wilkins, Len	pro. Oct 1945	1945-46	3	-	3	-	-	-
Wilkinson, Charles	Bournemouth & Bos.	1939-40	4	-	4	-	-	-
Wright, Robert	Charlton Athletic	1942-43	3	-	3	-	-	-
Young, Robert	Bournemouth & Bos.	1941-42	-	1	1	-	-	-

The Hampshire Cup Competitions 1887-1895.

With the formation of the Hampshire Football Association in 1887 and with it the Junior and Senior County Cup competitions, Saints entered upon the competitive arena of cup soccer for the first time. As a junior outfit Saints played their first ever cup-tie on a field at the rear of the Anchor Hotel at Redbridge, defeating a Totton side by 1-0, and from that game on Saints were not to look back. Seventeen games and fourteen victories later, Saints had dominated the Junior competition and with three consecutive titles the club won the trophy outright. Elevated to the senior competition in 1891, St. Mary's found themselves against the cream of the county's top sides, the Royal Engineers from Aldershot. They had won the Senior Cup in the previous two seasons and came face to face with Saints in the 1892 final. Saints won that final by 3-1 and succeeded in retaining the trophy the following season, beating a Medical Staff team 5-0 at the County Ground. By the time Saints had reached the 1893 final they had been unbeaten in 24 consecutive county cup games. However, the law of averages meant that one day they would have to suffer a defeat and it came at the hands of local rivals Freemantle who beat them 2-0 and thus a cup was prised from the hands of St. Mary's for the first time in six years. After another final defeat the following season Saints entered the 1894-95 season as a Southern League side, and a much stronger outfit swept aside all opposition in regaining the trophy. The 1895 final proved to be the last ever played for by a Saints senior side and the following season the club entered their reserve team XI.

A purely amateur organisation until the steady introduction of professionals in 1891, Saints relied basically on local talent to make up their side, together with the occasional recruit from the army hospital at Netley.

The teaching profession provided a number of the club's junior players. **Albert Fry** (b. Southampton 1860, d. Southampton 13 March 1937) a master at Taunton's school, and later headmaster at Foundry Lane, achieved a remarkable feat by scoring five times in one cup match. He usually occupied the full-back position but was so versatile that, on occasion, he even kept goal.

George Muir (b. Southampton, d. Southampton 29 March 1939) a member of the teacher training college in Winchester, and also later a headmaster in the town, gave the club valuable service before taking up the whistle. A Southern League official, George took charge of an amateur cup final before becoming a club director in 1914.

Army personnel who made brief appearances in the Saints colours included Sapper **John Arter** from the Royal Engineers and Corporal **W. Duff** a member of the Medical Staff Corps and previously with the Woolston Works team. (Others mentioned in Biographical section).

A dentist, **Charles Bromley**, was the club's chief goalgetter in the Junior Cup competition, scoring three times in three games. **Charles Deacon** (b. 1869, d. Southampton 21 October 1893) a clerk with the Southampton Telegraph Office, was one of the club's outstanding half-backs prior to the influx of professionals. Described by the local press as "the old warhorse", although only 24 years old at the time, he was a regular in the club's first eight years in existence. Charlie died tragically from a brain tumour, soon after giving up the game.

Monty Warn, an attacking left-winger, had the honour of scoring the club's winning goal in their first ever Junior final in 1887. After a spell with Cowes he returned to St. Mary's, retiring in 1892. Monty later became a Conservative agent in Shropshire.

Victor Barton the well-known Hampshire cricketer (b. Netley 6 October 1867, d. Southampton 23 March 1906) kept goal in the absence of **Ralph Ruffell** during the Senior Cup semi-final of 1893 and kept a clean sheet in a 2-0 victory over Portsmouth. Victor continued to assist the club over a number of years, turning out when needed in the reserve XI during the club's early Southern League days.

The Scottish influx into the side during the early County Cup days was headed by **R. McDonald** (d. Inverness 1930). An attacking inside-forward, he found the net four times in as many matches during the 1887-88 campaign before returning to his homeland. (**Ralph Aitken** appeared in a friendly in March 1891 and was the first Scottish international to wear the Saints colours). With **Fleming** and **McMillan** appearing in English cup-ties soon after, the Scottish ingredient increased and the first paid Scot, **Jack Angus**, was signed in 1893 and many more were to follow.

	Appearances			Goals		
	HJC	HSC	Total	HJC	HSC	Total
Angus, William James	-	7	7	-	5	5
Arter, John Thomas	5	-	5	1	-	1
Baker, Charles	-	4	4	-	1	1
Barton, Victor	-	1	1	-	-	-
Boyd, W.	-	1	1	-	-	-
Bromley, Charles E.	16	-	16	10	-	10
Bromley, Fred C.	6	3	9	6	3	9
Brown, R.	1	-	1	-	-	-
Carter, George	17	9	26	-	1	1
Cox, Walter	-	2	2	-	-	-
Crossley, J. F.	4	-	4	-	-	-
Deacon, Charles	14	5	19	2	1	3
Delamotte, F. A.	11	5	16	4	-	4
Denning, Arthur W.	1	-	1	-	-	-
Dollin, Albert Edwin	-	3	3	-	2	2
Dorkin, Jack W.	-	6	6	-	9	9
Duff, W.	2	-	2	-	-	-
Farwell, Arthur	11	8	19	4	3	7
Fry, Albert A.	14	1	15	7	-	7
Furby, William	-	1	1	-	-	-
Gandy, A.	6	-	6	1	-	1
Hamer, David Bowen	-	3	3	-	1	1
Hollands, Fred	-	4	4	-	1	1
Jeffery, William Walls	-	2	2	-	-	-
Kiddle, Robert Shenan	4	5	9	1	2	3
Littlehales, Alfred	-	4	4	-	4	4
McDonald, R.	4	-	4	4	-	4
Marshall, George	-	14	14	-	-	-
Mate, A.	1	-	1	-	-	-
Muir, George H.	7	-	7	-	-	-
Mulford, A. H.	-	3	3	-	-	-
Nicholls, Ernest Frederick	-	10	10	-	7	7
Offer, Henry Thomas	-	6	6	-	2	2
Price, T.	-	4	4	-	-	-
Rogers, Joseph	-	1	1	-	-	-
Rowthorn, A.	-	3	3	-	-	-
Ruffell, Daniel Ralph	17	9	26	-	-	-
Sommerville, J. L.	4	-	4	-	-	-
Stride, William Francis	10	11	21	-	-	-
Taylor, Ernest James	-	7	7	-	-	-
Thomson, W. J. G.	-	4	4	-	3	3
Varley, A.	5	-	5	-	-	-
Verney, George W.	10	12	22	1	2	3
Ward, Herbert Foster	-	7	7	-	4	4
Warn, Montgomery D.	17	-	17	6	-	6
Williams, G.	1	-	1	-	-	-
Williamson, H.	-	2	2	-	-	-

HJC: Hampshire Junior Cup   HSC: Hampshire Senior Cup

THE ALPHABET OF THE

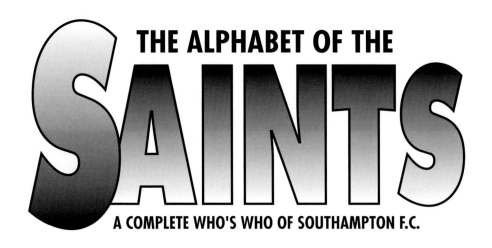

A COMPLETE WHO'S WHO OF SOUTHAMPTON F.C.

PRE-PUBLICATION
SUBSCRIBERS

The Saints in training 1913-14
Back: Ireland, Hollins, Steventon, Binder, McIntyre (Manager), Small, Andrews, F. Smith, Brooks. Front: McAlpine, Hadley, Kimpton, W. Smith, Denby.

1   THE FOOTBALL LEAGUE
2   F. G. L. ASKHAM, FCA, Chairman, Southampton F. C.
3   K. St. J. WISEMAN, Vice-Chairman, Southampton F. C.
4   JOHN CORBETT, Director, Southampton F. C.
5.   E. T. BATES, Director, Southampton F. C.
6   B. H. D. HUNT, Director, Southampton F. C.
7   I. L. GORDON, Director, Southampton F. C.
8   M. R. RICHARDS, FCA, Director, Southampton F. C.
9   IAN BRANFOOT, Team Manager, Southampton F. C.
10   BRIAN TRUSCOTT, Secretary, Southampton F. C.
11   BOB RUSSELL, Commercial Manager, Southampton F. C.
12   SOUTHAMPTON FOOTBALL CLUB
13   SOUTHAMPTON FOOTBALL CLUB
14   SOUTHAMPTON FOOTBALL CLUB
15   SOUTHAMPTON FOOTBALL CLUB
16   SOUTHAMPTON FOOTBALL CLUB
17   GARY CHALK
18   DUNCAN HOLLEY
19   PETER ASHTON, Chief Librarian, Southern Evening Echo
20   MIKE DAVAGE, Old Catton, Norwich
21   JIM CREASY, Malden, Surrey
22   IAN GARLAND, Chesham, Buckinghamshire
23   LEIGH EDWARDS, Bransgore, Christchurch
24   ANDREW MURRAY, Lordswood, Southampton
25   RAY MURSELL, Bitterne, Southampton
26   KEN PRIOR, Bitterne, Southampton
27   In Memory of MOLLY DAVAGE
28   SAMUEL CHALK, Eastleigh, Hampshire
29   JANICE, GUINNESS & MAX HEIGHWAY, Thurmaston, Leicester
30   DAVID F. STANSBRIDGE, Winchester, Hampshire
31   MICHAEL R. CHASE, Swanmore, Southampton
32   S.J. PEARCE, Chandlers Ford, Eastleigh, Hampshire
33   G.R. BATCHELOR, Burbage, Leicestershire
34   M.S. MURRAY, Shoreham-by-Sea, West Sussex
35   BRIAN MUNDY, Chandlers Ford, Eastleigh, Hampshire
36   DERRICK S. LEACH, Pamber Heath, Basingstoke, Hampshire
37   IAN DAVID WHITWORTH, Wakefield, West Yorkshire
38   TIM SCOTT
39   NIGEL JAMES COLLINS, Balsall Common, Coventry
40   ADRIAN CURTIS, Bitterne, Southampton
41   G.I. FORD, Merry Oak, Southampton
42   DAVID BRINDLEY, Rowner, Gosport, Hampshire
43   ROSS TAYLOR, Andover, Hampshire
44   F.C. SIBLEY, Blackfield, Southampton
45   J. SHIPPEY, Highcliffe. Christchurch, Dorset
46   DESMOND ELCOCK, Daventry, Northamptonshire
47   IAN RALPH WILLIS, Broadstone, Poole, Dorset

Harry Brophy scores on his Southampton debut against Tottenham Hotspur in the opening game of the season at the Dell on 27th August 1938.

48	LEE WRIGHT, Lytchett Matravers, Poole, Dorset
49	JEREMY BULLEN, Fair Oak, Eastleigh, Hampshire
50	'ON THE MARCH', Eastleigh, Hampshire
51	NEIL D. SKILTON, Fareham, Hampshire
52	RODNEY DATHAN, East End, Lymington, Hampshire
53	ANTHONY KERLEY, Eastleigh, Hampshire
54	NEIL WARWICK SMITH, Ashley, New Milton, Hampshire
55	G. MELLISH, Freemantle, Southampton
56	Mrs ANNE RICHARDS, Hythe, Southampton
57	MIKE MEREDITH, Loughborough, Leicestershire
58	D.D. RICKETTS, Regents Park, Southampton
59	Miss K.A. HAMMOND, Millbrook, Southampton
60	ROGER F. HARRIS, Maybush, Southampton
61	TONY WILLIAM HOPE, Old Basing, Basingstoke, Hampshire
62	PAUL DYKE, Strouden Park, Bournemouth, Dorset
63	DEREK BAKER, Eversley, Basingstoke, Hampshire
64	IVOR JENKINS, Taunton, Somerset
65	ROBERT JEX, Perivale, Middlesex
66	M.J. BENNETT, Andover, Hampshire
67	DAWN ADAMS, Owslebury, Winchester, Hampshire
68	COLIN A. ALCOCK, Haslemere, Surrey
69	H.F. BROPHY, Ravensden, Bedford
70	Miss F. HARDING, Winchester, Hampshire
71	S.F. SEDUNARY, Reading, Berkshire
72	TERENCE HENRY, Totton, Hampshire
73	ALISON FIANDER, Woodley, Reading, Berkshire
74	ALAN DENIS KING, Sholing, Southampton
75	PETER BRIAN HARDING, Romsey, Hampshire
76	BEAMER UPSCOTTY, Muswell Hill, London
77	MALCOLM HIGGINS, Hedge End, Southampton
78	ERIC DAY, Southerwicks, Corsham, Wiltshire
79	MARTYN THEAR, Hove, Sussex
80	A.P.C. RISTE, Warsash, Southampton
81	Miss J.M. TEAGUE, Queen's Park, Bournemouth, Dorset
82	KEVIN EDWARD BAKER, Southampton
83	GRAHAM KIRK, Winsor, Southampton
84	STUART KIRK, Winsor, Southampton
85	MARTIN R. DEAN, Hythe, Southampton
86	P.B. DEAN, Hythe, Southampton
87	VIVIENNE BROADWAY, Botley, Southampton
88	ANDREW SOFFE, Hordle, Lymington, Hampshire
89	K.J. RIDGWAY, Lancing, West Sussex
90	KEVIN HARDING, Hedge End, Southampton
91	SIMON J. STIRRETT, Old Calmore, Southampton
92	I. HARDEN, Lordswood, Southampton
93	MARTIN HOUSE, Romsey, Hampshire
94	JOANNE HAYNES, Eastleigh, Hampshire

Saints players greeting the crowd before the match against Fluminense in May 1948, at the start of their Brazilian tour.

95	DOROTHY SILLENCE, St. Denys, Southampton
96	MICHAEL JOHN LOOSEMORE, Highfield, Southampton
97	Miss KATHRYN BOWDEN, West End, Southampton
98	R. PAINTER, Bitterne Park, Southampton
99	DAVID R. TODD, Salisbury, Wiltshire
100	MICHAEL FREDERICK YOUNG, Hoeford, Gosport, Hampshire
101	STANLEY C. EDWARDSON, Shirley, Southampton
102	TONY GODFREY, Oakley, Basingstoke, Hampshire
103	RICHARD JOHN BUCKINGHAM-SMITH, Eastleigh, Hampshire
104	J.J. WHITE, Testbourne Meadows, Totton, Hampshire
105	MARK A. ROGERS, Romsey, Hampshire
106	BRIAN F. DAWKINS, Romsey, Hampshire
107	MICHAEL CLEMENT HALL, Bishopdown, Salisbury, Wiltshire
108	HUMPHREY FREDERICK SAINT, Salisbury, Wiltshire
109	ALAN CLIFTON WRIGHT, Hillingdon, Middlesex
110	T. STRUDWICK, New Milton, Hampshire
111	BRYAN WAYNE DAWKINS, Bitterne, Southampton
112	ROBERT WRIGHT, Fareham, Hampshire
113	W.H. LIGHT, Highwoods, Colchester, Essex
114	A. GOSLING, Pyrford Woods, Woking, Surrey
115	DAVID BASSIL, Lower Earley, Reading, Berkshire
116	Mr & Mrs T.S. BRUTY, Whitchurch, Hampshire
117	A.H. LEADBETTER, Calmore, Totton, Hampshire
118	DAVID JOHN GRAY, Bishopstoke, Eastleigh, Hampshire
119	TIM HILL, Bursledon, Southampton
120	CHRIS DAVAGE, Southampton
121	ALBERT DAVAGE, Bitterne, Southampton
122	GRAHAM WATFORD, Locksheath, Southampton
123	A.M. QUIGLEY, Merley, Wimborne, Dorset
124	S.R. QUIGLEY, Merley, Wimborne, Dorset
125	TREVOR GREEN, Queen Camel, Yeovil, Somerset
126	RICHARD BARRINGTON CLARKE, Bitterne, Southampton
127	D.A. BEVAN, Andover, Hampshire
128	DAVID JOHN HOWARD, Hartington, Buxton, Derbyshire
129	RAYMOND SHAW, Sutton-in-Ashfield, Nottinghamshire
130	ANDREW TAPPERN, Tilehurst, Reading
131	NIGEL OFFORD, Eastleigh, Hampshire
132	LISA HOLLEY, Hedge End, Southampton
133	ROY MARTIN, Thornhill, Southampton
134	LORRAINE MARTIN, Thornhill, Southampton
135	GEOFFREY MARTIN, Thornhill, Southampton
136	PAUL MARTIN, Thornhill, Southampton
137	DAVID STELLING, Knowle, Bristol
138	PAUL BAKER, Upper Shirley, Southampton
139	D. McGIBBON, Amersham, Buckinghamshire
140	C.G FRAY, Eastleigh, Hampshire
141	RAY & LESLEY ATKINS, Worcester

George Curtis (right) celebrates as Eric Day scores the equaliser against West Bromwich Albion on 23rd April 1949. Many in the 30,586 crowd (a Dell record until 1969) thought promotion was assured, but the Saints lost their final game at Chesterfield and missed out by a point.

142	DENNIS ARTHUR BULPITT, Bishopstoke, Eastleigh, Hampshire
143	JOHN WARREN, BEM, London W4
144	N.J. HARDING, Chandlers Ford, Eastleigh, Hampshire
145	A.M. EDWARDS, Newfound, Basingstoke, Hampshire
146	RAYMOND VINEY, Totton, Hampshire
147	MIKE ROBERTS, Islip, Kettering, Northamptonshire
148	MALCOLM P. LEWIS, Bitterne, Southampton
149	IAN BULLIVANT, Totton, Hampshire
150	DEAN MOULAND, Shirley, Southampton
151	HARRY PENK, Marchwood, Southampton
152	KEVIN STEVENS, Bournemouth, Dorset
153	GEOFF STEVENS, Bournemouth, Dorset
154	MIKE KIBBLE, Bournemouth, Dorset
155	STEVEN SAUNDERS, Christchurch, Dorset
156	PAUL GALBRAITH, Hedge End, Southampton
157	KEVEN JOHN QUICK, Shirley, Southampton
158	LARS-OLOF WENDLER, Hoganas, Sweden
159	CHRIS DYER, Slip End, Luton, Bedfordshire
160	ANTHONY G. WARE, Montacute, Somerset
161	T.J. THORNTON, Calmore, Totton, Hampshire
162	D.R.M. HOLLEY, Southampton
163	D.G.R. HOLLEY, Lymington, Hampshire
164	St. MARY's C.E. FIRST & MIDDLE SCHOOL, Southampton
165	REBECCA & BEN LEAR, Brockenhurst
166	MARTYN WARTSKI, Parkstone, Poole, Dorset
167	GORDON C. HISCOCKS, Melksham, Wiltshire
168	JAMES L. BROWNING, Romsey, Hampshire
169	PETER & ALISON HORN, Cadnam, Hampshire
170	D.W. STANLEY, Abbotts Barton, Winchester, Hampshire
171	RUTH MARTIN (nee Holley), Southampton
172	RAY GAIGER, Winchester, Hampshire
173	F.E. DUDLEY, Thorpe Bay, Essex
174	THE UGLY INSIDE
175	MARK & MARTIN ELLWOOD, Windsor, Berkshire
176	D.C. ROBERTS, Wantage, Oxon
177	M.C. ROBERTS, Wantage, Oxon
178	WILLIAM GEORGE LEVER, Compton Chamberlayne, Wiltshire
179	ROBERT OSBORNE, Totton, Hampshire
180	MICHAEL CONROY, Sparsholt, Hampshire
181	DAVID P. CROUCHER, Ashurst, Southampton
182	DEREK HYDE, Westbury on Trym, Bristol
183	ALAN J. POTTINGER, Stibbington, Hampshire
184	STUART VATCHER, Northbourne, Bournemouth
185	D.B. GRAY, Broadstone, Dorset
186	ALFRED CHURCHER, Sandal, Wakefield, West Yorkshire
187	IAN BELBIN, Bassett, Southampton
188	N.W. HUMBY, Ancells Farm, Fleet, Hampshire

George O'Brien (1959-66) meets Bill Rawlings (1919-28) at the Dell in November 1965. These two prolific forwards scored a combined total of 361 goals in 641 games for the Saints.

189 PETER DENNISON, West Cowes, Isle of Wight
190 MICHAEL FLEW, Bitterne Park, Southampton
191 ANDREW ROBERT FORD, Bisley, Woking, Surrey
192 Capt. D.B. HOLLEY, Devonport, Plymouth, Devon
193 ADRIAN NORMAN, Romsey, Hampshire
194 D.B. BRYETT, Laarbruch, Germany
195 GAVIN NEWELL, Brighton, East Sussex
196 JONATHON WARE, Yeovil, Somerset
197 JULIE WRIGHT, Bassett, Southampton
198 BRIAN TUBBS, Chandlers Ford, Eastleigh, Hampshire
199 M. STEVENS, Oakdale, Poole, Dorset
200 FRANK CHARLES SALTER, Harestock, Winchester
201 JOHN WARD, Fareham, Hampshire
202 WILLIAM B. KILMURRAY, Victoria, London
203 BARRY STREETER, Waterlooville, Portsmouth, Hampshire
204 CLIVE DAVIDSON, Midanbury, Southampton
205 JOHN HAMMILL, Five Oaks, St. Saviour, Jersey, Channel Islands
206 ALAN FINNEY, Portswood, Southampton
207 FREDERICK LEE, Ford, Plymouth, Devon
208 DEREK WHEATCROFT, Lenton, Nottingham
209 R.K. SHOESMITH, Cranham, Upminster, Essex
210 J. RINGROSE, Romford, Essex
211 BOB TANNER, Lock's Heath, Southampton
212 DAVID KEATS, Thornton Heath, Surrey
213 J.M. CADDY, Shirley, Southampton
214 GEORGE RATH, Teddington, Middlesex
215 CHRIS PAYNE, Ilford, Essex
216 DON McALLEN, Pennington, Lymington, Hampshire
217 NIGEL McALLEN, Pennington, Lymington, Hampshire
218 STEWART FELL, Radcliffe, Manchester
219 ANDREW TIMOTHY MARTIN, New Milton, Hampshire
220 J.A. HARRIS, Enfield, Middlesex
221 R.D.N. WELLS, Kingston upon Thames, Surrey
222 IAN GRIFFITHS, Wrexham, Clwyd
223 L.A. ZAMMIT, Fareham, Hampshire
224 COLIN WILCOX, Eastleigh, Hampshire
225 R.W. MARWICK, Coatbridge, Lanarkshire
226 ROGER TRIGGS, Gillingham, Kent
227 MELVIN HISCOCK, Emsworth, Hampshire
228 CRAIG & RYAN FULLER, Bisley, Surrey
229 JONNY STOKKELAND, Kvinesdal, Norway
230 CHRIS NEWMAN, Midanbury, Southampton
231 P.J. YOUNG, Ringwood, Hampshire
232 DAVID ADLEM, Eastville, Bristol
233 L.W. RICE, Dibden Purlieu, Southampton
234 S.F. WINDEBANK, Woolston, Southampton
235 GARTH I. DYKES, Leicester

Legendary Saints winger **Terry Paine** tangles with Crystal Palace's central defender **Mel Blyth** in April 1972 at Selhurst Park. The Saints won 3-2 with two goals from Mick Channon and another from Bobby Stokes.

236	JOHN WYATT, Totton, Southampton
237	DONALD NOBLE, Dunkeld, Perthshire
238	CLIVE I. WILLIAMS, Ashurst Bridge, Hampshire
239	PAUL WILKINSON, Hazel Grove, Stockport, Cheshire
240	JOHN FITZHUGH, Blaby, Leicester
241	M. WALDEN, Chandlers Ford, Eastleigh, Hampshire
242	TONY WRIGHT, Lymington, Hampshire
243	R.H. WHITE, Boscombe East, Bournemouth
244	W.D. PHILLIPS, Frogmore, Kingsbridge, Devon
245	DUNCAN WATT, Sleaford, Lincolnshire
246	BRIAN CLAYTON, Sholing, Southampton
247	JOHN MEATYARD, North Baddesley, Southampton
248	G.T. QUINN, Goxhill, South Humberside
249	KEVIN FOSTER, Stubbington, Fareham, Hampshire
250	IAIN BARCLAY, Stubbington, Fareham, Hampshire
251	MICHELLE THOMPSON, Larchwood, Totton, Southampton
252	ALAN HARDING, Swindon, Wiltshire
253	K.P. WOOD, Holbrook, Ipswich, Suffolk
254	A.D. SMALL, North Baddesley, Southampton
255	MICHAEL FEATHERSTONE, Enfield, Middlesex
256	CHRISTER SVENSSON, Odeshog, Sweden
257	DOUGLAS LAMMING, North Ferriby, North Humberside
258	NEIL FARMER, Millbrook, Southampton
259	DAVE JUSON, Freemantle, Southampton
260	JULIA PYBUS, Kings Somborne, Stockbridge, Hampshire
261	D. REEVES, Saris Green, Southampton
262	T. MARSHALL, Sholing Southampton
263	DAVID CONTRERAS, Ashington Park, New Milton, Hampshire
264	LEE CURTIS, Westham, Weymouth, Dorset
265	COLIN CAMERON, Sidcup, Kent
266	TIM BUTTIMORE, Bitteswell, Leicestershire
267	DAVID ARTHURS, Alsager, Staffordshire
268	ROBIN GOWERS, Fairstead, Chelmsford, Essex
269	FRANK SJOMAN, Helsinki, Finland
270	BENOIT AUDIBERT, Teddington, Middlesex
271	TONY HOWES, East Cowes, Isle of Wight
272	GWYNETH BELL, Highcliffe, Christchurch, Dorset
273	DAVID BROOKS, East Cowes, Isle of Wight
274	K.B. CUTLER, Dibden, Hythe, Southampton
275	R.C. HUMPHRIES MBE, Chandlers Ford, Eastleigh, Hampshire
276	DEREK MURRAY, Weybridge, Surrey
277	B. HOURSTON, St. Ola, Orkney
278	FREDERICK FURNESS, North Shields, Tyne & Wear
279	DAVID COYNE, Hampton, Middlesex
280	ALAN HINDLEY, Maghull, Merseyside
281	IAN JOHN STACEY, Speen, Newbury, Berkshire
282	ROBERT ELLIOTT, Romsey, Hampshire

Austin Hayes, *a promising young forward with the Saints during the late 70's whose life was tragically cut short by cancer. The Austin Hayes Memorial Trophy is now played for annually between a select eleven and Saints associate schoolboy team.*

283 STEVEN CHURCHER, Bishopstoke, Eastleigh, Hampshire
284 JOHN R. WINGFIELD, Waterlooville, Hampshire
285 NICHOLAS BARKER, Bitterne Park, Southampton
286 MICHAEL HAWKINS, Titchfield Common, Fareham, Hampshire
287 JANE WATT, Eastleigh, Hampshire
288 ANN CHALK, Eastleigh, Hampshire
289 JONATHAN RUDD, Cowes, Isle of Wight
290 ADRIAN SMITH, Bedford Park, Chiswick, London
291 DAMON ROBINSON, Sherfield-on-Loddon, Hampshire
292 THOMAS LEETE, Basingstoke, Hampshire
293 NEALE ADAMS, Hatch Warren, Basingstoke, Hampshire
294 S. ASHWELL, North Baddesley, Southampton
295 JOHN DAVIS, Basingstoke, Hampshire
296 DAVID LUMB, Bromley Cross, Bolton, Lancashire
297 W.B. LAIDLAW, Chandlers Ford, Hampshire
298 CHRISTOPHER HANCOCK, Saxon Meadows, Romsey, Hampshire
299 STEVE WESTON, Marley Mount, Sway, Lymington, Hampshire
300 ROBERT K. HALL, Totton, Southampton
301 ROBIN RICHARDSON, Eastleigh, Hampshire
302 M.J. CLIFFORD, West End, Southampton
303 M.F. FRY, Blackfield, Southampton
304 BRIAN SMITH, Eastleigh, Hampshire
305 PHIL STRUTHERS, Bentworth, Hampshire
306 JEFFREY WALTERS, Bishopstoke, Eastleigh, Hampshire
307 M.B.H. Le CHEMINANT, Chandlers Ford, Hampshire
308 D.W. EARLEY, Southampton
309 P. BAXTER, Tilehurst, Reading, Berkshire
310 RAYMOND BALL, Bitterne, Southampton
311 D.E. COLLINS, Rownham, Southampton
312 DEREK EDWARDS, Southampton
313 STEPHEN COSTELLO, Southampton
314 CHRIS GILFOY, Southampton
315 SAMUEL COLE, Southampton
316 STEWART EDGELER, Ardingly, West Sussex
317 ANDREW WEST, Donnington, Newbury, Berkshire
318 T.W. GRAHAM, Southampton
319 NICK BARKER, Petersfield, Hampshire
320 SIMON CORDEIRO, Fleet, Hampshire
321 ROB JONES, Sholing, Southampton
322 Mrs M.B. MERCER, Frimley, Camberley, Surrey
323 MALCOLM ROBERT WING, Millbrook, Southampton
324 L. GEARY, Andover, Hampshire
325 BOB MANNING, Sandhills, Thorner, Leeds, West Yorkshire
326 W.G.F. DIDHAM, Branksome Park, Poole, Dorset
327 D. HOLMES, Caversham, Reading, Berkshire
328 MARK YEATS, Winterslow, Salisbury, Wiltshire
329 P. GIBSON, Leatherhead, Surrey

The Saint who never was . . .
Yugoslavian central defender **Milos Drizic** *was brought over by manager Chris Nicholl in the late 1980's but his Saints career was more than short-lived as the British government refused him a work permit.*

330 GARETH M. DAVIES, Holyhead, Gwynedd
331 NICHOLAS AZERN, Bournemouth, Dorset
332 CLAIRE TWYNING, Shirley, Southampton
333 Mrs S. BEVIS, Park Gate, Southampton
334 Mrs M.R. WORTHY, Netley Abbey, Southampton
335 ANDREW COOPER, Bishopstoke, Eastleigh, Hampshire
336 DAVID WALTON, Corbridge, Northumberland
337 M.A. WYATT, Llanedeyrn, Cardiff, South Wales
338 PIERS ROBERT DAVIES, Aldermaston, Berkshire
339 HAROLD CLARKE, Milbourne Port, Sherborne, Dorset
340 DAVID L. WITT, Marchwood, Southampton
341 JOHN D. MASON, Rownhams, Hampshire
342 CHRISTOPHER WEBBER, Redlynch, Salisbury, Wiltshire
343 A.E. MARCHANT, Shirley, Southampton
344 MICHAEL BOWMAN, Hythe, Southampton
345 M.R. APPLETON, Moordown, Bournemouth, Dorset
346 JIMMY NOONE, Queniborough, Leicestershire
347 SAM HAYES, Camberley, Surrey
348 SIMON LEDGER, Camberley, Surrey
349 BRYN ELLIOTT, Southampton
350 J.R. O'DONNELL, Warsash, Southampton
351 PETER WHITLOCK, Fordingbridge, Hampshire
352 D.F.R. BULPITT, Marchwood, Southampton
353 TRICIA HAWKER, Whetstone, Leicester
354 JOHN McGUIGAN, Hamilton, Scotland
355 FRANK McGUIGAN, Hamilton Scotland
356 DAVID BREMNER, Hamilton, Scotland
357 JOHN LANGDON, Keyworth, Leicestershire
358 GERALD HILL, Blurton, Stoke-on-Trent, Staffordshire.
359 K. J. BOND, Pinehurst, Swindon, Wiltshire
360 BOBBY BASKCOMB, Worth Matravers, Dorset
361 LEE WARDLE, Coalville, Leicestershire
362 MARTIN TOPLEY (Printer), Leicestershire
363 LEIGH PEARCE, Quorn, Leicestershire
364 QUENTIN WOODHOUSE, Birstall, Leicestershire
365 BAS FORGHAM, Hugglescote, Coalville, Leicestershire
366 ROGER INGAMELLS, Beaumont Leys, Leicester
367 CHRIS DEWEY, Thurmaston, Leicester
368 TONY ROSSA, Anstey, Leicestershire
369 GERALD TOON, Scraptoft Lane, Leicester
370 EAMON C. HEIGHWAY, Thurmaston, Leicester
371 JULIA BYRNE, Clarendon Park, Leicester
372 JULIAN BASKCOMB, Clarendon Park, Leicester

ERRATA and ADDITIONS

Page 136

Bernard Gaughran was born in Dublin on 29 September 1915 and died in Dundalk 20 September 1977.

Page 248

George Moorhead was born in New Zealand in 1896 and not Lurgan, Co. Armagh. He died in Northern Ireland in 1976.

Page 310

The picture captioned Donald Slade should read Reg Slade.